Lecture Notes in Artificial Intelligence 9322

Subseries of Lecture Notes in Computer Science

More information about this series at http://www.springer.com/series/1244

Carsten Lutz · Silvio Ranise (Eds.)

Frontiers of Combining Systems

10th International Symposium, FroCoS 2015
Wroclaw, Poland, September 21–24, 2015
Proceedings

Editors
Carsten Lutz
Universität Bremen
Bremen
Germany

Silvio Ranise
Fondazione Bruno Kessler
Trento
Italy

ISSN 0302-9743
Lecture Notes in Artificial Intelligence
ISBN 978-3-319-24245-3
DOI 10.1007/978-3-319-24246-0

ISSN 1611-3349   (electronic)

ISBN 978-3-319-24246-0   (eBook)

Library of Congress Control Number: 2015948707

LNCS Sublibrary: SL7 – Artificial Intelligence

Printed on acid-free paper

Springer International Publishing AG Switzerland is part of Springer Science+Business Media
(www.springer.com)

Preface

These proceedings contain the papers selected for presentation at the *10th International Symposium on Frontiers of Combining Systems*, FroCoS 2015, held during September 21-24, 2015 in conjunction with the *International Conference on Automated Reasoning with Analytic Tableaux and Related Methods*, Tableaux 2015, in Wrocław, Poland. Previous FroCoS meetings were organized in Munich (Germany, 1996), Amsterdam (The Netherlands, 1998), Nancy (France, 2000), Santa Margherita Ligure (Italy, 2002), Cork (Ireland, 2004, as part of the International Joint Conference on Automated Reasoning, IJCAR), Vienna (Austria, 2005), Seattle (USA, 2006, as part of IJCAR), Liverpool (UK, 2007, co-located with the International Workshop on First-Order Theorem Proving, FTP), Sidney (Australia, 2008, as part of IJCAR), Trento (Italy, 2009), Edinburgh (UK, 2010, as part of IJCAR), Saarbrücken (Germany, 2011), Manchester (UK, 2012, as part of IJCAR), Nancy (France, 2013, in conjunction with Tableaux), and Vienna (Austria, 2014, as part of IJCAR).

Like previous events in the FroCoS series, FroCoS 2015 offered a common forum for research in the general area of combination, modularization, and integration of systems, with an emphasis on logic-based ones, and on their practical use. The development of techniques and methods for the combination and integration of dedicated formal systems, as well as for their modularization and analysis, is crucial to the development of systems in logic, computation, program development and verification, artificial intelligence, knowledge representation, and automated reasoning.

FroCoS 2015 received 34 submissions, which were evaluated on the basis of their significance, novelty, technical quality, and appropriateness to the FroCoS audience. After intensive reviewing and electronic discussions, 20 papers were selected for presentation at the symposium. Their topics include description logics, theorem proving and model building, decision procedures as well as their combination and application to verification, rewriting and constraint solving, reasoning in large theories, and transformations between symbolic systems. The symposium program included three invited talks:

- Andreas Herzig (Université Paul Sabatier, Toulouse, France): "*Knowledge and Action: How Should We Combine Their Logics?*"
- Philipp Rümmer (Uppsala University, Sweden): "*Free Variables and Theories: Revisiting Rigid E-unification*", and
- Thomas Sturm (Max-Planck-Institut für Informatik, Saarbrücken, Germany): "*From Complete Elimination Procedures to Subtropical Decisions over the Reals*".

It also shared Tableaux 2015's invited speaker, Oliver Ray, featured two shared sessions with Tableaux 2015, and the following tutorials:

- Till Mossakowski (University of Magdeburg, Germany): "The Distributed Ontology, Modeling, and Specification Language (DOL): Networks of Theories, Languages, and Logics"
- Cesare Tinelli (University of Iowa, USA): "A Taste of CVC4"
- Christoph Weidenbach (Max-Planck-Institut für Informatik, Saarbrücken, Germany): "Automated Reasoning Building Blocks."

We would like to thank all the people who invested their time and energy to make this year's symposium happen. In particular, we thank the authors for submitting their manuscripts and the attendees for contributing to the symposium discussion. We are also very grateful to the members of the Program Committee and to the external reviewers for carefully reviewing and discussing the submissions, and for their commitment to meet the strict deadlines.

We thank the people at Springer for their assistance with publishing these proceedings and for the generous financial support that allowed us to offer several student travel grants. Last but certainly not least, our thanks go to everybody who contributed to the organization of the event, most notably to Hans de Nivelle, General Chair of Tableaux 2015 and FroCoS 2015, for taking care of all the details of local organization.

September 2015
Carsten Lutz
Silvio Ranise

Organization

FroCoS Steering Committee

Franz Baader	President, FroCoS 1996 PC Co-chair, and Co-founder
Silvio Ghilardi	FroCoS 2009 PC Co-chair
Pascal Fontaine	FroCoS 2013 PC Co-chair
Silvio Ranise	FroCoS 2015 PC Co-chair
Renate Schmidt	FroCoS 2013 PC Co-chair
Viorica Sofronie-Stokkermans	FroCoS 2011 Conference Chair
Cesare Tinelli	FroCoS 2011 PC Chair

Program Committee

Program Chairs

Carsten Lutz	Universität Bremen, Germany
Silvio Ranise	Fondazione Bruno Kessler, Trento, Italy

Members

Alessandro Artale	Free University of Bolzano-Bozen, Italy
Franz Baader	TU Dresden, Germany
Clark Barrett	New York University, USA
Peter Baumgartner	National ICT of Australia, Australia
Christoph Benzmüller	Free University of Berlin, Germany
Thomas Bolander	Technical University of Denmark, Denmark
Torben Braüner	Roskilde University, Denmark
Sylvain Conchon	Université Paris-Sud, France
Clare Dixon	University of Liverpool, UK
François Fages	INRIA Paris-Rocquencourt, France
Pascal Fontaine	Université de Lorraine, Nancy, France
Didier Galmiche	Université de Lorraine, Nancy, France
Silvio Ghilardi	Università degli Studi di Milano, Italy
Jürgen Giesl	RWTH Aachen, Germany
Guido Governatori	National ICT of Australia, Australia
Roman Kontchakov	Birkbeck, University of London, UK
Till Mossakowski	University of Magdeburg, Germany
Christophe Ringeissen	INRIA Nancy-Grand Est, France
Renate Schmidt	University of Manchester, UK
Roberto Sebastiani	Università di Trento, Italy
Viorica Sofronie-Stokkermans	Universität Koblenz-Landau, Germany
Andrzej Szałas	University of Warsaw, Poland

René Thiemann   University of Innsbruck, Austria
Cesare Tinelli   University of Iowa, USA
Luca Viganò   King's College, London, UK
Christoph Weidenbach   Max-Planck Institut für Informatik,
                                Saarbrücken, Germany

Additional Reviewers

Codescu, Mihai   Larchey-Wendling, Dominique
Corzilius, Florian   Morawska, Barbara
Déharbe, David   Méry, Daniel
Ganesh, Vijay   Neuhaus, Fabian
Gao, Sicun   Nishida, Naoki
Gmeiner, Karl   Prabhakar, Pavithra
Gutiérrez Basulto, Víctor   Ryzhikov, Vladislav
Harrison, John   Scheibler, Karsten
Hernich, André   Schubert, Tobias
Hustadt, Ullrich   Sticksel, Christoph
Hutter, Dieter   Stratulat, Sorin
Iosif, Radu   Suda, Martin
Irfan, Ahmed   Tonetta, Stefano
Jovanović, Dejan   Trentin, Patrick
Khan, Muhammad S   Yamada, Akihisa
Kovtunova, Alisa

Abstracts of Invited Talks

Knowledge and Action: How Should we Combine Their Logics?

Andreas Herzig

University of Toulouse and CNRS,
IRIT, 118, Route de Narbonne, F-31062 Toulouse, France

The design of logical systems accounting for both knowledge and action is an important issue in AI and MAS. While there are fairly well-established logics of knowledge—essentially the modal logics S5 and S4.2—, there is much less consensus about logical formalisms for actions: there exists a plethora of rather expressive formal systems, including situation calculus, event calculus, fluent calculus, and dynamic logic. When one combines these formal systems with epistemic logic then one typically supposes that knowledge and actions are related through the principles of perfect recall and no miracles. The resulting many-dimensional logics often have high complexity or are undecidable.

In this talk, building on previous work with several colleagues [6, 2, 4, 5] I will advocate a combination that is based on a simple, STRIPS-like account of action: a dialect of Propositional Dynamic Logic PDL whose atomic programs are assignments of propositional variables. Its epistemic extension generalises the notion of visibility of a propositional variable by an agent, as proposed by van der Hoek, Wooldridge and colleagues [9, 8]. The model checking, satisfiability and validity problems of the resulting logic are all PSPACE complete. The logic allows to capture in a natural way several concepts that were studied in the literature, including logics of propositional control [3, 7] and epistemic boolean games [1].

References

1. Ågotnes, T., Harrenstein, P., van der Hoek, W., Wooldridge, M.: Boolean games with epistemic goals. In: Grossi, D., Roy, O., Huang, H. (eds.) Logic, Rationality, and Interaction - 4th International Workshop, LORI 2013, Hangzhou, China, October 9-12, 2013, Proceedings. Lecture Notes in Computer Science, vol. 8196, pp. 1–14. Springer (2013), http://dx.doi.org/10.1007/978-3-642-40948-6_1
2. Balbiani, P., Herzig, A., Troquard, N.: Dynamic logic of propositional assignments: a well-behaved variant of PDL. In: Kupferman, O. (ed.) Proceedings of the 28th Annual IEEE/ACM Symposium on Logic in Computer Science. pp. 143–152 (2013)
3. Gerbrandy, J.: Logics of propositional control. In: Proc. AAMAS'06. pp. 193–200 (2006)
4. Herzig, A.: Logics of knowledge and action: critical analysis and challenges. Journal of Autonomous Agents and Multi-Agent Systems pp. 1–35 (2014), to appear. Online July 2, 2014, doi : 10.1007/s10458-014-9267-z.

5. Herzig, A., Lorini, E., Maffre, F.: A poor man's epistemic logic based on propositional assignment and higher-order observation. In: Logic, Rationality, and Interaction - 5th International Workshop, LORI 2015, Taipeh, October, 2015, Proceedings (2015)
6. Herzig, A., Lorini, E., Troquard, N., Moisan, F.: A dynamic logic of normative systems. In: Proceedings of the 22nd International Joint Conference on Artificial Intelligence. pp. 228–233 (2011)
7. Hoek, W.v.d., Wooldridge, M.: On the logic of cooperation and propositional control. Artificial Intelligence 164(1-2), 81–119 (2005)
8. van der Hoek, W., Iliev, P., Wooldridge, M.: A logic of revelation and concealment. In: van der Hoek, W., Padgham, L., Conitzer, V., Winikoff, M. (eds.) Proceedings of the 11th International Conference on Autonomous Agents and Multiagent Systems. pp. 1115–1122. IFAAMAS (2012)
9. van der Hoek, W., Troquard, N., Wooldridge, M.: Knowledge and control. In: Sonenberg, L., Stone, P., Tumer, K., Yolum, P. (eds.) Proceedings of the 10th International Conference on Autonomous Agents and Multiagent Systems. pp. 719–726. IFAAMAS (2011)

Free Variables and Theories:
Revisiting Rigid E-Unification[*]

Peter Backeman and Philipp Rümmer

Uppsala University, Sweden

Abstract. The efficient integration of theory reasoning in first-order calculi with free variables (such as sequent calculi or tableaux) is a long-standing challenge. For the case of the theory of equality, an approach that has been extensively studied in the 90s is rigid E-unification, a variant of equational unification in which the assumption is made that every variable denotes exactly one term (rigid semantics). The fact that simultaneous rigid E-unification is undecidable, however, has hampered practical adoption of the method, and today there are few theorem provers that use rigid E-unification.

One solution is to consider incomplete algorithms for computing (simultaneous) rigid E-unifiers, which can still be sufficient to create sound and complete theorem provers for first-order logic with equality; such algorithms include rigid basic superposition proposed by Degtyarev and Voronkov, but also the much older subterm instantiation approach introduced by Kanger in 1963 (later also termed minus-normalisation). We introduce bounded rigid E-unification (BREU) as a new variant of E-unification corresponding to subterm instantiation. In contrast to general rigid E-unification, BREU is NP-complete for individual and simultaneous unification problems, and can be solved efficiently with the help of SAT; BREU can be combined with techniques like congruence closure for ground reasoning, and be used to construct theorem provers that are competitive with state-of-the-art tableau systems. We outline ongoing research how BREU can be generalised to other theories than equality.

---

[*] This work was partly supported by the Microsoft PhD Scholarship Programme and the Swedish Research Council.

From Complete Elimination Procedures to Subtropical Decisions over the Reals

Thomas Sturm

Max-Planck-Institut für Informatik, 66123 Saarbrücken, Germany
sturm@mpi-inf.mpg.de

Effective quantifier elimination procedures for first-order theories provide a powerful tool for generically solving a wide range of problems based on logical specifications. In contrast to general first-order provers, quantifier elimination procedures are based on a fixed set of admissible logical symbols with an implicitly fixed semantics. This admits the use of sub-algorithms from symbolic computation. We focus here on quantifier elimination for the reals and its applications giving examples from geometry [1, 6], verification [9], and the sciences [10, 11]. Beyond quantifier elimination we are going to discuss recent results on an incomplete decision procedure for the existential fragment of the reals [8], which has been successfully applied to the analysis of reaction systems in chemistry and in the life sciences [2]. We conclude with an overview on further quantifier-eliminable theories [7, 12, 5, 4, 3] that have been realized in our open-source computer logic software Redlog (www.redlog.eu).

References

1. Dolzmann, A., Sturm, T., Weispfenning, V.: A new approach for automatic theorem proving in real geometry. J. Autom. Reason. **21**(3) (1998) 357–380
2. Errami, H., Eiswirth, M., Grigoriev, D., Seiler, W.M., Sturm, T., Weber, A.: Detection of Hopf bifurcations in chemical reaction networks using convex coordinates. J. Comput. Phys. **291** (2015) 279–302
3. Lasaruk, A., Sturm, T.: Weak integer quantifier elimination beyond the linear case. In: Proc. CASC 2007. LNCS 4770. (2007)
4. Lasaruk, A., Sturm, T.: Weak quantifier elimination for the full linear theory of the integers. AAECC **18**(6) (2007) 545–574
5. Seidl, A.M., Sturm, T.: Boolean quantification in a first-order context. In: Proc. CASC 2003. TU München, Germany (2003) 329–345
6. Sturm, T.: Real Quantifier Elimination in Geometry. (1999)
7. Sturm, T.: Linear problems in valued fields. JSC **30**(2) (2000) 207–219
8. Sturm, T.: Subtropical real root finding. In: Proc. ISSAC 2015. (2015) 347–354
9. Sturm, T., Tiwari, A.: Verification and synthesis using real quantifier elimination. In: Proc. ISSAC 2011. (2011) 329–336
10. Sturm, T., Weber, A.: Investigating generic methods to solve Hopf bifurcation problems in algebraic biology. In: Proc. AB 2008. LNCS 5147. (2008) 200–215
11. Sturm, T., Weber, A., Abdel-Rahman, E.O., El Kahoui, M.: Investigating algebraic and logical algorithms to solve Hopf bifurcation problems in algebraic biology. MCS **2**(3) (2009) 493–515
12. Sturm, T., Weispfenning, V.: Quantifier elimination in term algebras. In: Proc. CASC 2002. TU München, Germany (2002) 285–300

Contents

Decision Procedures for Verification

Rewriting and Constraint Solving

Transformations between Symbolic Systems

Combination Methods

Reasoning in Large Theories

Invited Talk

Free Variables and Theories: Revisiting Rigid E-Unification*

Peter Backeman and Philipp Rümmer

Uppsala University, Sweden

Abstract. The efficient integration of theory reasoning in first-order calculi with free variables (such as sequent calculi or tableaux) is a long-standing challenge. For the case of the theory of equality, an approach that has been extensively studied in the 90s is rigid E-unification, a variant of equational unification in which the assumption is made that every variable denotes exactly one term (rigid semantics). The fact that simultaneous rigid E-unification is undecidable, however, has hampered practical adoption of the method, and today there are few theorem provers that use rigid E-unification.

One solution is to consider incomplete algorithms for computing (simultaneous) rigid E-unifiers, which can still be sufficient to create sound and complete theorem provers for first-order logic with equality; such algorithms include rigid basic superposition proposed by Degtyarev and Voronkov, but also the much older subterm instantiation approach introduced by Kanger in 1963 (later also termed minus-normalisation). We introduce bounded rigid E-unification (BREU) as a new variant of E-unification corresponding to subterm instantiation. In contrast to general rigid E-unification, BREU is NP-complete for individual and simultaneous unification problems, and can be solved efficiently with the help of SAT; BREU can be combined with techniques like congruence closure for ground reasoning, and be used to construct theorem provers that are competitive with state-of-the-art tableau systems. We outline ongoing research how BREU can be generalised to other theories than equality.

1 Introduction

The integration of efficient equality reasoning, and theory reasoning in general, in tableaux and sequent calculi is a long-standing challenge, and has led to a wealth of theoretically intriguing, yet surprisingly few practically satisfying solutions. Among others, a family of approaches related to the (undecidable) problem of computing *simultaneous rigid E-unifiers* have been developed, by utilising incomplete unification procedures in such a way that an overall complete first-order calculus is obtained [11,4,9]. Following the line of research started by Kanger [11], we recently introduced *simultaneous bounded rigid E-unification* (BREU) [2], a new version of rigid E-unification that is bounded in the sense that

---

* This work was partly supported by the Microsoft PhD Scholarship Programme and the Swedish Research Council.

C. Lutz and S. Ranise (Eds.): FroCoS 2015, LNAI 9322, pp. 3–13, 2015.
DOI: 10.1007/978-3-319-24246-0_1

variables only represent terms from finite domains, thus preserving decidability even for simultaneous E-unification problems. As demonstrated in [2], BREU can be used to design sound and complete calculi for first-order logic with equality, and to implement theorem provers that compare favourably to state-of-the-art tableau provers in terms of performance on problems with equality.

In this paper, we study the problem of generalising from BREU to bounded rigid unification modulo theories beyond equality. To this end, we first investigate different ways of defining semantics of BREU problems: BREU problems can be interpreted both syntactically and semantically, leading to two formalisms that differ in terms of expressiveness and complexity. We discuss how the semantic setting lends itself to generalisation rather naturally, in particular for theories that admit quantifier elimination. We conclude by outlining resulting challenges.

2 Background

2.1 Rigid E-Unification

We start by illustrating the rigid E-unification approach using the following problem from [4]:

$$\phi \;=\; \exists x, y, u, v. \; \begin{pmatrix} (a \approx b \;\to\; g(x, u, v) \approx g(y, f(c), f(d))) \;\wedge \\ (c \approx d \;\to\; g(u, x, y) \approx g(v, f(a), f(b))) \end{pmatrix}$$

To show validity of ϕ, a Gentzen-style proof (or, equivalently, a tableau) can be constructed, using free variables for x, y, u, v:

$$\frac{\dfrac{\mathcal{A}}{a \approx b \vdash g(X, U, V) \approx g(Y, f(c), f(d))} \quad \dfrac{\mathcal{B}}{c \approx d \vdash g(U, X, Y) \approx g(V, f(a), f(b))}}{\dfrac{\vdash (a \approx b \to g(X, U, V) \approx g(Y, f(c), f(d))) \wedge (c \approx d \to g(U, X, Y) \approx g(V, f(a), f(b)))}{\vdash \phi}}$$

To finish this proof, both $\mathcal{A}$ and $\mathcal{B}$ need to be closed by applying further rules, and substituting concrete terms for the variables. The substitution $\sigma_l = \{X \mapsto Y, U \mapsto f(c), V \mapsto f(d)\}$ makes it possible to close $\mathcal{A}$ through equational reasoning, and $\sigma_r = \{X \mapsto f(a), U \mapsto V, Y \mapsto f(b)\}$ closes $\mathcal{B}$, but neither closes both. Finding a substitution that closes both branches is known as *simultaneous rigid E-unification* (SREU), and has first been formulated in [8]:

Definition 1 (Rigid E-Unification). *Let E be a set of equations, and s, t be terms. A substitution σ is called a* rigid E-unifier *of s and t if $s\sigma \approx t\sigma$ follows from $E\sigma$ via ground equational reasoning. A simultaneous rigid E-unifier σ is a common rigid E-unifier for a set $(E_i, s_i, t_i)_{i=1}^n$ of rigid E-unification problems.*

In our example, two rigid E-unification problems have to be solved:

$$\begin{aligned} E_1 &= \{a \approx b\}, & s_1 &= g(X, U, V), & t_1 &= g(Y, f(c), f(d)), \\ E_2 &= \{c \approx d\}, & s_2 &= g(U, X, Y), & t_2 &= g(V, f(a), f(b)). \end{aligned}$$

We can observe that $\sigma_s = \{X \mapsto f(a), Y \mapsto f(b), U \mapsto f(c), V \mapsto f(d)\}$ is a simultaneous rigid E-unifier, and suffices to finish the proof of ϕ.

The SREU problem famously turned out undecidable [3], which makes the style of reasoning shown here problematic in automated theorem provers. Different solutions have been proposed to address this situation, including potentially non-terminating, but complete E-unification procedures [7], and terminating but incomplete algorithms that are nevertheless sufficient to create complete proof procedures [11,4,9]. The practical impact of such approaches has been limited; to the best of our knowledge, there is no (at least no actively maintained) theorem prover based on such explicit forms of SREU.

2.2 Subterm Instantiation and Bounded Rigid E-Unification

An early solution in the class of "terminating, but incomplete" algorithms for SREU was introduced as *dummy instantiation* in the seminal work of Kanger [11] (in 1963, i.e., even before the introduction of unification), and later studied under the names *subterm instantiation* and *minus-normalisation* [5,6]; the relationship to SREU was observed in [4]. In contrast to full SREU, subterm instantiation only considers E-unifiers where substituted terms are taken from some predefined finite set, which directly implies decidability. The impact of subterm instantiation on practical theorem proving was again limited, however, among others because no efficient search procedures for dummy instantiation were available [6].

In recent work, we have introduced *bounded rigid E-unification* (BREU), a new restricted version of SREU that captures the decision problem to be solved in the subterm instantiation method, and developed symbolic algorithms for computing bounded rigid E-unifiers [2,1]. We illustrate the application of BREU on the example from the previous section; for sake of presentation, BREU operates on formulae that are normalised by means of flattening (observe that ϕ and ϕ' are equivalent):

$$\phi' = \forall z_1, z_2, z_3, z_4.\ \Big(f(a) \not\approx z_1 \vee f(b) \not\approx z_2 \vee f(c) \not\approx z_3 \vee f(d) \not\approx z_4 \vee$$
$$\exists x, y, u, v.\ \forall z_5, z_6, z_7, z_8.\ \begin{pmatrix} g(x,u,v) \not\approx z_5 \vee g(y, z_3, z_4) \not\approx z_6 \vee \\ g(u, x, y) \not\approx z_7 \vee g(v, z_1, z_2) \not\approx z_8 \vee \\ ((a \not\approx b \vee z_5 \approx z_6) \wedge (c \not\approx d \vee z_7 \approx z_8)) \end{pmatrix}\Big)$$

A proof constructed for ϕ' has the same structure as the one for ϕ, with the difference that all function terms are now isolated in the antecedent:

$$\frac{\begin{array}{cc} \dfrac{\mathcal{A}'}{\ldots, g(X, U, V) \approx o_5, a \approx b \vdash o_5 \approx o_6} & \dfrac{\mathcal{B}'}{\ldots, g(U, X, Y) \approx o_7, c \approx d \vdash o_7 \approx o_8} \end{array}}{\begin{array}{c} \vdots \\ \hline f(a) \approx o_1 \vee f(b) \approx o_2 \vee f(c) \approx o_3 \vee f(d) \approx o_4 \vdash \exists x, y, u, v.\ \forall z_5, z_6, z_7, z_8.\ \ldots \\ \vdots \\ \hline \vdash \forall z_1, z_2, z_3, z_4.\ \ldots \end{array}} \quad (*)$$

To obtain a *bounded* rigid E-unification problem, we now restrict the terms considered for instantiation of X, Y, U, V to the symbols that were in scope when the variables were introduced (at $(*)$ in the proof): X ranges over constants $\{o_1, o_2, o_3, o_4\}$, Y over $\{o_1, o_2, o_3, o_4, X\}$, and so on. Since the problem is flat, those sets contain representatives of all existing ground terms at point $(*)$ in the proof. It is therefore possible to find a simultaneous E-unifier, namely the substitution $\sigma_b = \{X \mapsto o_1, Y \mapsto o_2, U \mapsto o_3, V \mapsto o_4\}$.

Despite the restriction to terms of only bounded size, the subterm instantiation strategy gives rise to a sound and complete calculus for first-order logic with equality [2]; intuitively, the calculus will eventually generate all required terms by repeated instantiation of quantified formulae. The finiteness of considered BREU problems, at any point during proof search, enables the use of efficient techniques from the SAT and SMT domain to check for the existence of unifiers.

2.3 Bounded Rigid E-Unification Formally

Given countably infinite sets C of constants (denoted by $c, d, \ldots$), V_b of bound variables (written $x, y, \ldots$), and V of free variables (denoted by $X, Y, \ldots$), as well as a finite set F of fixed-arity function symbols (written $f, g, \ldots$), the syntactic categories of *formulae* ϕ and *terms* t are defined by

$$\phi ::= \phi \wedge \phi \mid \phi \vee \phi \mid \neg\phi \mid \forall x.\phi \mid \exists x.\phi \mid t \approx t, \qquad t ::= c \mid x \mid X \mid f(t, \ldots, t).$$

We sometimes write $\phi \to \psi$ as shorthand notation for $\neg\phi \vee \psi$, and generally assume that bound variables x only occur underneath quantifiers $\forall x$ or $\exists x$. Semantics of terms and formulae without free variables is defined as is common using first-order structures (U, I) consisting of a non-empty universe U, and an interpretation function I.

We call constants and (free or bound) variables *atomic terms*, and all other terms *compound terms*. A *flat equation* is an equation between atomic terms, or an equation of the form $f(t_1, \ldots, t_n) \approx t_0$, where $t_0, \ldots, t_n$ are atomic terms. A substitution is a mapping of variables to terms, such that all but finitely many variables are mapped to themselves. Symbols $\sigma, \theta, \ldots$ denote substitutions, and we use post-fix notation $\phi\sigma$ or $t\sigma$ to denote application of substitutions. An *atomic substitution* is a substitution that maps variables only to atomic terms. We write $u[r]$ do denote that r is a subexpression of a term or formula u, and $u[s]$ for the term or formula obtained by replacing the subexpression r with s.

Definition 2 (Replacement Relation [13]). *The* replacement relation $\to_E$ *induced by a set of equations E is defined by: $u[l] \to u[r]$ if $l \approx r \in E$. The relation $\leftrightarrow_E^*$ represents the reflexive, symmetric and transitive closure of $\to_E$.*

Definition 3 (BREU). *A* bounded rigid E-unification (BREU) *problem is a triple $(\preceq, E, e)$, with $\preceq$ being a partial order over atomic terms such that for all variables X the set $\{s \mid s \preceq X\}$ is finite; E is a finite set of flat formulae; and $e = s \approx t$ is an equation between atomic terms (the target equation). An atomic substitution σ is called a* bounded rigid E-unifier *of s and t if $s\sigma \leftrightarrow_{E\sigma}^* t\sigma$ and $X\sigma \preceq X$ for all variables X.*

Definition 4 (Simultaneous BREU). *A simultaneous bounded rigid E-unification problem is a pair $(\preceq, (E_i, e_i)_{i=1}^n)$ such that each triple $(\preceq, E_i, e_i)$ is a bounded rigid E-unification problem. A substitution σ is a simultaneous bounded rigid E-unifier if it is a bounded rigid E-unifier for each problem $(\preceq, E_i, e_i)$.*

In the following, we say that a (possibly simultaneous) BREU problem is *syntactically solvable* if a bounded rigid E-unifier exists. As has been shown in [2], checking syntactic solvability is NP-hard, and can effectively be solved via an encoding to SAT, or with SMT-style reasoning.

Example 5. We revisit the example introduced in Sect. 2.1, which can be captured as the following simultaneous BREU problem $(\preceq, \{(E_1, e_1), (E_2, e_2)\})$:

$$E_1 = E \cup \{a \approx b\}, \quad e_1 = o_5 \approx o_6, \qquad E_2 = E \cup \{c \approx d\}, \quad e_2 = o_7 \approx o_8,$$

$$E = \left\{ \begin{array}{l} f(a) \approx o_1, f(b) \approx o_2, f(c) \approx o_3, f(d) \approx o_4, \\ g(X, U, V) \approx o_5, g(Y, o_3, o_4) \approx o_6, g(U, X, Y) \approx o_7, g(V, o_1, o_2) \approx o_8 \end{array} \right\}$$

with $a \prec b \prec c \prec d \prec o_1 \prec o_2 \prec o_3 \prec o_4 \prec X \prec Y \prec U \prec V \prec o_5 \prec o_6 \prec o_7 \prec o_8$.

A unifier for this problem is sufficient to close all goals of the tree up to equational reasoning; one solution is $\sigma = \{X \mapsto o_1, Y \mapsto o_2, U \mapsto o_3, V \mapsto o_4\}$.

The remainder of the paper considers the question how the notion of BREU can be carried over to other theories than just equality. As we will see, to this end it is useful to provide a more relaxed characterisation of BREU solvability.

3 Semantically Solving BREU

Definition 6 (Forest-Shaped BREU). *A BREU problem $(\preceq, (E_i, e_i)_{i=1}^n)$ is forest-shaped if (i) the order $\preceq$ forms a forest, that is, whenever $a \preceq b$ and $a' \preceq b$ it is the case that $a \preceq a'$ or $a' \preceq a$; and (ii) components (E_i, e_i) (for $i \in \{1, \ldots, n\}$) do not mix atomic terms from several branches of $\preceq$, that is, whenever (E_i, e_i) contains atomic terms s, t it is the case that $s \preceq t$ or $t \preceq s$.*

The BREU problem given in Example 5, and generally all BREU problems extracted from proofs (as defined in [2]) are forest-shaped; the structure of $\preceq$ will reflect the proof tree from which the BREU problem was derived. Importantly, forest-shaped problems can be reinterpreted as formulae by translating the order $\preceq$ to a prefix of quantifiers, and replacing equations E_i with Ackermann constraints. Without loss of generality, we assume that every equation in a set E_i of a BREU problem $(\preceq, (E_i, e_i)_{i=1}^n)$ contains a function symbol; equations $a \approx b$ between constants or variables can be rewritten to $f() \approx a, f() \approx b$ by introducing a fresh zero-ary function f.

Definition 7 (BREU Formula Encoding). *Suppose $B = (\preceq, (E_i, s_i \approx t_i)_{i=1}^n)$ is a forest-shaped simultaneous BREU problem, and S the (finite) set of atomic terms occurring in B, with $k = |S|$. Let further $S_b = \{x_1, \ldots, x_k\} \subseteq V_b$ be fresh bound variables (not occurring in B), and $\sigma : S \to S_b$ a bijection such that*

$\sigma(s) = x_i, \sigma(t) = x_j$ and $s \preceq t$ imply $i \leq j$. Then the formula $Q_1 x_1 . \ldots . Q_k x_k . \bigwedge_{j=1}^{n} G_j$ with

$$Q_i = \begin{cases} \forall & \text{if } \sigma^{-1}(x_i) \in C \text{ is a constant} \\ \exists & \text{otherwise} \end{cases}$$

$$G_j = \left(\bigwedge_{f(\bar{a}) \approx b, f(\bar{a}') \approx b' \in E_j} \sigma(\bar{a}) \approx \sigma(\bar{a}') \rightarrow \sigma(b) \approx \sigma(b') \right) \rightarrow \sigma(s_j) \approx \sigma(t_j)$$

is called a formula encoding of B.

Example 8. Consider the BREU problem $B = (\preceq, E, e)$ defined by

$$E = \{ f(X) \approx c, f(a) \approx a, f(b) \approx b \}, \qquad e = a \approx b, \qquad a \prec b \prec c \prec X .$$

To encode B as a formula, we fix fresh variables $x_1, \ldots, x_4$ and the mapping $\sigma = \{ a \mapsto x_1, b \mapsto x_2, c \mapsto x_3, X \mapsto x_4 \}$, and obtain

$$\forall x_1 . \forall x_2 . \forall x_3 . \exists x_4 . \ (x_4 \approx x_1 \rightarrow x_3 \approx x_1) \wedge (x_4 \approx x_2 \rightarrow x_3 \approx x_2) \rightarrow x_1 \approx x_2 . \quad (1)$$

Here, the assumption $x_4 \approx x_1 \rightarrow x_3 \approx x_1$ stems from the Ackermann constraint $X \approx a \rightarrow c \approx a$, and $x_4 \approx x_2 \rightarrow x_3 \approx x_2$ from $X \approx b \rightarrow c \approx b$; other Ackermann constraints are either tautologies, or equivalent to the two constraints given, and have been left out for sake of brevity.

The formula encoding of a BREU problem is a first-order formula with equality, but without functions symbols; the validity of the encoding is therefore decidable. It can also be observed that Def. 7 in principle admits multiple formula encodings for a BREU problem, but those different encodings are guaranteed to be equivalent, thanks to the fact that the BREU problem is forest-shaped.

We say that a BREU problem is *semantically solvable* if its formula encoding is valid. Semantic solvability is a weaker property than syntactic solvability (as in Def. 3). In particular, it can easily be checked that (1) is valid, but the problem B from Example 8 does not have any syntactic E-unifiers: such a unifier would have to map X to one of X, a, b, c, but in no case is it possible to conclude $a \approx b$.

Lemma 9. *If a (possibly simultaneous) forest-shaped BREU problem B has an E-unifier, then the formula encoding of B is valid.*

Proof. Any syntactic E-unifier defines how existential quantifiers in the formula encoding have to be instantiated to satisfy the formula. □

3.1 Semantic Solvability in a First-Order Calculus

The sequent calculus for first-order logic with equality introduced in [2] uses BREU to implement a global closure rule for free-variable proofs:

$$\cfrac{\cfrac{*}{\Gamma_1 \vdash \Delta_1} \quad \cdots \quad \cfrac{*}{\Gamma_n \vdash \Delta_n}}{\Gamma \vdash \Delta} \text{ BREU}$$

where $\Gamma_1 \vdash \Delta_1, \ldots, \Gamma_n \vdash \Delta_n$ are all open goals of the proof, $E_i = \{ t \approx s \in \Gamma_i \}$ are flat antecedent equations, $e_i = \bigvee \{ t \approx s \in \Delta_i \}$ are succedent equations, and the simultaneous BREU problem $(\preceq, (E_i, e_i)_{i=1}^{n})$ is solvable.

The rule uses a slightly generalised version of BREU in which a target constraint e_i can be a disjunction of equations; such problems can easily be translated to normal BREU at the cost of introducing additional function symbols. The order $\preceq$ in the rule is derived from the structure of a proof, and the BREU problem $(\preceq, (E_i, e_i)_{i=1}^n)$ is in particular forest-shaped. Given the alternative notion of semantic solvability, the question arises whether overall soundness and completeness of the first-order calculus from [2] are preserved when reformulating the BREU rule to be applicable whenever "the simultaneous BREU problem $(\preceq, (E_i, e_i)_{i=1}^n)$ is *semantically* solvable." We will call the new rule BREU$_{\text{SEM}}$.

The answer is positive in both cases. From Lem. 9, it follows directly that replacing BREU with BREU$_{\text{SEM}}$ preserves completeness of the calculus, because the weaker side condition only entails that BREU$_{\text{SEM}}$ might be applicable in more cases than BREU. Soundness cannot be concluded from the soundness proof given in [2] for the syntactic case, but we can instead find a simple inductive argument that the formula encoding of the BREU problem $(\preceq, (E_i, e_i)_{i=1}^n)$ constructed in BREU$_{\text{SEM}}$ is always an *under-approximation* of the root sequent of a proof. Thus, if the formula encoding is valid, also the validity of the root sequent follows:

Lemma 10. *Suppose $\Gamma \vdash \Delta$ is a sequent without free variables, and P a proof constructed from $\Gamma \vdash \Delta$. If B is the BREU problem constructed in an application of* BREU$_{\text{SEM}}$ *to P, then the formula encoding ϕ_B of B implies $\bigwedge \Gamma \to \bigvee \Delta$.*

3.2 The Complexity of Semantic Solvability

Example 8 illustrates that the notion of semantic solvability does not coincide with (and is therefore strictly weaker than) syntactic solvability; this implies that the use of the relaxed rule BREU$_{\text{SEM}}$ can sometimes lead to *shorter proofs* compared to the original rule BREU. The resulting gain in efficiency is offset, however, by the increased computational complexity of checking BREU solvability: in the syntactic case, this problem is NP-complete [2], whereas it turns out that semantic solvability is *PSPACE-complete*. For membership in PSPACE, observe that the formula encoding of a BREU problem can directly be mapped to a Quantified Boolean Formula (QBF), since it is only necessary to consider universes with as many individuals as the formula contains quantifiers.

Lemma 11 (PSPACE-hardness). *Checking whether a (possibly simultaneous) forest-shaped BREU problem has a valid formula encoding is PSPACE-hard.*

Proof. We show that QBF formulae ϕ can be translated to BREU problems B_ϕ, in such a way that the formula encoding of B_ϕ is equivalent to ϕ. Assume that $\phi = Q_1 x_1. \ldots . Q_k x_k. \psi$ is in prenex normal form, with $Q_i \in \{\exists, \forall\}$, and ψ is a Boolean formula over the variables $x_1, \ldots, x_k$ and connectives $\neg, \vee$.

To represent truth values, two constants $\mathbf{0}, \mathbf{1} \in C$ are introduced. Then, to handle the quantifiers, for each variable x_i with $Q_i = \exists$ a fresh free variable $X_i \in V$ is picked, and for each x_i with $Q_i = \forall$ a fresh variable $X_i \in V$ and a fresh constant $d_i \in C$. In addition, in the latter case we define two BREU sub-problems (E_i^0, e_i^0) and (E_i^1, e_i^1) with

$$E_i^0 = \{d_i \approx \mathbf{0}\}, \qquad e_i^0 = X_i \approx \mathbf{0}, \qquad E_i^1 = \{d_i \approx \mathbf{1}\}, \qquad e_i^1 = X_i \approx \mathbf{1} .$$

To represent the Boolean structure of ψ, like in [2] two function symbols f_{or} and f_{not} are introduced, which are axiomatised by equations $E_\mathbb{B} = \{f_{or}(\mathbf{0}, \mathbf{0}) \approx \mathbf{0}, f_{or}(\mathbf{0}, \mathbf{1}) \approx \mathbf{1}, f_{or}(\mathbf{1}, \mathbf{0}) \approx \mathbf{1}, f_{or}(\mathbf{1}, \mathbf{1}) \approx \mathbf{1}, f_{not}(\mathbf{0}) \approx \mathbf{1}, f_{not}(\mathbf{1}) \approx \mathbf{0}\}$. Each sub-formula θ of ψ is then encoded using a fresh constant c_θ and an equation e_θ:

$$
\begin{aligned}
e_\theta &= X_i \approx c_\theta && \text{if } \theta = x_i, \\
e_\theta &= f_{not}(c_{\theta_1}) \approx c_\theta && \text{if } \theta = \neg\theta_1, \\
e_\theta &= f_{or}(c_{\theta_1}, c_{\theta_2}) \approx c_\theta && \text{if } \theta = \theta_1 \vee \theta_2 .
\end{aligned}
$$

We write $E_\psi = \{e_\theta \mid \theta \text{ a sub-formula of } \psi\}$ for the set of all such equations.

Finally, the resulting (forest-shaped) BREU problem is

$$B_\phi = (\preceq, \{(E_i^0, e_i^0), (E_i^1, e_i^1) \mid i \in \{1, \ldots, k\}, Q_i = \forall\} \cup \{(E_\mathbb{B} \cup E_\psi, c_\psi \approx \mathbf{1})\})$$

with a total order $\preceq$ that satisfies $\{\mathbf{0}, \mathbf{1}\} \prec \{d_1, X_1\} \prec \cdots \prec \{d_k, X_k\} \prec \{c_\theta \mid \theta \text{ a sub-formula of } \psi\}$ as well as $d_i \prec X_i$ for all $Q_i = \forall$.

To see that ϕ and the formula encoding ϕ_E of B_ϕ are equivalent, we observe that the two formulae have essentially the same quantifier structure, with the difference that (i) ϕ_E starts with quantifiers $\forall x_{\mathbf{0}} \forall x_{\mathbf{1}}$ binding the truth values $\mathbf{0}, \mathbf{1}$; (ii) every quantifier $\exists x_i$ in ϕ is translated to a quantifier $\exists x_{X_i}$ in ϕ_E; (iii) universal quantifiers $\forall x_i$ are translated to $\forall x_{d_i} \exists x_{X_i}$, with the additional goals (E_i^0, e_i^0) and (E_i^1, e_i^1) expressing $x_{d_i} \approx x_{\mathbf{0}} \to x_{X_i} \approx x_{\mathbf{0}}$ and $x_{d_i} \approx x_{\mathbf{1}} \to x_{X_i} \approx x_{\mathbf{1}}$; and (iv) additional $\forall$-quantifiers are added to represent the propositional structure of the matrix ψ. (The somewhat elaborate translation of $\forall x_i$ ensures that universal quantifiers in ϕ_E effectively only range over truth values.) Equivalence of ϕ and ϕ_E follows from the fact that satisfying assignments of the existentially quantified variables can be mapped back and forth between ϕ and ϕ_E. $\qquad\square$

4   Towards Bounded Rigid Theory Unification

The notion of semantic solvability offers a natural path to generalise from BREU to Bounded Rigid T-Unification (BRTU), for theories T other than equality. The construction in particular applies to theories that admit quantifier elimination, including various forms of arithmetic. For sake of presentation, we assume that equality $\approx$ is still the only predicate in our logic, but we partition the set $F = F_i \cup F_u$ into a set F_i of interpreted T-functions, and a disjoint set F_u of uninterpreted functions. We further assume that the T-validity of first-order formulae ϕ without uninterpreted functions is decidable.

While the general definition of a BREU problem can be kept as in Def. 3 and 4, we redefine formula encodings to take theory symbols into account:

Definition 12 (BRTU Formula Encoding). *Suppose $B = (\preceq, (E_i, s_i \approx t_i)_{i=1}^n)$ is a forest-shaped simultaneous BREU problem, and S the (finite) set of atomic terms occurring in B, with $k = |S|$. Let further $S_b = \{x_1, \ldots, x_k\} \subseteq V_b$ be fresh bound variables (not occurring in B), and $\sigma : S \to S_b$ a bijection such that $\sigma(s) = x_i$, $\sigma(t) = x_j$ and $s \preceq t$ imply $i \leq j$. Then the formula $Q_1 x_1 \ldots . Q_k x_k . \bigwedge_{j=1}^n G_j^T$ with*

$$Q_i = \begin{cases} \forall & \text{if } \sigma^{-1}(x_i) \in C \text{ is a constant} \\ \exists & \text{otherwise} \end{cases}$$

$$G_j^T = \left(\begin{array}{c} \bigwedge_{\substack{f(\bar{a}) \approx b \in E_j \\ f \in F_i}} f(\sigma(\bar{a})) \approx \sigma(b) \wedge \\ \bigwedge_{\substack{f(\bar{a}) \approx b, f(\bar{a}') \approx b' \in E_j \\ f \in F_u}} \sigma(\bar{a}) \approx \sigma(\bar{a}') \to \sigma(b) \approx \sigma(b') \end{array} \right) \to \sigma(s_j) \approx \sigma(t_j)$$

is called a T-formula encoding of B.

Compared to Def. 7, the main change occurs in the definition of G_j^T, where now interpreted functions are kept instead of being replaced with Ackermann constraints. Similarly as before, we say that a BREU problem is *semantically T-solvable* if its T-formula encoding is valid in T.

Example 13. To illustrate the definition, we consider the theory $\mathcal{A}$ of linear (integer or rational) arithmetic, and the implication $f(0) \approx 0 \wedge f(X+1) \approx f(X)+1 \to f(1) \approx 1$, with X ranging over terms $\{0, 1, f(1)\}$. The literals $0, 1$ represent interpreted nullary function symbols, $+$ is an interpreted binary function symbol, and f is an uninterpreted function. Flattening the formula yields a well-formed BREU problem $B = (\preceq, E, e)$ with

$$E = \begin{cases} 0 \approx c_0, 1 \approx c_1, f(c_0) \approx c_0, f(c_1) = c_2, \\ X + c_1 \approx c_4, f(c_4) \approx c_6, f(X) \approx c_5, c_5 + c_1 \approx c_6 \end{cases}, \quad e = c_2 \approx c_1,$$

$$c_0 \prec c_1 \prec c_2 \prec X \prec c_4 \prec c_5 \prec c_6 .$$

Without taking theory $\mathcal{A}$ into account (treating $0, 1, +$ as uninterpreted functions), B is solvable neither syntactically nor semantically. The $\mathcal{A}$-formula encoding of B is obtained by eliminating f through Ackermann constraints (X is mapped to x_3, and constants c_i to x_i for $i \in \{0, 1, 2, 4, 5, 6\}$; redundant constraints are left out), and is a valid formula in theory $\mathcal{A}$:

$$\forall x_0, x_1, x_2. \exists x_3. \forall x_4, x_5, x_6.$$
$$\left(\begin{array}{l} 0 \approx x_0 \wedge 1 \approx x_1 \wedge x_3 + x_1 \approx x_4 \wedge x_5 + x_1 \approx x_6 \wedge \\ (x_0 \approx x_1 \to x_0 \approx x_2) \wedge (x_0 \approx x_4 \to x_0 \approx x_6) \wedge (x_0 \approx x_3 \to x_0 \approx x_5) \wedge \\ (x_1 \approx x_4 \to x_2 \approx x_6) \wedge (x_1 \approx x_3 \to x_2 \approx x_5) \wedge (x_4 \approx x_3 \to x_6 \approx x_5) \end{array} \right)$$
$$\to x_2 \approx x_1$$

5   Challenges and Conclusion

Since Lem. 10 carries over to any of the theories T considered in Sect. 4, the encoding from Def. 12 can in principle be used to implement sound calculi for first-order logic modulo T with bounded free-variable reasoning. For reasons of practicality, of course, various refinements of the overall approach are possible and advisable, along the lines of the procedures presented in [12,2]; among others, also procedures for ground reasoning in T can be integrated. For the special case of linear integer arithmetic, this style of reasoning was essentially implemented in the theorem prover PRINCESS [12]. There are several more conceptual challenges remaining, however:

Syntactically Solving BRTU. We have outlined how solvability of BREU can be characterised semantically, through an encoding as a formula, and then be generalised to theories other than equality. However, both steps have a severe impact on the computational complexity of checking solvability; checking semantic solvability for BRTU modulo linear integer arithmetic, for instance, necessitates a potentially doubly exponential validity check. A crucial question is whether a notion of (theory-dependent) syntactic solvability for BRTU exists, and to investigate the impact on the completeness of an overall proof procedure:

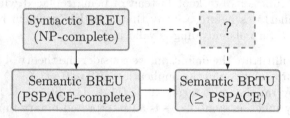

The Completeness of Proof Procedures. It is well-known that no complete calculi exist for first-order logic modulo various theories, for instance modulo linear arithmetic [10]. This leads to the question how the completeness of first-order calculi constructed with the help of BRTU can be characterised, and for which fragments completeness is indeed achieved. The question is partly addressed in [12], but only for linear integer arithmetic and in a setting where uninterpreted functions were replaced with uninterpreted predicates.

References

1. Backeman, P., Rümmer, P.: Efficient algorithms for bounded rigid E-Unification. In: Tableaux. LNCS. Springer (to appear, 2015)
2. Backeman, P., Rümmer, P.: Theorem proving with bounded rigid E-Unification. In: CADE. LNCS. Springer (to appear, 2015)
3. Degtyarev, A., Voronkov, A.: Simultaneous rigid E-Unification is undecidable. In: Kleine Büning, H. (ed.) CSL 1995. LNCS, vol. 1092, pp. 178–190. Springer, Heidelberg (1996)
4. Degtyarev, A., Voronkov, A.: What you always wanted to know about rigid E-Unification. J. Autom. Reasoning 20(1), 47–80 (1998)
5. Degtyarev, A., Voronkov, A.: Equality reasoning in sequent-based calculi. In: Handbook of Automated Reasoning, vol. 2. Elsevier and MIT Press (2001)

6. Degtyarev, A., Voronkov, A.: Kanger's Choices in Automated Reasoning. Springer (2001)
7. Fitting, M.C.: First-Order Logic and Automated Theorem Proving, 2nd edn. Graduate Texts in Computer Science. Springer, Berlin (1996)
8. Gallier, J.H., Raatz, S., Snyder, W.: Theorem proving using rigid e-unification equational matings. In: LICS, pp. 338–346. IEEE Computer Society (1987)
9. Giese, M.A.: A model generation style completeness proof for constraint tableaux with superposition. In: Egly, U., Fermüller, C. (eds.) TABLEAUX 2002. LNCS (LNAI), vol. 2381, pp. 130–144. Springer, Heidelberg (2002)
10. Halpern, J.Y.: Presburger arithmetic with unary predicates is Π_1^1 complete. Journal of Symbolic Logic 56 (1991)
11. Kanger, S.: A simplified proof method for elementary logic. In: Siekmann, J., Wrightson, G. (eds.) Automation of Reasoning 1: Classical Papers on Computational Logic 1957-1966, pp. 364–371. Springer, Heidelberg (1983). originally appeared in 1963
12. Rümmer, P.: A constraint sequent calculus for first-order logic with linear integer arithmetic. In: Cervesato, I., Veith, H., Voronkov, A. (eds.) LPAR 2008. LNCS (LNAI), vol. 5330, pp. 274–289. Springer, Heidelberg (2008)
13. Tiwari, A., Bachmair, L., Rueß, H.: Rigid E-Unification revisited. In: CADE. CADE-17, pp. 220–234. Springer, London (2000)

Description Logics

Decidable Description Logics of Context with Rigid Roles

Stephan Böhme and Marcel Lippmann

Institute for Theoretical Computer Science, Technische Universität Dresden
{stephan.boehme,marcel.lippmann}@tu-dresden.de

Abstract. To represent and reason about contextualized knowledge often two-dimensional Description Logics (DLs) are employed, where one DL is used to describe contexts (or possible worlds) and the other DL is used to describe the objects, i.e. the relational structure of the specific contexts. Previous approaches for DLs of context that combined pairs of DLs resulted in undecidability in those cases where so-called rigid roles are admitted, i.e. if parts of the relational structure are the same in all contexts. In this paper, we present a novel combination of pairs of DLs and show that reasoning stays decidable even in the presence of rigid roles. We give complexity results for various combinations of DLs including $\mathcal{ALC}$, $\mathcal{SHOQ}$, and $\mathcal{EL}$.

1 Introduction

Description logics (DLs) of context can be employed to represent and reason about contextualized knowledge [6,5,11,13,12]. Such contextualized knowledge naturally occurs in practice. Consider, for instance, the rôles[1] played by a person in different contexts. Person Bob, who works for the company Siemens, plays the rôle of an employee of Siemens while at work, i.e. in the work context, whereas he might play the rôle of a customer of Siemens in the context of private life. In this example, access restrictions to the data of Siemens might critically depend on the rôle played by Bob. Moreover, DLs capable of representing contexts are vital to integrate distributed knowledge as argued in [6,5].

In DLs, we use *concept names* (unary predicates) and *complex concepts* (using certain constructors) to describe subsets of an interpretation domain and *roles* (binary predicates) that are interpreted as binary relations over the interpretation domain. Thus, DLs are well-suited to describing contexts as formal objects with formal properties that are organized in relational structures, which are fundamental requirements for modeling contexts [15,16].

However, classical DLs lack expressive power to formalize furthermore that some individuals satisfy certain concepts and relate to other individuals depending on a specific context. Therefore, often two-dimensional DLs are employed [11,13,12]. The approach is to have one DL $\mathcal{L}_M$ as the *meta* or *outer logic* to represent the contexts and their relationships to each other. This logic

---

[1] We use the term "rôle" instead of "role" to avoid confusion with roles used in DLs.

C. Lutz and S. Ranise (Eds.): FroCoS 2015, LNAI 9322, pp. 17–32, 2015.
DOI: 10.1007/978-3-319-24246-0_2

is combined with the *object* or *inner logic* $\mathcal{L}_O$ that captures the relational structure within each of the contexts. Moreover, while some pieces of information depend on the context, other pieces of information are shared throughout all contexts. For instance, the name of a person typically stays the same independent of the actual context. To be able to express that, some concepts and roles are designated to be *rigid*, i.e. they are required to be interpreted the same in all contexts. Unfortunately, if rigid roles are admitted, reasoning in the above mentioned two-dimensional DLs of context turns out to be undecidable; see [11].

We propose and investigate a family of two-dimensional context DLs $\mathcal{L}_M[\![\mathcal{L}_O]\!]$ that meet the above requirements, but are a restricted form of the ones defined in [11] in the sense that we limit the interaction of $\mathcal{L}_M$ and $\mathcal{L}_O$. More precisely, in $\mathcal{L}_M[\![\mathcal{L}_O]\!]$ the outer logic can refer to the internal structure of each context, but not vice versa. That means that information is viewed in a top-down manner, i.e. information of different contexts is strictly capsuled and can only be accessed from the meta level. This means that we cannot express, for instance, that everybody who is employed by Siemens has a certain property in the context of private life. Interestingly, reasoning in $\mathcal{L}_M[\![\mathcal{L}_O]\!]$ stays decidable with such a restriction, even in the presence of rigid roles. In some sense this restriction is similar to what was done in [3,4,14] to obtain a decidable temporalized DL with rigid roles. Even though our techniques to show complexity results are similar to the ones employed for those temporalized DLs, we cannot simply reuse these results to reason in our context DLs, and more effort is needed to obtain tight complexity bounds.

For providing better intuition on how our formalism works, we examine the above mentioned example a bit further. Consider the following axioms:

$$\top \sqsubseteq [\![\exists\,\mathit{worksFor}.\{\mathit{Siemens}\}$$
$$\sqsubseteq \exists\,\mathit{hasAccessRights}.\{\mathit{Siemens}\}]\!] \tag{1}$$

$$\textsc{Work} \sqsubseteq [\![\mathit{worksFor}(\mathit{Bob},\mathit{Siemens})]\!] \tag{2}$$

$$[\![(\exists\,\mathit{worksFor}.\top)(\mathit{Bob})]\!] \sqsubseteq \exists\,\textsc{related}.(\textsc{Private} \sqcap [\![\mathit{HasMoney}(\mathit{Bob})]\!]) \tag{3}$$

$$\top \sqsubseteq [\![\exists\,\mathit{isCustomerOf}.\top \sqsubseteq \mathit{HasMoney}]\!] \tag{4}$$

$$\textsc{Private} \sqsubseteq [\![\mathit{isCustomerOf}(\mathit{Bob},\mathit{Siemens})]\!] \tag{5}$$

$$\textsc{Private} \sqcap \textsc{Work} \sqsubseteq \bot \tag{6}$$

$$\neg\textsc{Work} \sqsubseteq [\![\exists\,\mathit{worksFor}.\top \sqsubseteq \bot]\!] \tag{7}$$

The first axiom states that it holds true in all contexts that somebody who works for Siemens also has access rights to certain data. The second axiom states that Bob is an employee of Siemens in any work context. Furthermore, Axiom 3 says intuitively that in all contexts, in which Bob has a job, he will earn money, which is available in a private context. Then, Axioms 4 ensures that only people with money can be customers. Axiom 5 formalises that Bob is a customer of Siemens in any private context. Moreover, Axiom 6 ensures that the private contexts are disjoint from the work contexts. Finally, Axiom 7 states that the *worksFor* relation only exists in work contexts.

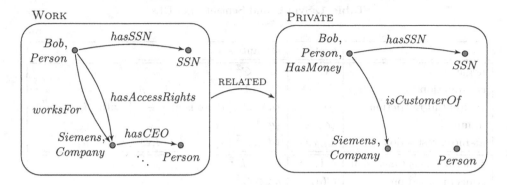

Fig. 1. Model of Axioms 1–7

A fundamental reasoning task is to decide whether the above mentioned axioms are *consistent* together, i.e. whether there is a common model. In our example, this is the case; Figure 1 depicts a model. In this model, we also have Bob's social security number linked to him using a rigid role *hasSSN*. We require this role to be rigid since Bob's social security number does not change over the contexts. Furthermore the axioms entail more knowledge such as for example that in any private context nobody will have access rights to work data of Siemens, i.e. PRIVATE $\sqsubseteq$ [∃ *hasAccessRights.*{*Siemens*} $\sqsubseteq \perp$].

The remainder of the paper is structured as follows. Next, we introduce syntax and semantics of our family of context DLs $\mathcal{L}_M[\![\mathcal{L}_O]\!]$. For this, we repeat some basic notions of DLs. In Section 3, we show decidability of the consistency problem in $\mathcal{L}_M[\![\mathcal{L}_O]\!]$ for $\mathcal{L}_M$ and $\mathcal{L}_O$ being DLs between $\mathcal{ALC}$ and $\mathcal{SHOQ}$. Even though our motivation are context DLs that are decidable in the presence of rigid roles, we still analyze the complexity of deciding consistency in all three cases (i.e. without rigid names, with rigid concepts and roles, and with rigid concepts only) to obtain a clearer picture of our logical formalism. Note that since it is well-known that rigid concepts can be simulated by rigid roles, there is no fourth case to consider. Thereafter, in Section 4 we investigate the complexity of deciding consistency in $\mathcal{L}_M[\![\mathcal{L}_O]\!]$ where $\mathcal{L}_M$ or $\mathcal{L}_O$ are $\mathcal{EL}$. Section 5 concludes the paper and lists some possible future work. Due to space constraints, the full proofs of our results can be found in the accompanying technical report [9].

2 Basic Notions

As argued in the introduction, our two-dimensional context DLs $\mathcal{L}_M[\![\mathcal{L}_O]\!]$ consist of combinations of two DLs: $\mathcal{L}_M$ and $\mathcal{L}_O$. First, we recall the basic definitions of DLs; for a thorough introduction to DLs, we refer the reader to [2].

Definition 1. *Let* $\mathsf{N_C}$, $\mathsf{N_R}$, *and* $\mathsf{N_I}$ *be non-empty, pairwise disjoint sets of* concept names, role names, *and* individual names, *respectively. Furthermore, let* $\mathsf{N} := (\mathsf{N_C}, \mathsf{N_R}, \mathsf{N_I})$. *The set of* concepts over N *is inductively defined starting*

Table 1. Syntax and Semantics of DLs

	syntax	semantics
negation	$\neg C$	$\Delta^{\mathcal{I}} \setminus C^{\mathcal{I}}$
conjunction	$C \sqcap D$	$C^{\mathcal{I}} \cap D^{\mathcal{I}}$
existential restriction	$\exists r.C$	$\{d \in \Delta^{\mathcal{I}} \mid \text{there is an } e \in C^{\mathcal{I}} \text{ with } (d,e) \in r^{\mathcal{I}}\}$
nominal	$\{a\}$	$\{a^{\mathcal{I}}\}$
at-most restriction	$\leqslant_n r.C$	$\{d \in \Delta^{\mathcal{I}} \mid \sharp\{e \in C^{\mathcal{I}} \mid (d,e) \in r^{\mathcal{I}}\} \leq n\}$
general concept inclusion	$C \sqsubseteq D$	$C^{\mathcal{I}} \subseteq D^{\mathcal{I}}$
concept assertion	$C(a)$	$a^{\mathcal{I}} \in C^{\mathcal{I}}$
role assertion	$r(a,b)$	$(a^{\mathcal{I}}, b^{\mathcal{I}}) \in r^{\mathcal{I}}$
role inclusion	$r \sqsubseteq s$	$r^{\mathcal{I}} \subseteq s^{\mathcal{I}}$
transitivity axiom	$\mathsf{trans}(r)$	$r^{\mathcal{I}} = (r^{\mathcal{I}})^+$

from concept names $A \in \mathsf{N_C}$ using the constructors in the upper part of Table 1, where $r, s \in \mathsf{N_R}$, $a, b \in \mathsf{N_I}$, $n \in \mathbb{N}$, and C, D are concepts over N. The lower part of Table 1 shows how axioms over N are defined.

Moreover, an RBox $\mathcal{R}$ over N is a finite set of role inclusions over N and transitivity axioms over N. A Boolean axiom formula over N is a Boolean combination of general concept inclusions (GCIs), concept and role assertion over N. Finally, a Boolean knowledge base (BKB) over N is a pair $\mathfrak{B} = (\mathcal{B}, \mathcal{R})$, where $\mathcal{B}$ is a Boolean axiom formula over N and $\mathcal{R}$ is an RBox over N.

Note that in this definition we refer to the triple N explicitly although it is usually left implicit in standard definitions. This turns out to be useful as we need to distinguish between the symbols used in $\mathcal{L}_M$ and $\mathcal{L}_O$. Sometimes we omit N, however, if it is clear from the context. As usual, we use the following abbreviations: $C \sqcup D$ (disjunction) for $\neg(\neg C \sqcap \neg D)$, $\top$ (top concept) for $A \sqcup \neg A$, where $A \in \mathsf{N_C}$ is arbitrary but fixed, $\bot$ (bottom concept) for $\neg\top$, $\forall r.C$ (value restriction) for $\neg\exists r.\neg C$, and $\geqslant_n s.C$ (at-least restriction) for $\neg(\leqslant_{n-1} s.C)$.

Which concept constructors and types of axioms are available depends on the specific DL used. In the DL $\mathcal{ALC}$, the only allowed concept constructors are negation, conjunction, and existential restriction. Thus disjunction, the top and bottom concept, and value restriction can be used as abbreviations. Moreover, no role inclusions and transitivity axioms are allowed in $\mathcal{ALC}$. If additional concept constructors or types of axioms are allowed, this is denoted by concatenating a corresponding letter: $\mathcal{O}$ means nominals, $\mathcal{Q}$ means at-most restrictions (qualified number restrictions), and $\mathcal{H}$ means role inclusions (role hierarchies). For instance, the DL $\mathcal{ALCHO}$ is the extension of $\mathcal{ALC}$ that also allows for nominals and role inclusions. The extension of $\mathcal{ALC}$ with transitivity axioms is denoted by $\mathcal{S}$. Hence, the DL allowing for all the concept constructors and types of axioms introduced here is called $\mathcal{SHOQ}$. The sub-Boolean DL $\mathcal{EL}$ is the fragment of $\mathcal{ALC}$ where only conjunction, existential restriction, and the top concept (which cannot be expressed as an abbreviation anymore due to the lack of negation) are admitted. We sometimes write $\mathcal{L}$-concept over N ($\mathcal{L}$-BKB over N, ...) for some DL $\mathcal{L}$ to make clear which DL is used.

The semantics of DLs are defined in a model-theoretic way.

Definition 2. *Let* N $= (N_C, N_R, N_I)$. *An* N-*interpretation is a pair* $\mathcal{I} = (\Delta^{\mathcal{I}}, \cdot^{\mathcal{I}})$, *where* $\Delta^{\mathcal{I}}$ *is a non-empty set (called* domain*), and* $\cdot^{\mathcal{I}}$ *is a mapping assigning a set* $A^{\mathcal{I}} \subseteq \Delta^{\mathcal{I}}$ *to every* $A \in N_C$, *a binary relation* $r^{\mathcal{I}} \subseteq \Delta^{\mathcal{I}} \times \Delta^{\mathcal{I}}$ *to every* $r \in N_R$, *and a domain element* $a^{\mathcal{I}} \in \Delta^{\mathcal{I}}$ *to every* $a \in N_I$. *The function* $\cdot^{\mathcal{I}}$ *is extended to concepts over* N *inductively as shown in the upper part of Table 1, where* $\sharp S$ *denotes the cardinality of the set* S.

Moreover, $\mathcal{I}$ *is a model of an axiom* α *over* N *if the condition in the lower part of Table 1 is satisfied, where* $\cdot^+$ *denotes the transitive closure of a binary relation. This is extended to Boolean axiom formulas over* N *in a straightforward way. We write* $\mathcal{I} \models \mathcal{B}$ *if* $\mathcal{I}$ *is a model of the Boolean axiom formula* $\mathcal{B}$ *over* N. *Furthermore,* $\mathcal{I}$ *is a model of an RBox* $\mathcal{R}$ *over* N *(written* $\mathcal{I} \models \mathcal{R}$*) if it is a model of each axiom in* $\mathcal{R}$.

Finally, $\mathcal{I}$ *is a model of the BKB* $\mathfrak{B} = (\mathcal{B}, \mathcal{R})$ *over* N *(written* $\mathcal{I} \models \mathfrak{B}$*) if it is a model of both* $\mathcal{B}$ *and* $\mathcal{R}$. *We call* $\mathfrak{B}$ consistent *if it has a model.*

We call $r \in N_R$ *transitive* (w.r.t. $\mathcal{R}$) if every model of $\mathcal{R}$ is a model of $\mathsf{trans}(r)$. Moreover, r is a *subrole* of $s \in N_R$ (w.r.t. $\mathcal{R}$) if every model of $\mathcal{R}$ is a model of $r \sqsubseteq s$. Finally, r is *simple w.r.t.* $\mathcal{R}$ if it has no transitive subrole. It is not hard to see that $r \in N_R$ is simple w.r.t. $\mathcal{R}$ iff $\mathsf{trans}(r) \notin \mathcal{R}$ and there do not exist roles $s_1, \ldots, s_k \in N_R$ such that $\{\mathsf{trans}(s_1), s_1 \sqsubseteq s_2, \ldots, s_{k-1} \sqsubseteq s_k, s_k \sqsubseteq r\} \subseteq \mathcal{R}$.[2]

Thus deciding whether $r \in N_R$ is simple can be decided in time polynomial in the size of $\mathcal{R}$. The problem of checking whether a given $\mathcal{SHQ}$-BKB $\mathfrak{B} = (\mathcal{B}, \mathcal{R})$ over N is consistent is undecidable in general [10]. One regains decidability with a syntactic restriction as follows: if $\leqslant_n r.C$ occurs in $\mathcal{B}$, then r must be simple w.r.t. $\mathcal{R}$. In the following, we make this restriction to the syntax of $\mathcal{SHQ}$ and all its extensions. This restriction is also the reason why there are no Boolean combinations of role inclusions and transitivity axioms allowed in the RBox $\mathcal{R}$ over N in the above definition. Otherwise the notion of a simple role would not make sense. For instance, it is not clear whether the role r should be considered simple in the Boolean combination of axioms $\mathsf{trans}(r) \vee r \sqsubseteq s$.

We are now ready to define the syntax of $\mathcal{L}_M[\![\mathcal{L}_O]\!]$. Throughout the paper, let O_C, O_R, and O_I be respectively sets of concept names, role names, and individual names for the object logic $\mathcal{L}_O$. Analogously, we define the sets M_C, M_R, and M_I for the meta logic $\mathcal{L}_M$. Without loss of generality, we assume that all those sets are pairwise disjoint. Moreover, let $O := (O_C, O_R, O_I)$ and $M := (M_C, M_R, M_I)$.

Definition 3. *A concept of the object logic* $\mathcal{L}_O$ *(o-concept) is an* $\mathcal{L}_O$-*concept over* O. *An* o-axiom *is an* $\mathcal{L}_O$-*GCI over* O, *an* $\mathcal{L}_O$-*concept assertion over* O, *or an* $\mathcal{L}_O$-*role assertion over* O. *The set of concepts of the meta logic* $\mathcal{L}_M$ *(m-concepts)*

---

[2] Note that this criterion of simple roles is enough since the considered DLs do not contain inverse roles.

is the smallest set such that (i) every $\mathcal{L}_M$-concept over M is an m-concept and (ii) $[\![\alpha]\!]$ is an m-concept if α is an o-axiom. The notion of an m-axiom is defined analogously. A Boolean m-axiom formula *is a Boolean combination of m-axioms.* Finally, a Boolean $\mathcal{L}_M[\![\mathcal{L}_O]\!]$-knowledge base ($\mathcal{L}_M[\![\mathcal{L}_O]\!]$-BKB) *is a triple* $\mathfrak{B} = (\mathcal{B}, \mathcal{R}_O, \mathcal{R}_M)$ *where* $\mathcal{R}_O$ *is an RBox over* O, $\mathcal{R}_M$ *an RBox over* M, *and* $\mathcal{B}$ *is a Boolean m-axiom formula.*

For the reasons above, role inclusions over O and transitivity axioms over O are not allowed to constitute m-concepts. However, we fix an RBox $\mathcal{R}_O$ over O that contains such o-axioms and holds in *all* contexts. The same applies to role inclusions over M and transitivity axioms over M, which are only allowed to occur in an RBox $\mathcal{R}_M$ over M.

The semantics of $\mathcal{L}_M[\![\mathcal{L}_O]\!]$ is defined by the notion of *nested interpretations*. These consist of O-interpretations for the specific contexts and an M-interpretation for the relational structure between them. We assume that all contexts speak about the same non-empty domain (*constant domain assumption*). As argued in the introduction, sometimes it is desired that concepts or roles in the object logic are interpreted the same in all contexts. Let $O_{\mathsf{Crig}} \subseteq O_{\mathsf{C}}$ denote the set of *rigid concepts*, and let $O_{\mathsf{Rrig}} \subseteq O_{\mathsf{R}}$ denote the set of *rigid roles*. We call concept names and role names in $O_{\mathsf{C}} \setminus O_{\mathsf{Crig}}$ and $O_{\mathsf{R}} \setminus O_{\mathsf{Rrig}}$ *flexible*. Moreover, we assume that individuals of the object logic are always interpreted the same in all contexts (*rigid individual assumption*).

Definition 4. *A* nested interpretation *is a tuple* $\mathcal{J} = (\mathbb{C}, \cdot^{\mathcal{J}}, \Delta, (\cdot^{\mathcal{I}_c})_{c \in \mathbb{C}})$, *where* $\mathbb{C}$ *is a non-empty set (called* contexts*) and* $(\mathbb{C}, \cdot^{\mathcal{J}})$ *is an* M*-interpretation.*

Moreover, for every $c \in \mathbb{C}$, $\mathcal{I}_c := (\Delta, \cdot^{\mathcal{I}_c})$ *is an* O*-interpretation such that we have for all* $c, c' \in \mathbb{C}$ *that* $x^{\mathcal{I}_c} = x^{\mathcal{I}_{c'}}$ *for every* $x \in O_{\mathsf{I}} \cup O_{\mathsf{Crig}} \cup O_{\mathsf{Rrig}}$.

We are now ready to define the semantics of $\mathcal{L}_M[\![\mathcal{L}_O]\!]$.

Definition 5. *Let* $\mathcal{J} = (\mathbb{C}, \cdot^{\mathcal{J}}, \Delta, (\cdot^{\mathcal{I}_c})_{c \in \mathbb{C}})$ *be a nested interpretation. The mapping* $\cdot^{\mathcal{J}}$ *is further extended to o-axioms as follows:* $[\![\alpha]\!]^{\mathcal{J}} := \{c \in \mathbb{C} \mid \mathcal{I}_c \models \alpha\}$.

Moreover, $\mathcal{J}$ *is a model of the m-axiom* β *if* $(\mathbb{C}, \cdot^{\mathcal{J}})$ *is a model of* β. *This is extended to Boolean m-axiom formulas in a straightforward way. We write* $\mathcal{J} \models \mathcal{B}$ *if* $\mathcal{J}$ *is a model of the Boolean m-axiom formula* $\mathcal{B}$. *Furthermore,* $\mathcal{J}$ *is a model of* $\mathcal{R}_M$ (*written* $\mathcal{J} \models \mathcal{R}_M$) *if* $(\mathbb{C}, \cdot^{\mathcal{J}})$ *is a model of* $\mathcal{R}_M$, *and* $\mathcal{J}$ *is a model of* $\mathcal{R}_O$ (*written* $\mathcal{J} \models \mathcal{R}_O$) *if* $\mathcal{I}_c$ *is a model of* $\mathcal{R}_O$ *for all* $c \in \mathbb{C}$.

Also, $\mathcal{J}$ *is a model of the* $\mathcal{L}_M[\![\mathcal{L}_O]\!]$-BKB $\mathfrak{B} = (\mathcal{B}, \mathcal{R}_O, \mathcal{R}_M)$ (*written* $\mathcal{J} \models \mathfrak{B}$) *if* $\mathcal{J}$ *is a model of* $\mathcal{B}$, $\mathcal{R}_O$, *and* $\mathcal{R}_M$. *We call* $\mathfrak{B}$ consistent *if it has a model.*

The consistency problem *in* $\mathcal{L}_M[\![\mathcal{L}_O]\!]$ *is the problem of deciding whether a given* $\mathcal{L}_M[\![\mathcal{L}_O]\!]$-BKB *is consistent.*

Note that besides the consistency problem there are several other reasoning tasks for $\mathcal{L}_M[\![\mathcal{L}_O]\!]$. The entailment problem, for instance, is the problem of deciding, given a BKB $\mathfrak{B}$ and an m-axiom β, whether $\mathfrak{B}$ *entails* β, i.e. whether all models of $\mathfrak{B}$ are also models of β. The consistency problem, however, is fundamental in the sense that most other standard decision problems (reasoning

Table 2. Complexity results for consistency in $\mathcal{L}_M[\![\mathcal{L}_O]\!]$

$\mathcal{L}_M$ \ $\mathcal{L}_O$	no rigid names		only rigid concepts		rigid roles	
	$\mathcal{EL}$	$\mathcal{ALC}$ – $\mathcal{SHOQ}$	$\mathcal{EL}$	$\mathcal{ALC}$ – $\mathcal{SHOQ}$	$\mathcal{EL}$	$\mathcal{ALC}$ – $\mathcal{SHOQ}$
$\mathcal{EL}$	const.	Exp	const.	NExp	const.	2Exp
$\mathcal{ALC}$ – $\mathcal{SHOQ}$	Exp	Exp	NExp	NExp	NExp	2Exp

tasks) can be polynomially reduced to it (in the presence of negation). For the entailment problem, note that it can be reduced to the *in*consistency problem: $\mathfrak{B} = (\mathcal{B}, \mathcal{R}_O, \mathcal{R}_M)$ entails β iff $(\mathcal{B} \wedge \neg\beta, \mathcal{R}_O, \mathcal{R}_M)$ is inconsistent. Hence, we focus in the present paper only on the consistency problem.

3   Complexity of the Consistency Problem

Our results for the computational complexity of the consistency problem in $\mathcal{L}_M[\![\mathcal{L}_O]\!]$ are listed in Table 2. In this section, we focus on the cases where $\mathcal{L}_M$ and $\mathcal{L}_O$ are DLs between $\mathcal{ALC}$ and $\mathcal{SHOQ}$. In Section 4, we treat the cases where $\mathcal{L}_M$ or $\mathcal{L}_O$ are $\mathcal{EL}$.

Since the lower bounds of context DLs treated in this section already hold for the fragment $\mathcal{EL}[\![\mathcal{ALC}]\!]$, they are shown in Section 4. For the upper bounds, let in the following $\mathfrak{B} = (\mathcal{B}, \mathcal{R}_O, \mathcal{R}_M)$ be a $\mathcal{SHOQ}[\![\mathcal{SHOQ}]\!]$-BKB. We proceed similar to what was done for the temporalized DL $\mathcal{ALC}$-LTL in [3,4] (and $\mathcal{SHOQ}$-LTL in [14]) and reduce the consistency problem to two separate decision problems. For the first problem, we consider the *outer abstraction*, which is the $\mathcal{SHOQ}$-BKB over M obtained by replacing each m-concept of the form $[\![\alpha]\!]$ occurring in $\mathcal{B}$ by a fresh concept name such that there is a 1–1 relationship between them.

Definition 6. *Let $\mathfrak{B} = (\mathcal{B}, \mathcal{R}_O, \mathcal{R}_M)$ be a $\mathcal{L}_M[\![\mathcal{L}_O]\!]$-BKB. Let b be the bijection mapping every m-concept of the form $[\![\alpha]\!]$ occurring in $\mathcal{B}$ to the concept name $A_{[\![\alpha]\!]} \in \mathsf{M}_C$, where we assume w.l.o.g. that $A_{[\![\alpha]\!]}$ does not occur in $\mathcal{B}$.*

1. *The Boolean $\mathcal{L}_M$-axiom formula $\mathcal{B}^b$ over M is obtained from $\mathcal{B}$ by replacing every occurrence of an m-concept of the form $[\![\alpha]\!]$ by $b([\![\alpha]\!])$. We call the $\mathcal{L}_M$-BKB $\mathfrak{B}^b = (\mathcal{B}^b, \mathcal{R}_M)$ the outer abstraction of $\mathfrak{B}$.*
2. *Given $\mathcal{J} = (\mathbb{C}, \cdot^{\mathcal{J}}, \Delta, (\cdot^{\mathcal{I}_c})_{c \in \mathbb{C}})$, its outer abstraction is the M-interpretation $\mathcal{J}^b = (\mathbb{C}, \cdot^{\mathcal{J}^b})$ where*
   - *for every $x \in \mathsf{M}_R \cup \mathsf{M}_I \cup (\mathsf{M}_C \setminus \mathsf{Im}(b))$, we have $x^{\mathcal{J}^b} = x^{\mathcal{J}}$, where $\mathsf{Im}(b)$ denotes the image of b, and*
   - *for every $A \in \mathsf{Im}(b)$, we have $A^{\mathcal{J}^b} = (b^{-1}(A))^{\mathcal{J}}$.*

For simplicity, for $\mathfrak{B}' = (\mathcal{B}', \mathcal{R}_O, \mathcal{R}_M)$ where $\mathcal{B}'$ is a subformula of $\mathcal{B}$, we denote by $(\mathfrak{B}')^b$ the outer abstraction of $\mathfrak{B}'$ that is obtained by restricting b to the m-concepts occurring in $\mathcal{B}'$.

Example 7. Let $\mathfrak{B}_{\text{ex}} = (\mathcal{B}_{\text{ex}}, \varnothing, \varnothing)$ with $\mathcal{B}_{\text{ex}} := C \sqsubseteq (\llbracket A \sqsubseteq \bot \rrbracket) \wedge (C \sqcap \llbracket A(a) \rrbracket)(c)$ be a $\mathcal{SHOQ}[\mathcal{SHOQ}]$-BKB. Then, b maps $\llbracket A \sqsubseteq \bot \rrbracket$ to $A_{\llbracket A \sqsubseteq \bot \rrbracket}$ and $\llbracket A(a) \rrbracket$ to $A_{\llbracket A(a) \rrbracket}$. Thus, the outer abstraction of $\mathfrak{B}_{\text{ex}}$ is

$$\mathfrak{B}_{\text{ex}}^{\text{b}} := \Big(C \sqsubseteq (A_{\llbracket A \sqsubseteq \bot \rrbracket}) \wedge (C \sqcap A_{\llbracket A(a) \rrbracket})(c), \ \varnothing \Big).$$

The following lemma makes the relationship between $\mathfrak{B}$ and its outer abstraction $\mathfrak{B}^{\text{b}}$ explicit. It is proved by induction on the structure of $\mathcal{B}$.

Lemma 8. *Let $\mathcal{J}$ be a nested interpretation such that $\mathcal{J}$ is a model of $\mathcal{R}_O$. Then, $\mathcal{J}$ is a model of $\mathfrak{B}$ iff $\mathcal{J}^{\text{b}}$ is a model of $\mathfrak{B}^{\text{b}}$.* $\qquad\square$

Note that this lemma yields that consistency of $\mathfrak{B}$ implies consistency of $\mathfrak{B}^{\text{b}}$. However, the converse does not hold as the following example shows.

Example 9. Consider again $\mathfrak{B}_{\text{ex}}$ of Example 7. Take any M-interpretation $\mathcal{H} = (\Gamma, \cdot^{\mathcal{H}})$ with $\Gamma = \{e\}$, $d^{\mathcal{H}} = e$, and $C^{\mathcal{H}} = A_{\llbracket A \sqsubseteq \bot \rrbracket}^{\mathcal{H}} = A_{\llbracket A(a) \rrbracket}^{\mathcal{H}} = \{e\}$.

Clearly, $\mathcal{H}$ is a model of $\mathfrak{B}_{\text{ex}}^{\text{b}}$, but there is no $\mathcal{J} = (\mathbb{C}, \cdot^{\mathcal{J}}, \Delta, (\cdot^{\mathcal{I}_c})_{c \in \mathbb{C}})$ with $\mathcal{J} \models \mathfrak{B}_{\text{ex}}$ since this would imply $\mathbb{C} = \Gamma$, and that $\mathcal{I}_e$ is a model of both $A \sqsubseteq \bot$ and $A(a)$, which is not possible.

Therefore, we need to ensure that the concept names in $\text{Im}(\text{b})$ are not treated independently. For expressing such a restriction on the model $\mathcal{I}$ of $\mathfrak{B}^{\text{b}}$, we adapt a notion of [3,4]. It is worth noting that this problem occurs also in much less expressive DLs as $\mathcal{ALC}$ or $\mathcal{EL}^{\bot}$ (i.e. $\mathcal{EL}$ extended with the bottom concept).

Definition 10. *Let $\mathcal{U} \subseteq \mathsf{N_C}$ and $\mathcal{Y} \subseteq \mathcal{P}(\mathcal{U})$. The N-interpretation $\mathcal{I} = (\Delta^{\mathcal{I}}, \cdot^{\mathcal{I}})$ weakly respects $(\mathcal{U}, \mathcal{Y})$ if $\mathcal{Y} \supseteq \mathcal{Z}$ where*

$$\mathcal{Z} := \{Y \subseteq \mathcal{U} \mid \text{there is some } d \in \Delta^{\mathcal{I}} \text{ with } d \in (C_{\mathcal{U},Y})^{\mathcal{I}}\}$$

and $C_{\mathcal{U},Y} := \bigsqcap_{A \in Y} A \sqcap \bigsqcap_{A \in \mathcal{U} \setminus Y} \neg A$. It respects $(\mathcal{U}, \mathcal{Y})$ if $\mathcal{Y} = \mathcal{Z}$.

The second decision problem that we use for deciding consistency is needed to make sure that such a set of concept names is admissible in the following sense.

Definition 11. *Let $\mathcal{X} = \{X_1, \ldots, X_k\} \subseteq \mathcal{P}(\text{Im}(\text{b}))$. We call $\mathcal{X}$ admissible if there exist O-interpretations $\mathcal{I}_1 = (\Delta, \cdot^{\mathcal{I}_1}), \ldots, \mathcal{I}_k = (\Delta, \cdot^{\mathcal{I}_k})$ such that*

- $x^{\mathcal{I}_i} = x^{\mathcal{I}_j}$ *for all $x \in \mathsf{O_I} \cup \mathsf{O_{Crig}} \cup \mathsf{O_{Rrig}}$ and all $i, j \in \{1, \ldots, k\}$, and*
- *every $\mathcal{I}_i$, $1 \leq i \leq k$, is a model of the $\mathcal{L}_O$-BKB $\mathfrak{B}_{X_i} = (\mathcal{B}_{X_i}, \mathcal{R}_O)$ over O where*

$$\mathcal{B}_{X_i} := \bigwedge_{\text{b}(\llbracket \alpha \rrbracket) \in X_i} \alpha \ \wedge \bigwedge_{\text{b}(\llbracket \alpha \rrbracket) \in \text{Im}(\text{b}) \setminus X_i} \neg\alpha.$$

Note that any subset $\mathcal{X}' \subseteq \mathcal{X}$ is admissible if $\mathcal{X}$ is admissible. Intuitively, the sets X_i in an admissible set $\mathcal{X}$ consist of concept names such that the corresponding o-axioms "fit together". Consider again Example 9. Clearly, the set $\{A_{\llbracket A \sqsubseteq \bot \rrbracket}, A_{\llbracket A(a) \rrbracket}\} \in \mathcal{P}(\text{Im}(\text{b}))$ *cannot* be contained in any admissible set $\mathcal{X}$.

Definition 12. *Let $\mathcal{X} \subseteq \mathcal{P}(\mathsf{Im}(\mathsf{b}))$. We call the $\mathcal{L}_M$-BKB $\mathfrak{B}^\mathsf{b}$ over M outer consistent with $\mathcal{X}$ if there exists a model of $\mathfrak{B}^\mathsf{b}$ that weakly respects $(\mathsf{Im}(\mathsf{b}), \mathcal{X})$.*

The next two lemmas show that the consistency problem in $\mathcal{L}_M[\mathcal{L}_O]$ can be decided by checking whether there is an admissible set $\mathcal{X}$ and the outer abstraction of the given $\mathcal{L}_M[\mathcal{L}_O]$-BKB is outer consistent with $\mathcal{X}$.

Lemma 13. *For every M-interpretation $\mathcal{H} = (\Gamma, \cdot^\mathcal{H})$, the following two statements are equivalent:*

1. *There exists a model $\mathcal{J}$ of $\mathfrak{B}$ with $\mathcal{J}^\mathsf{b} = \mathcal{H}$.*
2. *$\mathcal{H}$ is a model of $\mathfrak{B}^\mathsf{b}$ and the set $\{X_d \mid d \in \Gamma\}$ is admissible, where $X_d := \{A \in \mathsf{Im}(\mathsf{b}) \mid d \in A^\mathcal{H}\}$.* □

The following lemma is a simple consequence, where we exploit that outer consistency means that there exists a model that *weakly* respects $(\mathsf{Im}(\mathsf{b}), \mathcal{X})$.

Lemma 14. *The $\mathcal{L}_M[\mathcal{L}_O]$-BKB $\mathfrak{B}$ is consistent iff there is a set $\mathcal{X} \subseteq \mathcal{P}(\mathsf{Im}(\mathsf{b}))$ such that*

1. *$\mathcal{X}$ is admissible, and*
2. *$\mathfrak{B}^\mathsf{b}$ is outer consistent with $\mathcal{X}$.* □

To obtain a decision procedure for $\mathcal{SHOQ}[\mathcal{SHOQ}]$ consistency, we have to non-deterministically guess or construct the set $\mathcal{X}$, and then check the two conditions of Lemma 14. Beforehand, we focus on how to decide the second condition. For that, assume that a set $\mathcal{X} \subseteq \mathcal{P}(\mathsf{Im}(\mathsf{b}))$ is given.

Lemma 15. *Deciding whether $\mathfrak{B}^\mathsf{b}$ is outer consistent with $\mathcal{X}$ can be done in time exponential in the size of $\mathfrak{B}^\mathsf{b}$ and linear in size of $\mathcal{X}$.*

Proof. It is enough to show that deciding whether $\mathfrak{B}^\mathsf{b}$ has a model that weakly respects $(\mathsf{Im}(\mathsf{b}), \mathcal{X})$ can be done in time exponential in the size of $\mathfrak{B}^\mathsf{b}$ and linear in the size of $\mathcal{X}$. It is not hard to see that we can adapt the notion of a quasimodel respecting a pair $(\mathcal{U}, \mathcal{Y})$ of [14] to a quasimodel *weakly* respecting $(\mathcal{U}, \mathcal{Y})$. Indeed, one just has to drop Condition (i) in Definition 3.25 of [14]. Then, the proof of Lemma 3.26 there can be adapted such that our claim follows. This is done by dropping one check in Step 4 of the algorithm of [14]. □

Using this lemma, we provide decision procedures for $\mathcal{SHOQ}[\mathcal{SHOQ}]$ consistency. However, these depend also on the first condition of Lemma 14. We take care of this differently depending on which names are allowed to be rigid.

Consistency in $\mathcal{SHOQ}[\mathcal{SHOQ}]$ Without Rigid Names

In this section, we consider the case where no rigid concept names or role names are allowed. So we fix $O_{\mathsf{Crig}} = O_{\mathsf{Rrig}} = \varnothing$. The following theorem is a straightforward consequence of Lemmas 14 and 15. Its proof can be found in [9].

Theorem 16. *If* $O_{Crig} = O_{Rrig} = \varnothing$, *the consistency problem in* $\mathcal{SHOQ}[\mathcal{SHOQ}]$
is in EXP. □

Together with the lower bounds shown in Section 4, we obtain EXP-completeness
for the consistency problem in $\mathcal{L}_M[\mathcal{L}_O]$ for $\mathcal{L}_M$ and $\mathcal{L}_O$ being DLs between $\mathcal{ALC}$
and $\mathcal{SHOQ}$ if $O_{Crig} = O_{Rrig} = \varnothing$.

Consistency in $\mathcal{SHOQ}[\mathcal{SHOQ}]$ with Rigid Concept and Role Names

In this section, we consider the case where rigid concept and role names are
present. So we fix $O_{Crig} \neq \varnothing$ and $O_{Rrig} \neq \varnothing$.

Theorem 17. *If we have* $O_{Crig} \neq \varnothing$ *and* $O_{Rrig} \neq \varnothing$, *the consistency problem in*
$\mathcal{SHOQ}[\mathcal{SHOQ}]$ *is in* 2EXP.

Proof. Let $\mathfrak{B} = (\mathcal{B}, \mathcal{R}_O, \mathcal{R}_M)$ be a $\mathcal{SHOQ}[\mathcal{SHOQ}]$-BKB and $\mathfrak{B}^b = (\mathcal{B}^b, \mathcal{R}_M)$
its outer abstraction. We can decide consistency of $\mathfrak{B}$ using Lemma 14. For
that, we enumerate all sets $\mathcal{X} \subseteq \mathcal{P}(\mathsf{lm}(b))$, which can be done in time doubly
exponential in $\mathfrak{B}$. For each of these sets $\mathcal{X} = \{X_1, \dots, X_k\}$, we check whether
$\mathfrak{B}^b$ is outer consistent with $\mathcal{X}$, which can be done in time exponential in the
size of $\mathfrak{B}^b$ and linear in the size of $\mathcal{X}$. Then, we check $\mathcal{X}$ for admissibility using
the renaming technique of [3,4]. For every i, $1 \leq i \leq k$, every flexible concept
name A occurring in $\mathcal{B}^b$, and every flexible role name r occurring in $\mathcal{B}^b$ or $\mathcal{R}_O$, we
introduce copies $A^{(i)}$ and $r^{(i)}$. The $\mathcal{SHOQ}$-BKB $\mathfrak{B}^{(i)}_{X_i} = (\mathcal{B}^{(i)}_{X_i}, \mathcal{R}_O^{(i)})$ over O is
obtained from $\mathfrak{B}_{X_i}$ (see Definition 11) by replacing every occurrence of a flexible
name x by $x^{(i)}$. We define

$$\mathfrak{B}_{\mathcal{X}} := \left(\bigwedge_{1 \leq i \leq k} \mathcal{B}^{(i)}_{X_i}, \bigcup_{1 \leq i \leq k} \mathcal{R}_O^{(i)} \right).$$

It is not hard to verify (using arguments of [14]) that $\mathcal{X}$ is admissible iff $\mathfrak{B}_{\mathcal{X}}$
is consistent. Note that $\mathfrak{B}_{\mathcal{X}}$ is of size at most exponential in $\mathfrak{B}$ and can be
constructed in exponential time. Moreover, consistency of $\mathfrak{B}_{\mathcal{X}}$ can be decided in
time exponential in the size of $\mathfrak{B}_{\mathcal{X}}$ [14], and thus in time doubly exponential in
the size of $\mathfrak{B}$. □

Together with the lower bounds shown in Section 4, 2EXP-completeness is ob-
tained for the consistency problem in $\mathcal{L}_M[\mathcal{L}_O]$ for $\mathcal{L}_M$ and $\mathcal{L}_O$ being DLs between
$\mathcal{ALC}$ and $\mathcal{SHOQ}$ if $O_{Crig} \neq \varnothing$ and $O_{Rrig} \neq \varnothing$.

Consistency in $\mathcal{SHOQ}[\mathcal{SHOQ}]$ with Only Rigid Concept Names

In this section, we consider the case where rigid concept are present, but rigid
role names are not allowed. So we fix $O_{Crig} \neq \varnothing$ but $O_{Rrig} = \varnothing$.

Theorem 18. *If we have* $O_{Crig} \neq \varnothing$ *and* $O_{Rrig} = \varnothing$, *the consistency problem in*
$\mathcal{SHOQ}[\mathcal{SHOQ}]$ *is in* NEXP.

Proof. Let $\mathfrak{B} = (\mathcal{B}, \mathcal{R}_O, \mathcal{R}_M)$ be a $\mathcal{SHOQ}[\mathcal{SHOQ}]$-BKB and $\mathfrak{B}^b = (\mathcal{B}^b, \mathcal{R}_M)$ its outer abstraction. We can decide consistency of $\mathfrak{B}$ using Lemma 14. We first non-deterministically guess the set $\mathcal{X} = \{X_1, \dots, X_k\} \subseteq \mathcal{P}(\mathsf{Im}(b))$, which is of size at most exponential in $\mathfrak{B}$. Due to Lemma 15 we can check whether $\mathfrak{B}^b$ is outer consistent with $\mathcal{X}$ in time exponential in the size of $\mathfrak{B}^b$ and linear in the size of $\mathcal{X}$. It remains to check $\mathcal{X}$ for admissibility. For that let $O_{\mathsf{Crig}}(\mathcal{B}) \subseteq O_{\mathsf{Crig}}$ and $O_I(\mathcal{B}) \subseteq O_I$ be the sets of all rigid concept names and individual names occurring in $\mathcal{B}$, respectively. As done in [3,4] we non-deterministically guess a set $\mathcal{Y} \subseteq \mathcal{P}(O_{\mathsf{Crig}}(\mathcal{B}))$ and a mapping $\kappa \colon O_I(\mathcal{B}) \to \mathcal{Y}$ which also can be done in time exponential in the size of $\mathfrak{B}$. Using the same arguments as in [3,4] we can show that $\mathcal{X}$ is admissible iff

$$\widehat{\mathfrak{B}}_{X_i} := \left(\mathcal{B}_{X_i} \wedge \bigwedge_{a \in O_I(\mathcal{B})} \left(\bigsqcap_{A \in \kappa(a)} A \sqcap \bigsqcap_{A \in O_{\mathsf{Crig}}(\mathcal{B}) \setminus \kappa(a)} \neg A \right)(a), \mathcal{R}_O \right)$$

has a model that respects $(O_{\mathsf{Crig}}(\mathcal{B}), \mathcal{Y})$, for all $1 \leq i \leq k$. The $\mathcal{SHOQ}$-BKB $\widehat{\mathfrak{B}}_{X_i}$ is of size polynomial in the size of $\mathcal{B}$ and can be constructed in exponential time. We can check whether $\widehat{\mathfrak{B}}_{X_i}$ has a model that respects $(O_{\mathsf{Crig}}(\mathcal{B}), \mathcal{Y})$ in time exponential in the size of $\widehat{\mathfrak{B}}_{X_i}$ [3,4], and thus exponential in the size of $\mathfrak{B}$. □

Together with the lower bounds shown in Section 4, NExp-completeness is obtained for the consistency problem in $\mathcal{L}_M[\mathcal{L}_O]$ for $\mathcal{L}_M$ and $\mathcal{L}_O$ being DLs between $\mathcal{ALC}$ and $\mathcal{SHOQ}$ if $O_{\mathsf{Crig}} \neq \varnothing$ and $O_{\mathsf{Rrig}} = \varnothing$.

Summing up the results, we obtain the following corollary.

Corollary 19. *For all $\mathcal{L}_M$, $\mathcal{L}_O$ between $\mathcal{ALC}$ and $\mathcal{SHOQ}$, the consistency problem in $\mathcal{L}_M[\mathcal{L}_O]$ is*

- ExP-*complete if* $O_{\mathsf{Crig}} = \varnothing$ *and* $O_{\mathsf{Rrig}} = \varnothing$,
- NExp-*complete if* $O_{\mathsf{Crig}} \neq \varnothing$ *and* $O_{\mathsf{Rrig}} = \varnothing$, *and*
- 2Exp-*complete if* $O_{\mathsf{Crig}} \neq \varnothing$ *and* $O_{\mathsf{Rrig}} \neq \varnothing$. □

4   The Case of $\mathcal{EL}$: $\mathcal{L}_M[\mathcal{EL}]$ and $\mathcal{EL}[\mathcal{L}_O]$

In this section, we give some complexity results for context DLs $\mathcal{L}_M[\mathcal{L}_O]$ where $\mathcal{L}_M$ or $\mathcal{L}_O$ are $\mathcal{EL}$. We start with the case of $\mathcal{L}_M[\mathcal{EL}]$.

Theorem 20. *For all $\mathcal{L}_M$ between $\mathcal{ALC}$ and $\mathcal{SHOQ}$, the consistency problem in $\mathcal{L}_M[\mathcal{EL}]$ is* ExP-*complete if* $O_{\mathsf{Crig}} = \varnothing$ *and* $O_{\mathsf{Rrig}} = \varnothing$, *and* NExp-*complete otherwise.*

Proof sketch. The lower bound of ExP follows immediately from satisfiability in $\mathcal{ALC}$ [17]. For the case of rigid concept names, NExp-hardness is obtained by a careful reduction of the satisfiability problem in the temporalized DL $\mathcal{EL}$-LTL [8] (in the presence of rigid concept names). We exploit the fact that the lower bound for satisfiability in $\mathcal{EL}$-LTL holds already for a syntactically restricted fragment, i.e. $\mathcal{EL}$-LTL-formulas of the form $\Box\phi$ where ϕ is an $\mathcal{EL}$-LTL-formula that contains only X as temporal operator [7]. We obtain now an m-concept C_ϕ from ϕ by replacing $\mathcal{EL}$-axioms α by $[\![\alpha]\!]$, $\wedge$ by $\sqcap$, and subformulas of the form $X\psi$ by $\forall r.\psi \sqcap \exists r.\psi$ (with $r \in \mathsf{M_R}$ being arbitrary but fixed). It is not hard to verify that $\Box\phi$ is satisfiable iff $\top \sqsubseteq C_\phi \sqcap \exists r.\top$ is consistent.

The upper bounds of Exp in the case $\mathsf{O_{Crig}} = \mathsf{O_{Rrig}} = \varnothing$ follow immediately from Theorem 16. Next, we prove the upper bounds of NExp in the case of rigid names. We again use Lemma 14. First, we non-deterministically guess a set $\mathcal{X} \subseteq \mathcal{P}(\mathsf{Im}(\mathsf{b}))$ and construct the $\mathcal{EL}$-BKB $\mathcal{B}_\mathcal{X}$ over O as in the proof of Theorem 17, which is actually a conjunction of $\mathcal{EL}$-literals over O, i.e. of (negated) $\mathcal{EL}$-axioms over O. Consistency of $\mathcal{B}_\mathcal{X}$ can be reduced to consistency of a conjunction of $\mathcal{ELO}^\perp$-axioms over O, where $\mathcal{ELO}^\perp$ extends of $\mathcal{EL}$ with nominals and the bottom concept (see [9] for details). Since consistency of conjunctions of $\mathcal{ELO}^\perp$-axioms can be decided in polynomial time [1], we obtain our claimed upper bounds. $\quad\Box$

Next, we examine $\mathcal{EL}[\![\mathcal{L}_O]\!]$ where $\mathcal{L}_O$ is either $\mathcal{EL}$ or between $\mathcal{ALC}$ and $\mathcal{SHOQ}$. Instead of considering $\mathcal{EL}[\![\mathcal{L}_O]\!]$-BKBs, we allow only *conjunctions* of m-axioms. From a theoretical point of view, this restriction is interesting, as $\mathcal{EL}$ does not allow the constructors disjunction and negation to build concepts. Then, however, the consistency problem becomes trivial in the case of $\mathcal{EL}[\![\mathcal{EL}]\!]$ since all $\mathcal{EL}[\![\mathcal{EL}]\!]$-BKBs are consistent, as $\mathcal{EL}$ lacks any means of expressing contradictions. This restriction, however, does not yield a better complexity in the cases of $\mathcal{EL}[\![\mathcal{L}_O]\!]$, where $\mathcal{L}_O$ is between $\mathcal{ALC}$ and $\mathcal{SHOQ}$. For those context DLs, the complexity of the consistency problem turns out to be as hard as for $\mathcal{ALC}[\![\mathcal{L}_O]\!]$.

We show the lower bounds for the consistency problem in $\mathcal{EL}[\![\mathcal{ALC}]\!]$. We again distinguish the three cases of which names are allowed to be rigid. The next theorem is again a consequence of the complexity of the satisfiability problem in $\mathcal{ALC}$ [17].

Theorem 21. *If* $\mathsf{O_{Crig}} = \mathsf{O_{Rrig}} = \varnothing$, *the consistency problem in* $\mathcal{EL}[\![\mathcal{ALC}]\!]$ *is* Exp-*hard.* $\quad\Box$

For the case of rigid roles, we have lower bounds of 2Exp. The intuitive reason is that there is a limited interaction between the different contexts by means of rigid roles that allow to propagate information. In particular, even if $\mathcal{EL}$ is the outer logic, we can enforce that there are exponentially many different contexts by using object concept names serving as binary counter in the inner logic $\mathcal{ALC}$.

Theorem 22. *If* $\mathsf{O_{Crig}} \neq \varnothing$ *and* $\mathsf{O_{Rrig}} \neq \varnothing$, *the consistency problem in* $\mathcal{EL}[\![\mathcal{ALC}]\!]$ *is* 2Exp-*hard.*

Proof. To show the lower bound formally, we adapt the proof ideas of [3,4], and reduce the word problem for exponentially space-bounded alternating Turing machines (i.e. is a given word w accepted by the machine M) to the consistency problem in $\mathcal{EL}[\![\mathcal{ALC}]\!]$ with rigid roles, i.e. $\mathsf{O_{Rrig}} \neq \varnothing$. In [3,4], a reduction was provided to show 2Exp-hardness for the temporalized DL $\mathcal{ALC}$-LTL in the presence of rigid roles. Here, we mimic the properties of the time dimension that are important for the reduction using a role name $t \in \mathsf{M_R}$.

Our $\mathcal{EL}[\mathcal{ALC}]$-BKB is the conjunction of the $\mathcal{EL}[\mathcal{ALC}]$-BKBs introduced below. First, we ensure that we never have a "last" time point:

$$\top \sqsubseteq \exists t.\top$$

The $\mathcal{ALC}$-LTL-formula obtained in the reduction of [3,4] is a conjunction of $\mathcal{ALC}$-LTL-formulas of the form $\Box\phi$, where ϕ is an $\mathcal{ALC}$-LTL-formula. This makes sure that ϕ holds in all (temporal) worlds. For the cases where ϕ is an $\mathcal{ALC}$-axiom, we can simply express this by:

$$\top \sqsubseteq [\![\phi]\!]$$

This captures all except for two conjuncts of the $\mathcal{ALC}$-LTL-formula of the reduction of [3,4]. There, a k-bit binary counter using concept names $A'_0, \ldots, A'_{k-1}$ was attached to the individual name a, which is incremented along the temporal dimension. We can express something similar in $\mathcal{EL}[\mathcal{ALC}]$, but instead of incrementing the counter values along a sequence of t-successors, we have to go backwards since $\mathcal{EL}$ does allow for branching but does not allow for value restrictions, i.e. we cannot make sure that all t-successors behave the same. More precisely, if the counter value n is attached to a in context c, the value $n + 1$ (modulo 2^k) must be attached to a in all of c's t-predecessors.

First, we ensure which bits must be flipped:

$$\bigwedge_{i<k} \Big(\exists t.([\![A'_0(a)]\!] \sqcap \ldots \sqcap [\![A'_{i-1}(a)]\!] \sqcap [\![A'_i(a)]\!]) \sqsubseteq [\![(\neg A'_i)(a)]\!] \Big)$$

$$\bigwedge_{i<k} \Big(\exists t.([\![A'_0(a)]\!] \sqcap \ldots \sqcap [\![A'_{i-1}(a)]\!] \sqcap [\![(\neg A'_i)(a)]\!]) \sqsubseteq [\![A'_i(a)]\!] \Big)$$

Next, we ensure that all other bits stay the same:

$$\bigwedge_{0<i<k} \bigwedge_{j<i} \Big(\exists t.([\![(\neg A'_j)(a)]\!] \sqcap [\![A'_i(a)]\!]) \sqsubseteq [\![A'_i(a)]\!] \Big)$$

$$\bigwedge_{0<i<k} \bigwedge_{j<i} \Big(\exists t.([\![(\neg A'_j)(a)]\!] \sqcap [\![(\neg A'_i)(a)]\!]) \sqsubseteq [\![(\neg A'_i)(a)]\!] \Big)$$

Note that due to the first m-axiom above, we enforce every context to have a t-successor. By the other m-axioms, we make sure that we enforce a t-chain of length 2^k. As in [3,4], it is not necessary to initialize the counter. Since we decrement the counter along the t-chain (modulo 2^k), every value between 0 and $2^k - 1$ is reached.

The conjunction of all the $\mathcal{EL}[\mathcal{ALC}]$-BKBs above yields an $\mathcal{EL}[\mathcal{ALC}]$-BKB $\mathcal{B}$ that is consistent iff w is accepted by M. $\Box$

Using similar ideas as in the proof of Theorem 22, we obtain NExp-hardness in the case where only rigid concept names are admitted.

Theorem 23. *If $O_{\mathsf{Crig}} \neq \varnothing$ and $O_{\mathsf{Rrig}} = \varnothing$, the consistency problem in $\mathcal{EL}[\mathcal{ALC}]$ is NExp-hard.*

Proof. To show the lower bound, we again adapt the proof ideas of [3,4], and reduce an exponentially bounded version of the domino problem to the consistency problem in $\mathcal{EL}[\mathcal{ALC}]$ with rigid concepts, i.e. $O_{Crig} \neq \varnothing$ and $O_{Rrig} = \varnothing$. In [3,4], a reduction was provided to show NExp-hardness of $\mathcal{ALC}$-LTL in the presence of rigid concepts. As in the proof of Theorem 22, we mimic the properties of the time dimension that are important for the reduction using a role name $t \in M_R$.

Our $\mathcal{EL}[\mathcal{ALC}]$-BKB is the conjunction of the $\mathcal{EL}[\mathcal{ALC}]$-BKBs introduced below. We proceed in a similar way as in the proof of Theorem 22. First, we ensure that we never have a "last" time point:

$$\top \sqsubseteq \exists t.\top$$

Next, note that since $\square$ distributes over conjunction, most of the conjuncts of the $\mathcal{ALC}$-LTL-formula of the reduction of [3,4] can be rewritten as conjunctions of $\mathcal{ALC}$-LTL-formulas of the form $\square\alpha$, where α is an $\mathcal{ALC}$-axiom. As argued in the proof of Theorem 22, this can equivalently be expressed by $\top \sqsubseteq [\![\alpha]\!]$.

In [3,4], a $(2n + 2)$-bit binary counter is employed using concept names $Z_0, \ldots, Z_{2n+1}$. This counter is attached to an individual name a, which is incremented along the temporal dimension. This can be expressed in $\mathcal{EL}[\mathcal{ALC}]$ as shown in the proof of Theorem 22:

$$\bigwedge_{i<2n+2} \Big(\exists t.([\![Z_0(a)]\!] \sqcap \ldots \sqcap [\![Z_{i-1}(a)]\!] \sqcap [\![Z_i(a)]\!]) \sqsubseteq [\![(\neg Z_i)(a)]\!] \Big)$$

$$\bigwedge_{i<2n+2} \Big(\exists t.([\![Z_0(a)]\!] \sqcap \ldots \sqcap [\![Z_{i-1}(a)]\!] \sqcap [\![(\neg Z_i)(a)]\!]) \sqsubseteq [\![Z_i(a)]\!] \Big)$$

$$\bigwedge_{0<i<2n+2} \bigwedge_{j<i} \Big(\exists t.([\![(\neg Z_j)(a)]\!] \sqcap [\![Z_i(a)]\!]) \sqsubseteq [\![Z_i(a)]\!] \Big)$$

$$\bigwedge_{0<i<2n+2} \bigwedge_{j<i} \Big(\exists t.([\![(\neg Z_j)(a)]\!] \sqcap [\![(\neg Z_i)(a)]\!]) \sqsubseteq [\![(\neg Z_i)(a)]\!] \Big)$$

Note that due to the first m-axiom above, we enforce that every context has a t-successor. By the other m-axioms, we make sure that we enforce a t-chain of length 2^{2n+2}. As in [3,4], it is not necessary to initialize the counter. Since we decrement the counter along the t-chain (modulo 2^{2n+2}), every value between 0 and $2^{2n+2} - 1$ is reached.

In [3,4], an $\mathcal{ALC}$-LTL-formula is used to express that the value of the counter in shared by all domain elements belonging to the current (temporal) world. This is expressed using a disjunction, which we can simulate as follows:

$$\bigwedge_{0 \leq i \leq 2n+1} \Big([\![Z_i(a)]\!] \sqsubseteq [\![\top \sqsubseteq Z_i]\!] \ \wedge \ [\![(\neg Z_i)(a)]\!] \sqsubseteq [\![Z_i \sqsubseteq \bot]\!] \Big)$$

Next, there is a concept name N, which is required to be non-empty in every (temporal) world. We express this using a role name $r \in O_R$:

$$\top \sqsubseteq [\![(\exists r.N)(a)]\!]$$

It is only left to express the following $\mathcal{ALC}$-LTL-formula of [3,4]:

$$\Box\left(\bigvee_{d\in D}(\top \sqsubseteq d')\right)$$

For readability, let $D = \{d_1, \ldots, d_k\}$. We use non-convexity of $\mathcal{ALC}$ as follows to express this:

$$\top \sqsubseteq [\![(d'_1 \sqcup \cdots \sqcup d'_k)(a)]\!] \;\wedge\; \bigwedge_{1\leq i\leq k}\left([\![d'_i(a)]\!] \sqsubseteq [\![\top \sqsubseteq d'_i]\!]\right)$$

The conjunction of all the $\mathcal{EL}[\![\mathcal{ALC}]\!]$-BKBs above yields an $\mathcal{EL}[\![\mathcal{ALC}]\!]$-BKB $\mathcal{B}$ that is consistent iff the exponentially bounded version of the domino problem has a solution.   □

Summing up the results of this section together with the upper bounds of Section 3, we obtain the following corollary.

Corollary 24. *For all $\mathcal{L}_O$ between $\mathcal{ALC}$ and $\mathcal{SHOQ}$, the consistency problem in $\mathcal{EL}[\![\mathcal{L}_O]\!]$ is*

- EXP-*complete if* $O_{\mathsf{Crig}} = \varnothing$ *and* $O_{\mathsf{Rrig}} = \varnothing$;
- NEXP-*complete if* $O_{\mathsf{Crig}} \neq \varnothing$ *and* $O_{\mathsf{Rrig}} = \varnothing$; *and*
- 2EXP-*complete if* $O_{\mathsf{Crig}} \neq \varnothing$ *and* $O_{\mathsf{Rrig}} \neq \varnothing$.   □

5 Conclusions

We have introduced and investigated a family of two-dimensional context DLs $\mathcal{L}_M[\![\mathcal{L}_O]\!]$ capable of representing information on contexts (using a DL $\mathcal{L}_O$) and the relation between them (using a DL $\mathcal{L}_M$). In these context DLs, the consistency problem is decidable even in the presence of rigid names. We have investigated the complexity of the context DLs built from the classical DLs $\mathcal{EL}$, $\mathcal{ALC}$, and $\mathcal{SHOQ}$, where we considered three different cases: (i) no rigid names, (ii) only rigid concepts, and (iii) both rigid concepts and roles are admitted. Our results are depicted in Table 2. Interestingly, the consistency problem in $\mathcal{EL}[\![\mathcal{L}_O]\!]$, where $\mathcal{L}_O$ is between $\mathcal{ALC}$ and $\mathcal{SHOQ}$, is as hard as in $\mathcal{SHOQ}[\![\mathcal{SHOQ}]\!]$: it ranges from EXP-complete (Case (i)) over NEXP-complete (Case (ii)) to 2EXP-complete (Case (iii)). However, for the logics $\mathcal{L}_M[\![\mathcal{EL}]\!]$, where $\mathcal{L}_M$ is between $\mathcal{ALC}$ and $\mathcal{SHOQ}$, the consistency problem is EXP-complete in Case (i) and NEXP-complete in the Cases (ii) and (iii), i.e. there is no jump in the complexity if rigid roles are admitted.

For future work, we would like to consider DLs admitting inverse roles, which are also useful for representing information about and within contexts. As argued in [16], also temporal information is often required to represent information about contexts faithfully. We think that our decision procedures can be adapted to deal with temporalized context DLs such as LTL$[\![\mathcal{L}_M[\![\mathcal{L}_O]\!]]\!]$. Moreover, besides consistency and other standard reasoning tasks, there are also reasoning tasks specific to contexts and rôles that we want to investigate in future, such as to check whether an object is allowed to play two rôles (at the same time).

Acknowledgements. The authors wish to thank Stefan Borgwardt for helpful discussions on the proofs of the lower bounds of the context DLs $\mathcal{EL}[\![\mathcal{L}_O]\!]$. The first author was supported by the DFG in the RTG 1907 (RoSI). The second author was partially supported by the DFG in the CRC 912 (HAEC).

References

1. Baader, F., Brandt, S., Lutz, C.: Pushing the $\mathcal{EL}$ envelope. In: Proc. IJCAI 2005, pp. 364–369 (2005)
2. Baader, F., Calvanese, D., McGuinness, D.L., Nardi, D., Patel-Schneider, P.F. (eds.): The Description Logic Handbook: Theory, Implementation, and Applications, 2nd edn. Cambridge University Press (2007)
3. Baader, F., Ghilardi, S., Lutz, C.: LTL over description logic axioms. In: Proc. KR 2008, pp. 684–694 (2008)
4. Baader, F., Ghilardi, S., Lutz, C.: LTL over description logic axioms. ACM Trans. Comput. Log. 13(3) (2012)
5. Bao, J., Voutsadakis, G., Slutzki, G., Honavar, V.: Package-based description logics. In: Stuckenschmidt, H., Parent, C., Spaccapietra, S. (eds.) Modular Ontologies. LNCS, vol. 5445, pp. 349–371. Springer, Heidelberg (2009)
6. Borgida, A., Serafini, L.: Distributed description logics: Assimilating information from peer sources. Journal of Data Semantics 2800, 153–184 (2003)
7. Borgwardt, S., Thost, V.: LTL over $\mathcal{EL}$ axioms. LTCS-Report 15-07, Chair of Automata Theory, TU Dresden (2015), see http://lat.inf.tu-dresden.de/research/reports.html.
8. Borgwardt, S., Thost, V.: Temporal query answering in the description logic $\mathcal{EL}$. In: Proc. IJCAI 2015, pp. 2819–2825 (2015)
9. Böhme, S., Lippmann, M.: Description logics of context with rigid roles revisited. LTCS-Report 15-04, Chair of Automata Theory, TU Dresden (2015). see http://lat.inf.tu-dresden.de/research/reports.html
10. Horrocks, I., Sattler, U., Tobies, S.: Practical reasoning for very expressive description logics. Journal of the IGPL 8(3), 239–263 (2000)
11. Klarman, S., Gutiérrez-Basulto, V.: $\mathcal{ALC}_{\mathcal{ALC}}$: A context description logic. In: Janhunen, T., Niemelä, I. (eds.) JELIA 2010. LNCS, vol. 6341, pp. 208–220. Springer, Heidelberg (2010)
12. Klarman, S., Gutiérrez-Basulto, V.: Two-dimensional description logics for context-based semantic interoperability. In: Proc. AAAI 2011 (2011)
13. Klarman, S., Gutiérrez-Basulto, V.: Two-dimensional description logics of context. In: Proc. DL 2011 (2011)
14. Lippmann, M.: Temporalised Description Logics for Monitoring Partially Observable Events. Ph.D. thesis, TU Dresden, Germany (2014)
15. McCarthy, J.: Generality in artificial intelligence. Communications of the ACM 30(12), 1030–1035 (1987)
16. McCarthy, J.: Notes on formalizing context. In: Proc. IJCAI 1993, pp. 555–562 (1993)
17. Schild, K.: A correspondence theory for terminological logics: Preliminary report. In: Proc. IJCAI 1991, pp. 466–471 (1991)

Adding Threshold Concepts to the Description Logic $\mathcal{EL}$

Franz Baader[1], Gerhard Brewka[2], and Oliver Fernández Gil[2,*]

[1] Theoretical Computer Science, TU Dresden, Germany
baader@tcs.inf.tu-dresden.de
[2] Department of Computer Science, University of Leipzig, Germany
{brewka,fernandez}@informatik.uni-leipzig.de

Abstract. We introduce an extension of the lightweight Description Logic $\mathcal{EL}$ that allows us to define concepts in an approximate way. For this purpose, we use a graded membership function, which for each individual and concept yields a number in the interval $[0,1]$ expressing the degree to which the individual belongs to the concept. Threshold concepts $C_{\sim t}$ for $\sim \in \{<,\leq,>,\geq\}$ then collect all the individuals that belong to C with degree $\sim t$. We generalize a well-known characterization of membership in $\mathcal{EL}$ concepts to construct a specific graded membership function deg, and investigate the complexity of reasoning in the Description Logic $\tau\mathcal{EL}(deg)$, which extends $\mathcal{EL}$ by threshold concepts defined using deg. We also compare the instance problem for threshold concepts of the form $C_{>t}$ in $\tau\mathcal{EL}(deg)$ with the relaxed instance queries of Ecke et al.

1 Introduction

Description logics (DLs) [3] are a family of logic-based knowledge representation formalisms, which can be used to represent the conceptual knowledge of an application domain in a structured and formally well-understood way. They allow their users to define the important notions of the domain as concepts by stating necessary and sufficient conditions for an individual to belong to the concept. These conditions can be atomic properties required for the individual (expressed by concept names) or properties that refer to relationships with other individuals and their properties (expressed as role restrictions). The expressivity of a particular DL is determined by what sort of properties can be required and how they can be combined.

The DL $\mathcal{EL}$, in which concepts can be built using concept names as well as the concept constructors conjunction ($\sqcap$), existential restriction ($\exists r.C$), and the top concept ($\top$), has drawn considerable attention in the last decade since, on the one hand, important inference problems such as the subsumption problem are polynomial in $\mathcal{EL}$, even with respect to expressive terminological axioms [7]. On the other hand, though quite inexpressive, $\mathcal{EL}$ can be used to define biomedical ontologies, such as the large medical ontology SNOMED CT.[1] In $\mathcal{EL}$ we can, for

---

* Supported by DFG Graduiertenkolleg 1763 (QuantLA).
[1] see http://www.ihtsdo.org/snomed-ct/

© Springer International Publishing Switzerland 2015
C. Lutz and S. Ranise (Eds.): FroCoS 2015, LNAI 9322, pp. 33–48, 2015.
DOI: 10.1007/978-3-319-24246-0_3

example, define the concept of a *happy man* as a male human that is healthy and handsome, has a rich and intelligent wife, a son and a daughter, and a friend:

$$\text{Human} \sqcap \text{Male} \sqcap \text{Healthy} \sqcap \text{Handsome} \sqcap$$

$$\exists\text{spouse.}(\text{Rich} \sqcap \text{Intelligent} \sqcap \text{Female}) \sqcap \quad\quad\quad (1)$$

$$\exists\text{child.Male} \sqcap \exists\text{child.Female} \sqcap \exists\text{friend.}\top$$

For an individual to belong to this concept, all the stated properties need to be satisfied. However, maybe we would still want to call a man happy if most, though not all, of the properties hold. It might be sufficient to have just a daughter without a son, or a wife that is only intelligent but not rich, or maybe an intelligent and rich spouse of a different gender. But still, not too many of the properties should be violated.

In this paper, we introduce a DL extending $\mathcal{EL}$ that allows us to define concepts in such an approximate way. The main idea is to use a *graded membership function*, which instead of a Boolean membership value 0 or 1 yields a membership degree from the interval $[0, 1]$. We can then require a happy man to belong to the $\mathcal{EL}$ concept (1) with degree at least .8. More generally, if C is an $\mathcal{EL}$ concept, then the *threshold concept* $C_{\geq t}$ for $t \in [0, 1]$ collects all the individuals that belong to C with degree at least t. In addition to such upper threshold concepts, we will also consider lower threshold concepts $C_{\leq t}$ and allow the use of strict inequalities in both. For example, an unhappy man could be required to belong to the $\mathcal{EL}$ concept (1) with a degree less than .2.

The use of membership degree functions with values in the interval $[0, 1]$ may remind the reader of fuzzy logics. However, there is no strong relationship between this work and the work on fuzzy DLs [6] for two reasons. First, in fuzzy DLs the semantics is extended to fuzzy interpretations where concept and role names are interpreted as fuzzy sets and relations, respectively. The membership degree of an individual to belong to a complex concept is then computed using fuzzy interpretations of the concept constructors (e.g., conjunction is interpreted using an appropriate triangular norm). In our setting, we consider crisp interpretations of concept and role names, and directly define membership degrees for complex concepts based on them. Second, we use membership degrees to obtain new concept constructors, but the threshold concepts obtained by applying these constructors are again crisp rather than fuzzy.

In the next section, we will formally introduce the DL $\mathcal{EL}$, and then recall the well-known characterization of element-hood in $\mathcal{EL}$ concepts via existence of homomorphisms between $\mathcal{EL}$ description graphs (which can express both $\mathcal{EL}$ concepts and interpretations in a graphical way). In Section 3, we then extend $\mathcal{EL}$ by new threshold concept constructors, which are based on an arbitrary, but fixed graded membership function. We will impose some minimal requirements on such membership functions, and show the consequences that these conditions have for our threshold logic. In Section 4, we then introduce a specific graded membership function *deg*, which satisfies the requirements from the previous sections. Its definition is a natural extension of the homomorphism characterization of crisp membership in $\mathcal{EL}$. Basically, an individual is punished (in the sense that its membership degree is lowered) for each missing property in a uniform way. More sophisticated versions of this function, which weigh the absence of different properties in a different way, may be useful in practice. However, they are easy to define and considering them would only add clutter, but no new insights, to our investigation (in Section 5) of the computational properties of the threshold logic obtained by using this function.

In Section 6 we compare our graded membership function with similarity measures on $\mathcal{EL}$ concepts. In fact, from a technical point of view, the graded membership function introduced in Section 4 is akin to the similarity measures for $\mathcal{EL}$ concepts introduced in [14,15], though only [15] directly draws its inspirations from the homomorphism characterization of subsumption in $\mathcal{EL}$. We show that a variant of the relaxed instance query approach of [10] can be used to turn a similarity measure into a graded membership function. It turns out that, applied to a simple instance $\bowtie^1$ of the framework for constructing similarity measures in [14], this approach actually yields our membership function deg. In addition, we can show that the relaxed instance queries of [14] can be expressed as instance queries w.r.t. threshold concepts of the form $C_{>t}$. However, the new DL introduced in this paper is considerably more expressive than just such threshold concepts since we also allow the use of comparison operators other than $>$ in threshold concepts, and the threshold concepts can be embedded in complex $\mathcal{EL}$ concepts.

This paper is an extended version of [16]. Due to the space constraints, we cannot provide all technical details and proofs in this paper. They can be found in the technical report [1].

2   The Description Logic $\mathcal{EL}$

We start by defining syntax and semantics of $\mathcal{EL}$. Starting with finite sets of concept names N_C and role names N_R, the set $\mathcal{C}_{\mathcal{EL}}$ of $\mathcal{EL}$ concept descriptions is obtained by using the concept constructors *conjunction* $(C \sqcap D)$, *existential restriction* $(\exists r.C)$ and *top* $(\top)$, in the following way:

$$C ::= \top \mid A \mid C \sqcap C \mid \exists r.C$$

where $A \in N_C$, $r \in N_R$ and $C \in \mathcal{C}_{\mathcal{EL}}$.

An *interpretation* $\mathcal{I} = (\Delta^{\mathcal{I}}, \cdot^{\mathcal{I}})$ consists of a non-empty domain $\Delta^{\mathcal{I}}$ and an interpretation function $\cdot^{\mathcal{I}}$ that assigns subsets of $\Delta^{\mathcal{I}}$ to each concept name and binary relations over $\Delta^{\mathcal{I}}$ to each role name. The interpretation function $\cdot^{\mathcal{I}}$ is inductively extended to concept descriptions in the usual way:

$$\top^{\mathcal{I}} := \Delta^{\mathcal{I}},$$
$$(C \sqcap D)^{\mathcal{I}} := C^{\mathcal{I}} \cap D^{\mathcal{I}},$$
$$(\exists r.C)^{\mathcal{I}} := \{x \in \Delta^{\mathcal{I}} \mid \exists y.\, (x, y) \in r^{\mathcal{I}} \wedge y \in C^{\mathcal{I}}\}.$$

Given $C, D \in \mathcal{C}_{\mathcal{EL}}$, we say that C is *subsumed by* D (denoted as $C \sqsubseteq D$) iff $C^{\mathcal{I}} \subseteq D^{\mathcal{I}}$ for every interpretation $\mathcal{I}$. These two concept descriptions are *equivalent* (denoted as $C \equiv D$) iff $C \sqsubseteq D$ and $D \sqsubseteq C$. Finally, C is *satisfiable* iff $C^{\mathcal{I}} \neq \emptyset$ for some interpretation $\mathcal{I}$.

Our definition of graded membership will be based on graphical representations of concepts and interpretations, and on homomorphisms between such representations. For this reason, we recall these notions together with the pertinent results. They are all taken from [4,12,2].

Definition 1 ($\mathcal{EL}$ Description Graphs). *An $\mathcal{EL}$ description graph is of the form $G = (V_G, E_G, \ell_G)$ where:*

- V_G *is a set of nodes.*
- $E_G \subseteq V_G \times \mathsf{N_R} \times V_G$ *is a set of edges labelled by role names,*
- $\ell_G : V_G \rightarrow 2^{\mathsf{N_C}}$ *is a function that labels nodes with sets of concept names.*

An $\mathcal{EL}$ *description tree* T is a description graph that is a tree with a distinguished element v_0 representing its root. In [4], it was shown that every $\mathcal{EL}$ concept description C can be translated into a corresponding description tree T_C and vice versa. Furthermore, every interpretation $\mathcal{I} = (\Delta^{\mathcal{I}}, \cdot^{\mathcal{I}})$ can be translated into an $\mathcal{EL}$ description graph $G_{\mathcal{I}} = (V_{\mathcal{I}}, E_{\mathcal{I}}, \ell_{\mathcal{I}})$ in the following way [2]:

- $V_{\mathcal{I}} = \Delta^{\mathcal{I}}$,
- $E_{\mathcal{I}} = \{(vrw) \mid (v, w) \in r^{\mathcal{I}}\}$,
- $\ell_{\mathcal{I}}(v) = \{A \mid v \in A^{\mathcal{I}}\}$ for all $v \in V_{\mathcal{I}}$.

Example 1. The $\mathcal{EL}$ concept description

$$C := A \sqcap \exists r.(A \sqcap B \sqcap \exists r.\top) \sqcap \exists r.A$$

yields the $\mathcal{EL}$ description tree T_C depicted on the left-hand side in Figure 1. The description graph on the right-hand side corresponds to the following interpretation:

- $\Delta^{\mathcal{I}} := \{a_1, a_2, a_3\}$,
- $A^{\mathcal{I}} := \{a_1, a_2\}$ and $B^{\mathcal{I}} := \{a_2, a_3\}$,
- $r^{\mathcal{I}} := \{(a_1, a_2), (a_2, a_3), (a_3, a_1)\}$.

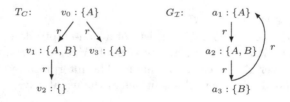

Fig. 1. $\mathcal{EL}$ description graphs.

Next, we generalize homomorphisms between $\mathcal{EL}$ description trees [4] to arbitrary graphs.

Definition 2 (Homomorphisms on $\mathcal{EL}$ Description Graphs). *Let $G = (V_G, E_G, \ell_G)$ and $H = (V_H, E_H, \ell_H)$ be two $\mathcal{EL}$ description graphs. A mapping $\varphi : V_G \to V_H$ is a* homomorphism *from G to H iff the following conditions are satisfied:*

1. *$\ell_G(v) \subseteq \ell_H(\varphi(v))$ for all $v \in V_G$, and*
2. *$vrw \in E_G$ implies $\varphi(v)r\varphi(w) \in E_H$.*

This homomorphism is an isomorphism *iff it is bijective, equality instead of just inclusion holds in 1., and biimplication instead of just implication holds in 2.*

In Example 1, the mapping φ with $\varphi(v_i) = a_{i+1}$ for $i = 0, 1, 2$ and $\varphi(v_3) = a_2$ is a homomorphism. Homomorphisms between $\mathcal{EL}$ description trees can be used to characterize subsumption in $\mathcal{EL}$.

Theorem 1 ([4]). *Let C, D be $\mathcal{EL}$ concept descriptions and T_C, T_D the corresponding $\mathcal{EL}$ description trees. Then $C \sqsubseteq D$ iff there exists a homomorphism from T_D to T_C that maps the root of T_D to the root of T_C.*

The proof of this result can be easily adapted to obtain a similar characterization of *element-hood* in $\mathcal{EL}$, i.e., whether $d \in C^\mathcal{I}$ for some $d \in \Delta^\mathcal{I}$.

Theorem 2. *Let $\mathcal{I}$ be an interpretation, $d \in \Delta^\mathcal{I}$, and C an $\mathcal{EL}$ concept description. Then, $d \in C^\mathcal{I}$ iff there exists a homomorphism φ from T_C to $G_\mathcal{I}$ such that $\varphi(v_0) = d$.*

In Example 1, the existence of the homomorphism φ defined above thus shows that $a_1 \in C^\mathcal{I}$. Equivalence of $\mathcal{EL}$ concept descriptions can be characterized via the existence of isomorphisms, but for this the concept descriptions first need to be normalized by removing redundant existential restrictions. To be more precise, the *reduced form* of an $\mathcal{EL}$ concept description is obtained by applying the rewrite rule $\exists r.C \sqcap \exists r.D \longrightarrow \exists r.C$ if $C \sqsubseteq D$ as long as possible. This rule is applied modulo associativity and commutativity of $\sqcap$, and not only on the top-level conjunction of the description, but also under the scope of existential restrictions. Since every application of the rule decreases the size of the description, it is easy to see that the reduced form can be computed in polynomial time. We say that an $\mathcal{EL}$ concept description is *reduced* iff this rule does not apply to it. In our Example 1, the reduced form of C is the reduced description $A \sqcap \exists r.(A \sqcap B \sqcap \exists r.\top)$.

Theorem 3 ([12]). *Let C, D be $\mathcal{EL}$ concept descriptions, C^r, D^r their reduced forms, and T_{C^r}, T_{D^r} the corresponding $\mathcal{EL}$ description trees. Then $C \equiv D$ iff there exists an isomorphism between T_{C^r} and T_{D^r}.*

3 The Logic $\tau\mathcal{EL}(m)$

Our new logic will allow us to take an arbitrary $\mathcal{EL}$ concept C and turn it into a threshold concept. To this end we introduce a family of constructors that are based on the membership degree of individuals in C. For instance, the threshold concept $C_{>.8}$ represents the individuals that belong to C with degree $> .8$. The semantics of the new threshold concepts depends on a (graded) membership function m. Given an interpretation $\mathcal{I}$, this function takes a domain element $d \in \Delta^{\mathcal{I}}$ and an $\mathcal{EL}$ concept C as input, and returns a value between 0 and 1, representing the extent to which d belongs to C in $\mathcal{I}$.

The choice of the membership function obviously has a great influence on the semantics of the threshold concepts. In Section 4 we will propose one specific such function deg, but we do not claim this is the only reasonable way to define such a function. Rather, the membership function is a parameter in defining the logic. To highlight this dependency, we call the logic $\tau \mathcal{EL}(m)$.

Nevertheless, membership functions are not arbitrary. There are two properties we require such functions to satisfy:

Definition 3. *A graded membership function m is a family of functions that contains for every interpretation $\mathcal{I}$ a function $m^{\mathcal{I}} : \Delta^{\mathcal{I}} \times \mathcal{C}_{\mathcal{EL}} \to [0,1]$ satisfying the following conditions (for $C, D \in \mathcal{C}_{\mathcal{EL}}$):*

$$M1 : d \in C^{\mathcal{I}} \Leftrightarrow m^{\mathcal{I}}(d, C) = 1 \ \text{ for all } d \in \Delta^{\mathcal{I}},$$
$$M2 : C \equiv D \Leftrightarrow \text{ for all } d \in \Delta^{\mathcal{I}} : m^{\mathcal{I}}(d, C) = m^{\mathcal{I}}(d, D).$$

Property *M1* requires that the value 1 is a distinguished value reserved for proper containment in a concept. Property *M2* requires equivalence invariance. It expresses the intuition that the membership value should not depend on the syntactic form of a concept, but only on its semantics. Note that the right to left implication in *M2* already follows from *M1*.

We now turn to the syntax of $\tau \mathcal{EL}(m)$. Given finite sets of concept names $\mathsf{N_C}$ and role names $\mathsf{N_R}$, $\tau \mathcal{EL}(m)$ *concept descriptions* are defined as follows:

$$\widehat{C} ::= \top \mid A \mid \widehat{C} \sqcap \widehat{C} \mid \exists r.\widehat{C} \mid E_{\sim q}$$

where $A \in \mathsf{N_C}$, $r \in \mathsf{N_R}$, $\sim \ \in \{<, \leq, >, \geq\}$, $q \in [0,1] \cap \mathbb{Q}$, E is an $\mathcal{EL}$ concept description and $\widehat{C}$ is a $\tau \mathcal{EL}(m)$ concept description. Concepts of the form $E_{\sim q}$ are called *threshold concepts*.

The semantics of the new threshold concepts is defined in the following way:

$$[E_{\sim q}]^{\mathcal{I}} := \{d \in \Delta^{\mathcal{I}} \mid m^{\mathcal{I}}(d, E) \sim q\}.$$

The extension of $\cdot^{\mathcal{I}}$ to more complex concepts is defined as in $\mathcal{EL}$ by additionally considering the semantics of the newly introduced threshold concepts.

Requiring property *M1* has the following consequences for the semantics of threshold concepts:

Proposition 1. *For every $\mathcal{EL}$ concept description E we have*

$$E_{\geq 1} \equiv E \quad \text{and} \quad E_{<1} \equiv \neg E,$$

where the semantics of negation is defined as usual, i.e., $[\neg E]^{\mathcal{I}} := \Delta^{\mathcal{I}} \setminus E^{\mathcal{I}}$.

The second equivalence basically says that $\tau\mathcal{EL}(m)$ can express negation of $\mathcal{EL}$ concept descriptions. This does not imply that $\tau\mathcal{EL}(m)$ is closed under negation since the threshold constructors can only be applied to $\mathcal{EL}$ concept descriptions. Thus, negation cannot be nested using these constructors. A formal proof that $\tau\mathcal{EL}(deg)$ for the membership function deg introduced in the next section cannot express full negation can be found in [1]. However, atomic negation (i.e., negation applied to concept names) can obviously be expressed. Consequently, unlike $\mathcal{EL}$ concept descriptions, not all $\tau\mathcal{EL}(m)$ concept descriptions are satisfiable. A simple example is the concept description $A_{\geq 1} \sqcap A_{<1}$, which is equivalent to $A \sqcap \neg A$.

4   The Membership Function *deg*

To make things more concrete, we now introduce a specific membership function, denoted deg. Given an interpretation $\mathcal{I}$, an element $d \in \Delta^{\mathcal{I}}$, and an $\mathcal{EL}$ concept description C, this function is supposed to measure to which degree d satisfies the conditions for membership expressed by C. To come up with such a measure, we use the homomorphism characterization of membership (see Theorem 2) as starting point. Basically, we consider all partial mappings from T_C to $G_{\mathcal{I}}$ that map the root of T_C to d and respect the edge structure of T_C. For each of these mappings we then calculate to which degree it satisfies the homomorphism conditions, and take the degree of the best such mapping as the membership degree $deg^{\mathcal{I}}(d, C)$. We consider partial mappings rather than total ones since one of the violations of properties demanded by C could be that a required role successor does not exist at all.

To formalize this idea, we first define the notion of *partial tree-to-graph homomorphisms* from description trees to description graphs. In this definition, the node labels are ignored (they will be considered in the next step).

Definition 4. *Let $T = (V_t, E_t, \ell_t, v_0)$ and $G = (V_g, E_g, \ell_g)$ be a description tree (with root v_0) and a description graph, respectively. A partial mapping $h : V_t \to V_g$ is a partial tree-to-graph homomorphism (ptgh) from T to G iff the following conditions are satisfied:*

1. $\mathsf{dom}(h)$ *is a sub-tree of T with root v_0, i.e., $v_0 \in \mathsf{dom}(h)$ and if $(v, r, w) \in E_t$ and $w \in \mathsf{dom}(h)$, then $v \in \mathsf{dom}(h)$;*
2. *for all edges $(v, r, w) \in E_t$, $w \in \mathsf{dom}(h)$ implies $(h(v), r, h(w)) \in E_g$.*

In order to measure how far away from a homomorphism according to Definition 2 such a *ptgh* is, we define the notion of a *weighted* homomorphism between a finite $\mathcal{EL}$ description tree and an $\mathcal{EL}$ description graph.

Definition 5. *Let T be a finite $\mathcal{EL}$ description tree, G an $\mathcal{EL}$ description graph and $h : V_T \mapsto V_G$ a ptgh from T to G. We define the weighted homomorphism induced by h from T to G as a function $h_w : \mathsf{dom}(h) \to [0, 1]$ as follows. For a* *given $v \in \mathsf{dom}(h)$, let $k^*(v)$ be the number of successors of v in T, and $v_1, \ldots, v_k$ the k $(0 \le k \le k^*(v))$ children of v in T such that $v_i \in \mathsf{dom}(h)$. Then*

$$h_w(v) := \begin{cases} 1 & \text{if } |\ell_T(v)| + k^*(v) = 0 \\ \dfrac{|\ell_T(v) \cap \ell_G(h(v))| + \sum_{1 \le i \le k} h_w(v_i)}{|\ell_T(v)| + k^*(v)} & \text{otherwise.} \end{cases}$$

It is easy to see that h_w is well-defined. In fact, T is a finite tree, which ensures that the recursive definition of h_w is well-founded. In addition, the first case in the definition ensures that division by zero is avoided. Using value 1 in this case is justified since then no property is required. In the second case, missing concept names and missing successors decrease the weight of a node since then the required name or successor contributes to the denominator, but not to the numerator. Required successors that are there are only counted if they are successors for the correct role, and then they do not contribute with value 1 to the numerator, but only with their weight (i.e., the degree to which they match the requirements for this successor).

When defining the value of the membership function $deg^{\mathcal{I}}(d, C)$, we do not use the concept C directly, but rather its reduced form C^r. This will ensure that deg satisfies property *M2* (see Proposition 2 below).

Definition 6. *Let $\mathcal{I} = (\Delta^{\mathcal{I}}, \cdot^{\mathcal{I}})$ be an interpretation, d an element of $\Delta^{\mathcal{I}}$, and C an $\mathcal{EL}$ concept description with reduced form C^r. In addition, let $\mathcal{H}(T_{C^r}, G_{\mathcal{I}}, d)$ be the set of all ptghs from T_{C^r} to $G_{\mathcal{I}}$ with $h(v_0) = d$. The set $\mathcal{V}^{\mathcal{I}}(d, C^r)$ of all relevant values is defined as*

$$\mathcal{V}^{\mathcal{I}}(d, C^r) := \{q \mid h_w(v_0) = q \text{ and } h \in \mathcal{H}(T_{C^r}, G_{\mathcal{I}}, d)\}.$$

Then we define $deg^{\mathcal{I}}(d, C) := \max \mathcal{V}^{\mathcal{I}}(d, C^r)$.

If the interpretation $\mathcal{I}$ is infinite, there may exist infinitely many *ptghs* from T_{C^r} to $G_{\mathcal{I}}$ with $h(v_0) = d$. Therefore, it is not immediately clear whether the maximum in the above definition actually exists, and thus whether $deg^{\mathcal{I}}(d, C)$ is well-defined. To prove that the maximum exists also for infinite interpretations, we show that the set $\mathcal{V}^{\mathcal{I}}(d, C^r)$ is actually a finite set. For this purpose, we introduce canonical interpretations induced by *ptghs*.

Definition 7 (Canonical Interpretation). *Let $\mathcal{I} = (\Delta^{\mathcal{I}}, \cdot^{\mathcal{I}})$ be an interpretation, C an $\mathcal{EL}$ concept description and h be a ptgh from T_{C^r} to $G_{\mathcal{I}}$. The canonical interpretation $\mathcal{I}_h$ induced by h is the one having the description tree $T_{\mathcal{I}_h} = (V_{\mathcal{I}_h}, E_{\mathcal{I}_h}, v_0, \ell_{\mathcal{I}_h})$ with*

$$V_{\mathcal{I}_h} := \mathsf{dom}(h),$$
$$E_{\mathcal{I}_h} := \{vrw \in E_{T_{C^r}} \mid v, w \in \mathsf{dom}(h)\}$$
$$\ell_{\mathcal{I}_h}(v) := \ell_{T_{C^r}}(v) \cap \ell_{\mathcal{I}}(h(v)) \text{ for all } v \in \mathsf{dom}(h).$$

Lemma 1. *Let $\mathcal{I}$ be an interpretation, $d \in \Delta^{\mathcal{I}}$ and C an $\mathcal{EL}$ concept description. Then the following two properties hold:*

1. *there are only finitely many different canonical interpretations induced by ptghs $h \in \mathcal{H}(T_{C^r}, G_{\mathcal{I}}, d)$;*
2. *for every $h \in \mathcal{H}(T_{C^r}, G_{\mathcal{I}}, d)$, the identity mapping $i^{\mathcal{I}_h} : \mathrm{dom}(h) \to V_{\mathcal{I}_h}$ with $i^{\mathcal{I}_h}(v) = v$ for all $v \in \mathrm{dom}(h)$ is a ptgh from T_C to $T_{\mathcal{I}_h}$ that satisfies $h_w(v_0) = i_w^{\mathcal{I}_h}(v_0)$.*

The first statement is an easy consequence of the fact that the description tree for a canonical interpretation has nodes from the finite set of nodes of T_{C^r} and labels from the finite set of concept and role names. The second fact is not hard to show, and it obviously implies that the set $\mathcal{V}^{\mathcal{I}}(d, C^r)$ is finite. Consequently, $deg^{\mathcal{I}}(d, C)$ is well-defined. Moreover, as an easy consequence of the proof of Lemma 1 we can show that the same value can be obtained by considering the corresponding canonical interpretation. To be more precise:

Lemma 2. *Let $\mathcal{I} = (\Delta^{\mathcal{I}}, \cdot^{\mathcal{I}})$ be an interpretation, $d \in \Delta^{\mathcal{I}}$ and C an $\mathcal{EL}$ concept description. Let h be a ptgh from T_{C^r} to $G_{\mathcal{I}}$ such that $h(v_0) = d$ and $deg^{\mathcal{I}}(d, C) = h_w(v_0)$. In addition, let $\mathcal{I}_h$ be the corresponding canonical interpretation. Then, $deg^{\mathcal{I}_h}(v_0, C) = deg^{\mathcal{I}}(d, C)$.*

If the interpretation $\mathcal{I}$ is finite, $deg^{\mathcal{I}}(d, C)$ for $d \in \Delta^{\mathcal{I}}$ and an $\mathcal{EL}$ concept description C can actually be computed in polynomial time. The polynomial time algorithm described in [1] is inspired by the polynomial time algorithm for checking the existence of a homomorphism between $\mathcal{EL}$ description trees [5,4], and similar to the algorithm for computing the similarity degree between $\mathcal{EL}$ concept descriptions introduced in [15]. Finally, it remains to show that deg satisfies the properties required for a membership function.

Proposition 2. *The function deg satisfies M1 and M2.*

In fact, *M1* is easy to show and *M2* follows from the fact that we use the reduced form of a concept description rather than the description itself. Otherwise, *M2* would not hold. For example, consider the concept description $C := \exists r.A \sqcap \exists r.(A \sqcap B)$, which is equivalent to its reduced form $C^r = \exists r.(A \sqcap B)$. Let d be an individual that has a single r-successor belonging to A, but not to B. Then using C instead of C^r would yield membership degree $3/4$, whereas the use of C^r yields the degree $1/2$.

5   Reasoning in $\tau\mathcal{EL}(deg)$

We start with investigating the complexity of terminological reasoning (subsumption, satisfiability) in $\tau\mathcal{EL}(deg)$, and then turn to assertional reasoning (consistency, instance). In the following, we assume that all concept descriptions E occurring in threshold concepts $E_{\sim q}$ are reduced (i.e., $E^r = E$), and thus we can directly use E when computing membership degrees. This is without loss of generality since the reduced form of an $\mathcal{EL}$ concept description can be computed in polynomial time.

Terminological Reasoning. In contrast to $\mathcal{EL}$, where every concept description is satisfiable, we have seen in Section 3 that there are unsatisfiable $\tau\mathcal{EL}(deg)$ concept descriptions, such as $A_{\geq 1} \sqcap A_{<1}$. Thus, the satisfiability problem is non-trivial in $\tau\mathcal{EL}(deg)$. In fact, by a simple reduction from the well-known NP-complete problem ALL-POS ONE-IN-THREE 3SAT [11], we can show that testing $\tau\mathcal{EL}(deg)$ concept descriptions for satisfiability is actually NP-hard. The main idea underlying this reduction is that, for any three distinct concept names A_i, A_j, A_k, an individual belongs to $(A_i \sqcap A_j \sqcap A_k)_{\leq 1/3} \sqcap (A_i \sqcap A_j \sqcap A_k)_{\geq 1/3}$ iff it belongs to exactly one of these three concepts. This also yields coNP-hardness of subsumption in $\tau\mathcal{EL}(deg)$ since unsatisfiability can be reduced to subsumption: $\widehat{C}$ is not satisfiable iff $\widehat{C} \sqsubseteq A_{\geq 1} \sqcap A_{<1}$.

Lemma 3. *In $\tau\mathcal{EL}(deg)$, satisfiability is NP-hard and subsumption is coNP-hard.*

Before proving an NP upper bound for satisfiability, we show that the homomorphism characterization of membership in an $\mathcal{EL}$ concept can be extended to $\tau\mathcal{EL}(deg)$. For this, we first extend $\mathcal{EL}$ description graphs to $\tau\mathcal{EL}(deg)$ description graphs. This is done by allowing the node labelling function to assign, in addition, threshold concepts as labels.

Definition 8. *Let $\widehat{H} = (V_H, E_H, \widehat{\ell}_H)$ be a $\tau\mathcal{EL}(deg)$ description graph and $\mathcal{I}$ an interpretation with associated $\mathcal{EL}$ description graph $G_{\mathcal{I}} = (V_{\mathcal{I}}, E_{\mathcal{I}}, \ell_{\mathcal{I}})$. The mapping $\phi : V_H \to V_{\mathcal{I}}$ is a τ-homomorphism from $\widehat{H}$ to $G_{\mathcal{I}}$ iff*

1. *ϕ is a homomorphism from $\widehat{H}$ to $G_{\mathcal{I}}$ according to Definition 2, where threshold concepts in labels are ignored,*
2. *for all $v \in V_H$: if $E_{\sim q} \in \widehat{\ell}_H(v)$, then $\phi(v) \in [E_{\sim q}]^{\mathcal{I}}$.*

If the interpretation $\mathcal{I}$ is finite, then the existence of a τ-homomorphism can be checked in polynomial time. Intuitively, for the first condition one just needs to check for the existence of a classical homomorphism, and for the second one needs to compute membership degrees. Both can be done in polynomial time. Similar to $\mathcal{EL}$, the existence of a τ-homomorphism characterizes membership in $\tau\mathcal{EL}(deg)$ concept descriptions.

Theorem 4. *Let $\mathcal{I}$ be an interpretation, $d \in \Delta^{\mathcal{I}}$, and $\widehat{C}$ a $\tau\mathcal{EL}(deg)$ concept description. Then, $d \in \widehat{C}^{\mathcal{I}}$ iff there exists a τ-homomorphism ϕ from $T_{\widehat{C}}$ to $G_{\mathcal{I}}$ such that $\phi(v_0) = d$.*

This theorem can be used to prove a bounded model property for $\tau\mathcal{EL}(deg)$ concept descriptions.

Lemma 4. *Let $\widehat{C}$ be a $\tau\mathcal{EL}(deg)$ concept description of size $\mathsf{s}(\widehat{C})$. If $\widehat{C}$ is satisfiable, then there exists an interpretation $\mathcal{J}$ such that $\widehat{C}^{\mathcal{J}} \neq \emptyset$ and $|\Delta^{\mathcal{J}}| \leq \mathsf{s}(\widehat{C})$.*

Proof sketch. Since $\widehat{C}$ is satisfiable, there is an interpretation $\mathcal{I}$ and some $d \in \Delta^{\mathcal{I}}$ such that $d \in \widehat{C}^{\mathcal{I}}$. Therefore, there exists a τ-homomorphism ϕ from $T_{\widehat{C}}$ to $G_{\mathcal{I}}$

with $\phi(v_0) = d$. The idea is to use ϕ and small fragments of $\mathcal{I}$ to build $\mathcal{J}$ and a τ-homomorphism from $T_{\widehat{C}}$ to $G_{\mathcal{J}}$, and then apply Theorem 4 to $\widehat{C}$ and $\mathcal{J}$.

The interpretation $\mathcal{J}$ is built in two steps. We first use as base interpretation $\mathcal{I}_0$ the interpretation associated to the description tree $T_{\widehat{C}}$, where we ignore labels of the form $E_{\sim q}$. Then the identity mapping ϕ_{id} is a homomorphism from $T_{\widehat{C}}$ to $G_{\mathcal{I}_0}$. However, this interpretation and homomorphism need not satisfy Condition 2 of Definition 8. To repair this, we extend $\mathcal{I}_0$ to $\mathcal{J}$ by adding appropriate canonical interpretations. To be more precise, for a given node v in $\mathcal{I}_0$ that has $E_{\sim q}$ in its label, we know that $\phi(v) \in [E_{\sim q}]^{\mathcal{I}}$, i.e. $deg^{\mathcal{I}}(\phi(v), E) \sim q$. By Lemma 2, we do not need all of $\mathcal{I}$ to obtain the degree $deg^{\mathcal{I}}(\phi(v), E)$. It is sufficient to use the fragment corresponding to the canonical interpretation. The interpretation $\mathcal{J}$ satisfying $\widehat{C}$ is obtained from $\mathcal{I}_0$ by plugging in such canonical interpretations where ever it is required by threshold concepts in labels of nodes (see [1] for details).

Since the size of $\mathcal{I}_0$ is bounded by the size of $\widehat{C}$ (without counting the threshold concepts) and since the size of a canonical interpretation added to satisfy a threshold concept $E_{\sim q}$ in $\widehat{C}$ is bounded by the size of E, this yields the required bound for the size of $\mathcal{J}$.   □

This lemma yields a standard guess-and-check NP-algorithm to decide satisfiability of $\widehat{C}$: first guess an interpretation $\mathcal{J}$ of size at most $\mathsf{s}(\widehat{C})$, and then check (in polynomial time) whether there exists a τ-homomorphism from $T_{\widehat{C}}$ to $G_{\mathcal{J}}$.

A coNP-upper bound for subsumption cannot directly be obtained from the fact that satisfiability is in NP. In fact, though we have $\widehat{C} \sqsubseteq \widehat{D}$ iff $\widehat{C} \sqcap \neg \widehat{D}$ is unsatisfiable, this equivalence cannot be used directly since $\neg \widehat{D}$ need not be a $\tau\mathcal{EL}(deg)$ concept description. Nevertheless, we can extend the ideas used in the proof of Lemma 4 to obtain a bounded model property for satisfiability of concepts of the form $\widehat{C} \sqcap \neg \widehat{D}$.

Lemma 5. *Let $\widehat{C}$ and $\widehat{D}$ be $\tau\mathcal{EL}(deg)$ concept descriptions of respective sizes $\mathsf{s}(\widehat{C})$ and $\mathsf{s}(\widehat{D})$. If $\widehat{C} \sqcap \neg \widehat{D}$ is satisfiable, then there exists an interpretation $\mathcal{J}$ such that $\widehat{C}^{\mathcal{J}} \setminus \widehat{D}^{\mathcal{J}} \neq \emptyset$ and $|\Delta^{\mathcal{J}}| \leq \mathsf{s}(\widehat{C}) \times \mathsf{s}(\widehat{D})$.*

Proof sketch. We first apply the construction used in the proof of Lemma 4 to construct, for a given interpretation $\mathcal{I}$ with $\widehat{C}^{\mathcal{I}} \setminus \widehat{D}^{\mathcal{I}} \neq \emptyset$, an interpretation $\mathcal{J}_0$ such that $\widehat{C}^{\mathcal{J}_0} \neq \emptyset$ and $|\Delta^{\mathcal{J}_0}| \leq \mathsf{s}(\widehat{C})$. This construction is such that $G_{\mathcal{J}_0}$ is tree-shaped and there is a homomorphism φ from $G_{\mathcal{J}_0}$ to $G_{\mathcal{I}}$ with $\varphi(v_0) = d$. We then use φ to extend $\mathcal{J}_0$ to $\mathcal{J}$ such that $v_0 \notin \widehat{D}^{\mathcal{J}}$ holds. Starting with the root v_0, we consider all the nodes in $\Delta^{\mathcal{J}_0}$ in a top-down manner.

First, assume that $\widehat{D}$ contains a top-level conjunct of the form $E_{\leq q}$ such that $d = \varphi(v_0) \notin [E_{\leq q}]^{\mathcal{I}}$, but $v_0 \in [E_{\leq q}]^{\mathcal{J}_0}$. Then we attach to v_0 a canonical interpretation that yields for d the same membership degree as $\mathcal{I}$ to ensure that, in the extended interpretation, v_0 no longer belongs to $E_{\leq q}$.

Now, consider the case where $\widehat{D}$ contains a top-level conjunct $\widehat{F} = \exists r.\widehat{F}'$ such that $d = \varphi(v_0) \notin \widehat{F}^{\mathcal{I}}$, but $v_0 \in \widehat{F}^{\mathcal{J}_0}$. Then there is an r-successor v of v_0 that satisfies $v \in [\widehat{F}']^{\mathcal{J}_0}$, but since $\varphi(v)$ is an r-successor of $\varphi(v_0)$ in $\mathcal{I}$, we also have

$\varphi(v) \notin [\widehat{F'}]^{\mathcal{I}}$. We can now recursively apply the construction to v. Overall, the construction terminates and considers every node in $\Delta^{\mathcal{J}_0}$ only once since $G_{\mathcal{J}_0}$ is tree-shaped. Since the number of nodes in $\Delta^{\mathcal{J}_0}$ is bounded by $\mathsf{s}(\widehat{C})$ and the size of each of the added canonical interpretations is bounded by $\mathsf{s}(\widehat{D})$, we obtain the desired bound on the size of $\mathcal{J}$.   □

The lemma yields an obvious guess-and-check NP-algorithm for non-subsumption, which shows that subsumption is in co-NP. Overall, we thus have shown:

Theorem 5. *In $\tau\mathcal{EL}(deg)$, satisfiability is NP-complete and subsumption coNP-complete.*

Assertional Reasoning. Information about specific individuals can be expressed in an ABox. An *ABox* $\mathcal{A}$ is a finite set of *assertions* of the form $\widehat{C}(a)$ or $r(a,b)$, where $\widehat{C}$ is a $\tau\mathcal{EL}(deg)$ concept description, $r \in \mathsf{N_R}$, and a,b are individual names. In addition to concept and role names, an interpretation $\mathcal{I}$ now assigns domain elements $a^{\mathcal{I}}$ to individual names a. The assertion $\widehat{C}(a)$ is satisfied by $\mathcal{I}$ iff $a^{\mathcal{I}} \in \widehat{C}^{\mathcal{I}}$, and $r(a,b)$ is satisfied by $\mathcal{I}$ iff $(a^{\mathcal{I}}, b^{\mathcal{I}}) \in r^{\mathcal{I}}$. The interpretation $\mathcal{I}$ is a *model* of $\mathcal{A}$ iff $\mathcal{I}$ satisfies all assertions in $\mathcal{A}$. The ABox $\mathcal{A}$ is *consistent* iff it has a model, and the individual a is an *instance* of the concept $\widehat{C}$ in $\mathcal{A}$ (written as $\mathcal{A} \models \widehat{C}(a)$) iff $a^{\mathcal{I}} \in \widehat{C}^{\mathcal{I}}$ holds in all models of $\mathcal{A}$.

Since satisfiability can obviously be reduced to consistency, and subsumption to the instance problem, the lower bounds shown above also hold for assertional reasoning. Regarding upper bounds, the consistency problem can be tackled in a similar way as the satisfiability problem. As shown in [13], $\mathcal{EL}$ ABoxes can be translated into $\mathcal{EL}$ description graphs and consistency can be characterized using homomorphisms between description graphs. Again, this characterization can be extended to $\tau\mathcal{EL}(deg)$, and can be used to prove an appropriate bounded model property with a polynomial bound. Similar to our treatment of subsumption, this can then be used to obtain a bounded model property for non-instance ($\mathcal{A} \not\models \widehat{C}(a)$)). However, there the bound on the model has the size of $\widehat{C}$ in the exponent. For this reason, we obtain a coNP upper bound for the instance problem only if we consider data complexity [8], where the size of the query concept $\widehat{C}$ is assumed to be constant.

Theorem 6. *In $\tau\mathcal{EL}(deg)$, consistency is NP-complete, and instance checking is coNP-complete w.r.t. data complexity.*

The instance problem becomes simpler if we consider only $\mathcal{EL}$ ABoxes and *positive $\tau\mathcal{EL}(deg)$ concept descriptions*, i.e., concept descriptions $\widehat{C}$ that only contain threshold concepts of the form $E_{\geq t}$ or $E_{>t}$. Basically, given an $\mathcal{EL}$ ABox, a positive $\tau\mathcal{EL}(deg)$ concept description $\widehat{C}$, and an individual a, one considers the interpretation $\mathcal{I}$ corresponding to the description graph of $\mathcal{A}$, and then checks whether there is a τ-homomorphism ϕ from $T_{\widehat{C}}$ to $G_{\mathcal{I}}$ with $\phi(v_0) = a$ (see [1] for details).

Proposition 3. *For positive $\tau\mathcal{EL}(deg)$ concept descriptions and $\mathcal{EL}$ ABoxes, the instance problem can be decided in polynomial time.*

6   Concept Similarity and Relaxed Instance Queries

In its most general form, a concept similarity measure (CSM) $\bowtie$ is a function that maps each pair of concepts C, D (of a given DL) to a value $C \bowtie D \in [0, 1]$ such that $C \bowtie C = 1$. Intuitively, the higher the value of $C \bowtie D$ is, the more similar the two concepts are supposed to be. Such measures can in principle be defined for arbitrary DLs, but here we restrict the attention to CSMs between $\mathcal{EL}$ concepts, i.e., a CSM is a mapping $\bowtie : \mathcal{C}_{\mathcal{EL}} \times \mathcal{C}_{\mathcal{EL}} \to [0, 1]$.

Ecke et al. [10,9] use CSMs to relax instance queries, i.e., instead of requiring that an individual is an instance of the query concept, they only require that it is an instance of a concept that is "similar enough" to the query concept.

Definition 9 ([10,9]). *Let $\bowtie$ be a CSM, $\mathcal{A}$ an $\mathcal{EL}$ ABox, and $t \in [0, 1)$. The individual $a \in \mathsf{N}_\mathsf{I}$ is a* relaxed instance *of the $\mathcal{EL}$ query concept Q w.r.t. $\mathcal{A}$, $\bowtie$, and the threshold t iff there exists an $\mathcal{EL}$ concept description X such that $Q \bowtie X > t$ and $\mathcal{A} \models X(a)$. The set of all individuals occurring in $\mathcal{A}$ that are relaxed instances of Q w.r.t. $\mathcal{A}$, $\bowtie$, and t is denoted by $\mathsf{Relax}_t^{\bowtie}(Q, \mathcal{A})$.*

We apply the same idea on the semantic level of an interpretation rather than the ABox level to obtain graded membership functions from similarity measures.

Definition 10. *Let $\bowtie$ be a CSM. Then, for each interpretation $\mathcal{I}$, we define the function $m_{\bowtie}^{\mathcal{I}} : \Delta^{\mathcal{I}} \times \mathcal{C}_{\mathcal{EL}} \to [0, 1]$ as*

$$m_{\bowtie}^{\mathcal{I}}(d, C) := \max\{C \bowtie D \mid D \in \mathcal{C}_{\mathcal{EL}} \text{ and } d \in D^{\mathcal{I}}\}.$$

For an arbitrary CSM $\bowtie$, the maximum in this definition need not exist since D ranges over infinitely many concept descriptions. However, two properties that are satisfied by many similarity measures considered in the literature are sufficient to obtain well-definedness for $m_{\bowtie}$. The first is equivalence invariance:

- The CSM $\bowtie$ is *equivalence invariant* iff $C \equiv C'$ and $D \equiv D'$ implies $C \bowtie D = C' \bowtie D'$ for all $C, C', D, D' \in \mathcal{C}_{\mathcal{EL}}$.

To formulate the second property, we need to recall that the *role depth* of an $\mathcal{EL}$ concept description C is the maximal nesting of existential restrictions in C; equivalently, it is the height of the description tree T_C. The *restriction C_k of C to role depth k* is the concept description whose description tree is obtained from T_C by removing all the nodes (and edges leading to them) whose distance from the root is larger than k.

- The CSM $\bowtie$ is *role-depth bounded* iff $C \bowtie D = C_k \bowtie D_k$ for all $C, D \in \mathcal{C}_{\mathcal{EL}}$ and any k that is larger than the minimal role depth of C, D.

Role-depth boundedness implies that, in Definition 10, we can restrict the maximum computation to concepts D whose role depth is at most $d+1$, where d is the role depth of C. Since it is well-known that, up to equivalence, $\mathcal{C}_{\mathcal{EL}}$ contains only finitely many concept descriptions of any fixed role depth, these two properties yield well-definedness for $m_{\bowtie}$. For $m_{\bowtie}$ to be a graded membership function, it also needs to satisfy the properties *M1* and *M2*. To obtain these two properties for $m_{\bowtie}$, we must require that $\bowtie$ satisfies the following additional property:

- The CSM $\bowtie$ is *equivalence closed* iff the following equivalence holds:
  $C \equiv D$ iff $C \bowtie D = 1$.

Proposition 4. *Let $\bowtie$ be an equivalence invariant, role-depth bounded, and equivalence closed CSM. Then $m_\bowtie$ is a well-defined graded membership function.*

Consequently, an equivalence invariant, role-depth bounded, and equivalence closed CSM $\bowtie$ induces a DL $\tau\mathcal{EL}(m_\bowtie)$. Computing instances of threshold concepts of the form $Q_{>t}$ in this logic corresponds to answering relaxed instance queries w.r.t. $\bowtie$.

Proposition 5. *Let $\bowtie$ be an equivalence invariant, role-depth bounded, and equivalence closed CSM, $\mathcal{A}$ an $\mathcal{EL}$ ABox, and $t \in [0,1)$. Then*

$$\mathrm{Relax}_t^\bowtie(Q, \mathcal{A}) = \{a \mid \mathcal{A} \models Q_{>t}(a) \text{ and } a \text{ occurs in } \mathcal{A}\},$$

where the semantics of the threshold concept $Q_{>t}$ is defined as in $\tau\mathcal{EL}(m_\bowtie)$.

Lehman and Turhan [14] introduce a framework (called *simi framework*) that can be used to define a variety of similarity measures between $\mathcal{EL}$ concepts satisfying the properties required by our Propositions 4 and 5. Here, we consider only one instance of this framework and show that the similarity measure obtained this way induces our graded membership function *deg*.

Lehman and Turhan first define a directional measure and then combine the values obtained by comparing the concepts in both directions with this directional measure.

Definition 11 ([14]). *Let C, D be two $\mathcal{EL}$ concept descriptions. If one of these two concepts is equivalent to $\top$, then we define $simi_d(\top, D) := 1$ for all D and $simi_d(D, \top) := 0$ for $D \not\equiv \top$. Otherwise, let $top(C), top(D)$ respectively be the set of concept names and existential restrictions in the top-level conjunction of C, D. We define*

$$simi_d(C, D) := \frac{\displaystyle\sum_{C' \in top(C)} \max\{simi_a(C', D') \mid D' \in top(D)\}}{|top(C)|}, \quad \text{where}$$

$simi_a(A, A) := 1, \quad simi_a(A, B) := 0$ *for* $A, B \in \mathsf{N_C}, A \neq B$,
$simi_a(\exists r.E, A) := simi_a(A, \exists r.E) := 0$ *for* $A \in \mathsf{N_C}$,
$simi_a(\exists r.E, \exists r.F) := simi_d(E, F), \quad simi_a(\exists r.E, \exists s.F) := 0$ *for* $r, s \in \mathsf{N_R}, r \neq s$.

The bidirectional similarity measure $\bowtie^1$ is then defined as

$$C \bowtie^1 D := \min\{simi_d(C^r, D^r), simi_d(D^r, C^r)\}.$$

It is easy to show that $\bowtie^1$ is equivalence invariant, role-depth bounded, and equivalence closed. Note that equivalence invariance depends on the fact that we apply $simi_d$ to the reduced forms of C, D. Since $\bowtie^1$ satisfies the properties required by Propositions 4, it induces a graded membership function $m_{\bowtie^1}$. We can show that this function coincides with the graded membership function introduced in Section 4 (see [1] for the proof).

Theorem 7. *For all interpretations $\mathcal{I}$, $d \in \Delta^{\mathcal{I}}$, and $\mathcal{EL}$ concept descriptions Q we have $m_{\bowtie^1}^{\mathcal{I}}(d, Q) = deg^{\mathcal{I}}(d, Q)$.*

Proposition 5 thus implies that answering of relaxed instance queries w.r.t. $\bowtie^1$ is the same as computing instances for threshold concepts of the form $Q_{>}t$ in $\tau\mathcal{EL}(deg)$. Since such concepts are positive, Proposition 3 yields the following corollary.

Corollary 1. *Let $\mathcal{A}$ be an $\mathcal{EL}$ ABox, Q an $\mathcal{EL}$ query concept, a an individual name, and $t \in [0, 1)$. Then it can be decided in polynomial time whether $a \in$ $\mathsf{Relax}_t^{\bowtie^1}(Q, \mathcal{A})$ or not.*

Note that Ecke et al. [10,9] show only an NP upper bound w.r.t. data complexity for this problem, albeit for a larger class of instances of the *simi* framework.

7 Conclusion

We have introduced a family of DLs $\tau\mathcal{EL}(m)$ parameterized with a graded membership function m, which extends the popular lightweight DL $\mathcal{EL}$ by threshold concepts that can be used to approximate classical concepts. Inspired by the homomorphism characterization of membership in $\mathcal{EL}$ concepts, we have defined a particular membership function deg and have investigated the complexity of reasoning in $\tau\mathcal{EL}(deg)$. It turns out that the higher expressiveness takes its toll: whereas reasoning in $\mathcal{EL}$ can be done in polynomial time, it is NP- or coNP-complete in $\tau\mathcal{EL}(deg)$, depending on which inference problem is considered. We have also shown that concept similarity measures satisfying certain properties can be used to define graded membership functions. In particular, the function deg can be constructed in this way from a particular instance of the *simi* framework of Lehmann and Turhan [14]. Nevertheless, our direct definition of deg based on homomorphisms is important since the partial tree-to-graph homomorphisms used there are the main technical tool for showing our decidability and complexity results.

While introduced as formalism for defining concepts by approximation, a possible use-case for $\tau\mathcal{EL}(deg)$ is relaxation of instance queries, as motivated and investigated in [10,9]. Compared to the setting considered in [10,9], $\tau\mathcal{EL}(deg)$ yields a considerably more expressive query language since we can combine threshold concepts using the constructors of $\mathcal{EL}$ and can also forbid that thresholds are reached. Restricted to the setting of relaxed instance queries, our approach actually allows relaxed instance checking in polynomial time. On the other hand, [10,9] can also deal with other instances of the *simi* framework.

An important topic for future research is to consider graded membership functions $m_{\bowtie}$ that are induced by other instances of *simi*. We conjecture that these instances can also be defined directly by an appropriate adaptation of our homomorphism-based definition. The hope is then that our decidability and complexity results can be generalized to these functions. Another important topic for future research is to add TBoxes. While acyclic TBoxes can already be handled by our approach through unfolding, we would like to treat them directly by an adaptation of the homomorphism-based approach to avoid a possible exponential blowup due to unfolding. For cyclic and general TBoxes, homomorphisms probably need to be replaced by simulations [2,9].

References

1. Baader, F., Brewka, G., Fernández Gil, O.: Adding threshold concepts to the description logic $\mathcal{EL}$. LTCS-Report LTCS-15-09, TU Dresden, Germany (2015). See http://lat.inf.tu-dresden.de/research/reports.html
2. Baader, F.: Terminological cycles in a description logic with existential restrictions. In: Proc. IJCAI 2003 (2003)
3. Baader, F., Calvanese, D., McGuinness, D.L., Nardi, D., Patel-Schneider, P.F. (eds.): The Description Logic Handbook. Cambridge University Press (2003)
4. Baader, F., Küsters, R., Molitor, R.: Computing least common subsumers in description logics with existential restrictions. In: Proc. IJCAI 1999 (1999)
5. Baader, F., Küsters, R., Molitor, R.: Computing least common subsumers in description logics with existential restrictions. LTCS-Report LTCS-98-09. RWTH Aachen, Germany (1998).
   See http://lat.inf.tu-dresden.de/research/reports.html
6. Borgwardt, S., Distel, F., Peñaloza, R.: The limits of decidability in fuzzy description logics with general concept inclusions. Artificial Intelligence 218 (2015)
7. Brandt, S.: Polynomial time reasoning in a description logic with existential restrictions, GCI axioms, and - what else? In: Proc. ECAI 2004 (2004)
8. Donini, F.M., Lenzerini, M., Nardi, D., Schaerf, A.: Deduction in concept languages: From subsumption to instance checking. J. Log. Comput. 4(4) (1994)
9. Ecke, A., Peñaloza, R., Turhan, A.Y.: Similarity-based relaxed instance queries. Journal of Applied Logic (in press, 2015)
10. Ecke, A., Peñaloza, R., Turhan, A.: Answering instance queries relaxed by concept similarity. In: Proc. KR 2014 (2014)
11. Garey, M.R., Johnson, D.S.: Computers and Intractability: A Guide to the Theory of NP-Completeness. W. H. Freeman (1979)
12. Küsters, R.: Non-Standard Inferences in Description Logics. LNCS (LNAI), vol. 2100. Springer, Heidelberg (2001)
13. Küsters, R., Molitor, R.: Approximating most specific concepts in description logics with existential restrictions. AI Commun. 15(1) (2002)
14. Lehmann, K., Turhan, A.-Y.: A framework for semantic-based similarity measures for $\mathcal{ELH}$-concepts. In: del Cerro, L.F., Herzig, A., Mengin, J. (eds.) JELIA 2012. LNCS, vol. 7519, pp. 307–319. Springer, Heidelberg (2012)
15. Suntisrivaraporn, B.: A similarity measure for the description logic EL with unfoldable terminologies. In: Proc. INCoS 2013 (2013)
16. Baader, F., Brewka, G., Fernández Gil, O.: Adding threshold concepts to the description logic $\mathcal{EL}$. In: Proc. DL 2015 (2015)

Reasoning in Expressive Description Logics under Infinitely Valued Gödel Semantics*

Stefan Borgwardt[1] and Rafael Peñaloza[2]

[1] Theoretical Computer Science, TU Dresden, Germany
Stefan.Borgwardt@tu-dresden.de
[2] KRDB Research Centre, Free University of Bozen-Bolzano, Italy
rafael.penaloza@unibz.it

Abstract. Fuzzy Description Logics (FDLs) combine classical Description Logics with the semantics of Fuzzy Logics in order to represent and reason with vague knowledge. Most FDLs using truth values from the interval $[0, 1]$ have been shown to be undecidable in the presence of a negation constructor and general concept inclusions. One exception are those FDLs whose semantics is based on the infinitely valued Gödel t-norm (G). We extend previous decidability results for the FDL G-$\mathcal{ALC}$ to deal with complex role inclusions, nominals, inverse roles, and qualified number restrictions. Our novel approach is based on a combination of the known crispification technique for finitely valued FDLs and an automata-based procedure for reasoning in G-$\mathcal{ALC}$.

1 Introduction

Description Logics (DLs) are a well-studied family of knowledge representation formalisms [1]. They constitute the logical backbone of the standard Semantic Web ontology language OWL 2,[1] and its profiles, and have been successfully applied to represent the knowledge of many and diverse application domains, particularly in the bio-medical sciences. DLs describe the domain knowledge using *concepts* (such as Patient) that represent sets of individuals, and *roles* (hasChild) that represent connections between individuals. *Ontologies* are collections of axioms formulated over these concepts and roles, which restrict the possible interpretations. The typical axioms considered in DLs are *assertions*, like alice:Patient, providing knowledge about specific individuals; *general concept inclusions (GCIs)*, such as Patient ⊑ Human, which express subset relations between concepts; and *role inclusions* hasChild ∘ hasChild ⊑ hasGrandchild between (chains of) roles. Different DLs are characterized by the constructors allowed to formulate complex concepts, roles, and axioms.

$\mathcal{ALC}$ [30] is a prototypical DL of intermediate expressivity that uses as concept constructors: conjunction (Patient⊓Female), negation (¬Smoker), existential

---

* This work was partially supported by DFG grant BA 1122/17-1 'FuzzyDL', CRC 912 'HAEC', and the Cluster of Excellence 'cfAED', and developed while R. Peñaloza was affiliated with TU Dresden and the Center for Advancing Electronics Dresden.
[1] http://www.w3.org/TR/owl2-overview/

restriction (∃hasChild.HeavySmoker), and value restriction (∀hasChild.Male), and allows assertions and GCIs. The DL underlying the OWL 2 DL standard is called $\mathcal{SROIQ}$ and additionally provides, among others, role inclusions, number restrictions (⩾3 hasChild.Adult), nominals ({alice}), and inverse roles (hasChild⁻). The complexity of common reasoning problems, such as consistency of ontologies or subsumption between concepts, has been extensively studied for these DLs, and ranges from ExpTime to (co-)2-NExpTime [26, 29, 33].

Fuzzy Description Logics (FDLs) have been introduced as extensions of classical DLs to represent and reason with vague knowledge. The main idea is to use truth values from the interval [0, 1] instead of only *true* and *false*. In this way, one can give a more fine-grained semantics to inherently vague concepts like LowFrequency or HighConcentration, which can be found in biomedical ontologies like SNOMED CT[2] and Galen.[3] Different FDLs are characterized not only by the constructors they allow, but also by the way these constructors are interpreted. To interpret conjunction in complex concepts like

$$\exists \text{hasHeartRate.LowFrequency} \sqcap$$
$$\exists \text{hasBloodAlcohol.HighConcentration,}$$

a popular approach is to use so-called *t-norms* [27]. The semantics of the other logical constructors can then be derived from these t-norms in a principled way, as suggested in [20]. Following the principles of mathematical fuzzy logic, existential and value restrictions are interpreted as suprema and infima of truth values, respectively. However, to avoid problems with infinitely many truth values, reasoning in fuzzy DLs is often restricted to so-called *witnessed models* [21], in which these suprema (infima) are required to be maxima (minima); i.e. the truth value of the restriction is witnessed by at least one domain element.

Unfortunately, most FDLs become undecidable when the logic uses GCIs and negation under witnessed model semantics [2, 13, 18]. One of the few exceptions are FDLs using the *Gödel* t-norm, which is defined as min{x, y}, to interpret conjunctions [12]. In the absence of an involutive negation constructor and negated assertions, such FDLs are even trivially equivalent to classical DLs [13]. However, in the presence of the involutive negation, reasoning becomes more complicated. Despite not being as well-behaved as finitely valued FDLs, which use a finite total order of truth values instead of the infinite interval [0, 1], it was shown using an automata-based approach that reasoning in Gödel extensions of $\mathcal{ALC}$ exhibits the same complexity as in the classical case, i.e. it is ExpTime-complete [12]. A major drawback of this approach is that it always has an exponential runtime, even when the input ontology has a simple form.

In the present paper, we present a combination of the automata-based construction for $\mathcal{ALC}$ from [12] and automata-based algorithms and reduction techniques developed for more expressive finitely valued FDLs [5, 6, 10, 11, 14, 15, 31]. We exploit the forest model property of classical DLs [17, 25] to encode order relationships between concepts in a fuzzy interpretation in a manner similar to

---

[2] http://www.ihtsdo.org/snomed-ct/
[3] http://www.opengalen.org/

the Hintikka trees from [12]. However, instead of using automata to determine the existence of such trees, we reduce the fuzzy ontology directly into a classical $\mathcal{ALCOQ}$ ontology, which enables us to use optimized reasoners for classical DLs. In addition to the *cut-concepts* of the form $\boxed{C \geqslant p}$ for a fuzzy concept C and a value p, which are used in the reductions for finitely valued DLs [6, 10, 31], we employ *order concepts* $\boxed{C \leqslant D}$ expressing relationships between fuzzy concepts. The details of these concepts are explained in Section 4. In contrast to the reductions for finitely valued Gödel FDLs [6, 7], our reduction does not produce an exponential blowup in the nesting depth of concepts in the input ontology.

Although our reduction deals with the Gödel extension of $\mathcal{SROIQ}$, it is not correct if all three constructors nominals ($\mathcal{O}$), inverse roles ($\mathcal{I}$), and number restrictions ($\mathcal{Q}$) are present in the ontology, since then one cannot restrict reasoning to forest-shaped models [32]. However, it is correct for $\mathcal{SRIQ}$, $\mathcal{SROQ}$, and $\mathcal{SROI}$, and we obtain several complexity results that match the currently best known upper bounds for reasoning in (sublogics of) these DLs. In particular, we show that reasoning in Gödel extensions of $\mathcal{SRIQ}$ is 2-ExpTime-complete, and for $\mathcal{SHOI}$ and $\mathcal{SHIQ}$ it is ExpTime-complete. Full proofs of all presented results can be found in [16].

2 Preliminaries

We consider vague statements taking truth degrees from the subset $[0, 1]$ of the reals, where the *Gödel t-norm* $\min\{x, y\}$ is used to interpret logical conjunction. The semantics of implications is given by the *residuum* of this t-norm; i.e.,

$$x \Rightarrow y := \begin{cases} 1 & \text{if } x \leqslant y, \\ y & \text{otherwise.} \end{cases}$$

We use both the *residual negation* $x \mapsto (x \Rightarrow 0)$ and the *involutive negation* $x \mapsto (1 - x)$ in the rest of this paper.

We recall some basic definitions from [12]. An *order structure* S is a finite set containing at least the numbers $0, 0.5$, and 1, endowed with an involutive unary operation $\mathsf{inv} \colon S \to S$ such that $\mathsf{inv}(x) = 1 - x$ for all $x \in S \cap [0, 1]$. A *total preorder* over S is a transitive and total binary relation $\preccurlyeq \subseteq S \times S$. For $x, y \in S$, we write $x \equiv y$ if $x \preccurlyeq y$ and $y \preccurlyeq x$. Notice that $\equiv$ is an equivalence relation on S. The total preorders considered in [12] have to satisfy additional properties, e.g. that 0 and 1 are always the least and greatest elements, respectively. These properties can be found in our reduction in the axioms of $\mathsf{red}(\mathcal{U})$ (see Section 4).

We now define the fuzzy description logic $\mathsf{G}\text{-}\mathcal{SROIQ}$. Let $\mathsf{N_I}$, $\mathsf{N_C}$, and $\mathsf{N_R}$ be three mutually disjoint sets of *individual names*, *concept names*, and *role names*, respectively, where $\mathsf{N_R}$ contains the *universal role* r_u. The set of *(complex) roles* is $\mathsf{N_R^-} := \mathsf{N_R} \cup \{r^- \mid r \in \mathsf{N_R}\}$; the elements of the form r^- are called *inverse roles*. Since there are several syntactic restrictions based on which roles appear in which role axioms, we start by defining role hierarchies. A *role hierarchy* $\mathcal{R}_h$ is a finite set of *(complex) role inclusions* of the form $\langle w \sqsubseteq r \geqslant p \rangle$, where $r \neq r_u$

is a role name, $w \in (\mathsf{N_R^-})^+$ is a non-empty *role chain* not including the universal role,[4] and $p \in (0, 1]$. Such a role inclusion is called *simple* if $w \in \mathsf{N_R^-}$. We extend the notation $\cdot^-$ to inverse roles r^- and role chains $w = r_1 \dots r_n$ by setting $(r^-)^- := r$ and $w^- := r_n^- \dots r_1^-$.

We recall the regularity condition from [5,23]. Let $\prec$ be a strict partial order on $\mathsf{N_R^-}$ such that $r \prec s$ iff $r^- \prec s$. A role inclusion $\langle w \sqsubseteq r \geqslant p \rangle$ is $\prec$-*regular* if

- w is of the form rr or r^-, or
- w is of the form $r_1 \dots r_n$, $rr_1 \dots r_n$, or $r_1 \dots r_n r$, and for all $1 \leqslant i \leqslant n$ it holds that $r_i \prec r$.

A role hierarchy $\mathcal{R}_h$ is *regular* if there is a strict partial order $\prec$ as above such that each role inclusion in $\mathcal{R}_h$ is $\prec$-regular. A role name r is *simple* (w.r.t. $\mathcal{R}_h$) if for each $\langle w \sqsubseteq r \geqslant p \rangle \in \mathcal{R}_h$ we have that w is of the form s or s^- for a simple role s. This notion is well-defined since the regularity condition prevents any cyclic dependencies between role names in $\mathcal{R}_h$. An inverse role r^- is *simple* if r is simple. In the following, we always assume that we have a regular role hierarchy $\mathcal{R}_h$.

Concepts in G-$\mathcal{SROIQ}$ are built from concept names using the constructors listed in the upper part of Table 1, where C, D denote concepts, p is a rational number from $[0, 1]$, $n \in \mathbb{N}$, $a \in \mathsf{N_I}$, $r \in \mathsf{N_R^-}$, and $s \in \mathsf{N_R^-}$ is a simple role. The restriction to simple roles in at-least restrictions is necessary to ensure decidability [24]. We also use the common DL constructors $\top := \bar{1}$ (top concept), $\bot := \bar{0}$ (bottom concept), $C \sqcup D := \neg(\neg C \sqcap \neg D)$ (disjunction), and $\leqslant n \, s.C := \neg(\geqslant(n+1) \, s.C)$ (at-most restriction).

Note that we use the involutive negation to define at-most restrictions. In [7], they are defined using the residual negation: $\leqslant n \, s.C := (\geqslant(n+1) \, s.C) \to \bot$. This has the effect that the value of $\leqslant n \, r.C$ is always either 0 or 1 (see the semantics below). However, this discrepancy in definitions is not an issue since our reduction can handle both cases. The use of rational truth constants $\bar{p}$ is not standard in FDLs, but it allows us to simulate *fuzzy nominals* [4] of the form $\{p_1/a_1, \dots, p_n/a_n\}$ with $p_i \in [0, 1]$ and $a_i \in \mathsf{N_I}$, $1 \leqslant i \leqslant n$, via $(\{a_1\} \sqcap \overline{p_1}) \sqcup \dots \sqcup (\{a_n\} \sqcap \overline{p_n})$.

The semantics of G-$\mathcal{SROIQ}$ is based on G-*interpretations* $\mathcal{I} = (\Delta^{\mathcal{I}}, \cdot^{\mathcal{I}})$ over a non-empty *domain* $\Delta^{\mathcal{I}}$, which assign to each individual name $a \in \mathsf{N_I}$ an element $a^{\mathcal{I}} \in \Delta^{\mathcal{I}}$, to each concept name $A \in \mathsf{N_C}$ a fuzzy set $A^{\mathcal{I}} \colon \Delta^{\mathcal{I}} \to [0, 1]$, and to each role name $r \in \mathsf{N_R}$ a fuzzy binary relation $r^{\mathcal{I}} \colon \Delta^{\mathcal{I}} \times \Delta^{\mathcal{I}} \to [0, 1]$. This interpretation is extended to complex concepts and roles as defined in the last column of Table 1, for all $d, e \in \Delta^{\mathcal{I}}$.

We restrict all reasoning problems to *witnessed* G-interpretations [21], which intuitively require the suprema and infima in the semantics to be maxima and minima, respectively. Formally, a G-interpretation $\mathcal{I}$ is *witnessed* if, for every $d \in \Delta^{\mathcal{I}}$, $n \geqslant 0$, $r \in \mathsf{N_R^-}$, simple $s \in \mathsf{N_R^-}$, and concept C, there are

---

4   For ease of presentation, we omit the composition symbol $\circ$ from role chains.

Table 1. Syntax and semantics of G-$\mathcal{SROIQ}$

Name	Syntax	Semantics ($C^{\mathcal{I}}(d)$ / $r^{\mathcal{I}}(d,e)$)
concept name	A	$A^{\mathcal{I}}(d) \in [0,1]$
truth constant	$\overline{p}$	p
conjunction	$C \sqcap D$	$\min\{C^{\mathcal{I}}(d), D^{\mathcal{I}}(d)\}$
implication	$C \to D$	$C^{\mathcal{I}}(d) \Rightarrow D^{\mathcal{I}}(d)$
negation	$\neg C$	$1 - C^{\mathcal{I}}(d)$
existential restriction	$\exists r.C$	$\displaystyle\sup_{e \in \Delta^{\mathcal{I}}} \min\{r^{\mathcal{I}}(d,e), C^{\mathcal{I}}(e)\}$
value restriction	$\forall r.C$	$\displaystyle\inf_{e \in \Delta^{\mathcal{I}}} r^{\mathcal{I}}(d,e) \Rightarrow C^{\mathcal{I}}(e)$
nominal	$\{a\}$	$\begin{cases} 1 & \text{if } d = a^{\mathcal{I}} \\ 0 & \text{otherwise} \end{cases}$
at-least restriction	$\geqslant n\, s.C$	$\displaystyle\sup_{\substack{e_1,\dots,e_n \in \Delta^{\mathcal{I}} \\ \text{pairwise different}}} \min_{i=1}^{n} \min\{s^{\mathcal{I}}(d,e_i), C^{\mathcal{I}}(e_i)\}$
local reflexivity	$\exists s.\mathsf{Self}$	$r^{\mathcal{I}}(d,d)$
role name	r	$r^{\mathcal{I}}(d,e) \in [0,1]$
inverse role	r^-	$r^{\mathcal{I}}(e,d)$
universal role	r_u	1

$e, e', e_1, \dots, e_n \in \Delta^{\mathcal{I}}$ such that $e_1, \dots, e_n$ are pairwise different,

$$(\exists r.C)^{\mathcal{I}}(d) = \min\{r^{\mathcal{I}}(d,e), C^{\mathcal{I}}(e)\},$$
$$(\forall r.C)^{\mathcal{I}}(d) = r^{\mathcal{I}}(d,e') \Rightarrow C^{\mathcal{I}}(e'), \text{ and}$$
$$(\geqslant n\, s.C)^{\mathcal{I}}(d) = \min_{i=1}^{n} \min\{s^{\mathcal{I}}(d,e_i), C^{\mathcal{I}}(e_i)\}.$$

As we have seen already in the role inclusions, the axioms of G-$\mathcal{SROIQ}$ extend classical axioms by stating a degree in $(0,1]$ to which the axioms hold. Moreover, we can compare the degrees of arbitrary *classical assertions* of the form $a{:}C$ or $(a,b){:}r$ for $a, b \in \mathsf{N_I}$, $r \in \mathsf{N_R}$, and a concept C. An *order assertion* [12] is of the form $\langle \alpha \bowtie p \rangle$ or $\langle \alpha \bowtie \beta \rangle$ for classical assertions α, β, $\bowtie \in \{<, \leqslant, =, \geqslant, >\}$, and $p \in [0,1]$. An *ordered ABox* is a finite set of order assertions and *individual (in)equality assertions* of the form $a \approx b$ ($a \not\approx b$) for $a, b \in \mathsf{N_I}$. A *general concept inclusion (GCI)* is of the form $\langle C \sqsubseteq D \geqslant p \rangle$ for concepts C, D and $p \in (0,1]$. A *TBox* is a finite set of GCIs. A *disjoint role axiom* is of the form $\langle \mathsf{dis}(r,s) \geqslant p \rangle$ for two simple roles $r, s \in \mathsf{N_R^-}$ and $p \in (0,1]$. A *reflexivity axiom* is of the form $\langle \mathsf{ref}(r) \geqslant p \rangle$ for a role $r \in \mathsf{N_R^-}$ and $p \in (0,1]$. An *RBox* $\mathcal{R} = \mathcal{R}_h \cup \mathcal{R}_a$ consists of a role hierarchy $\mathcal{R}_h$ and a finite set $\mathcal{R}_a$ of disjoint role and reflexivity axioms. An *ontology* $\mathcal{O} = (\mathcal{A}, \mathcal{T}, \mathcal{R})$ consists of an ABox $\mathcal{A}$, a TBox $\mathcal{T}$, and an RBox $\mathcal{R}$.

A G-interpretation $\mathcal{I}$ *satisfies* (or is a *model* of)

- an order assertion $\langle \alpha \bowtie \beta \rangle$ if $\alpha^{\mathcal{I}} \bowtie \beta^{\mathcal{I}}$ (where $p^{\mathcal{I}} := p$, $(a{:}C)^{\mathcal{I}} := C^{\mathcal{I}}(a^{\mathcal{I}})$, and $((a,b){:}r)^{\mathcal{I}} := r^{\mathcal{I}}(a^{\mathcal{I}}, b^{\mathcal{I}}))$;
- an (in)equality assertion $a \approx b$ $(a \not\approx b)$ if $a^{\mathcal{I}} = b^{\mathcal{I}}$ $(a^{\mathcal{I}} \neq b^{\mathcal{I}})$;
- a GCI $\langle C \sqsubseteq D \geqslant p \rangle$ if $C^{\mathcal{I}}(d) \Rightarrow D^{\mathcal{I}}(d) \geqslant p$ holds for all $d \in \Delta^{\mathcal{I}}$;
- a role inclusion $\langle r_1 \ldots r_n \sqsubseteq r \geqslant p \rangle$ if $(r_1 \ldots r_n)^{\mathcal{I}}(d_0, d_n) \Rightarrow r^{\mathcal{I}}(d_0, d_n) \geqslant p$ holds for all $d_0, d_n \in \Delta^{\mathcal{I}}$, where

$$(r_1 \ldots r_n)^{\mathcal{I}}(d_0, d_n) := \sup_{d_1, \ldots, d_{n-1} \in \Delta^{\mathcal{I}}} \min_{i=1}^{n} r_i^{\mathcal{I}}(d_{i-1}, d_i);$$

- a disjoint role axiom $\langle \mathsf{dis}(r,s) \geqslant p \rangle$ if $\min\{r^{\mathcal{I}}(d,e), s^{\mathcal{I}}(d,e)\} \leqslant 1 - p$ holds for all $d, e \in \Delta^{\mathcal{I}}$;
- a reflexivity axiom $\langle \mathsf{ref}(r) \geqslant p \rangle$ if $r^{\mathcal{I}}(d,d) \geqslant p$ holds for all $d \in \Delta^{\mathcal{I}}$;
- an ontology if it satisfies all its axioms.

An ontology is *consistent* if it has a (witnessed) model.

We can simulate other common role axioms in G-$\mathcal{SROIQ}$ [7, 22] by those we introduced above:

- transitivity axioms $\langle \mathsf{tra}(r) \geqslant p \rangle$ by $\langle rr \sqsubseteq r \geqslant p \rangle$;
- symmetry axioms $\langle \mathsf{sym}(r) \geqslant p \rangle$ by $\langle r^- \sqsubseteq r \geqslant p \rangle$;
- asymmetry axioms $\langle \mathsf{asy}(s) \geqslant p \rangle$ by $\langle \mathsf{dis}(s, s^-) \geqslant p \rangle$;
- irreflexivity axioms $\langle \mathsf{irr}(s) \geqslant p \rangle$ by $\langle \exists s.\mathsf{Self} \sqsubseteq \neg \overline{p} \geqslant 1 \rangle$; and
- negated role assertions $\langle (a,b){:}\neg r \geqslant p \rangle$ by $\langle (a,b){:}r \leqslant 1 - p \rangle$.

For an ontology $\mathcal{O}$, we denote by $\mathsf{rol}(\mathcal{O})$ the set of all roles occurring in $\mathcal{O}$, together with their inverses; by $\mathsf{ind}(\mathcal{O})$ the set of all individual names occurring in $\mathcal{O}$, and by $\mathsf{sub}(\mathcal{O})$ the closure under negation of the set of all subconcepts occurring in $\mathcal{O}$. We consider $\neg\neg C$ to be equal to C, and thus $\mathsf{sub}(\mathcal{O})$ is of quadratic size in the size of $\mathcal{O}$. We denote by $\mathcal{V}_{\mathcal{O}}$ the closure under the involutive negation $x \mapsto 1 - x$ of the set of all truth degrees appearing in $\mathcal{O}$ (either in axioms or in truth constants), together with 0, 0.5, and 1. This set is of linear size.

Other common reasoning problems for FDLs, such as concept satisfiability and subsumption can be reduced to consistency [12]: the subsumption between C and D to degree q w.r.t. a TBox $\mathcal{T}$ and an RBox $\mathcal{R}$ is equivalent to the inconsistency of $(\{\langle a{:}C \to D < q \rangle\}, \mathcal{T}, \mathcal{R})$, and the satisfiability of C to degree q w.r.t. $\mathcal{T}$ and $\mathcal{R}$ is equivalent to the consistency of $(\{\langle a{:}C \geqslant q \rangle\}, \mathcal{T}, \mathcal{R})$.

The letter $\mathcal{I}$ in G-$\mathcal{SROIQ}$ denotes the presence of inverse roles and the universal role. If such roles are not allowed, the resulting logic is written as G-$\mathcal{SROQ}$. Likewise, the name G-$\mathcal{SRIQ}$ indicates the absence of nominals, and G-$\mathcal{SROI}$ that of at-least and at-most restrictions. Replacing the letter $\mathcal{R}$ with $\mathcal{H}$ indicates that RBoxes are restricted to simple role inclusions, ABoxes are restricted to order assertions, and local reflexivity is not allowed; however, the letter $\mathcal{S}$ indicates that transitivity axioms are still allowed. Hence, in G-$\mathcal{SHOIQ}$ we can use role inclusions of the forms $\langle r \sqsubseteq s \geqslant p \rangle$ and $\langle rr \sqsubseteq r \geqslant p \rangle$. Disallowing axioms of the first type removes the letter $\mathcal{H}$, while the absence of transitivity axioms is denoted by replacing $\mathcal{S}$ with $\mathcal{ALC}$.

Classical DLs are obtained from the above definitions by restricting the set of truth values to 0 and 1. The semantics of a classical concept C is then viewed as a set $C^{\mathcal{I}} \subseteq \Delta^{\mathcal{I}}$ instead of the characteristic function $C^{\mathcal{I}} : \Delta^{\mathcal{I}} \to \{0, 1\}$, and likewise for roles. In this setting, all axioms (also order assertions) are restricted to be of the form $\langle \alpha \geqslant 1 \rangle$, and usually this is simply written as α, e.g. $C \sqsubseteq D$ instead of $\langle C \sqsubseteq D \geqslant 1 \rangle$. We also use $C \equiv D$ to abbreviate $C \sqsubseteq D$ and $D \sqsubseteq C$. Furthermore, the implication constructor $C \to D$, although usually not included in classical DLs, can be expressed via $\neg C \sqcup D$.

In this paper, we provide a reduction from a G-$\mathcal{SROIQ}$ ontology to a classical $\mathcal{ALCOQ}$ ontology. For all sublogics of G-$\mathcal{SROIQ}$ that do not contain the constructors $\mathcal{O}$, $\mathcal{I}$, and $\mathcal{Q}$ at the same time, the reduction preserves consistency. Before we describe the main reduction, however, we provide a characterization of role hierarchies using (weighted) finite automata.

3 Automata for Complex Role Inclusions

Let $\mathcal{O} = (\mathcal{A}, \mathcal{T}, \mathcal{R})$ be a G-$\mathcal{SROIQ}$ ontology. We extend the idea from [23] of using finite automata to characterize all role chains that imply a given role w.r.t. $\mathcal{R}_h$. Here, we use a kind of weighted automata [19], which use as input symbols the roles in $\mathrm{rol}(\mathcal{O})$, and compute a weight for any given input word.

Definition 1 (WFA). A weighted finite automaton (WFA) is a quadruple $\mathbf{A} = (Q, q_{\mathrm{ini}}, \mathrm{wt}, q_{\mathrm{fin}})$, consisting of a non-empty set Q of states, an initial state $q_{\mathrm{ini}} \in Q$, a transition weight function $\mathrm{wt} \colon Q \times (\mathrm{rol}(\mathcal{O}) \cup \{\varepsilon\}) \times Q \to [0, 1]$, and a final state $q_{\mathrm{fin}} \in Q$. Given an input word $w \in \mathrm{rol}(\mathcal{O})^*$, a run of $\mathbf{A}$ on w is a non-empty sequence of pairs $\mathbf{r} = (w_i, q_i)_{0 \leqslant i \leqslant m}$ such that $(w_0, q_0) = (w, q_{\mathrm{ini}})$, $(w_m, q_m) = (\varepsilon, q_{\mathrm{fin}})$, and for each i, $1 \leqslant i \leqslant m$, it holds that $w_{i-1} = x_i w_i$ for some $x_i \in \mathrm{rol}(\mathcal{O}) \cup \{\varepsilon\}$. The weight of such a run is $\mathrm{wt}(\mathbf{r}) := \min_{i=1}^{m} \mathrm{wt}(q_{i-1}, x_i, q_i)$. The behavior of $\mathbf{A}$ on w is $(\|\mathbf{A}\|, w) := \sup_{\mathbf{r} \text{ run of } \mathbf{A} \text{ on } w} \mathrm{wt}(\mathbf{r})$.

We often denote by $q \xrightarrow{x, p} q' \in \mathbf{A}$ the fact that $\mathrm{wt}(q, x, q') = p$. Further, for a state q of $\mathbf{A}$, we denote by $\mathbf{A}^q$ the automaton resulting from $\mathbf{A}$ by making q the initial state.

Following [23], we now construct, for each role r, a WFA $\mathbf{A}_r$ that recognizes all role chains that "imply" r w.r.t. $\mathcal{R}_h$ (with associated degrees). This construction proceeds in several steps. The first automaton $\mathbf{A}_r^0$ contains the initial state i_r, the final state f_r, and the transition $i_r \xrightarrow{r, 1} f_r$, as well as the following transitions for each $\langle w \sqsubseteq r \geqslant p \rangle \in \mathcal{R}$:

- if $w = rr$, then $f_r \xrightarrow{\varepsilon, p} i_r$;
- if $w = r_1 \dots r_n$ with $r_1 \neq r \neq r_n$, then $i_r \xrightarrow{r_1, 1} q_w^1 \xrightarrow{r_2, 1} \dots \xrightarrow{r_n, 1} q_w^n \xrightarrow{\varepsilon, p} f_r$;
- if $w = rr_1 \dots r_n$, then $f_r \xrightarrow{r_1, 1} q_w^1 \xrightarrow{r_2, 1} \dots \xrightarrow{r_n, 1} q_w^n \xrightarrow{\varepsilon, p} f_r$; and
- if $w = r_1 \dots r_n r$, then $i_r \xrightarrow{r_1, 1} q_w^1 \xrightarrow{r_2, 1} \dots \xrightarrow{r_n, 1} q_w^n \xrightarrow{\varepsilon, p} i_r$,

where all states q_w^i are distinct. Here and in the following, all transitions that are not explicitly mentioned have weight 0.

The WFA $\mathbf{A}_r^1$ is now defined as $\mathbf{A}_r^0$ if there is no role inclusion of the form $\langle r^- \sqsubseteq r \geqslant p \rangle \in \mathcal{R}$; otherwise, $\mathbf{A}_r^1$ is the disjoint union of $\mathbf{A}_r^0$ and a mirrored copy of $\mathbf{A}_r^0$, where i_r is the only initial state, f_r is the only final state, and the following transitions are added for the copy f_r' of f_r and the copy i_r' of i_r:

$i_r \xrightarrow{\varepsilon,p} f_r'$, $f_r' \xrightarrow{\varepsilon,p} i_r$, $f_r \xrightarrow{\varepsilon,p} i_r'$, and $i_r' \xrightarrow{\varepsilon,p} f_r$.

Finally, we define the WFA $\mathbf{A}_r$ by induction on $\prec$ as follows:

- if r is minimal w.r.t. $\prec$, then $\mathbf{A}_r := \mathbf{A}_r^1$;
- otherwise, $\mathbf{A}_r$ is the disjoint union of $\mathbf{A}_r^1$ with a copy $\mathbf{A}_s^{1'}$ of $\mathbf{A}_s^1$ for each transition $q \xrightarrow{s,1} q'$ in $\mathbf{A}_r^1$ with $s \neq r$.[5] For each such transition, we add ε-transitions with weight 1 from q to the initial state of $\mathbf{A}_s^{1'}$ and from the final state of $\mathbf{A}_s^{1'}$ to q'.
- The automaton $\mathbf{A}_{r^-}$ is a mirrored copy of $\mathbf{A}_r$.

The difference to the construction in [23] is only the inclusion of the appropriate weights for each considered role inclusion. As shown in [23], the size of each $\mathbf{A}_r$ is bounded exponentially in the length of the longest chain $r_1 \prec \cdots \prec r_n$ for which there are role inclusions $\langle u_i r_{i-1} v_i \sqsubseteq r_i \geqslant p_i \rangle \in \mathcal{R}$ for all i, $2 \leqslant i \leqslant n$.

The following generalization of [23, Proposition 9] describes the promised characterization of the role inclusions in $\mathcal{R}$ in terms of the behavior of the automata $\mathbf{A}_r$. A detailed proof can be found in [16].

Lemma 2. *A* G-*interpretation* $\mathcal{I}$ *satisfies all role inclusions in* $\mathcal{R}$ *iff for every* $r \in \mathsf{rol}(\mathcal{O})$, *every* $w \in \mathsf{rol}(\mathcal{O})^+$, *and all* $d, e \in \Delta^{\mathcal{I}}$, *we have*

$$w^{\mathcal{I}}(d, e) \Rightarrow r^{\mathcal{I}}(d, e) \geqslant (\|\mathbf{A}_r\|, w).$$

Intuitively, the degree to which the interpretation of w must be "included" in the interpretation of r is determined by the behavior of $\|\mathbf{A}_r\|$ on w.

For the universal role r_u, we define $\mathbf{A}_{r_u}$ as above based on the role inclusions $\langle r_u^- \sqsubseteq r_u \geqslant 1 \rangle$, $\langle r_u r_u \sqsubseteq r_u \geqslant 1 \rangle$, and $\langle r \sqsubseteq r_u \geqslant 1 \rangle$ for all $r \in \mathsf{rol}(\mathcal{O})$. Hence, $\mathbf{A}_{r_u}$ accepts any (non-empty) word $w \in \mathsf{rol}(\mathcal{O})^+$ with degree 1, and it is easy to see that Lemma 2 also holds for r_u.

4   The Reduction

We now describe the reduction from $\mathcal{O}$ to a classical $\mathcal{ALCOQ}$ ontology $\mathsf{red}(\mathcal{O})$. This reduction always uses nominals, even in the logic G-$\mathcal{SRIQ}$. However, if number restrictions are not allowed (e.g. in G-$\mathcal{SROI}$), then $\mathsf{red}(\mathcal{O})$ is an $\mathcal{ALCO}$ ontology. For ease of presentation, we consider here only the FDL G-$\mathcal{SROQ}$ without (local) reflexivity statements of the form $\exists r.\mathsf{Self}$ or $\langle \mathsf{ref}(r) \geqslant p \rangle$. In the presence of these constructors and inverse roles, the reduction contains some

---

[5] Note that all transitions labeled with roles have weight 0 or 1.

additional concepts and axioms, but the main ideas remain the same. The full construction can be found in [16].

We first extend the set $\mathsf{sub}(\mathcal{O})$ by all nominals $\{a\}$, $a \in \mathsf{ind}(\mathcal{O})$, (and their negations) to be able to distinguish all named domain elements. We further add all "concepts" of the form $\forall \mathbf{A}_r^q.C$ ($\exists \mathbf{A}_r^q.C$) for all $\forall r.C$ ($\exists r.C$) occurring in $\mathcal{O}$ and all states q of $\mathbf{A}_r$. These concepts help to transfer the constraints imposed by the existential and value restrictions along all role chains that imply the possibly non-simple role r. The semantics of $\forall \mathbf{A}.C$ is defined as follows:

$$(\forall \mathbf{A}.C)^{\mathcal{I}}(d) := \inf_{w \in \mathsf{rol}(\mathcal{O})^*} \inf_{e \in \Delta^{\mathcal{I}}} \min\{(\|\mathbf{A}\|, w), w^{\mathcal{I}}(d, e)\} \Rightarrow C^{\mathcal{I}}(e),$$

where $\varepsilon^{\mathcal{I}}(d, e) := 1$ if $d = e$, and $\varepsilon^{\mathcal{I}}(d, e) := 0$ otherwise. Intuitively, it behaves like a value restriction, but instead of considering only the role r, we consider any role chain w, weighted by the behavior of $\mathbf{A}$ on w. Recall that for $\mathbf{A}_r$, this behavior represents the degree to which w implies r w.r.t. $\mathcal{R}_h$ (see Lemma 2).

The idea is that in our reduction we do not need to explicitly represent all role connections, but only a "skeleton" of connections which are necessary to satisfy the witnessing conditions for role restrictions. The restrictions for all implied role connections are then handled by the concepts $\forall \mathbf{A}_r.C$ and $\exists \mathbf{A}_r.C$ by simulating the transitions of $\mathbf{A}_r$; each transition corresponds to a role connection to a new domain element. Note that we do not need to introduce concepts of the form $\geqslant n \, \mathbf{A}_r.C$ since all roles in at-least restrictions must be simple, i.e. there can be no role chains of length > 1 that imply them (at least not with a degree > 0).

The main idea of the reduction is that instead of precisely defining the interpretation of all concepts at each domain element, it suffices to consider a total preorder on them. For example, if an axiom restricts the value of $C \to D$ at each domain element to be $\geqslant 0.5$, then we do not have to find the exact values of C and D, but only to ensure that either $C^{\mathcal{I}}(d) \leqslant D^{\mathcal{I}}(d)$ or else $D^{\mathcal{I}}(d) \geqslant 0.5$. This information is encoded by total preorders over the order structure $\mathcal{U}$ that is defined below. The other main insight for our reduction is that we consider only (quasi-)forest-shaped models of $\mathcal{O}$ [17]. In such a model, the domain elements identified by individual names serve as the roots of several tree-shaped structures. The roots themselves may be arbitrarily interconnected by roles. Due to nominals, there may also be role connections from any domain element back to the roots. Note that complex role inclusions may actually imply role connections between arbitrary domain elements, but the underlying tree-shaped "skeleton" is what is important for reasoning purposes (for details, see [17] and our correctness proof in [16]). This dependence on forest-shaped models is the reason why our reduction works only for G-$\mathcal{SROI}$, G-$\mathcal{SROQ}$, and G-$\mathcal{SRIQ}$—even classical $\mathcal{ALCOIQ}$ does not have the forest model property [32].

We now define the order structure $\mathcal{U}$ as follows:

$$\mathcal{U}_{\mathcal{A}} := \mathcal{V}_{\mathcal{O}} \cup \{a{:}C \mid a \in \mathsf{ind}(\mathcal{O}), \ C \in \mathsf{sub}(\mathcal{O})\} \cup$$
$$\{(a, b){:}s \mid a, b \in \mathsf{ind}(\mathcal{O}), \ r \in \mathsf{rol}(\mathcal{O}), \ s \in \{r, \neg r\}\}$$
$$\mathcal{U} := \mathcal{U}_{\mathcal{A}} \cup \mathsf{sub}(\mathcal{O}) \cup \mathsf{sub}_{\uparrow}(\mathcal{O}) \cup$$
$$\{s, \ (*, a){:}s \mid a \in \mathsf{ind}(\mathcal{O}), \ r \in \mathsf{rol}(\mathcal{O}), \ s \in \{r, \neg r\}\},$$

where $\mathsf{sub}_\uparrow(\mathcal{O}) := \{\langle C \rangle_\uparrow \mid C \in \mathsf{sub}(\mathcal{O})\}$ and the function inv is defined by $\mathsf{inv}(C) := \neg C$, $\mathsf{inv}(a\!:\!C) := a\!:\!\neg C$, $\mathsf{inv}(*,a)\!:\!r := (*,a)\!:\!\neg r$, etc.

Total preorders on assertions in $\mathcal{U}_\mathcal{A}$ are used to describe the behavior of the named root elements in the forest-shaped model. For example, if the order is such that $a\!:\!C > (a,b)\!:\!r$, the idea is that in the corresponding G-model $\mathcal{I}$ of $\mathcal{O}$ the value of C at a is strictly greater that the value of the r-connection from a to b, i.e. $C^\mathcal{I}(a^\mathcal{I}) > r^\mathcal{I}(a^\mathcal{I}, b^\mathcal{I})$. For each domain element of $\mathcal{I}$, total preorders on the elements of $\mathsf{sub}(\mathcal{O})$ describe the degrees of all relevant concepts in a similar way. The elements of $\mathsf{sub}_\uparrow(\mathcal{O})$ are used to refer to degrees of concepts at the unique predecessor element in the tree-shaped parts of the interpretation. For convenience, we also define $\langle p \rangle_\uparrow := p$ for all $p \in \mathcal{V}_\mathcal{O}$. The elements $r \in \mathsf{rol}(\mathcal{O})$ represent the values of the role connections from the predecessor. The special elements $(*,a)\!:\!r$ describe role connections between arbitrary domain elements (represented by $*$) and the named elements in the roots.

In order to describe total preorders over $\mathcal{U}$ with a classical $\mathcal{ALCOQ}$ ontology, we use special concept names of the form $\boxed{\alpha \leqslant \beta}$ for $\alpha, \beta \in \mathcal{U}$. This differs from previous reductions for finitely valued FDLs [7,9,31] in that we not only consider *cut-concepts* of the form $\boxed{p \leqslant C}$ with $p \in \mathcal{V}_\mathcal{O}$, but also relationships between different concepts.[6] We use the abbreviations $\boxed{\alpha \geqslant \beta} := \boxed{\beta \leqslant \alpha}$, $\boxed{\alpha < \beta} := \neg\boxed{\alpha \geqslant \beta}$, and similarly for $=$ and $>$. Furthermore, we define the complex expressions

- $\boxed{\alpha \geqslant \min\{\beta,\gamma\}} := \boxed{\alpha \geqslant \beta} \sqcup \boxed{\alpha \geqslant \gamma}$,
- $\boxed{\alpha \leqslant \min\{\beta,\gamma\}} := \boxed{\alpha \leqslant \beta} \sqcap \boxed{\alpha \leqslant \gamma}$,
- $\boxed{\alpha \geqslant \beta \Rightarrow \gamma} := (\boxed{\beta \leqslant \gamma} \rightarrow \boxed{\alpha \geqslant 1}) \sqcap (\boxed{\beta > \gamma} \rightarrow \boxed{\alpha \geqslant \gamma})$,
- $\boxed{\alpha \leqslant \beta \Rightarrow \gamma} := \boxed{\beta \leqslant \gamma} \sqcup \boxed{\alpha \leqslant \gamma}$,

and extend these notions to $\boxed{\alpha \bowtie \beta \Rightarrow \gamma}$ etc., for $\bowtie \in \{<,=,>\}$, analogously.

In our reduction, we additionally use the special concept name AN to identify the *anonymous* domain elements, i.e. those which are not of the form $b^\mathcal{I}$ for any $b \in \mathsf{ind}(\mathcal{O})$. The reduction uses only one classical role name $\mathfrak{r}$, which simulates the tree structure of the fuzzy interpretation; the actual values of the fuzzy roles in this tree are expressed using the elements in $\mathcal{U}$. The reduced ontology $\mathsf{red}(\mathcal{O})$ consists of the parts $\mathsf{red}(\mathcal{U})$, $\mathsf{red}(\mathcal{A})$, $\mathsf{red}(\mathsf{AN})$, $\mathsf{red}(\uparrow)$, $\mathsf{red}(\mathcal{R})$, $\mathsf{red}(\mathcal{T})$, and $\mathsf{red}(C)$ for all $C \in \mathsf{sub}(\mathcal{O})$, which we define in the following. We emphasize again that $\mathsf{red}(\mathcal{O})$ is formulated in $\mathcal{ALCOQ}$, whenever $\mathcal{O}$ is in G-$\mathcal{SRIQ}$ or G-$\mathcal{SROQ}$, and in $\mathcal{ALCO}$ if $\mathcal{O}$ is a G-$\mathcal{SROI}$ ontology. This is due to the fact that we always use nominals to distinguish the named from the anonymous part of the forest-shaped model, and the inverse of $\mathfrak{r}$ is not needed in the reduction (see [16] for details).

The first part of $\mathsf{red}(\mathcal{O})$ is

$$\mathsf{red}(\mathcal{U}) := \{\boxed{\alpha \leqslant \beta} \sqcap \boxed{\beta \leqslant \gamma} \sqsubseteq \boxed{\alpha \leqslant \gamma} \mid \alpha,\beta,\gamma \in \mathcal{U}\} \cup$$
$$\{\top \sqsubseteq \boxed{\alpha \leqslant \beta} \sqcup \boxed{\beta \leqslant \alpha} \mid \alpha,\beta \in \mathcal{U}\} \cup$$
$$\{\top \sqsubseteq \boxed{0 \leqslant \alpha} \sqcap \boxed{\alpha \leqslant 1} \mid \alpha \in \mathcal{U}\} \cup$$
$$\{\top \sqsubseteq \boxed{\alpha \bowtie \beta} \mid \alpha,\beta \in \mathcal{V}_\mathcal{O}, \ \alpha \bowtie \beta\} \cup$$
$$\{\boxed{\alpha \leqslant \beta} \sqsubseteq \boxed{\mathsf{inv}(\beta) \leqslant \mathsf{inv}(\alpha)} \mid \alpha,\beta \in \mathcal{U}\}.$$

---

[6] For the rest of this paper, the expressions $\boxed{\alpha \leqslant \beta}$ denote classical concept names.

These axioms ensure that at each domain element the relation "$\leqslant$" forms a total preorder compatible with the values in $\mathcal{V}_\mathcal{O}$, and that inv is an antitone operator. To describe the behavior of the named elements, we use the following axioms:

$$\text{red}(\mathcal{A}) := \{c:\boxed{\alpha \bowtie \beta} \mid \langle \alpha \bowtie \beta \rangle \in \mathcal{A}\} \cup \{a \approx b \in \mathcal{A}\} \cup \{a \not\approx b \in \mathcal{A}\} \cup$$
$$\{(a,b):\mathfrak{r} \mid a,b \in \text{ind}(\mathcal{O})\} \cup \{\boxed{\alpha \bowtie \beta} \sqsubseteq \forall \mathfrak{r}.\boxed{\alpha \bowtie \beta} \mid \alpha, \beta \in \mathcal{U}_\mathcal{A}\} \cup$$
$$\{a:\boxed{a:C = C} \mid a \in \text{ind}(\mathcal{O}), \ C \in \text{sub}(\mathcal{O})\} \cup$$
$$\{a:\boxed{(a,b):r = (*,b):r} \mid a,b \in \text{ind}(\mathcal{O}), \ r \in \text{rol}(\mathcal{O})\},$$

where c is an arbitrary individual name. The first two lines are responsible for enforcing that the ABox is satisfied and that information about the behavior of the named individuals is available throughout the whole model. The remaining axioms describe various equivalences for named individuals, e.g. that $(a,b):r$ and $(*,b):r$ should have the same value when evaluated at a.

The next axiom defines the concept AN of all *anonymous* elements, i.e. those that are not designated by an individual name:

$$\text{red}(\text{AN}) := \Big\{ \neg \text{AN} \equiv \bigsqcup_{a \in \text{ind}(\mathcal{O})} \{a\} \Big\}.$$

The following axioms ensure that the order of an element in a tree-shaped part of the model is known at each of its successors via the elements of $\text{sub}_\uparrow(\mathcal{O})$:

$$\text{red}(\uparrow) := \{ \boxed{\alpha \bowtie \beta} \sqsubseteq \forall \mathfrak{r}.(\text{AN} \rightarrow \boxed{\langle \alpha \rangle_\uparrow \bowtie \langle \beta \rangle_\uparrow}) \mid \alpha, \beta \in \mathcal{V}_\mathcal{O} \cup \text{sub}(\mathcal{O})\}.$$

We now come to the reduction of the RBox:

$$\text{red}(\mathcal{R}) := \{\top \sqsubseteq \boxed{(a,b):r \Rightarrow (a,b):s \geqslant p} \sqcap \boxed{r \Rightarrow s \geqslant p} \mid$$
$$\langle r \sqsubseteq s \geqslant p \rangle \in \mathcal{R}, \ a,b \in \text{ind}(\mathcal{O}) \cup \{*\}\} \cup$$
$$\{\top \sqsubseteq \boxed{\min\{(a,b):r, (a,b):s\} \leqslant 1 - p} \sqcap \boxed{\min\{r,s\} \leqslant 1 - p} \mid$$
$$\langle \text{dis}(r,s) \geqslant p \rangle \in \mathcal{R}, \ a,b \in \text{ind}(\mathcal{O}) \cup \{*\}\}$$

These axioms ensure that the various elements of $\mathcal{U}$ that represent the values of role connections, such as $(a,b):r$ and r, respect the axioms in $\mathcal{R}$. Although simple role inclusions $\langle r \sqsubseteq s \geqslant p \rangle$ are handled by the automata $\mathbf{A}_r$, we include them also here. The reason is that the reduction of at-least restrictions below does not need to use these automata since only simple roles can occur in them.

The GCIs in $\mathcal{T}$ can be translated in a straightforward manner:

$$\text{red}(\mathcal{T}) := \{\top \sqsubseteq \boxed{p \leqslant C \Rightarrow D} \mid \langle C \sqsubseteq D \geqslant p \rangle \in \mathcal{T}\}$$

We now come to the reductions of the concepts. Intuitively, each $\text{red}(C)$ with $C \in \text{sub}(\mathcal{O})$ describes the semantics of C in terms of its order relationships to other elements of $\mathcal{U}$. Note that the semantics of the involutive negation

$\neg C = \mathsf{inv}(C)$ is already handled by the operator inv (see $\mathsf{red}(\mathcal{U})$ above):

$$\mathsf{red}(\top) := \{\top \sqsubseteq \boxed{\top \geqslant 1}\}$$
$$\mathsf{red}(\{a\}) := \{\{a\} \sqsubseteq \boxed{1 \leqslant \{a\}}, \ \neg\{a\} \sqsubseteq \boxed{\{a\} \leqslant 0}\}$$
$$\mathsf{red}(\overline{p}) := \{\top \sqsubseteq \boxed{\overline{p} = p}\}$$
$$\mathsf{red}(\neg C) := \emptyset$$
$$\mathsf{red}(C \sqcap D) := \{\top \sqsubseteq \boxed{C \sqcap D = \min\{C, D\}}\}$$
$$\mathsf{red}(C \to D) := \{\top \sqsubseteq \boxed{C \to D = C \Rightarrow D}\}$$

The reductions of role restrictions are more involved. In particular, in the case of value and existential restrictions we have to deal with non-simple roles, for which we employ the automata $\mathbf{A}_r$ from the previous section:

$$\mathsf{red}(\forall r.C) := \{\top \sqsubseteq \boxed{(\forall r.C) \leqslant (\forall \mathbf{A}_r.C)},$$
$$\top \sqsubseteq \exists \mathfrak{r}.\big(\mathsf{AN} \sqcap \boxed{\langle \forall r.C\rangle_\uparrow \geqslant r \Rightarrow C}\big) \sqcup$$
$$\bigsqcup_{a \in \mathsf{ind}(\mathcal{O})} \big(\exists \mathfrak{r}.\{a\} \sqcap \boxed{(\forall r.C) \geqslant (*, a):r \Rightarrow a:C}\big)\}$$

The second axiom of $\mathsf{red}(\forall r.C)$ ensures the existence of a witness for $\forall r.C$ at each domain element. For example, assume that the preorder represented by the concepts $\boxed{\alpha \leqslant \beta}$ at some domain element d satisfies $0.5 < \forall r.C < 1$. The first possibility is that the above axiom creates an anonymous element e that is connected to d via $\mathfrak{r}$, and hence by $\mathsf{red}(\mathsf{AN})$ we know that e satisfies $0.5 < \langle \forall r.C\rangle_\uparrow < 1$. The axiom further requires that $\langle \forall r.C\rangle_\uparrow \geqslant r \Rightarrow C$, which implies that $\langle \forall r.C\rangle_\uparrow \geqslant C$ and $r > C$. We will see below that the reduction of $\forall \mathbf{A}_r.C$ further ensures that $\langle \forall r.C\rangle_\uparrow \leqslant r \Rightarrow C$, and thus we get $\langle \forall r.C\rangle_\uparrow = C$. Hence, e can be seen as an abstract representation of the witness of $\forall r.C$ at d; the precise value of the r-connection between d and e (represented by the element r) is irrelevant, as long as it is strictly greater than the value of C at e. The other disjuncts of this axiom deal with the possibility that a named domain element acts as the witness for the value restriction in a similar way.

Together with the first axiom of $\mathsf{red}(\forall r.C)$, the following axioms ensure that no other r-successor of d violates the lower bound on $r \Rightarrow C$ given by $\forall r.C$ at d:

$$\mathsf{red}(\forall \mathbf{A}^q.C) := \{\top \sqsubseteq \boxed{(\forall \mathbf{A}^q.C) \leqslant C} \mid q \text{ is final}\} \cup \bigcup_{q \xrightarrow{x,p} q' \in \mathbf{A}} \mathsf{red}_{x,p,q'}(\forall \mathbf{A}^q.C)$$

$$\mathsf{red}_{\varepsilon,p,q'}(\forall \mathbf{A}^q.C) := \{\top \sqsubseteq \boxed{(\forall \mathbf{A}^q.C) \leqslant p \Rightarrow (\forall \mathbf{A}^{q'}.C)}\}$$
$$\mathsf{red}_{s,p,q'}(\forall \mathbf{A}^q.C) :=$$
$$\{\top \sqsubseteq \forall \mathfrak{r}.\big(\mathsf{AN} \to \boxed{\langle \forall \mathbf{A}^q.C\rangle_\uparrow \leqslant \min\{p, s\} \Rightarrow (\forall \mathbf{A}^{q'}.C)}\big)\} \cup$$
$$\{\exists \mathfrak{r}.\{a\} \sqsubseteq \boxed{(\forall \mathbf{A}^q.C) \leqslant \min\{p, (*, a):s\} \Rightarrow a:(\forall \mathbf{A}^{q'}.C)} \mid a \in \mathsf{ind}(\mathcal{O})\}$$

Recall that $\mathbf{A}_r$ in particular contains the transition $i_r \xrightarrow{r,1} f_r$ from the initial state i_r to the final state f_r. By the first axiom in $\mathsf{red}(\forall r.C)$ and the first axiom in $\mathsf{red}_{r,1,f_r}(\forall \mathbf{A}_r.C)$, the witness e satisfies $\langle \forall r.C \rangle_\uparrow \leqslant \langle \forall \mathbf{A}_r.C \rangle_\uparrow \leqslant r \Rightarrow (\forall \mathbf{A}_r^{f_r}.C)$ Since f_r is final, we further have $(\forall \mathbf{A}_r^{f_r}.C) \leqslant C$ by $\mathsf{red}(\forall \mathbf{A}_r^{f_r}.C)$, and hence $\langle \forall r.C \rangle_\uparrow \leqslant r \Rightarrow C$, as claimed above.

Using arbitrary runs through the automaton $\mathbf{A}_r$, we can ensure that no other r-successor of d violates the value restriction. For example, if $r^{\mathcal{I}}(d, e_1) = 0.3$ and $r^{\mathcal{I}}(e_1, e_2) = 0.5$ for two other (anonymous) domain elements e_1, e_2, and we further have the role inclusion $\langle rr \sqsubseteq r \geqslant 0.7 \rangle$, then we know that $r^{\mathcal{I}}(d, e_2)$ must be at least 0.5. Although this r-connection is not explicitly represented in our forest-based encoding, concepts of the form $\forall \mathbf{A}_r^q.C$ are appropriately transferred from d via e_1 to e_2 in order to ensure that the value of C at e_2 satisfies $0.5 < (\forall r.C)^{\mathcal{I}}(d) \leqslant r^{\mathcal{I}}(d, e_2) \Rightarrow C^{\mathcal{I}}(e_2)$. In this example, since we know only that $r^{\mathcal{I}}(d, e_2) \geqslant 0.5$, it must be ensured that $C^{\mathcal{I}}(e_2) \geqslant r^{\mathcal{I}}(d, e_2)$.

The reduction for existential restrictions can be defined similarly to that for value restrictions, but replacing $\geqslant$ with $\leqslant$ (and vice versa) and $\Rightarrow$ with min.

We now come to the final component of $\mathsf{red}(\mathcal{O})$:

$$\mathsf{red}(\geqslant n\, r.C) := \{\top \sqsubseteq \bigsqcup_{m=0}^{n} \bigsqcup_{\substack{S \subseteq \mathsf{ind}(\mathcal{O}) \\ |S| = n-m}} \bigsqcap \mathsf{red}_{m,S,\leqslant}(\geqslant n\, r.C),$$

$$\mathsf{AN} \sqsubseteq \neg \bigsqcup_{m=0}^{n} \bigsqcup_{\substack{S \subseteq \mathsf{ind}(\mathcal{O}) \\ |S| = n-m}} \bigsqcap \mathsf{red}_{m,S,<}(\geqslant n\, r.C)\} \cup$$

$$\{a{:}\neg{\geqslant} n\, \mathfrak{r}.((\mathsf{AN} \sqcap \boxed{\langle \geqslant n\, r.C \rangle_\uparrow < \min\{r, C\}}) \sqcup$$

$$(\neg\mathsf{AN} \sqcap \boxed{(a{:}{\geqslant} n\, r.C) < \min\{(a, *){:}r, C\}})) \mid a \in \mathsf{ind}(\mathcal{O})\}$$

$$\mathsf{red}_{m,S,\lhd}(\geqslant n\, r.C) := \{{\geqslant} m\, \mathfrak{r}.(\mathsf{AN} \sqcap \boxed{\langle \geqslant n\, r.C \rangle_\uparrow \lhd \min\{r, C\}})\} \cup$$

$$\{\exists \mathfrak{r}.(\{a\} \sqcap \neg\{b\}) \mid a, b \in S,\ a \neq b\} \cup$$

$$\{\boxed{(\geqslant n\, r.C) \lhd \min\{(*, a){:}r, a{:}C\}} \mid a \in S\}$$

The reduction of at-least restrictions works similarly to the one of value restrictions: the first axiom ensures the existence of the n required witnesses, while the second one ensures that no n different elements can exceed the value of the at-least restriction. Unfortunately, the number of named successors cannot be counted using a classical at-least restriction in our encoding, since these named successors do not know about the degree of the role connection from an anonymous element; otherwise they would have to store a possibly infinite amount of information since they may have infinitely many anonymous role predecessors. For this reason, the above axioms first guess how many $(n - m)$ and which (S) named elements are connected to the current domain element to the appropriate degrees (given by $(*, a){:}r$). The assertions in $\mathsf{red}(\geqslant n\, r.C)$ express a restriction similar to that of the second GCI for named domain elements.

The proof of the following correctness result can be found in [16]. As mentioned before, this holds only for logics with the forest model property [17]. However, it is not affected by the presence or absence of (local) reflexivity.

Lemma 3. *In* G-$\mathcal{SRIQ}$, G-$\mathcal{SROQ}$, *or* G-$\mathcal{SROI}$, $\mathcal{O}$ *has a* G-*model iff* red($\mathcal{O}$) *has a classical model.*

We now analyze the complexity of the reduction. As in [23], the construction of the automata $\mathbf{A}_r$ causes an exponential blowup in the size of $\mathcal{R}$, which cannot be avoided [26]. Independent of this, our reduction also involves an exponential blowup in the (binary encoding of) the largest number n involved in a number restriction in $\mathcal{O}$, and in the number of individual names occurring in $\mathcal{O}$, since the number of disjuncts in each GCI from red($\geqslant n\, r.C$) is linear in $n \cdot 2^{|\mathrm{ind}(\mathcal{O})|}$. However, we can avoid this blowup if we remove either nominals or number restrictions [16]. Hence, we obtain the following complexity results.

Theorem 4. *Deciding consistency is*

- 2-EXPTIME-*complete in* G-$\mathcal{SRIQ}$,
- *in* 2-EXPTIME *in* G-$\mathcal{SROI}$ *and* G-$\mathcal{SROQ}$, *and*
- EXPTIME-*complete in all FDLs between* G-$\mathcal{ALC}$ *and* G-$\mathcal{SHOI}$ *or* G-$\mathcal{SHIQ}$.

Proof. The consistency of the $\mathcal{ALCOQ}$ ontology red($\mathcal{O}$) is decidable in exponential time in the size of red($\mathcal{O}$) [17]. The first upper bounds thus follow from the fact that the size of red($\mathcal{O}$) is exponential in the size of $\mathcal{O}$. 2-EXPTIME-hardness holds already for G-$\mathcal{SRIQ}$ without involutive negation and only assertions of the form $\langle \alpha \geqslant p \rangle$ since in this case reasoning in G-$\mathcal{SRIQ}$ is equivalent to reasoning in classical $\mathcal{SRIQ}$ [13, 26].

Without complex role inclusions, i.e. restricting to simple role inclusions and transitivity axioms, the size of the automata $\mathbf{A}_r$ is polynomial in the size of $\mathcal{R}$ [23]. The other exponential blowup can be avoided by disallowing nominals or number restrictions. Hence, for G-$\mathcal{SHOI}$ and G-$\mathcal{SHIQ}$, the size of red($\mathcal{O}$) is polynomial in the size of $\mathcal{O}$, and the lower bound follows again from the reduction in [13] and EXPTIME-hardness of consistency in classical $\mathcal{ALC}$ [29]. □

To the best of our knowledge, it is still open whether consistency in $\mathcal{SROI}$ and $\mathcal{SROQ}$ is 2-EXPTIME-hard, even in the classical case [17, 28]; the best known lower bound is the EXPTIME-hardness of $\mathcal{ALC}$ [29]. We also leave open the complexity of G-$\mathcal{SHOQ}$, which is EXPTIME-complete in the classical case [17,29].

5 Conclusions

Using a combination of techniques developed for infinitely valued Gödel extensions of $\mathcal{ALC}$ [12] and for finitely valued Gödel extensions of $\mathcal{SROIQ}$ [6,7,14,15], we derived several tight complexity bounds for consistency in sublogics of G-$\mathcal{SROIQ}$. Our reduction circumvents the best-case exponential behavior of the automata-based approach in [12] and avoids the exponential blowup in the nesting depth of concepts of the reductions in [6,7]. However, it introduces an exponential blowup in the size of the binary encoding of numbers in number restrictions and the number of individual names occurring in the ontology. Beyond the complexity results, an important benefit of our approach is that it does not need the development of a specialized fuzzy DL reasoner, but can use any state-of-the-art reasoner for classical $\mathcal{ALCOQ}$. For that reason, this new reduction aids in closing the gap between efficient classical and fuzzy DL reasoners.

A promising direction for future research is to integrate our reduction directly into a classical tableaux procedure. Observe that the axioms in red(C) are already closely related to the rules employed in (classical and fuzzy) tableaux algorithms (see, e.g. [3,8,23]). For example, the concept $\forall r.C$ in a node leads to the creation of an r-successor node that witnesses the value of $\forall r.C$, i.e., that satisfies the inequations in red($\forall r.C$). Such a tableaux procedure would need to deal with total preorders in each node, possibly using an external solver.

On the theoretical side, we want to prove 2-NExpTime-completeness of reasoning in G-$\mathcal{SROIQ}$. As a prerequisite, we would have to eliminate the dependency on the forest-shaped structure of interpretations. It may be possible to adapt the tableaux rules from [22] for this purpose. It also remains open whether consistency in G-$\mathcal{SHOQ}$ is ExpTime-complete, as for its classical counterpart.

As done in [7], we can also combine our reduction with the one for infinitely valued Zadeh semantics. While not based on a t-norm, it is one of the most widely used semantics for fuzzy applications. It also shares many properties of the classical semantics, and hence is a natural choice for simple applications.

References

1. Baader, F., Calvanese, D., McGuinness, D.L., Nardi, D., Patel-Schneider, P.F. (eds.): The Description Logic Handbook: Theory, Implementation, and Applications, 2nd edn. Cambridge University Press (2007)
2. Baader, F., Peñaloza, R.: On the undecidability of fuzzy description logics with GCIs and product t-norm. In: Tinelli, C., Sofronie-Stokkermans, V. (eds.) FroCoS 2011. LNCS, vol. 6989, pp. 55–70. Springer, Heidelberg (2011)
3. Baader, F., Sattler, U.: An overview of tableau algorithms for description logics. Studia Logica 69(1), 5–40 (2001)
4. Bobillo, F., Delgado, M., Gómez-Romero, J.: A crisp representation for fuzzy $\mathcal{SHOIN}$ with fuzzy nominals and general concept inclusions. In: da Costa, P.C.G., d'Amato, C., Fanizzi, N., Laskey, K.B., Laskey, K.J., Lukasiewicz, T., Nickles, M., Pool, M. (eds.) URSW 2005 - 2007. LNCS (LNAI), vol. 5327, pp. 174–188. Springer, Heidelberg (2008)
5. Bobillo, F., Delgado, M., Gómez-Romero, J.: Optimizing the crisp representation of the fuzzy description logic $\mathcal{SROIQ}$. In: da Costa, P.C.G., d'Amato, C., Fanizzi, N., Laskey, K.B., Laskey, K.J., Lukasiewicz, T., Nickles, M., Pool, M. (eds.) URSW 2005 - 2007. LNCS (LNAI), vol. 5327, pp. 189–206. Springer, Heidelberg (2008)
6. Bobillo, F., Delgado, M., Gómez-Romero, J., Straccia, U.: Fuzzy description logics under Gödel semantics. Int. J. Approx. Reason. 50(3), 494–514 (2009)
7. Bobillo, F., Delgado, M., Gómez-Romero, J., Straccia, U.: Joining Gödel and Zadeh fuzzy logics in fuzzy description logics. Int. J. Uncertain. Fuzz. 20(4), 475–508 (2012)

8. Bobillo, F., Straccia, U.: Fuzzy description logics with general t-norms and datatypes. Fuzzy Set. Syst. 160(23), 3382–3402 (2009)
9. Bobillo, F., Straccia, U.: Reasoning with the finitely many-valued Łukasiewicz fuzzy description logic $\mathcal{SROIQ}$. Inform. Sciences 181, 758–778 (2011)
10. Bobillo, F., Straccia, U.: Finite fuzzy description logics and crisp representations. In: Bobillo, F., et al. (eds.) URSW 2008-2010/UniDL 2010. LNCS, vol. 7123, pp. 99–118. Springer, Heidelberg (2013)
11. Borgwardt, S.: Fuzzy DLs over finite lattices with nominals. In: Proc. DL 2014. CEUR-WS, vol. 1193, pp. 58–70 (2014)
12. Borgwardt, S., Distel, F., Peñaloza, R.: Decidable Gödel description logics without the finitely-valued model property. In: Proc. KR 2014, pp. 228–237. AAAI Press (2014)
13. Borgwardt, S., Distel, F., Peñaloza, R.: The limits of decidability in fuzzy description logics with general concept inclusions. Artif. Intell. 218, 23–55 (2015)
14. Borgwardt, S., Peñaloza, R.: The complexity of lattice-based fuzzy description logics 2(1), 1–19 (2013)
15. Borgwardt, S., Peñaloza, R.: Finite lattices do not make reasoning in $\mathcal{ALCOI}$ harder. In: Bobillo, F., Carvalho, R.N., Costa, P.C.G., d'Amato, C., Fanizzi, N., Laskey, K.B., Laskey, K.J., Lukasiewicz, T., Nickles, M., Pool, M. (eds.) URSW 2011-2013. LNCS, vol. 8816, pp. 122–141. Springer, Heidelberg (2014)
16. Borgwardt, S., Peñaloza, R.: Infinitely valued Gödel semantics for expressive description logics. LTCS-Report 15-11, Chair for Automata Theory, TU Dresden, Germany (2015). see http://lat.inf.tu-dresden.de/research/reports.html.
17. Calvanese, D., Eiter, T., Ortiz, M.: Regular path queries in expressive description logics with nominals. In: Proc. IJCAI 2009, pp. 714–720. AAAI Press (2009)
18. Cerami, M., Straccia, U.: On the (un)decidability of fuzzy description logics under Łukasiewicz t-norm. Inform. Sciences 227, 1–21 (2013)
19. Droste, M., Kuich, W., Vogler, H.: Handbook of Weighted Automata. 1st edn. Springer (2009)
20. Hájek, P.: Metamathematics of Fuzzy Logic (Trends in Logic). Springer (2001)
21. Hájek, P.: Making fuzzy description logic more general. Fuzzy Set. Syst. 154(1), 1–15 (2005)
22. Horrocks, I., Kutz, O., Sattler, U.: The even more irresistible $\mathcal{SROIQ}$. In: Proc. KR 2006, pp. 57–67. AAAI Press (2006)
23. Horrocks, I., Sattler, U.: Decidability of $\mathcal{SHIQ}$ with complex role inclusion axioms 160(1-2), 79–104 (2004)
24. Horrocks, I., Sattler, U., Tobies, S.: Practical reasoning for very expressive description logics 8(3), 239–263 (2000)
25. Kazakov, Y.: A polynomial translation from the two-variable guarded fragment with number restrictions to the guarded fragment. In: Alferes, J.J., Leite, J. (eds.) JELIA 2004. LNCS (LNAI), vol. 3229, pp. 372–384. Springer, Heidelberg (2004)
26. Kazakov, Y.: $\mathcal{RIQ}$ and $\mathcal{SROIQ}$ are harder than $\mathcal{SHOIQ}$. In: Proc. KR 2008, pp. 274–284. AAAI Press (2008)
27. Klement, E.P., Mesiar, R., Pap, E.: Triangular Norms. Trends in Logic, Studia Logica Library. Springer (2000)
28. Ortiz, M., Šimkus, M.: Reasoning and query answering in description logics. In: Eiter, T., Krennwallner, T. (eds.) Reasoning Web 2012. LNCS, vol. 7487, pp. 1–53. Springer, Heidelberg (2012)

29. Schild, K.: A correspondence theory for terminological logics: Preliminary report. In: Proc. IJCAI 1991, pp. 466–471. Morgan Kaufmann (1991)
30. Schmidt-Schauß, M., Smolka, G.: Attributive concept descriptions with complements. Artif. Intell. 48(1), 1–26 (1991)
31. Straccia, U.: Transforming fuzzy description logics into classical description logics. In: Alferes, J.J., Leite, J. (eds.) JELIA 2004. LNCS (LNAI), vol. 3229, pp. 385–399. Springer, Heidelberg (2004)
32. Tobies, S.: The complexity of reasoning with cardinality restrictions and nominals in expressive description logics. J. Artif. Intell. Res. 12, 199–217 (2000)
33. Tobies, S.: Complexity Results and Practical Algorithms for Logics in Knowledge Representation. Ph.D. thesis, RWTH Aachen, Germany (2001)

Theorem Proving and Model Building

NRCL - A Model Building Approach
to the Bernays-Schönfinkel Fragment

Gábor Alagi[1,2,3] and Christoph Weidenbach[3]

[1] Saarbrücken Graduate School of Computer Science, Germany
[2] Saarland University, Saarbrücken, Germany
[3] Max-Planck-Institut für Informatik, Saarbrücken, Germany
{galagi,weidenbach}@mpi-inf.mpg.de

Abstract. We combine constrained literals for model representation with key concepts from first-order superposition and propositional conflict-driven clause learning (CDCL) to create the new calculus *Non-Redundant Clause Learning* (NRCL) deciding the Bernays-Schönfinkel fragment. We use first-order literals constrained by disequalities between tuples of terms for compact model representation. From superposition, NRCL inherits the abstract redundancy criterion and the monotone model operator. CDCL adds the dynamic, conflict-driven search for a model. As a result, NRCL finds a false clause modulo the current model candidate effectively. It guides the derivation of a first-order ordered resolvent that is never redundant. Similar to 1UIP-learning in CDCL, the learned resolvent induces backtracking and, by blocking the previous conflict state via propagation, it enforces progress towards finding a model or a refutation. The non-redundancy result also implies that only finitely many clauses can be generated by NRCL on the Bernays-Schönfinkel fragment, which proves termination.

1 Introduction

The Bernays-Schönfinkel fragment (BS) is an important decidable fragment of first-order logic, which has many applications, including knowledge representation and ontological reasoning, hardware verification, logic programming, and planning.

Over the years a number of calculi have attempted to provide an efficient solution for BS problems. These approaches range from the early *SEM* and *Mace* systems [26] to the recent state-of-the-art solvers like *iProver* [11] and *Darwin* [5], but even general purpose first-order theorem provers provide specialized techniques for this fragment, like specialized splitting techniques for *SPASS* introduced in [13] and [10], or the *generalisation* technique in *Vampire* [21]. Dedicated calculi that try to lift the ideas of CDCL (Conflict-Driven Clause Learning) [24, 6] are *Model Evolution* [5], *DPLL(SX)* [22], and *SGGS* [7].

In this paper, we introduce a new calculus for solving BS problems with problem-driven partial model building. Due to space limitations, we omit most proofs and technical details. We refer the interested reader to the extended version of this paper [1]. Our approach builds first-order candidate models instead

© Springer International Publishing Switzerland 2015
C. Lutz and S. Ranise (Eds.): FroCoS 2015, LNAI 9322, pp. 69–84, 2015.
DOI: 10.1007/978-3-319-24246-0_5

of approximations, uses constrained literals for model representation, and learns new non-redundant clauses to guide the search. Our calculus, called NRCL or *Non-Redundant Clause Learning*, inherits the concepts of non-redundant inferences from superposition [3, 20, 27] and problem-driven partial model building from CDCL.

Compared to the existing approaches, we use a more expressive and implicit constraint language, our search is guided by backjumping and learning non-redundant clauses, and our model representation is more compact, in general. In addition, compared to all existing approaches, we can prove that all our learned clauses are non-redundant and this way, for the first time, establish a calculus that combines the search with respect to a dynamically changing (partial) model with an overall notion of redundancy.

In the rest of the paper, we first introduce some basic definitions and notions in Section 2, followed by a description of our calculus in Section 3, and we establish its soundness in Section 4. After introducing some regularity conditions, we provide our key result, *non-redundant clause learning*, and prove termination of NRCL in Section 5. In Section 6, we compare our calculus to the existing literature. Finally, Section 7 provides a summary and outlines future work.

2   Preliminaries

Basic Definitions. We assume the reader is familiar with first-order logic, its syntax, and its semantics. In particular, we handle the Bernays-Schönfinkel fragment, which allows no function symbols except for finitely many constants in the clausal normal forms.

We denote the finite *signature* by Σ, the *set of predicate symbols* by Pr, and call the finite set of constants the *domain*, denoted by $\mathcal{D}$. We denote the set of all first-order atoms over a signature Σ and a possibly infinite set of variables X by $\mathcal{A}_\Sigma(\mathrm{X})$. In particular, the set of ground atoms is denoted by $\mathcal{A}_\Sigma$, a short-hand for $\mathcal{A}_\Sigma(\emptyset)$. For a literal L, $|L|$ denotes the atom contained in L. In general, we denote the ground instances of an *expression* - a term, literal, or clause - e over the domain $\mathcal{D}$ by the notation gnd(e).

W.l.o.g., we assume that each independent expression is variable disjoint, and we call a variable *fresh* if it does not occur in any expression - e.g. clause or clause set - of the current context.

We consider *substitutions* in the usual way, and for a substitution σ, dom(σ) denotes the *domain* of σ, i.e. the finite set of variables with $x \neq x\sigma$, and rng(σ) denotes the *range* of σ, i.e. the image of dom(σ) w.r.t. σ. We assume the reader is familiar with *most general unifiers*, and mgu denotes the result of unifying two or more expressions or substitutions. We use the short-hand $\exists\sigma = \mathrm{mgu}(e_1, e_2)$ to both state the existence of a most general unifier and bind σ to it.

For expressions or substitutions e_1, e_2, we say e_2 *can be matched against* e_1, or e_2 *is more general than* e_1, and write $e_1 \geq e_2$, if and only if there is a substitution σ such that $e_1 = e_2\sigma$.

We represent a first-order interpretation I with the set $\{A \in \mathcal{A}_\Sigma \mid I \models A\}$. We define *satisfiability* and *semantic consequence* as usual. In particular, we consider the problem of deciding whether a finite clause set N over a BS language Σ without equality is satisfiable. This problem is known to be NEXPTIME-complete [18].

Dismatching Constraints. We use conjunctions of disequations between tuples of terms as constraints. We call these constraints *dismatching constraints*, and they provide a means to describe subsets of ground instances of expressions, e.g. sequences of constrained literals are used later on for model representation.

Dismatching constraints are equivalent with *implicit generalizations*, which maintain lists of literals with fresh variables representing exceptions for the literals constrained. This constraint language has applications in inductive learning, logic programming and term rewriting. For more details see e.g. [9][17]. Compared to implicit generalizations, dismatching constraints extract the arguments of the literals and represent the restrictions more compactly, which also allows more simplification. The name *dismatching constraints* was chosen following the example of *iProver* [15].

We chose these constraints for a balance between expressiveness and simplicity, for the existing literature, and for compactness. However, NRCL is compatible with any constraint language allowing the operations discussed below.

Definition 2.1 (Dismatching Constraint). *A dismatching constraint π is of the form $\bigwedge_{i \in \mathcal{I}} \vec{s}_i \neq \vec{t}_i$, where $\mathcal{I}$ is a finite set of indices, and for each $i \in \mathcal{I}$, $\vec{s}_i$ and $\vec{t}_i$ are tuples of terms of the same dimension.*

We define $\mathrm{lvar}(\pi)$ and $\mathrm{rvar}(\pi)$ as the set of the left-hand side and right-hand side variables of π, respectively. Furthermore, we assume that $\mathrm{lvar}(\pi) \cap \mathrm{rvar}(\pi) = \emptyset$, and for each $i, j \in \mathcal{I}$, $\vec{t}_i$ and $\vec{t}_j$ are variable disjoint whenever i differs from j.

We further extend the set of constraints with the constants $\top$, $\bot$ representing the tautological and the unsatisfiable constraint, respectively.

Furthermore, we maintain a strict normal form, defined below, which already assumes most inexpensive simplifications. We note that any dismatching constraint can be normalized in polynomial time, see [1] for details. Thus, w.l.o.g. we assume that the constraints are always in normal form, and the result of any operation is transformed into normal form implicitly.

Definition 2.2 (Normal Form). *We say a constraint $\pi = \bigwedge_{i \in \mathcal{I}} \vec{s}_i \neq \vec{t}_i$ is in normal form iff (i) each $\vec{s}_i$ contains only variables, and (ii) no variable occurs more than once in any left-hand side $\vec{s}_i$.*

Finally, the semantics of dismatching constraints is given below. We note that, although the definition assumes an arbitrary variable set V, the notion of satisfiability depends only on $\mathrm{lvar}(\pi)$.

Definition 2.3. *A solution of a constraint $\pi = \bigwedge_{i \in \mathcal{I}} \vec{s}_i \neq \vec{t}_i$ over some variable set V, which contains $\mathrm{lvar}(\pi)$ but contains no variable from $\mathrm{rvar}(\pi)$, is a ground substitution $\delta : V \to \mathcal{D}$ such that no $\vec{t}_i$ can be matched against the respective $\vec{s}_i\delta$, i.e. no $\vec{s}_i\delta$ is an instance of the respective $\vec{t}_i$.*

In particular, if $\pi = \top$, any such grounding substitution is a solution, and $\pi = \bot$ has no solution at all.

As usual, π is called satisfiable *and* unsatisfiable *if it has a solution or no solution, respectively.*

As an example, consider the constraint $\pi = ((x, y) \neq (v, v) \wedge y \neq a)$ over the domain $\mathcal{D} = \{a, b\}$. Then π is satisfiable and the only solution of π (over $V = \{x, y\}$) is the ground substitution $\sigma = \{x \leftarrow a, y \leftarrow b\}$, since y can only be b and the first subconstraint represents $x \neq y$.

Constrained Literals. Next, we define literals constrained with dismatching constraints in normal form, and give their semantics as sets of ground literals.

Definition 2.4 (Constrained Literal). *We call a pair $(L; \pi)$ of a literal L and a dismatching constraint π such that both* $\mathrm{lvar}(\pi) \subseteq \mathrm{var}(L)$ *and* $\mathrm{rvar}(\pi) \cap \mathrm{var}(L) = \emptyset$ *hold a* constrained literal.

The semantics is given by defining the set of covered literals, *denoted by* $\mathrm{gnd}(L; \pi)$*, as the set of all ground instances $L\delta$ such that δ is a solution of π w.r.t.* $\mathrm{var}(L)$*.*

Then, a ground literal L' is covered *by a constrained literal $(L; \pi)$ iff $L' \in \mathrm{gnd}(L; \pi)$. Finally, we say that a constrained literal $(L; \pi)$ is* empty *iff $\mathrm{gnd}(L; \pi)$ is empty.*

It is easy to see that $(L; \pi)$ is empty if and only if π is unsatisfiable, and that given a solution δ of π over $\mathrm{lvar}(\pi)$, for any extension δ' of δ to $\mathrm{var}(L)$, $L\delta' \in \mathrm{gnd}(L; \pi)$ holds.

As an example for cover-sets, consider $(P(x, y); (x, y) \neq (v, v) \wedge x \neq a \wedge y \neq b)$. Then the set of covered literals over the domain $\mathcal{D}_2 = \{a, b\}$ is $\{P(b, a)\}$, while over $\mathcal{D}_3 = \{a, b, c\}$, it is $\{P(b, a), P(c, a), P(b, c)\}$.

Constrained Clauses. We represent a collection of ground clauses by a *constrained clause $(C; \pi)$*. Extending the notations and semantics for constrained literals to constrained clauses is straightforward. Furthermore, we use the notation $(C; \sigma; \pi)$ for the constrained clause $(C\sigma; \pi)$, whenever we wish to syntactically distinguish C and σ. We note that during resolving away literals from C, we might get a state where $\mathrm{lvar}(\pi)$ contains variables not occurring in C. For semantic purposes, these *free variables* are considered existential variables, and we eliminate them through instantiation. See Section 8 of the extended paper [1] for further details.

Operations. In the context of our calculus, three operations on constrained literals are of significance: *conjunction*, *difference*, and *testing the emptiness of a constrained literal*. They correspond to the intersection, set-theoretic difference, and emptiness of the corresponding cover-sets, respectively.

Conjunction and relative difference can be computed in linear time, while deciding emptiness is known to be co-NP-complete [17]. For a detailed handling of the operations, see the extended paper [1].

We note that the operations are indeed complex, but so is checking subsumption and subsumption resolution in first-order theorem provers, and even *iProver* calls CDCL iteratively. Yet, these techniques are efficient in practice, which we consider an indication that an efficient implementation of NRCL is possible.

Model Candidate. In the course of this paper, we represent a *(partial) model candidate*, also called a *(partial) model assumption*, as a sequence Γ of annotated constrained literals. Following the terminology of CDCL, we also call such a sequence a *trail* in the context of NRCL. We call the elements of a trail *assignments*, as they define truth-values for ground atoms.

Literals in Γ are either *decision* or *deduced literals*. Decisions are annotated with unique positive integers, with $(L; \pi)^i$ representing the ith decision in Γ. Deduced literals are annotated with their reasons, a clause from the current clause set. In the following, α denotes an arbitrary annotation, C a reason clause, and k, l, i integers.

Furthermore, we only consider *strongly consistent* sequences, i.e. we assume for any trail Γ that for all different $(L; \pi), (L'; \pi') \in \Gamma$, $\text{gnd}(|L|; \pi) \cap \text{gnd}(|L'|; \pi')$ is empty. This ensures that each ground atom is defined by at most one literal from Γ, and there are no conflicting assignments in Γ.

We note that this approach to define truth-values for groups of ground atoms represented by constrained literals can be also seen as providing a propositional abstraction and an abstract partial interpretation. In this context, our calculus can be considered as a fine-grained abstraction-refinement algorithm, which interleaves refinement and abstract model search, and lets the clauses and decision heuristics guide these implicit steps.

A trail Γ induces a partial interpretation, which lifts the standard CDCL notions of *true*, *false*, or *undefined* under Γ. In particular, a ground literal L' is *defined by* a constrained literal $(L; \pi) \in \Gamma$, iff $|L'| \in \text{gnd}(|L|; \pi)$. If such an $(L; \pi)$ exists, we also say that Γ *defines* L'. Then, the value of the defined ground literal L' is *true* iff L' and L has the same polarity.

Non-ground literals are treated as unit clauses, and a set of ground clauses represented by the constrained clause $(C; \pi)$ is *true* or *false* in Γ, if all of the covered ground instances are *true*, or *false*, respectively. The notion of *defined by* Γ extends to constrained clauses similarly, i.e. $(C; \sigma)$ is defined w.r.t. Γ iff for each $C' \in \text{gnd}(C; \sigma)$, at least one $L' \in C'$ is defined under Γ.

The partial interpretation can be extended to a total interpretation called the *induced interpretation* and given as $I_\Gamma = \cup \{\text{gnd}(L; \pi) \mid (L; \pi) \in \Gamma^+\}$, where Γ^+ denotes the set of positive constrained literals in Γ. This interpretation serves as a minimal model defined by the positive literals, and it is used in the rule *Success* and the relevant proofs.

We call the annotation of a decision in Γ the *level* of this decision literal. Then, the *level* $\text{lvl}(L)$ of a defined ground literal L w.r.t. Γ is the level of the last decision in Γ before the constrained literal defining L, and zero if no such decision exists. We call the largest level the *top-level*, and also *the level of the trail*. The empty trail is considered to have the level zero.

Following the terminology of CDCL, we call a ground clause *assertive* iff it is false w.r.t. the current trail and contains exactly one top-level literal. We say a first-order clause C or a constrained clause $(C\sigma; \pi)$ *is assertive* iff $\text{gnd}(C)$, and $\text{gnd}(C\sigma; \pi)$ contains at least one assertive ground clause, respectively.

Induced Ordering. Below, we define the ordering induced by the current trail, which is used to define abstract redundancy in Section 5. This dynamic ordering captures the local correlation between the atoms and literals in the search, and shifts the focus on the recent behavior of the calculus. In the following, let $<$ denote a given well-founded total ordering over ground expressions - atoms, literals and clauses -, and let Γ denote a strongly consistent trail.

Definition 2.5. *The* abstraction function defined by Γ *is the function* def : $\mathcal{A}_\Sigma \to \Gamma \cup \{\bot\}$ *which assigns to each ground atom the constrained literal defining it, and $\bot$ if no such literal exists.*

We call elements of $\Gamma \cup \{\bot\}$ the abstract atoms *defined by Γ. Then,* def *is extended to ground literals and clauses by assigning the corresponding negated abstract atom to a negative literal, and the disjunction of the corresponding abstract literals to a clause, respectively.*

Definition 2.6. The precedence ordering $<_p^\Gamma$ $(<_p)$ *defined by Γ is the ordering over the constrained literals in Γ defined by their position in Γ, i.e. $(L_1; \pi_1) <_p (L_2; \pi_2)$ iff $\Gamma = \Gamma_1, (L_1; \pi_1)^{\alpha_1}, \Gamma_2, (L_2; \pi_2)^{\alpha_2}, \Gamma_3$ for some $\Gamma_1, \Gamma_2, \Gamma_3$, and α_1, α_2.*

We extend this ordering to $\Gamma \cup \{\bot\}$ with $\bot$ as maximal element. Finally, this ordering can be extended to abstract literals and clauses in the usual manner.

Definition 2.7. The ordering $<_\Gamma^{atom}$ *induced by Γ is defined over $\mathcal{A}_\Sigma$ and given as follows: $P <_\Gamma^{atom} Q$ iff either (i) $\mathrm{def}(P) <_p \mathrm{def}(Q)$, or (ii) $\mathrm{def}(P) = \mathrm{def}(Q)$ and $P < Q$ holds.*

This ordering is extended to ground literals in the usual way, resulting in the literal ordering $<_\Gamma^{lit}$.

Finally, we extend it to ground clauses: $C <_\Gamma C'$ iff either (i) $\mathrm{def}(C) <_p \mathrm{def}(C')$, or (ii) $\mathrm{def}(C) = \mathrm{def}(C')$ and C $(<_\Gamma^{lit})_{mul} C'$ hold, where $(<_\Gamma^{lit})_{mul}$ denotes the multiset extension of the literal ordering.

This ordering extends the atom and literal orderings, and we call it the ordering induced by Γ.

Proposition 2.8. $<_\Gamma$ *is well-defined, total on ground clauses, and a well-founded ordering.*

3   Calculus

States. We present our calculus as a set of rules over so-called *states*, tuples of the form $(\Gamma; N; U; k; s)$ where Γ denotes the trail, N the given clause set, U the set of learned clauses, k a non-negative integer - unless terminating with *Success* -, and s a *state indicator*. The latter can be $\top$, $\bot$, or $(C; \sigma; \pi)$.

$\top$ indicates the conflict search phase, if $k \geq 0$, or that Γ defines a model for N, if $k = -1$. $\bot$ means the empty clause has been learned, i.e. the unsatisfiability of N has been established. Finally, an indicator of the form $(C; \sigma; \pi)$ represents a set of clause instances falsified by the current trail Γ, and indicates the conflict resolution phase of our calculus.

As a starting state, we propose the initial state $(\epsilon; N; \emptyset; 0; \top)$, where ϵ stands for the empty trail, and N is the set of input clauses. However, we note that our definitions and results are independent from this state, and any *sound* state (see Definition 4.1) can be chosen as a starting state.

An Outline of NRCL. The calculus NRCL attempts to find a model through a series of both arbitrary and deduced assignments. Analogously to propositional SAT solvers, we apply *Propagate* to find literals implied by existing assignments, and once it is exhausted, we add arbitrary literals, so-called *decisions* to the trail with *Decide*. We restrict decisions to constrained instances of clause literals from N to avoid defining irrelevant atoms, and achieve earlier termination.

When adding new assignments onto the trail, the conditions of the rules ensure that each step is *sound* and *effective*, i.e. each ground literal defined by the added literal is indeed a consequence in the case of *Propagate*, was undefined before, and at least one such ground literal exists.

We call this phase *conflict search* and it ends with either a model of the original clause set, or with finding a clause C with some instances given in the form $(C; \sigma; \pi)$ falsified by the current trail. In the latter case, we initiate *conflict resolution* with *Conflict*, which identifies a set of clause instances contradicting the current model assumption. We also refer to this set as the *conflict-set*.

Then, we traverse the trail, ignoring irrelevant assignments via *Skip*, and resolving the current false clause with relevant reason clauses with *Resolve*. Ideally, this phase ends with learning a new assertive clause with *Backjump*, and backtracking to a state where this clause is not yet falsified. We note that unsatisfiability is established through learning the empty clause $\bot$.

On Factorization. As opposed to propositional SAT solving, where every clause can be considered already exhaustively factorized, in our case some ground instances might be still subject to factorization, which constitutes an additional challenge when trying to maintain important invariants, like the soundness of states defined in the next section.

On the one hand, during conflict search we have to avoid situations when a clause would be falsified by the decision immediately without allowing the use of factorization. This case is captured in the following definition. We note that instead of a blocked decision, we can always pick a stricter unblocked decision, e.g. an undefined ground literal in the worst case.

Definition 3.1. *We say that* a decision $(L; \pi)$ is blocked in Γ by a clause C, if C has a ground instance $C\sigma$ with $L_1, L_2 \in C\sigma$ such that for $\Gamma' = \Gamma, (L; \pi)$ (i) $C\sigma$ is false under Γ', (ii) $(L; \pi)$ is undefined in Γ, (iii) $\neg L_1, \neg L_2 \in \text{gnd}(L; \pi)$, and (iv) $L_1 \neq L_2$ all hold.

As an example, consider $\mathcal{D} = \{a, b, c\}$, $\Gamma = \{(\neg Q(x, y); \top)^1\}$, and a clause set containing $\neg P(x) \vee \neg P(y) \vee Q(x, y)$. Then $(P(x); \top)$, and $(P(x); x \neq c)$ are both blocked decisions in Γ, as witnessed by $\neg P(a) \vee \neg P(b) \vee Q(a, b)$.

On the other hand, during resolution, we need the option to factorize the current false clause with *Factorize*, and also to learn a clause blocking the last decision instead of learning an assertive clause.

Involved Operations. A short remark on the usage of the operations over constrained expressions: Conjunction is used whenever we try to unify two constrained literals, e.g. during learning a new clause via resolution, or finding candidates for propagation. Difference is needed when we remove already defined literals ensuring that a new assignment only defines new values. Finally, emptiness is tested overall in the calculus to ensure that a new assignment indeed defines the value of at least one ground atom.

Closures. We extend our language with *constrained closures* of literals of the form $(L \cdot \sigma; \pi)$, where $L \cdot \sigma$ is the *closure* representing $L\sigma$. This is an extension of the existing notation, and a form of book-keeping to make it easier to define the rules for clause learning.

For all other purposes, $L \cdot \sigma$ is identified with $L\sigma$, and all definitions over constrained literals can be extended to constrained closures accordingly. Decisions are always considered having empty closures, and the literal L is also a short-hand for $L \cdot \emptyset$. For further details, see [1].

Rules. Below, we present the rules of our calculus in a generic style as a state transition system, similarly to [19]. We note that in the rules π_1, π_2 is often used as a short-hand for $\pi_1 \wedge \pi_2$, if it is unambiguous. Furthermore, blocking is considered only w.r.t. the current clause set $N \cup U$ in the rest of the paper.

The strategy for completeness is discussed in Section 5, while technical details are addressed in the extended paper [1]. In particular, candidate clauses and substitutions for the rules can be found by combining standard indexing structures for testing simultaneous unifiability.

Propagate. $(\Gamma; N; U; k; \top) \Rightarrow (\Gamma, (L \cdot \sigma; \pi)^{C \vee L}; N; U; k; \top)$
if $k \geq 0$, and for $(C \vee L) \in (N \cup U)$, σ, and π all the followings hold: (i) $(C\sigma; \pi)$ is false under Γ, (ii) $(L\sigma; \pi)$ is undefined in Γ, and (iii) $(L\sigma; \pi)$ is not empty.

Decide. $(\Gamma; N; U; k; \top) \Rightarrow (\Gamma, (L; \pi)^{k+1}; N; U; k+1; \top)$
if $k \geq 0$, and for L, π all the followings hold: (i) $(L; \pi)$ is undefined in Γ, (ii) $(L; \pi)$ is not blocked in Γ, (iii) $(L; \pi)$ is not empty (iv) $\exists (C \vee L') \in N$ such that $|L| \geq |L'|$.

Conflict. $(\Gamma; N; U; k; \top) \Rightarrow (\Gamma; N; U; k; (C; \sigma; \pi))$
if $k \geq 0$, and for $\bot \neq C \in (N \cup U)$, σ, and π, (i) $(C\sigma; \pi)$ is false under Γ, and (ii) $(C\sigma; \pi)$ is not empty.

Success. $(\Gamma; N; U; k; \top) \Rightarrow (\Gamma; N; U; -1; \top)$ if $k \geq 0$, and $I_\Gamma \models N$.

Failure. $(\Gamma; N; U; k; \top) \Rightarrow (\Gamma; N; U; 0; \bot)$ if $\bot \in (N \cup U)$.

We note that the last condition in *Success* can be replaced by demanding that the rules *Propagate*, *Decide* and *Conflict* are exhausted and $\bot \notin (N \cup U)$. Then, after terminating, every undefined ground atom can be considered having arbitrary truth-values, or simply *false*, the way it is defined in I_Γ.

Skip. $(\Gamma, (L' \cdot \sigma'; \pi')^{C'}; N; U; k; (C; \sigma; \pi)) \Rightarrow (\Gamma; N; U; k; (C; \sigma; \pi))$
if there is no $L \in C$ such that (i) $\exists \eta = \mathrm{mgu}(L'\sigma', \neg L\sigma)$, and (ii) $(C\sigma\eta; \pi\eta, \pi'\eta)$ is not empty.

Resolve. $(\Gamma, (L' \cdot \sigma'; \pi')^{C' \vee L'}; \mathrm{N}; \mathrm{U}; k; (C \vee L; \sigma; \pi)) \Rightarrow$
$(\Gamma, (L' \cdot \sigma'; \pi')^{C' \vee L'}; \mathrm{N}; \mathrm{U}; k; ((C \vee C')\eta_0; \sigma^*; \pi\eta, \pi'\eta))$
if for L', σ, π' and $C' \vee L'$, all the followings hold: (i) $((C \vee L)\sigma; \pi)$ is not assertive, or $k = 0$, (ii) $\exists \eta = \mathrm{mgu}(L'\sigma', \neg L\sigma)$, and let $\eta_0 = \mathrm{mgu}(L', \neg L)$, and σ^* such that $\sigma\sigma'\eta = \eta_0\sigma^*$, and (iii) $((C \vee L)\sigma\eta; \pi\eta, \pi'\eta)$ is not empty.

Factorize. $(\Gamma, \ell; \mathrm{N}; \mathrm{U}; k; (C \vee L_1 \vee L_2; \sigma; \pi)) \Rightarrow (\Gamma, \ell; \mathrm{N}; \mathrm{U}; k; ((C \vee L_1)\eta_0; \sigma^*; \pi\eta))$
if $\ell = (L' \cdot \sigma'; \pi')^\alpha$ for some L', σ', π', and annotation α, and the followings hold:
(i) $\exists \eta = \mathrm{mgu}\{L_1\sigma, L_2\sigma, L'\sigma'\}$, and let $\eta_0 = \mathrm{mgu}(L_1, L_2)$, and σ^* such that $\sigma\eta = \eta_0\sigma^*$, and (ii) $((C \vee L_1)\sigma\eta; \pi\eta, \pi'\eta)$ is not empty.

We note that in both the case of *Resolve* and *Factorize* dropping the used trail-literal is not desired as the new conflict might still be resolvable or factorizable with it.

Backjump. $(\Gamma_1, \Gamma_2; \mathrm{N}; \mathrm{U}; k; (C; \sigma; \pi)) \Rightarrow (\Gamma_1; \mathrm{N}; \mathrm{U} \cup \{C\}; k'; \top)$
if $0 \le k' \le k$, $k' = \mathrm{lvl}(\Gamma_1)$, and one of the following condition-sets hold: (1) $k = 0$, and $C = \bot$; or (2) $k > 0$, $(C\sigma; \pi)$ is assertive, and C has no false instance under Γ_1; or (3) $k > 0$, the right-most element of Γ_2 is the top-level decision, $(C\sigma; \pi)$ is not assertive, *Factorize* cannot be applied, and C has no false instance under Γ_1.

In case (1), we say that *the empty clause $\bot$ is learned*. In case (2), we say *a new assertive clause is learned*, and in case (3) *a new blocking clause is learned*.

It is clear that $k' = 0$ or $k' < k$ in case (1) and (2), (3), respectively. The optimal choice for k' is the smallest level for which the learned clause can be used in *Propagate*. Such a k' might not always exist for the learned clause C, largely due to the instances of C not covered by $(C\sigma; \pi)$. In these cases the optimal choice for k' is the largest level for which C has no false instance.

Example. As an example, we present a derivation over $\mathcal{D} = \{a, b, c\}$ and from the clause set
$$\mathrm{N} = \{ \ C_1 : \neg P(c, x, x), \ C_2 : \neg P(x, y, z) \vee \neg P(u, w, t) \vee Q(x, u),$$
$$C_3 : \neg P(x, y, z) \vee \neg Q(a, x), \ C_4 : \neg Q(x, b) \vee \neg P(x, y, z) \ \}$$
The run below is by no means optimal - any sensible heuristic would choose the negative assignment for P outright -, but it is a valid derivation, and serves well as a demonstration for the syntactic behavior.

$$(\epsilon; \mathrm{N}; \emptyset; 0; \top) \overset{Propagate}{\Rightarrow} ((\neg P(c, x, x); \top)^{C_1}; \mathrm{N}; \emptyset; 0; \top) \overset{Decide}{\Rightarrow}$$

$$((\neg P(c, x, x); \top)^{C_1}, (P(x, y, z); x \ne c)^1; \mathrm{N}; \emptyset; 1; \top) \overset{Propagate}{\Rightarrow}$$

$$((\neg P(c, x, x); \top)^{C_1}, (P(x, y, z); x \ne c)^1, (\neg Q(a, x); x \ne c)^{C_3}; \mathrm{N}; \emptyset; 1; \top) \overset{ConflictC_2}{\Rightarrow}$$

$$(\dots; \mathrm{N}; \emptyset; 1; (\neg P(x, y, z) \vee \neg P(u, w, t) \vee Q(x, u); \{x \leftarrow a\}; u \ne c)) \overset{Resolve}{\Rightarrow}$$

$$(\dots; \mathrm{N}; \emptyset; 1; (\neg P(a, y, z) \vee \neg P(u, w, t) \vee \neg P(u, y', z'); \emptyset; u \ne c)) \overset{Skip}{\Rightarrow}$$

$$(\dots, (P(x, y, z); x \ne c)^1; \mathrm{N}; \emptyset; 1; (\neg P(a, y, z) \vee \neg P(u, w, t) \vee \neg P(u, y', z'); \emptyset; u \ne c))$$

$$\overset{Factorize}{\Rightarrow} (\dots, (P(x, y, z); x \ne c)^1; \mathrm{N}; \emptyset; 1; (\neg P(a, y, z) \vee \neg P(u, w, t); \emptyset; u \ne c))$$

$$\overset{Factorize}{\Rightarrow} ((\neg P(c, x, x); \top)^{C_1}, (P(x, y, z); x \neq c)^1; N; \emptyset; 1; (\neg P(a, y, z); \emptyset; \top))$$

$$\overset{Backjump(2)}{\Rightarrow} ((\neg P(c, x, x); \top)^{C_1}; N; \{\neg P(a, y, z)\}; 0; \top) \Rightarrow \dots$$

NRCL eventually finds a model, see [1] for the complete derivation.

4   Soundness

Next, we address soundness. The following state invariant defines a consistency notion for states.

Definition 4.1. *A state $(\Gamma; N; U; k; s)$ is called* well-formed *iff (i) if $k \geq 0$ then Γ contains exactly k decisions, (ii) for each i from $1, 2, \dots, k$, there is a unique $(L; \pi)^i \in \Gamma$, (iii) the decisions occur in Γ in the order of their levels, (iv) if $\Gamma = \Gamma_1, (L; \pi)^i, \Gamma_2, (L, \pi)^i$ satisfies the conditions of* Decide *w.r.t. Γ_1, N, and U, and (v) if $\Gamma = \Gamma_1, (L \cdot \sigma; \pi)^{C \vee L}, \Gamma_2, (C\sigma; \pi)$ is false under Γ_1, and $(L\sigma; \pi)$ satisfies the conditions for* Propagate *w.r.t. Γ_1 and $C \vee L$.*

A state $(\Gamma; N; U; k; s)$ is sound *iff (i) Γ is a consistent sequence of constrained literals, (ii) Γ is well-formed, (iii) $N \models U$, (iv) if $s = \bot$ then $\bot \in N \cup U$, (v) $k = -1$ implies $I_\Gamma \models N$, and (vi) if $s = (C; \sigma; \pi)$ then $(C\sigma; \pi)$ is false under Γ, $N \models C$, and $(C\sigma; \pi)$ is not empty.*

Then, a rule is called sound *iff it preserves the soundness of its left-hand side state.*

It is easy to see that the initial state $(\epsilon; N; \emptyset; 0; \top)$ is always sound. Furthermore, soundness is an invariant.

Theorem 4.2. *The rules of NRCL are sound.*

A direct consequence of Theorem 4.2 is that any state reached from a sound initial state is also sound. In the rest of the paper, we call derivations from a sound initial state *runs* of our calculus.

Theorem 4.3 (Soundness). *The calculus NRCL is sound, i.e. if a run terminates with the* Failure, *or* Success *rules, then the starting set N is unsatisfiable, and satisfiable, respectively. Furthermore, in the latter case the trail upon termination defines a model of N.*

5   Termination and Completeness

In this section, we define a sufficient strategy for proving termination, formulate our main result regarding non-redundant clause learning, and finally we show termination and completeness as a consequence.

Regular Runs. First, we define a strategy for NRCL in the form of *regular runs*, which is sufficient to prove both non-redundant clause learning and termination.

Definition 5.1. *A sound state* $(\Gamma; N; U; k; s)$ *is* regular *iff the followings hold: (i) If* $\Gamma = \Gamma', (L \cdot \sigma; \pi)^\alpha$, *then no clause from* $N \cup U$ *is false w.r.t.* Γ'. *(ii) For all decomposition* $\Gamma = \Gamma_1, (L; \pi)^i, \Gamma_2$ *with decision* $(L; \pi)^i$, Propagate *is exhausted w.r.t.* Γ_1 *and* $N \cup U$.

We note that the last assignment on the trail might still make some clauses false, and the initial state $(\epsilon; N; \emptyset; 0; \top)$ is always regular.

Definition 5.2. *We call a run* regular *iff the followings hold: (i) The starting state is regular. (ii) During conflict search, rules are always applied in this order exhaustively:* Failure, Success, Conflict, Propagate, Decide. *(Or* Failure, Conflict, Propagate, Decide, Success, *if we test success through exhausted conflict search.) (iii) In conflict resolution* Backjump *is always applied as soon as possible, and the new subsequent state is a regular state.*

Lemma 5.3. *Regular runs preserve regularity, i.e. every state in a regular run is regular.*

Regular runs entail properties similar to standard invariants of CDCL solvers, which are exploited in the non-redundancy and termination proofs.

Redundancy and Clause Learning. We define redundancy w.r.t. the induced ordering $<_\Gamma$ in the standard way. While this definition depends on the dynamically changing ordering $<_\Gamma$, it is still meaningful as it allows the removal of clauses which are redundant w.r.t. any possible induced ordering.

Definition 5.4. *A ground clause* C *is* redundant *w.r.t. a ground clause set* N *(and* $<_\Gamma$) *iff* $C \in N$, *or there is an* $S \subseteq N^{<_\Gamma C} : S \models C$.

A first-order clause C *is* redundant *w.r.t. the first-order clause set* N *(and* $<_\Gamma$) *iff for each* $C' \in \text{gnd}(C) : C'$ *is redundant w.r.t.* $\text{gnd}(N)$. *If redundancy does not hold, we call the corresponding clause* non-redundant, *or* irredundant.

As a consequence of the definitions, many important first-order redundancy criterions hold w.r.t. any possible $<_\Gamma$. In particular, the classic *subsumption, subsumption resolution*, and *tautology deletion* are such *admissible* criterions, as shown in the extended paper [1].

Next, we show that each learned clause is non-redundant w.r.t. the current clause set and induced ordering. It means, on the one hand, that forward redundancy elimination is unnecessary for these clauses, and, on the other hand, each clause we learn can be considered as making progress.

Theorem 5.5 (Non-redundant Clause Learning). *Let* Γ *denote the trail at a conflict in a regular run,* $<_\Gamma$ *the induced ordering, and assume the clause* C *is learned via the* Backjump *rule, and let* N *and* U *be the starting clause set and the set of learned clauses before the conflict, respectively.*

Then, C *is not redundant w.r.t.* $N \cup U$ *and* $<_\Gamma$.

Proof: (Sketch) The proof uses case distinction, and relies on the definitions of induced ordering and regular runs, and the conditions of the rules. See the extended paper [1] for details. **Qed.**

Decision Procedure. Just as most related calculi, NRCL is a decision procedure for BS as well, under the regularity conditions of Definition 5.2. In the following, we assume the finiteness of N, Σ and $\mathcal{D}$, and we present below the lemmas and propositions leading to termination. This result together with soundness, shown in Theorem 4.3, already implies completeness.

Proposition 5.6. *A regular run is never stuck, i.e. it terminates with the terminal rules, or one of the other rules is applicable.*

Lemma 5.7. *A conflict search phase of a regular run always terminates, i.e. it leads either to a conflict or to termination.*

Lemma 5.8. *A conflict resolution phase of a regular run always terminates, i.e. it leads to the application of* Backjump *after finitely many steps.*

Lemma 5.9. *A regular run can only learn finitely many new clauses.*

Proof: (Sketch) Our proof uses Higman's Lemma [12]. It states that given an infinite sequence of words over a finite alphabet, there is always an index and a subsequent index such that the first word is *embedded* into the latter, i.e. after deleting some letters from the second word we can get the first one.

In our setting, the finite set of ground literals over Σ serves as the finite alphabet, and the sequence of learned non-redundant ground instances as the word sequence. Then embedding translates to subsumption.

Thus, given an infinite sequence of learned clauses, the corresponding infinite sequence of non-redundant ground instances, which exists by Theorem 5.5, contains two clauses such that the one learned earlier subsumes the other. A contradiction to non-redundancy. See [1] for the full proof. **Qed.**

Theorem 5.10 (Termination). *A regular run always terminates.*

Corollary 5.11 (Decision Procedure). *Regular runs provide a decision procedure for the Bernays-Schönfinkel fragment.*

I.e. every regular run terminates after finitely many steps with Failure, *or* Success, *for an unsatisfiable, or satisfiable clause set N, respectively.*

6   Related Work

In this section, we compare NRCL to existing systems and calculi. Many of these techniques are capable of handling full first-order logic. Here, we only focus on their behavior on the Bernays-Schönfinkel fragment. Due to space constraints, we focus on the aspects most relevant to our calculus. For a more thorough comparison, see [1].

The finite model finder *Paradox* [8] grounds the problem and passes it to a CDCL-based SAT solver. In comparison, NRCL works directly with the original clauses and not with the exponentially larger set of ground instances, and we learn more general first-order clauses, instead of single ground instances.

Model Evolution [5] lifts DPLL - the ancestor of CDCL, a calculus using backtracking instead of backjumping and clause learning -, and was later extended with clause learning [4]. It represents a model with a set of first-order literals, called *context*, and detects conflicts using syntactic concepts weaker then the full-fledged semantics based on the induced interpretation. This potentially leads to longer derivations before detecting a false clause. Compared to *Model Evolution*, NRCL relies on the full-fledged semantics, uses more compact model representation (see the experiment below), and we learn only non-redundant clauses. It is not clear if the latter holds for *Model Evolution*, especially the admissibility of the classic criterions needs in-depth considerations.

DPLL(SX) [22] attempts to lift CDCL to BS in a similar manner, has a similar rule set, and uses substitution sets represented by BDDs instead of constraints, which provides an explicit model representation. First, our constraint language is dual to the one of *DPLL(SX)* and provides for some model classes more compact representations, see below. Second, DPLL(SX) lacks the concept for blocking, and applies an explicit refine rule instead. As a side effect, it learns nothing from conflicts which lead to blocking clauses, and in these cases it abandons conflict resolution and refines the last decision. Finally, we also address redundancy, and exploit the non-redundancy result to show termination, which we consider a valuable addition.

The most recent calculus *SGGS* [7] uses conjunctions of atoms of the form $x \neq y$, and $top(x) \neq f$ as constraints, represents models with sequences of constrained clauses with selected literals, and uses a given initial interpretation I as semantic guidance for the calculus. *SGGS* keeps extending the sequence to satisfy more and more clauses, and handles contradictions via resolution and constraint splitting. NRCL utilizes a more expressive constraint language, which results in less fragmentation and potentially a smaller representation size. This also allows to learn more general clauses. We consider our model representation to be more explicit, as determining which literal is responsible for an assignment is more straightforward. Finally, our calculus learns new non-redundant clauses and uses backjumping.

iProver [11][14] generates a propositional approximation of the clause set by instantiating all the variables with constants, and passes it on to a CDCL-based SAT solver. Unsatisfiability of the approximation entails the unsatisfiability of the original problem. On the other hand, if an abstract model is generated, it is used to guide the calculus to add proper instances of the original clauses, which refines the propositional abstraction. Compared to *iProver*, our approach is fine-grained, as the evaluation and refinement of our implicit abstraction happen interleaved with the other reasoning steps. Furthermore, we work directly with the original clause set, and our trail always corresponds to a consistent first-order model candidate.

NRCL contributes to the state-of-the-art solvers in terms of model representation. Considering the sole constrained literal
$$(P(x_1, \ldots, x_k); x_1 \neq x_2, \ldots, x_{k-1} \neq x_k)$$
already demonstrates that NRCL can be exponentially more compact w.r.t. increasing k than the respective substitution set representation in $DPLL(SX)$, and at least quadratically more compact than the respective context in *Model Evolution*.

In addition to the theoretical argument, we also ran a small experiment for models represented by literals of similar form. We have not yet implemented NRCL. However, the below problem is solved by any regular run in NRCL without backjumping. The clause set
$$Q(x, x), \neg Q(a_1, a_2), \neg Q(a_2, a_3), \ldots, \neg Q(a_{n-1}, a_n),$$
$$\neg P(x_1, x_1, x_3, \ldots, x_k), \ldots, \neg P(x_1, x_2, \ldots, x_{k-1}, x_{k-1}),$$
$$\neg Q(x, z) \vee Q(x, y) \vee Q(y, z), P(x_1, \ldots, x_k) \vee Q(x_1, x_2) \vee \ldots \vee Q(x_{k-1}, x_k)$$
has a model where the positive atoms are represented by the constrained literals $(P(x_1, \ldots, x_k); x_1 \neq x_2, \ldots, x_{k-1} \neq x_k)$ and $(Q(x, x); \top)$. NRCL directly finds this model, by exhaustively applying propagation, making a single decision on $P(x_1, \ldots, x_k)$ and finally setting all undefined $Q(x, y)$ literals to false. A decision on some $Q(x_i, x_{i+1})$ leads to a similar behavior and model.

We ran the the available state-of-the-art provers $Darwin$[1] (1.4.5) and *iProver* (0.8.1) on this set. The experiments were carried out on a Debian Linux (4.7.2-5) Intel (Xeon E5-2680, 2.7GHZ) computer with 256GB physical memory. For $n = 7$ and $k = 5, 7, 9$, *Darwin* needs $0.2, 8.1, 518$ seconds to find a model, respectively. For $k = 7$ and $n = 7, 10, 13$, it is $8.1, 62, 347$ seconds, respectively. For $k = 9$ and $n = 7, 10, 13, 16, 19, 22$, *iProver* needs $0, 0.2, 21, 39, 116, 718$ seconds, respectively.

For *Darwin*, these results show an exponentially growing solution time w.r.t. k (the arity of P) or n (the domain size). *iProver* is robust against increasing k but not against increasing n, where it also shows an exponential growth. This shows that our model representation is not subsumed by either calculus.

Finally, the technique introduced in [13] for *SPASS* employs a combination of restricted superposition on Horn clauses, and *labelled splitting* [10] on non-Horn clauses. Compared to this approach, NRCL maintains a model candidate, it is restricted to learn clauses only at conflicts and only non-redundant ones, does not rely on Horn clauses, and the implicit branchings through decisions and backjumps are more elaborate and guided by the model search, compared to the splitting techniques employed by first-order theorem provers. However, we note that for some problem classes finite superposition saturation is still superior to explicit model generation, see e.g. superposition for knowledge bases in [25].

7   Conclusion

In this paper, we proposed the decision procedure NRCL for the Bernays-Schönfinkel fragment. Our approach represents a model candidate as a set of

---
[1] The implementation of *Model Evolution*

constrained literals, and derives a model or a proof of unsatisfiability through a series of decisions, propagations, and learning new clauses.

Compared to earlier work in this direction, we investigated the standard redundancy notion w.r.t. the ordering induced by the current trail. One of our main contributions over existing work is that, by design, we can prove our learned clauses to be non-redundant, i.e., any learned clause makes progress towards finding a model or a refutation, because it eliminates at least one potential model. In general, we consider this a key property for automated reasoning.

Projecting NRCL to propositional logic proves this property for CDCL with respect to our notion of redundancy. Our notion also admits techniques like subsumption and subsumption resolution, which are important in both SAT solving and first-order theorem proving. We see this as a strong indication that a future implementation will contribute to the state of the art.

As future research, the immediate goal is to implement NRCL. This includes developing suitable and efficient term indexing structures, detecting and exploiting redundancy, and defining concrete and efficient heuristics.

Our long-term goal is to extend this calculus beyond Bernays-Schönfinkel. The next step into this direction is to enrich our calculus with function symbols and sorts to handle the *non-cyclic fragment* introduced in [16]. This class still has the finite Herbrand model property, thus, our results will directly extend to this fragment. Further goals are to consider other decidable fragments, to treat equality, and finally to extend our work to finite model finding.

Acknowledgments. We thank our reviewers for their constructive and helpful comments.

References

[1] Alagi, G., Weidenbach, C.: NRCL - A Model Building Approach to the Bernays-Schönfinkel Fragment (Full Paper). CoRR, abs/1502.05501 (2015). http://arxiv.org/abs/1502.05501

[2] Armando, A., Baumgartner, P., Dowek, G. (eds.): IJCAR 2008. LNCS (LNAI), vol. 5195. Springer, Heidelberg (2008)

[3] Bachmair, L., Ganzinger, H.: Resolution theorem proving. In: Robinson and Voronkov (eds.) [23], pp. 19–99

[4] Baumgartner, P., Fuchs, A., Tinelli, C.: Lemma Learning in the model evolution calculus. In: Hermann, M., Voronkov, A. (eds.) LPAR 2006. LNCS (LNAI), vol. 4246, pp. 572–586. Springer, Heidelberg (2006)

[5] Baumgartner, P., Tinelli, C.: The model evolution calculus. In: Baader, F. (ed.) CADE 2003. LNCS (LNAI), vol. 2741, pp. 350–364. Springer, Heidelberg (2003)

[6] Biere, A., Heule, M., van Maaren, H., Walsh, T. (eds.): Handbook of Satisfiability. Frontiers in Artificial Intelligence and Applications, vol. 185. IOS Press (2009)

[7] Bonacina, M.P., Plaisted, D.A.: SGGS theorem proving: an exposition. In: Notes of the Fourth Workshop on Practical Aspects in Automated Reasoning (PAAR) (2014)

[8] Claessen, K., Srensson, N.: New Techniques that Improve MACE-style finite model finding. In: Model Computation - Principles, Algorithms, Applications (2003)

[9] Comon, H.: Disunification: A survey. In: Computational Logic - Essays in Honor of Alan Robinson, pp. 322–359 (1991)

[10] Fietzke, A., Weidenbach, C.: Labelled splitting. Ann. Math. Artif. Intell. 55(1–2), 3–34 (2009)

[11] Ganzinger, H., Korovin, K.: New directions in instantiation-based theorem proving. In: LICS, pp. 55–64. IEEE Computer Society (2003)

[12] Higman, G.: Ordering by Divisibility in Abstract Algebras. Proceedings of the London Mathematical Society 2(1), 326–336 (1952)

[13] Hillenbrand, T., Weidenbach, C.: Superposition for bounded domains. In: Bonacina, M.P., Stickel, M.E. (eds.) Automated Reasoning and Mathematics. LNCS, vol. 7788, pp. 68–100. Springer, Heidelberg (2013)

[14] Korovin, K.: iProver - An instantiation-based theorem prover for first-order logic (system description). In: Armando et al. [2], pp. 292–298

[15] Korovin, K.: Inst-Gen – A modular approach to instantiation-based automated reasoning. In: Voronkov, A., Weidenbach, C. (eds.) Programming Logics. LNCS, vol. 7797, pp. 239–270. Springer, Heidelberg (2013)

[16] Korovin, K.: Non-cyclic sorts for first-order satisfiability. In: Fontaine, P., Ringeissen, C., Schmidt, R.A. (eds.) FroCoS 2013. LNCS, vol. 8152, pp. 214–228. Springer, Heidelberg (2013)

[17] Lassez, J.-L., Marriott, K.: Explicit Representation of Terms Defined by Counter Examples. J. Autom. Reasoning 3(3), 301–317 (1987)

[18] Lewis, H.R.: Complexity Results for Classes of Quantificational Formulas. J. Comput. Syst. Sci. 21(3), 317–353 (1980)

[19] Nieuwenhuis, R., Oliveras, A., Tinelli, C.: Abstract DPLL and abstract DPLL nodulo theories. In: Baader, F., Voronkov, A. (eds.) LPAR 2004. LNCS (LNAI), vol. 3452, pp. 36–50. Springer, Heidelberg (2005)

[20] Nieuwenhuis, R., Rubio, A.: Paramodulation-based theorem proving. In: Robinson and Voronkov [23], pp. 371–443

[21] Pérez, J.A.N., Voronkov, A.: Proof Systems for Effectively Propositional Logic. In: Armando et al. [21], pp. 426–440

[22] Piskac, R., de Moura, L.M., Bjørner, N.: Deciding Effectively Propositional Logic Using DPLL and Substitution Sets. J. Autom. Reasoning 44(4), 401–424 (2010)

[23] Robinson, J.A., Voronkov, A. (eds.): Handbook of Automated Reasoning, vol. 2. Elsevier and MIT Press (2001)

[24] Silva, J.P.M., Sakallah, K.A.: Conflict analysis in search algorithms for satisfiability. In: ICTAI, pp. 467–469 (1996)

[25] Suda, M., Weidenbach, C., Wischnewski, P.: On the saturation of YAGO. In: Giesl, J., Hähnle, R. (eds.) IJCAR 2010. LNCS, vol. 6173, pp. 441–456. Springer, Heidelberg (2010)

[26] Tammet, T.: Finite model building: improvements and comparisons. In: Model Computation: Principles, Algorithms, Applications (2003)

[27] Weidenbach, C.: Combining superposition, sorts and splitting. In: Robinson and Voronkov [23], pp. 1965–2013

First-Order Logic Theorem Proving and Model Building via Approximation and Instantiation

Andreas Teucke[1,2] and Christoph Weidenbach[1]

[1] Max-Planck Institut for Informatics, Campus E1 4 66123 Saarbrücken Germany
[2] Graduate School of Computer Science, Saarbrücken, Germany

Abstract. In this paper we consider first-order logic theorem proving and model building via approximation and instantiation. Given a clause set we propose its approximation into a simplified clause set where satisfiability is decidable. The approximation extends the signature and preserves unsatisfiability: if the simplified clause set is satisfiable in some model, so is the original clause set in the same model interpreted in the original signature. A refutation generated by a decision procedure on the simplified clause set can then either be lifted to a refutation in the original clause set, or it guides a refinement excluding the previously found unliftable refutation. This way the approach is refutationally complete. We do not step-wise lift refutations but lift conflicting cores, finite unsatisfiable clause sets representing at least one refutation. The approach is dual to many existing approaches in the literature.

1 Introduction

The Inst-Gen calculus by Ganzinger and Korovin [6] and its implementation in iProver has shown to be very successful. The calculus is based on an under-approximation - instantiation - refinement loop. A given first-order clause set is under-approximated by finite grounding and afterwards a SAT-solver is used to test unsatisfiability. If the ground clause set is unsatisfiable then a refutation for the original clause set is found. If it is satisfiable, the model generated by the SAT-solver is typically not a model for the original clause set. If it is not, it is used to instantiate the original clauses such that the found model is ruled out for the future.

In this paper we define a calculus that is dual to the Inst-Gen calculus. A given first-order clause set is over-approximated into a decidable fragment of first-order logic: a monadic, shallow, linear Horn (MSLH) theory [14]. If the over-approximated clause set is satisfiable, so is the original clause set. If it is unsatisfiable, the found refutation is typically not a refutation for the original clause set. If it is not, the refutation is analyzed to instantiate the original clause set such that the found refutation is ruled out for the future. The MSLH fragment properly includes first-order ground logic, but is also expressive enough to represent minimal infinite models.

In addition to developing a new proof method for first-order logic the representation of first order models constitutes our second motivation for studying the

© Springer International Publishing Switzerland 2015
C. Lutz and S. Ranise (Eds.): FroCoS 2015, LNAI 9322, pp. 85–100, 2015.
DOI: 10.1007/978-3-319-24246-0_6

new calculus and the particular MSLH approximation. It is meanwhile accepted that a model-based guidance can significantly improve an automated reasoning calculus. The propositional CDCL calculus [9] is one prominent example for this insight. In first-order logic, (partial) model operators typically generate inductive models for which almost all interesting properties become undecidable, in general. One way out of this problem is to generate a model for an approximated clause set, such that important properties with respect to the original clause set are preserved. In the case of our calculus and approximation, a found model can be effectively translated into a model for the original clause set. So our result is also a first step towards model-based guidance in first-order logic automated reasoning.

As an example for our calculus, consider the first-order Horn clauses

$S(x) \rightarrow P(x, g(x)); S(a); S(b); S(g(x)); \neg P(a, g(b)); \neg P(g(x), g(g(x)))$

that are approximated (Section 2) into the MSLH theory $S(x), R(y) \rightarrow T(f_P(x, y)); S(x) \rightarrow R(g(x)); S(a); S(b); S(g(x)); \neg T(f_P(a, g(b))); \neg T(f_P(g(x), g(g(x))))$ where the relation P is encoded by the function f_P and the non-linear occurrence of x in the first clause is approximated by the introduction of the additional variable y. The approximated clause set has two refutations: one using $\neg T(f_P(a, g(b)))$ and the second using $\neg T(f_P(g(x), g(g(x))))$ plus the rest of the clauses, respectively. While the first refutation cannot be lifted, the second one is liftable to a refutation of the original clause set (Section 3). Actually, we do not consider refutations, but conflicting cores (Definition 9). Conflicting cores are finite, unsatisfiable clause sets where variables are considered to be shared among clauses and rigid such that any instantiation preserves unsatisfiability. Conflicting cores can be effectively generated out of refutations via instantiation of (copies of) the input clauses involved in the refutation. For the above second refutation the conflicting core of the approximated clause set is $S(g(x)), R(g(g(x))) \rightarrow T(f_P(g(x), g(g(x)))); S(g(x)) \rightarrow R(g(g(x))); S(g(x)); \neg T(f_P(g(x), g(g(x))))$.

In case the first refutation is selected for lifting, it fails, so the original clause set is refined (Section 4). The refinement replaces the first clause with

$S(a) \rightarrow P(a, g(a)); S(b) \rightarrow P(b, g(b))$ and $S(g(x)) \rightarrow P(g(x), g(g(x)))$.

The approximation of the resulting new clause set does no longer enable a refutation using $\neg T(f_P(a, g(b)))$. Therefore, the refutation using $\neg T(f_P(g(x), g(g(x))))$ is found after refinement. In case the original clause set contains a non-Horn clause, one positive literal is selected by the approximation.

The paper is now organized as follows. Section 2 introduces some basic notions and the approximation relation $\Rightarrow_{APR}$ that transforms any first-order clause set into an MSLH theory. The lifting of conflicting cores is described in Section 3 and the respective abstraction refinement in Section 4 including soundness and completeness results. The paper ends with a summary including a discussion on future and related work, Section 5.

2 Linear Shallow Monadic Horn Approximation

We consider a standard first-order language without equality where Σ denotes the signature. The symbols x, y denote variables, a, b constants, f, g, h are functions and s, t terms. Predicates are denoted by S, P, Q, R, literals by E, clauses by C, D, and sets of clauses by N, M. The term $t[s]_p$ denotes that the term t has the subterm s at position p. The notion is extended to atoms, clauses, and multiple positions. A predicate with exactly one argument is called monadic. For the sake of presentation, propositional atoms are considered as ground monadic atoms. A literal is either an atom or an atom preceded by $\neg$ and it is then called positive or negative, respectively. A term is complex if it is not a variable and shallow if it has at most depth one. It is called linear if there are no duplicate variable occurrences. A literal, where every term is shallow, is also called shallow. A clause is a multiset of literals which we write as an implication $\Gamma \to \Delta$ where the atoms in Δ denote the positive literals and the atoms in Γ the negative literals. If Γ is empty we omit $\to$, e.g., we write $P(x)$ instead of $\to P(x)$ whereas if Δ is empty $\to$ is always shown. If a clause has at most one positive literal, it is a Horn clause. If there are no variables, then terms, atoms and clauses are called ground, respectively. A substitution σ is a mapping from variables into terms denoted by pairs $\{x \mapsto t\}$. If for some term t (literal E, clause C, clause set N), $t\sigma$ ($E\sigma$, $C\sigma$, $N\sigma$) is ground, then σ is a grounding substitution.

A Herbrand interpretation I is a - possibly infinite - set of positive ground literals and I is said to satisfy a clause $C = \Gamma \to \Delta$, denoted by $I \vDash C$, if $\Delta\sigma \cap I \neq \emptyset$ or $\Gamma\sigma \not\subseteq I$ for every grounding substitution σ. An interpretation I is called a model of N if I satisfies N, $I \vDash N$, i.e., $I \vDash C$ for every $C \in N$. Models are considered *minimal* with respect to set inclusion. A set of clauses N is satisfiable, if there exists a model that satisfies N. Otherwise the set is unsatisfiable.

Definition 1 (Approximation). *Given a relation $\Rightarrow$ on clause sets: (1) $\Rightarrow$ is called an over-approximation if for all N and N' with $N \Rightarrow N'$ satisfiability of N' implies satisfiability of N, (2) $\Rightarrow$ is called an under-approximation if for all N and N' with $N \Rightarrow N'$, unsatisfiability of N' implies unsatisfiability of N.*

Next we introduce our concrete over-approximation $\Rightarrow_{\mathrm{APR}}$ that maps a clause set N to an MSLH clause set N'. Starting from a clause set N the transformation is parameterized by a single monadic projection predicate T, fresh to N and for each non-monadic predicate P a projection function f_P fresh to N. We establish on the fly a parent relation between the approximated clause(s) and the parent clause. We call the transitive closure of the parent relation the ancestor relation. The ancestor relation is needed for defining lifting and refinement.

Definition 2. *Given a predicate P, projection predicate T, and projection function f_P, define the injective function $\mu_P^T(P(t_1, \ldots, t_n)) := T(f_P(t_1, \ldots, t_n))$ and $\mu_P^T(Q(s_1, \ldots, s_m)) := Q(s_1, \ldots, s_m)$ for any atom with a predicate symbol different from P. The function is extended to clauses, clause sets and interpretations. Given a signature Σ with non-monadic predicates $P_1, \ldots, P_n$, define $\mu_\Sigma^T(N) = \mu_{P_1}^T(\ldots (\mu_{P_n}^T(N)) \ldots)$ and $\mu_\Sigma^T(\mathcal{I}) = \mu_{P_1}^T(\ldots (\mu_{P_n}^T(\mathcal{I})) \ldots)$.*

Monadic. $N \Rightarrow_{\text{MO}} \mu_P^T(N)$

provided P is a non-monadic predicate in the signature of N; for all $C \in N$ with $C \neq \mu_P^T(C)$, the clause C is the parent of $\mu_P^T(C)$

Horn. $N \cup \{\Gamma \to E_1, \ldots, E_n\} \Rightarrow_{\text{HO}} N \cup \{\Gamma \to E_i\}$

provided $n > 1$ and $1 \leq i \leq n$; $\Gamma \to E_1, \ldots, E_n$ is the parent of $\Gamma \to E_i$

Shallow. $N \cup \{\Gamma \to E[s]_p\} \Rightarrow_{\text{SH}} N \cup \{S(x), \Gamma_1 \to E[x]_p\} \cup \{\Gamma_2 \to S(s)\}$

provided s is a complex term, p not a top position, x and S fresh, and $\Gamma_1 \cup \Gamma_2 = \Gamma$, $\{Q(y) \in \Gamma \mid y \in \text{vars}(E[x]_p)\} \subseteq \Gamma_1$, $\{Q(y) \in \Gamma \mid y \in \text{vars}(s)\} \subseteq \Gamma_2$; the clause $\Gamma \to E[s]_p$ is the parent of $S(x), \Gamma_1 \to E[x]_p$ and $\Gamma_2 \to S(s)$

Linear. $N \cup \{\Gamma \to E[x]_{p,q}\} \Rightarrow_{\text{LI}} N \cup \{\Gamma\{x \mapsto x'\}, \Gamma \to E[x']_q\}$

provided x' is fresh, the positions p, q denote different occurrences of x in E; $\Gamma \to E[x]_{p,q}$ is the parent of $\Gamma\{x \mapsto x'\}, \Gamma \to E[x']_q$

In the Shallow transformation, Γ_1 and Γ_2 can be almost arbitrarily chosen as long as they "add up" to Γ. The goal, however, is to minimize the set of common variables $\text{vars}(\Gamma_2, s) \cap \text{vars}(\Gamma_1, E[x]_p)$. If the intersection is empty, the Shallow transformation is satisfiability equivalent. The conditions on Γ_1 and Γ_2 ensure that freshly introduced $S(x)$ atoms are not separated from the respective positive atom $E[x]_p$ in subsequent shallow transformation applications. This is will be required for Lemma 8. In the Linear transformation, the duplication of literals in Γ is not needed if x does not occur in them.

Definition 3 ($\Rightarrow_{\text{APR}}$). *We define $\Rightarrow_{\text{APR}}$ as the priority rewrite system [1] consisting of $\Rightarrow_{\text{MO}}$, $\Rightarrow_{\text{HO}}$, $\Rightarrow_{\text{SH}}$ and $\Rightarrow_{\text{LI}}$ with priority $\Rightarrow_{\text{MO}} > \Rightarrow_{\text{HO}} > \Rightarrow_{\text{SH}} > \Rightarrow_{\text{LI}}$.*

Lemma 4 ($\Rightarrow_{\text{APR}}$ **is a Terminating Over-Approximation**). *The approximation rules are terminating over-approximations: (i) $\Rightarrow_{\text{APR}}$ terminates (ii) the Monadic transformation is an over-approximation (iii) the Horn transformation is an over-approximation (iv) the Shallow transformation is an over-approximation (v) the Linear transformation is an over-approximation*

Proof. (i) The transformations can be considered sequentially, because of the imposed rule preference. The Monadic transformation strictly reduces the number of non-monadic atoms. The Horn transformation strictly reduces the number of non-Horn clauses. The Shallow transformation strictly reduces the multiset of term depths of the newly introduced clauses compared to the removed parent clause. The Linear transformation strictly reduces the number of duplicate variable occurrences in positive literals. Hence $\Rightarrow_{\text{APR}}$ terminates.

(ii) Let $N_0 \Rightarrow_{\text{MO}} N_1 = \mu_P(N_0)$. Then, $N_0 = \mu_P^{-1}(N_1)$. Let $\mathcal{I}$ be a model of N_1 and $C \in N_0$. Since $\mu_P(C) \in N_1$, $\mathcal{I} \models \mu_P(C)$ and thus, $\mu_P^{-1}(\mathcal{I}) \models C$. Hence, $\mu_P^{-1}(\mathcal{I})$ is a model of N_0. Therefore, the Monadic transformation is an over-approximation. Actually, it is also a satisfiability preserving transformation.

(iii) Let $N_0 = N \cup \{\Gamma \to E_1, \dots, E_n\} \Rightarrow_{\text{HO}} N \cup \{\Gamma \to E_i\}$, where $N \cup \{\Gamma \to E_i\}$ is satisfiable. The clause $\Gamma \to E_i$ subsumes the clause $\Gamma \to E_1, \dots, E_n$. Hence, for any model $\mathcal{I}$, $\mathcal{I} \models N \cup \{\Gamma \to E_1, \dots, E_n\}$ if $\mathcal{I} \models N \cup \{\Gamma \to E_i\}$. Therefore, the Horn transformation is an over-approximation.

(iv) Let $N_0 = N \cup \{\Gamma \to E[s]_p\} \Rightarrow_{\text{SH}} N \cup \{S(x), \Gamma_1 \to E[x]_p; \Gamma_2 \to S(s)\} = N_1$. Let $\mathcal{I}$ be a model of N_1 and C be a ground instance of a clause in N_0. If C is an instance of a clause in N, then $\mathcal{I} \models C$. Otherwise $C = (\Gamma \to E[s]_p)\sigma$ for some ground substitution σ. Then $S(s)\sigma, \Gamma_1\sigma \to E[s]_p\sigma = (S(x), \Gamma_1 \to E[x]_p)\{x \mapsto s\}\sigma$ and $\Gamma_2\sigma \to S(s)\sigma = (\Gamma_2 \to S(s))\sigma$. Since $\mathcal{I} \models N_1$, $\mathcal{I}$ also satisfies the resolvent $\Gamma_1\sigma, \Gamma_2\sigma \to E[s]_p\sigma$, which equals C modulo condensation. Hence $\mathcal{I} \models N_0$. Therefore, the Shallow transformation is an over-approximation.

(v) Let $N_0 = N \cup \{\Gamma \to E[x]_{p,q}\} \Rightarrow_{\text{LI}} N \cup \{\Gamma\{x \mapsto x'\}, \Gamma \to E[x']_q\} = N_1$. Let $\mathcal{I}$ be a model of N_1 and C be a ground instance of a clause in N_0. If C is an instance of a clause in N, then $\mathcal{I} \models C$. Otherwise $C = (\Gamma \to E[x]_{p,q})\sigma$ for some ground substitution σ. Then, $(\Gamma\{x \mapsto x'\}, \Gamma \to E[x']_q)\{x' \mapsto x\}\sigma = (\Gamma, \Gamma \to E[x]_q)\sigma$, which equals C modulo condensation. Thus, $\mathcal{I} \models C$ because $\mathcal{I} \models (\Gamma\{x \mapsto x'\}, \Gamma \to E[x']_q)\{x' \mapsto x\}\sigma$. Hence $\mathcal{I} \models N_0$. Therefore, Linear transformation is an over-approximation. $\qquad\square$

Corollary 5. *If $N \Rightarrow_{\text{APR}}^* N'$ and N' is satisfied by a model $\mathcal{I}$, then $\mu_\Sigma^{-1}(\mathcal{I})$ is a model of N.*

In addition to being an over-approximation, the minimal model (with respect to set inclusion) of the eventual approximation generated by $\Rightarrow_{\text{APR}}$ preserves the skeleton term structure of the original clause set, if it exists. The refinement introduced in Section 4 instantiates clauses. Thus it always makes progress towards finding a model or a refutation.

Definition 6 (Term Skeleton). *The term skeleton of term t, $skt(t)$, is defined as (1) $skt(x) = x'$, where x' is a fresh variable (2) $skt(f(s_1, \dots, s_n)) = f(skt(s_1), \dots, skt(s_n))$.*

Lemma 7. *Let N_0 be a monadic clause set and N_k be its approximation via $\Rightarrow_{\text{APR}}$. Let N_k be satisfiable and $\mathcal{I}$ be a minimal model for N_k. If $P(s) \in \mathcal{I}$ and P is a predicate in N_0, then there exists a clause $C = \Gamma \to \Delta, P(t) \in N_0$ and a substitution σ such that $s = skt(t)\sigma$ and for each variable x and predicate S with $C = S(x), \Gamma' \to \Delta, P(t[x]_p)$ and $s|_p = s''$, $S(s'') \in \mathcal{I}$.*

Proof. By induction on the length of the approximation $N_0 \Rightarrow_{\text{APR}}^* N_k$.

For the base $N_k = N_0$, assume there is no $C \in N_k$ with $C\sigma = \Gamma \to \Delta, P(s)$, where for each variable x and predicate S with $C = S(x), \Gamma' \to \Delta, P(t[x]_p)$ and $s|_p = s''$, $S(s'') \in \mathcal{I}$. Then $\mathcal{I} \setminus \{P(s)\}$ is still a model of N_k and therefore $\mathcal{I}$ was not minimal. A contradiction.

Let $N_0 \Rightarrow_{\text{APR}} N_1 \Rightarrow_{\text{APR}}^* N_k$, $P(s) \in \mathcal{I}$ and P is a predicate in N_0 and hence also in N_1. By the induction hypothesis on $N_1 \Rightarrow_{\text{APR}}^* N_k$, there exist a clause $C = \Gamma \to \Delta, P(t) \in N_1$ and a substitution σ such that $s = skt(t)\sigma$ and $S(s'') \in \mathcal{I}$ for each variable x and predicate S with $C = S(x), \Gamma' \to \Delta, P(t[x]_p)$

and $s|_p = s''$. The first approximation rule application is either a Linear, a Shallow or a Horn transformation, considered below by case analysis.

Horn Case. Let $\Rightarrow_{APR}$ be a Horn transformation that replaces $\Gamma'' \to \Delta', Q(t')$ with $\Gamma'' \to Q(t')$. If $C \neq \Gamma'' \to Q(t')$, then $C \in N_0$ fulfills the claim. Otherwise, $\Gamma \to \Delta, P(t) = \Gamma'' \to Q(t')$ and hence $P(t) = Q(t')$ and $\Gamma = \Gamma''$. For $\Gamma'' \to \Delta', Q(t') \in N_0$, $s = skt(t)\sigma = skt(t')\sigma$ and $S(s'') \in \mathcal{I}$ for each variable x and predicate S with $S(x) \in \Gamma''$, $Q(t') = Q(t'[x]_p)$ and $s|_p = s''$.

Linear Case. Let $\Rightarrow_{APR}$ be a linear transformation that replaces $C_0 = \Gamma'' \to E[x]_{p,q}$ with $C_1 = \Gamma'', \Gamma''\{x \mapsto x'\} \to E[x']_q$. If $C \neq C_1$, then $C \in N_0$ fulfills the claim. Otherwise, $C_0 = \Gamma'' \to P(t)\{x' \mapsto x\} \in N_0$ fulfills the claim because $s = skt(t)\sigma = skt(t\{x' \mapsto x\})\sigma$ and $\Gamma'' \subseteq \Gamma''$, $\Gamma''\{x \mapsto x'\}$.

Shallow Case. Let $\Rightarrow_{APR}$ be a shallow transformation that replaces $C_0 = \Gamma'' \to E[s']_p$ with $C_1 = S(x), \Gamma_1 \to E[x]_p$ and $C_2 = \Gamma_2 \to S(s')$. Since S is fresh, $C \neq C_2$. If $C \neq C_1$, then $C \in N_0$ fulfills the claim. Otherwise, $C = C_1 = S(x), \Gamma_1 \to P(t[x]_p)$ and hence, $s = skt(t[x]_p)\sigma$ and $S(s'') \in \mathcal{I}$ for $s|_p = s''$. Then by the induction hypothesis, there exist a clause $C_S = \Gamma_S \to \Delta_S, S(t_S) \in N_1$ and a substitution σ_S such that $s'' = skt(t_S)\sigma_S$ and for each variable x and predicate S' with $C_S = S'(x), \Gamma'_S \to \Delta_S, P(t_S[x]_q)$ and $s''|_q = s'''$, $S'(s''') \in \mathcal{I}$. By construction, $C_S = C_2$. Thus, $s'' = skt(s')\sigma_S$ and $s = skt(t[x]_p)\sigma$ imply there exists a σ'' such that $s = skt(t[s']_p)\sigma''$. Furthermore, because $\Gamma_1 \cup \Gamma_2 = \Gamma''$, if $C_0 = S'(x), \Gamma''' \to P(t[s']_p)[x]_q$, then either $S'(x) \in \Gamma_1$ and thus $S'(s'''') \in \mathcal{I}$, where $s|_q = s''''$, or $S'(x) \in \Gamma_2$ and thus $S'(s'''') \in \mathcal{I}$, where $(s[s'']_p)|_q = s''''$. Hence, $C_0 \in N_0$ fulfills the claim.   □

Note that for Lemma 7 the clause set N_k may contain predicates that have been introduced by the Shallow transformation and are therefore not contained in N_0.

Lemma 8. *Let $N \Rightarrow^*_{APR} N'$, where N' is a normal form, and $\mathcal{I}$ be a minimal model for N'. If $\mu_\Sigma(P(s_1, \ldots, s_n)) \in \mathcal{I}$ and P is a predicate in N, then there is a clause $\Gamma \to \Delta, P(t_1, \ldots, t_n) \in N$ and a substitution σ such that $s_i = skt(t_i)\sigma$ for all i.*

Proof. Because of the rule priority of $\Rightarrow_{APR}$, $N \Rightarrow^*_{MO} \mu_\Sigma(N) \Rightarrow^*_{APR} N'$.

Let $P(s) \in \mathcal{I}$ and P be a monadic predicate in N. Since P is monadic, P is a predicate in $\mu_\Sigma(N)$. Hence by Lemma 7, there exists a clause $\Gamma \to \Delta, P(t) \in \mu_\Sigma(N)$ and a substitution σ such that $s = skt(t)\sigma$. Then, $\mu_\Sigma^{-1}(\Gamma \to \Delta, P(t)) \in N$ fulfills the claim.

Let $T(f_p(s_1, \ldots, s_n)) \in \mathcal{I}$. T is monadic and a predicate in $\mu_\Sigma(N)$. Hence by Lemma 7, there exists a clause $\Gamma \to \Delta, T(t) \in \mu_\Sigma(N)$ and substitution σ such that $f_p(s_1, \ldots, s_n) = skt(t)\sigma$. Therefore, $t = f_p(t_1, \ldots, t_n)$ with $s_i = skt(t_i)\sigma$ for all i. Then, $\mu_\Sigma^{-1}(\Gamma \to \Delta, T(f_p(t_1, \ldots, t_n))) \in N$ fulfills the claim.   □

The above lemma also holds if satisfiability of N' is dropped and $\mathcal{I}$ is replaced by the superposition partial minimal model operator [15].

3 Lifting a Conflicting Core

When lifting a refutation of an MSLH approximation, we do not lift single inference steps, but an unsatisfiable clause set called the conflicting core.

Definition 9 (Conflicting Core). *A finite clause set $N^\perp$ is a conflicting core if for all grounding substitutions τ the clause set $N^\perp\tau$ is unsatisfiable. $N^\perp$ is a conflicting core of N if in addition every clause $C \in N^\perp$ is an instance of a clause in N.*

Given an MSLH approximation N_k of N and a conflicting core $N_k^\perp$ of N_k, using the lifting lemmas provided in this section we attempt to lift $N_k^\perp$ step-wise to a conflicting core $N^\perp$ of N. In case of success this shows the unsatisfiability of N. In case an approximation step cannot be lifted, the original clause set is refined by instantiation, explained in Section 4.

Let N_k be an unsatisfiable MSLH approximation. Since N_k belongs to a decidable first-order fragment, we expect an appropriate decision procedure to generate a proof of unsatisfiability for N_k, e.g., by ordered resolution with selection [14]. A conflicting core can be generated out of a resolution refutation by applying the substitutions of the proof to the used input clauses as follows.

We require a variable renaming such that all input clauses from N_k used in the refutation are variable disjoint. Begin with the singleton set containing the pair of the empty clause and the empty substitution. Then recursively choose a pair (C, σ) from the set where $C \notin N_k$. There exists a step in the refutation that generated this clause. Because N_k is Horn, the clause is generated by a resolution inference. It is the resolvent of some C_1 and C_2 with mgu τ. Replace (C, σ) by $(C_1, \tau\sigma)$ and $(C_2, \tau\sigma)$. The procedure terminates in linear time in the size of the refutation. For each pair (C, σ), collect the clause $C\sigma$, resulting in a conflicting core $N_k^\perp$ of N_k.

For example, let $N = \{P(x, x');\ P(y, a), P(z, b) \to\}$. N is unsatisfiable and a possible ground refutation is resolving $P(b, a), P(a, b) \to$ with $P(b, a)$ and $P(a, b)$. From this refutation, we construct the conflicting core $N_{ba}^\perp = \{P(b, a);\ P(a, b);\ P(b, a), P(a, b) \to\}$. An alternative refutation is to resolve $P(x, x')$ and $P(y, a), P(z, b) \to$ with substitution $\{x \mapsto y; x' \mapsto a\}$ and then the resolvent and $P(x, x')$ with substitution $\{x \mapsto z; x' \mapsto b\}$. Here, we construct the conflicting core $N_{yz}^\perp = \{P(y, a);\ P(z, b);\ P(y, a), P(z, b) \to\}$. Note that $N_{yz}^\perp$ is more general than $N_{ba}^\perp$ since $N_{yz}^\perp\{y \mapsto b; z \mapsto a\} = N_{ba}^\perp$. A conflicting core is minimal in that it represents the most general clauses corresponding to the refutation from that it is generated.

In order to lift a Linear transformation the remaining and the newly introduced variable need to be instantiated with the same term. For example, let $N = \{P(x, x);\ P(y, a), P(z, b) \to\}$. Then $N' = \{P(x, x');\ P(y, a), P(z, b) \to\}$ is a Linear transformation of N and and $N^\perp = \{P(a, a);\ P(b, b);\ P(a, a), P(b, b) \to\}$ is a ground conflicting core of N'. Since $P(a, a)$ and $P(b, b)$ are instances of $P(x, x)$ lifting succeeds and $N^\perp$ is also a core of N.

Lemma 10 (Lifting the Linear Transformation). *Let $N_k = N \cup \{C\} \Rightarrow_{\mathrm{LI}} N_{k+1} = N \cup \{C'\}$ where $C = \Gamma \to E[x]_{p,q}$ and $C' = \Gamma\{x \mapsto x'\}, \Gamma \to E[x']_q$.*

Let $N_{k+1}^{\perp}$ be a conflicting core of N_{k+1} and $C'\sigma_1, \ldots, C'\sigma_m$ be all clauses in $N_{k+1}^{\perp}$ that are instances of C'. If $x\sigma_j = x'\sigma_j$ for $1 \leq j \leq m$, then $N_{k+1}^{\perp} \setminus \{C'\sigma_1, \ldots, C'\sigma_m\} \cup \{C\sigma_1, \ldots, C\sigma_m\} = N_k^{\perp}$ is a conflicting core of N_k.

Proof. Let σ be any grounding substitution and $\mathcal{I}$ be any interpretation. Then, $\mathcal{I} \nvDash N_{k+1}^{\perp}\sigma$ and there exists a clause $C^{\perp} \in N_{k+1}^{\perp}\sigma$ such that $\mathcal{I} \nvDash C^{\perp}$. If $C^{\perp}$ is not an instance of C', then $C^{\perp}$ is a clause in $N_k^{\perp}\sigma$. Thus, $\mathcal{I} \nvDash N_k^{\perp}\sigma$. If $C^{\perp}$ is an instance of C', then $C^{\perp} = C'\sigma_j\sigma$ for some $1 \leq j \leq m$. Because $x\sigma_j = x'\sigma_j$, $C'\sigma_j\sigma$ and $C\sigma_j\sigma$ are equal modulo condensation. Thus, $\mathcal{I} \nvDash N_k^{\perp}\sigma$. Therefore, $N_k^{\perp}$ is a conflicting core of N_k.   □

A Shallow transformation introduces a new predicate S, which is removed in the lifting step. We take all clauses with S-atoms in the conflicting core and generate any possible resolutions on these S-atoms. The resolvents, which don't contain the S-atom anymore, then replace their parent clauses in the core. Lifting succeeds if all resolvents are instances of the original clause in the Shallow transformation.

For example, let $N = \{P(x), Q(y) \rightarrow R(g(x, f(y))); R(g(a, f(b))) \rightarrow; P(a); Q(b)\}$. Then $N' = \{Q(y) \rightarrow S(f(y)); S(x'), P(x) \rightarrow R(g(x, x')); R(g(a, f(b))) \rightarrow; P(a); Q(b)\}$ is a Shallow transformation of N and $N'^{\perp} = \{Q(b) \rightarrow S(f(b)); S(f(b)), P(a) \rightarrow R(g(a, f(b))); R(g(a, f(b))) \rightarrow; P(a); Q(b)\}$ is a conflicting core of N'. By replacing $S(f(b)), P(a) \rightarrow R(g(a, f(b)))$ and $Q(b) \rightarrow S(f(b))$ with their resolvent, $N'^{\perp}$ lifts to $\{P(a), Q(b) \rightarrow R(g(a, f(b))); R(g(a, f(b))) \rightarrow; P(a); Q(b)\}$, a conflicting core of N.

Lemma 11 (Lifting the Shallow Transformation). *Let $N_k = N \cup \{C\} \Rightarrow_{\text{SH}} N_{k+1} = N \cup \{C_1, C_2\}$ where $C = \Gamma \rightarrow E[s]_p$, $C_1 = S(x), \Gamma_1 \rightarrow E[x]_p$ and $C_2 = \Gamma_2 \rightarrow S(s)$. Let $N_{k+1}^{\perp}$ be a conflicting core of N_{k+1} and N_S be the set of all resolvents of clauses in $N_{k+1}^{\perp}$ on the S-atom. If all clauses in N_S are instances of C modulo condensation, then $N_k^{\perp} = \{D \in N_{k+1}^{\perp} \mid D$ not an instance of C_1 or $C_2\} \cup N_S$ is a conflicting core of N_k.*

Proof. Let σ be any grounding substitution and $\mathcal{I}$ be any interpretation. Then, $\mathcal{I} \nvDash N_{k+1}^{\perp}\sigma$ and there exists $C^{\perp} \in N_{k+1}^{\perp}\sigma$ such that $\mathcal{I} \nvDash C^{\perp}$. If $C^{\perp}$ is not an instance of C_1 or C_2, then $C^{\perp} \in N_k^{\perp}\sigma$. Thus, $\mathcal{I} \nvDash N_k^{\perp}\sigma$. Otherwise, assume $C_1\tau_1 \ldots, C_1\tau_m$ and $C_2\rho_1, \ldots, C_2\rho_n$ are the only clauses in $N_k^{\perp}\sigma$ false under $\mathcal{I}$. Let $\mathcal{I}' := \mathcal{I} \setminus \{S(x)\tau_1, \ldots, S(x)\tau_m\} \cup \{S(s)\rho_1, \ldots, S(s)\rho_n\}$, i.e., we change the truth value for S-atoms such that the clauses unsatisfied under $\mathcal{I}$ are satisfied under $\mathcal{I}'$. Because $\mathcal{I}$ and $\mathcal{I}'$ only differ on S-atoms, there exists a clause $D \in N_k^{\perp}\sigma$ that is false under $\mathcal{I}'$ and contains an S-atom. Let $D = C_1\sigma'$. Since $\mathcal{I} \vDash D$, $S(x)\sigma'$ was added to $\mathcal{I}'$ by some clause $C_2\rho_j$, where $S(s)\rho_j = S(x)\sigma'$. Let R be the resolvent of $C_2\rho_j$ and $C_1\sigma'$ on $S(s)\rho_j$ and $S(x)\sigma'$. Then, $\mathcal{I} \nvDash R$ because $\mathcal{I} \nvDash C_2\rho_j$ and $\mathcal{I} \cup \{S(s)\rho_j\} \nvDash C_1\sigma'$. Thus, $\mathcal{I} \nvDash N_k^{\perp}\sigma$. For $D = C_2\sigma'$, the proof is analogous. Therefore, $N_k^{\perp}$ is a conflicting core of N_k.   □

Because the Horn transformation only keeps a single literal per non-Horn clause, a single conflicting core corresponds to an incomplete proof of the original problem. For example, if the clause $\rightarrow E_1, E_2$ is approximated as E_1 and a proof uses $E_1\sigma$ and $E_1\tau$, then repeating the refutation with $\rightarrow E_1, E_2$ leads to the clause $\rightarrow E_2\sigma, E_2\tau$ instead of $\bot$.

Without loss of generality and to ease the below arguments, we assume that any non-Horn clause has exactly two positive literals: $\Gamma \rightarrow E_1, E_2$. Any clause with more positive literals is preprocessed by renaming pairs of positive literals using fresh predicates.

For the lifting, we require that $\Gamma \rightarrow E_1, E_2$ was approximated both ways resulting in an approximation with $\Gamma \rightarrow E_1$ and another with $\Gamma \rightarrow E_2$. If neither approximation is satisfiable, there exist conflicting cores for both. From each core, all instances $(\Gamma \rightarrow E_1)\tau_i$ and $(\Gamma \rightarrow E_2)\rho_j$ are replaced by a sort of Cartesian product: $\Gamma\tau_i, \Gamma\rho_j \rightarrow E_1\tau_i, E_2\rho_j$. Lifting succeeds if all products are instances of the original clause $\Gamma \rightarrow E_1, E_2$ modulo condensation.

For example, let $N = \{P(x), Q(y); Q(a), Q(b) \rightarrow; P(a) \rightarrow\}$. Its two Horn transformations are $\{P(x); Q(a), Q(b) \rightarrow; P(a) \rightarrow\}$ and $\{Q(y); Q(a), Q(b) \rightarrow; P(a) \rightarrow\}$. $N_1^\perp = \{P(a); P(a) \rightarrow\}$ and $N_2^\perp = \{Q(a), Q(b) \rightarrow; Q(a); Q(b)\}$ are respective conflicting cores. By combining them, we get $N^\perp = \{P(a), Q(a); P(a), Q(b); P(a) \rightarrow; Q(a), Q(b) \rightarrow\}$, a conflicting core of N.

Lemma 12 (Lifting the Horn Transformation). *Let $N_k = N \cup \{C\} \Rightarrow_{\mathrm{HO}} N \cup \{C_1\}$ and $N_k \Rightarrow_{\mathrm{HO}} N \cup \{C_2\}$ where $C = \Gamma \rightarrow E_1, E_2$, $C_1 = \Gamma \rightarrow E_1$ and $C_2 = \Gamma \rightarrow E_2$. Respectively, let $N_1^\perp$ and $N_2^\perp$ be their conflicting cores, and $C_1\tau_1, \ldots, C_1\tau_m$ and $C_2\rho_1, \ldots, C_2\rho_n$ be all clauses in $N_1^\perp$ and $N_2^\perp$ that are instances of C_1 and C_2. Define $N_H = \{\Gamma\tau_i, \Gamma\rho_j \rightarrow E_1\tau_i, E_2\rho_j \mid 1 \le i \le m, 1 \le j \le n\}$. If every clause in N_H is an instance of C modulo condensation, then $N_k^\perp = N_1^\perp \setminus \{C_1\tau_1, \ldots, C_1\tau_m\} \cup N_2^\perp \setminus \{C_2\rho_1, \ldots, C_2\rho_n\} \cup N_H$ is a conflicting core of N_k.*

Proof. Let σ be any grounding substitution and $\mathcal{I}$ be any interpretation. Then, $\mathcal{I} \nvDash N_1^\perp\sigma$ and $\mathcal{I} \nvDash N_2^\perp\sigma$. There exist $C_1^\perp \in N_1^\perp$ and $C_2^\perp \in N_2^\perp$ such that $\mathcal{I} \nvDash C_1^\perp$ and $\mathcal{I} \nvDash C_2^\perp$. If $C_l^\perp$ is not an instance of C_l for some l, then $C_l^\perp \in N_k^\perp\sigma$. Thus, $\mathcal{I} \nvDash N_k^\perp\sigma$. Otherwise, $C_1^\perp = C_1\tau_i\sigma$ and $C_2^\perp = C_2\rho_j\sigma$ for some i and j. Then, $\mathcal{I} \nvDash (\Gamma\tau_i, \Gamma\rho_j \rightarrow E_1\tau_i, E_2\rho_j)\sigma$, which is in $N_H\sigma$. Thus, $\mathcal{I} \nvDash N_k^\perp\sigma$. Therefore, $N_k^\perp$ is a conflicting core of N_k. $\qquad\square$

Lastly, there exists a special case, where a single core is sufficient. If the core is a conflicting core for each transformation case, then each instance only needs to be combined with itself, which guarantees a successful lifting. For example, let $N = \{P(a, b) \rightarrow; P(x, b), P(a, y)\}$. Then $N_1 = \{P(a, b) \rightarrow; P(x, b)\}$ and $N_2 = \{P(a, b) \rightarrow; P(a, y)\}$ are Horn transformations of N. $N^\perp = \{P(a, b) \rightarrow; P(a, b)\}$ is a conflicting core of both N_1 and N_2. The lifting to $N^\perp = \{P(a, b) \rightarrow; P(a, b), P(a, b)\}$ is a conflicting core of N.

Since the Monadic transformation is satisfiability preserving, lifting always succeeds by replacing any $T(f_P(t_1, \ldots, t_n))$ atoms in the core by $P(t_1, \ldots, t_n)$. For example, let $N = \{P(x, x'); P(y, a), P(z, b) \rightarrow\}$. Then $N' = \{T(f_P(x, x')); T(f_P(y, a)), T(f_P(z, b)) \rightarrow\}$ is a Monadic transformation of N and a conflicting core is $N'^\perp = \{T(f_P(y, a)); T(f_P(z, b)); T(f_P(y, a)), T(f_P(z, b)) \rightarrow\}$. Reverting the atoms gives $N^\perp = \{P(y,a);\ P(z,b);\ P(y,a), P(z,b) \to\}$, a conflicting core of N.

Lemma 13 (Lifting the Monadic Transformation). *Let* $N \Rightarrow_{MO} \mu_P(N)$ *where* P *is a non monadic predicate in* N. *If* $N^\perp$ *is a conflicting core of* $\mu_P(N)$ *then* $\mu_P^{-1}(N^\perp)$ *is a conflicting core of* N.

By definition, if $N^\perp$ is a conflicting core of N, then $N^\perp\tau$ is also a conflicting core of N for any τ. Sometimes a conflicting core, where no lifting lemma applies, can be instantiated into a core, where one does. This then still implies a successful lifting.

For example, let $N = \{P(x,x);\ P(y,a), P(z,b) \to\}$. Then $N' = \{P(x,x');$ $P(y,a), P(z,b) \to\}$ is a Linear transformation of N and and $N'^\perp = \{P(y,a);$ $P(b,b);\ P(y,a), P(b,b) \to\}$ is a conflicting core of N'. Because for $P(y,a) = P(x,x')\sigma$, $x\sigma = y$, $x'\sigma = a$, Lemma 10 is not applicable. However, Lemma 10 can be applied on $N^\perp\{y \mapsto a\} = \{P(a,a);\ P(b,b);\ P(a,a), P(b,b) \to\}$.

4   Approximation Refinement

In the previous section, we have presented the lifting process. If, however, in one of the lifting steps the conditions of the corresponding lemma cannot be met, lifting fails. A failed lifting lemma always means that some approximated clause is not an instance of the parent clause in a transformation step. Because the clauses also have overlapping skeleton term structures, there exists at least one variable in the original clause that the approximation instantiates twice in a non-unifiable way. This results in two conflicting substitutions.

For example, let $N = \{P(x,x);\ P(y,a), P(z,b) \to\}$ and $N' = \{P(x,x');$ $P(y,a),\ P(z,b) \to\}$, its Linear transformation. $\{P(a,a), P(a,b) \to;\ P(a,a);$ $P(a,b)\}$ is a ground conflicting core of N'. Because $P(x,x)$ and $P(a,b)$ cannot be unified, lifting fails. $\{x \mapsto a\}$ and $\{x \mapsto b\}$ are the conflicting substitutions.

The refinement then always replaces the original clause in N with a set of specific instances, which are determined by the conflicting substitutions.

Definition 14 (Specific Instances). *Let* C *be a clause and* σ_1 *and* σ_2 *be two substitutions such that the respective literals in* $C\sigma_1$ *and* $C\sigma_2$ *cannot be simultaneously unified. Then, the* specific instances *of* C *with respect to* σ_1 *and* σ_2 *are clauses* $C\tau_1, \ldots, C\tau_n$ *such that (i) any ground instance of* C *is an instance of some* $C\tau_i$ *and (ii) no* $C\tau_i$ *shares ground instances with both* $C\sigma_1$ *and* $C\sigma_2$.

The existence of a finite set of specific instances is guaranteed for conflicting substitutions [7]. The first property ensures that if we replace C in N with specific instances, the models of N stay the same. The second property ensures that the approximation of the refined set no longer produces the same conflict because by Lemma 8 the changes to the skeleton term structure carry over to the approximation.

Continuing from the previous example. The specific instances of $P(x,x)$ are $P(a,a)$ and $P(b,b)$. In the approximation of the refinement $N'' = \{P(a,a);$

$P(b, b)$; $P(y, a), P(z, b) \rightarrow$}, the conflicting clause $P(a, b)$ is not an instance anymore. Hence, the previous conflicting core $N^\perp$ cannot be found again. The refinement loop then restarts with the refined clause set.

Since lifting fails at some step except for Monadic transformation, we describe the refinement for Linear, Shallow and Horn transformation separately.

A Linear transformation enables more instantiations of the approximated clause than the original, that is, two variables that were the same can now be instantiated differently.

Definition 15 (Linear Approximation Refinement). *Let* $N \Rightarrow_{APR}^*$ $N_k \Rightarrow_{LI} N_{k+1}$ *where* $C = \Gamma \rightarrow E[x]_{p,q}$ *is approximated by* $C_1 = \Gamma\{x \mapsto x'\}, \Gamma \rightarrow E[x']_q$. *Let* $N_{k+1}^\perp$ *be a conflicting core of* N_{k+1} *with some* $C_1\sigma \in N_{k+1}^\perp$ *such that* $x\sigma$ *and* $x'\sigma$ *cannot be unified. Let* $C \in N$ *be the ancestor of* $C' \in N_{k+1}$. $N \setminus \{C\} \cup \{C\tau_1, \ldots, C\tau_n\}$ *is the* linear approximation refinement *of* N, *where the* $C\tau_i$ *are the specific instances of* C *with respect to the substitutions* $\{x \mapsto x\sigma\}$ *and* $\{x \mapsto x'\sigma\}$.

The Shallow transformation is similar to the Linear transformation, because it also creates cases where the same variable is instantiated differently. As mentioned before, the Shallow transformation can always be lifted if the set of common variables $vars(\Gamma_2, s) \cap vars(\Gamma_1, E[x]_p)$ is empty. Otherwise, each variable in the intersection potentially introduces instantiations that are not liftable.

For example, let $N = \{P(f(x, g(x))); P(f(a, g(b)) \rightarrow\}$ and $N' = \{S(g(y)); S(z) \rightarrow P(f(x, z)); P(f(a, g(b)) \rightarrow\}$, the Shallow transformation of N. $\{S(g(b)); S(g(b)) \rightarrow P(f(a, g(b))); P(f(a, g(b)) \rightarrow\}$ is a conflicting core of N'. Because $P(f(a, g(b)))$ and $P(f(x, g(x)))$ cannot be unified, lifting fails. $\{x \mapsto a\}$ and $\{x \mapsto b\}$ are the conflicting substitutions. The specific instances of $P(f(x, g(x)))$ are $P(f(f(x, y), g(f(x, y)))); P(f(g(x), g(g(x)))); P(f(a, g(a)))$ and $P(f(b, g(b)))$. In the approximation of the refinement, the conflicting clause $P(f(a, g(b)))$ is not a possible resolvent anymore.

Definition 16 (Shallow Approximation Refinement). *Let* $N \Rightarrow_{APR}^* N_k$ $\Rightarrow_{SH} N_{k+1}$ *where* $C = \Gamma \rightarrow E[s]_p$ *is approximated by* $C_1 = S(x), \Gamma_1 \rightarrow E[x]_p$ *and* $C_2 = \Gamma_2 \rightarrow S(s)$. *Let* $N_{k+1}^\perp$ *be a conflicting core of* N_{k+1} *with* $C_1\sigma_1 \in N_{k+1}^\perp$ *and* $C_2\sigma_2 \in N_{k+1}^\perp$ *such that their resolvent* C_R *is not unifiable with* C. *Let* $C \in N$ *be the ancestor of* C_1. $N \setminus \{C\} \cup \{C\tau_1, \ldots, C\tau_n\}$ *is the* shallow approximation refinement *of* N, *where the* $C\tau_i$ *are the specific instances of* C *with respect to the substitutions* σ_1 *and* σ_2.

The Horn approximation refinement works in an analogous way to the Shallow approximation refinement with the difference that the two clauses come from two conflicting cores instead of the same. Similarly, if the set of common variables $vars(E_1) \cap vars(E_2)$ is not empty, each variable in the intersection potentially introduces instantiations that are not liftable.

For example, let $N = \{P(x), Q(x); P(a) \rightarrow; P(b) \rightarrow; Q(a), Q(b) \rightarrow\}$. $\{P(x); P(a) \rightarrow; P(b) \rightarrow; Q(a), Q(b) \rightarrow\}$ and $\{Q(y); P(a) \rightarrow; P(b) \rightarrow; Q(a), Q(b) \rightarrow\}$ are the Horn transformations of N. $N_1^\perp = \{P(a); P(a) \rightarrow\}$ and $N_2^\perp = \{Q(a); Q(b);$

$Q(a), Q(b) \to \}$ are respective conflicting cores. Because the product $P(a), Q(b)$ cannot be unified with $P(x), Q(x)$, lifting fails. $\{x \mapsto a\}$ and $\{x \mapsto b\}$ are the conflicting substitutions. The specific instances of $P(x), Q(x)$ are $P(a), Q(a)$ and $P(b), Q(b)$. In the approximation of the refinement, the conflicting clause $P(a), Q(b)$ is not a possible product anymore.

Definition 17 (Horn Approximation Refinement). Let $N \Rightarrow^*_{\mathrm{APR}} N_k = N' \cup \{C\}$, $N_k \Rightarrow_{\mathrm{HO}} N' \cup \{C_1\}$ and $N_k \Rightarrow_{\mathrm{HO}} N' \cup \{C_2\}$ where $C = \Gamma \to E_1, E_2$, $C_1 = \Gamma \to E_1$ and $C_2 = \Gamma \to E_2$. Let $N_1^\perp$ and $N_2^\perp$ be conflicting cores of each case respectively with $C_1\sigma_1 \in N_1^\perp$ and $C_2\sigma_2 \in N_2^\perp$ such that their product is not unifiable with C. Let $C \in N$ be the ancestor of C_1 and C_2. The Horn approximation refinement of N is the clause set $N \setminus \{C\} \cup \{C\tau_1, \ldots, C\tau_n\}$ where the $C\tau_i$ are the specific instances of C with respect to the substitutions σ_1 and σ_2.

While the lifting lemmas require instances, the refinements check for unifiability. If all clauses are unifiable, but the respective lifting lemma does not apply because some clause C is not an instance, apply the most general unifier for C to the core. Repeat until either the lifting lemma applies or some instance is not unifiable.

Theorem 18 (Completeness). Let N_0 be an unsatisfiable clause set and N_k its MSLH approximation. Then, there exists a conflicting core of N_k that can be lifted to N_0.

Proof. by induction on the number k of approximation steps. The case $k = 0$ is obvious. For $k > 0$, let $N_0 \Rightarrow^*_{\mathrm{APR}} N_{k-1} \Rightarrow_{\mathrm{APR}} N_k$. By the inductive hypothesis, there is a conflicting core $N_{k-1}^\perp$ of N_{k-1} which can be lifted to N_0. The final approximation rule application is either a Linear, a Shallow, a Horn or a Monadic transformation, considered below by case analysis.

Linear Case. Let $N_{k-1} = N' \cup \{C\} \Rightarrow_{\mathrm{LI}} N_k = N' \cup \{C'\}$ with $C = \Gamma \to E[x]_{p,q}$ and $C' = \Gamma\{x \mapsto x'\}, \Gamma \to E[x']_q$. Let $C\sigma_1, \ldots, C\sigma_n$ be the instances of C in $N_{k-1}^\perp$. $N_{k-1}^\perp \setminus \{C\sigma_1, \ldots, C\sigma_n\} \cup \{C'\{x' \mapsto x\}\sigma_j \mid 1 \le j \le n\}$ is a conflicting core of N_k. By Lemma 10, it can be lifted to $N_{k-1}^\perp$ and by the inductive hypothesis, can be lifted to a conflicting core of N_0.

Shallow Case. Let $N \Rightarrow^*_{\mathrm{APR}} N_{k-1} = N' \cup \{C\} \Rightarrow_{\mathrm{SH}} N_k = N' \cup \{C_1, C_2\}$ with $C = \Gamma \to E[s]_p$, $C_1 = S(x), \Gamma_1 \to E[x]_p$ and $C_2 = \Gamma_2 \to S(s)$. Assume $C\sigma$ is the only instances of C in $N_{k-1}^\perp$. $N_k^\perp = N_{k-1}^\perp \setminus \{C\sigma\} \cup \{(C_1\{x \mapsto s\}\sigma, C_2\sigma\}$ is a conflicting core of N_k. By Lemma 11, $N_k^\perp$ can be lifted to $N_{k-1}^\perp$. Now, let $C\sigma_1, \ldots, C\sigma_n$ be the instances of C in $N_{k-1}^\perp$ with $n > 1$. Let $C_0 \in N_0$ be the ancestor of C and $N_0' = N_0 \setminus \{C_0\} \cup \{C_0\sigma_1, \ldots, C_0\sigma_n\}$. $N_{k-1}^\perp$ is also a conflicting core for the corresponding approximation $N_k' = N' \cup \{C\sigma_1, \ldots, C\sigma_n\}$. For each $C\sigma_i$, $N_{k-1}^\perp$ contains only one instance such that the above case applies. Thus, there is a core for approximation of each $C\sigma_i$ that can be lifted to $N_{k-1}^\perp$.

Horn Case. Let $N_{k-1} = N' \cup \{C\}$ with $C = \Gamma \to E_1, E_2$. Assume $C\sigma$ is the only instances of C in $N_{k-1}^\perp$. $N_{k_1}^\perp = N_{k-1}^\perp \setminus \{C\sigma\} \cup \{(\Gamma \to E_1)\sigma\}$ is a conflicting core of $N_{k_1} = N' \cup \{(\Gamma \to E_1)\}$. $N_{k_2}^\perp$, constructed analogously for

$\Gamma \to E_2$, is a conflicting core of N_{k_2}. By Lemma 12, $N_{k_1}^{\perp}$ and $N_{k_2}^{\perp}$ can be lifted to $N_{k-1}^{\perp}$.Giunchiglia Now, let $C\sigma_1, \ldots, C\sigma_n$ be the instances of C in $N_{k-1}^{\perp}$ with $n > 1$. Let $C_0 \in N_0$ be the ancestor of C and $N_0' = N_0 \setminus \{C_0\} \cup \{C_0\sigma_1, \ldots, C_0\sigma_n\}$. $N_{k-1}^{\perp}$ is also a conflicting core for the corresponding approximation $N_k' = N' \cup \{C\sigma_1, \ldots, C\sigma_n\}$. For each $C\sigma_i$, $N_{k-1}^{\perp}$ contains only one instance such that the above case applies. Thus, there are cores for each possible approximation of the $C\sigma_i$ such that they can be lifted to $N_{k-1}^{\perp}$.

Monadic Case. Let $N_{k-1} \Rightarrow_{\mathrm{MO}} N_k = \mu_P(N_{k-1})$ where P is a non-monadic predicate in N_{k-1} $N_k^{\perp} = \mu_P(N_{k-1}^{\perp})$ is a conflicting core of N_k. By Lemma 13, $N_k^{\perp}$ can be lifted to $N_{k-1}^{\perp}$. $\qquad\square$

The above lemma considers static completeness, i.e., it does not tell how the conflicting core that can eventually be lifted is found. One way is to enumerate all refutations of N_k in a fair way. A straightforward fairness criterion is to enumerate the refutations by increasing term depth of the clauses used in the refutation. Since the decision procedure on the MSLH fragment [14] generates only finitely many different non-redundant clauses not exceeding a concrete term depth with respect to the renaming of variables, eventually the liftable refutation will be generated.

5 Summary

We have presented a sound and complete calculus for first-order logic without equality based on an over-approximation/refinement loop. The refinement by instantiation introduced in Section 4 may generate up to exponentially many clauses in the depth of the terms that caused a lifting step to fail. The Horn approximation together with its lifting cannot make use of dependencies between the split positive literals. Although worst case both problems cannot be avoided by any first-order calculus, we would like to have more flexibility in the over-approximation/refinement loop to deal with them.

Consider the example $N = \{P(x, z), Q(y, z) \to R(x, f(y)); P(a, a); P(a, b); Q(b, a), Q(b, b); R(a, f(b)) \to\}$ and $N' = \{Q(y, z) \to S(f(y)); S(y), P(x, z) \to R(x, y); P(a, a); P(a, b); Q(b, a), Q(b, b); R(a, f(b)) \to\}$, a Shallow transformation of N. $\{S(f(b)), P(a, a) \to R(a, f(b)); Q(b, a) \to S(f(b)); S(f(b)), P(a, b) \to R(a, f(b)); Q(b, b) \to S(f(b)); P(a, a); P(a, b); Q(b, a), Q(b, b); R(a, f(b)) \to\}$ is a conflicting core of N'. Lifting it fails because the resolvents $P(a, a), Q(b, b) \to R(a, f(b))$ and $P(a, b), Q(b, a) \to R(a, f(b))$ are not instances of $P(x, z), Q(y, z) \to R(x, f(y))$. However, if we ignore these two resolvents the remaining resolvents $P(a, a), Q(b, a) \to R(a, f(b))$ and $P(a, b), Q(b, b) \to R(a, f(b))$ still constitute the conflicting core $\{P(a, a), Q(b, a) \to R(a, f(b)); P(a, b), Q(b, b) \to R(a, f(b)); P(a, a); P(a, b); Q(b, a), Q(b, b); R(a, f(b)) \to\}$ of N. So the lifting condition for the Shallow transformation can be refined that way. Even though Lemma 11 fails, not all conflicting clauses are actually required for lifting. A similar situation can occur during Horn lifting, Lemma 12, where not all combinations of the clauses from the two branches are instances of the split clause, but a subset of the combinations that are instances still build a conflicting core.

While the calculus describes lifting in a step by step approach, in practice the conditions for Linear and Shallow lifting can be checked on the fly. While constructing the conflicting core the instantiations of linearized variables can be immediately checked. Analogously, the above suggested refinement for the Shallow transformation can be checked while constructing the conflicting core. In particular, by considering the resolution inferences on the freshly introduced S-atoms.

While the MSLH fragment requires Horn clauses, there exist other fragments that do not. Without the Horn restriction, the over-approximation/refinement loop can likely handle non-Horn clauses in a more flexible way than the fixed exponential cost in the number of Horn transformations of our current Horn lifting. However, alternative decidable non-Horn fragments have to support via approximation the presented lifting and refinement principle. We are currently looking for such alternative fragments.

In "A theory of abstractions" [3] Giunchiglia and Walsh do not define an actual approximation but a general framework to classify and compare approximations, which are here called abstractions. They informally define abstractions as "the process of mapping a representations of a problem" that "helps deal with the problem in the original search space by preserving certain desirable properties" and "is simpler to handle". In their framework an abstraction is a mapping between formal systems, i.e., a triple of a language, axioms and deduction rules, which satisfy one of the following conditions: An increasing abstraction (TI) f maps theorems only to theorems, i.e., if α is a theorem, then $f(\alpha)$ is also a theorem, while a decreasing abstraction (TD) maps only theorems to theorems, i.e., if $f(\alpha)$ is a theorem, then α was also a theorem. Furthermore, they define dual definitions for refutations, where not theorems but formulas that make a formal system inconsistent are considered. An increasing abstraction (NTI) then maps inconsistent formulas only to inconsistent formulas and vice versa for decreasing abstractions (NTD).

They list several examples of abstractions such as ABSTRIPS by Sacerdott [11], a GPS planning method by Newell and Simon [8], Plaisted's theory of abstractions [10], propositional abstractions exemplified by Giunchiglia [2], predicate abstractions by Plaisted [10] and Tenenberg [13], domain abstractions by Hobbs [4] and Imielinski [5] and ground abstractions introduced by Plaisted [10]. With respect to their notions the approximation described in this paper is an abstraction where the desirable property is the over-approximation and the decidability of the fragment makes it simpler to handle. More specifically in the context of [3] the approximation is an NTI abstraction for refutation systems, i.e., it is an abstraction that preserves inconsistency of the original.

In Plaisted [10] three classes of abstractions are defined. The first two are ordinary and weak abstractions, which share the condition that if C subsumes D then every abstraction of D is subsumed by some abstraction of C. However, our approximation falls in neither class as it violates this condition via the Horn approximation. For example Q subsumes P, Q, but the Horn approximation P of P, Q is not subsumed by any approximation of Q. The third class are generalization functions, which do not change the problem but abstract the resolution rule of inference.

The theorem prover iProver uses the Inst-Gen [6] method, where a first-order problem is abstracted with a SAT problem by replacing every variable by the fresh constant $\bot$. The approximation is solved by a SAT solver and its answer is lifted to the original by equating abstracted terms with the set they represent, e.g., if $P(\bot)$ is true in a model returned by the SAT solver, then all instantiations of the original $P(x)$ are considered true as well. Inst-Gen abstracts using an under-approximation of the original clause set. In case the lifting of the satisfying model is inconsistent, the clash is resolved by appropriately instantiating the involved clauses, which mimics an inference step. This is the dual of our method with the roles of satisfiability and unsatisfiability switched. A further difference, however, is that Inst-Gen only finds finite models after approximation, while our approximation also discovers infinite models. For example the simple problem $\{P(a), \neg P(f(a)), P(x) \rightarrow P(f(f(x))), P(f(f(x))) \rightarrow P(x)\}$ has the satisfying model where P is the set of even numbers. However, iProver's approximation can never return such a model as any $P(f^n(\bot))$ will necessarily abstract both true and false atoms and therefore instantiate new clauses infinitely. Our method on the other hand will produce the approximation $\{P(a), \neg P(f(a)), S(y) \rightarrow P(f(y)), P(x) \rightarrow S(f(x)), P(f(f(x))) \rightarrow P(x)\}$, which is saturated after inferring $\neg S(a)$.

In summary, we have presented the first sound and complete calculus for first-order logic based on an over-approximation-refinement loop. There is no implementation so far, but the calculus is at least practically useful if a clause set is close to the MSLH fragment in the sense that only a few refinement loops are needed for finding the model or a liftable refutation. The approximation relation is already implemented and applying it to all satisfiable non-equality problems in the TPTP version 6.1 [12] results in a success rate of 38%, i.e., for all these problems the approximation is not too crude and directly delivers the result without any needed refinement.

Our result is also a first step towards a model-based guidance of first-order reasoning. We proved that a model of the approximated clause set is also a model for the original clause set. For model guidance, we need this property also for partial models. For example, in the sense that if a clause is false with respect to a partial model operator on the original clause set, it is also false with respect to a partial model operator on the approximated clause set. This property does not hold for the standard superposition partial model operator applied to the MSLH approximation suggested in this paper. It is subject to future research whether there exist partial model operators that both fit a suitable approximation resulting in a decidable fragment and preserve false clauses over the approximation.

Acknowledgments. We thank our reviewers for their helpful and constructive comments.

References

1. Baeten, J.C.M., Bergstra, J.A., Klop, J.W., Weijland, W.P.: Term-rewriting systems with rule priorities. Theor. Comput. Sci. 67(2&3), 283–301 (1989)
2. Giunchiglia, F., Giunchiglia, E.: Building complex derived inference rules: A decider for the class of prenex universal-existential formulas. In: ECAI, pp. 607–609 (1988)
3. Giunchiglia, F., Walsh, T.: A theory of abstraction. Artif. Intell. 57(2–3), 323–389 (1992)
4. Hobbs, J.R.: Granularity. In: Proceedings of the Ninth International Joint Conference on Artificial Intelligence, pp. 432–435. Morgan Kaufmann (1985)
5. Imielinski, T.: Domain abstraction and limited reasoning. In: Proceedings of the 10th International Joint Conference on Artificial Intelligence, vol. 2, pp. 997–1003. Morgan Kaufmann Publishers Inc., San Francisco (1987)
6. Korovin, K.: Inst-Gen - A modular approach to instantiation-based automated reasoning. In: Voronkov, A., Weidenbach, C. (eds.) Programming Logics. LNCS, vol. 7797, pp. 239–270. Springer, Heidelberg (2013)
7. Lassez, J.-L., Marriott, K.: Explicit representation of terms defined by counter examples. J. Autom. Reason. 3(3), 301–317 (1987)
8. Newell, A.: Human Problem Solving. Prentice-Hall, Inc., Upper Saddle River (1972)
9. Nieuwenhuis, R., Oliveras, A., Tinelli, C.: Solving sat and sat modulo theories: From an abstract davis–putnam–logemann–loveland procedure to dpll(t). Journal of the ACM 53, 937–977 (2006)
10. Plaisted, D.A.: Theorem proving with abstraction. Artif. Intell. 16(1), 47–108 (1981)
11. Sacerdott, E.D.: Planning in a hierarchy of abstraction spaces. In: Proceedings of the 3rd International Joint Conference on Artificial Intelligence, IJCAI 1973, pp. 412–422. Morgan Kaufmann Publishers Inc., San Francisco (1973)
12. Sutcliffe, G.: The TPTP Problem Library and Associated Infrastructure: The FOF and CNF Parts, v3.5.0. Journal of Automated Reasoning 43(4), 337–362 (2009)
13. Tenenberg, J.: Preserving consistency across abstraction mappings. In: Proceedings of the 10th IJCAI, International Joint Conference on Artificial Intelligence, pp. 1011–1014 (1987)
14. Weidenbach, C.: Towards an automatic analysis of security protocols in first-order logic. In: Ganzinger, H. (ed.) CADE 1999. LNCS (LNAI), vol. 1632, pp. 314–328. Springer, Heidelberg (1999)
15. Weidenbach, C.: Combining superposition, sorts and splitting. In: Robinson, A., Voronkov, A. (eds.) Handbook of Automated Reasoning, vol. 2, chapter 27, pp. 1965–2012. Elsevier (2001)

An Expressive Model for Instance Decomposition Based Parallel SAT Solvers

Tobias Philipp

Knowledge Representation and Reasoning Group
Technische Universität Dresden, 01062 Dresden, Germany

Abstract. SAT solvers are highly efficient programs that decide the satisfiability problem for propositional formulas in conjunctive normal form. Contemporary SAT solvers combine many advanced techniques such as clause sharing and inprocessing. Clause sharing is a form of cooperation in parallel SAT solvers based on clause learning, whereas inprocessing simplifies formulas in a satisfiability-preserving way. In this paper, we present the instance decomposition formalism ID that models parallel SAT solvers with label-based clause sharing and inprocessing. We formally prove soundness of ID and show that the concept of labels can be used to ensure satisfiability-preserving operations. Moreover, we develop a new proof format for SAT solvers based on this approach, which is derived from ID.

1 Introduction

The satisfiability problem (SAT) is one of the most prominent problems in theoretical computer science and has many applications in software verification [6], planning [29, 41], bioinformatics [31] and scheduling [15]. Modern SAT solvers based on the DPLL algorithm [8] use many advanced techniques like *clause learning* [36], *non-chronological backtracking* [45], *restarts* [14], *clause removal* [2,10], *preprocessing* [9,32], *inprocessing* [4,28,44], efficient *data structures* [24,38] and advanced *decision heuristics* [1,2,20,38]. These improvements in the last decades led to a spectacular performance of conflict-driven satisfiability solvers.

Parallelization is a promising approach to solve *hard instances* (see [37,43] for an overview of parallel SAT solving). In this paper, we consider the *instance decomposition approach* [21], that decomposes the *solution space*, i.e. the set of models, by creating a sequence of formulas $F_1, \ldots, F_n$ for a given input formula F such that a model of the formula F_i is a model of the input formula F. Moreover, if the formulas $F_1, \ldots, F_n$ are unsatisfiable, then F is unsatisfiable as well. The formulas $F_1, \ldots, F_n$ are then solved in parallel. This means that the solvers are competing in finding a model of the input formula, and cooperating in proving its unsatisfiability. Figure 1 illustrates this form of cooperation: The input formula F is divided into the formula F_0 and F_1 by assigning the propositional variables x to *true* and *false*, respectively. The assignment of variables to truth values is realized by adding the facts x and $\neg x$, respectively, to the formulas. The formula F_1 is again divided into F_{10} and F_{11} by assigning the variables y to *true* and *false*

© Springer International Publishing Switzerland 2015
C. Lutz and S. Ranise (Eds.): FroCoS 2015, LNAI 9322, pp. 101–116, 2015.
DOI: 10.1007/978-3-319-24246-0_7

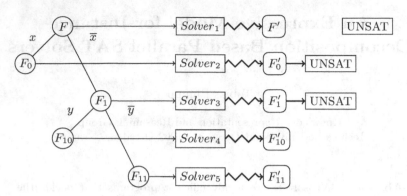

Fig. 1. Illustration of a state in an instance decomposition based SAT solver, where the input formula F is distributed among five solver incarnations together with the partitioning constraints. $Solver_2$ and $Solver_3$ have both proven the unsatisfiability of their assigned formulas, and propagate these results to the *root solver*, which then reports UNSAT.

respectively. In the considered case, Solver 2 solves F_0 and Solver 3 solves F_1 and both terminate in the answer that their assigned formulas are unsatisfiable. From these results, we can infer that our input formula F is unsatisfiable and we can terminate. Instance decomposition is applied in the solvers PCASSO [26] and Treengeling [4], which have achieved impressive performance, showing that the approach can compete with state-of-the-art parallel SAT solvers. According to [33], instance decomposition is the approach that scales best.

An additional improvement in PCASSO [26] is clause sharing among *all* solver incarnations by using *position-based tagging* [30]. In general, learned clauses may depend on the partitioning constraints, and in this case clause sharing can make a satisfiable formula unsatisfiable. However, in position-based tagging, clause sharing is restricted to clauses that are labeled as safe, i.e. those that do not depend on partition constraints. In particular, when a solver working on the formula F_i imports a safe clause C, it is guaranteed that the formula F_i entails the clause C. However, formula simplification techniques such as *blocked clause elimination* [27], *variable elimination* [9,46], and *equivalence elimination* [19] do not preserve logical equivalence. Therefore, sharing safe clauses among solver incarnations does not preserve equivalence any more, which was the idea of safe clauses [30]. Consequently, solvers like PCASSO do not apply any formula simplification techniques.

We propose to formalize the computations performed in complex SAT solvers in a similar way than in [34] to understand and to reason about these systems. Moreover, we can implement certifying algorithms, that compute witnesses of the results, based on our formalism [13,17]. Such witnesses received attention as SAT solvers can be buggy [7], and recent SAT competitions included certified UNSAT tracks.

Our contributions are:

- We have developed the *instance decomposition model* ID that models parallel SAT solvers based on the instance decomposition approach with *label-based clause sharing* and inprocessing. In particular, we have generalized the notion of safe clauses such that we can include clause elimination procedures that change the semantics of formulas. To the best of our knowledge, combining clause sharing and inprocessing is new in this approach.
- We have shown soundness of our model.
- Our formalism can be used as an *execution trace* of parallel SAT solvers, which is useful for certifying unsatisfiability results. In this paper we propose a new format based on TraceCheck [5] for unsatisfiability proofs from parallel SAT solvers based on instance decomposition. The format is based on the notion of *labeled, extended resolution refutations* that merge the proofs constructed by the parallel solvers into a single derivation.

Structure. We present propositional logic, partition and label functions in Sect. 2. In Sect. 3, we develop the formalism ID and afterwards our new proof format in Sect. 4. Finally, we conclude in Sect. 5.

2 Background

2.1 The Satisfiability Problem

We assume a fixed infinite set $\mathcal{V}$ of Boolean *variables*. A *literal* L is a variable A (*positive literal*) or a negated variable $\neg A$ (*negative literal*). The *complement* $\overline{L}$ of a positive (negative, resp.) literal L is the negative (positive, resp.) literal with the same variable as L. In SAT, we deal with finite clause multisets called *formulas* representing a generalized conjunction. Each *clause* C is a finite set of literals that represents a generalized disjunction. The set of all formulas is denoted with $\mathcal{L}$.

The semantics of formulas is built on interpretations. An *interpretation* I is a set of literals that for all variables A contains exactly one of A or $\neg A$, and can be understood as a mapping from the set $\mathcal{V}$ of all Boolean variables to the set $\{\top, \bot\}$ of truth values.

The interpretation I *satisfies* the literal L, in symbols, $I \models L$, if and only if $L \in I$. It *satisfies* the clause C, in symbols $I \models C$, if and only if there is a literal $L \in C$ such that $I \models L$. For a formula F, the interpretation I *satisfies* the formula F, in symbols $I \models F$, if and only if for every clause $C \in F$ we find that the interpretation I satisfies the clause C. A *model* I of a formula F is an interpretation I that satisfies the formula F, i.e. $I \models F$. If there is such an interpretation I, the formula F is *satisfiable*. Otherwise, the formula F is *unsatisfiable*. Given a formula F, the *satisfiability problem (SAT)* is the problem whether the formula F is satisfiable. Two formulas F and F' are *equisatisfiable*, in symbols $F \equiv_{\mathsf{sat}} F'$, if and only if either both are satisfiable or both are unsatisfiable. In this paper, we will often relate formulas by the *entailment relation*: The formula F *entails* the formula F' if and only if every model of the formula F is a model of the formula F'. Two formulas F and F' are *equivalent*, in symbols $F \equiv F'$, if and only if the formula F entails the formula F' and vice versa. The *solution space* of a formula F, denoted by $\mathsf{SolutionSpace}(F)$, is the set of models of F.

2.2   Partition Functions in SAT Solvers

Partition functions are the core of instance decomposition based parallel SAT solvers. XOR and scattering functions have been proposed for instance decompositions, and are recursively applied [22]. The *XOR function* of the formula F and a sequence of literals $L_1, \ldots, L_n$ are the formulas $(F \,\dot{\cup}\, F_{\mathsf{even}})$ and $(F \,\dot{\cup}\, F_{\mathsf{odd}})$, where F_{even} (F_{odd}) is a formula that is satisfied by an interpretation I iff the number of literals in $L_1, \ldots, L_n$ mapped to *true* under I is even (odd, resp.). For a sequence of conjunctions of literals T_i, $i \in \{1, \ldots, n-1\}$, the *scattering function* [21] produces the following formulas:

$$
F_i = \begin{cases} F \,\dot{\cup}\, T_1 & \text{if } i = 1 \\ F \,\dot{\cup}\, \{\overline{T_1}, \ldots, \overline{T_{i-1}}, T_i\} & \text{if } 1 < i < n \\ F \,\dot{\cup}\, \{\overline{T_1}, \ldots, \overline{T_{n-1}}\} & \text{if } i = n \end{cases}
$$

If the set of variables occurring in the conjunction of literals T_i are pairwise disjoint, then the scattering function is a *tabu scattering function*. Tabu scattering is used in the parallel SAT solver PCASSO [26]. XOR and scattering functions are subsumed by the following definition:

Definition 1. *A partition function is a function $p_n(F) = (F_1, \ldots, F_n)$ where $n > 0$ and $F \equiv F_1 \vee \ldots \vee F_n$. The set of all plain partitions of formulas $\mathsf{PlainPa}$ is defined as*

$$\mathsf{PlainPa} = \{p_n(F) \mid F \text{ is a formula and } p_n \text{ is a partition}\}$$

The set of all recursive partitions of formulas RecPa is inductively defined as follows: if F is a formula and p_n is a partition, then $p_n(F) \in \mathsf{RecPa}$. If we know $(F_1, \ldots, F_n) \in \mathsf{RecPa}$ and $p_m(F_i) = (G_1, \ldots, G_m)$ is a partition function, then $(F_1, \ldots, F_{i-1}, F_i, G_1, \ldots, G_m, F_{i+1}, \ldots, F_n) \in \mathsf{RecPa}$. □

Partitions provide a way to cooperate in deciding the satisfiability of a formula: A *cooperation tree for* $F_0, \ldots, F_n$ is a binary relation $E \subseteq \{0, \ldots, n\} \times \{0, \ldots, n\}$ such that *1.* the formula F_0 is satisfiable if and only if the formula F_i is satisfiable for some $i \in \{1, \ldots, n\}$, and *2.* the formula F_i is satisfiable if and only if the formula F_j is satisfiable for some $j \in \{1, \ldots, n\}$ with $(i, j) \in E$ and F_i is not a leaf node, i.e. there is at least one j such that $(i, j) \in E$. The first condition corresponds to the intuition that the input formula is the root of the tree.

Example 1 (Partition Functions). Consider the two tabu scattering functions $p_2(F) = ((F \,\dot{\cup}\, \{\{x\}\}), (F \,\dot{\cup}\, \{\{\overline{x}\}\}))$ and $p'_2(F) = ((F \,\dot{\cup}\, \{\{y\}\}), (F \,\dot{\cup}\, \{\{\overline{y}\}\}))$, and the formulas $F, F_0, F_1, F_{10}, F_{11}$ where $p_2(F) = (F_0, F_1)$ and additionally

$p'_2(F_1) = (F_{10}, F_{11})$. The partition functions compute the formulas below, forming a *tree-shaped structure* of these formulas:

$$F_\epsilon = \{\{x, y\}\}$$
$$F_0 = \{\{x, y\}, \{x\}\}$$
$$F_1 = \{\{x, y\}, \{\overline{x}\}\}$$
$$F_{10} = \{\{x, y\}, \{\overline{x}\}, \{y\}\}$$
$$F_{11} = \{\{x, y\}, \{\overline{x}\}, \{\overline{y}\}\}$$

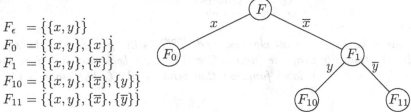

Proposition 1 below presents properties of partition functions: Consider a formula F and a partitioning function $p_n(F) = (F_1, \ldots, F_n)$. If the formula F_i is satisfiable, then we know that the formula F is satisfiable (Prop. 1.1). Likewise, the formulas $F_1, \ldots, F_n$ are unsatisfiable if and only if the formula F is unsatisfiable (Prop. 1.2). The formula F_i entails the input formula F (Prop. 1.3) for every $i \in \{1, \ldots, n\}$ and the union of the solution space of the formulas F_i is the solution space of the input formula F (Prop. 1.4). Proposition 1.5 states that every partition function induces a cooperation tree. The Prop. 1.6, 1.7, and 1.8 state that scattering functions, tabu scattering functions and XOR functions are partition functions. Moreover, recursively defined partition are partition functions (Prop. 1.9). In particular this means that we can model the iterative partitioning approach, if we restrict ourselves to plain partition functions.

Proposition 1 (Partition Functions). *Let p_n be a partition function and $F, F_1, \ldots, F_n$ formulas such that $p_n(F) = (F_1, \ldots, F_n)$.*

Basic Properties
1. *If F_i is satisfiable, then F is satisfiable.*
2. *F is satisfiable iff F_i is satisfiable for some $i \in \{1, \ldots, n\}$.*
3. *$F_i \models F$ for every $i \in \{1, \ldots, n\}$.*
4. *SolutionSpace$(F_1) \cup \ldots \cup$ SolutionSpace$(F_n) =$ SolutionSpace(F).*
5. *$\{(0, i) \mid i \in \{1, \ldots, n\}\}$ is a cooperation tree for $F_0, \ldots, F_n$ with $F_0 = F$.*

Partition Functions
6. *The XOR function is a partitioning function.*
7. *Scattering functions are partitioning functions.*
8. *Tabu scattering functions are partitioning functions.*
9. *Recursive partitions are plain partitions and vice versa:* PlainPa = RecPa.

Proof. For details, see [40]. □

2.3 Label Functions

Label functions provide an efficient way to decide equisatisfiability, and we use them to control clause sharing. This is important because parallel SAT solvers share clauses among the solver incarnations if importing shared clauses preserve satisfiability. We consider a finite set of *labels*, denoted by Labels.

Definition 2. *A label function ℓ is a pair (ℓ_C, ℓ_F)*

$$\ell_C : \mathbb{N} \times \mathsf{Clauses} \mapsto 2^{\mathsf{Labels}}$$
$$\ell_F : \mathbb{N} \mapsto 2^{\mathsf{Labels}}$$

where Clauses *is the set of all clauses, and* 2^{Labels} *is the powerset of the set of all labels. We typically drop the indices* C *and* F. *Let* ℓ *be a label function, then* $\ell[i, C \to L]$ *denotes the label function that behaves like* ℓ, *but maps* (i, C) *to* L. □

Intuitively, a label function ℓ assigns each solver incarnation $Solver_i$ a finite set of labels $\ell(i)$, and each clause C of the solver incarnation $Solver_i$ a finite set of labels $\ell(i, C)$. In the sharing model in the next section, we allow $Solver_i$ to import the clause C from the $Solver_j$, if $\ell(F_j, C) \subseteq \ell(F_i)$, i.e. if the label of the clause C is a subset of the label of the solver incarnation $Solver_i$. The *Boolean label function* [23] is a simple label function with the two labels safe and unsafe, and is defined by the formulas of the solver incarnations $F_1, \dots, F_n$ as follows:

$$\ell(j, C) = \begin{cases} \{\mathsf{safe}\} & \text{if } C \in F_i \text{ for all } i \in \{1, \dots, n\} \\ \{\mathsf{unsafe}\} & \text{otherwise} \end{cases} \quad \text{for all } j \in \{1, \dots, n\}$$

$$\ell(i) \quad = \{\mathsf{safe}\} \text{ for all } i \in \{1, \dots, n\}$$

Example 2 (Boolean label function). Consider the following two satisfiable formulas $F_1 = \{\{x, y\}, \{\overline{x}\}\}$ and $F_2 = \{\{x, y\}, \{\overline{y}\}\}$, which are solved by the solver incarnations $Solver_1$ and $Solver_2$. Then $\ell_C(1, \{x, y\}) = \ell_C(2, \{x, y\}) = \{\mathsf{safe}\}$, $\ell_C(1, \overline{x}) = \ell_C(2, \overline{y}) = \{\mathsf{unsafe}\}$ and $\ell_F(1) = \ell_F(2) = \{\mathsf{safe}\}$. Since we have $\ell_C(1, \{\overline{x}\}) = \ell_C(2, \{\overline{y}\}) = \{\mathsf{unsafe}\}$ the solver incarnation $Solver_1$ cannot import the clause $\overline{y}$ from the solver incarnation $Solver_2$ since $\ell_C(2, \overline{y}) = \{\mathsf{unsafe}\}$ and $\{\mathsf{unsafe}\} \not\subseteq \{\mathsf{safe}\} = \ell_F(1)$. Indeed, the formula $F_1 \cup \{\overline{y}\}$ is unsatisfiable. □

The *position-based label function* [30] is determined by the tree-like structure that is obtained by applying the scattering functions iteratively. We represent the tree-structure of the formulas by the indices: An index is a word w in the *index language* L, where $L \subseteq \Sigma^*$, and the language L is closed under prefixes, i.e. whenever $ua \in L$ where $u \in \Sigma^*$ and $a \in \Sigma$, then $u \in L$. The empty word ϵ is contained in every index language L. Initially, we require that $F_u \subseteq F_{uv}$ holds for all $uv \in L$ for the tree representation, but we do not require that this subset relation is preserved by computations of the SAT solver. The position-based label assigns each formula its position in the tree as a label, and each clause the position of the nearest label of the root:

$$\ell(u, C) = v \text{ where } v \text{ is the shortest prefix of } u \text{ such that } C \in F_v$$
$$\ell(u) \quad = \{v \mid v \text{ is a prefix of } u\}$$

Example 3 (Position-based label function). We consider the index language over the alphabet $\Sigma = \{0, 1\}$. Consider the formulas $F_\epsilon, F_0, F_1, F_{10}, F_{11}$ and the tree-shaped structure of these formulas from Example 1:

The position-based label function is then:

$$
\begin{array}{ll}
\ell_\mathsf{F}(\epsilon) = \{\epsilon\} & \ell_\mathsf{C}(w, \{x, y\}) = \{\epsilon\} \text{ for } w \in \{0, 1, 10, 11\} \\
\ell_\mathsf{F}(0) = \{\epsilon, 0\} & \ell_\mathsf{C}(0, \{x\}) = \{0\} \\
\ell_\mathsf{F}(1) = \{\epsilon, 1\} & \ell_\mathsf{C}(w, \{\overline{x}\}) = \{1\} \text{ for } w \in \{1, 10, 11\} \\
\ell_\mathsf{F}(10) = \{\epsilon, 1, 10\} & \ell_\mathsf{C}(10, \{y\}) = \{10\} \\
\ell_\mathsf{F}(11) = \{\epsilon, 1, 11\} & \ell_\mathsf{C}(11, \{\overline{y}\}) = \{11\}
\end{array}
$$

The position-based label functions denote clauses as safe for a subtree.   □

We call label functions that support clause sharing as consistent. The idea is that, given a label function ℓ, and a sequence of formula $F_1, \ldots, F_n$, clause sharing preserves the satisfiability of each formula. A clause C can be shared from formula F_j to the formula F_i, if $\ell_\mathsf{C}(j, C) \subseteq \ell_\mathsf{F}(i)$.

Definition 3 (Label Consistency). *A label function ℓ is consistent for the formulas $F_1, \ldots, F_n$ if and only if for all $i \in \{1, \ldots, n\}$ it holds that*

$$
F_i \equiv_\mathsf{sat} F_i \,\dot\cup\, \{C \in F_j \mid \ell_\mathsf{C}(j, C) \subseteq \ell_\mathsf{F}(i), \text{ and } 1 \le j \le n\}.
$$

□

The following example demonstrates that some label functions are not consistent for a sequence of formulas:

Example 4. Consider the two satisfiable formulas $F_1 = \{\{x\}\}$ and $F_2 = \{\{\overline{x}\}\}$, and the label function ℓ with $\ell(1, \{x\}) = \ell(2, \{\overline{x}\}) = \ell(1) = \ell(2) = \emptyset$. However, $F_1 \not\equiv_\mathsf{sat} F_1 \,\dot\cup\, \{\{\overline{x}\}\}$. Consequently, the label function ℓ is inconsistent for the formulas F_1, F_2.   □

Proposition 2 below presents properties of label functions. The addition of labels for a clause preserves label consistency (Prop. 2.1), and the deletion of a label of a solver incarnation preserves label consistency Prop. 2.2. Proposition 2.3 states that clause sharing preserves label consistency. Moreover, clause sharing preserves the satisfiability for consistent label functions (Prop. 2.4). The Boolean label function and the position-based label function are consistent (Prop. 2.5, Prop. 2.6). Proposition 2.7 states that resolvents can be added without loosing label consistency, when the label of the resolvent is equal to the union of the labels the resolvent depends on. Likewise, we can add the empty clause to a formula if it is unsatisfiable without loosing label consistency, if the label of the empty clause is the set of all labels (Prop. 2.8). Clause elimination techniques preserve label consistency (Prop. 2.9).

Proposition 2. *Let $F_1, \ldots, F_n$ be formulas, ℓ a consistent label function for $F_1, \ldots, F_n$, and L a finite set of labels.*

Basic properties

1. *If $\ell(i, C) \subseteq L$, then $\ell[i, C \to L]$ is consistent for $F_1, \ldots, F_n$.*
2. *If $L \subseteq \ell(i)$, then $\ell[i \to L]$ is consistent for $F_1, \ldots, F_n$.*
3. *If $\ell(j, C) \subseteq \ell(i)$ and $C \in F_j$, then $\ell[i, C \to \ell(j, C)]$ is consistent for $F_1, \ldots, F_{i-1}, F_i \,\dot{\cup}\, \{C\}, F_{i+1}, \ldots, F_n$.*
4. *If $\ell(j, C) \subseteq \ell(i)$ and $C \in F_j$, then $F_i \equiv_{\mathsf{sat}} F_i \,\dot{\cup}\, \{C\}$.*

Consistent label functions

5. *The Boolean label function is consistent.*
6. *The position-based label function is consistent.*

Interplay resolution and consistent label functions

7. *If D is a resolvent of $C, C' \in F_i$, then $\ell[i, D \to \ell(i, C) \cup \ell(i, C')]$ is consistent for $F_1, \ldots, F_{i-1}, F_i \,\dot{\cup}\, \{D\}, F_{i+1}, \ldots, F_n$.*
8. *If F_i is unsatisfiable, then the label function $\ell[i, \emptyset \to \ell(i)]$ is consistent for $F_1, \ldots, F_{i-1}, F_i \,\dot{\cup}\, \{\emptyset\}, F_{i+1}, \ldots, F_n$.*

Interplay inprocessing and consistent label functions

9. *If $F_i' \subseteq F_i$ and $F_i' \equiv_{\mathsf{sat}} F_i$, then label function ℓ is consistent for $F_1, \ldots, F_{i-1}, F_i', F_{i+1}, \ldots, F_n$.*

Proof. For details, see [40]. □

3   The Instance Decomposition Model ID

We use the notion of system transition systems to describe the behavior of the instance decomposition based solvers. Formally, a *state transition system* is a tuple $(\Delta, \rightsquigarrow)$ where Δ is the set of *states* and $\rightsquigarrow \,\subseteq \Delta \times \Delta$ is the *state transition relation*. Given a state transition system $(\Delta, \rightsquigarrow)$, we define $\overset{0}{\rightsquigarrow} = \{(x, x) \mid x \in \Delta\}$, $\overset{n}{\rightsquigarrow} = \{(x, z) \mid (x, y) \in \overset{n-1}{\rightsquigarrow} \text{ and } (y, z) \in \rightsquigarrow\}$ for all $n \in \mathbb{N}_{>0}$ and $\overset{*}{\rightsquigarrow} = \bigcup_{i \in \mathbb{N}} \overset{i}{\rightsquigarrow}$. Instead of $(x, y) \in \rightsquigarrow$, we write $x \rightsquigarrow y$.

We model parallel SAT solvers based on the instance decomposition approach with label-based clause sharing as follows: A state of a sequential SAT solver $Solver_i$ is a formula F_i and the solver $Solver_i$ maintains the part of the label function $\ell(i, C)$ for all clauses $C \in F_i$. Then, the state of computation in instance decomposition based solvers is the tuple $(F_0, \ldots, F_n, \ell, E)$, where E is a cooperation tree that is obtained by partitioning the input formula.

An *instance decomposition system with multiplicity* $n + 1$ is a state transition system whose set of states consists of the final states $\{\mathsf{SAT}, \mathsf{UNSAT}\}$ and

$$\{(F_0, \ldots, F_n, \ell, E) \mid F_i \text{ are formulas}, E \subseteq \{1, \ldots, n\} \text{ and } \ell \text{ is a label function}\}.$$

The initial state is the tuple $\mathsf{init}_{p_n, E, \ell}(F_0) = (F_0, F_1, \ldots, F_n, \ell, E)$, where p_n is a partition function such that $p_n(F_0) = (F_1, \ldots, F_n)$, E is a cooperation tree for

SAT-rule:	$(F_0, \ldots, F_n, \ell, E) \rightsquigarrow_{\text{SAT}} \text{SAT}$ iff F_i is satisfiable for some $i \in \{0, \ldots, n\}$.
UNSAT-rule:	$(F_0, \ldots, F_n, \ell, E) \rightsquigarrow_{\text{UNSAT}_1} \text{UNSAT}$ iff $\emptyset \in F_0$, i.e. F_0 is unsatisfiable.
LOCUNSAT-rule:	$(F_0, \ldots, F_{i-1}, F_i, F_{i+1}, \ldots, F_n, \ell, E) \rightsquigarrow_{\text{UNSAT}_3}$ $(F_0, \ldots, F_{i-1}, F_i \cup \{\emptyset\}, F_{i+1}, \ell[i, \emptyset \rightarrow \ell(i)], E)$ iff $\emptyset \in F_j$ for all $j \in \{0, \ldots, n\}$ with $(i, j) \in E$, and there exists a $j \in \{0, \ldots, n\}$ with $(i, j) \in E$.
LR-rule:	$(F_0, \ldots, F_{i-1}, F_i, F_{i+1}, \ldots, F_n, \ell, E) \rightsquigarrow_{\text{LR}}$ $(F_0, \ldots F_{i-1}, F_i', F_{i+1}, \ldots, F_n, \ell[i, C \rightarrow \ell(i, D) \cup \ell(i, D')], E)$ iff C is a resolvent of $D, D' \in F_i$, $F_i' = F_i \cup \{C\}$.
DEL-rule:	$(F_0, \ldots, F_{i-1}, F_i, F_{i+1}, \ldots, F_n, \ell, E) \rightsquigarrow_{\text{DEL}}$ $(F_0, \ldots, F_{i-1}, F_i', F_{i+1}, \ldots, F_n, \ell, E)$ iff $F_i \equiv_{\text{sat}} F_i'$, $F_i' \subseteq F_i$.
SHARE-rule:	$(F_0, \ldots, F_n, \ell, E) \rightsquigarrow_{\text{SHARE}}$ $(F_0, \ldots, F_{i-1}, F_i', F_{i+1}, \ldots F_n, \ell[i, C \rightarrow \ell(j, C)], E)$ iff $F_i' = F_i \cup \{C\}$, $C \in F_j$ and $\ell(j, C) \subseteq \ell(F_i)$.

Fig. 2. The rules of the instance decomposition formalism ID. These definitions apply to all formulas $F_1, \ldots, F_n, F_1', \ldots, F_n'$, clauses C and $i \in \{1, \ldots, n\}$.

$F_0, \ldots, F_n$ and ℓ is a consistent label function for the formulas $F_0, \ldots, F_n$. Note that the first component of the initial state is the input formula. The transition relation of the instance decomposition system is composed of the relations presented in Figure 2:

$$\rightsquigarrow_{\text{ID}} := \{\text{SAT, UNSAT, LOCUNSAT, LR, DEL, SHARE}\}.$$

We have two termination rules: The SAT-rule terminates the computation in the final state SAT if the i'th solver founds that its working formula F_i is satisfiable. Likewise, the UNSAT-rule terminates the computation in the final state UNSAT if the formula F_0 contains the empty clause, i.e. F_0 is unsatisfiable. We have two cooperation rules: The LOCUNSAT-rule allows to add the empty clause to the formula F_i when all its children in the cooperating tree are known to be unsatisfiable, which is the case if $\emptyset \in F_j$ with $(i, j) \in E$ for all $j \in \{1, \ldots, n\}$, and the solver incarnation $Solver_i$ is a non-leaf node in the cooperation tree E. The SHARE-rule models label-based clause sharing: The solver incarnation $Solver_i$ can import the clause C from the solver incarnation $Solver_j$, if we have that $\ell(j, C) \subseteq \ell(i)$. We model clause learning with labels with the LR-rule (*labeled resolution*) that adds a resolvent C from the clauses D, D' and sets the label of the clause C to the union over the labels of the two clauses D, D'. Clause forgetting and clause elimination techniques are modeled with the DEL-rule that replaces a formula F_i with a subset of the formula F_i, if this operation preserves satisfiability.

A SAT calculus $(\Delta, \rightsquigarrow, \text{init})$ is *sound* if and only if for all formulas F we have that $\text{init}(F) \overset{*}{\rightsquigarrow} \text{SAT}$ implies that the formula F is satisfiable, and whenever $\text{init}(F) \overset{*}{\rightsquigarrow} \text{UNSAT}$ the formula F is unsatisfiable. Intuitively, soundness means that every answer in the system is correct. A state $x \in \Delta$ is *reachable* in the calculus if there is a formula F such that $\text{init}(F) \overset{*}{\rightsquigarrow} x$.

For showing soundness of this sharing model, we will first establish the invariants:

Lemma 1 (Invariants). *Let F_0 be the input formula, p_n a partitioning, E a cooperation tree for p_n and ℓ be a consistent label function for the formulas $F_0, \ldots, F_n$. Assume $\text{init}_{p_n, E, \ell} = (F_0, F_1, \ldots, F_n, \ell, E) \rightsquigarrow_m (F_0', \ldots, F_n', \ell', E)$. Then the following properties hold:*

1. *$F_i \equiv_{\text{sat}} F_i'$ for every $i \in \{0, \ldots, n\}$,*
2. *ℓ' is a consistent label for $F_0', \ldots, F_n'$, and*
3. *E is a cooperation tree for $F_0', \ldots, F_n'$.*

Proof. We prove the claims by induction on the number m of transition steps. For the base case $m = 0$, the claims trivially holds. For the induction step, assume that the claim holds for the state $(F_1, \ldots, F_n, \ell, E)$ and that $(F_1, \ldots, F_n, \ell, E) \rightsquigarrow_R (F_1', \ldots, F_n', \ell', E)$ for some rule R in the instance decomposition model ID. Note that $R \notin \{\text{SAT}, \text{UNSAT}\}$. We distinguish between the applied rule R:

- LOCUNSAT-rule: Since E is a cooperation tree, we know that the formula F_i must be unsatisfiable. Then we know that $F_i \equiv F_i \,\dot\cup\, \{\emptyset\}$. Then 1. is satisfied since equivalent formulas are equisatisfiable. 2. follows straightforward from Prop. 2.8. Invariant 3. follows straightforward from 1.
- LR-rule: 1. follows from the fact that resolvents are entailed by its formula, and equivalent formulas as equisatisfiable. 2. follows straightforward from Prop. 2.7. Invariant 3. is an immediate consequence of 1.
- SHARE-rule: 1. follows straightforward from Prop. 2.4. Invariant 2. follows straightforward from Prop. 2.3. and invariant 3. follows from 1.
- DEL-rule: 1. is clear by the definition of the DEL-rule. 2. holds immediately by Prop. 2.9. Invariant 3. is an immediate consequence of 1.   □

We can now show the following theorem, that states that the formalism ID computes correct answers:

Theorem 1. *The instance decomposition formalism ID is sound.*

Proof. Let F_0 be the input formula, $p_n(F_0) = (F_1, \ldots, F_n)$ be a partitioning, E be some corresponding cooperation tree, and ℓ be a consistent label for the formulas $F_0, \ldots, F_n$. Assume

$$(F_0, \ldots, F_n, \ell, E) \overset{*}{\rightsquigarrow}_{\text{ID}} (F_0', \ldots, F_n', \ell', E) \rightsquigarrow_{\text{ID}} \text{SAT (UNSAT, resp.)}$$

We divide the proof into two parts: First, we prove that the output SAT is correct, secondly we prove that the output UNSAT is correct.

- SAT: Then, F_i' is satisfiable for some $i \in \{0, \ldots, n\}$. Since E is a cooperation tree for the formulas $F_0', \ldots, F_n'$, we know that the formula F_0' must be satisfiable. Since the formulas F_0 and F_0' are equisatisfiable by Prop. 2.1, we know that the input formula F_0 is satisfiable.
- UNSAT: In this case, the formula F_0' is unsatisfiable and since the formulas F_0 and F_0' are equisatisfiable by Prop. 2.1, we know that the input formula F_0 is unsatisfiable.

Hence, the instance decomposition formalism ID is sound.   □

The theorem above states that we can use clause elimination techniques like blocked clause elimination or variable elimination as inprocessing in solvers like PCASSO.

4 Proof Format

Satisfiability solvers became highly complex procedures, and even intensively-tested systems were not absent of bugs [7]. These reliability problems required that SAT solvers emit unsatisfiability proofs, which are independently verifiable certificates for the unsatisfiability of formulas. The idea was mentioned in early work on Stålmarck's algorithm [16]. In this section, we present a proof format for instance decomposition based SAT solvers.

CDCL-style SAT solvers are based on systematic backtrack-search augmented with *clause learning* [42]. Each time a conflicting assignment is detected, a new clause is added to the formula to redirect the search. For unsatisfiable formulas, the SAT solver repeats this process until the empty clause is learned. Resolution refutations [5, 11] were a straightforward idea for unsatisfiability proofs, but are huge and hard to construct in contemporary SAT solvers. Beame et al. characterized learned clauses as trivial resolution derivations [3], which can be efficiently checked by *reverse unit propagation* (RUP) [3,12]. Goldberg et al. proposed *clausal proofs* [13], which are sequences of learned clauses, based on this criterion. Clausal proofs based on *resolution asymmetric tautologies* (RAT) [28] can be used for SAT solvers that apply pre- and inprocessing [9,28]. Heule et al. developed the drat-trim [47] tool based on *backward checking* [18], which efficiently checks unsatisfiability proofs, as well as the mechanically verified checker written in the ACL2 theorem prover [48]. An alternative approach to unsatisfiability proofs are *mechanically-verified* SAT solvers [35,39].

For simplicity, we consider resolution proofs because then we can easily infer the labels for clauses, whereas in clausal proofs the label is not necessarily unique. In the following, we will consider only position-based tagging as label functions. Our proof format is derived from the instance decomposition model (UNSAT-, LOCUNSAT-, and LR-rule) and is built upon the following observation:

Proposition 3. *Let F_0 be the input formula, p_n be a partitioning, E be a cooperation tree for p_n and ℓ be the position-based tagging function for the formulas $F_0, \ldots, F_n$. If*

$$\text{init}_{p_n, E, \ell} = (F_0, F_1, \ldots, F_n, \ell, E) \rightsquigarrow_m (F_0', \ldots, F_n', \ell', E) \rightsquigarrow_{\text{UNSAT}} \text{UNSAT},$$

then $\ell(\emptyset, F_0) = \emptyset$.

Proof. We show the claim by proving the following by induction over the length of derivation m: If $C \in F_u$, then $\ell(u, C) \subseteq \ell(u)$. For the base case $m = 0$, the claim follows from the definition of position-based tagging. For the induction step, assume that the claim holds for the state $(F_1, \ldots, F_n, \ell, E)$ and that $(F_1, \ldots, F_n, \ell, E) \rightsquigarrow_R (F_1', \ldots, F_n', \ell', E)$ for some rule R in the instance decomposition model ID. Note that $R \notin \{\text{SAT}, \text{UNSAT}\}$. We distinguish between the applied rule R:

- LOCUNSAT-rule: In this case, we add the empty clause to F_i and assign the label of the new clause to $\ell(i)$. Consequently, the claim holds.
- LR-rule: Follows straightforward from the definition of labeled resolvent and inductive reasons.
- SHARE-rule: Follows straightforward from the third condition of the rule.
- DEL-rule: Follows straightforward from monotonicity of our claim.

Consequently, we find $\ell(C, 0) \subseteq \ell(0)$ for every clause $C \in F_0$. In particular, this holds for the empty clause. □

The above statement relates unsatisfiability proofs to labeled resolvents as follows: An unsatisfiability proof is a sequence of labeled clauses to the empty clause with no associated labels. The empty clause with no labels attached corresponds to a clause that does not depend on any partitioning constraint. Additionally, we drop labels if a subtree in the partitioning is proven to be unsatisfiable (LOCUNSAT-rule):

Definition 4. *A labeled and extended resolution derivation of C_n in F is a finite sequence of labeled clauses $(C_i \mid 1 \leq i \leq n)$ such that one of the following holds for every $1 \leq i \leq n$:*

- $C_i \in F$,
- *C_i is a labeled resolvent from two previous clauses C_j and C_k where $j < i$ and $k < n$, or*
- *C_i is the empty clause with label u and for every $a \in \Sigma$ there is the empty clause labeled with ua.* □

Proposition 4. *If p is a cooperation tree and there is a labeled and extended resolution derivation of the empty clause in $F_0 \ldots F_n$, then F_0 is unsatisfiable.*

Proof. The claim follows from the corresponding soundness results from the instance decomposition model. □

Therefore, a proof checking system has to verify that *1.* input clauses have been consistently labeled, *2.* input clauses have been correctly partitioned, and *3.* resolvents and their labels have been correctly computed. Condition *1.* and *2.* can easily be checked, if we consider specific partitioning and labeling functions. Proof validators like `TraceCheck` [5] have implemented *3.* but labels were not considered. Therefore, implementing a proof validator based on labeled and extended resolution refutations is feasible. In particular, we do not need to separate resolution steps performed in the different SAT solvers in the proposed proof format, i.e. we basically merge the proof constructed from the parallel solvers into a single proof.

5 Conclusion

Parallel SAT solvers employ many advanced techniques, but not every combination of advanced techniques is sound. In particular, the combination of clause sharing and inprocessing can make a formula unsatisfiable.

Consequently, a SAT solver can incorrectly report the unsatisfiability of a formula. *Fuzzing* [7] is a technique that allows SAT solver engineers to test and empirically verify sound combinations of techniques. One of the reasons for this methodology is the lack of tools to study such advanced combinations. Moreover, useful combinations that involve complicated constraints might be missed with the purely experimental approach. We therefore propose to formalize modern parallel SAT solvers to understand the interplay of advanced techniques, and to reason about them. In this paper, we developed a formal model in terms of state transition systems. The instance decomposition formalism ID models parallel solvers with label-based clause sharing and inprocessing. The solver PCASSO can be modeled as an instance of the model ID. Clause sharing is restricted to ensure that clauses that depend on partition constraints are only imported if this preserves the satisfiability of the formula. We have shown that ID is sound.

We have also studied label functions in more detail to control clause sharing in a satisfiability-preserving way. Originally, label functions were introduced as a *tractable*, sound, but incomplete method to decide entailment [23], which is known to be co$\mathcal{NP}$-*complete*. However, we have shown how to add clause elimination techniques, which was stated as a research question in [25].

Another important aspect is that the formalism can also be used as an *execution trace*, that can be used for unsatisfiability proofs from parallel SAT solvers. For this purpose, we developed the notion of *labeled, extended resolution derivation*.

As future work, we identify two interesting challenges: How can we combine clause addition and elimination techniques in instance decomposition based SAT solvers? How can we construct clausal proofs?

Acknowledgment. I want to thank Norbert Manthey for explaining me some details of SAT solving.

References

1. Audemard, G., Lagniez, J.-M., Mazure, B., Saïs, L.: On freezing and reactivating learnt clauses. In: Sakallah, K.A., Simon, L. (eds.) SAT 2011. LNCS, vol. 6695, pp. 188–200. Springer, Heidelberg (2011)
2. Audemard, G., Simon, L.: Predicting learnt clauses quality in modern SAT solvers. In: Boutilier, C. (ed.) IJCAI 2009, pp. 399–404. Morgan Kaufmann Publishers Inc., Pasadena (2009)
3. Beame, P., Kautz, H., Sabharwal, A.: Towards understanding and harnessing the potential of clause learning. Journal of Artificial Intelligene Research 22(1), 319–351 (2004)
4. Biere, A.: Lingeling, Plingeling, PicoSAT and PrecoSAT at SAT Race 2010. FMV Report Series Technical Report 10/1, Johannes Kepler University, Linz, Austria (2010)
5. Biere,   A.:   BooleForce   and   TraceCheck   (2014). http://fmv.jku.at/booleforce
6. Biere, A., Cimatti, A., Clarke, E.M., Fujita, M., Zhu, Y.: Symbolic model checking using SAT procedures instead of BDDs. In: Irwin, M.J. (ed.) DAC 1999, pp. 317–320. ACM (1999)
7. Brummayer, R., Biere, A.: Fuzzing and delta-debugging SMT solvers. In: Workshop SMT 2010, pp. 1–5. ACM (2009)
8. Davis, M., Logemann, G., Loveland, D.: A machine program for theorem-proving. Communications of the ACM 5(7), 394–397 (1962)
9. Eén, N., Biere, A.: Effective preprocessing in SAT through variable and clause elimination. In: Bacchus, F., Walsh, T. (eds.) SAT 2005. LNCS, vol. 3569, pp. 61–75. Springer, Heidelberg (2005)
10. Eén, N., Sörensson, N.: An extensible SAT-solver. In: Giunchiglia, E., Tacchella, A. (eds.) SAT 2003. LNCS, vol. 2919, pp. 502–518. Springer, Heidelberg (2004)
11. Gelder, A.V.: Extracting (easily) checkable proofs from a satisfiability solver that employs both preorder and postorder resolution. In: ISAIM 2002 (2002)
12. Gelder, A.V.: Verifying RUP proofs of propositional unsatisfiability. In: ISAIM 2008 (2008)
13. Goldberg, E., Novikov, Y.: Verification of proofs of unsatisfiability for CNF formulas. In: DATE 2003, pp. 10886–10891. IEEE Computer Society, Washington, DC (2003)
14. Gomes, C.P., Selman, B., Crato, N., Kautz, H.: Heavy-tailed phenomena in satisfiability and constraint satisfaction problems. Journal of Automated Reasoning 24(1–2), 67–100 (2000)
15. Großmann, P., Hölldobler, S., Manthey, N., Nachtigall, K., Opitz, J., Steinke, P.: Solving periodic event scheduling problems with SAT. In: Jiang, H., Ding, W., Ali, M., Wu, X. (eds.) IEA/AIE 2012. LNCS, vol. 7345, pp. 166–175. Springer, Heidelberg (2012)
16. Harrison, J.: Stålmarck's algorithm as a HOL derived rule. In: von Wright, J., Harrison, J., Grundy, J. (eds.) TPHOLs 1996. LNCS, vol. 1125, pp. 221–234. Springer, Heidelberg (1996)
17. Heule, M., Manthey, N., Philipp, T.: Validating unsatisfiability results of clause sharing parallel SAT solvers. In: Berre, D.L. (ed.) POS 2014. EPiC Series, vol. 27, pp. 12–25. EasyChair (2014)
18. Heule, M.J.H., Hunt Jr., W.A., Wetzler, N.: Trimming while checking clausal proofs. In: Jobstmann, B., Ray, S. (eds.) FMCAD 2013, pp. 181–188. IEEE (2013)

19. Heule, M.J.H., Järvisalo, M., Biere, A.: Efficient CNF simplification based on binary implication graphs. In: Sakallah, K.A., Simon, L. (eds.) SAT 2011. LNCS, vol. 6695, pp. 201–215. Springer, Heidelberg (2011)
20. Huang, J.: The effect of restarts on the efficiency of clause learning. In: Veloso, M. (ed.) IJCAI 2007, pp. 2318–2323. Morgan Kaufmann Publishers Inc., San Francisco (2007)
21. Hyvärinen, A.E.J., Junttila, T.A., Niemelä, I.: A distribution method for solving SAT in grids. In: Biere, A., Gomes, C.P. (eds.) SAT 2006. LNCS, vol. 4121, pp. 430–435. Springer, Heidelberg (2006)
22. Hyvärinen, A.E.J., Junttila, T., Niemelä, I.: Partitioning SAT instances for distributed solving. In: Fermüller, C.G., Voronkov, A. (eds.) LPAR-17. LNCS, vol. 6397, pp. 372–386. Springer, Heidelberg (2010)
23. Hyvärinen, A.E.J., Junttila, T.A., Niemelä, I.: Incorporating learning in grid-based randomized SAT solving. In: Dochev, D., Pistore, M., Traverso, P. (eds.) AIMSA 2008. LNCS (LNAI), vol. 5253, pp. 247–261. Springer, Heidelberg (2008)
24. Hölldobler, S., Manthey, N., Saptawijaya, A.: Improving resource-unaware SAT solvers. In: Fermüller, C.G., Voronkov, A. (eds.) LPAR-17. LNCS, vol. 6397, pp. 519–534. Springer, Heidelberg (2010)
25. Irfan, A., Lanti, D., Manthey, N.: Modern cooperative parallel SAT solving. In: POS 2013 (2013)
26. Irfan, A., Lanti, D., Manthey, N.: PCASSO a parallel cooperative sat SOlver. In: Balint, A., Belov, A., Heule, M.J.H., Järvisalo, M. (eds.) Proceedings of SAT Challenge 2013. Department of Computer Science Series of Publications B, vol. B-2013-1, pp. 64–65. University of Helsinki, Helsinki (2013)
27. Järvisalo, M., Biere, A., Heule, M.: Blocked clause elimination. In: Esparza, J., Majumdar, R. (eds.) TACAS 2010. LNCS, vol. 6015, pp. 129–144. Springer, Heidelberg (2010)
28. Järvisalo, M., Heule, M.J.H., Biere, A.: Inprocessing rules. In: Gramlich, B., Miller, D., Sattler, U. (eds.) IJCAR 2012. LNCS, vol. 7364, pp. 355–370. Springer, Heidelberg (2012)
29. Kautz, H.A., Selman, B.: Planning as satisfiability. In: Neumann, B. (ed.) ECAI 1992. pp. 359– 363 (1992)
30. Lanti, D., Manthey, N.: Sharing information in parallel search with search space partitioning. In: Nicosia, G., Pardalos, P. (eds.) LION 7. LNCS, vol. 7997, pp. 52–58. Springer, Heidelberg (2013)
31. Lynce, I., Marques-Silva, J.: SAT in bioinformatics: Making the case with haplotype inference. In: Biere, A., Gomes, C.P. (eds.) SAT 2006. LNCS, vol. 4121, pp. 136–141. Springer, Heidelberg (2006)
32. Manthey, N.: Coprocessor 2.0 – A flexible CNF simplifier. In: Cimatti, A., Sebastiani, R. (eds.) SAT 2012. LNCS, vol. 7317, pp. 436–441. Springer, Heidelberg (2012)
33. Manthey, N.: Towards Next Generation Sequential and Parallel SAT Solvers. Ph.D. thesis, Technische Universität Dresden, Informatik Fakultät (2015)
34. Manthey, N., Philipp, T., Wernhard, C.: Soundness of inprocessing in clause sharing SAT solvers. In: Järvisalo, M., Van Gelder, A. (eds.) SAT 2013. LNCS, vol. 7962, pp. 22–39. Springer, Heidelberg (2013)
35. Marić, F.: Formalization and implementation of modern SAT solvers. Journal of Automated Reasoning 43(1), 81–119 (2009)
36. Marques Silva, J.P., Sakallah, K.A.: Grasp: A search algorithm for propositional satisfiability. IEEE Transactions on Computers 48(5), 506–521 (1999)

37. Martins, R., Manquinho, V., Lynce, I.: An overview of parallel SAT solving. Constraints 17(3), 304–347 (2012)
38. Moskewicz, M.W., Madigan, C.F., Zhao, Y., Zhang, L., Malik, S.: Chaff: engineering an efficient SAT solver. In: DAC 2001, pp. 530–535. Association for Computing Machinery, Las Vegas (2001)
39. Oe, D., Stump, A., Oliver, C., Clancy, K.: versat: A verified modern SAT solver. In: Kuncak, V., Rybalchenko, A. (eds.) VMCAI 2012. LNCS, vol. 7148, pp. 363–378. Springer, Heidelberg (2012)
40. Philipp, T.: Expressive Models for Parallel Satisfiability Solvers. Master thesis, Technische Universität Dresden, Informatik Fakultät (2013)
41. : Engineering efficient planners with SAT. In: Raedt, L.D., Bessière, C., Dubois, D., Doherty, P., Frasconi, P., Heintz, F., Lucas, P.J.F. (eds.) ECAI 2012. Frontiers in Artificial Intelligence and Applications, pp. 684–689. IOS Press (2012)
42. Silva, J.P.M., Sakallah, K.A.: GRASP - a new search algorithm for satisfiability. In: ICCAD 1996, pp. 220–227. IEEE Computer Society, Washington (1996)
43. Singer, D.: Parallel resolution of the satisfiability problem: A survey. In: Talbi, E.G. (ed.) Parallel Combinatorial Optimization, chap. 5, pp. 123–148. Wiley Interscience (2006)
44. Soos, M.: CryptoMiniSat 2.5.0. In: SAT Race Competitive Event Booklet (2010)
45. Stallman, R.M., Sussman, G.J.: Forward reasoning and dependency-directed backtracking in a system for computer-aided circuit analysis. Artificial Intelligence 9(2), 135–196 (1977)
46. Subbarayan, S., Pradhan, D.K.: NiVER: Non-increasing variable elimination resolution for preprocessing SAT instances. In: H. Hoos, H., Mitchell, D.G. (eds.) SAT 2004. LNCS, vol. 3542, pp. 276–291. Springer, Heidelberg (2005)
47. Wetzler, N., Heule, M.J.H., Hunt Jr., W.A.: DRAT-trim: Efficient checking and trimming using expressive clausal proofs. In: Sinz, C., Egly, U. (eds.) SAT 2014. LNCS, vol. 8561, pp. 422–429. Springer, Heidelberg (2014)
48. Wetzler, N., Heule, M.J.H., Hunt Jr., W.A.: Mechanical verification of SAT refutations with extended resolution. In: Blazy, S., Paulin-Mohring, C., Pichardie, D. (eds.) ITP 2013. LNCS, vol. 7998, pp. 229–244. Springer, Heidelberg (2013)

Decision Procedures

Weakly Equivalent Arrays

Jürgen Christ and Jochen Hoenicke*

Department of Computer Science,
University of Freiburg
{christj,hoenicke}@informatik.uni-freiburg.de

Abstract. The (extensional) theory of arrays is widely used to model systems. Hence, efficient decision procedures are needed to model check such systems. In this paper, we present an efficient decision procedure for the theory of arrays. We build upon the notion of *weak equivalence*. Intuitively, two arrays are weakly equivalent if they only differ at finitely many indices. We formalise this notion and show how to exploit weak equivalences to decide formulas in the quantifier-free fragment of the theory of arrays. We present a novel data structure to represent *all* weak equivalence classes induced by a formula in linear space (in the number of array terms). Experimental evidence shows that this technique is competitive with other approaches.

1 Introduction

Arrays are widely used to model systems. In software model checking, for example, the heap of a program can be modelled by an array that represents the main memory. A software model checker using such a model can check for illegal accesses to memory or even memory leaks by constructing verification conditions that require reasoning about the theory of arrays. McCarthy [10] laid the foundations for this theory. He defined a store and a select operation and the corresponding select-over-store axioms stating that the store operation changes an array at only one position. Current decision procedures use a series of instantiations of McCarthy's axioms to prove a formula.

This is similar to solving a formula in the equality theory by repeatedly instantiating transitivity axioms. However, modern solvers based on DPLL($\mathcal{T}$) [9] combine propositional reasoning with a dedicated decision procedure for reasoning about theories. For example, a solver for the theory of equalities reasons about equality chains and creates lemmas on the fly that summarise transitivity for a long chain of equalities. These lemmas are only created if they are in conflict with the equality literals currently set in the DPLL solver. This removes some burden from the DPLL engine, as fewer lemmas are needed. The dedicated decision procedure is usually faster than adding a lot of small lemmas and deriving new ones by unit resolution in the DPLL engine. Also it reduces the literals that have to be created overall.

* This work is supported by the German Research Council (DFG) as part of the Transregional Collaborative Research Center "Automatic Verification and Analysis of Complex Systems" (SFB/TR14 AVACS).

C. Lutz and S. Ranise (Eds.): FroCoS 2015, LNAI 9322, pp. 119–131, 2015.
DOI: 10.1007/978-3-319-24246-0_8

We propose a new dedicated decision procedure for the extensional theory of arrays. Instead of using McCarthy's select-over-store axiom, the procedure creates instances of an extended select-over-store lemma that reasons over a chain of store operations. New lemmas are only created if the currently decided equalities are in conflict with the theory of arrays or to propagate an undecided equality literal on existing terms. The main advantage of using a chain of store operations is that no new array select terms need to be created for the intermediate arrays in the chain. This reduces the number of new terms and the number of new literals that need to be created.

McCarthy's store operation produces an array that differs from the original one at only one index. This is generalised by the notion of *weak equivalence* where two arrays differ only at finitely many indices. We use the notion of weak equivalence to define an extended select-over-store axiom that reasons about a chain of stores. We present a new data structure based on congruence closure to quickly detect which arrays are weakly equivalent and which lemmas need to be created.

Our contributions are:

- we show how to exploit weak equivalences to derive extended lemmas in the theory of arrays (Section 4),
- we present a dedicated decision procedure for quantifier-free formulas in the theory of arrays that produces (almost) no new terms, and we show its completeness by explicitly constructing a model (Section 5),
- we present an extension of this procedure to the theory of arrays with difference function [4] (Section 6),
- we present a new data structure for representing weak equivalence in linear space and polynomial time (Section 7).

The algorithms are implemented in our solver SMTInterpol [6]. While our solver is primarily designed to be used in interpolant generation, we will not cover this topic in this paper.

Related Work Since the proposal of the theory of arrays by McCarthy [10] several decision procedures have been proposed. We can identify two basic branches: *rewrite-based* and *instantiation-based* techniques.

Armando et al. [1] used rewriting techniques to solve the theory of arrays. They showed how to construct simplification orderings to achieve completeness. The benchmarks used in this paper test specific properties of the array operators like commutativity of stores if the indices differ. While these benchmarks require a lot of instantiations of McCarthy's axioms, they are easy for the decision procedure presented in this paper since the properties tested by these benchmarks are properties satisfied by the weak equivalence relation presented in this paper.

Bruttomesso et al. [4] present a rewrite based decision procedure to reason about arrays. This approach exploits some key properties of the store operation that are also captured by the weak equivalence relation described in this paper. Contrary to our method, the rewrite based approach is not designed for

Nelson–Oppen style theory combination and thus not easily integratable into an existing SMT solver.

A decision procedure for the theory of arrays based on instantiating McCarthy's axioms is given by de Moura and Bjørner [11]. The decision procedure saturates several rules that instantiate array axioms under certain conditions. Several filters are proposed to minimise the number of instantiations.

Closest to our work is the decision procedure published by Brummayer and Biere [3], which combines array theory with bitvector theory. Similar to our approach, their decision procedure for arrays derives new extended select-over-store lemmas. They do not use weak equivalence graphs and their handling of extensionality is geared towards bitvector theory.

Stump et al. [14] use a similar notion of weak equivalence, which they call partial equality. For each partial equality they track the set of indices where arrays differ. Contrary to the technique presented in this paper, they do not have a compact (linear space) representation of all partial equalities.

2 Notation

We assume the notation of sorted first-order logic. A theory is defined by a *signature* Σ and a *set of axioms*. The signature lists the *sorts* and *function symbols*. A function symbol has an arity $\sigma_1 \times \cdots \times \sigma_n \to \sigma_0$ where σ_i are sorts. We assume that the signature contains the sort bool and for every sort σ the equality symbol $=$ with arity $\sigma \times \sigma \to$ bool with its usual interpretation. A *model* maps every sort σ interpreted by this model to a non-empty domain $\mathcal{D}_\sigma$ and every constant or function symbol into the corresponding domain. A theory $\mathcal{T}$ is *stably infinite* for a sort if and only if every satisfiable quantifier-free formula is satisfied in a model of $\mathcal{T}$ with an infinite universe for that sort.

The theory of arrays $\mathcal{T}_A$ defines a parametric sort $\sigma \Rightarrow \tau$ for an index sort σ and an element sort τ. The signature of $\mathcal{T}_A$ contains the select function $\cdot[\cdot]$ and the store function $\cdot\langle\cdot \lhd \cdot\rangle$, where $a[i]$ returns the element stored in array a at index i and $a\langle i \lhd v\rangle$ returns a new array that stores the same values as a except that it stores v at index i. Every model of the theory of arrays satisfies the select-over-store axioms proposed by McCarthy [10]:

$$\forall a\, i\, v.\ a\langle i \lhd v\rangle[i] = v \tag{idx}$$

$$\forall a\, i\, j\, v.\ i \neq j \implies a\langle i \lhd v\rangle[j] = a[j] \tag{select-over-store}$$

Additionally we consider the extensional variant of the theory of arrays. Then, every model also has to satisfy the extensionality axiom:

$$\forall a\, b.\ a = b \vee \exists i.\ a[i] \neq b[i] \tag{ext}$$

We use a, b, c to denote array-valued variables, i, j, k to denote index variables, and v, w to denote element variables. We use P to denote a path in a graph. A path in a graph is a sequence of edges.

In the remainder of this paper, we consider quantifier-free $\mathcal{T}_A$-formulae. Furthermore we fix the theories to be stably infinite for the index sort and require that the element sort contains at least two different values[1].

3   A Motivating Example

It is well known that stores with different indices commute. This observation led to a whole set of parametric benchmarks [1]. We will use the version consisting of two stores as an example.

$$b = a\langle i \lhd v \rangle \land c = a\langle j \lhd w \rangle \land i \neq j \land b\langle j \lhd w \rangle \neq c\langle i \lhd v \rangle \qquad (0)$$

This formula is unsatisfiable in the extensional theory of arrays. To prove unsatisfiability of this formula we instantiate (ext). Skolemizing the existential quantifier with the fresh index k, we get $b\langle j \lhd w \rangle = c\langle i \lhd v \rangle \lor b\langle j \lhd w \rangle[k] \neq c\langle i \lhd v \rangle[k]$. Furthermore, we instantiate (idx) for every store term in the formula. Next, we instantiate (select-over-store) for the read terms introduced by the instantiation of the extensionality axiom. We get

$$k = j \lor b\langle j \lhd w \rangle[k] = b[k] \quad \text{and} \quad k = i \lor c\langle i \lhd v \rangle[k] = c[k] \qquad (1)$$

Since $b = a\langle i \lhd v \rangle$, the read term $b[k]$ gives rise to another instantiation and similarly for $c = a\langle j \lhd w \rangle$:

$$k = i \lor a\langle i \lhd v \rangle[k] = a[k] \quad \text{and} \quad k = j \lor a\langle j \lhd w \rangle[k] = a[k] \qquad (2)$$

The final step in the proof of unsatisfiability involves a case split on the value of k. We have to consider three cases: If $k = i$, then $k \neq j$ and we use the left part of (1) and the (idx) instantiations $a\langle i \lhd v \rangle[i] = v$ and $c\langle i \lhd v \rangle[i] = v$ to derive the conflict. A symmetric argument holds for $k \neq i$ and $k = j$. The final case is $k \neq i \land k \neq j$. In this case we need all four (select-over-store) instantiations to derive the conflict.

A lot of effort was needed above to prove a trivial property about the store operation. A number of terms were created that are not present in the original formula, e. g., $a\langle i \lhd v \rangle[k]$. Even worse, if k differs from the store indices i and j, we needed four axiom instantiations to prove that the value at index k did not change. These axiom instantiations were also the source for the case splits.

A more direct approach to the array theory is to consider chains of store operations. In fact, both $b\langle j \lhd w \rangle$ and $c\langle i \lhd v \rangle$ are modifications of the array a. Thus, they can only differ at the indices i, j that appear in the store terms. To check for equality of these two arrays, it is thus sufficient to check the values stored at indices i and j. As we will see in the remainder of the paper, our procedure derives an instance of a generalised extensionality axiom

$$\begin{pmatrix} b = a\langle i \lhd v \rangle \land a\langle j \lhd w \rangle = c \land i \neq j \\ \land\, a\langle i \lhd v \rangle[i] = v \land v = c\langle i \lhd v \rangle[i] \\ \land\, b\langle j \lhd w \rangle[j] = w \land w = a\langle j \lhd w \rangle[j] \end{pmatrix} \implies b\langle j \lhd w \rangle = c\langle i \lhd v \rangle.$$

---

[1] Note that $\mathcal{T}_A$ is stably infinite for the array sort under these conditions. Thus, $\mathcal{T}_A$ can be used in a Nelson–Oppen style theory combination.

Even though this lemma looks more complicated than the instantiations shown above it can be used to refute the formula above without any case splits using just the instantiations of axiom (idx).

4   Weak Equivalences over Arrays

For quantifier-free input, arrays that are connected via a sequence of $\cdot\langle \cdot \lhd \cdot \rangle$ can only differ at finitely many indices. We call such arrays *weakly equivalent*. In this section we formally define weak equivalence as an equivalence relation on the set $\mathcal{A}$ of array terms occurring in the input formula. From this we derive new equalities on index, element or array terms.

Let V denote the set of index, element and array terms that occur in the formula and need to be considered by the array theory, defined as

$$V = \mathcal{A} \cup \{a[i], a\langle i \lhd v\rangle[i], i, v \mid a\langle i \lhd v\rangle \in \mathcal{A}\} \cup \{a[i], i \mid a[i] \text{ occurs in input}\}$$

Our algorithm starts with an equivalence relation $\sim\ \subseteq V \times V$ representing equality on the terms in V. From this the algorithm derives weak equivalences, i. e., which array terms are equal on all but finitely many indices. Finally, it derives new equalities on value and array terms that have to hold in the array theory.

The array $a\langle i \lhd v\rangle$ is weakly equivalent to a because it differs at most at index i. Also two equal arrays are weakly equivalent. The transitive closure is the weak equivalence relation. To make the store indices explicit we build a weak equivalence graph, where the vertices are the array terms $\mathcal{A}$ and the edges are labelled with the indices used in store terms.

Definition 1 (weak equivalence). *Given an equivalence relation $\sim$, the weak equivalence graph G^W contains the vertices $\mathcal{A}$ and the labelled undirected edges:*

1. $a \leftrightarrow b$ if $a \sim b$, and

2. $a \overset{i}{\leftrightarrow} b$ if a has the form $b\langle i \lhd \cdot\rangle$ or b has the form $a\langle i \lhd \cdot\rangle$.

We write $a \overset{(P)}{\leftrightarrow} b$ if there exists a path P between nodes a and b in G^W. In this case, we call a and b weakly equivalent. The weak equivalence class of a is defined as $\text{WeakEQ}(a) := \{b \mid \exists P.\ a \overset{(P)}{\leftrightarrow} b\}$.

For a path P we define $\text{Stores}\,(P)$ as the set of all indices corresponding to edges of the form $\overset{i}{\leftrightarrow}$, i. e., $\text{Stores}\,(P) := \{i \mid \exists a\, b.\ a \overset{i}{\leftrightarrow} b \in P\}$.

Example 1. Consider Formula (0) on page 119. The formula induces the equivalence relation $\{b \sim a\langle i \lhd v\rangle, c \sim a\langle j \lhd w\rangle\}$. The weak equivalence graph for this example is shown in Figure 1. Let P denote the path from $b\langle j \lhd w\rangle$ to $c\langle i \lhd v\rangle$ in the weak equivalence graph. Then, $\text{Stores}\,(P) = \{i, j\}$. Thus, arrays $b\langle j \lhd w\rangle$ and $c\langle i \lhd v\rangle$ can only differ in at most the values stored at the indices i and j.

$$b\langle j \lhd w\rangle \overset{j}{\longleftrightarrow} b \longleftrightarrow a\langle i \lhd v\rangle \overset{i}{\longleftrightarrow} a \overset{j}{\longleftrightarrow} a\langle j \lhd w\rangle \overset{i}{\longleftrightarrow} c \longleftrightarrow c\langle i \lhd v\rangle$$

Fig. 1. Weak equivalence graph for $b \sim a\langle i \lhd v\rangle, c \sim a\langle j \lhd w\rangle$ in Example 1.

If $a \overset{(P)}{\Leftrightarrow} b$ for a path P holds, then for all indices i that are different from any index occurring in Stores (P), the values $a[i]$ and $b[i]$ must be equal. We capture this by the following definition.

Definition 2 (weak equivalence on i). *Two arrays a and b are called weakly equivalent on i if and only if they are connected by a path that does not contain an edge $\overset{j}{\leftrightarrow}$ where $j \sim i$. We denote weak equivalence on i by $a \approx_i b$ and define it as $a \approx_i b := \exists P. \, a \overset{(P)}{\Leftrightarrow} b \wedge \forall j \in$ Stores $(P). \, j \not\sim i$.*

Example 2. Consider again Formula (0) and the corresponding weak equivalence graph from Figure 1. Then, $b\langle j \lhd w\rangle \approx_i a\langle i \lhd v\rangle$ since the path between these two arrays only contains a store edge labelled with j and $i \not\sim j$. Furthermore, $a\langle j \lhd w\rangle \approx_j c\langle i \lhd v\rangle$ since the only store edge connecting these two arrays is labelled with i.

Note that the definition of weakly equivalent on i depends on the index variables not related by the equivalence relation. Using this definition, we can propagate equalities between shared selects if the arrays are weakly equivalent on the index of the select.

Lemma 1 (read-over-weakeq). *Let $\sim$ be an equivalence relation. Let $a[i]$ and $b[j]$ be two selects such that $i \sim j$ and $a \approx_i b$. Then, $\sim$ satisfies the array axioms only if $a[i] \sim b[j]$ holds.*

Proof (Sketch). Induction over the length of the path P witnessing $a \approx_i b$. $\qquad \square$

This lemma tells us that if two arrays are weakly equivalent on i they store the same value at index i. The reverse is not necessarily true. In the example above neither $b\langle j \lhd w\rangle \approx_i c\langle i \lhd v\rangle$ nor $b\langle j \lhd w\rangle \approx_j c\langle i \lhd v\rangle$ hold. Therefore, we define a weaker relation, which we call weak congruence on i.

Definition 3 (weak congruence on i). *Let $\sim$ be an equivalence relation over V. Arrays a and b are weakly congruent on i if and only if $\sim$ guarantees that they store the same value at index i. We denote weak congruence on i by $\cong_i$ and define*

$$a \cong_i b := a \approx_i b \vee (\exists a' \, b' \, j \, k. \, a \approx_i a' \wedge i \sim j \wedge a'[j] \sim b'[k] \wedge k \sim i \wedge b' \approx_i b).$$

We use weak congruences to decide extensionality. If a and b are weak congruent on all indices, then $a = b$ should be propagated. This naïve approach would require checking every index in the formula. To minimise the number of indices we need to consider, we start with a path in the weak equivalence graph.

Lemma 2 (weakeq-ext). *Let $\sim$ be an equivalence relation. Let a and b be two arrays with $a \overset{(P)}{\Leftrightarrow} b$. If for all indices $i \in \text{Stores}\,(P)$ we have $a \cong_i b$, then $\sim$ satisfies the array axioms only if $a \sim b$ holds.*

Proof. Follows from Lemma 1, Definition 3 and (ext). □

Example 3. Consider again Formula (0). Axiom (idx) implies $a\langle i \lhd v\rangle[i] = v = c\langle i \lhd v\rangle[i]$ and likewise for j. Therefore, we now consider the equivalence relation $\{b \sim a\langle i \lhd v\rangle, c \sim a\langle j \lhd w\rangle, a\langle i \lhd v\rangle[i] \sim c\langle i \lhd v\rangle[i], a\langle j \lhd w\rangle[j] \sim b\langle j \lhd w\rangle[j]\}$. Example 2 showed $b\langle j \lhd w\rangle \approx_i a\langle i \lhd v\rangle$ and $a\langle j \lhd w\rangle \approx_j c\langle i \lhd v\rangle$. Then by definition, $b\langle j \lhd w\rangle \cong_i c\langle i \lhd v\rangle$ and $b\langle j \lhd w\rangle \cong_j c\langle i \lhd v\rangle$ hold. Since only i and j occur as store indices on the path from $b\langle j \lhd w\rangle$ to $c\langle i \lhd v\rangle$, Lemma 2 implies $b\langle j \lhd w\rangle \sim c\langle i \lhd v\rangle$.

5   A Decision Procedure Based on Weak Equivalences

Our overall procedure consists of two steps. The first step is a preprocessing step instantiating the axioms (idx) for all $a\langle i \lhd v\rangle$ occurring in the formula. The preprocessing step adds at most one select term $a\langle i \lhd v\rangle[i]$ for every store. The created instance of (idx) is interpolation friendly as it contains only the symbols a, i, v that already appeared in the input term $a\langle i \lhd v\rangle$.

The second step of our decision procedure is running DPLL($\mathcal{T}$) [9]. The input formula including the instantiations of the idx axioms is converted into a propositional formula, called the *propositional core*, by introducing a propositional variable for every atom occurring in the formula. The DPLL($\mathcal{T}$) algorithm enumerates candidate solutions of the propositional core, which are given as valuations of the atoms occurring in the formula. To support Nelson–Oppen theory combination, the valuation contains also a truth value of the equality atom $v = w$ for every pair $v, w \in V$. Then a separate theory solver for every supported theory checks if the valuation of the atoms is consistent with the axioms of the theories. If the theory solver finds a conflict it returns a set of atoms whose current valuation violates the theory axioms. The negation of these atoms form a valid clause in the theory and this clause is added to the propositional core. The DPLL($\mathcal{T}$) algorithm repeats until all possible valuations of the atoms have been tried or a valuation is found that is consistent with all theories.

The solver for the theory of arrays only considers the equality atoms $v = w$ for $v, w \in V$. These form an equivalence relation $\sim \subseteq V \times V$ (the congruence theory solver will ensure this). If $\sim$ is inconsistent with the array axioms the lemma returned by the algorithm is a disjunction of equalities and disequalities.

We propagate new equalities from weak equivalence relations and weak congruence relations based on Lemmas 1 and 2. These relations depend on the equivalence relation $\sim$, which represents logical equality ($=$). We now define a function Cond($\cdot$) that takes a path in the weak equivalence graph and computes a condition (a conjunction of equalities and disequalities) under which a weak equivalence or weak congruence holds. Likewise we define a function $\text{Cond}_i(\cdot)$

for a path that ensures weak equivalence on i. First we give the definition for a single edge. If the edge in the weak equivalence graph represents an equality, the condition reflects this equality. For an edge between a and $a\langle j \lhd \cdot\rangle$, no condition is needed for weak equivalence. However, $\mathrm{Cond}_i(\cdot)$ should ensure that i does not occur on the path, so $i \neq j$ needs to hold.

$$\mathrm{Cond}(a \leftrightarrow b) := a = b \qquad\qquad \mathrm{Cond}_i(a \leftrightarrow b) := a = b$$

$$\mathrm{Cond}(a \overset{j}{\leftrightarrow} b) := \mathrm{true} \qquad\qquad \mathrm{Cond}_i(a \overset{j}{\leftrightarrow} b) := i \neq j$$

We can extend these definitions to paths by conjoining the conditions for all edges on that path. By abuse of notation, we overload $\mathrm{Cond}(\cdot)$ such that it computes the condition under which two arrays are weakly equivalent on i resp. weakly congruent on i. We compute $\mathrm{Cond}(a \approx_i b)$ using some path that witnesses $a \approx_i b$ (the definition is not unique if there are several paths).

$$\mathrm{Cond}(a \approx_i b) := \mathrm{Cond}_i(P) \text{ where } a \overset{(P)}{\leftrightarrow} b \wedge \forall j \in \mathrm{Stores}\,(P)\,.\, i \not\sim j$$

Finally, to define $\mathrm{Cond}(a \cong_i b)$, we use the definition of $\cong_i$.

$$\mathrm{Cond}(a \cong_i b) := \begin{cases} \mathrm{Cond}(a \approx_i b) & \text{if } a \approx_i b \\ \begin{aligned}&\mathrm{Cond}(a \approx_i a') \wedge i = j \\ &\wedge\, a'[j] = b'[k] \\ &\wedge\, k = i \wedge \mathrm{Cond}(b' \approx_i b)\end{aligned} & \text{if } \begin{aligned}&a \approx_i a' \wedge i \sim j \wedge a'[j] \sim b'[k] \\ &\wedge\, k \sim i \wedge b' \approx_i b\end{aligned} \end{cases}$$

Example 4. Consider again Formula 0 with the equivalence relation $\sim$ from Example 3. Then we have $b\langle j \lhd w\rangle \approx_i a\langle i \lhd v\rangle$ and $\mathrm{Cond}(b\langle j \lhd w\rangle \approx_i a\langle i \lhd v\rangle) \equiv i \neq j \wedge b = a\langle i \lhd v\rangle$. Similarly, we get $\mathrm{Cond}(a\langle j \lhd w\rangle \approx_j c\langle i \lhd v\rangle) \equiv a\langle j \lhd w\rangle = c \wedge i \neq j$.

As seen in Example 3, $b\langle j \lhd w\rangle \cong_i c\langle i \lhd v\rangle$ holds since $b\langle j \lhd w\rangle \approx_i a\langle i \lhd v\rangle$, $a\langle i \lhd v\rangle[i] = v = c\langle i \lhd v\rangle[i]$. Thus, (if we remove the trivial conjunct $i = i$)

$$\mathrm{Cond}(b\langle j \lhd w\rangle \cong_i c\langle i \lhd v\rangle) \equiv i \neq j \wedge b = a\langle i \lhd v\rangle \wedge a\langle i \lhd v\rangle[i] = c\langle i \lhd v\rangle[i].$$

Our algorithm is given in Figure 2. It takes an equivalence relation $\sim$ and returns either "sat" if $\sim$ satisfies the array axioms, or a lemma that explains why the array axioms are not satisfied. If $\sim$ satisfies the conditions for Lemma 1, the algorithm creates the corresponding lemma and returns it in Line 2. If $\sim$ satisfies the conditions for Lemma 2, it creates the corresponding lemma and returns it in Line 4. If neither of these conditions is satisfied, $\sim$ satisfies the array axioms and the algorithm returns in Line 5.

The resulting decision procedure is sound and complete for the extensional theory of arrays assuming sound and complete decision procedures for the index and element theories.

Theorem 1. *If the algorithm in Figure 2 returns (unsat, F), then F is valid.*

Proof. Follows from Lemma 1 and 2. □

ARRAY-THEORY($\sim$)

    // Input: Equivalence relation $\sim \subseteq V \times V$
    // Output: Either (unsat, F), where F is a formula valid for the array theory
           that is not satisfied by $\sim$, or sat.
1   **if** $\exists a, b, i, j \in V.a[i], b[j] \in V \wedge a \approx_i b \wedge i \sim j \wedge a[i] \not\sim b[j]$ **then**
2   **return** (unsat, $i \neq j \vee \neg \operatorname{Cond}(a \approx_i b) \vee a[i] = b[j]$)
3   **if** $\exists a, b \in V.\ \exists P.a \overset{(P)}{\leftrightarrow} b, a \not\sim b, \forall i \in \operatorname{Stores}(P).\ a \cong_i b$ **then**
4   **return** (unsat, $\neg \operatorname{Cond}(P) \vee \bigvee_{i \in \operatorname{Stores}(P)} \neg \operatorname{Cond}(a \cong_i b) \vee a = b$)
5   **return** sat

Fig. 2. Consistency checking algorithm for the array theory.

Theorem 2. *If the algorithm in Figure 2 returns sat, then there exists a model $\mathcal{M}$ of the array theory assigning values to V such that $\mathcal{M}(v) = \mathcal{M}(w)$ iff $v \sim w$.*

Proof (Sketch). For the non-array sorts we choose arbitrary domains containing at least one element for every equivalence class of $\sim$. We map each non-array term $v \in V$ to its equivalence class. We assume that for an element sort τ the domain contains at least two elements Fst_τ and Snd_τ. For every sort σ that is used as index sort, we assume D_σ contains an infinite supply of fresh domain elements. We write $\ulcorner X \urcorner$ to denote a fresh element for X, i.e., an element of D_σ that is different from all equivalence classes of $v \in V$ and of all other fresh elements.

For an array sort, we define $\mathcal{D}_{\sigma \Rightarrow \tau}$ as the set of functions from $\mathcal{D}_\sigma$ to $\mathcal{D}_\tau$. For an array term $a \in \mathcal{A}$ of sort $\sigma \Rightarrow \tau$, we define $\mathcal{M}(a) : D_\sigma \to D_\tau$ where

$$\mathcal{M}(a)(\jmath) := \begin{cases} \mathcal{M}(b[i]) & \text{if } b[i] \in V, \mathcal{M}(i) = \jmath, \text{and } a \approx_i b \\ Snd_\tau & \text{if } \jmath = \ulcorner \operatorname{WeakEQ}(a) \urcorner \\ Fst_\tau & \text{otherwise} \end{cases}$$

The values Fst_τ and Snd_τ are used to ensure that two arrays that are not connected in the weak equivalence graph are distinct, i. e., they store different values for at least one index. In the definition above, this index is a fresh index representing the whole weak equivalence class. Also note that the first case of the definition is unique, since the condition in Figure 2, Line 1 does not hold.

The functions $\cdot[\cdot]$ resp. $\cdot\langle \cdot \lhd \cdot \rangle$ are interpreted by function application and function update. The full proof requires to show that the value assigned to a shared variable is consistent with its interpretation in the array theory, e. g., for $a[j] \in V\ \mathcal{M}(a)(\mathcal{M}(j)) = \mathcal{M}(a[j])$ holds and that $\mathcal{M}(v) = \mathcal{M}(w)$ holds iff $v \sim w$. See [5] for details. $\quad\square$

Our proof shows that the cardinality of the element domain can be chosen arbitrarily as long as it contains at least two elements. Thus our procedure even works with theories that are not stably infinite on some domains [13]. If the element theory is stably infinite we do not have to add for every $a\langle i \lhd v \rangle$ the select $a[i]$ to V. Instead, we assume $a[i]$ to be different from any other $b[i]$

unless $a \approx_i b$. This reduces the number of shared terms and, thus, the number of possible instantiations. With this modification, we have to modify the model construction from the proof of Theorem 2.

Theorem 3. *Assume a stably infinite element theory. Let*

$$V = \mathcal{A} \cup \{a\langle i \lhd v\rangle[i], i, v \mid a\langle i \lhd v\rangle \in \mathcal{A}\} \cup \{a[i], i \mid a[i] \text{ occurs in input}\}.$$

If the algorithm in Figure 2 returns sat, then there exists a model $\mathcal{M}$ of the array theory assigning values to V such that $\mathcal{M}(v) = \mathcal{M}(w)$ iff $v \sim w$.

Proof (Sketch). We redefine the generation of the model $\mathcal{M}$ in the proof of Theorem 2. Let $\mathrm{WeakEQ}_i(a) := \{b \mid b \approx_i a\}$ denote the set of array terms that are weakly equivalent on i to a. Let $\mathrm{Stores}\,(\mathrm{WeakEQ}(a)) := \{i \mid \exists b v. b\langle i \lhd v\rangle \in \mathrm{WeakEQ}(a)\}$ be the set of all store indices occurring in the weak equivalence class of a. We construct $\mathcal{M}_A$ in the following way.

$$\mathcal{M}_A(a)(\text{J}) := \begin{cases} \mathcal{M}(b[i]) & \text{if } b[i] \in V, \mathcal{M}(i) = \text{J, and } a \approx_i b \\ \ulcorner \mathrm{WeakEQ}_j(a)\urcorner & \text{if } \mathcal{M}(j) = \text{J}, j \in \mathrm{Stores}\,(\mathrm{WeakEQ}(a)) \text{ and} \\ & \quad \text{there is no } b[i] \in V \text{ with } \mathcal{M}(i) = \text{J}, a \approx_i b \\ \mathit{Snd}_\tau & \text{if } \text{J} = \ulcorner \mathrm{WeakEQ}(a)\urcorner \\ \mathit{Fst}_\tau & \text{otherwise} \end{cases}$$

The difference between this model and the one constructed in the proof of Theorem 2 is the case where $a\langle i \lhd w\rangle$, but not $a[i]$ occurs in the formula (more precisely, there is no $b[j] \in V$ such that $a \approx_i b$ and $i \sim j$). In this case, we set $a[i]$ to a fresh value $\ulcorner \mathrm{WeakEQ}_j(a)\urcorner$. See [5] for more details. $\square$

This optimisation reduces the amount of work without any extra cost. Furthermore, it is widely applicable. In fact, the non-bitvector logics defined in SMTLIB [2] only allow array sorts where the element theory is stably infinite. Thus, only the terms corresponding to instantiations of Axiom (idx) are required.

6   Extension to $\mathcal{T}_{A x Diff}$

Bruttomesso et al. [4] closed $\mathcal{T}_A$ under Craig interpolation [8]. Their extension, $\mathcal{T}_{A x Diff}$, adds to the signature the function $\mathrm{diff}(a, b)$ that takes arrays a and b and returns an index. The extensionality axiom is replaced by

$$\forall a\, b.\ a = b \vee a[\mathrm{diff}(a, b)] \neq b[\mathrm{diff}(a, b)] \qquad \text{(ext-diff)}$$

This axiom specifies the semantics of $\mathrm{diff}(a, b)$. If a and b differ, then $\mathrm{diff}(a, b)$ and $\mathrm{diff}(b, a)$ specify indices at which a and b store different values. If $a = b$ holds, then $\mathrm{diff}(a, b)$ and $\mathrm{diff}(b, a)$ can be arbitrary. Note that $\mathrm{diff}(a, b)$ might be different from $\mathrm{diff}(b, a)$ in both cases.

To accommodate for $\mathrm{diff}(\cdot, \cdot)$ terms in the input, we add another step to our preprocessor. This step instantiates axiom (ext-diff) for every $\mathrm{diff}(a, b)$ term occurring in the input. Note that this creates select terms of the form $a[\text{diff}(a, b)]$ which will be automatically added to the set of shared terms V. Besides these new select terms no new terms are created.

We use the algorithm presented in Figure 2 to solve the preprocessed formula. In the cases where the algorithms returns (unsat, F), F is still a valid lemma. If the algorithm returns sat, we have to create an interpretation for diff. For array terms, we can use the model construction from the proof of Theorem 2, or the one from the modified version in Theorem 3.

Theorem 4 (completeness for $\mathcal{T}_{AxDiff}$). *Assume the axiom (ext-diff) has been instantiated by the preprocessor for every* $\text{diff}(a, b)$ *in the input formula. If the algorithm in Figure 2 returns sat, then there exists a model* $\mathcal{M}$ *of* $\mathcal{T}_{AxDiff}$ *assigning values to* V *such that* $\mathcal{M}(v) = \mathcal{M}(w)$ *iff* $v \sim w$.

Proof (Sketch). The model construction for arrays is the same as the construction used in the proof of Theorem 2 or, in case the element theory is stably infinite, the one used in the proof of Theorem 3. We now give a model for diff.

$$
\mathcal{M}(\text{diff})(a, b) := \begin{cases} \mathcal{M}(\text{diff}(a', b')) & \text{if } \text{diff}(a', b') \text{ occurs in the input} \\ & \text{and } a \sim a' \text{ and } b \sim b' \\ \ulcorner\text{WeakEQ}(a)\urcorner & \text{if } a \not\approx_W b \\ \mathcal{M}_A(i) & \text{if } a \approx_W b \text{ and } a \not\approx_i b \\ & \text{for some } i \in \text{Stores}\,(\text{Path}\,(a, b)) \\ Fst_\sigma & \text{otherwise} \end{cases}
$$

Note that the last case is only reached when the arrays equal. See [5] for more details. $\square$

7 Implementation and Evaluation

This section presents an efficient implementation of the algorithm from Figure 2. We represent the weak equivalence classes and the weak equivalence on i classes by a data structure whose size is linear in the number of array terms in the input formula.

We represent the weak equivalence relation and the weak equivalence on i relations in a forest structure, similarly to the representation of an equivalence graph in congruence solvers [12]. Every vertex corresponds to an array term. A vertex is the root of its weak equivalence class if it does not have an outgoing edge. Otherwise, the outgoing edge points towards (but not necessarily onto) the representative. These edges build a spanning tree for every equivalence class. The edges point from a child node to the parent node.

We have to distinguish between strong equivalence, weak equivalence, and weak equivalence on i. The strong equivalence classes are already handled by the equality solver. In our implementation of the array solver we treat them as indivisible and create a single node for every strong equivalence class. To represent the weak equivalence relations the nodes have up to two outgoing edges, a

struct NODE
   p : NODE
   pi : INDEX
   s : NODE

GET-REP(n : NODE)
  if $n.p = $ NIL **then** n
  else   GET-REP($n.p$)

MAKE-REP(n : NODE)
  if $n.p \neq $ NIL **then**
    MAKE-REP($n.p$)
    $n.p.p := n$ ⎫ invert
    $n.p.pi := n.pi$ ⎬ primary edge
    $n.p := $ NIL   ⎭
    MAKE-REP$_i$(n)

GET-REP$_i$(n : NODE, i : INDEX)
  if $n.p = $ NIL **then** n
  elseif $n.pi \neq i$ **then** GET-REP$_i$($n.p, i$)
  elseif $n.s = $ NIL **then** n
  else   GET-REP$_i$($n.s, i$)

MAKE-REP$_i$(n : NODE)
  if $n.s \neq $ NIL **then**
    if $n.s.pi \neq n.pi$ **then**
      $n.s := n.s.p$ move towards representative
      MAKE-REP$_i$(n)
    else
      MAKE-REP$_i$($n.s$)
      $n.s.s := n$ ⎫ invert secondary
      $n.s := $ NIL ⎭ edge

Fig. 3. Data structure and functions to represent weak equivalence relations. A NODE structure is created for every strong equivalence class on arrays. It contains two outgoing edges p, s pointing towards the representative of the weak equivalence classes. The functions GET-REP and GET-REP$_i$ are used to find the representative of the weak equivalence (resp. weak equivalence on i) class. The functions MAKE-REP and MAKE-REP$_i$ invert the edges to make a node the representative of its weak equivalence classes.

primary p and a secondary s, see Figure 3. The edges come from a store operation and correspond to the edges $\overset{i}{\leftrightarrow}$ in the weak equivalence graph. The index of the primary edge is stored in the pi field. The primary edge points towards the representative of the weak equivalence class. Every primary edge p connects the node representing (the strong equivalence class of) a store $a\langle j \lhd v \rangle$ with the node representing a and the corresponding index in the pi field is j. Note, however, that the direction of the edge can be arbitrary, as we invert the edges during the execution of the algorithm. If the primary edge is missing the node is the representative of its weak equivalence class. The procedure GET-REP(a) implements the algorithm that finds the representative.

While the primary edge is enough to represent the weak equivalence relation, we need another edge to represent weak equivalence on i. The representative of weak equivalence on i is usually found by following the primary edges. However, if the store of the primary edge is on the index i, the secondary edge is followed instead. If the secondary edge is missing the node is the representative of its weak equivalence on i class. The root node that has no outgoing primary edge must also not have any outgoing secondary edge and is the representative of all its weak equivalence on i classes. The procedure GET-REP$_i$(a, i) implements the algorithm that finds the representative on i.

The helper function MAKE-REP changes the representative of a weak equivalence class by inverting the primary edges. Similarly, the function MAKE-REP$_i$

ADD-SECONDARY(S : INDEX SET, a, b : NODE)
    if $a = b$ **then**
        return
    if $a.pi \notin S \wedge$ GET-REP$_i(a, a.pi) \neq b$ **then**
        MAKE-REP$_i(a)$
        $a.s := b$
    ADD-SECONDARY($S \cup \{a.pi\}, a.p, b$)

ADD-STORE(a, b : NODE, i : INDEX)
    MAKE-REP(b)
    if GET-REP(a) $= b$ **then**
        ADD-SECONDARY($\{i\}, a, b$)
    else
        $b.p := a$
        $b.pi := i$

Fig. 4. The algorithm ADD-STORE adds a new store edge to the data structure updating the weak equivalence classes. In the else case a new primary edge is added to merge two disjoint weak equivalence classes. Otherwise, ADD-SECONDARY inserts new secondary edges to merge the necessary weak equivalence on i classes.

inverts the secondary edges to change the representative of the weak equivalence on $n.pi$ class. It does not take the index as argument as it will always use $n.pi$. Note that the first method may temporarily violate the invariant that the representative does not have an outgoing secondary edge. To restore the invariant it calls the second method at the end.

Thus, the equivalence classes are represented as follows. Two arrays a and b are weakly equivalent iff GET-REP(a) = GET-REP(b) and they are weakly equivalent on i ($a \approx_i b$) iff GET-REP$_i(a, i)$ = GET-REP$_i(b, i)$.

The algorithm proceeds by inserting the store edges one by one, similarly to the algorithm presented in [12]. The algorithm that inserts a store edge is given in Figure 4. The algorithm first inverts the outgoing edges of one node to make it the representative of its weak equivalence class. If the other side of the store edge lies in a different weak equivalence class, the store can be inserted as a new primary edge.

If the nodes are already weakly equivalent, the procedure ADD-SECONDARY is called. This procedure follows the path from the other array a to the array b that was made the representative. For every node on this path it checks if a secondary edge needs to be added. If the primary edge of the node is labelled with a store on i, the algorithm first checks if the node is weakly equivalent on i with b due to the new store edge. This is the case if no store on i occurred on the path so far and the new store is also on an index different from i. We use the set S to collect these forbidden indices. Then if b is not already the representative of the weak equivalence on i class, the outgoing secondary edges are reversed and a new secondary edge is added.

The complexity of the procedure ADD-STORE is worst case quadratic in the size of the weak equivalence class. This stems from MAKE-REP$_i$ being linear in the size and being called a linear number of times by MAKE-REP. The overall complexity is cubic in the number of stores in the input formula. The space requirement, however, is only linear. In our current implementation in SMTInterpol this procedure was not a bottleneck so far.

The secondary edges are not directly between the arrays that are connected by a store. Instead the outgoing secondary edge for the weak equivalence on i

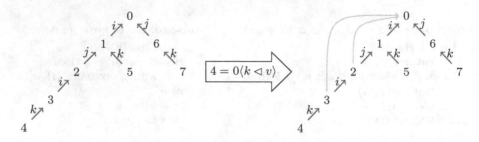

Fig. 5. Weak equivalence classes represented by a graph using primary and secondary edges. The short direct edges are primary edges, the long bent edges are secondary edges. Each primary edge represents a store edge between the connected nodes and is labelled by the index of the store. The secondary edges in the right graph were created by a store edge on index k between node 0 and 4 as described in Example 5.

class has to be placed at the root of the subtree of the weak equivalence tree where the primary edge has the index i. In fact, since a single store can connect the weak equivalence on i classes for multiple indices, there can be multiple secondary edges corresponding to the same store.

To reconstruct a weak equivalence paths, the data structure needs to associate each edge with the store that created it. Due to the fact that the secondary edges are not directly between the involved arrays the algorithm is slightly complicated. To find a weak equivalence on i path between two node, the first step is to determine the secondary edges between these nodes. It is guaranteed that the arrays involved in the secondary edge are connected by primary edges on indices different from i. Then a path of primary edges can be created that connect these endpoints. Finally, equality paths that connects the arrays involved in the end points of primary and secondary edges are produced by the equality solver.

Example 5. Figure 5 shows an example of the data structure where the primary edges are labelled by the index of the corresponding store. This data structure represents only one weak equivalence class with the representative node 0. The resulting data structure after adding a store with index k between nodes 0 and 4 is shown on the right. Since nodes 0 and 4 were already in the same weak equivalence class, secondary edges were added.

These secondary edges are needed to connect the weak equivalence on i and on j classes. Figure 6(a) shows how the first secondary edge connects the two weak equivalence on i classes rooted at nodes 0 resp. 3. This is necessary since there is now a new path using the edge from 4 to 0. Note that no secondary edge is added to node 1, since nodes 1, 2, and 5 are still not weakly equivalent on i to the other nodes. Figure 6(b) shows the connection between the two weak equivalence on j classes rooted at nodes 0 resp. 2. The weak equivalence on j class rooted at node 6 is not affected by a new edge between nodes 0 and 4 since these nodes are on a different path.

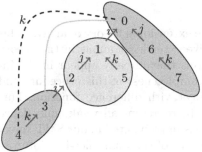

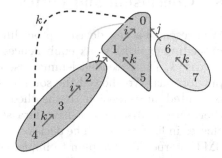

(a) Merging weak equivalence on i.   (b) Merging weak equivalence on j.

Fig. 6. Secondary edges merge weak equivalence on i classes.

Solver	Total (1042)	QF_AX	QF_ALIA (97)	QF_AUFLIA
Yices 2	92.67 (1042)	4.05	63.45 (97)	25.17
SMTInterpol				
(reset)	769.21 (1042)	70.96	468.24 (97)	230.01
(restart)	2663.03 (1042)	607.63	894.62 (97)	1160.78
Z3	5276.94 (1042)	27.77	5152.12 (97)	97.05
MathSAT	8626.92 (1023)	23.34	8507.60 (78)	95.98
CVC4	11121.47 (1022)	49.35	9402.96 (77)	1669.16

Table 1. Summary of the results of the divisions QF_AX, QF_ALIA, and QF_AUFLIA from the SMT-COMP 2014. The columns show the time in seconds and in parenthesis the number of benchmarks solved. In QF_AX and QF_AUFLIA all solvers solved all 335 resp. 610 benchmarks. To measure the start-up overhead of Java we also ran the benchmark in a single virtual machine using the **(reset)** command of SMT-LIB 2.5.

We implemented this decision procedure in our SMT solver SMTInterpol [6]. During SMTCOMP 2014, SMTInterpol could solve all array benchmarks in the division QF_AX, QF_ALIA, and QF_AUFLIA. Table 1 shows the summary of the results. In this competition, SMTInterpol (1042 out of 1042 in 2663 seconds) is runner up to Yices 2[2]. Since SMTInterpol is written in Java the start-up overhead for trivial benchmarks is significant. Without the start-up overhead we could run all benchmarks in a single script using the **(reset)** command (with the same benchmark scrambling) in 769 seconds[3]. Our solver performed best in the QF_ALIA benchmark set that is dominated by industrial benchmarks (82 %). The other benchmark sets contain mainly crafted benchmarks. For some of the crafted benchmarks it is possible to solve them by preprocessor techniques, which are not used in our solver.

---

[2] We are not aware of a publication describing the array decision procedure of Yices 2, but according to its developer it uses a similar technique.

[3] See https://www.starexec.org/starexec/secure/details/job.jsp?id=8631 for details (Login is public, password is public).

8   Conclusion and Future Work

We presented a new decision procedure for the extensional theory of arrays. This procedure exploits weak equivalences to derive extended lemmas in the theory of arrays. The extended lemmas use only terms that already appear in the input formula. We showed the soundness and completeness of this procedure and presented an extension to the theory of arrays with difference function. Furthermore we discussed a new data structure to represent all weak equivalence classes in linear space. The decision procedure is implemented in our SMT solver SMTInterpol [6]. We plan to implement a variant of the quantifier-free interpolation for arrays [4] based on the lemmas generated by this decision procedure as an extension of proof tree preserving interpolation [7].

References

1. Armando, A., Bonacina, M.P., Ranise, S., Schulz, S.: New results on rewrite-based satisfiability procedures. ACM Trans. Comput. Log. 10(1) (2009)
2. Barrett, C., Stump, A., Tinelli, C.: The SMT-LIB Standard: 2.0. In: SMT (2010)
3. Brummayer, R., Biere, A.: Lemmas on demand for the extensional theory of arrays. JSAT 6(1-3), 165–201 (2009)
4. Bruttomesso, R., Ghilardi, S., Ranise, S.: Quantifier-free interpolation of a theory of arrays. Logical Methods in Computer Science 8(2) (2012)
5. Christ, J., Hoenicke, J.: Weakly equivalent arrays. CoRR mabs/1405.6939 (2014). http://arxiv.org/abs/1405.6939
6. Christ, J., Hoenicke, J., Nutz, A.: SMTInterpol: An interpolating SMT solver. In: Donaldson, A., Parker, D. (eds.) SPIN 2012. LNCS, vol. 7385, pp. 248–254. Springer, Heidelberg (2012)
7. Christ, J., Hoenicke, J., Nutz, A.: Proof tree preserving interpolation. In: Piterman, N., Smolka, S.A. (eds.) TACAS 2013. LNCS, vol. 7795, pp. 124–138. Springer, Heidelberg (2013)
8. Craig, W.: Three uses of the Herbrand-Gentzen theorem in relating model theory and proof theory. J. Symb. Log. 22(3), 269–285 (1957)
9. Ganzinger, H., Hagen, G., Nieuwenhuis, R., Oliveras, A., Tinelli, C.: DPLL(T): Fast decision procedures. In: Alur, R., Peled, D.A. (eds.) CAV 2004. LNCS, vol. 3114, pp. 175–188. Springer, Heidelberg (2004)
10. McCarthy, J.: Towards a mathematical science of computation. In: IFIP Congress, pp. 21–28 (1962)
11. de Moura, L., Bjørner, N.: Generalized, efficient array decision procedures. In: FMCAD, pp. 45–52 (2009)
12. Nieuwenhuis, R., Oliveras, A.: Proof-producing congruence closure. In: Giesl, J. (ed.) RTA 2005. LNCS, vol. 3467, pp. 453–468. Springer, Heidelberg (2005)
13. Ranise, S., Ringeissen, C., Zarba, C.G.: Combining data structures with nonstably infinite theories using many-sorted logic. In: Gramlich, B. (ed.) FroCos 2005. LNCS (LNAI), vol. 3717, pp. 48–64. Springer, Heidelberg (2005)
14. Stump, A., Barrett, C.W., Dill, D.L., Levitt, J.R.: A decision procedure for an extensional theory of arrays. In: LICS, pp. 29–37. IEEE Computer Society (2001)

A Decision Procedure for Regular Membership and Length Constraints over Unbounded Strings*

Tianyi Liang[1], Nestan Tsiskaridze[1], Andrew Reynolds[2],
Cesare Tinelli[1], and Clark Barrett[3]

[1] Department of Computer Science, The University of Iowa
[2] École Polytechnique Fédérale de Lausanne
[3] Department of Computer Science, New York University

Abstract. We prove that the quantifier-free fragment of the theory of character strings with regular language membership constraints and linear integer constraints over string lengths is decidable. We do that by describing a sound, complete and terminating tableaux calculus for that fragment which uses as oracles a decision procedure for linear integer arithmetic and a number of computable functions over regular expressions. A distinguishing feature of this calculus is that it provides a completely algebraic method for solving membership constraints which can be easily integrated into multi-theory SMT solvers. Another is that it can be used to generate symbolic solutions for such constraints, that is, solved forms that provide simple and compact representations of entire sets of complete solutions. The calculus is part of a larger one providing the theoretical foundations of a high performance theory solver for string constraints implemented in the SMT solver CVC4.

1 Introduction

The study of word algebra and regular expressions has a long history in mathematics and computer science. There has been much renewed interest lately for these topics within the software verification and computer security communities because of the increasing importance of reasoning about character strings and regular expressions when proving safety properties or trying to detect security violations in programs that process string values.

To support these applications, several systems have been developed recently that check the satisfiability of constraints over a rich set of string operations including string equalities and inequalities, string length, regular language membership, and additional functions over strings besides string concatenation [34, 1, 19, 30]. A lot of this work focuses on generally (refutation) incomplete methods to detect the unsatisfiability of these constraints, a practical approach for making progress in program analysis applications. A major difficulty in providing complete methods is that any reasonably comprehensive theory of character strings is undecidable [7, 23, 27]. However, several more restricted, but

---

* This work was partially funded by NSF grants #1228765 and #1228768.

C. Lutz and S. Ranise (Eds.): FroCoS 2015, LNAI 9322, pp. 135–150, 2015.
DOI: 10.1007/978-3-319-24246-0_9

still quite useful, theories of strings do have a decidable satisfiability problem. These include any theories of fixed-length strings, which are trivially decidable because their domains are finite, but also some fragments over unbounded strings (e.g., word equations [22, 25]). Recent research has focused on identifying decidable fragments suitable for program analysis and, more crucially, on developing efficient solvers for them.

In previous work, we described a comprehensive approach, based on algebraic techniques and described abstractly as a calculus, to reason efficiently about quantifier-free formulas in a rich theory of unbounded strings with length and regular language membership [19]. And based on that approach, we constructed an efficient string solver, fully integrated into the multi-theory SMT solver CVC4. The calculus developed in that work is both refutation and solution sound but refutation incomplete.

Contribution and Significance. We have developed an improved version of the calculus presented in [19] that is also complete and terminating over a restriction of the general language to membership and length constraints. In this paper, we present a simplified version of that calculus which can be used to prove that the fragment in question is decidable. Strictly speaking, this decidability result is not new, as it is implicitly implied by some recent results from Abdulla *et al.* [1], although that work does not mention the result. We provide a full proof based on the calculus presented here. This contribution is significant not only because of the importance of the fragment but also for the following reasons. First, contrary to previous approaches for solving membership constraints which rely on reductions to finite state automata problems, our approach is completely algebraic and works directly with regular expressions. This facilitates the creation of efficient *incremental* solvers which can be more easily incorporated into modern SMT solvers since they do not rely on eager conversion to automata problems. Second, our completeness argument shows how to produce *symbolic solutions* for satisfiable problems with regular membership constraints, that is, intensional representations of (possibly infinite) sets of concrete solutions. This is useful for security analysis applications like filter generation and automatic exploit generation (AEG), where any assignment satisfying the constraints generated from a program is a security exploit. A symbolic solution enables AEG applications, for example, to generate fewer, more general exploits, thus also reducing the number of exploits that would need to be examined by a user.

Although our eventual goal is overall efficiency in practice, the calculus presented here focuses (for simplicity) on proving the decidability result. As a consequence, it uses a few auxiliary functions that apply generally inefficient eager (but algebraic) conversions from and to regular expressions. We plan to present in future work a version of the calculus that lifts these conversions to a set of additional derivation rules, making them amenable to lazy and selective application based on search heuristics.

1.1   Related Work

There have been a number of different approaches for solving string constraints with regular expressions. The earliest and perhaps most established approach is based on reductions to automata decision problems. One of these was implemented in the system DPRLE, used to check programs against SQL injection vulnerabilities [13]. The approach followed in that system has the strong limitation of imposing an upper bound on the length of string variables, a hard to overcome drawback shared by various later works. This approach was later improved by the same author with a method for generating automata lazily from the input problem which does not requiring any *priori* length bounds [14]. At the same time, a comprehensive set of algorithms and data structures for performing fast automata operations was developed to support constraint solving over strings, for instance in [12].

Current automata-based approaches to reason about regular expressions can be divided in two classes depending on whether their transitions processing a single character a time (e.g., [9, 33]) or a set of them (e.g., [31, 32, 14]). Most of the tools based on these approaches offer very limited support to reason about constraints mixing strings and other data types. Also, automata refinement may constitute a performance bottleneck, even though it is very useful in solving membership constraints. Further discussion can be found in [10, 18]. Other approaches for solving regular expression constraints are based on reductions to other theories, such as bit-vectors [15] or linear integer arithmetic constraints [29], [7], and using constraint solvers for those theories.

Three notable systems that solve regular membership constraints are REX [32, 31], MONA [11] and the Java String Analyzer (JSA) [8]. REX too is based on automata. In contrast to the work described in [14] where each transitions covers an integer interval, Rex encodes strings as symbolic finite automata (SFA) first. Each SFA transition uses a logical predicate over linear arithmetic to represent a set of character-level candidates. This allows REX to encode transitions as SMT constraints which it then sends to an SMT solver for a model. This approach provides an efficient encoding for solving membership constraints, however, it currently does not support mixed constraints over additional theories.

MONA is a solver for monadic second-order logic with built-in support for string constraints. Although MONA is an automata-based, it uses Multi Terminal BDDs to represent automata. This kind of implementation requires sophisticated engineering techniques (see [16]) which make it difficult to build in additional theories to support solving of combined constraints. PISA [28] is another string solver based monadic second-order logic. However, the language of PISA is rather restrictive, e.g., no binary operations between two variables are allowed.

JSA is geared specifically to Java string constraints. It first translates them to a flow graph, and then analyzes the graph by converting it to a context-free language. This language is approximated with the Mohri-Nederhof algorithm to a regular one and encoded as a multi-level automaton. Compared to our work, JSA focuses exclusively on Java string analysis, approximation, and automaton conversion, while our approach does not depend on any particular language, and solves string constraints natively with no approximations.

It is well-known that regular languages are closed under common operations (e.g., concatenation, union, intersection, complementation); however, the complexity of performing most of these operations is high as a consequence of the high complexity of the corresponding membership problem. For example, membership in the intersection of two regular languages is PSPACE-complete [17]. Thus, in practice many procedure implementing regular language operations are approximate (e.g., [6, 26]). In contrast, the calculus we present here does not approximate.

Our calculus decides a fragment that combines regular membership constraints with string length constraints. To the best of our knowledge, there are no explicit claims about the decidability of this fragment. The work in [1] implies that the fragment is indeed decidable, although the paper contains no proof, or mention, of this. The method described in that paper replaces all characters in regular expressions with a single arbitrary character, and reduces the expression to their Parikh images [24], generating a set of *semi-linear* integer constraints which can then be checked for satisfiability using any linear arithmetic solver. Since our approach does not use rely on approximations it can build a model directly when the constraints are satisfiable. This part of work our has some similarities with the Parikh image described in [4], although we developed it independently.

1.2   Formal Preliminaries

We work in the context of many-sorted first-order logic with equality ($\approx$). We assume the reader is familiar with the notions of many-sorted signature, term, literal, formula, free variable, interpretation, and satisfiability of a formula in an interpretation (see, e.g., [5] for more details). A *theory* is a pair $T = (\Sigma, \mathbf{I})$ where Σ is a signature and $\mathbf{I}$ is a class of Σ-interpretations, the *models* of T, that is closed under variable reassignment. If $\mathcal{I}$ is an interpretation and t is a term, we denote by $t^{\mathcal{I}}$ the value of t in $\mathcal{I}$. A Σ-formula φ is *T-satisfiable* (resp., *T-unsatisfiable*) if it is satisfied by some (resp., no) interpretation in $\mathbf{I}$. A set Γ of formulas *entails in* T a Σ-formula φ, written $\Gamma \models_T \varphi$, if every interpretation in $\mathbf{I}$ that satisfies all formulas in Γ satisfies φ as well. The set Γ is *satisfiable in* T if $\Gamma \not\models_T \bot$ where $\bot$ is the universally false atom. If e is a term or a formula, we denote by $\mathcal{V}(e)$ the set of e's free variables, extending the notation to sets of terms or formulas as expected. Two Σ-formulas φ and ψ are *T-equisatisfiable* if for every model $\mathcal{I}$ of T that satisfies one, there is a model of T that satisfies the other and differs from $\mathcal{I}$ at most over the free variables not shared by φ and ψ.

2   A Theory of Strings and Regular Language Membership

We consider a theory T_{LR} of strings with length and regular language membership constraints over a signature Σ_{LR} with three sorts, Str, Int, and Lan, and an infinite set of variables for each of these sorts. This theory is essentially the theory of a single many-sorted structure and its models differ only on how the variables are

ϵ : Str $\_ \cdot \_$: Str $\times$ Str $\to$ Str c : Str for all $c \in \mathcal{A}$ $|\_|$: Str $\to$ Int

Ch : Lan $\_ \cdot \_$: Lan $\times$ Lan $\to$ Lan $\_ \sqcup \_$: Lan $\times$ Lan $\to$ Lan $\_^*$: Lan $\to$ Lan

$\varnothing$: Lan $\_$ in $\_$: Str $\times$ Lan $\_ \sqcap \_$: Lan $\times$ Lan $\to$ Lan $\ulcorner \_ \urcorner$: Str $\to$ Lan

Fig. 1. Basic set of string and regular expression function and predicate symbols.

$(\_)^{(\_)}$: Lan $\times$ Int $\to$ Lan   sh : Lan $\times$ Lan $\times$ Lan $\to$ Lan

Fig. 2. Additional regular expression function symbols.

interpreted. All models of T_{LR} interpret Int as the set of integer numbers, Str as the language $\mathcal{W}$ of all words over some fixed finite alphabet $\mathcal{A}$ of *characters*, and Lan as the power set of $\mathcal{W}$. The signature includes: the usual symbols of linear integer arithmetic, interpreted as expected; all the elements of $\mathcal{W}$ as constant symbols, or *string constants*, interpreted as themselves; and all the function symbols given in Figure 1 with their rank. In that figure, the two $\cdot$ symbols denote word concatenation and language concatenation, respectively; $|\_|$ denotes word length; and $\ulcorner \_ \urcorner$ denotes the singleton set constructor, mapping each word $w \in \mathcal{W}$ to the language $\{w\}$; the symbols ϵ, Ch, $\varnothing$, and in respectively denote the empty word, the language of one-character words, the empty language, and the language membership predicate; the symbols $\sqcup$, $\sqcap$, and $(\_)^*$ respectively denote language union, intersection and Kleene closure.

We call a *string term* any term of sort Str or of the form $|s|$; an *arithmetic term* any term of sort Int all of whose occurrences of $|\_|$ are applied to a variable; and a *regular expression* any *variable-free* term of sort Lan. A string term is *atomic* if it is a variable or a string constant. An *arithmetic constraint* is a (dis)equality $(\neg)u \approx v$ or an inequality $u \geq v$ where u and v are arithmetic terms. A *membership constraint* is a literal of the form $(\neg)(s \in r)$ where s is a string term and r is a regular expression. A T_{LR}-*constraint* is an arithmetic or a membership constraint. Note that we do not consider here equalities between terms of sort Str. Also note that if x is a string variable, $|x|$ is both a string and an arithmetic term. By the definition of T_{LR}, a regular expression r is interpreted as the same language in every model of T_{LR}. We call that the *language generated by* r and denote it by $\mathcal{L}(r)$.

Expanding the Language. The calculus we present later is able to compute a *solved form* for a satisfiable input set of T_{LR}-constraints with string variables $x_1, \ldots, x_n$. This solved form consists of a set $\{x_i \text{ in } q_i\}_{i=1,\ldots,n}$ of membership constraints where, for all i, q_i is a *solved-form* term, a term of sort Lan over integer variables and a signature that includes string constants, the symbols Ch, $\cdot$ and $\ulcorner \_ \urcorner$ from Figure 1, and the two function symbols from Figure 2. Note that the latter two symbols are not in the (input) language of T_{LR}-constraints; they are used only in solved forms. We expand the models of T_{LR} to these two symbols so that the following holds.

- For all integers n and regular expressions r, $\mathcal{L}(r^n) = \{\epsilon\}$ if $n \leq 0$ and $\mathcal{L}(r^n) = \mathcal{L}(r \cdot r^{n-1})$ otherwise.

$$(s_1 \cdot s_2) \cdot s_3 \;\to\; s_1 \cdot (s_2 \cdot s_3) \qquad\qquad s \cdot \epsilon \to s \qquad \epsilon \cdot s \to s$$

$$|s_1 \cdot s_2| \;\to\; |s_1| + |s_2| \qquad\qquad |c| \to 1 \qquad |\epsilon| \to 0$$

$$r_1 \cdot (r_2 \sqcup r_3) \;\to\; (r_1 \cdot r_2) \sqcup (r_1 \cdot r_3) \qquad \ulcorner\epsilon\urcorner \cdot r \to r \qquad \varnothing \cdot r \to \varnothing$$

$$(r_1 \sqcup r_2) \cdot r_3 \;\to\; (r_1 \cdot r_3) \sqcup (r_2 \cdot r_3) \qquad r \cdot \ulcorner\epsilon\urcorner \to r \qquad r \cdot \varnothing \to \varnothing$$

$$\ulcorner s_1 \urcorner \cdot \ulcorner s_2 \urcorner \;\to\; \ulcorner s_1 \cdot s_2 \urcorner \qquad\qquad r^{**} \to r^* \qquad \ulcorner\epsilon\urcorner^* \to \ulcorner\epsilon\urcorner$$

$$r \sqcup r \;\to\; r \qquad\qquad (r \sqcup \ulcorner\epsilon\urcorner)^* \to r^* \qquad \varnothing^* \to \ulcorner\epsilon\urcorner$$

$$r_1 \sqcap r_2 \;\to\; \pi(r_1, r_2) \qquad\qquad \varnothing \sqcup r \to r \qquad \varnothing \sqcap r \to \varnothing$$

Fig. 3. Term normalization rules, defined modulo commutativity of $\sqcup$ and $\sqcap$; $\pi(r_1, r_2)$ is the regular expression computed by the function π defined in Figure 8.

- For all regular expressions r, r', q, $\mathcal{L}(\mathsf{sh}(r, r', q)) = \{w_1 w_1' \cdots w_n w_n' \in \mathcal{L}(q) \mid n > 0, \; w_1 \cdots w_n \in \mathcal{L}(r), \; w_1' \cdots w_n' \in \mathcal{L}(r')\}.$[1]

Intuitively, the strings generated by $\mathsf{sh}(r, r', q)$ can be obtained by *shuffling* together a word w generated by r and a word w' generated by r', as long as the resulting word is in the language generated by q. Shuffling is achieved by breaking w and w' arbitrarily into n segments and merging the two lists of segments together.

Notational Conventions. We use c, d to denote *character constants*, that is, string constants of length one; l for arbitrary string constants; x for string variables; s, t for string terms; z for integer variables; u, v for arithmetic terms; and q, r for regular expressions. We will omit applications of the $\ulcorner\_\urcorner$ operator, treating (variable-free) terms of sort Str as the corresponding regular expression. When convenient, we will treat a multi-character constant l as the term $c \cdot l'$ where c is the first character of l and l' is the rest of l. We will write $\models_{\mathsf{LR}}$ instead of $\models_{T_{\mathsf{LR}}}$.

3   A Calculus for Constraint Satisfiability in T_{LR}

We are interested in checking the satisfiability in T_{LR} of finite sets of T_{LR}-constraints as defined in Section 2. In this section, we describe a tableaux-style calculus that can be used to construct a decision procedure for this problem.

Configurations. The calculus applies to a finite set of T_{LR}-constraints with the goal of determining their T_{LR}-satisfiability. It consists of derivation rules that operate over *configurations*. A configuration is either the distinguished configuration unsat or a tuple of the form $\langle A, R, V \rangle$, where: A is a set of arithmetic constraints and implications of the form $z_1 \approx 0 \Rightarrow z_2 \approx 0$; R is a set of *positive* membership constraints; and V is a set of membership constraints in solved form.

Informally, the sets A and R initially store a T_{LR}-equisatisfiable variant of the input set and progressively receive additional constraints derived by the calculus;

---

[1]   Any of the words $w_1, \ldots, w_n, w_1', \ldots, w_n'$ in the definition of sh could be empty. We use juxtaposition to denote word concatenation at the semantic level.

$$\text{A-Conflict}\ \frac{A \models_{\mathsf{LIA}} \bot}{\text{unsat}} \qquad \text{EmptyS}\ \frac{\epsilon \text{ in } r \in R \quad \text{not } \varepsilon(r)}{\text{unsat}} \qquad \text{EmptyR}\ \frac{s \text{ in } \varnothing \in R}{\text{unsat}}$$

$$\text{Assign-1}\ \frac{R = R,\ x \text{ in } l}{A := A,\ |x| \approx |l|\!\downarrow \quad R := (R\{x \mapsto l\})\!\downarrow \quad V := V,\ x \text{ in } l}$$

$$\text{Assign-2}\ \frac{R = R,\ x \text{ in } r \quad x \notin \mathcal{V}(R) \quad \text{top}(r) \notin \{\sqcup, \varnothing\} \quad \gamma(r) = (q, u, A)}{A := A,\ |x| \approx u\!\downarrow,\ A\!\downarrow \quad R := R \quad V := V,\ x \text{ in } q}$$

$$\text{Consume-1}\ \frac{R = R,\ c \text{ in } r}{R := R,\ \epsilon \text{ in } (\partial_c\, r)\!\downarrow} \qquad \text{Consume-2}\ \frac{R = R,\ c \cdot s \text{ in } r}{R := R,\ s \text{ in } (\partial_c\, r)\!\downarrow}$$

$$\text{Split}\ \frac{R := R,\ x \cdot s \text{ in } r}{\|_{(r_1, r_2) \in \beta(r)}\ R := R,\ x \text{ in } r_1\!\downarrow,\ s \text{ in } r_2\!\downarrow}$$

$$\text{Inter}\ \frac{R := R,\ s \text{ in } r_1,\ s \text{ in } r_2}{R := R,\ s \text{ in } (r_1 \sqcap r_2)\!\downarrow} \qquad \text{Union}\ \frac{R := R,\ s \text{ in } r_1 \sqcup r_2}{R := R,\ s \text{ in } r_1 \quad \| \quad R := R,\ s \text{ in } r_2}$$

Fig. 4. Derivation Rules. $R\{x \mapsto l\}$ is the result of applying the substitution $\{x \mapsto l\}$ to every term in R; $\text{top}(r)$ is the top symbol of term r.

V, which is initially empty, represents the solution computed so far (each string variable in V is associated with a set of possible values using solved-form terms).

By standard transformations, one can convert any finite set of T_{LR}-constraints into a T_{LR}-equisatisfiable set $A \cup R$ where R is a set of positive membership constraints [2] and A is a set of arithmetic constraints that includes a constraint of the form $|x| \geq 0$ for every string variable $x \in \mathcal{V}(A)$ and contains no string variables that do not occur in R. We assume that all terms in such configurations are irreducible by the rewrite system in Figure 3 which can be shown to be equivalence-preserving and terminating over Σ_{LR}-terms.[3] The rewrite system uses the auxiliary function π, closely based on one by Lu [21], which maps two regular expressions r_1 and r_2 to a regular expression that generates the same language as $r_1 \sqcap r_2$ (i.e., $\mathcal{L}(\pi(r_1, r_2)) = \mathcal{L}(r_1 \sqcap r_2)$) but contains no occurrences of $\sqcap$. If t is a Σ_{LR}-term, we denote by $t\!\downarrow$ any normal form of t with respect to the rewrite system in Figure 3, and extend this notation to sets of Σ_{LR}-terms as expected. We call a term t *normalized* if $t = t\!\downarrow$.

Without loss of generality, *we will consider for our calculus only starting configurations* $\langle A, R, \emptyset \rangle$ *where A, R are as above.*

The calculus assumes the availability of a procedure for checking entailment in the (decidable) theory of linear integer arithmetic ($\models_{\mathsf{LIA}}$). The only significant deviation we require is that the procedure be able to accept terms of the form $|x|$, where x is a string variable, by treating the whole term as an arithmetic variable.

---

[2] Each negative membership constraint $s \notin r$ can be replaced by $s \in r^c$ where r^c is a regular expression generating the complement of $\mathcal{L}(r)$. This replacement is effective although current procedures for computing r^c are generally inefficient in practice.

[3] The system is not confluent but we do not need it to be.

In essence, the calculus models a solver for T_{LR}-constraints that is based on the cooperation of a standard subsolver for linear arithmetic constraints and a novel subsolver that processes membership constraints natively, without reduction to automata problems. This is done by processing regular expressions by means of algebraic manipulations and non-deterministic choices. The two subsolvers communicate by exchanging linear arithmetic constraints over string lengths.

Derivation Rules. The rules of the calculus are provided in Figure 4 in *guarded assignment form* where fields A, R, and V store, in order, the components of a current configuration $\langle A, R, V \rangle$. A derivation rule applies to a current configuration C if all of the rule's premises hold for C *and* the resulting configuration is different from C. A rule's conclusion describes how each component of C is changed, if at all. In the rules, we write S, t as an abbreviation for $S \cup \{t\}$. Rules with two or more conclusions separated by the symbol ‖ are non-deterministic branching rules.

The derivation rules rely on several computable functions and predicates, described below and defined formally in Figures 5, 6, 7, 8, and 9, which apply to ⊓-free regular expressions.

- The family of functions $(\partial_c)_{c \in \mathcal{A}}$ computes the *partial derivative* of the input with respect to character c. Concretely, $\partial_c(r)$ is a regular expression whose language is the set of all words w (including the empty one) such that $cw \in \mathcal{L}(r)$.

- The predicate ε holds exactly for those regular expressions whose language contains the empty string ϵ.

- The function γ produces three outputs from a normalized regular expression r with top symbol other than $\varnothing$ or $\sqcup$: a solved-form term q, an arithmetic term u, and a set A of arithmetic constraints over the (integer) variables in q and u. Intuitively, u and A together express constraints on the possible lengths of the words in $\mathcal{L}(r)$.

- The function β returns a finite set of regular expression pairs. Each pair $(r_1, r_2) \in \beta(r)$ is such that $\mathcal{L}(r) = \mathcal{L}(r_1 \cdot r_2)$. Moreover, $\beta(r)$ is exhaustive in the sense that for every pair of words w_1, w_2 such that $w_1 w_2 \in \mathcal{L}(r)$, there is a pair $(r_1, r_2) \in \beta(r)$ such that $w_1 \in \mathcal{L}(r_1)$ and $w_2 \in \mathcal{L}(r_2)$.

The definition of the partial derivative functions is due to Antimirov [2]; the functions γ and β are novel. Given these auxiliary predicates and functions, the calculus rules should be self-explanatory, with the possible exception of Assign-2. This rule considers a membership constraint $(x \text{ in } r)$ where r is not a union and (by construction) contains no occurrences of $\varnothing$ and ⊓. If x occurs in no other membership constraints in the R component of the configuration, the rule uses γ to compute a solution form of $(x \text{ in } r)$ and stores it in the V component.

Derivation Trees and Derivations. The rules in this calculus are used to construct derivation trees. A *derivation tree* is a tree where each node is a configuration and each non-root node is obtained from its parent node by applying

$$\varepsilon(r) \quad \text{iff} \quad (r = r_1 \cdot r_2 \text{ and } \varepsilon(r_1) \text{ and } \varepsilon(r_2)) \quad \text{or} \quad r = \epsilon \quad \text{or} \quad r = r_1^* \quad \text{or}$$
$$(r = r_1 \sqcup r_2 \text{ and } \varepsilon(r_1)) \quad \text{or} \quad (r = r_1 \sqcup r_2 \text{ and } \varepsilon(r_2))$$

Fig. 5. Definition of predicate ε.

$$\partial_c \varnothing = \varnothing \qquad \partial_c(r_1 \sqcup r_2) = \partial_c r_1 \sqcup \partial_c r_2 \qquad\qquad \partial_c(c \cdot s) = s$$
$$\partial_c \epsilon = \varnothing \qquad \partial_c(r_1 \cdot r_2) = (\partial_c r_1 \cdot r_2) \sqcup \partial_c r_2 \quad \text{if } \varepsilon(r_1)$$
$$\partial_c \, \mathsf{Ch} = \epsilon \qquad \partial_c(r_1 \cdot r_2) = \partial_c r_1 \cdot r_2 \quad \text{if not } \varepsilon(r_1)$$
$$\partial_c(r^*) = (\partial_c r) \cdot r^* \qquad \partial_c(d \cdot s) = \varnothing \quad \text{if } c \neq d$$

Fig. 6. Definition of partial derivative function ∂_c.

one of the derivation rules. We call the root of a derivation tree an *initial* configuration. A branch of a derivation tree is *saturated* if no rules apply to its leaf, it is *closed* if it ends with unsat. A derivation tree is *closed* if all of its branches are closed.

A derivation tree *derives* from a derivation tree T if it is obtained from T by the application of exactly one of the derivation rules to one of T's leaves. A *derivation* is a sequence $(T_i)_{i \geq 0}$ of derivation trees such that T_0 is a one-node tree whose root is an initial configuration and T_{i+1} derives from T_i for all $i \geq 0$.

Let S be a set of Σ_{LR}-constraints. A *refutation of set* S is a derivation that starts with a one-node tree with a configuration $\langle A, R, \emptyset \rangle$ where $A \cup R$ is T_{LR}-equisatisfiable with S, and ends with a closed tree.

Example 1. Consider the satisfiable initial configuration with $\mathsf{A} = \emptyset$, $\mathsf{V} = \emptyset$, and $\mathsf{R} = \{bc \cdot x \text{ in } ((aa \sqcup b)^* \cdot c)^* \sqcup a \cdot c^*\}$ where x is a variable of sort String and a, b, c are characters. A derivation in the calculus can start with an application of the Union rule. In the branch $bc \cdot x$ in $a \cdot c^*$, Consume-2 will apply and replace the constraint with $c \cdot x$ in $\varnothing$ which then will be closed by EmptyR. In the branch $bc \cdot x$ in $((aa \sqcup b)^* \cdot c)^*$, Consume-2 will be applied twice: once for b, resulting in $\mathsf{R} = \{c \cdot x \text{ in } (aa \sqcup b)^* \cdot c \cdot ((aa \sqcup b)^* \cdot c)^*\}$; and once for c, resulting in $\mathsf{R} = \{x \text{ in } ((aa \sqcup b)^* \cdot c)^*\}$. Now, by applying Assign-2 to the resulting configuration, we will have the following saturated configuration:

$$\mathsf{A} = \{z_1 \geq 0, \, z_2 \geq 0, \, z_3 \geq 0, \, z_4 \geq 0, \, z_1 \approx 0 \Rightarrow z_2 \approx 0\} \quad \mathsf{R} = \emptyset \quad \mathsf{V} = \{x \text{ in } q_2\}$$
$$\cup \, \{z_2 \approx z_3 + z_4, \, |x| \approx 2 * z_3 + z_4 + z_1\}$$

where $q_2 = \mathsf{sh}(q_1, c^{z_1}, r_1)$, $q_1 = \mathsf{sh}((aa)^{z_3}, b^{z_4}, r_2)$, $r_1 = ((aa \sqcup b)^* \cdot c)^{z_1}$, $r_2 = (aa \sqcup b)^{z_2}$, and $z_1, \dots, z_4$ are fresh variables of sort Int. The set in A is satisfiable, for instance with the variable assignment $\{z_1 \mapsto 1, z_2 \mapsto 2, z_3 \mapsto 1, z_4 \mapsto 1, |x| \mapsto 4\}$. Given this assignment one can evaluate—deterministically—the term q_2 inside out and obtain $q_2 = \{aabc, baac\}$ after evaluating q_1 to $\{aab, baa\}$. At this point, any element of q_2 is a solution for x in the original problem. As we show later, any other satisfying assignment for A will lead to a ground expression for q_2 that is guaranteed to generate a non-empty language of solutions for x. □

Example 2. Suppose we start with the unsatisfiable configuration with $\mathsf{A} = \{|x| \approx 2 * k + 1\}$, $\mathsf{R} = \{x \cdot x \text{ in } r\}$, and $\mathsf{V} = \emptyset$ where $r = (aaaa)^*$ and a

$$\beta(\varnothing) = \emptyset \qquad\qquad \beta(c) = \{(c, \epsilon), (\epsilon, c)\} \qquad\qquad \beta(r_1 \sqcup r_2) = \beta(r_1) \cup \beta(r_2)$$
$$\beta(\epsilon) = \{(\epsilon, \epsilon)\} \qquad \beta(\mathsf{Ch}) = \{(\mathsf{Ch}, \epsilon), (\epsilon, \mathsf{Ch})\}$$
$$\beta(r^*) = \beta(\epsilon) \cup \{(r^* \cdot r_1, r_2 \cdot r^*) \mid (r_1, r_2) \in \beta(r)\}$$
$$\beta(r_1 \cdot r_2) = \{(r_{11}, r_{12} \cdot r_2) \mid (r_{11}, r_{12}) \in \beta(r_1)\} \cup \{(r_1 \cdot r_{21}, r_{22}) \mid (r_{21}, r_{22}) \in \beta(r_2)\}$$

Fig. 7. Definition of splitting function β.

$$\pi(r, r') = \pi'(r, r', \emptyset) \qquad \pi'(r, r', C) = y_{r,r'} \text{ if } y_{r,r'} \in C \qquad \pi'(r, \varnothing, C) = \varnothing$$
$$\pi'(\epsilon, r, C) = \epsilon \text{ if } \varepsilon(r) \qquad \pi'(\epsilon, r, C) = \varnothing \text{ if not } \varepsilon(r) \qquad \pi'(\varnothing, r, C) = \varnothing$$
$$\pi'(r, \epsilon, C) = \epsilon \text{ if } \varepsilon(r) \qquad \pi'(r, \epsilon, C) = \varnothing \text{ if not } \varepsilon(r) \qquad \pi'(r, r, C) = r$$
$$\pi'(r, r', C) = r_1^* \cdot r_1' \text{ if } v_{r,r'} \notin C \text{ and } \varepsilon(r) \text{ and } \varepsilon(r') \text{ where}$$
$$(r_1, r_1') = \rho_{v_{r,r'}}(\epsilon \sqcup \bigsqcup_{c \in \mathcal{A}} c \cdot \pi'(\partial_c r, \partial_c r', C')), \quad C' = C \cup \{v_{r,r'}\}$$
$$\pi(r, r', C) = r_1^* \cdot r_1' \text{ if } v_{r,r'} \notin C \text{ and not } (\varepsilon(r) \text{ and } \varepsilon(r')) \text{ where}$$
$$(r_1, r_1') = \rho_{v_{r,r'}}(\bigsqcup_{c \in \mathcal{A}} c \cdot \pi'(\partial_c r, \partial_c r', C')), \quad C' = C \cup \{v_{r,r'}\}$$

$$\rho_y(\varnothing) = (\varnothing, \varnothing) \qquad \rho_y(y) = (\epsilon, \varnothing) \qquad \rho_y(r) = (\epsilon, r) \text{ if } y \notin \mathcal{V}(r)$$
$$\rho_y(r) = (r_1 \cdot r_{21}, r_{22}) \text{ if } y \in \mathcal{V}(r), \ r = r_1 \cdot r_2, \text{ and } (r_{21}, r_{22}) = \rho_y(r_2)$$
$$\rho_y(r) = (r_{11} \sqcup r_{21}, r_{12} \sqcup r_{22}) \text{ if } y \in \mathcal{V}(r), \ r = r_1 \sqcup r_2, \text{ and } (r_{i1}, r_{i2}) = \rho_y(r_i)$$

Fig. 8. Definition of intersection function π.

is a character. One possibility is to apply the Split rule. Since $\beta(r) = \{(\epsilon, \epsilon),$ $(r \cdot a, aaa \cdot r), (r \cdot a, aaa \cdot r), (r \cdot aa, aa \cdot r), (r \cdot aaa, a \cdot r)\}$, four branches will be created. In the first branch, $\mathsf{R} = \{x \text{ in } \epsilon\}$. The rule Assign-1 can be applied, adding x in ϵ to V and $|x| \approx 0$ to A. After that, the branch can be closed by A-Conflict. In the second branch, $\mathsf{R} = \{x \text{ in } r \cdot a, x \text{ in } aaa \cdot r\}$ to which Inter can be applied, replacing the constraints in R with x in $\varnothing$. Then the branch can be closed by EmptyS. Something, similar can be done on the fourth branch. In the third branch, R can become $\{x \text{ in } aa \cdot r\}$ by Inter. Then $|x| \approx 2 + 4 * z$ and $z \geq 0$ can be added to A by Assign-2, with z a fresh integer variable. That branch can be closed by A-Conflict, yielding a refutation of the input problem.   □

4   Calculus Correctness

We prove the correctness of the calculus in by showing that (i) it has no infinite derivations; (ii) its rules preserve satisfiability in T_{LR}; (iii) every saturated branch in a derivation tree determines a model of T_{LR} that satisfies the initial configuration. Together with the termination of the auxiliary functions and procedures used by the calculus, this implies the decidability of the quantifier-free satisfiability problem for T_{LR}.[4]

---

[4] For space constraints, the most of the proofs of these results are omitted. The interested reader is referred to the longer version of this paper [20] for the missing proofs.

$$\gamma(r) = \gamma'(r, \emptyset)$$

$$\gamma'(l, A) = (l, |l|\Downarrow, A) \qquad\qquad \gamma'(\mathsf{Ch}, A) = (\mathsf{Ch}, 1, A)$$

$$\gamma'(r_1 \cdot r_2, A) = (q_1 \cdot q_2, u_1 + u_2, A_1 \cup A_2) \text{ where } (q_i, u_i, A_i) = \gamma'(r_i, A) \text{ for } i = 1, 2$$

$$\gamma'(r^*, A) = (q, u, B \cup \{z_1 \geq 0\}) \text{ where } (q, u, B) = \gamma'(r^{z_1}, A)$$

$$\gamma'(l^z, A) = (l^z, z \times |l|\Downarrow, A) \qquad \gamma'(\mathsf{Ch}^z, A) = (\mathsf{Ch}^z, z, A)$$

$$\gamma'((r_1 \sqcup r_2)^z, A) = (\mathsf{sh}(q_1, q_2, (r_1 \sqcup r_2)^z), u_1 + u_2, B)$$

$$\text{where } B = A_1 \cup A_2 \cup \{z \approx z_1 + z_2, z_1 \geq 0, z_2 \geq 0\}$$
$$(q_i, u_i, A_i) = \gamma'(r_i^{z_i}, A) \text{ for } i = 1, 2$$

$$\gamma'((r_1 \cdot r_2)^z, A) = (\mathsf{sh}(q_1, q_2, (r_1 \cdot r_2)^z), u_1 + u_2, A_1 \cup A_2)$$

$$\text{where } (q_i, u_i, A_i) = \gamma'(r_i^z, A) \text{ for } i = 1, 2$$

$$\gamma'((r^*)^z, A) = \gamma'(q, u, B \cup \{z \approx 0 \Rightarrow z_1 \approx 0, z_1 \geq 0\}) \text{ where } (q, u, B) = \gamma'(r^{z_1}, A)$$

Fig. 9. Definition of function γ. The letters z_1 and z_2 denote fresh integer variables variables variables variables variables.

4.1 Termination

Proving the termination of the auxiliary functions and predicates is a simple exercise.

Proposition 1. *The function π is well defined and computable over the set of all regular expressions. The predicate ε and the functions ∂_c, β and γ are well defined and computable over the set of all $\sqcap$-free regular expressions.*

By Proposition 1, every rule is effective. To prove the termination of the calculus it suffices to define a well-founded ordering of configurations and show that every rule application produces a smaller configuration along that ordering.

Proposition 2. *Every derivation in the calculus is finite.*

Proof (Sketch). One can show that every application of a derivation rule to a leaf of a derivation tree produces smaller configurations with respect to a well-founded relation $\succ$ over configurations which implies that no derivation tree can be grown indefinitely.

The relation $\succ$ is defined as follows. To each configuration $\langle A, R, V \rangle$ we associate a tuple $(\mathcal{V}(R), \mathrm{ms}(R), \mathrm{occ}(R))$ where $\mathrm{ms}(R)$ is the *multiset* $\{s \mid s \text{ in } r \in \mathsf{R}\}$ and $\mathrm{occ}(R)$ is the number of occurrences of $\sqcup$ in R. Let $\succ_{\mathsf{Str}}$ be the ordering over string terms such that $s \succ_{\mathsf{Str}} t$ iff s has a greater term size than t, with the convention that ϵ has size 0. Let $\succ_{\mathrm{lex}}$ be the lexicographic extension of the following orderings to tuples like $(\mathcal{V}(R), \mathrm{ms}(R), \mathrm{occ}(R))$ above: the set inclusion ordering; the multiset ordering extending $\succ_{\mathsf{Str}}$; the $>$ ordering over natural numbers. Finally, define $\succ$ where (i) $\langle A_1, R_1, V_1 \rangle \succ \langle A_2, R_2, V_2 \rangle$ iff $(\mathcal{V}(R_1), \mathrm{ms}(R_1), \mathrm{occ}(R_1)) \succ_{\mathrm{lex}} (\mathcal{V}(R_2), \mathrm{ms}(R_2), \mathrm{occ}(R_2))$ and (ii) $\langle A, R, V \rangle \succ \mathsf{unsat}$. The well foundedness of $\succ$ follows by standard results (see e.g., [3]). $\qquad\square$

4.2   Correctness

To prove the correctness of the calculus we use the following properties of the various auxiliary functions.

Lemma 1 (Correctness of Normalization). *Every rule in Figure 3 preserves term equivalence in T_{LR}.*

Lemma 2 (Correctness of π). *For any regular expressions r_1 and r_2, $\pi(r_1, r_2)$ contains no occurrences of $\sqcap$. Moreover, $\mathcal{L}(\pi(r_1, r_2)) = \mathcal{L}(r_1 \sqcap r_2)$.*

Lemma 3. *For all normalized regular expressions r and for all characters $c \in \mathcal{A}$, the following hold:*

1. *$\varepsilon(r)$ iff $\epsilon \in \mathcal{L}(r)$;*
2. *$\mathcal{L}(\partial_c r) = \{w \mid cw \in \mathcal{L}(r)\}$;*
3. *for all $(r_1, r_2) \in \beta(r)$, $\mathcal{L}(r_1 \cdot r_2) = \mathcal{L}(r)$;*
4. *for all $w_1 w_2 \in \mathcal{L}(r)$, there is a $(r_1, r_2) \in \beta(r)$ s.t. $w_1 \in \mathcal{L}(r_1)$ and $w_2 \in \mathcal{L}(r_2)$.*

Lemma 4. *Let x be a string variable, let r be a normalized regular expression with $\mathrm{top}(r) \notin \{\varnothing, \sqcup\}$, let A be a set of arithmetic constraints, and let $(r_\gamma, u_\gamma, A_\gamma) = \gamma(r)$.*

1. *The constraint set $S := \{x \text{ in } r\} \cup A$ is satisfied by a model $\mathcal{I}$ of T_{LR} iff the set $S_\gamma := \{x \text{ in } r_\gamma, |x| \approx u_\gamma\} \cup A \cup A_\gamma$ is satisfied by a model $\mathcal{I}_\gamma$ of T_{LR} where $\mathcal{I}$ and $\mathcal{I}_\gamma$ agree on the variables of S.*
2. *All models $\mathcal{I}$ of T_{LR} satisfying A_γ are such that for all $w \in r_\gamma^{\mathcal{I}}$, the length of w equals $u_\gamma^{\mathcal{I}}$.*

We say that a configuration $\langle A, R, V \rangle$ is satisfied by an interpretation $\mathcal{I}$ if the set $A \cup R \cup V$ is satisfied by $\mathcal{I}$. We consider unsat to be satisfied by no interpretation.

Lemma 5. *For every rule of the calculus, the premise configuration is satisfied by a model $\mathcal{I}_p$ of T_{LR} iff one of its conclusion configurations is satisfied by a model $\mathcal{I}_c$ of T_{LR} where $\mathcal{I}_p$ and $\mathcal{I}_c$ agree on the variables shared by the two configurations.*

Using the previous lemma in the left-to-right direction together with a structural induction argument on derivation trees, one can readily show that the root of every closed derivation tree is unsatisfiable. From this, the *refutation soundness* of the calculus easily follows.

Proposition 3 (Refutation Soundness). *Every set of T_{LR}-constraints that has a refutation is T_{LR}-unsatisfiable.*

Thanks to earlier lemmas and the one below one can also prove that the calculus is *solution sound*.

Lemma 6. *If* $\langle A, R, V \rangle$ *is a saturated leaf of a derivation tree with root* $\langle A_0, R_0, \emptyset \rangle$ *then for every (string) variable* x *in* R_0 *there is a constraint of the form* $(x \text{ in } q)$ *in* V.

Proposition 4 (Solution Soundness). *For every saturated leaf* $\langle A, R, V \rangle$ *of a derivation tree with root* $\langle A_0, R_0, \emptyset \rangle$ *there is a model* $\mathcal{I}$ *of* T_{LR} *that satisfies* $A_0 \cup R_0$ *and is such that* $x^{\mathcal{I}} \in q^{\mathcal{I}}$ *for all* $(x \text{ in } q) \in V$.

Proof. Let $K := \langle A, R, V \rangle$ be as above. It is not difficult to show based the derivation rules that $\mathcal{V}(A_0 \cup R_0) \subseteq \mathcal{V}(A \cup R \cup V)$ and $A_0 \subseteq A$. Moreover, every integer variable of V is in A, by definition of γ, and each string variable of R occurs in V exactly once.

The set R contains at most constraints of the form $(\epsilon \text{ in } r)$ with $\epsilon \in \mathcal{L}(r)$; otherwise, one of the derivation rules would apply to K, against the assumption that it is saturated. This makes R trivially satisfiable. The set A is satisfiable as well, otherwise A-Conflict would apply. Let $\mathcal{J}$ be a model of T_{LR} satisfying A and let $(x \text{ in } q)$ be any element of V. We claim that the set $q^{\mathcal{J}}$ is nonempty and contains only words of length $|x|^{\mathcal{J}}$. In fact, if $(x \text{ in } q)$ was added to V by Assign-1, then q is a literal l and $|x| \approx |l|\!\downarrow \in A$. If $(x \text{ in } q)$ was added to V by Assign-2, then $\gamma(r) = (q, u_\gamma, A_\gamma)$ for some r, where $A_\gamma \subseteq A$ and $|x| \approx u_\gamma \in A$. Since $\mathcal{J}$ satisfies A_γ, by Lemma 4(2), all words in $q^{\mathcal{J}}$, if any, are of length $u_\gamma^{\mathcal{J}}$ which is the same as $|x|^{\mathcal{J}}$. To argue that $q^{\mathcal{J}}$ is non-empty, by Lemma 4(2), it is enough to argue that $\mathcal{L}(r)$ is nonempty. This can be seen by observing that, by definition of the the rewrite rules in Figure 3, and by Lemma 1 and Lemma 2, r is guaranteed to contain no occurrences of $\emptyset$ or $\sqcap$, and containing such symbols is a necessary condition for a regular expression to have an empty language. The statement of the lemma follows by the generality of $(x \text{ in } q)$. $\square$

Proposition 5 (Refutation Completeness). *Every set of* T_{LR}*-constraints unsatisfiable in* T_{LR} *has a refutation.*

Proof. Contrapositively, suppose that the set of T_{LR}-constraints does not have a refutation. Then, by Proposition 2, it must have a derivation that generates a tree with a saturated branch. By Proposition 4 the set is satisfiable in T_{LR}. $\square$

4.3   Decidability

Proposition 6 (Decidability). *The* T_{LR}*-satisfiability of quantifier-free* Σ_{LR}*-formulas with no regular expression variables is decidable.*

Proof. By standard methods, the T_{LR}-satisfiability of quantifier-free Σ_{LR}-formulas with no variables of sort Lan can be effectively reduced to the T_{LR}-satisfiability of T_{LR}-constraints. The existence of a terminating procedure to check such constraints is a consequence of Proposition 1 and Proposition 2. The correctness of the procedure is a consequence of Propositions 3 and 5. $\square$

5   Conclusion and Further Work

We have presented an algebraic approach for solving regular membership constraints and linear length constraints in the theory of strings. This approach works directly on regular expressions without the need to translate them to automata. Moreover, it does not require imposing *a priori* bounds on string variables. We have proved that our approach is sound, complete and terminating, thus it is a decision procedure for this fragment. In addition, when the constraints are satisfiable, our approach provides a model—in fact a generator of a set of models. Therefore, it has all the properties required for integration into an SMT solver.

In ongoing work, we are investigating a possible extension of our procedure to word equations over unbounded strings. Although the satisfiability of sets of word equations is also decidable, the decidability of the combined language is still an open problem. We hope to find a fragment that is sufficiently expressive for real-world problems, while also being decidable, or at least effective for solving problems in practice.

Additionally, we have identified two bottlenecks in the calculus presented here: the computation of the intersection and the complement operations over regular expressions. Therefore, we plan to focus on developing approaches for computing these operations that are efficient in practice. We are also working on an extension to symbolic regular expressions, specifically, regular expressions that contain string variables.

References

[1] Abdulla, P.A., Atig, M.F., Chen, Y.-F., Holík, L., Rezine, A., Rümmer, P., Stenman, J.: String constraints for verification. In: Biere, A., Bloem, R. (eds.) CAV 2014. LNCS, vol. 8559, pp. 150–166. Springer, Heidelberg (2014)

[2] Antimirov, V.: Partial derivatives of regular expressions and finite automaton constructions. Theor. Comput. Sci. 155(2), 291–319 (1996)

[3] Baader, F., Nipkow, T.: Term Rewriting and All That. Cambridge University Press (1998)

[4] Badban, B., Dashti, M.: Semi-linear parikh images of regular expressions via reduction. In: Hliněný, P., Kučera, A. (eds.) MFCS 2010. LNCS, vol. 6281, pp. 653–664. Springer, Heidelberg (2010)

[5] Barrett, C., Sebastiani, R., Seshia, S., Tinelli, C.: Satisfiability modulo theories. In: Biere, A., Heule, M.J.H., van Maaren, H., Walsh, T. (eds.) Handbook of Satisfiability, vol. 185, chapter 26, pp. 825–885. IOS Press, February 2008

[6] Berry, G., Sethi, R.: From regular expressions to deterministic automata. Theor. Comput. Sci. 48(1), 117–126 (1986)

[7] Bjørner, N., Tillmann, N., Voronkov, A.: Path feasibility analysis for string-manipulating programs. In: Kowalewski, S., Philippou, A. (eds.) TACAS 2009. LNCS, vol. 5505, pp. 307–321. Springer, Heidelberg (2009)

[8] Christensen, A.S., Møller, A., Schwartzbach, M.I.: Precise analysis of string expressions. In: Cousot, R. (ed.) SAS 2003. LNCS, vol. 2694, pp. 1–18. Springer, Heidelberg (2003)

[9] Fu, X., Chih Li, C.: A string constraint solver for detecting web application vulnerability. In: Proceedings of the 22nd International Conference on Software Engineering and Knowledge Engineering, SEKE 2010. Knowledge Systems Institute Graduate (2010)

[10] Ghosh, I., Shafiei, N., Li, G., Chiang, W.-F.: JST: An automatic test generation tool for industrial Java applications with strings. In: Proceedings of the 2013 International Conference on Software Engineering, ICSE 2013, pp. 992–1001. IEEE Press, Piscataway (2013)

[11] Henriksen, J.G., Jensen, J.L., Jørgensen, M.E., Klarlund, N., Paige, R., Rauhe, T., Sandholm, A.: Mona: Monadic second-order logic in practice. In: Brinksma, E., Steffen, B., Cleaveland, W.R., Larsen, K.G., Margaria, T. (eds.) TACAS 1995. LNCS, vol. 1019, pp. 89–110. Springer, Heidelberg (1995)

[12] Hooimeijer, P., Veanes, M.: An evaluation of automata algorithms for string analysis. In: Jhala, R., Schmidt, D. (eds.) VMCAI 2011. LNCS, vol. 6538, pp. 248–262. Springer, Heidelberg (2011)

[13] Hooimeijer, P., Weimer, W.: A decision procedure for subset constraints over regular languages. In: Proceedings of the 2009 ACM SIGPLAN Conference on Programming Language Design and Implementation, pp. 188–198. ACM (2009)

[14] Hooimeijer, P., Weimer, W.: Solving string constraints lazily. In: Proceedings of the IEEE/ACM International Conference on Automated Software Engineering, pp. 377–386. ACM (2010)

[15] Kiezun, A., Ganesh, V., Guo, P.J., Hooimeijer, P., Ernst, M.D.: HAMPI: a solver for string constraints. In: Proceedings of the Eighteenth International Symposium on Software Testing and Analysis, pp. 105–116. ACM (2009)

[16] Klarlund, N., Møller, A.: MONA implementation secrets. In: Yu, S., Păun, A. (eds.) CIAA 2000. LNCS, vol. 2088, pp. 182–194. Springer, Heidelberg (2001)

[17] Kozen, D.: Lower bounds for natural proof systems. In: FOCS, pp. 254–266. IEEE Computer Society (1977)

[18] Li, G., Ghosh, I.: PASS: String solving with parameterized array and interval automaton. In: Bertacco, V., Legay, A. (eds.) HVC 2013. LNCS, vol. 8244, pp. 15–31. Springer, Heidelberg (2013)

[19] Liang, T., Reynolds, A., Tinelli, C., Barrett, C., Deters, M.: A dPLL(T) theory solver for a theory of strings and regular expressions. In: Biere, A., Bloem, R. (eds.) CAV 2014. LNCS, vol. 8559, pp. 646–662. Springer, Heidelberg (2014)

[20] Liang, T., Tsiskaridze, N., Reynolds, A., Tinelli, C., Barrett, C.: A decision procedure for regular membership and length constraints over unbounded strings. Technical report, Department of Computer Science, The University of Iowa (2015). http://www.cs.uiowa.edu/~tinelli/papers.html

[21] Lu, K.Z.M.: XHaskell - Adding Regular Expression Type to Haskell. PhD thesis, National University of Singapore (2009)

[22] Makanin, G.S.: The problem of solvability of equations in a free semigroup. English Rransl. in Math USSR Sbornik 32, 147–236 (1977)

[23] Matiyasevich, Y.V.: Hilbert's tenth problem and paradigms of computation. In: Cooper, S.B., Löwe, B., Torenvliet, L. (eds.) CiE 2005. LNCS, vol. 3526, pp. 310–321. Springer, Heidelberg (2005)

[24] Parikh, R.J.: On context-free languages. J. ACM 13(4), 570–581 (1966)

[25] Plandowski, W.: Satisfiability of word equations with constants is in pspace. J. ACM 51(3), 483–496 (2004)

[26] Rosu, G., Viswanathan, M.: Testing extended regular language membership incrementally by rewriting. In: Nieuwenhuis, R. (ed.) RTA 2003. LNCS, vol. 2706, pp. 499–514. Springer, Heidelberg (2003)

[27] Schulz, K. (ed.): Word Equations and Related Topics. Springer-Verlag New York, Inc., New York (1990)

[28] Tateishi, T., Pistoia, M., Tripp, O.: Path- and index-sensitive string analysis based on monadic second-order logic. ACM Trans. Softw. Eng. Methodol. 33, 1–33 (2013)

[29] Tillmann, N., de Halleux, J.: Pex–white box test generation for.NET. In: Beckert, B., Hähnle, R. (eds.) TAP 2008. LNCS, vol. 4966, pp. 134–153. Springer, Heidelberg (2008)

[30] Trinh, M.-T., Chu, D.-H., Jaffar, J.: S3: A symbolic string solver for vulnerability detection in web applications. In: Yung, M., Li, N. (eds.) Proceedings of the 21st ACM Conference on Computer and Communications Security (2014)

[31] Veanes, M.: Applications of symbolic finite automata. In: Konstantinidis, S. (ed.) CIAA 2013. LNCS, vol. 7982, pp. 16–23. Springer, Heidelberg (2013)

[32] Veanes, M., Bjørner, N., de Moura, L.: Symbolic automata constraint solving. In: Fermüller, C.G., Voronkov, A. (eds.) LPAR-17. LNCS, vol. 6397, pp. 640–654. Springer, Heidelberg (2010)

[33] Yu, F., Alkhalaf, M., Bultan, T.: STRANGER: An automata-based string analysis tool for PHP. In: Esparza, J., Majumdar, R. (eds.) TACAS 2010. LNCS, vol. 6015, pp. 154–157. Springer, Heidelberg (2010)

[34] Zheng, Y., Zhang, X., Ganesh, V.: Z3-str: A z3-based string solver for web application analysis. In: Proceedings of the 2013 9th Joint Meeting on Foundations of Software Engineering, ESEC/FSE 2013, pp. 114–124. ACM, New York (2013)

Adapting Real Quantifier Elimination Methods for Conflict Set Computation

Maximilian Jaroschek[1], Pablo Federico Dobal[1,2,3], and Pascal Fontaine[3,*]

[1] Max Planck Institute for Informatics, Saarbrücken, Germany
[2] Universität des Saarlandes, Saarbrücken, Germany
[3] INRIA, Université de Lorraine and LORIA, Nancy, France

Abstract. The satisfiability problem in real closed fields is decidable. In the context of satisfiability modulo theories, the problem restricted to conjunctive sets of literals, that is, sets of polynomial constraints, is of particular importance. One of the central problems is the computation of good explanations of the unsatisfiability of such sets, i.e. obtaining a small subset of the input constraints whose conjunction is already unsatisfiable. We adapt two commonly used real quantifier elimination methods, cylindrical algebraic decomposition and virtual substitution, to provide such conflict sets and demonstrate the performance of our method in practice.

Keywords: SMT, real quantifier elimination, cylindrical algebraic decomposition, virtual substitution, conflict set.

1 Introduction

Among the reasons for the current success of Satisfiability Modulo Theory (SMT, we refer to [1] for more information) solvers is the ability to handle large formulas in an expressive language. Since arithmetic is pervasive in applications of SMT, this language should include some kind of arithmetic theory. Linear arithmetic (on reals and integers) was one of the first theories considered for SMT [22], and integrated in practice into SMT solvers [2,14]. Non-linear arithmetic is also mentioned in the fundamental combination of theories paper [22]. Although many applications do require non-linear arithmetic reasoning — our motivating application was the verification of a clock synchronization algorithm [3] — it is considered in practice only since quite recently (e.g. [19]), and few solvers integrate non-linear arithmetic reasoning capabilities. Up to now, no technique is accepted as the right way to integrate non-linear reasoning capabilities into SMT solvers.

The theory of real closed fields (reals with order, addition, and multiplication) has however been extensively studied in the area of symbolic computation, and

---

* This work has been supported by the ANR/DFG project STU 483/2-1 SMArT, project ANR-13-IS02-0001 of the Agence Nationale de la Recherche, by the European Union Seventh Framework Programme under grant agreement no. 295261 (MEALS), by the Région Lorraine, and by the STIC AmSud MISMT

© Springer International Publishing Switzerland 2015
C. Lutz and S. Ranise (Eds.): FroCoS 2015, LNAI 9322, pp. 151–166, 2015.
DOI: 10.1007/978-3-319-24246-0_10

mature tools exist to handle sets of constraints in this language, e.g. [16,4]. The results presented here aim at adapting those tools so that they can be integrated into an SMT framework. Indeed, whereas developing dedicated techniques for non-linear arithmetic within SMT is crucial, a lesson from linear arithmetic is that mature (external) tools should also be adapted for cooperation with SMT solvers. For instance, a reasonably efficient linear programming tool suitably incorporated into the SMT solver CVC4 provided an impressive improvement of efficiency compared to the dedicated SMT techniques alone [20].

To integrate a theory reasoner in an SMT framework, some features are valuable (see Section 1.4.1 in [1]). Since we envision fast and incomplete techniques tightly integrated within SMT, backed up by a complete and robust but also heavy engine, it is not of foremost importance for this engine to be incremental and backtrackable: it will only be called as a last resort on a full assignment when the heuristic solver failed to show unsatisfiability. However, a critical feature is that the complete engine provides models, both for feedback to the user but also for model-based combination with other theories [12,13]. Adapting established real closed field decision procedures to produce models has been the subject of a previous work [21]. The other critical feature is to be able, from an unsatisfiable set of constraints, to extract a small conflict set. Without this ability, the cooperation of the SMT solver and the engine would most probably fail because the SMT solver would enumerate an exponential number of slightly different assignments, successively submitted to the engine. The engine would reject them one by one, but they would essentially be unsatisfiable for the same reason. With small conflict set production, all these assignments are blocked by the strong conflict clause added within the SMT solver in just one call to the external engine.

We here focus on the computation of small conflict sets from unsatisfiable sets of non-linear constraints. Two commonly used real quantifier elimination methods, namely cylindrical algebraic decomposition and virtual substitution, are considered. They basically share a feature that provides the key to efficiently compute conflict sets: a finite set of test points is generated in the process. These test points falsify some of the input constraints. If the tentative conflict set contains enough constraints so that at least one of them is false for each test point, it is indeed a conflict set.

Section 2 briefly describes the two decision procedures for sets of polynomial constraints on the reals, Section 3 presents the small conflict set extraction method, and experimental results are discussed in Section 4.

2   Real Quantifier Elimination

Given a quantified formula ϕ, quantifier elimination is the process of finding an equivalent, quantifier-free formula ϕ'. Whether or not quantifier elimination is possible in theory and practice in general depends on the considered formal system and the underlying theory.

For first-order logic formulas over the reals it is well known that quantifier elimination is possible. This was first proven by Tarski in 1951 [23], but the first successful algorithmic approach to the problem was developed by Collins in 1974 [8]. To formally define the problem, consider a quantifier-free first-order formula $\varphi(x_1, \ldots, x_n, u_1, \ldots, u_m)$ over the reals in the variables $x_1, \ldots, x_n$, $u_1, \ldots, u_m$. Given the formula

$$\phi \equiv Q_1 x_1, \ldots Q_n x_n : \varphi(x_1, \ldots, x_n, u_1, \ldots, u_m),$$

with $Q_i \in \{\forall, \exists\}$ for $1 \leq i \leq n$, the quantifier-elimination problem consists in finding a quantifier-free first-order formula $\phi'(u_1, \ldots, u_m)$ such that ϕ' is logically equivalent to ϕ. It was proven independently by Weispfenning [24] and Davenport and Heintz [11] that solving the quantifier elimination problem over real closed fields can require double exponential space.

Subsequently we describe two widely used real quantifier elimination methods. Both approaches are based on the same general idea which we discuss first before going into details about the specifics for each method. Our goal is to give a comprehensible and intuitive introduction to these procedures and not to describe them in thorough technical detail. References to more in depth treatments of the subjects are given for the interested reader.

While these methods work in a general context, our focus lies on input formulas found in the SMT setting with only existential quantifiers and no free variables:

$$\phi \equiv \exists x_1, \ldots \exists x_n : \varphi(x_1, \ldots, x_n), \tag{1}$$

It is clear that then either `true` or `false` is a quantifier-free equivalent of ϕ. Over the reals, quantifier-free formulas are Boolean combinations of polynomial expressions of the form $p(x_1, \ldots, x_n) \bowtie 0$ where p is a polynomial in $\mathbb{R}[x_1, \ldots, x_n]$ and $\bowtie$ is a relation symbol in $\{<, \leq, =, \neq, >, \geq\}$. Given a point $(a_1, \ldots, a_n) \in \mathbb{R}^n$, we can see if φ holds for this point by substituting a_i for x_i for all $1 \leq i \leq n$. If we were able to perform the substitution for all points in $\mathbb{R}^n$ in finite time, we could easily see if ϕ holds or not.

The approach of the two quantifier elimination methods *cylindrical algebraic decomposition* (CAD) and *virtual substitution* (VS) is to reduce the set of infinitely many points in $\mathbb{R}^n$ to a finite set of test points, i.e. to find a finite subset T of $\mathbb{R}^n$ such that ϕ holds over $\mathbb{R}^n$ if and only if it holds over T.

2.1 Cylindrical Algebraic Decomposition

Cylindrical algebraic decomposition [8] is the most widely used real quantifier elimination method to date. It is based on a simple observation: given a finite, non-empty set P of polynomials in n variables, one can define an equivalence relation on $\mathbb{R}^n$ that decomposes the space into finitely many connected cells such that all the given polynomials are sign invariant in each cell.

Definition 1. *Let P be a non-empty set of polynomials in $\mathbb{R}[x_1, \ldots, x_n]$. For $a, b \in \mathbb{R}^n$ we say that a is equivalent to b if there exists a path $\gamma : [0, 1] \to \mathbb{R}^n$ from a to b such that for all $s, t \in [0, 1]$ and all $p \in P$ we have that*

$$\operatorname{sgn}(p(\gamma(s))) = \operatorname{sgn}(p(\gamma(t))).$$

The term cell *refers to the preimage of an equivalence class under the canonical homomorphism which maps a point to its equivalence class. We call the set of all cells an (algebraic) decomposition of* $\mathbb{R}^n$.

Example 1. To illustrate the basic idea, we consider the bivariate case, and the following set of polynomials.

$$P = \{\underbrace{x^2 + y^2 - 1}_{p_1}, \underbrace{x^2 - y + 1/2}_{p_2}\}$$

The first polynomial defines three connected, sign invariant cells in $\mathbb{R}^2$ given by

$$\{(a,b) \in \mathbb{R}^2 \mid p_1 < 0\}, \{(a,b) \in \mathbb{R}^2 \mid p_1 = 0\}, \{(a,b) \in \mathbb{R}^2 \mid p_1 > 0\},$$

and similarly, p_2 also decomposes $\mathbb{R}^2$ into three cells when not taking p_1 into account. The combination of the cells induced by p_1 and the cells induced by p_2 gives rise to a new decomposition where the original cells either persist, collapse into common cells or form new cells via intersection. The decomposition of $\mathbb{R}^2$ induced by P consists of 5 different cells in total, as illustrated in Figure 1.

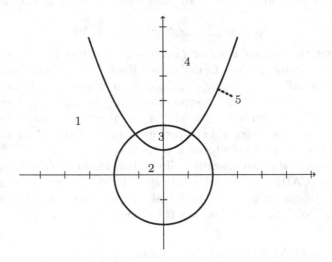

Fig. 1. The sign invariant cells of Example 1. Note that cell no. 5 is given by the union of the varieties of p_1 and p_2.

To study a quantified formula ϕ, we want to collect in a set P all the polynomial expressions in ϕ and then compute a sample point for each cell in the decomposition induced by P. While it seems easy to identify the different sign invariant cells simply by inspection of the plot of the varieties in Figure 1, it is a non-trivial task for a computer and for more involved polynomial systems (in more than two variables).

To facilitate the algorithmic identification of different cells, new polynomials are added to P so that the decomposition becomes cylindrical in the following sense:

Definition 2. *A decomposition of $\mathbb{R}^n$ is called cylindrical if $n = 1$ or if there exists a projection $\pi : \mathbb{R}^n \to \mathbb{R}^{n-1}$ that acts on the elements of $\mathbb{R}^n$ by removing one of their coordinates such that the following two conditions hold:*

1. *For two cells $C_1, C_2 \subset \mathbb{R}^n$, either $\pi(C_1) = \pi(C_2)$ or $\pi(C_1) \cap \pi(C_2) = \emptyset$.*
2. *The decomposition of $\mathbb{R}^{n-1}$ induced by the images under π of the cells in the decomposition of $\mathbb{R}^n$ is cylindrical.*

We call a set of polynomials $P \subset R[x_1, \dots, x_n]$ cylindrical if the decomposition of $\mathbb{R}^n$ induced by P is cylindrical.

Again, this can easily be illustrated by an example.

Example 2. (Example 1 continued.) The decomposition induced by P as in Example 1 is not cylindrical. We can, however, refine it by adding four linear polynomials to the set. Let $c = \sqrt{0.5(\sqrt{7} - 2)}$ (c is such that $p_1(\pm c) = p_2(\pm c)$) and set

$$P' = P \cup \{x + 1, x + c, x - c, x - 1\}.$$

P' is cylindrical and the decomposition is illustrated in Figure 2. It consists of 47 different cells.

Starting from a set of sample points from each cell in the induced decomposition of $\mathbb{R}$ (represented by the dots on the horizontal axis in the figure), we can easily find all cells in $\mathbb{R}^2$ "above" a fixed cell in $\mathbb{R}$ by keeping the x_1 value fixed and looking for roots of any polynomial in P with that x_1 value. In the picture, this corresponds to moving along the dotted line and looking for sign changes.

The full CAD algorithm works in three major steps. We start with a formula ϕ of the form (1) and collect the contained polynomials in a set $P_n \subset \mathbb{R}[x_1, \dots, x_n]$. The first step, the projection phase, recursively adds new elements to P_n such that its induced decomposition becomes cylindrical. We denote this superset of P_n by $\mathrm{cadp}(P_n)$. If $n = 1$, then P_1 is always cylindrical, so $\mathrm{cadp}(P_1) := P_1$. For $n > 1$, we compute a set P_{n-1} which contains all polynomials in $Q_n := P_n \cap \mathbb{R}[x_1, \dots, x_{n-1}]$ as well as the image $P_n \setminus Q_n$ under a so called projection operator and return $\mathrm{cadp}(P_n) := P_n \cup \mathrm{cadp}(P_{n-1})$. The projection operator is a map such that $\mathrm{cadp}(P_n)$ is cylindrical if $\mathrm{cadp}(P_{n-1})$ is. Intuitively it adds polynomials in $\mathbb{R}[x_1, \dots, x_{n-1}]$ to P_{n-1} that correspond to asymptotes orthogonal to the projection direction, intersections and self intersections of the algebraic curves defined by the polynomials in $P_n \setminus Q_n$. In Example 2, $x \pm 1$ corresponds to the vertical asymptotes of the algebraic curve given by p_1 and $x \pm c$ corresponds to the intersection of the two curves given by p_1 and p_2.

In the second step, the extension phase, sample points of the cells in the decomposition of $\mathbb{R}$ induced by P_1 are obtained by computing the roots of the polynomials in P_1 and points from the intervals between these roots. The cells

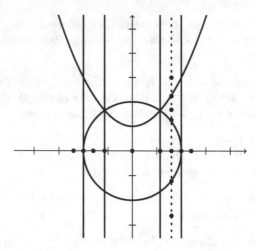

Fig. 2. A cylindrical algebraic decomposition of $\mathbb{R}^2$ induced by the polynomials in Example 2.

of $\mathbb{R}$ are extended to cells of $\mathbb{R}^2$ by keeping the x_1 values of the sample points fixed and computing the roots of the polynomials in P_2 regarded as univariate polynomials in x_2. This step is iterated to obtain the cells in $\mathbb{R}^3$, $\mathbb{R}^4$ etc. In the last step, the sample points of the cells in $\mathbb{R}^n$ are plugged into the the polynomials in P and ϕ is evaluated.

It was shown by Brown and Davenport [5] that the complexity of CAD is double exponential in the number of variables. Many improvements of the base algorithm like the ones found in [9,6,7], however, allow for solving moderately sized systems via CAD.

2.2   Virtual Substitution

The virtual substitution technique takes a more symbolic view on the roots of a polynomial. It was introduced by Weispfenning in 1988, see [25], and several improvements and generalizations have been developed since. It is not as prevalent as CAD due to its current degree limitations in practice, but usually performs much better in terms of computing time.

To get a good understanding of VS, consider first univariate polynomials and a special form of the quantifier-free formula ϕ that contains no strict inequalities but only Boolean combinations of expressions of the form $p(x) \bowtie 0$ with $\bowtie \in \{\leq, =, \geq\}$. Similarly to CAD, VS decomposes the space into connected cells. However, while CAD does not really exploit the literals but only the polynomials appearing in them, the cells in VS are constructed such that the truth value of ϕ (rather than the signs of the images of the polynomials) remains invariant in each cell.

Let $p_1, p_2 \in \mathbb{R}[x]$ and $\phi = p_1 \geq 0 \wedge p_2 \geq 0$. The real roots $r_1, \ldots, r_k$ of p_1 given in ascending order decompose $\mathbb{R}$ into finitely many intervals

$$(-\infty, r_1], (r_1, r_2], \ldots, (r_{k-1}, r_k], (r_k, +\infty).$$

The real roots of p_2 then refine this decomposition such that in each interval, the truth values of the inequalities and equations in ϕ do not change within an interval.

Example 3. Let $p_1 = 10^{-1}(x + 5)(x + 2)(x - 6)$ and $p_2 = x^2 - 9$ and $\Phi = \exists x : p_1 \geq 0 \wedge p_2 \leq 0$. Then the truth invariant decomposition induced by the real roots of p_1 and p_2 consists of the intervals

$$(-\infty, -5], (-5, -3], (-3, -2], (-2, 3], (3, 6], (6, +\infty).$$

By plugging in the upper interval bounds (and evaluating the polynomials at $+\infty$), we see that $\phi \equiv \mathbf{true}$ via the test point $x = -3$.

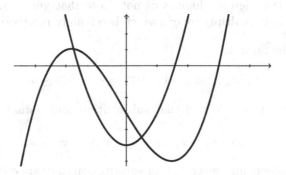

Fig. 3. Plot of the polynomials in Example 3.

When dealing with multivariate polynomials in $\mathbb{R}[x_1, \ldots, x_n]$, the idea is to choose one variable x_i and view the polynomials as univariate in x_i. Then we are in the univariate setting where we can (symbolically) compute the interval decomposition. Here, the interval bounds are not real numbers but expressions in the variables $x_1, \ldots, x_{i-1}, x_{i+1}, \ldots, x_n$.

Example 4. Let $p_1 = x_1 x_2 - 1$ and $p_2 = x_1 - 3$ and $\phi = \exists x_1 \exists x_2 : p_1 \geq 0 \wedge p_2 \leq 0$. As univariate polynomials in $\mathbb{R}(x_1)[x_2]$, p_2 either vanishes identically or has no roots. The polynomial p_1 has either no roots or a root at x_1^{-1}. We substitute this root expression for x_2 and get

$$p_1(x_1^{-1}/x_2) = x_1 x_1^{-1} - 1 = 0, \quad p_2(x_1^{-1}/x_2) = x_1 - 3.$$

This substitution is only possible if we require that $x_1 \neq 0$. Therefore, after the substitution, ϕ becomes

$$\exists x_1 : 0 \geq 0 \wedge x_1 - 3 \leq 0 \wedge x_1 \neq 0,$$

and one quantifier has been removed. Continuing the process will give $\Phi \equiv$ **true** via the test point $(3, \frac{1}{3})$.

In the example, the root expression has to be substituted into all polynomial constraints, but it is also necessary to ensure that the substitution term is valid. Here, this is achieved by adding a constraint to the formula to prevent division by zero. Such additional constraints are called *guards* of the substitution term. Also, substitution in the above example generates a (quantified) Boolean combination of polynomial constraints; this is not always the case. Indeed substitution can lead for instance to rational functions. In virtual substitution, this problem is circumvented by a more sophisticated substitution process.

Assume that after the substitution the resulting formula contains a relation of the form $p/q \bowtie 0$ with p and q coprime polynomials in $\mathbb{R}[x_1, \ldots, x_k]$. In order to remove the denominator, we can multiply the relation by q. We do not know, however, if in the subsequent substitution steps we derive values for $x_1, \ldots, x_k$ such that q would evaluate to a strictly positive or negative number and thus whether the relation sign $\bowtie$ changes or not. Note that guards prevent q to be zero. A way out is to multiply by q^2 (which is certainly positive) rather than q.

Example 5. In the formula

$$\exists x_1 \exists x_2 : x_1 x_2 - 1 \geq 0 \wedge x_2 + x_1 - 3 \leq 0.$$

we substitute x_2 by x_1^{-1} via virtual substitution and obtain the equivalent formula

$$\exists x_1 : x_1 + x_1^2(x_1 - 3) \leq 0 \wedge x_1 \neq 0.$$

In the full VS algorithm, several other substitution rules are necessary to avoid non-polynomial expressions. These are detailed in [25] for virtual substitution for polynomials of degree at most two. Also included are rules that allow strict inequalities by substitution of ϵ-terms. In theory, the method can be extended to an arbitrary but fixed degree bound, see [27], but there are still obstacles to overcome for higher degree implementations.

Virtual substitution performs significantly better in theory and practice compared to CAD. As shown in [26], VS is double exponential in the number of quantifier alternations but only single exponential in the number of quantified variables for a fixed quantifier type. Since the input in the SMT setting does not contain quantifier alternations, virtual substitution is significantly better compared to cylindrical algebraic decomposition for these formulas in terms of theoretical complexity.

3   Finding Conflict Sets

In order to benefit from the interplay between SAT-solvers and special theory solvers, it is required from the theory solver to provide small conflict sets. The input to the theory solver is a conjunction of literals and if this conjunction is not satisfiable, an answer in the form of a (hopefully small) subset of the input literals that is unsatisfiable itself should be returned. We call this answer a conflict set. Such a conflict set should ideally be as small as possible. A minimum conflict set is a conflict set with minimum size, whereas a minimal conflict set does not contain unnecessary literals, that is, all its subsets are satisfiable. A minimum conflict set is minimal, but a minimal conflict set might not have the smallest size. The procedure here is not guaranteed to produce minimum or even minimal conflict sets, but we will show in Section 4 that it is efficient at finding small conflict sets. We now describe how virtual substitution and cylindrical algebraic decomposition can be adapted to provide such answers.

3.1 Conflict Sets and Linear Programming

The problem can be stated as follows: given an unsatisfiable quantified formula ϕ of the form

$$\phi = \exists x_1 \ldots \exists x_n : \bigwedge_{1 \leq i \leq m} p_i \bowtie_i 0, \tag{2}$$

with $p_i \in \mathbb{R}[x_1, \ldots, x_n]$ and $\bowtie_i \in \{<, \leq, =, \neq, >, \geq\}$, find a subset $I \subset \{1, \ldots, m\}$ as small as possible such that the formula

$$\phi' = \exists x_1 \ldots \exists x_n : \bigwedge_{i \in I} p_i \bowtie_i 0,$$

is unsatisfiable.

As was stated in the beginning of Section 2, virtual substitution and cylindrical algebraic decomposition share the same basic idea of finding a finite set T of test points that suffice to determine the unsatisfiability of ϕ. The key to the problem of finding a conflict set is a reformulation of the problem in terms of these test points. For that, denote by r_i the ith polynomial constraint in ϕ for $i \in \{0, \ldots, m\}$ and for each i let $e_i : T \to \{0, 1\}$ be such that $e_i(a) = 0$ if r_i holds at a and 1 otherwise. Applying CAD or VS to ϕ will result in $T = \{t_1, \ldots, t_k\}$ such that for each $t \in T$ there exists an i with $e_i(t) = 1$. Now let v_i be the vector $(e_i(t_1), e_i(t_2), \ldots, e_i(t_k))$. Then the problem of finding the smallest conflict set can be restated as a linear optimization problem.[1] Considering a vector $w \in \{0, 1\}^m$, it is indeed equivalent to minimizing $w_1 + \cdots + w_m$ under the linear constraints

$$Mw \geq \mathbf{1},$$

where M is the matrix that contains the v_i as columns and $\mathbf{1} = (1, \ldots, 1)$. We will refer to matrices M constructed in this way as *evaluation matrices*. If the vector w is as desired, then an entry 1 at the ith position means that r_i is part of the computed conflict set.

---

[1] Alternatively, since $e_i(t_k)$ is either 0 or 1 for each i and k, the problem can be recast into propositional logic, and reduces then to finding the smallest implicant of a set of clauses, that is, the smallest set of literals implying all clauses.

Note that our reformulation yields a 0-1-linear integer programming problem of the form

$$\min_{bw}\{w \in \{0,1\}^m \mid Mw \geq \mathbf{1}\}, \text{ with } b = \mathbf{1} = (1,\ldots,1), M \in \{0,1\}^{k \times m}, \quad (3)$$

and we can use highly optimized linear programming techniques to find an optimal or approximate solution.

This is only one of the benefits that the reformulation provides us. Another one is that the information necessary to construct the matrix M, i.e. the test points and images under the evaluation functions e_i, is already computed during the quantifier elimination. We will further investigate this fact in the next section.

We can easily deduce that solving the linear optimization problem is not harder than solving the original minimum conflict set problem:

Theorem 1. *Let $\mathcal{A}$ be an algorithm that solves the problem of finding a minimum conflict set. Then there exists a polynomial time algorithm $\mathcal{B}$ that transforms a matrix with entries in $\{0,1\}$ into a system of polynomials such that $\mathcal{A} \circ \mathcal{B}$ is an algorithm for solving linear optimization problems of the form (3)*

Proof. For a given matrix $M \in \{0,1\}^{k \times m}$, we show how to construct an equivalent conflict set problem in polynomial time, i.e. a formula ϕ whose minimum conflict set immediately yields a solution to the linear programming problem (3). Let ϕ be the quantified formula given by

$$\phi = \exists x : \bigwedge_{i \in \{1,\ldots,m\}} p_i = 0,$$

with

$$p_i = \prod_{j=1}^{k} (x - j)^{1-M(j,i)}.$$

One can easily check that the indices of the constraints in any minimum conflict set give rise to a solution of the linear programming problem. Multiplication of polynomials can be done in polynomial time, which proves the claim.   □

3.2   Conflict Sets and Quantifier Elimination Optimization

One of the main reasons why CAD and VS perform reasonably fast in practice is that since their initial development, many improvements have been made to speed up the computation. For CAD, many of these improvements take the form of specialized projection operators that reduce the number of cells that are constructed in the projection phase for certain kinds of input. Another major contribution was the development of *partial cylindrical algebraic decomposition* by Collins and Hong in [9]. In the case of virtual substitution, many improvements focus on the simplification of the quantifier free formula after every substitution step. Most notably, this includes the work of Sturm and Dolzmann in [15,17].

While some of the improvements do not have an effect on the computation of conflict sets as presented in Section 3.1, others will reduce the amount of available information for the evaluation matrix. There are basically two scenarios for information loss, which we describe with the help of two showcase improvements for CAD and VS.

In the partial CAD method, the following rule is used to avoid unnecessary cell construction. Note that we do not state it in full generality but adapt the rule to our framework.

Let ϕ be of the form (2) with polynomials in $\mathbb{R}[x_1, \ldots, x_n]$. If $p \in \mathbb{R}[x_1, \ldots, x_k]$ appears in ϕ with $k < n$ and there is a cell C in the CAD of $\mathbb{R}^k$ induced by the polynomials in ϕ in which one of the constraints depending only on p evaluates to `false`, then the cells above C do not have to be constructed.

Assume $(a_1, \ldots, a_k) \in \mathbb{R}^k$ lies in such a cell with a constraint containing p_i evaluating to `false` and further assume we compute the CAD without the aforementioned rule. This means that in the evaluation matrix we get ℓ rows corresponding to test points $(a_1, \ldots, a_k, *, \ldots, *)$ with $\ell \geq 1$ and all entries of the ith column are equal to 1 at the positions of these rows. On the other hand, if we compute the partial CAD, these rows will be missing in the evaluation matrix. However, we can add one row that corresponds to the test point $(a_1, \ldots, a_k)$ and we know that it will contain at least one non-zero entry at position i. At positions that correspond to polynomial constraints in more than the first k variables we insert the value 0. With this strategy, we can compensate for missing rows in the evaluation matrix. It is important to note that in this setting, we do not necessarily get a minimal conflict set even if we look for an optimal solution in (3).

A second reason for missing information can be found in the simplification strategies used in virtual substitution. If these strategies can determine at some point in the computation that the current quantifier-free formula (obtained for instance after some substitution steps) is a tautology or a contradiction, the remaining variables will not be substituted in the current substitution branch. An example for such a situation is a formula of the form

$$x_k \geq 0 \wedge \cdots \wedge x_k < 0 \wedge \ldots$$

which is obviously a contradiction and instead of continuing the substitution process, one can return `false` for this substitution branch. This scenario is similar to the one before in that an unknown number of rows in the evaluation matrix is missing. In contrast to the partial CAD improvement however, the truth value of the substitution branch is derived not from a single constraint but from a subset of the constraints in the formula.

In order to preserve compatibility with the conflict set computation, we therefore require that the simplification mechanism itself is able to determine a *local* conflict set, i.e. a conflict set of the quantifier-free formula on which the simplification mechanism acts. We then can extend this to a *global* conflict set.

The global conflict set should contain the union of all the local conflict sets and the corresponding columns can be removed from the evaluation matrix, together with all rows where these columns have non-zero entries.

4   Finding Conflict Sets via Redlog

We implemented our method in the package Redlog, part of the open source computer algebra system Reduce [18]. We have adapted the available CAD and VS implementations as well as parts of the simplification facilities for quantifier-free formulas to explicitly provide the test point evaluations and local conflict sets. Our method is such that it requires only little changes to the highly optimized Redlog code. In other methods, see e.g. [10], the implementations of CAD and VS are built from the ground up for use in SMT solving.

To provide a reasonably large and meaningful test set, we used the quantifier-free real arithmetic (QF_NRA) benchmarks from the SMT-LIB library. Our method expects a set of literals as input, so we use the veriT SMT-solver to generate, for each SMT-LIB benchmark, one complete assignment of atoms in the formula. This assignment is satisfiable in the theory of real linear arithmetic considering multiplication as an uninterpreted predicate. This set is further simplified using a preprocessor (which would eventually also have to be considered in the conflict clause production). This preprocessor only does trivial rewriting. Since Redlog is a generic tool and is not tuned for SMT-LIB like formulas, it greatly benefits from this simple cleaning phase. Finally, among the obtained formulas, some are satisfiable, and are not considered here. The test set thus obtained contains 6076 formulas that are proved unsatisfiable by Redlog. Figure 4 provides an idea of the size of formulas: a point (x, y) on the curve means that there are x formulas with a size smaller than y. The benchmarks as well as a distribution of Redlog featuring conflict set computation can be obtained on http://www.loria.fr/~pdobal/.[2] All our experiments use a 600 seconds timeout on a computer with an Intel i7-4600U CPU at 2.10GHz and 16 GB of RAM running Linux.

The scatter plot on Figure 6 gives a comparative view of the problem and conflict set sizes, whereas Figure 5 provides the distribution of the conflict set sizes: the method is suitable to provide small conflict sets. Even if most inputs contain tens or hundreds of constraints, just a few conflict sets have more than ten constraints. Semiautomatic inspection of the conflict sets exhibits that some of these are not minimal, i.e. they contain literals that are not necessary for unsatisfiability. For integration within SMT, it will be necessary to evaluate whether it is more efficient to reduce the conflict set size using other techniques or to keep these perfectible conflict sets as they are.

Figure 7 provides a comparative graph of the running times of Redlog with and without conflict set generation. Conflict set generation is not exactly the non-conflict set producing algorithm with an additional phase: some features of the original (non-conflict set producing) algorithm have to be turned off.

---

[2] 7947 formulas are provided, including the ones with a satisfiable or unknown status.

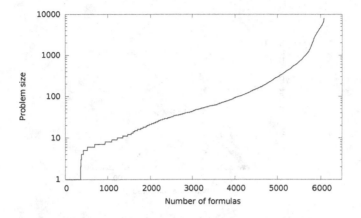

Fig. 4. Problem size (in number of constraints) repartition.

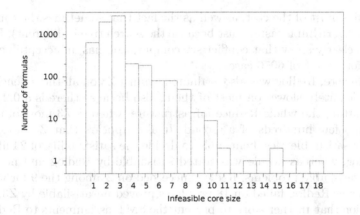

Fig. 5. Number of formulas for a given conflict set size (in number of constraints).

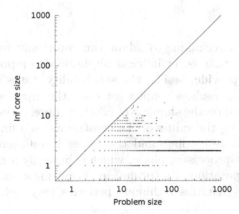

Fig. 6. Size of formulas vs. size of conflict sets (in number of constraints).

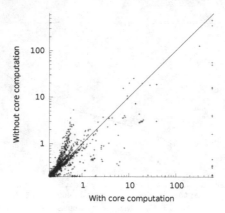

Fig. 7. Computing time (in seconds) with and without conflict set generation.

This explains most of the cost, as well as the fact that sometimes the conflict set generating algorithm is faster (just because the search tree is different). However the results clearly show that conflict set computation has an acceptable cost; it fails only for 22 out of 6076 cases.

As a side note, Redlog was also evaluated against Z3 on all these benchmarks. Redlog is definitely slower on most of them, also because there is a 0.2 seconds cost for starting the whole Reduce infrastructure, whereas Z3 most of the time answers in a few hundreds of a second. It also appears that Z3 is extremely effective for satisfiable files, being able to decide the satisfiability of 24 files more than Redlog, whereas no file was stated satisfiable by Redlog and not by Z3. On the unsatisfiable problems, Redlog succeeded on 2 among the 9 for which Z3 failed, whereas Redlog failed on 18 problems proved unsatisfiable by Z3. This is an indication that further work to present the SMT assignments to Redlog in a better way could lead to good results when using Redlog as a back-end.

5   Conclusion

We introduced here a technique to adapt two commonly used real quantifier elimination methods, that is, cylindrical algebraic decomposition and virtual substitution, to also provide, besides the satisfiability status of a set of polynomial constraints on the reals, a conflict set when the input set is unsatisfiable. This technique is based on the simple, yet effective, observation that both methods amount to checking the values of the constraints on a finite number of test points. Collecting the test points and the values is sufficient to compute the conflict sets in a post-processing phase, which is basically a linear optimization problem, or the computation of a (prime) implicant for a set of clauses. Experimental results show that this technique performs very well to produce small conflict sets.

Quantifier elimination methods also come with their lot of heuristics, and these are not all seamlessly compatible with our technique. Here, some of those heuristics were turned off, and some were adapted to tag the constraints used by the heuristics as mandatory for the conflict set. This is responsible for non-minimality of the produced conflict sets. Although we can observe experimentally that the produced conflict sets are small, it will certainly be beneficial to better analyze the heuristics for finer conflict set production.

In their applications, SMT solvers are used to check large and mostly easy computer generated formulas, whereas Redlog was mostly conceived for hard problems of moderate size. In order to succeed the integration of Redlog as a complete back-end for non-linear constraints within SMT, it is necessary to improve the heuristic simplification preprocessing phase, which is currently extremely basic. Another non-trivial issue is to take into account this preprocessing phase for the conflict computation.

Acknowledgements. We would like to thank the reviewers for their valuable suggestions and comments on this paper. Furthermore, the expertise of Thomas Sturm and Marek Košta on Redlog was of much benefit to the authors.

References

1. Barrett, C., Sebastiani, R., Seshia, S.A., Tinelli, C.: Satisfiability modulo theories. In: Biere, A., Heule, M.J.H., van Maaren, H., Walsh, T. (eds.) Handbook of Satisfiability. Frontiers in Artificial Intelligence and Applications, vol. 185, chapter 26, pp. 825–885. IOS Press, February 2009
2. Barrett, C.W.: Checking validity of quantifier-free formulas in combinations of first-order theories. PhD thesis, Stanford University (2003)
3. Barsotti, D., Nieto, L.P., Tiu, A.: Verification of clock synchronization algorithms: experiments on a combination of deductive tools. Form. Asp. Comput. 19(3), 321–341 (2007)
4. Brown, C.W.: Qepcad b: A program for computing with semi-algebraic sets using cads. SIGSAM Bulletin 37, 97–108 (2003)
5. Brown, C.W., Davenport, J.H.: The complexity of quantifier elimination and cylindrical algebraic decomposition. In: Proceedings of the 2007 International Symposium on Symbolic and Algebraic Computation, ISSAC 2007, pp. 54–60. ACM, New York (2007)
6. Brown, C.W., Kosta, M.: Constructing a single cell in cylindrical algebraic decomposition. J. Symb. Comput. 70, 14–48 (2015)
7. Chen, C., Moreno Maza, M.: An incremental algorithm for computing cylindrical algebraic decompositions. In: Feng, R., Lee, W.-S., Sato, Y. (eds.) Computer Mathematics, pp. 199–221. Springer, Heidelberg (2014)
8. Collins, G.E.: Quantifier elimination for real closed fields by cylindrical algebraic decomposition–preliminary report. SIGSAM Bull. 8(3), 80–90 (1974)
9. Collins, G.E., Hong, H.: Partial cylindrical algebraic decomposition for quantifier elimination. Journal of Symbolic Computation 12(3), 299–328 (1991)
10. Corzilius, F., Loup, U., Junges, S., Ábrahám, E.: SMT-RAT: An SMT-compliant nonlinear real arithmetic toolbox. In: Cimatti, A., Sebastiani, R. (eds.) SAT 2012. LNCS, vol. 7317, pp. 442–448. Springer, Heidelberg (2012)

11. Davenport, J.H., Heintz, J.: Real quantifier elimination is doubly exponential. Journal of Symbolic Computation 5(1), 29–35 (1988)
12. de Moura, L.M., Bjørner, N.: Model-based theory combination. Electronic Notes in Theoretical Computer Science 198(2), 37–49 (2008)
13. de Oliveira, D.C.B., Déharbe, D., Fontaine, P.: Combining decision procedures by (model-)equality propagation. Science of Computer Programming 77(4), 518–532 (2012)
14. Detlefs, D., Nelson, G., Saxe, J.B.: Simplify: A theorem prover for program checking. Technical Report HPL-2003-148, Hewlett Packard Laboratories, July 23, 2003
15. Dolzmann, A.: Algorithmic strategies for applicable real quantifier elimination. PhD thesis, Universität Passau, Innstrasse 29, 94032 Passau (2000)
16. Dolzmann, A., Sturm, T.: Redlog: Computer algebra meets computer logic. SIGSAM Bull. 31(2), 2–9 (1997)
17. Dolzmann, A., Sturm, T.: Simplification of quantifier-free formulae over ordered fields. Journal of Symbolic Computation 24(2), 209–231 (1997)
18. Hearn, A.C., Schöpf, R.: Reduce User's Manual, Free Version, October 2014
19. Jovanović, D., de Moura, L.: Solving non-linear arithmetic. In: Gramlich, B., Miller, D., Sattler, U. (eds.) IJCAR 2012. LNCS, vol. 7364, pp. 339–354. Springer, Heidelberg (2012)
20. King, T., Barrett, C., Tinelli, C.: Leveraging linear and mixed integer programming for SMT. In: Claessen, K., Kuncak, V. (eds.) Formal Methods In Computer-Aided Design (FMCAD), Austin, TX, October, pp. 24:139–24:146. FMCAD Inc. (2014)
21. Kosta, M., Sturm, T., Dolzmann, A.: Better answers to real questions. CoRR, abs/1501.05098 (2015)
22. Nelson, G., Oppen, D.C.: Simplifications by cooperating decision procedures. ACM Transactions on Programming Languages and Systems 1(2), 245–257 (1979)
23. Tarski, A.: A decision method for elementary algebra and geometry. Rand report. Rand Corporation, 1948. Republished as A Decision Method for Elementary Algebra and Geometry, 2nd edn. University of California Press, Berkeley (1951)
24. Weispfenning, V.: The complexity of linear problems in fields. Journal of Symbolic Computation 5(1–2), 3–27 (1988)
25. Weispfenning, V.: A new approach to quantifier elimination for real algebra. Technical Report MIP-9305, FMI, Universität Passau, Germany, July 1993
26. Weispfenning, V.: Quantifier elimination for real algebra – the quadratic case and beyond. AAECC 8, 85–101 (1993)
27. Weispfenning, V.: Quantifier elimination for real algebra – the cubic case. In: Proceedings of the International Symposium on Symbolic and Algebraic Computation, pp. 258–263. ACM, New York (1994)

Decision Procedures for Verification

A New Acceleration-Based Combination Framework for Array Properties

Francesco Alberti[1], Silvio Ghilardi[2], and Natasha Sharygina[3]

[1] Fondazione Centro San Raffaele, Milan, Italy
[2] Università degli Studi di Milano, Milan, Italy
[3] Università della Svizzera Italiana, Lugano, Switzerland

Abstract. This paper presents an acceleration-based combination framework for checking the satisfiability of classes of quantified formulæ of the theory of arrays. We identify sufficient conditions for which an 'accelerability' result can be used as a black-box module inside such satisfiability procedures. Besides establishing new decidability results and relating them to results from recent literature, we discuss the application of our combination framework to the problem of checking the safety of imperative programs with arrays.

1 Introduction

The theory of arrays is one of the most relevant theories for software verification, this is the reason why current research in automated reasoning dedicated so much effort in establishing decision and complexity results for it. From a logical perspective, arrays can be modeled just by adding free function symbols to some fragment of arithmetic. If quantified formulæ are concerned, however, satisfiability becomes intractable when free unary function symbols are added to mild fragments of arithmetic [16]. Since applications require the use of quantifiers, e.g. in order to express invariants of program loops, it becomes crucial to identify sufficiently expressive tractable quantified fragments of the theory of arrays.

Various decidability (and sometimes also complexity) results for such fragments are known from the literature. These results are often orthogonal to each other, rely on rather different techniques, and finding common generalizations is a hard task. Let us mention for instance two contributions from recent literature, namely the decidability results for SIL-fragments in [15] and those for flat mono-sorted fragments in [4]. The flat mono-sorted fragment of [4] is decidable via an SMT-based combination method involving an extra quantifier-elimination step; on the contrary the SIL-fragment of [15] is decided by a procedure that requires back and forth conversions between logic and automata. The SIL-decidable fragment of [15] has a heavy syntactic limitation on consequents of guards: such consequents must be difference bound constraints. On the other hand, the main limitation of the flat mono-sorted fragment in [4], inherited by an analogous limitation from [10], is the impossibility of applying dereference to terms which are not variables in the consequents of guards. This limitation typically prevents

© Springer International Publishing Switzerland 2015
C. Lutz and S. Ranise (Eds.): FroCoS 2015, LNAI 9322, pp. 169–185, 2015.
DOI: 10.1007/978-3-319-24246-0_11

applications to programs where terms like $a[i]$ and $a[i+1]$ are *both* used as, for instance, in array updates.

The technique used in [15] exploits previous acceleration results for difference bound constraints; acceleration (i.e. the definability of the transitive closure of special classes of relations [6–9, 11, 12]) plays an important role in several model-checking approaches which are, in a sense, orthogonal to the SMT-inspired model-checking methods. The curious fact is that acceleration results, previously established using counter automata, were transferred in [15] to array theories via another further conversion from array logic to counter automata formalism.

The contribution of this paper is the definition of a new framework for checking the satisfiability of quantified array formulæ. The principal feature of our framework is that it can exploit and combine acceleration results as *black box* modules. Indeed, the main questions we answer in this paper, in a combination spirit, are the following: *can we use acceleration results as they are, i.e., as black box modules inside decision procedures for array fragments?* What are the *formal conditions* that such 'acceleration modules' have to satisfy in order to be combined as black box modules? Formally, we will answer these two questions with the Definitions 1-2 and with Theorem 3. In particular, the algorithm of Theorem 3 supplies a simple 'guess-and-group' preprocessing step putting current SMT-solvers in the condition of importing acceleration modules. Decidability results like those in [4] and [15] follow as immediate consequences, and further decidable array property fragments can be designed by mere combination.

A remark about acceleration is in order. In our earlier work [2,4], we adopted acceleration techniques into SMT-based software model-checking; to this aim, we investigated what in this paper will be called 'vertical' acceleration, i.e., acceleratability of array relations expressed via specific (syntactically characterized) formulæ in the theory of arrays. In this paper the aim is different, because acceleratability in the underlying arithmetic is used as an ingredient for designing satisfiability procedures at the more complex level of array formulæ. We will refer to this acceleration as 'horizontal' acceleration.

A Running Example. Consider the program of Fig. 1. We want to prove that the assertion in location 4 cannot be violated. The formal proof we produce is *precise*, it does not rely on any form of abstraction or of over-approximation. To do this we need two forms of acceleration: (i) we need *vertical* acceleration (i.e. acceleration at the level of the theory of arrays) to summarize the two loops; (ii) we need *horizontal* acceleration (i.e. acceleration at the level of the underlying arithmetic) in order to discharge the proof obligation coming from (i).

The program in Fig. 1 has two array variables, a_1, a_2, and an integer variable, I. An error path violating the assertion should comprise the following steps: (1) an initialization step leading to initial values $a_1^{(1)}, a_2^{(1)}, I^{(1)}$; (2) n executions of the loop in location 2 leading from $a_1^{(1)}, a_2^{(1)}, I^{(1)}$ to updated values $a_1^{(2)}, a_2^{(2)}, I^{(2)}$; (3) the exit step from the loop in location 2 and the execution of the instruction in location 3, leading from $a_1^{(2)}, a_2^{(2)}, I^{(2)}$ to updated values $a_1^{(3)}, a_2^{(3)}, I^{(3)}$; (4) m executions of the loop in location 4 leading from $a_1^{(3)}, a_2^{(3)}, I^{(3)}$ to updated values

```
            int a₁[N+1]; int a₂[N+1]; int I;
         1  I = 0; a₁[I] = 0; a₂[I] = 0;
                         ⎧ a₁[I + 1] = a₁[I] + 1;  ⎫
         2  while (I < N) ⎨ a₂[I + 1] = I + 1;     ⎬
                         ⎩ I++;                    ⎭
         3  I = 0;
                         ⎧ assert(a₁[I+1] = a₂[I+1]); ⎫
         4  while (I < N) ⎨ I++;                       ⎬
                         ⎩                             ⎭
```

Fig. 1. Running example.

(α_1) $\quad I^{(1)} = 0 \;\wedge\; a_1^{(1)}[I^{(1)}] = 0 \;\wedge\; a_2^{(1)}[I^{(1)}] = 0$

(α_2)
$$
\begin{pmatrix}
\forall i \left(\begin{array}{c} I^{(1)} \leq i < I^{(1)} + n \;\rightarrow\; i < N \;\wedge\; a_1^{(2)}[i+1] = a_1^{(2)}[i] + 1 \;\wedge\; \\ \wedge\; a_2^{(2)}[i+1] = i+1 \end{array} \right) \wedge \\
\wedge\; \forall i \left(I^{(1)} + n + 1 \leq i \leq N \;\rightarrow\; a_1^{(2)}[i] = a_1^{(1)}[i] \;\wedge\; a_2^{(2)}[i] = a_2^{(1)}[i] \right) \wedge \\
\wedge\; \forall i \left(0 \leq i \leq I^{(1)} \;\rightarrow\; a_1^{(2)}[i] = a_1^{(1)}[i] \;\wedge\; a_2^{(2)}[i] = a_2^{(1)}[i] \right) \\
\wedge\; I^{(2)} = I^{(1)} + n
\end{pmatrix}
$$

(α_3) $\quad I^{(2)} \geq N \;\wedge\; I^{(3)} = 0 \;\wedge\; a_1^{(3)} = a_1^{(2)} \;\wedge\; a_2^{(3)} = a_2^{(2)}$

(α_4)
$$
\begin{pmatrix}
\forall i \left(I^{(3)} \leq i < I^{(3)} + m \;\rightarrow\; i < N \;\wedge\; a_1^{(3)}[i+1] = a_2^{(3)}[i+1] \right) \wedge \\
\wedge\; a_1^{(4)} = a_1^{(3)} \;\wedge\; a_2^{(4)} = a_2^{(3)} \;\wedge \\
\wedge\; I^{(4)} = I^{(3)} + m
\end{pmatrix}
$$

(α_5) $\quad a_1^{(4)}[I^{(4)} + 1] \neq a_2^{(4)}[I^{(4)} + 1]$

Fig. 2. Proof obligation.

$a_1^{(4)}, a_2^{(4)}, I^{(4)}$; (5) the satisfiability of the error exit condition from the loop in location 4 by the final values $a_1^{(4)}, a_2^{(4)}, I^{(4)}$. Thus, the error path is feasible iff the conjunction of the formulæ $(\alpha_1) - (\alpha_5)$ from Fig. 2 is satisfiable.

The formulæ (α_2) and (α_4) are computed following mechanical patterns for 'vertical' array acceleration (see Section 5 for more). The satisfiability test of the conjunction $(\alpha_1) \wedge \cdots \wedge (\alpha_5)$ is not handled by current SMT-solvers and it is not trivial indeed, because quantifiers and some form of induction are involved (to make first order logic conversion, read array equalities like $a_1^{(3)} = a_1^{(4)}$ as $\forall i \; (a_1^{(3)}[i] = a_1^{(4)}[i])$). In order to discharge the proof obligation consisting of the satisfiability test of the conjunction of the formulæ $(\alpha_1) - (\alpha_5)$, the method we propose in Theorems 3-4 below relies on acceleration results for fragments of plain arithmetic. Roughly speaking, the idea is the following.

Take for instance the consequent of the first guard of (α_2): such a consequent comes from the loop body of location 2 in Fig. 1. The instructions describing such loop can be converted into a logical formula relating the values of the program variables $\mathtt{I}, \mathtt{a}_1, \mathtt{a}_2$ before a single execution of the loop with the corresponding values $\overline{\mathtt{I}}, \overline{\mathtt{a}_1}, \overline{\mathtt{a}_2}$ after the single execution of the loop. If, in such a logical formula, we abstract out the terms $\mathtt{I}, \mathtt{a}_1[\mathtt{I}], \mathtt{a}_2[\mathtt{I}], \overline{\mathtt{a}_1}[\mathtt{I}], \overline{\mathtt{a}_2}[\mathtt{I}]$ with the fresh variables $i, e_1, e_2, \bar{e}_1, \bar{e}_2$ and the terms $\mathtt{I}+1, \mathtt{a}_1[\mathtt{I}+1], \mathtt{a}_2[\mathtt{I}+1], \overline{\mathtt{a}_1}[\mathtt{I}+1], \overline{\mathtt{a}_2}[\mathtt{I}+1]$ with the corresponding primed variables $i', e_1', e_2', \bar{e}_1', \bar{e}_2'$ we get a purely arithmetical relation $\phi(i, e_1, e_2, \bar{e}_1, \bar{e}_2, i', e_1', e_2', \bar{e}_1', \bar{e}_2')$ between 5-tuples of variables. If this relation is acceleratable, we can replace (up to satisfiability) the first guard of (α_2) with the arithmetical formula expressing the fact that the relation denoted by ϕ is composed with itself $(\mathtt{I}^{(1)} + n) - \mathtt{I}^{(1)} = n$ times. In this way, we get a reduction of the proof obligation of Fig. 2 to plain Presburger arithmetic. Of course, the above description of the reduction is very loose and quite incomplete, we shall turn to this Example in Section 5 and run it in full details. Here we just observe that accelerations in fragments of arithmetic are used as *black boxes* during the *horizontal* phase of the reduction (this phase is computing accelerations inside array intervals, whereas vertical acceleration computes acceleration between array variables as wholes).

Plan of the Paper. Section 2 fixes notations; in Section 3 we introduce acceleratable fragments and in Section 4 we use them in decision procedures for quantified array formulæ. In Section 5 we show applications to reachability problems for array programs. Section 6 concludes. For space reasons, additional material (including some proofs) has been moved to the online available full version [5].

2   Notation

We work in a decidable fragment of arithmetic (typically Presburger arithmetic, but given the modularity of our approach, we can consider even more expressive fragments like [17]); we expand the related language with *free constants* and *free unary function symbols*. When we speak about truth or about validity, *we refer to the structures having as reduct the standard model of the integers* with the natural interpretation of the arithmetic symbols. In order to make our language more manageable, we may enrich it with definable function and predicate symbols (see any textbook in mathematical logic, like [18] for the notion of a definable predicate or function symbol). A *purely arithmetical* formula is a formula that does not contain free function symbols (notice however that such a formula may contain *parameters*, i.e. free constants).

It is convenient to partition the set of variables we use into two disjoint sets $\mathcal{V} = \{x, y, z, w, \ldots, i, j, \ldots\}$ and $\mathcal{V}' = \{x', y', z', w', \ldots, i', j', \ldots\}$, where $\mathcal{V}'$ contains precisely a 'primed' copy of each variable in $\mathcal{V}$. *Renaming substitutions* are bijections σ on variables respecting primed copies (i.e. we have $\sigma(x)' = \sigma(x')$ for all x). Free constants are indicated with letters $c, d, \ldots$, terms with letters $t, u, \ldots$ and formulæ with letters $\phi, \psi, \ldots$. Underlined or bold letters usually denote tuples (of variables, constants, terms) of unspecified length. With $\underline{t} = \underline{u}$

we mean component-wise equality, i.e. $\bigwedge_i t_i = u_i$, where it is implicitly assumed that $\underline{t}, \underline{u}$ have the same length and that $\underline{t} = t_1, \ldots, t_n$ and $\underline{u} = u_1, \ldots, u_n$. The notation $\phi(\underline{x}), t(\underline{x})$ indicates that *at most* the variables $\underline{x}$ occur free in ϕ, t.

When we talk about arrays we assume that they are modeled as unary free function symbols to be denoted with letters $a, b, \ldots$. Read operation (i.e. function application) is denoted with $[-]$; $\mathbf{a}, \mathbf{b}$ stands for tuples of array variables. If $\mathbf{a} = a_1, \ldots, a_n$ and $\underline{t} = t_1, \ldots, t_n$, then $\mathbf{a}[\underline{t}]$ stands for $a_1[t_1], a_2[t_2], \ldots, a_n[t_n]$;[1] however, if $\underline{t}$ is a single term, we may use $\mathbf{a}[t]$ for $a_1[t], \ldots, a_n[t]$. Notations like $\phi(\underline{x}, \mathbf{a}[\underline{t}])$ mean that $\phi(\underline{x}, \underline{y})$ is purely arithmetical and that the tuple of distinct variables $\underline{y}$ has been component-wise replaced by the length-matching tuple of terms $\mathbf{a}[\underline{t}]$.

Arrays are equipped with length; for simplicity, we assume that length is the same for all arrays we consider; we represent it by a free constant N. In our intended models, for every array a, *we assume that $a[x]$ is equal to a conventional value (say, 0) for any x outside the interval* $[0, N]$. When we discuss satisfiability of array fragments, we are only interested in sub-intervals of $[0, N]$, hence we use notations like $t \in [u_1, u_2]$ to mean the conjunction $0 \leq u_1 \leq t \leq u_2 \leq N$; similarly, $t \in [u_1, u_2)$ means $t \in [u_1, u_2 - 1]$. We may also use standard notation for relativized quantifiers, e.g. $\forall i \in [u_1, u_2] \, \psi$ abbreviates $\forall i \, (i \in [u_1, u_2) \rightarrow \psi)$.

3 Acceleratable Fragments

A formula $\phi(\underline{x}, \underline{x}')$ denotes a relation among tuples; $\phi^n(\underline{x}, \underline{x}')$ is the formula representing the composition of the relation denoted by ϕ with itself n-times. More precisely, we have

$$\phi^1(\underline{x}, \underline{x}') : \ \equiv \phi(\underline{x}, \underline{x}'); \qquad \phi^{n+1}(\underline{x}, \underline{x}') : \ \equiv \exists \underline{x}^\sharp \, (\phi^n(\underline{x}, \underline{x}^\sharp) \wedge \phi(\underline{x}^\sharp, \underline{x}')).$$

Definition 1. *A purely arithmetical formula $\phi(\underline{x}, \underline{x}')$, is said to be* acceleratable *iff there exists (and one can actually compute) a formula $\phi^*(\underline{x}, \underline{x}', j)$ such that for all $n \in \mathbb{N}$*

$$\models \phi^n(\underline{x}, \underline{x}') \leftrightarrow \phi^*(\underline{x}, \underline{x}', \bar{n}) \tag{1}$$

where $\bar{n}$ is the n-th numeral, i.e. it is $S(\cdots S(0) \cdots)$, where S - the successor symbol - is applied n-times.[2]

Definition 2. *A set of purely arithmetical formulæ Γ is said to be an* acceleratable fragment *iff every $\phi \in \Gamma$ is acceleratable and Γ is closed under conjunctions and renaming substitutions. An acceleratable fragment Γ is said to be* normal *iff it contains the formulæ $x' = x + 1$ and $y' = x'$ for every variables x, y.*

Closure under conjunctions of acceleratable fragments is a crucial condition: we need it in the 'grouping' step of the modular algorithm of Theorem 3; normality is required in the applications from Section 5. We supply below, using relevant results from the literature, some important examples of acceleratable fragments.

---

[1] This is different from previous papers of ours.

[2] Sometimes we shall write n instead of $\bar{n}$ if confusion does not arise.

Theorem 1. [9,11] Difference Bounds Constraints, *i.e. conjunctions of formulae of the kind*

$$x - x' \bowtie \bar{n}, \quad x - y \bowtie \bar{n}, \quad x' - y' \bowtie \bar{n}$$

(where $n \in \mathbb{Z}$ and $\bowtie \in \{\leq, \geq\}$) are a normal acceleratable fragment.

Theorem 2. [7] Octagons, *i.e. conjunctions of formulae of the kind*

$$x \pm x' \bowtie \bar{n}, \quad x \pm y \bowtie \bar{n}, \quad x' \pm y' \bowtie \bar{n}, \quad 2x \bowtie \bar{n}, \quad 2x' \bowtie \bar{n}$$

(where $n \in \mathbb{Z}$ and $\bowtie \in \{\leq, \geq\}$) are a normal acceleratable fragment.

Another class is introduced in Proposition 1 below. This class (called the class of iteratable formulæ) is ubiquitous; in essence, the idea of an iteratable formula is based on the simple idea of combining (a generalized form of) variable increments with non-deterministic updates; the formal definition of an iteratable formula requires nevertheless some technicalities to match Definition 2.

We recall the notion of an iterator from [2]. Given a m-tuple of terms

$$\mathbf{u}(\underline{x}) := u_1(x_1, \ldots, x_m), \ldots, u_m(x_1, \ldots, x_m) \tag{2}$$

containing the m variables $\underline{x} = x_1, \ldots, x_m$, we indicate with $\mathbf{u}^n$ the term expressing the n-times composition of (the function denoted by) $\mathbf{u}$ with itself. Formally, we have $\mathbf{u}^0(\underline{x}) := \underline{x}$ and

$$\mathbf{u}^{n+1}(\underline{x}) := u_1(\mathbf{u}^n(\underline{x})), \ldots, u_m(\mathbf{u}^n(\underline{x})) \ .$$

Definition 3. *A tuple of terms $\mathbf{u}$ like (2) is said to be an* iterator *iff there is an m-tuple of $m+1$-ary terms $\mathbf{u}^*(\underline{x}, y) := u_1^*(x_1, \ldots, x_m, y), \ldots, u_m^*(x_1, \ldots, x_m, y)$ such that for any natural number $n \geq 0$ it happens that the formula*

$$\mathbf{u}^n(\underline{x}) = \mathbf{u}^*(\underline{x}, \bar{n}) \tag{3}$$

is valid.[3] The ordered tuple of (distinct) variables $(x_1, \ldots, x_m)$ is said to be the domain *of the iterator $\mathbf{u}$ and $\mathbf{u}$ is said to be an m-ary iterator.*

Example 1. The canonical example is when we have $m = 1$ and $\mathbf{u} := u_1(x_1) := x_1 + 1$; this is an iterator with $u_1^*(x_1, y) := x_1 + y$. □

Example 2. The previous example can be modified, by choosing $\mathbf{u}$ to be $x_1 + \bar{k}$, for some integer $k \neq 0$: then we have $u_1^*(x_1, y) := x_1 + k * y$ (where $k * y$ is the sum $y + \cdots + y$ of k copies of y). □

Example 3. Sometimes we need to use definable functions to build $\mathbf{u}^*$. Take $\mathbf{u}$ to be $\bar{n} - x_1$; then we have $u_1^*(x_1, y) := (\mathbf{if}\ y \equiv 0\ (mod\ 2)\ \mathbf{then}\ x_1\ \mathbf{else}\ \bar{n} - x_1)$. □

---

[3] Recall that in this paper 'validity' means validity in the class of our intended structures - those having the standard model of arithmetic as reduct.

Example 4. Finite monoid affine transformations [12] supply another interesting example. Let v be a vector from $\mathbb{Z}^m$ and let M be a $m \times m$ integer matrix generating a finite monoid (i.e. we have that $M^{k+l} = M^k$ for some $k, l > 0$). Putting $\mathbf{u}(\underline{x}) := M\underline{x} + v$, we get an iterator (the definition of $\mathbf{u}^*(\underline{x}, y)$ requires the identification of a rather complex - but straightforward - definable function, see [12]).   □

Definition 4. *A formula $\phi(\underline{x}, \underline{x}')$ is said to be* iteratable *iff there is a finite set I_ϕ of iterators such that:*

(0) *the variables $\underline{x}, \underline{x}'$ are partitioned as $\underline{z}, \underline{z}', \underline{w}'$ (notice that the unprimed variables $\underline{w}$ do not occur in ϕ);*
(i) *the domain of every $\mathbf{u} \in I_\phi$ is included in $\underline{z}$;*
(ii) *every $z \in \underline{z}$ belongs to the domain of at least one $\mathbf{u} \in I_\phi$;*
(ii) *if $(z_{i_1}, \ldots, z_{i_s}) \subseteq \underline{z}$ is the domain of $\mathbf{u} = (u_1, \ldots, u_s) \in I_\phi$, then*

$$\phi(\underline{x}, \underline{x}') \to z'_{i_j} = u_j(z_{i_1}, \ldots, z_{i_s}) \tag{4}$$

is valid for all $j = 1, \ldots, s$.

Thus, in iteratable formulae, the 'updates' z_i' are deterministic and expressed via an iterator; the reason why we allow I_ϕ to be a set (not just a singleton) is because we want to ensure closure under conjunctions of iteratable formulæ. The typical example of an iteratable formula is a formula of the kind

$$\underline{z}' = \mathbf{u}(\underline{z}) \land \psi(\underline{z}, \underline{z}', \underline{w}') \tag{5}$$

where ψ is arbitrary and $\mathbf{u}$ is an iterator with domain $\underline{z}$. Notice that, when taking iterated composition of the relation denoted by the above formula with itself, the variables $\underline{w}'$ are non-deterministically chosen at each step.

Proposition 1. *The set of iteratable formulæ form a normal acceleratable fragment.*

Proof. For the full proof, see [5]. Here we just give the explicit definition of the accelerated formula ϕ^* for an iteratable ϕ. Suppose that free variables occurring in ϕ are partitioned as $z_1, \ldots, z_n, z_1', \ldots, z_n', \underline{w}'$; to make our notation more compact, we let $\underline{z} := z_1, \ldots, z_n$ and $\underline{x} := \underline{z}, \underline{w}$. The formula $\phi^*(\underline{x}, \underline{x}', j)$ is given by

$$\underline{z}' = \mathbf{v}(\underline{z}, j) \land \forall k \in [0, j) \, \exists \tilde{\underline{w}} \left(\begin{array}{l} (k = j-1 \to \tilde{\underline{w}} = \underline{w}') \land \\ \land\ \phi(\mathbf{v}(\underline{z}, k), \mathbf{v}(\underline{z}, k+1), \tilde{w}) \end{array} \right) \tag{6}$$

where the tuple of terms $\mathbf{v}(\underline{z}, k) := v_1(\underline{z}, k), \ldots, v_n(\underline{z}, k)$ is obtained as follows. For every $z_l \in \underline{z}$, choose some iterator $\mathbf{u}^l \in I_\phi$ such that z_l is in the domain of $\mathbf{u}^l$: if z_l occurs at the h-th place in such a domain, we let v_l be $(\mathbf{u}^l)_h^*(\underline{z}, k)$. In other words: we compute the iteration $(\mathbf{u}^l)^*$ of $\mathbf{u}^l$ according to (3), take its h-component, and apply it to $\underline{z}$ and k (actually, $(\mathbf{u}^l)^*$ will be applied to k and to the subset of $\underline{z}$ which is the domain of $\mathbf{u}^l$, however it is compatible with our notational conventions to display more variables than those actually occurring in a syntactic expression).   □

Example 5. Consider the following formula ϕ (this example will be used for the proof obligation of Fig. 2 - variables are numbered so to make this application easier to recognize):

$$i' = i{+}1 \ \wedge \ i < N \ \wedge \ (x_1^{(2)})' = x_1^{(2)}{+}1 \ \wedge \ (x_2^{(2)})' = i{+}1 \ \wedge \ (x_1^{(3)})' = (x_1^{(2)})' \ \wedge$$
$$\wedge \ (x_2^{(3)})' = (x_2^{(2)})' \ \wedge \ (x_1^{(3)})' = (x_2^{(3)})' \ \wedge \ (x_1^{(4)})' = (x_1^{(3)})' \ \wedge \ (x_2^{(4)})' = (x_2^{(3)})'$$

To show that ϕ is iteratable, let us put

$$\underline{z} := \ i, x_1^{(2)}, \qquad \underline{w}' := \ (x_2^{(2)})', (x_1^{(3)})', (x_2^{(3)})', (x_1^{(4)})', (x_2^{(4)})' \ ;$$

an iterator $\mathbf{u}(\underline{z})$ such that $\phi \models \underline{z}' = \mathbf{u}(\underline{z})$ is given by

$$i' = i{+}1, \ \ (x_1^{(2)})' = x_1^{(2)}{+}1 \ .$$

As a consequence, the formula $\phi^*(\underline{z}, \underline{z}', \underline{w}', j)$, according to (6), can be written as

$$i' = i{+}j \ \wedge \ (x_1^{(2)})' = x_1^{(2)}{+}j \ \wedge \ \forall k \ \in [0, j) \ \exists \underline{\tilde{w}} \ ((k = j{-}1 \rightarrow \underline{\tilde{w}} = \underline{w}') \wedge \tilde{\phi}_k) \ \ (7)$$

where $\tilde{\phi}_k$ (omitting the trivial literals $i + k + 1 = i + k + 1$ and $x_1^{(2)} + k + 1 = x_1^{(2)} + k + 1$) is the following formula

$$\tilde{\phi}_k \equiv \ \ \ i{+}k < N \ \wedge \ \tilde{x}_2^{(2)} = i{+}k{+}1 \ \wedge \ \tilde{x}_1^{(3)} = x_1^{(2)}{+}k{+}1 \ \wedge$$
$$\wedge \ \tilde{x}_2^{(3)} = \tilde{x}_2^{(2)} \ \wedge \ \tilde{x}_1^{(3)} = \tilde{x}_2^{(3)} \ \wedge \ \tilde{x}_1^{(4)} = \tilde{x}_1^{(3)} \ \wedge \ \tilde{x}_2^{(4)} = \tilde{x}_2^{(3)}$$

Notice that formula (6) introduces quantifiers; this does not matter because the underlying fragment of arithmetic we work with is assumed to be fully decidable. In practice, fragments used in verification - like difference logic and Presburger arithmetic - admit quantifier elimination and, if we eliminate quantifiers from (7), we can simplify it to

$$i' = i{+}j \ \wedge \ (x_1^{(2)})' = x_1^{(2)}{+}j \ \wedge \ i + j < N \ \wedge \ (x_2^{(2)})' = i{+}j \ \wedge \ (x_1^{(3)})' = x_1^{(2)}{+}j \wedge$$
$$\wedge \ (x_2^{(3)})' = i{+}j \ \wedge \ x_1^{(2)} = i \ \wedge \ (x_1^{(4)})' = x_1^{(2)}{+}j \ \wedge \ (x_2^{(4)})' = i{+}j$$

$$(8)$$

Thus (8) represents the formula $\phi^*(\underline{z}, \underline{z}', \underline{w}', j)$, up to equivalence. □

4 Acceleration Modules in Satisfiability Procedures

Let Γ be an acceleratable fragment; a Γ-*guard* is a formula of the kind

$$\forall i \ (\ i \in [t, u) \rightarrow \phi(i, \mathbf{a}[i], \mathbf{a}[i + 1]) \ ) \tag{9}$$

such that the formula $i' = i{+}1 \wedge \phi(i, \underline{y}, \underline{y}')$ belongs to Γ and t, u are ground terms (recall that we expanded the language with free constants, hence ground terms may contain them). Notice that, since Γ is closed under renaming substitutions, the choice of the tuple $i, \underline{y}, i', \underline{y}'$ is immaterial.

Theorem 3. *Let Γ be an acceleratable fragment; then, any Boolean combination of ground formulae and Γ-guards is decidable for satisfiability.*

Proof. Since the negation of a Γ-guard can be converted into a ground formula by Skolemization, it is sufficient to check the satisfiability of a conjunction

$$L_1 \wedge \cdots \wedge L_n \wedge G_1 \wedge \cdots \wedge G_m \tag{10}$$

of ground literals and Γ-guards. We design a satisfiability algorithm below.

STEP I [Guess an ordering]. Let S be the set of *ground* terms occurring in (10);[4] guess a partition on S and an ordering $C_1 < \cdots < C_l$ of the equivalence classes. For each equivalence class C_i, introduce a fresh constant c_i; then add to the current formula the literals of the form $c_i = t$ (varying $t \in C_i$) and of the form $c_i < c_{i+1}$.

STEP II [Cleaning] We call a constant c_h an *out-of-bound* constant in case h is bigger (resp. smaller) than the index of the constant corresponding to the equivalence class of N (resp. of 0); a term t is out-of-bound iff the free constant c_k representing the equivalence class of t is out-of-bound. Dereference terms $a_j[t]$, where t is out-of-bound, are replaced by the conventional value 0. Guards whose antecedent is of the kind $i \in [t, u)$, where t is out-of-bound or u is out-of-bound or u is in the same equivalence class as N, are removed (by our conventions from Section 2, these guards are tautological, having an inconsistent antecedent). Similarly, guards whose antecedent is of the kind $i \in [c_h, c_k)$ for $h \geq k$ are removed too.

STEP III [Grouping the guards]. In this step, we rewrite guards. The new guards will be of the kind

$$\forall i\, (i \in [c_k, c_{k+1}) \rightarrow \psi_k(i, \mathbf{a}[i], \mathbf{a}[i+1]))$$

where $k + 1$ is less or equal to the index of the constant corresponding to the equivalence class of N and k is bigger or equal to the index of the constant corresponding to the equivalence class of 0. The formula ψ_k is obtained by taking the conjunction of the relevant consequents of the guards from (10). In other words, if (10) contains the guard $\forall i\, (i \in [t, u) \rightarrow \phi(i, \mathbf{a}[i], \mathbf{a}[i+1]))$ and the equivalence class of c_k follows the equivalence class of t and the equivalence class of u follows the equivalence class of c_{k+1}, then ϕ is included among the conjuncts of ψ_k. Since acceleratable fragments are closed under conjunctions, the new guards we obtain are still Γ-guards.

STEP IV [Reduction to Pure Arithmetic]. Let

$$G \wedge \bigwedge_{k=1}^{l} \forall i\, (i \in [c_k, c_{k+1}) \rightarrow \psi_k(i, \mathbf{a}[i], \mathbf{a}[i+1])) \tag{11}$$

---

[4] We must include $0, N$ among such terms; however, to economize the guessing step, besides $0, N$, we can limit ourselves to terms t occurring in sub-expression of the form $a[t], i \in [t, u), i \in [u, t)$.

be the formula we obtain after STEP III. Here G is a conjunction of ground literals (including the literals added in STEP I) and the quantified formulae are Γ-guards. By the definition of a Γ-guard, the formulæ

$$\phi_k(i, i', \underline{y}, \underline{y}') :\equiv i' = i + 1 \wedge \psi_k(i, \underline{y}, \underline{y}') \tag{12}$$

are in Γ. We now replace (11) by the formula

$$G(\underline{d}_1/\mathbf{a}[c_1], \ldots, \underline{d}_l/\mathbf{a}[c_l]) \wedge \bigwedge_{k=1}^{l} \phi_k^*(c_k, c_{k+1}, \underline{d}_k, \underline{d}_{k+1}, c_{k+1} - c_k) \tag{13}$$

where $\underline{d}_1, \ldots, \underline{d}_l$ are tuples of fresh constants and $G(\underline{d}_1/\mathbf{a}[c_1], \ldots, \underline{d}_l/\mathbf{a}[c_l])$ is obtained from G by replacing component-wise, for each $k = 1, \ldots, l$ and for each t lying in the same equivalence class as c_k, the tuple $\mathbf{a}[t]$ by the tuple $\underline{d}_k$.

We claim that the formulæ (13) are equi-satisfiable with the original formula (10). Clearly, it is sufficient to show that (13) is equi-satisfiable to (11). Suppose that (13) is satisfiable: this means that we can assign integer numbers to the free constants occurring in (13), so to make the statement (13) true. We use the same letters to denote a free constant, the number assigned to it and the corresponding numeral. From the fact that $\phi_k^*(c_k, c_{k+1}, \underline{d}_k, \underline{d}_{k+1}, c_{k+1} - c_k)$ is true (for the given choice of the $c_k, c_{k+1}, \underline{d}_k, \underline{d}_{k+1}$), we can infer that $\phi_k^{c_{k+1}-c_k}(c_k, c_{k+1}, \underline{d}_k, \underline{d}_{k+1})$ holds by Definition 1. By (12) and the definition of relation composition, we get tuples $\underline{d}_k := \underline{d}_{c_k}, \underline{d}_{c_k+1}, \underline{d}_{c_k+2} \cdots, \underline{d}_{c_k+(c_{k+1}-c_k)} := \underline{d}_{k+1}$ such that

$$\psi_k(c_k, \underline{d}_{c_k}, \underline{d}_{c_k+1}), \ \psi_k(c_k + 1, \underline{d}_{c_k+1}, \underline{d}_{c_k+2}), \ \ldots, \ \psi_k(c_{k+1} - 1, \underline{d}_{c_{k+1}-1}, \underline{d}_{c_{k+1}})$$

all hold. Thus, we define the interpretations of the unary integer functions $\mathbf{a}$, by letting $\mathbf{a}(n) := 0$ for $n > N$ and $n < 0$ and for $c_k \leq n \leq c_{k+1}$ by taking $\mathbf{a}(n)$ to be $\underline{d}_n$. Formula (11) holds by construction. Similar considerations, read in the opposite sense, show that the satisfiability of (11) implies the satisfiability of (13). □

Remark 1 (Complexity). Since this is a modular procedure, its complexity can only be evaluated relatively to the complexities of the acceleration module and of the underlying arithmetic solver. To this aim, notice that Steps I-II introduce a linear guessing followed by linear manipulations and that Step III produces a quadratically long formula (11). After these steps, the complexity relies entirely on the complexity of the acceleration module and on the complexity of the arithmetic solver: if we suppose that the former requires space $f_S(n)$ and time $f_T(n)$ to produce the accelerated formula (13) out of (11) and that the latter requires space $g_S(m)$ and time $g_T(m)$ for its satisfiability checks, the cost of the whole procedure requires space bounded by $g_S(f_S(O(n^2)))$ and time bounded by $2^{O(n^2)} \cdot g_T(f_T(O(n^2)))$ (we need exponential time to go through all possible linear orderings).

We underline that in examples coming from practical verification problems, the expensive guess of STEP I is not needed, because the few consistent guessings are suggested by the problem itself, as witnessed by the example below.

Example 6. We consider the proof obligation of Fig. 2. We first need to rewrite all universally quantified guards in it in such a way that they match the pattern given by (9). Thus, sub-formulae like $\forall i \; (t \leq i \leq u \; \rightarrow \; \gamma(i, \mathbf{a}[i]))$ must be rewritten as $(t \leq u \rightarrow \gamma(t, \mathbf{a}[t])) \wedge \forall i \; (i \in [t, u) \; \rightarrow \; \gamma(i+1, \mathbf{a}[i+1]))$; similarly, array equations of the form $\mathbf{a} = \mathbf{b}$ are rewritten to $\mathbf{a}[0] = \mathbf{b}[0] \wedge \forall i \; (i \in [0, N) \rightarrow \mathbf{a}[i+1] = \mathbf{b}[i+1])$. After these rewritings, we can observe that all guards occurring in Fig. 2 are Γ-guards, where Γ is the acceleratable fragment of Proposition 1 (one may equivalently use the fragment of Theorem 1 instead). To see this, let us abstract out $a_1^{(k)}[i], a_1^{(k)}[i+1]$ with $x_1^{(k)}, (x_1^{(k)})'$ and $a_2^{(k)}[i], a_2^{(k)}[i+1]$ with $x_2^{(k)}, (x_2^{(k)})'$ ($k = 1, \ldots, 4$). Then, let us consider for instance the first guard of (α_2): the formula to be checked to belong to the acceleratable fragment is

$$i' = i + 1 \wedge i < N \wedge (x_1^{(2)})' = x_1^{(2)} + 1 \wedge (x_2^{(2)})' = i + 1$$

and it is clear that this formula fits Proposition 1 (and Theorem 1 too). Thus, we can run the algorithm of Theorem 3 to check the unsatisfiability of the conjunction of the formulæ (α_1) − (α_5). As for STEP I, consider the partition

$$\{0, \mathtt{I}^{(1)}, \mathtt{I}^{(3)}\} \; < \; \{\mathtt{I}^{(3)} + m, \mathtt{I}^{(4)}\} \; < \; \{\mathtt{I}^{(4)} + 1\} \; < \; \{N, \mathtt{I}^{(2)}, \mathtt{I}^{(1)} + n\} \; < \; \{\mathtt{I}^{(1)} + n + 1\}$$

(other partitions are either analogous to this one or do not admit a consistent ordering). We call c_1, c_2, c_3, c_4, c_5, respectively, the fresh constants denoting a generic element of the above classes of the partition (notice that c_5 is out-of-bound). STEP II eliminates the second guard from (α_2). STEP III produces a formula which is the conjunction of the ground literals from Fig. 3 with three Γ-guards $\gamma_{12}, \gamma_{23}, \gamma_{34}$ (relative to the intervals $[c_1, c_2), [c_2, c_3), [c_3, c_4)$, respectively), also displayed in Fig. 3.

Going to STEP IV, we now consider the formula (13); the acceleration formulæ replacing the Γ-guards $\gamma_{12}, \gamma_{23}, \gamma_{34}$ can be drawn from Example 5 (strictly speaking, Example 5 analyzes only γ_{12}, but the other two Γ-guards are analyzed in the same way). Thus formula (13) becomes equivalent to the conjunction of the literals from Fig. 3 together with the additional literals from Fig. 4. To improve readability, in Fig. 4 we do not replace terms $\mathbf{a}[t]$ with fresh constants depending on the equivalence class of t like in (13) (as a consequence, we shall need below congruence closure besides arithmetic to check inconsistency). To conclude the unsatisfiability test of the proof obligation from Fig. 2 it is then sufficient to observe that the following unsatisfiable subset can be extracted from the literals in Fig. 3-4:

$$a_1^{(4)}[\mathtt{I}^{(4)} + 1] \neq a_2^{(4)}[\mathtt{I}^{(4)} + 1], \qquad c_3 = \mathtt{I}^{(4)} + 1, \qquad c_1 = 0,$$
$$a_1^{(4)}[c_3] = a_1^{(2)}[c_2] + (c_3 - c_2), \qquad c_1 = \mathtt{I}^{(1)}, \qquad a_1^{(2)}[0] = a_1^{(1)}[0],$$
$$a_1^{(2)}[c_2] = a_1^{(2)}[c_1] + (c_2 - c_1), \qquad a_1^{(1)}[\mathtt{I}^{(1)}] = 0, \qquad a_2^{(4)}[c_3] = c_2 + (c_3 - c_2). \quad \square$$

The decidable class covered by Theorem 3 includes some remarkable classes known to be decidable from the literature: in particular, it covers the SIL-fragments of [15] and the flat mono-sorted fragments of [4]. We point out, however, that some other known decidable classes are still orthogonal to the classes

---

Literals:

$I^{(1)} = 0$, $a_1^{(1)}[I^{(1)}] = 0$, $a_2^{(1)}[I^{(1)}] = 0$, $a_1^{(2)}[0] = a_1^{(1)}[0]$, $a_2^{(2)}[0] = a_2^{(1)}[0]$,

$I^{(2)} = I^{(1)} + n$, $I^{(2)} \geq N$, $I^{(3)} = 0$, $a_1^{(3)}[0] = a_1^{(2)}[0]$, $a_2^{(3)}[0] = a_2^{(2)}[0]$,

$I^{(4)} = I^{(3)} + m$, $a_1^{(4)}[0] = a_1^{(3)}[0]$, $a_2^{(4)}[0] = a_2^{(3)}[0]$, $a_1^{(4)}[I^{(4)}+1] \neq a_2^{(4)}[I^{(4)}+1]$,

$c_1 = 0$, $c_1 = I^{(1)}$, $c_1 = I^{(3)}$, $c_1 < c_2$, $c_2 = I^{(3)} + m$, $c_2 = I^{(4)}$, $c_2 < c_3$, $c_3 = I^{(4)}+1$,

$c_3 < c_4$, $c_4 = N$, $c_4 = I^{(2)}$, $c_4 = I^{(1)} + n$, $c_4 < c_5$, $c_5 = I^{(1)} + n + 1$.

Guards:

$$\gamma_{12} \equiv \quad \forall i \in [c_1, c_2) \begin{pmatrix} i < N \wedge \ a_1^{(2)}[i+1] = a_1^{(2)}[i] + 1 \ \wedge \ a_2^{(2)}[i+1] = i+1 \ \wedge \\ \wedge \ a_1^{(3)}[i+1] = a_1^{(2)}[i+1] \ \wedge \ a_2^{(3)}[i+1] = a_2^{(2)}[i+1] \wedge \\ \wedge \ a_1^{(3)}[i+1] = a_2^{(3)}[i+1] \wedge \\ \wedge \ a_1^{(4)}[i+1] = a_1^{(3)}[i+1] \ \wedge \ a_2^{(4)}[i+1] = a_2^{(3)}[i+1] \end{pmatrix}$$

$$\gamma_{23} \equiv \quad \forall i \in [c_2, c_3) \begin{pmatrix} i < N \wedge \ a_1^{(2)}[i+1] = a_1^{(2)}[i] + 1 \ \wedge \ a_2^{(2)}[i+1] = i+1 \ \wedge \\ \wedge \ a_1^{(3)}[i+1] = a_1^{(2)}[i+1] \ \wedge \ a_2^{(3)}[i+1] = a_2^{(2)}[i+1] \ \wedge \\ \wedge \ a_1^{(4)}[i+1] = a_1^{(3)}[i+1] \ \wedge \ a_2^{(4)}[i+1] = a_2^{(3)}[i+1] \end{pmatrix}$$

$$\gamma_{34} \equiv \quad \forall i \in [c_3, c_4) \begin{pmatrix} i < N \wedge \ a_1^{(2)}[i+1] = a_1^{(2)}[i] + 1 \ \wedge \ a_2^{(2)}[i+1] = i+1 \ \wedge \\ \wedge \ a_2^{(3)}[i+1] = a_2^{(2)}[i+1] \ \wedge \ a_1^{(3)}[i+1] = a_1^{(2)}[i+1] \ \wedge \\ \wedge \ a_1^{(4)}[i+1] = a_1^{(3)}[i+1] \ \wedge \ a_2^{(4)}[i+1] = a_2^{(3)}[i+1] \end{pmatrix}$$

Fig. 3. Literals and Guards after STEP III (see Example 6).

---

presented in this paper. Since a comprehensive comparison is rather technical and require more space, we defer it to [5].

5   Applications to Imperative Programs

In this section we show how to use our results in order to establish decidability of safety problems for a class of imperative programs handling arrays. We will consider programs with *flat* control-flow graph with loops represented by acceleratable formulæ. This section provides just initial assesments: future more extensive work may comprise the exploitation of generalized notions like iterators/selectors [2] and the adoption of compiler-oriented optimization features [1,14] which lie outside the scope of this work.

Henceforth **v** will denote the variables of the programs we analyze. Formally, $\mathbf{v} = \mathbf{a}, I$ where, according to our conventions, **a** is a tuple of array variables (modeled as free unary function symbols in our framework) and I is an integer variable to be used as a counter to scan arrays (we omit further integer variables for simplicity, but see Remark 2 below). As stated in Section 2, we work in a

---

Literals from γ_{12}:

$c_2 = c_1 + (c_2 - c_1),$ $\qquad$ $\mathbf{a}_1^{(2)}[c_2] = \mathbf{a}_1^{(2)}[c_1] + (c_2 - c_1),$ $\quad$ $\mathbf{a}_2^{(2)}[c_2] = c_1 + (c_2 - c_1),$

$\mathbf{a}_1^{(3)}[c_2] = \mathbf{a}_1^{(2)}[c_1] + (c_2 - c_1),$ $\quad$ $\mathbf{a}_1^{(4)}[c_2] = \mathbf{a}_1^{(2)}[c_1] + (c_2 - c_1),$ $\quad$ $c_1 + (c_2 - c_1) < N,$

$\mathbf{a}_2^{(3)}[c_2] = c_1 + (c_2 - c_1),$ $\qquad$ $\mathbf{a}_2^{(4)}[c_2] = c_1 + (c_2 - c_1),$ $\qquad$ $\mathbf{a}_1^{(2)}[c_1] = c_1 \,.$

Literals from γ_{23}:

$c_3 = c_2 + (c_3 - c_2),$ $\qquad$ $\mathbf{a}_1^{(2)}[c_3] = \mathbf{a}_1^{(2)}[c_2] + (c_3 - c_2),$ $\quad$ $\mathbf{a}_2^{(2)}[c_3] = c_2 + (c_3 - c_2),$

$\mathbf{a}_1^{(3)}[c_3] = \mathbf{a}_1^{(2)}[c_2] + (c_3 - c_2),$ $\quad$ $\mathbf{a}_1^{(4)}[c_3] = \mathbf{a}_1^{(2)}[c_2] + (c_3 - c_2),$ $\quad$ $c_2 + (c_3 - c_2) < N,$

$\mathbf{a}_2^{(3)}[c_3] = c_2 + (c_3 - c_2),$ $\qquad$ $\mathbf{a}_2^{(4)}[c_3] = c_2 + (c_3 - c_2) \,.$

Literals from γ_{34}:

$c_4 = c_3 + (c_4 - c_3),$ $\qquad$ $\mathbf{a}_1^{(2)}[c_4] = \mathbf{a}_1^{(2)}[c_3] + (c_4 - c_3),$ $\quad$ $\mathbf{a}_2^{(2)}[c_4] = c_3 + (c_4 - c_3),$

$\mathbf{a}_1^{(3)}[c_4] = \mathbf{a}_1^{(2)}[c_3] + (c_4 - c_3),$ $\quad$ $\mathbf{a}_1^{(4)}[c_4] = \mathbf{a}_1^{(2)}[c_3] + (c_4 - c_3),$ $\quad$ $c_3 + (c_4 - c_3) < N,$

$\mathbf{a}_2^{(3)}[c_4] = c_3 + (c_4 - c_3),$ $\qquad$ $\mathbf{a}_2^{(4)}[c_4] = c_3 + (c_4 - c_3) \,.$

Fig. 4. (STEP IV) Literals whose conjunction is the formula $\bigwedge_{k=1}^{3} \phi_k^*$ from (13) (see Example 6).

decidable fragment of arithmetic, extended with free constants and free unary function symbols. A *state-formula* is a formula $\alpha(\mathbf{v})$ representing a (possibly infinite) set of configurations of the program under analysis. A *transition formula* is a formula of the kind $\tau(\mathbf{v}, \overline{\mathbf{v}})$ where $\overline{\mathbf{v}}$ is a renaming of the tuple $\mathbf{v}$ (we prefer not to use here the standard model-checking notation $\mathbf{v}'$ for $\overline{\mathbf{v}}$, because we already used the primed notation in the previous sections in a different context).

Definition 5 (Programs). *Given a set of variables $\mathbf{v}$, a program is a triple $\mathcal{P} = (L, \Lambda, E)$, where (i) $L = \{l_1, \ldots, l_n\}$ is a set of* program locations *among which we distinguish an initial location l_{init} and an error location l_{error}; (ii) Λ is a finite set of transition formulæ $\{\tau_1(\mathbf{v}, \overline{\mathbf{v}}), \ldots, \tau_r(\mathbf{v}, \overline{\mathbf{v}})\}$ and (iii) $E \subseteq L \times \Lambda \times L$ is a set of* actions.

We indicate by $src, \mathcal{L}, tgt$ the three projection functions on E; that is, for $e = (l_i, \tau_j, l_k) \in E$, we have $src(e) = l_i$ (this is called the 'source' location of e), $\mathcal{L}(e) = \tau_j$ (this is called the 'label' of e) and $tgt(e) = l_k$ (this is called the 'target' location of e).

Definition 6 (Program paths). *A* program path *(in short,* path*) of $\mathcal{P} = (L, \Lambda, E)$ is a sequence $\rho \in E^n$, i.e., $\rho = e_1, e_2, \ldots, e_n$, such that for every e_i, e_{i+1}, we have $tgt(e_i) = src(e_{i+1})$. We denote with $|\rho|$ the length of the path. An* error path *is a path ρ with $src(e_1) = l_{\mathsf{init}}$ and $tgt(e_{|\rho|}) = l_{\mathsf{error}}$. A path ρ is a* feasible path *if $\bigwedge_{j=1}^{|\rho|} \mathcal{L}(e_j)^{(j)}$ is satisfiable, where $\mathcal{L}(e_j)^{(j)}$ represents*

$\tau_{i_j}(\mathbf{v}^{(j-1)}, \mathbf{v}^{(j)})$, with $\mathcal{L}(e_j) = \tau_{i_j}$. The (unbounded) reachability problem *for a program* $\mathcal{P}$ *is to detect if* $\mathcal{P}$ *admits a feasible error path.*

One word about the notation $\tau_{i_j}(\mathbf{v}^{(j-1)}, \mathbf{v}^{(j)})$ used above: when we use tuples of variables like $\mathbf{v}^{(j)}$, we mean that we simultaneously employ many disjointed renamed copies (written $\mathbf{v}^{(1)}, \mathbf{v}^{(2)}, \mathbf{v}^{(3)}, \ldots$) of the tuple $\mathbf{v}$. Obviously, $\tau_{i_j}(\mathbf{v}^{(j-1)}, \mathbf{v}^{(j)})$ indicates the formula obtained from $\tau_{i_j}(\mathbf{v}, \overline{\mathbf{v}})$ by replacing $\mathbf{v}$ by $\mathbf{v}^{(j-1)}$ and $\overline{\mathbf{v}}$ by $\mathbf{v}^{(j)}$.

We first give the definition of a flat^0-program, i.e. of a program with only self-loops for which each location belongs to at most one loop.

Definition 7 (flat^0-**program**). *A program* $\mathcal{P}$ *is a* flat^0-*program if for every path* $\rho = e_1, \ldots, e_n$ *of* $\mathcal{P}$ *it holds that for every* $j < k$ *(*$j, k \in \{1, \ldots, n\}$*), if* $src(e_j) = tgt(e_k)$ *then* $e_j = e_{j+1} = \cdots = e_k$.

We shall consider below only programs whose transitions are of two kinds:

(i) *quantifier-free* formulae $\tau(\mathbf{v}, \overline{\mathbf{v}})$: these formulæ can be used only as labels for actions which are not self-loops (i.e. whose source and target locations do not coincide);

(ii) transitions used as labels in *self-loops*: these transitions must be of the following kind

$$(\forall i \neq I{+}1 \; \mathbf{a}[i] = \overline{\mathbf{a}}[i]) \wedge \gamma(I, \mathbf{a}[I], \mathbf{a}[I+1], \overline{\mathbf{a}}[I+1]) \wedge \overline{I} = I{+}1 \quad (14)$$

where γ is quantifier-free and arithmetical over $\mathbf{a}[I], \mathbf{a}[I+1], \overline{\mathbf{a}}[I+1]$.

Formula (14) says that the loop modifies just the entry $I{+}1$ of each array $\mathbf{a}$. It is general enough to include instructions of the following kind

```
while(δ(I, a[I], a[I + 1])){  a[I + 1] := t(I, a[I], a[I + 1]);  I++;  }
```

where δ is a guard expressed via a quantifier-free formula arithmetical over $\mathbf{a}[I], \mathbf{a}[I+1]$ and where the terms $\mathbf{t}$ are also arithmetical over $\mathbf{a}[I], \mathbf{a}[I+1]$.

Remark 2. Additional integer variables can be modeled as arrays as follows. Suppose we have an integer variable C and that inside the loop we want to update it as $C := \mathbf{u}(I, C, \mathbf{a}[I], \mathbf{a}[I+1])$. Then we can introduce a fresh array variable c; this variable is (partially) initialized as $c[I] := C$ before the loop, it is returned as $C := c[I]$ after the loop and it is updated inside the loop as $c[I+1] := \mathbf{u}(I, c[I], \mathbf{a}[I], \mathbf{a}[I+1])$.

Assumption. *We assume from now on that our programs are* flat^0-*programs and that their transitions are subject to the above restrictions* (i) *and* (ii).

This assumption is not yet sufficient for decidability, though. To gain decidability, we put further conditions on guards and updates. Let us consider the list of variables $I, e, \overline{e}, I', e', \overline{e}'$ where the variables $e, \overline{e}$ are meant to abstract out $\mathbf{a}[I], \overline{\mathbf{a}}[I]$ and the variables $\mathbf{e}', \overline{\mathbf{e}}'$ to abstract out $\mathbf{a}[I+1], \overline{\mathbf{a}}[I+1]$. We call *arithmetic projections* of $\mathcal{P}$ the formulæ

$$I' = I + 1 \ \wedge \ \gamma(I, \overline{\mathbf{e}}, \mathbf{e}', \overline{\mathbf{e}}') \tag{15}$$

extracted from the self-loops instructions (14) occurring in $\mathcal{P}$. We give some sufficient practical (relatively simple) conditions so that the simultaneous acceleration of the formulæ (14) occurring in a path of $\mathcal{P}$ meets the hypothesis of Theorem 3. One needs to pay attention to the fact that the update of $\mathbf{a}[I+1]$ is recursive; this is why the variables $\overline{\mathbf{e}}$ abstracting out $\overline{\mathbf{a}}[I]$ have been preferred to[5] the $\mathbf{e}$ (abstracting out $\mathbf{a}[I]$) when defining arithmetic projections.

Theorem 4. *The unbounded reachability problem for $\mathcal{P}$ is decidable if there is a normal acceleratable fragment containing all arithmetic projections of $\mathcal{P}$.*

Proof. (Sketch, see [5] for details). For a transition relation $\tau(\mathbf{v}, \overline{\mathbf{v}})$ given by (14), the transition $\tau^*(\mathbf{v}, \overline{\mathbf{v}}, \overline{n})$ expressing the n-times composition of τ with itself is given by:

$$\begin{pmatrix} \forall i \in [I, I+n) & \gamma(i, \overline{\mathbf{a}}[i], \mathbf{a}[i+1], \overline{\mathbf{a}}[i+1]) & \wedge \\ \forall i \in [0, I+1) & \overline{\mathbf{a}}[i] = \mathbf{a}[i] & \wedge \\ \forall i \in [I+n+1, N+1) & \overline{\mathbf{a}}[i] = \mathbf{a}[i] & \wedge \\ \overline{I} = I + n & & \end{pmatrix} \tag{16}$$

Let now Γ be a normal acceleratable fragment containing all arithmetic projections of $\mathcal{P}$: the key observation is that (16) (after little rewriting) *is a conjunction of ground literals and Γ-guards*. This allows to check the satisfiability of all formulæ expressing the feasibility of an error path.   □

Example 7. We apply the procedures of Theorem 4 to the example of Fig. 1. The relevant error path comprises the execution of the instruction in location 1, n executions of the loop in location 2, the exit condition from this loop together with execution of the instruction in location 3, m executions of the loop in location 4 and the error exit condition from that loop. If we apply formulæ (16) for acceleration, we get the proof obligation of Fig. 2 (with little simplifications improving readability). Example 6 shows that the conjunction of the formulæ from Fig. 2 is inconsistent, hence the program of Fig. 1 is safe.   □

6   Conclusions and Future Work

In this paper we presented a new framework for deciding the satisfiability of quantified formulæ with arrays. Such framework allows for the integration of acceleration results satisfying the conditions identified in Definitions 1-2, and exploits them as black-box modules, as described by the algorithm of Theorem 3.

---

[5] Notice that $\mathbf{a}[I] = \overline{\mathbf{a}}[I]$ is nevertheless a logical consequence of (14).

The framework can also be applied in a software model-checking scenario, where it can be proven that the safety of a new class of programs with arrays can be decided by integrating our new results with acceleration procedures.

On the practical side, in our experience [2–4], the tools get remarkable benefits from acceleration/decidability results, both whenever the results are used directly in decisions procedures like that of Theorem 4 and when they are used indirectly, via abstraction and instantiation, like in [2]. Implementing the results of this work is an interesting and substantial future project which we intent to pursue building upon our tools BOOSTER [3] and MCMT [13].

References

1. Aho, A.V., Lam, M.S., Sethi, R., Ullman, J.: Compilers: Principles, Techniques, and Tools. Addison-Wesley Educational Publishers, Incorporated (2007)
2. Alberti, F., Ghilardi, S., Sharygina, N.: Definability of accelerated relations in a theory of arrays and its applications. In: Fontaine, P., Ringeissen, C., Schmidt, R.A. (eds.) FroCoS 2013. LNCS, vol. 8152, pp. 23–39. Springer, Heidelberg (2013)
3. Alberti, F., Ghilardi, S., Sharygina, N.: Booster: an acceleration-based verification framework for array programs. In: Cassez, F., Raskin, J.-F. (eds.) ATVA 2014. LNCS, vol. 8837, pp. 18–23. Springer, Heidelberg (2014)
4. Alberti, F., Ghilardi, S., Sharygina, N.: Decision procedures for flat array properties. In: TACAS, pp. 15–30 (2014)
5. Alberti, F., Ghilardi, S., Sharygina, N.: A new acceleration-based combination framework for array properties, Avalilable from authors' webpages (2015)
6. Boigelot, B.: On iterating linear transformations over recognizable sets of integers. Theor. Comput. Sci. 309(1), 413–468 (2003)
7. Bozga, M., Gîrlea, C., Iosif, R.: Iterating octagons. In: Kowalewski, S., Philippou, A. (eds.) TACAS 2009. LNCS, vol. 5505, pp. 337–351. Springer, Heidelberg (2009)
8. Bozga, M., Iosif, R., Konečný, F.: Fast acceleration of ultimately periodic relations. In: Touili, T., Cook, B., Jackson, P. (eds.) CAV 2010. LNCS, vol. 6174, pp. 227–242. Springer, Heidelberg (2010)
9. Bozga, M., Iosif, R., Lakhnech, Y.: Flat parametric counter automata. Fundamenta Informaticae (91), 275–303 (2009)
10. Bradley, A.R., Manna, Z., Sipma, H.B.: What's decidable about arrays? In: Emerson, E.A., Namjoshi, K.S. (eds.) VMCAI 2006. LNCS, vol. 3855, pp. 427–442. Springer, Heidelberg (2006)
11. Comon, H., Jurski, Y.: Multiple counters automata, safety analysis and presburger arithmetic. In: Vardi, M.Y. (ed.) CAV 1998. LNCS, vol. 1427, pp. 268–279. Springer, Heidelberg (1998)
12. Finkel, A., Leroux, J.: How to compose Presburger-accelerations: Applications to broadcast protocols. In: Agrawal, M., Seth, A.K. (eds.) FSTTCS 2002. LNCS, vol. 2556, pp. 145–156. Springer, Heidelberg (2002)
13. Ghilardi, S., Ranise, S.: MCMT: A model checker modulo theories. In: Giesl, J., Hähnle, R. (eds.) IJCAR 2010. LNCS, vol. 6173, pp. 22–29. Springer, Heidelberg (2010)
14. Gurfinkel, A., Chaki, S., Sapra, S.: Efficient predicate abstraction of program summaries. In: Bobaru, M., Havelund, K., Holzmann, G.J., Joshi, R. (eds.) NFM 2011. LNCS, vol. 6617, pp. 131–145. Springer, Heidelberg (2011)

15. Habermehl, P., Iosif, R., Vojnar, T.: A logic of singly indexed arrays. In: Cervesato, I., Veith, H., Voronkov, A. (eds.) LPAR 2008. LNCS (LNAI), vol. 5330, pp. 558–573. Springer, Heidelberg (2008)
16. Halpern, J.Y.: Presburger arithmetic with unary predicates is Π_1^1 complete. J. Symbolic Logic 56(2), 637–642 (1991)
17. Semënov, A.L.: Logical theories of one-place functions on the set of natural numbers. Izvestiya: Mathematics 22, 587–618 (1984)
18. Shoenfield, J.R.: Mathematical logic. Association for Symbolic Logic, Urbana, IL, 2001. Reprint of the 1973 second printing

Decidability of Verification of Safety Properties of Spatial Families of Linear Hybrid Automata

Werner Damm[1], Matthias Horbach[2], and Viorica Sofronie-Stokkermans[2]

[1] Carl von Ossietzky University, Oldenburg, Germany
[2] University Koblenz and Max-Planck-Institut für Informatik, Saarbrücken, Germany

Abstract. We consider systems composed of an unbounded number of uniformly designed linear hybrid automata, whose dynamic behavior is determined by their relation to neighboring systems. We present a class of such systems and a class of safety properties whose verification can be reduced to the verification of (small) families of "neighboring" systems of bounded size, and identify situations in which such verification problems are decidable, resp. fixed parameter tractable. We illustrate the approach with an example from coordinated vehicle guidance.

1 Introduction

Verification of families of interacting systems is very important nowadays: Consider for instance families of autonomous cars performing cooperative maneuvers for collision avoidance, lane changing, overtaking, and passing intersections relying on an internal digital representation of the environment – capturing relative distance and speed of surrounding vehicles through on board sensors, sensor fusion, and vehicle2vehicle communication. While prototype realizations of such highly automated driving functions have been demonstrated (cf. e.g. HaveIT project), the challenge in deploying such solutions rests in proving their safety.

In this paper, we propose a general mathematical model capturing the essence of such interacting systems as *spatial families of hybrid automata* and provide efficient verification methods for proving safety when abstracting the dynamics to linear hybrid automata. The main contributions can be summarized as follows:

- We identify a class of systems composed of dynamically communicating uniformly defined linear hybrid automata and a class of safety properties for which the verification of the whole system can be reduced to the verification of subsystems of bounded size of "neighboring" components.
- We identify situations when verification is decidable/fixed parameter tractable.
- We analyze the complexity of parametric verification resp. synthesis.

Related work: Our work generalizes previous results on verification of classes of systems such as [1,21,7,5,17] in supporting the much richer system model of linear hybrid automata. The compositional approach [12] addresses the same application class, but does not provide complexity results. [10] searches for strategies controlling all vehicles, and employs heuristic methods to determine strategies for coordinated vehicle movements. An excellent survey of alternative methods

© Springer International Publishing Switzerland 2015
C. Lutz and S. Ranise (Eds.): FroCoS 2015, LNAI 9322, pp. 186–202, 2015.
DOI: 10.1007/978-3-319-24246-0_12

for controlling all vehicles to perform collision-free driving tasks is given in [9]. Both methods share the restriction of the analysis to a small number of vehicles, whereas we consider an unbounded number of systems. In [6], a temporal logic to reason about systems of automata is provided; the logic we use is similar. In [19,20] a small model theorem for *finite* families of automata with constant derivatives (with a parametric bound on the number of components) is established. Our approach allows us to consider families with an *unbounded* or *infinite* number of components which are *parametric linear hybrid automata*. In [19,20], the discrete transitions refer to changes in exactly one system (thus no global updates of sensors can be modeled). We allow for parallel mode switches and global topology updates. In [25], robust finite abstractions with bounded estimation errors are provided for reducing the synthesis of winning strategies for LTL objectives to finite state synthesis; the approach is used for an aerospace control application. [29] proposes a quantified differential dynamic logic for specifying and verifying distributed hybrid systems but the focus is not on providing decidability results or small model property results. There are various approaches to the parametric verification of individual hybrid automata, cf. [2], the development of a dynamic hybrid logic [28], and of tools like [8,11]. A survey of existing decidability and undecidability results can be found in [31,4]. Our current work stands in the tradition of [31,4,32], where we studied linear hybrid systems in which both mode changes and the dynamics can be parametrized.

Paper Structure. In Sect. 2 we present our model of spatial families of hybrid automata with its semantics. In Sect. 3 we introduce the verification properties we consider. The notions are illustrated on a running example of cars on a highway. In Sect. 4 we present classes of decidable and tractable logical theories, which we use in Sect. 5 for solving the verification tasks and proving modularity and complexity results. In Sect. 6 we discuss our tests with our system H-PILoT. Details, including further examples and proofs, can be found in [3].

2   Spatial Families of Hybrid Automata

We study families $\{S(i) \mid i \in I\}$ consisting of an unbounded number of similar systems. To describe them, we have to specify the properties of the component systems and their interaction. We model the systems $S(i)$ using hybrid automata and describe their interaction using structures $(I, \{p : I \to I\}_{p \in P})$ where I is a countably infinite set and $P = P_S \cup P_N$ is a finite set of unary function symbols which model the way the systems perceive other systems using sensors in P_S, or by neighborhood connections (e.g. established by communication channels) in P_N. We use highway control as a running example.

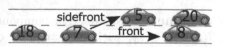

Fig. 1. Traffic situation

Example 1. Let I be a set of car identities, including the special constant nil.

(1) A car can observe other cars through sensors; these are modeled by a finite application-dependent set P_S of functions $p : I \to I$, where $p(i) = j$ represents

the fact that i's p-sensor observes car j. We choose P_S to include back, front, sidefront, sideback with obvious interpretations: In Fig. 1, we have sidefront(7) = 5, back(7) = 18, front(7) = 8. If sensor $p \in P$ of car i sees no car then $p(i)$ = nil.

(2) Car platoons of length at most n can be modeled e.g. by choosing a set of neighborhood connections P_N including leader, follower$_1$, ... follower$_n$, next, prev. Car i is leader if leader(i) = i; if leader(j)=$i{\neq}j$, j=follower$_k$(i) for some $k \leq n$.

Definition 1 ((Linear) hybrid automata [2]). *A hybrid automaton (HA) S* = $(X, Q, \text{Init}, \text{flow}, \text{Inv}, E, \text{guard}, \text{jump})$ *consists of: (1) finite sets* $X = \{x_1, \ldots, x_n\}$ *(real-valued variables) and Q (control modes); a finite multiset E with elements in* $Q \times Q$ *(control switches); (2) families* Init = $\{\text{Init}_q \mid q \in Q\}$ *and* Inv = $\{\text{Inv}_q \mid q \in Q\}$ *of predicates over X, defining the initial states and invariant conditions for each control mode, and* flow = $\{\text{flow}_q \mid q \in Q\}$ *of predicates over* $X \cup \dot{X}$ *specifying the dynamics in each control mode, where* $\dot{X} = \{\dot{x}_1, \ldots, \dot{x}_n\}$, *(̇$x_i$ is the derivative of* x_i*); (3) families* $\{\text{guard}_e \mid e \in E\}$ *of guards (predicates over X) and* $\{\text{jump}_e \mid e \in E\}$ *of jump conditions (predicates over* $X \cup X'$*) for the control switches, where* $X' = \{x'_1, \ldots, x'_n\}$ *is a copy of X.*

A linear hybrid automaton (LHA) is a HA in which for every $q \in Q, e \in E$*:* (i) Inv$_q$, Init$_q$, jump$_e$ *and* guard$_e$ *are convex linear predicates[1] and (ii)* flow$_q$ *is a convex linear predicate (with only non-strict inequalities) over* $\dot{X}$.

A *state* of S is a pair (q, a), where $q \in Q$ and $a{=}(a_1, \ldots, a_n)$, where $a_i{\in}\mathbb{R}$ is a value for $x_i{\in}X$. A state $s = (q, a)$ is *admissible* (resp. *initial*) if Inv$_q$ (resp. Init$_q$) is true when each x_i is replaced by a_i. A state can change by a jump (instantaneous transition that changes the control mode and the values of the variables according to the jump conditions), or by a flow (evolution in a mode q where the values of the variables change according to the flow$_q$).

The Language. To describe the families $\{S(i) \mid i \in I\}$, the topology $(I, \{p : I \to I\}_{p \in P})$ and its updates, and the safety properties we are interested in, we use a two-sorted first-order language $\mathcal{L}_{\text{p,n}}$ of a theory of pointers (sort p) for representing the indices, with a constant nil and unary function symbols in P (sort p $\to$ p) and in a set X (sort p $\to$ n) and a theory $\mathcal{T}_n$ (sort n) for describing properties of the values of the continuous variables of the systems e.g. the theory $\mathbb{R}$ of real numbers, or linear real arithmetic $LI(\mathbb{R})$). We consider first-order formulae in the language $\mathcal{L}_{\text{p,n}}$. Variables of sort p are denoted with indexed versions of i, j, k; variables of sort n are denoted $x_1, \ldots, x_n$.

Component Systems. The component systems are similar[2] hybrid automata $\{S(i) \mid i \in I\}$, with the same set of control modes Q and the same mode switches $E \subseteq Q \times Q$, and whose real valued variables $X_{S(i)}$ are partitioned into a set $X(i) = \{x(i) \mid x \in X\}$ of variables describing the states of the system $S(i)$ and a set $X_P(i) = \{x_p(i) \mid x \in X, p \in P\}$ describing the state of the neighbors

---

[1] A convex linear predicate is a finite conjunction of linear inequalities over $\mathbb{R}$.

[2] The results can be adapted to the situation when a finite number of types of systems are given and the description of each $S(i)$ is of one of these types.

$\{p(i) \mid p \in P\}$ of i, where $X = \{x_1, \ldots, x_n\}$. We assume that all sets $X(i), i \in I$ are disjoint. Every component system $S(i)$ has the form:

$$S(i) = (X(i) \cup X_P(i), Q, \mathsf{flow}(i), \mathsf{Inv}(i), \mathsf{Init}(i), E, \mathsf{guard}(i), \mathsf{jump}(i))$$

where – with the notations in Def. 1 – for every $q \in Q$ and $e \in E$ $\mathsf{flow}_q(i)$, $\mathsf{Inv}_q(i)$, $\mathsf{Init}_q(i)$, $\mathsf{guard}_e(i)$, $\mathsf{jump}_e(i)$ are conjunctions of formulae of the form $\mathcal{E} \vee C$, where C is a predicate over $X_{S(i)}$ (for $\mathsf{Inv}(i), \mathsf{Init}(i), \mathsf{guard}(i)$), or over $X_{S(i)} \cup \dot{X}_{S(i)}$ (for $\mathsf{flow}(i)$) resp. over $X_{S(i)} \cup X_i'$ (for $\mathsf{jump}(i)$) and $\mathcal{E}$ is a disjunction of equalities of the form $i = \mathsf{nil}$ and $p(i) = \mathsf{nil}$ if $x_p(i)$ occurs in C. All these formulae can also be regarded as $\mathcal{L}_{\mathsf{p},\mathsf{n}}$-formulae; for all $i \in I$ they differ only in the variable index. We consider two possibilities for $x_p(i)$:

(a) $x_p(i)$ is at any moment the value of $x(p(i))$, the value of variable x for the system $S(p(i))$ and is controlled by suitable flow/jump conditions of $S(p(i))$;
(b) $x_p(i)$ is the value of $x(p(i))$ which was sensed by the sensor in the last measurement, and does not change between measurements.

$S(i)$ is *linear* if (i) $\mathsf{flow}(i)$ contains only variables in $\dot{X}_{S(i)}$ and (ii) $\mathsf{flow}(i)$, $\mathsf{Inv}(i)$, $\mathsf{Init}(i)$, $\mathsf{guard}(i)$, $\mathsf{jump}(i)$ are conjunctions of formulae $\mathcal{E} \vee C$, as above, where C is a linear inequality (non-strict for flows). We also consider systems of *parametric* LHA, in which some coefficients in the linear inequalities (and also bounds for invariants, guards or jumps) are parameters in a set Par.

Example 2. Consider the following model of a system of cars: The controlled variables are the position and the lane of the car, so $X = \{\mathsf{pos}, \mathsf{lane}\}$. The car can drive on lane 1 or 2. Its sensors provide information about the car in front and back on the same lane $(\mathsf{front}, \mathsf{back})$ and about the closest cars on the other lane $(\mathsf{sidefront}, \mathsf{sideback})$. Thus, $P = \{\mathsf{back}, \mathsf{front}, \mathsf{sideback}, \mathsf{sidefront}\}$. Each car is modeled by a hybrid automaton with set of continuous variables $\{\mathsf{pos}(i), \mathsf{lane}(i)\} \cup \{\mathsf{pos}_p(i), \mathsf{lane}_p(i) \mid p \in P\}$ and modes $Q = \{\mathsf{Appr}, \mathsf{Rec}\}$. We assume that $x_p(i) = x(p(i))$ (variant (a) above). $\mathsf{Par} = \{d, d', D, D'\}$. As initial states, we allow all states where $\mathsf{pos}_{\mathsf{front}}(i) - \mathsf{pos}(i) \geq d'$ if $\mathsf{front}(i) \neq \mathsf{nil}$, and where the respective mode invariant is satisfied.

In mode Appr, car i keeps the velocity high enough to approach the car ahead. $\mathsf{Inv}_{\mathsf{Appr}}$ is $(1 \leq \mathsf{lane}(i) \leq 2) \wedge (\mathsf{front}(i){=}\mathsf{nil} \vee \mathsf{pos}_{\mathsf{front}}(i) - \mathsf{pos}(i) \geq d)$;
$\mathsf{flow}_{\mathsf{Appr}}$ is $\mathsf{lane}(i) = 0 \wedge (\mathsf{front}(i) = \mathsf{nil} \vee \dot{\mathsf{pos}}_{\mathsf{front}}(i) \leq \dot{\mathsf{pos}}(i)) \wedge (0 \leq \dot{\mathsf{pos}}(i) \leq 100)$.

In mode Rec, car i maintains a lower velocity to fall back.
$\mathsf{Inv}_{\mathsf{Rec}}$ is $(1 \leq \mathsf{lane}(i) \leq 2) \wedge (\mathsf{front}(i){=}\mathsf{nil} \vee \mathsf{pos}_{\mathsf{front}}(i) - \mathsf{pos}(i) \leq D)$;
$\mathsf{flow}_{\mathsf{Rec}}$ is $\mathsf{lane}(i) = 0 \wedge 0 \leq \dot{\mathsf{pos}}(i) \wedge (\mathsf{front}(i) = \mathsf{nil} \vee \dot{\mathsf{pos}}(i) \leq \dot{\mathsf{pos}}_{\mathsf{front}}(i))$.

A mode switch (without resets) can happen if there is a car ahead $(\mathsf{front}(i) \neq \mathsf{nil})$ and the distance to that car leaves a predefined range, i.e. $\mathsf{pos}_{\mathsf{front}}(i) - \mathsf{pos}(i) \leq D'$ (switch from Appr to Rec) or $\mathsf{pos}_{\mathsf{front}}(i) - \mathsf{pos}(i) \geq d'$ (switch back).

Another mode switch to mode Appr, which changes between lanes 1 and 2 with reset $\mathsf{lane}'(i){=}3{-}\mathsf{lane}(i)$, can happen when the car in front is too close $(\mathsf{front}(i) \neq \mathsf{nil} \wedge \mathsf{pos}_{\mathsf{front}}(i) - \mathsf{pos}(i) \leq D')$ and there is space to start the maneuver: $\mathsf{back}(i) = \mathsf{nil} \vee \mathsf{pos}(i) - \mathsf{pos}_{\mathsf{back}}(i) \geq d'$ and similarly for $\mathsf{sideback}(i)$ and $\mathsf{sidefront}(i)$.

Topology. We model the topology of the family of systems and its updates using an automaton Top with one mode, having as read-only-variables all variables in $\{x(i) \mid x \in X, i \in I\}$ and as write variables $\{p(i) \mid p \in P, i \in I\}$, where $P = P_S \cup P_N$. The initial states Init are described using $\mathcal{L}_{p,n}$-formulae. The jumps can represent updates of the sensor values $p(i), p \in P_S$ for a single system $S(i)$, but also synchronized global updates of the sensors $p \in P_S$ or neighborhood connections $p \in P_N$ for subsets of systems with a certain property (described by a formula): This can be useful when modeling systems of systems with an external controller (e.g. systems of car platoons) and entails a simultaneous update of an unbounded set of variables.[3] Therefore, the description of the mode switches (topology updates) in Top is of a global nature and is done using $\mathcal{L}_{p,n}$-formulae. The update rules for $p \in P$, $\mathsf{Update}(p, p')$, are conjunctions of implications:

$$\forall i (i \neq \mathsf{nil} \wedge \phi_k^p(i) \to F_k^p(p'(i), i)), \qquad k \in \{1, \ldots, m\} \tag{1}$$

which describe how the values of the pointer p change depending on a set of mutually exclusive conditions $\{\phi_1^p(i), \ldots, \phi_m^p(i)\}$. The $\phi_k^p(i)$ and $F_k^p(j, i)$ are formulae over the 2-sorted language $\mathcal{L}_{p,n}$ without any occurrence of unary functions in P'; if $p \in P_S$ (p represents a sensor), they also do not contain functions in P. Under the condition $\phi_k^p(i)$, the existence of a value for $p'(i)$ such that $F_k^p(p'(i), i)$ holds must be guaranteed. The variables $\{x(i) \mid x \in X, i \in I\}$ can be used in the guards of $\mathsf{Update}(p, p')$, but cannot be updated by Top. If $x_p(i)$ stores the value of $x(p(i))$ at the update of p (case (b) on page 189), then the update rules also change $x_p(i)$, so $F_k^p(p'(i), i)$ must contain $x'_p(i) = x(p'(i))$ as a conjunct.

Example 3. For the example in Ex. 2, consider the following formulae:
- $\mathsf{ASL}(j, i)$: $j \neq \mathsf{nil} \wedge \mathsf{lane}(j) = \mathsf{lane}(i) \wedge \mathsf{pos}(j) > \mathsf{pos}(i)$ which expresses the fact that j is ahead of i on the same lane, and
- $\mathsf{Closest}_f(j, i)$: $\mathsf{ASL}(j, i) \wedge \forall k (\mathsf{ASL}(k, i) \to \mathsf{pos}(k) \geq \mathsf{pos}(j))$, which expresses the fact that j is ahead of i and there is no car between them.

The rule for updating the front sensor of all cars with a given property Prop and of no other car is described by rule $\mathsf{Update}(\mathsf{front}, \mathsf{front}')$:

$$\forall i (i \neq \mathsf{nil} \wedge \mathsf{Prop}(i) \wedge \neg \exists j (\mathsf{ASL}(j, i)) \to \mathsf{front}'(i) = \mathsf{nil})$$
$$\forall i (i \neq \mathsf{nil} \wedge \mathsf{Prop}(i) \wedge \exists j (\mathsf{ASL}(j, i)) \to \mathsf{Closest}_f(\mathsf{front}'(i), i))$$
$$\forall i (i \neq \mathsf{nil} \wedge \neg \mathsf{Prop}(i) \to \mathsf{front}'(i) = \mathsf{front}(i))$$

If $\mathsf{Prop}(i) = (i = i_0)$, only the front sensor of car i_0 is updated. For car platoons, $\mathsf{Prop}(i)$ can be $\mathsf{leader}(i) = i_0$; we obtain a coordinated update for all platoon members. If $\mathsf{Prop}(i) = \mathsf{true}$, $\mathsf{Update}(\mathsf{front}, \mathsf{front}')$ describes a global update.

The initial states can e.g. be the states in which all sensor pointers have the correct value, as if they had just been updated. For front this is expressed by:

$$\forall i (i \neq \mathsf{nil} \wedge \mathsf{Prop}(i) \wedge \neg \exists j (\mathsf{ASL}(j, i)) \to \mathsf{front}(i) = \mathsf{nil})$$
$$\forall i (i \neq \mathsf{nil} \wedge \mathsf{Prop}(i) \wedge \exists j (\mathsf{ASL}(j, i)) \to \mathsf{Closest}_f(\mathsf{front}(i), i))$$

---

[3] Our choice allows us to uniformly represent various types of topology updates, from purely local ones to global updates, without loss of generality.

Example 4. Consider a car platoon as in Ex. 1(2). The situation when car i_0 (not a leader) leaves the platoon can e.g. be described by $\text{next}'(i_0) = \text{nil}$ and:
$$\text{prev}(i_0) \neq \text{nil} \to \text{next}'(\text{prev}(i_0)) = \text{next}(i_0)$$
$$\forall i (i \neq i_0 \wedge i \neq \text{prev}(i_0) \to \text{next}'(i) = \text{next}(i))$$

Timed Topology Automata. If we want to ensure that the component systems update the information about their neighbors sufficiently often, we can use additional clock variables $\{c_p(i) \mid i \in I, p \in P\}$, satisfying flow conditions of the form $\dot{c}_p(i) = 1$. Every topology update involving a set of systems and pointer field p has the effect that the clocks $c_p(i)$ for all systems i in that set are set to 0 (added to the conclusion to the topology updates). (Thus, in Ex. 3 the consequence of the update rules would contain as a conjunct the formula $c'_{\text{front}}(i) = 0$.) In addition, we can require that for every system i the interval between two updates of $p \in P$ is at most $\Delta t(i)$. Then Init_{Top} contains $\forall i\, c_p(i) = 0$ as a conjunct; the invariant of the mode of Top contains $\forall i\, 0 \leq c_p(i) \leq \Delta t(i)$; and if $c_p(i) = \Delta t(i)$ a topology update for system i must take place.

Definition 2 (Spatial Family of Hybrid Automata). *A* spatial family of hybrid automata (SFHA) *is a family of the form* $S = (\text{Top}, \{S(i) \mid i \in I\})$, *where* $\{S(i) \mid i \in I\}$ *is a system of similar hybrid automata and* Top *is a topology automaton. If for every* $i \in I$, $S(i)$ *is a linear hybrid automaton, we talk about a* spatial family of linear hybrid automata (SFLHA). *If the topology automaton is timed, we speak of a* spatial family of timed (linear) hybrid automata (SFT(L)HA). *An SFLHA* S *is* decoupled *if the real-valued variables in the guard of a mode switch of* $S(i)$ *can only be reset in a jump by* $S(i)$ *or by* Top.

Example 5. If, for every $i \in I$, $x_p(i) = x(p(i))$ (variant (a) on page 189) and $x_p(i)$ is used in the guard of a mode switch of $S(i)$, then in order to ensure that S is decoupled, no jump of $S(p(i))$ should reset $x(p(i))$. If $x_p(i)$ is the value sensed by the sensor p in the last measurement (variant (b)), then S is always decoupled.

A state $s=(q,a)$ of S consists of $q=(q_i)_{i \in I} \in Q^I$ and a tuple a of values of the variables of all components; initial states of S are the initial state of Top whose restriction to the variables of $S(i)$ are initial states of $S(i)$. A state change (s, s') is a flow (jump) if its restriction to the variables of $S(i)$ is a flow (resp. jump or flow of length 0) for all $i \in I$. A run of S is a sequence $s_0, s_1, \ldots$ where (i) s_0 is an initial state of S, (ii) each pair (s_j, s_{j+1}) is a jump, a flow or a topology update, and (iii) each flow is followed by a jump or topology update.

Notation. Sequences $i_1, \ldots, i_k$ of variables of sort p are denoted with $\bar{i}$, sequences $x_1, \ldots, x_n$ (resp. $\dot{x}_1, \ldots, \dot{x}_n$) with $\bar{x}$ (resp. $\bar{\dot{x}}$). The sequence $x_1(i), \ldots, x_n(i)$ of all variables of $S(i)$ is denoted with $\bar{x}(i)$, and $\dot{x}_1(i), \ldots, \dot{x}_n(i)$ with $\bar{\dot{x}}(i)$. To refer to the value of $x(i)$ at time t, we write $x(i,t)$. The sequence $x_1(i,t), \ldots, x_n(i,t)$ of values of variables of system S_i at a time t is denoted $\bar{x}(i,t)$.

3   Verification Tasks

The properties of SFLHA we consider are specified in a logic which combines first-order logic over the language $\mathcal{L}_{p,n}$ and temporal logic: Formulae are constructed inductively from atoms using temporal operators and quantification over variables of pointer sort. Since runs of the system define valuations of variables for each point in time, the semantics of such formulae is defined canonically, see e.g. [13]. We consider *safety properties* of the form:

$$\Phi_{entry} \rightarrow \Box\Phi_{safe},$$

which state that for every run of the composed system, if Φ_{entry} holds at the beginning of the run then Φ_{safe} is always true.

Example 6. Collision freedom can be expressed using the formula

$$\Phi_{safe}^g : \forall i, j(i\neq\text{nil} \wedge j\neq\text{nil} \wedge \text{lane}(i)=\text{lane}(j) \wedge \text{pos}(i)>\text{pos}(j) \rightarrow \text{pos}(i) - \text{pos}(j)\geq d_s)$$

for suitably chosen constant $d_s > 0$ (global safety) or by referring only to the "neighbors", using $\Phi_{safe}^l = \bigwedge_{p\in P} \Phi_{safe}^p$, where e.g. Φ_{safe}^{front} is:

$$\forall i(i \neq \text{nil} \wedge \text{front}(i) \neq \text{nil}\rightarrow\text{pos}(\text{front}(i)) - \text{pos}(i) \geq d_s).$$

We identify a class of general safety properties (with what we call exhaustive entry conditions, see Def. 3) which can be reduced to invariant checking for certain *mode reachable* states (Def. 4). We then show that for decoupled SFLHA we can reduce checking invariance for mode reachable states of Φ_{safe} to satisfiability checking in suitable logical theories, which are combinations of $LI(\mathbb{R})$ possibly extended with functions x_i satisfying additional properties (boundedness, continuity, boundedness conditions for the slope), and theories of pointers for modeling the information provided by the sensors. Using results in Sect. 4, in Sect. 5 we identify situations in which the analysis of safety properties $\Phi_{entry} \rightarrow \Box\Phi_{safe}$ can be precisely reduced to a neighborhood of bounded size of the systems for which Φ_{safe} could fail. This allows us to prove a small model property and to identify safety properties which are decidable resp. fixed parameter tractable.

3.1   Safety Properties

Safety of LHA is in general undecidable; classes of LHA and safety properties which are decidable have been identified in several papers. In [4] we discuss such approaches and propose weaker conditions guaranteeing decidability. The approach described here continues this line of research. The choice of the class of safety properties we consider is based on the observation that industrial styleguides for designing hybrid automata make sure that modes are entered in an "inner envelope", chosen such that modes cannot be left before a fixed minimal dwelling time; this avoids immediate context switching. In [4] we showed that using inner envelopes for LHA allows us to reduce safety checking to invariant checking and the proof of bounded liveness properties to checking bounded unfoldings.

Definition 3. *Safety properties with* exhaustive entry conditions *have the form* $\Phi_{\mathsf{entry}} \to \Box\Phi_{\mathsf{safe}}$ *where* $\Phi_{\mathsf{entry}} = \forall i_1, \ldots, i_m \phi_{\mathsf{entry}}(\overline{x}(i_1), \ldots, \overline{x}(i_m))$ *is a formula in the language* $\mathcal{L}_{\mathsf{p},\mathsf{n}}$ *such that: (i) If* Φ_{entry} *holds in a state* s, s *is an initial state of* S; *(ii) For every jump or topology update* (s, s'), Φ_{entry} *holds in* s'.

Remark. Condition (i) guarantees that we make minimal restrictions on initial states: runs can start in any state satisfying Φ_{entry}. The formula Φ_{entry} can be seen as a description of certain "inner envelopes" of the modes. Condition (ii) expresses the fact that a jump leads into a state satisfying Φ_{entry} (in the inner envelope of the target mode).

For instance, if $\mathsf{Init}_{\mathsf{top}}$ describes the fact that the information about all variables detected by sensors in P_S is precise, then condition (ii) imposes the restriction that sensors have to be globally updated after any jump or local topology update, which is clearly too restrictive. We can instead require that the initial states contain all states in which the positions indicated by sensors are within a given margin ε of error (the entry condition Φ_{entry} could describe such states).

Example 7. *In the running example, where* lane *can be updated by a jump (from value 1 to 2 or vice versa) if the margin of error is* ε, *in order to guarantee (ii) we need to ensure that (a)* Top *is a timed topology automaton where the interval* Δt *between sensor updates is small enough and (b) after lane changes the sensors of the systems affected by the change are simultaneously updated.*

We prove that checking safety properties with exhaustive entry conditions for decoupled SFHA can be reduced to checking whether the safety property Φ_{safe} is invariant under certain jumps, flows, and topology updates.

Definition 4. *Let* $S = (\mathsf{Top}, \{S(i) \mid i \in I\})$ *be an SFHA. A state* s *(resp. state change* (s, s')) *where* $s = (q, a)$ *of* S, *s.t.* $q = (q_i)_{i \in I}$, *is* globally mode reachable *(GMR, for short) if there exists a state* (q, a') *of* S *such that* a' *satisfies* Φ_{entry} *and there is a flow in* S *from* (q, a') *to* (q, a).

Theorem 1. *A decoupled SFLHA* $S = (\mathsf{Top}, \{S(i) \mid i \in I\})$ *satisfies a safety property with exhaustive entry conditions* $\Phi_{\mathsf{entry}} \to \Box\Phi_{\mathsf{safe}}$, *iff the following hold:*

(1) All states satisfying Φ_{entry} *satisfy* Φ_{safe}.
(2) Φ_{safe} *is preserved under all flows starting from a state satisfying* Φ_{entry}.
(3) Φ_{safe} *is preserved under all GMR jumps.*
(4) Φ_{safe} *is preserved under all GMR topology updates.*

3.2 Reduction to Satisfiability Checking

We show that for decoupled SFLHA S we can reduce checking conditions (i) and (ii) in Def. 3 to satisfiability tests. We consider safety properties $\Phi_{\mathsf{entry}} \to \Box\Phi_{\mathsf{safe}}$ with exhaustive entry conditions, where $\Phi_{\mathsf{entry}} = \forall i_1 \ldots i_m \phi_{\mathsf{entry}}(\overline{x}(i_1), \ldots, \overline{x}(i_m))$ and $\Phi_{\mathsf{safe}} = \forall i_1 \ldots i_n \phi_{\mathsf{safe}}(\overline{x}(i_1), \ldots, \overline{x}(i_n))$, where ϕ_{entry} and ϕ_{safe} are quantifier-free. We show that checking them can be reduced to checking whether for all combinations of modes $q = (q_i)_{i \in I}$ certain formulae $F_q^{\mathsf{init}}, F_q^{\mathsf{flow}}, F_q^{\mathsf{jump}}, F_q^{\mathsf{top}}$ are unsatisfiable. We first show that for decoupled SFLHA we do not need to consider parallel jumps.

Lemma 2 *Let $S = (\text{Top}, \{S(i) \mid i \in I\})$ be a decoupled SFHA.*

(1) Φ_{safe} is invariant under all (GMR) jumps in S iff it is invariant under all (GMR) jumps which reset the variables of a finite family of systems in S.

(2) Φ_{safe} is invariant under all (GMR) jumps involving a finite family of systems in S iff it is invariant under all (GMR) jumps in any component of S.

Theorem 3. *For a decoupled SFHA S, conditions (i) and (ii) in Def. 3 hold iff:*

(i) $\Phi_{\text{entry}}(\overline{x}) \wedge \left(\neg(\bigvee_{q \in Q} \text{Init}_q(\overline{x}_{i_0})) \vee \neg \text{Init}_{\text{top}}(\overline{x})\right) \models \bot.$

(ii) for all $(q_i)_{i \in I} \in Q^I, e \in E, i_0 \in I \ (\forall i \text{Inv}_{q_i}(\overline{x}_i)) \wedge \text{Update}(p, p') \wedge \neg \Phi'_{\text{entry}}(\overline{x}) \models \bot,$ where Φ'_{entry} arises from Φ_{entry} by replacing p with p', and $(\forall i \text{Inv}_{q_i}(\overline{x}_i)) \wedge \text{guard}_e(\overline{x}_{i_0}) \wedge \text{jump}_e(\overline{x}_{i_0}, \overline{x}'_{i_0}) \wedge \forall j (j \neq i_0 \to \overline{x}'(j) = \overline{x}(j)) \wedge \neg \Phi_{\text{entry}}(\overline{x}') \models \bot.$

Theorem 4. *Let $\mathcal{S}$ be a decoupled SFLHA. The following hold (where $c_1, \ldots, c_n$ are Skolem constants obtained from the negation of Φ_{safe}):*

(1) The entry states of $\mathcal{S}$ satisfy Φ_{safe} iff for all $q = (q_i)_{i \in I} \in Q^I$ the formula

$$F_q^{\text{entry}} : \Phi_{\text{entry}} \wedge \neg \phi_{\text{safe}}(\overline{x}(c_1), \ldots, \overline{x}(c_n)) \text{ is unsatisfiable.}$$

(2) Φ_{safe} is invariant under flows starting in a state satisfying Φ_{entry} iff for all $q = (q_i)_{i \in I} \in Q^I$ the formula F_q^{flow}:

$$t_0 < t_1 \wedge \Phi_{\text{entry}} \wedge \forall i_1, \ldots, i_n \phi_{\text{safe}}(\overline{x}(i_1, t_0), \ldots, \overline{x}(i_n, t_0)) \wedge \forall i \, \text{Flow}_{q_i}(\overline{x}(i, t_0), \overline{x}(i, t_1))$$
$$\wedge \neg \phi_{\text{safe}}(\overline{x}(c_1, t_1), \ldots, \overline{x}(c_n, t_1)),$$

is unsatisfiable, where if $\text{flow}_q(i) = \bigwedge \left(\mathcal{E}_f \vee \sum_{k=1}^n a_k^q(i) \dot{x}_k(i) \leq a^q(i)\right)$ then:

$$\text{Flow}_{q_i}(\overline{x}(i, t_0), \overline{x}(i, t_1)) := \bigwedge \left(\mathcal{E}_f \vee \sum_{k=1}^n a_k^{q_i}(i)(x_k(i, t_1) - x_k(i, t_0)) \leq a^{q_i}(i)(t_1 - t_0)\right) \wedge$$
$$\forall i \left(\text{Inv}_{q_i}(\overline{x}(i, t_0)) \wedge \text{Inv}_{q_i}(\overline{x}(i, t_1))\right).$$

(3) Φ_{safe} is invariant under GMR jumps in S iff for all $q = (q_i)_{i \in I} \in Q^I$ the following formula $F^{\text{jump}q}_e(i_0)$ is unsatisfiable for every $i_0 \in I$ and $e = (q_{i_0}, q'_{i_0}) \in E$, s.t. if $p(i_0)$ occurs in guard_e it is not nil:

$$t_0 < t_1 \wedge \forall j_1 \ldots j_n \phi_{\text{entry}}(\overline{x}(j_1, t_0), \ldots, \overline{x}(j_1, t_0)) \wedge \forall i \text{Flow}_{q_i}(\overline{x}(i, t_0), \overline{x}(i, t_1))$$
$$\wedge \forall i_1, \ldots, i_n \phi_{\text{safe}}(\overline{x}(j_1, t_1), \ldots, \overline{x}(i_n, t_1))$$
$$\wedge \text{guard}_e(\overline{x}(i_0, t_1)) \wedge \text{jump}_e(\overline{x}(i_0, t_1), \overline{x}'(i_0)) \wedge \text{Inv}_{q'_{i_0}}(\overline{x}'(i_0, t_1))$$
$$\wedge \forall j (j \neq i_0 \to \overline{x}'(j) = \overline{x}(j)) \wedge \neg \phi_{\text{safe}}(\overline{x}'(c_1), \ldots, \overline{x}'(c_n)).$$

(4) Φ_{safe} is invariant under GMR topology updates for pointers in a set P_1 iff for all $q = (q_i)_{i \in I} \in Q^I$ the following formula F_q^{top} is unsatisfiable:

$$t_0 < t_1 \wedge \forall j_1 \ldots j_n \phi_{\text{entry}}(\overline{x}(j_1, t_0), \ldots, \overline{x}(j_1, t_0)) \wedge \forall i \text{Flow}_{q_i}(\overline{x}(i, t_0), \overline{x}(i, t_1))$$
$$\wedge \forall i_1, \ldots, i_n \phi_{\text{safe}}(\overline{x}(j_1, t_1), \ldots, \overline{x}(i_n, t_1)) \wedge$$
$$\wedge \bigwedge_{p \in P_1} \text{Update}(p, p') \wedge \neg \phi'_{\text{safe}}(\overline{x}(c_1), \ldots, \overline{x}(c_n))$$

where ϕ'_{safe} is obtained from ϕ_{safe} by replacing every $p \in P_1$ with p'.

4   Automated Reasoning

We present classes of theories for which decidable fragments relevant for the verification tasks above exist. We use the following complexity results for fragments of linear arithmetic: The satisfiability over $\mathbb{R}$ of conjunctions of linear inequalities can be checked in PTIME [22]. The problem of checking the satisfiability of sets of clauses in $LI(\mathbb{R})$ is in NP [33]. The satisfiability of any conjunction of Horn disjunctive linear (HDL) constraints[4] over $\mathbb{R}$ [23] and the satisfiability of any conjunction of Ord-Horn constraints[5] over $\mathbb{R}$ [27] can be decided in PTIME.

Local Theory Extensions. Let $\mathcal{T}_0$ be a base theory with signature Σ_0. We consider extensions $\mathcal{T}_1 := \mathcal{T}_0 \cup \mathcal{K}$ of $\mathcal{T}_0$ with new function symbols in a set Σ_1 of *extension functions* whose properties are axiomatized with a set $\mathcal{K}$ of *augmented clauses*, i.e. of axioms of the form $\forall x_1 \ldots x_n (\Phi(x_1, \ldots, x_n) \vee C(x_1, \ldots, x_n))$, where $\Phi(x_1, \ldots, x_n)$ is a *first-order formula in signature* Σ_0 and $C(x_1, \ldots, x_n)$ *is a* clause *containing extension functions*. $\mathcal{T}_0 \subseteq \mathcal{T}_0 \cup \mathcal{K}$ is a *local extension* [30,16] if for every set G of ground $\Sigma_0 \cup \Sigma_1 \cup \Sigma_c$-clauses (where Σ_c is a set of additional constants), if G is unsatisfiable w.r.t. $\mathcal{T}_0 \cup \mathcal{K}$ then unsatisfiability can be detected using the set $\mathcal{K}[G]$ consisting of those instances of $\mathcal{K}$ in which the terms starting with extension functions are ground terms occurring in $\mathcal{K}$ or G. Stably local extensions are defined similarly, with the difference that $\mathcal{K}[G]$ is replaced with $\mathcal{K}^{[G]}$, the set of instances of $\mathcal{K}$ in which the variables are instantiated with ground terms starting with extension functions which occur in $\mathcal{K}$ or G.

Theorem 5 ([30]). *If $\mathcal{T}_0 \subseteq \mathcal{T}_0 \cup \mathcal{K}$ is a (stably) local extension and G is a set of (augmented) ground clauses then we can reduce the problem of checking whether G is satisfiable w.r.t. $\mathcal{T}_0 \cup \mathcal{K}$ to a satisfiability test w.r.t. $\mathcal{T}_0$: We purify $\mathcal{K}[G] \cup G$ (resp. $\mathcal{K}^{[G]} \cup G$) by introducing (bottom-up) new constants c_t for subterms $t = f(g_1, \ldots, g_n)$ with $f \in \Sigma$, g_i ground $\Sigma_0 \cup \Sigma_c$-terms; replacing the terms t with the constants c_t; and adding the definitions $c_t = t$ to a set D. Similarly for stably local extensions. We denote by $\mathcal{K}_0 \cup G_0 \cup D$ the set of formulae obtained this way. Then G is satisfiable w.r.t. $\mathcal{T}_0 \cup \mathcal{K}$ iff $\mathcal{K}_0 \cup G_0 \cup \mathsf{Con}_0$ is satisfiable w.r.t. $\mathcal{T}_0$, where $\mathsf{Con}_0 = \{(\bigwedge_{i=1}^n c_i = d_i) \to c = d \mid f(c_1, \ldots, c_n) = c, f(d_1, \ldots, d_n) = d \in D\}$.*

If $\mathcal{K}[G]$ is finite and if the set $\mathcal{K}_0 \cup G_0 \cup \mathsf{Con}_0$ belongs to a decidable fragment $\mathcal{F}$ of $\mathcal{T}_0$, then the satisfiability of G w.r.t. $\mathcal{T}_1$ is decidable. As the size of $\mathcal{K}_0 \cup G_0 \cup N_0$ is polynomial in the size of G (for a given $\mathcal{K}$), locality allows us to express the complexity of the ground satisfiability problem w.r.t. $\mathcal{T}_1$ as a function of the complexity of the satisfiability of $\mathcal{F}$-formulae w.r.t. $\mathcal{T}_0$.

Many update rules define local theory extensions.

Theorem 6 ([18,14]). *Let $\mathcal{T}_0$ be a base theory with signature Σ_0 and $\Sigma \subseteq \Sigma_0$. Consider a family $\mathsf{Update}(\Sigma, \Sigma')$ of update axioms of the form:*

$$\forall \overline{x}(\phi_i^f(\overline{x}) \to F_i^f(f'(\overline{x}), \overline{x})) \quad i = 1, \ldots, m, \quad f \in \Sigma \tag{2}$$

which describe how the values of the Σ-functions change, depending on a finite set $\{\phi_i^f \mid i \in I\}$ of Σ_0-formulae and using Σ_0-formulae F_i^f such that (i) $\phi_i(\overline{x}) \wedge \phi_j(\overline{x}) \models_{\mathcal{T}_0} \bot$ for $i \neq j$ and (ii) $\mathcal{T}_0 \models \forall \overline{x}(\phi_i(\overline{x}) \to \exists y(F_i(y, \overline{x})))$ for all $i \in I$. Then the extension of $\mathcal{T}_0$ with axioms $\mathsf{Update}(\Sigma, \Sigma')$ is local.

---

[4] A Horn-disjunctive linear constraint is a disjunction $d_1 \vee \cdots \vee d_n$ where each d_i is a linear inequality or disequation, and the number of inequalities does not exceed one.

[5] Ord-Horn constraints are implications $\bigwedge_{i=1}^n x_i \leq y_i \to x_0 \leq y_0$, ($x_i, y_i$ are variables).

Theories of Pointers [24]. Consider the language $\mathcal{L}_{p,n}$ with sorts p (pointer) and n (scalar) introduced before, with set of unary pointer (numeric) fields P (P_n), and with a constant nil of sort p. The only predicate of sort p is equality; the signature Σ_n of sort n depends on the theory $\mathcal{T}_n$ modeling the scalar domain. A *guarded* p-*positive extended clause* is a clause of the form:

$$C := \forall i_1 \ldots i_n \ \mathcal{E}(i_1, \ldots, i_n) \vee \mathcal{C}(\overline{s}_i(i_1), \ldots, \overline{s}_i(i_n)) \tag{3}$$

where $\mathcal{C}$ is a $\mathcal{T}_n$-formula over terms of sort n and $\mathcal{E}$ is the disjunction of all equality atoms of the form $i = \text{nil}, f_n(i) = \text{nil}, \ldots, f_2(\ldots f_n(i)) = \text{nil}$ for all terms $f_1(f_2(\ldots f_n(i)))$ occurring in C.

Theorem 7 ([14]). *Every set $\mathcal{K}$ of guarded p-positive extended clauses defines a stably local extension of $\mathcal{T}_n \cup \text{Eq}_p$, where Eq_p is the theory of equality of sort p.*

5 Verification: Decidability and Complexity

We consider safety properties with extensive entry conditions of the form $\Phi_{\text{entry}} \rightarrow \Box \Phi_{\text{safe}}$. We make the following assumptions:

Assumption 1: $S = (\text{Top}, \{S(i) \mid i \in I\})$ is a decoupled SFLHA.
Assumption 2: Φ_{safe} and Φ_{entry} are sets of guarded p-positive extended clauses of the form $\forall i_1, \ldots, i_n \mathcal{E} \vee \mathcal{C}$, such that $\mathcal{C}$ is a conjunction of linear inequalities.
Assumption 3: $\text{Update}(p, p')$ are (A) of form (2) in Thm. 6 or (B) contain only formulae $\forall i(i \neq \text{nil} \wedge \phi \rightarrow F(p'(i), i))$ where (i) $\phi = \forall j_1, \ldots, j_m \psi(i, j_1, \ldots, j_m)$ with $m \geq 0$ and all free variables in $F(p'(i), i)$ occur below p', or (ii) $\phi = \exists \overline{j} \psi(i, \overline{j})$ and $i \neq \text{nil} \wedge \psi(i, \overline{j}) \rightarrow F(i', i)$ is a guarded p-positive extended clause $\mathcal{E} \vee \mathcal{C}$, where $\mathcal{C}$ is a conjunction of linear inequalities.
Assumption 4: The numeric constraints in the description of S (including the conditions $\phi_k^p \rightarrow F_k^p(j, i)$ obtained from $\phi_k^p \rightarrow F_k^p(p'(i), i)$ in $\text{Update}(p, p')$ by replacing all occurrences of $p'(i)$ with j) and the numerical constraints in Φ_{safe} and Φ_{entry} are all HDL constraints or all Ord-Horn constraints.

We prove that under Assumptions 1–3 the problems are decidable, and analyze their complexity.

Verification of Safety Properties. We analyze the complexity of verifying safety properties with exhaustive entry conditions, by analyzing the complexity of checking the satisfiability of the formulae F_q^{entry}, F_q^{jump}, F_q^{flow} and F_q^{top}. Since the number of systems to be considered is unbounded, a naive approach to analyzing the satisfiability of these formulae for all tuples $q = (q_i)_{i \in I} \in Q^I$ can be problematic. We identify situations which allow us to limit the analysis to a "neighborhood" of the systems for which ϕ_{safe} fails. For this we use the specific form of the axioms we consider.

Theorem 8. *The following theory extensions are stably local for all $(q_i)_{i \in I} \in Q^I$:*
(1) $\mathbb{R} \cup \text{Eq}_p \subseteq \mathbb{R} \cup \Phi_{\text{entry}}$ (under Assumption 2).
(2) $\mathbb{R} \cup \text{Eq}_p \subseteq \mathbb{R} \cup \{\Phi_{\text{safe}}(\overline{x}(t_0)) \wedge \forall i \, (\text{Flow}_{q_i}(\overline{x}(i, t_0), \overline{x}(i, t_1)))\}$ (Assumptions 1,2).

(3) $\mathbb{R} \cup \mathsf{Eq}_\mathsf{p} \subseteq \mathbb{R} \cup \{\Phi_{\mathsf{entry}}(\overline{x}(t_0)) \wedge \forall i\,(\mathsf{Flow}_{q_i}(\overline{x}(i,t_0),\overline{x}(i,t_1))) \wedge \Phi_{\mathsf{safe}}(\overline{x}(t_1)) \wedge$
$\quad \mathsf{guard}_e(\overline{x}(i_0,t_1)) \wedge \mathsf{jump}_e(\overline{x}(i_0,t_1),\overline{x}'(i_0)) \wedge \mathsf{Inv}_{q'_{i_0}}(\overline{x}'(i_0,t_1))\}$ *for every* $i_0 \in I$
and $e \in E$ *s.t. if* $p(i_0)$ *occurs in* guard_e *it is not* nil *(under Assumptions 1,2).*

(4) $\mathbb{R} \cup \mathsf{Eq}_\mathsf{p} \subseteq \mathbb{R} \cup \{\Phi_{\mathsf{entry}}(\overline{x}(t_0)) \wedge \forall i\,(\mathsf{Flow}_{q_i}(\overline{x}(i,t_0),\overline{x}(i,t_1))) \wedge \Phi_{\mathsf{safe}}(\overline{x}(t_1))\} \subseteq$
$\quad \mathbb{R} \cup \{\Phi_{\mathsf{entry}}(\overline{x}(t_0)) \wedge \Phi_{\mathsf{safe}}(\overline{x}(t_0)) \wedge \forall i\,(\mathsf{Flow}_{q_i}(\overline{x}(i,t_0),\overline{x}(i,t_1)))\} \cup \mathsf{Update}(\mathsf{p},\mathsf{p}')$
(under Assumptions 1,2,3). (The last extension is local.)

Let $G = \neg\phi_{\mathsf{safe}}(\overline{x}(c_1),\ldots,\overline{x}(c_n))$. By Assumption 2, G consists of a conjunction of linear inequalities and a set of pointer disequalities, containing clauses of the form $g \neq$ nil for every ground term g of sort p occurring in G below a pointer or scalar field. From Thm. 8 we obtain the following decidability results:

Theorem 9 (Entry States). $\mathsf{F}_q^{\mathsf{entry}}$ *is satisfiable for some* $q \in Q^I$ *iff there exists a finite set* I_{entry} *of indices (with size polynomial in the number of terms of sort* p *in* Φ_{safe}*) and* $q_0 = (q_i)_{i \in I_{\mathsf{entry}}}$ *such that:*

$$F_{q_0}^{\mathsf{entry}} : \bigwedge_{j_1 \ldots j_m \in I_{\mathsf{entry}}} \phi_{\mathsf{entry}}(x_{j_1},\ldots x_{j_m}) \wedge G \quad \text{is satisfiable.}$$

For every $q_0 \in Q^{I_{\mathsf{entry}}}$*, the satisfiability of the formula* $F_{q_0}^{\mathsf{entry}}$ *is decidable (in NP).*

Proof. By Thm. 8(1), $\mathcal{K}_{\mathsf{entry}} = \Phi_{\mathsf{entry}}$ defines a stably local theory extension of $\mathbb{R} \cup \mathsf{Eq}_\mathsf{p}$, so in order to check whether $\mathsf{F}_q^{\mathsf{entry}}$ is satisfiable it is sufficient to check whether $\mathcal{K}_{\mathsf{entry}}^{[G]} \wedge G$ is satisfiable. The latter happens iff there exists a finite set I_{entry} of indices (corresponding to the set of all ground terms of sort p in $\mathcal{K}_{\mathsf{entry}}^{[G]}$ after instantiation) and a tuple $q_0 = (q_i)_{i \in I_{\mathsf{entry}}}$ such that $F_{q_0}^{\mathsf{entry}}$ is satisfiable; decidability and complexity is proved by carefully analyzing the properties of this set of instances.

Example 8. Consider the running example, with entry states being the initial states for the tuple $q = (q_i)_{i \in I}$ consisting of the Appr modes for all systems:

$\mathsf{Init}_q := \forall i(i \neq \mathsf{nil} \wedge \mathsf{front}(i) \neq \mathsf{nil} \to \mathsf{pos}(\mathsf{front}(i)) - \mathsf{pos}(i) \geq d')$
$\qquad\qquad$ for a given constant $d' > 0$

$\mathsf{Init}_{\mathsf{top}} := \bigwedge_{p \in P_S} \mathsf{Update}(p,p)$, where $\mathsf{Update}(\mathsf{front},\mathsf{front})$ consists of the formulae:

$\quad i \neq \mathsf{nil} \wedge \neg \exists j(\mathsf{ASL}(j,i)) \to \mathsf{front}(i) = \mathsf{nil}$
$\quad i \neq \mathsf{nil} \wedge \exists j(\mathsf{ASL}(j,i)) \quad \to \mathsf{Closest}_\mathsf{f}(\mathsf{front}(i),i)$

where $\mathsf{ASL}(j,i)$: $j \neq \mathsf{nil} \wedge \mathsf{lane}(j) = \mathsf{lane}(i) \wedge \mathsf{pos}(j) > \mathsf{pos}(i)$ and $\mathsf{Closest}_\mathsf{f}(j,i)$: $\mathsf{ASL}(j,i) \wedge \forall k(\mathsf{ASL}(k,i) \to \mathsf{pos}(k) \geq \mathsf{pos}(j))$, so it clearly satisfies Assumption 3 (A).

Let $\Phi_{\mathsf{safe}}^g = \forall i,j(i \neq \mathsf{nil} \wedge j \neq \mathsf{nil} \wedge \mathsf{pos}(i) > \mathsf{pos}(j) \wedge \mathsf{lane}(i) = \mathsf{lane}(j) \to \mathsf{pos}(i) - \mathsf{pos}(j) \geq d_s)$. We check the satisfiability of $\mathsf{Init}_q \wedge \mathsf{Init}_{\mathsf{top}} \wedge G$, where $G = \neg\Phi_{\mathsf{safe}}^g$ is:

$i_0 \neq \mathsf{nil} \wedge j_0 \neq \mathsf{nil} \wedge \mathsf{lane}(i_0) = \mathsf{lane}(j_0) \wedge \mathsf{pos}(i_0) > \mathsf{pos}(j_0) \wedge \mathsf{pos}(i_0) - \mathsf{pos}(j_0) < d_s$.
We instantiate $\mathsf{Init}_q \wedge \mathsf{Init}_{\mathsf{top}}$. E.g., by instantiating i in Init_q with j_0 we obtain:

$\quad j_0 \neq \mathsf{nil} \wedge \mathsf{front}(j_0) \neq \mathsf{nil} \wedge \mathsf{lane}(\mathsf{front}(j_0)) = \mathsf{lane}(j_0) \to \mathsf{pos}(\mathsf{front}(j_0)) - \mathsf{pos}(j_0) \geq d'$;

the instantiation of the prenex form of the second axiom in the update rule, in which i is replaced with j_0, and j and k (in $\mathsf{Closest_f}$) with i_0 is:

$$j_0 \neq \mathsf{nil} \wedge i_0 \neq \mathsf{nil} \wedge \mathsf{lane}(i_0) = \mathsf{lane}(j_0) \wedge \mathsf{pos}(i_0) > \mathsf{pos}(j_0)$$
$$\rightarrow \mathsf{front}(j_0) \neq \mathsf{nil} \wedge \mathsf{lane}(\mathsf{front}(j_0)) = \mathsf{lane}(j_0) \wedge \mathsf{pos}(\mathsf{front}(j_0)) > \mathsf{front}(j_0)$$
$$\wedge \, (i_0 \neq \mathsf{nil} \wedge \mathsf{lane}(i_0) = \mathsf{lane}(j_0) \wedge \mathsf{pos}(i_0) > \mathsf{pos}(j_0) \rightarrow \mathsf{pos}(i_0) > \mathsf{pos}(\mathsf{front}(j_0)))$$

After the hierarchical reduction we obtain a set of clauses which is clearly unsatisfiable if $d' \geq d_s$.

Theorem 10 (Flows). *Under Assumptions 1,2, F_q^{flow} is satisfiable for some $q \in Q^I$ iff there exists a finite set $I_{\mathsf{flow}} \subseteq I$ (corresponding to all ground terms of sort p in G), and $q_0 = (q_i)_{i \in I_{\mathsf{flow}}}$ s.t. $F_{q_0}^{\mathsf{flow}}$ – obtained from F_q^{flow} by instantiating the variables of sort p with elements in I_{flow} – is satisfiable. For every $q_0 = (q_i)_{i \in I_{\mathsf{flow}}}$ the satisfiability of $F_{q_0}^{\mathsf{flow}}$ is decidable (in NP).*

Theorem 11 (Jumps). *Under Assumptions 1, 2, $F^{\mathsf{jump}}{}_e^q(i_0)$ is satisfiable for some $i_0 \in I, e \in E$ and $q = (q_i)_{i \in I} \in Q^I$ iff there exist $i_0 \in I$ and $e \in E$ and a finite set I_{jump} consisting of i_0 together with all ground terms of sort p occurring in G, and $q_0 = (q_i)_{i \in I_{\mathsf{jump}}}$, such that $F^{\mathsf{jump}}{}_{e_0}^{q_0}$ – obtained from $F^{\mathsf{jump}}{}_e^q(i_0)$ by instantiating the variables of sort p with conjunction terms in I_{jump} – is satisfiable. The problem is decidable (and in NP).*

Theorem 12 (Topology Updates). *Under Assumptions 2,3, for checking the satisfiability of the formula F^{top} we need to consider only those instances of these formulae where the terms of pointer sort are in a finite set I_{update} containing all ground terms of pointer sort of $\neg\phi'_{\mathsf{safe}}(\overline{x}(j_1), \ldots, \overline{x}(j_n))$, and additionally all Skolem constants c_p, $p \in P$ which occur from Skolemization in the instances of $\mathsf{Update}(p, p')$. The problem is decidable (and in NP).*

Example 9. Consider the topology updates in Ex. 3. Invariance of Φ_{safe}^g under these updates can be proved as in Ex. 8. It can be easily shown that Φ_{safe}^l is not invariant. We now consider a variant $\overline{\Phi}^l_{\mathsf{safe}}$ of Φ^l_{safe} where:

$$\overline{\Phi}^{\mathsf{front}}_{\mathsf{safe}} : \forall i \big(i \neq \mathsf{nil} \wedge \mathsf{front}(i) \neq \mathsf{nil} \wedge \mathsf{lane}(i) = \mathsf{lane}(\mathsf{front}(i)) \rightarrow \mathsf{pos}(\mathsf{front}(i)) - \mathsf{pos}(i) > d_s\big)$$

In order to prove that $\overline{\Phi}^{\mathsf{front}}_{\mathsf{safe}}$ is preserved by topology updates, we prove that $\overline{\Phi}^{\mathsf{front}}_{\mathsf{safe}} \wedge \mathsf{Update}(p, p') \wedge G$ is unsatisfiable, where $G = \neg\overline{\Phi}^{\mathsf{front}'}_{\mathsf{safe}}$ is the ground clause $i_0 \neq \mathsf{nil} \wedge \mathsf{front}'(i_0) \neq \mathsf{nil} \wedge \mathsf{lane}(i_0) = \mathsf{lane}(\mathsf{front}'(i_0)) \wedge \mathsf{pos}(\mathsf{front}'(i_0)) - \mathsf{pos}(i_0) \leq d_s$.

The extension: $\mathbb{R} \cup \overline{\Phi}^{\mathsf{front}}_{\mathsf{safe}} \subseteq \mathbb{R} \cup \overline{\Phi}^{\mathsf{front}}_{\mathsf{safe}} \cup \mathsf{Update}(\mathsf{front}, \mathsf{front}')$ is local. We determine $\mathsf{Update}(\mathsf{front}, \mathsf{front}')[G]$, where $\mathsf{st}(K, G) = \{\mathsf{front}'(i_0)\}$. After instantiation and purification (replacing $\mathsf{front}'(i_0)$ with f') we obtain:

$$i_0 \neq \mathsf{nil} \wedge \neg\exists j(\mathsf{ASL}(j, i_0)) \rightarrow f' = \mathsf{nil}$$
$$i_0 \neq \mathsf{nil} \wedge \exists j(\mathsf{ASL}(j, i_0)) \rightarrow \mathsf{Closest}_f(f', i_0)$$

with the notations in Ex. 3. Transforming these formulas into prenex form and skolemizing the existential quantifier, we obtain (with Skolem constant c_0):

$$C_1 : i_0 \neq \mathsf{nil} \wedge \neg\mathsf{ASL}(c_0, i_0) \rightarrow f' = \mathsf{nil} \qquad C_2 : i_0 \neq \mathsf{nil} \wedge \mathsf{ASL}(j, i_0) \rightarrow \mathsf{Closest}(f', i_0).$$

The formula C_1 is ground. To check the satisfiability of $\Phi_{\mathsf{safe}} \cup C_2 \cup G_1$ where $G_1 = C_1 \wedge G_0$ (where G_0 is $i_0 \neq \mathsf{nil} \wedge f' \neq \mathsf{nil} \wedge \mathsf{lane}(i_0) = \mathsf{lane}(f') \wedge \mathsf{pos}(f') - \mathsf{pos}(i_0) \leq d_s$), it is sufficient to check the satisfiability of $\Phi_{\mathsf{safe}}[G_1] \cup C_2[G_1] \cup G_1$.

From Theorems 9, 10, 11 and 12 we obtain a small model property.

Theorem 13 (Small Model Property). *Under Assumptions 1–3, a decoupled SFLHA S satisfies a safety property with exhaustive entry conditions iff the property holds in all subsystems of S of the form $S_0 = (\mathsf{Top}, \{S(i) \mid i \in I_0\})$, where I_0 is the set of all indices corresponding to ground terms in $G = \neg\Phi_{\mathsf{safe}}$ occurring in the instances of the formulae $F_q^{\mathsf{init}[G]}, F_q^{\mathsf{flow}[G]}, F_q^{\mathsf{jump}[G]}, F_q^{\mathsf{top}[G]}$ ($|I_0|$ is polynomial in the number of terms of sort p occurring in Φ_{safe}; the degree of the polynomial depends on the number of free variables in the update axioms).*

Theorem 14. *Under Assumptions 1–4, the following hold for every conjunction* $\mathsf{Def} : \bigwedge_{p(t)\in T_1} p(t){=}\mathsf{nil} \wedge \bigwedge_{p(t)\in T_2} p(t){\neq}\mathsf{nil}$, *where $T_1 \cup T_2 = \{p(t) \mid t$ subterm of sort p of $G, p{\in}P, p(t)$ not in $G\}$ and every $q \in Q^{I_{\mathsf{entry}}}$ (resp. $Q^{I_{\mathsf{flow}}}$ or $Q^{I_{\mathsf{update}}}$):*

(1) The satisfiability of $F_q^{\mathsf{entry}} \wedge \mathsf{Def}$ can be checked in PTIME.

(2) The satisfiability of $F_q^{\mathsf{flow}} \wedge \mathsf{Def}$ can be checked in PTIME.

(2) The satisfiability of $F^{\mathsf{jump}q} \wedge \mathsf{Def}$ can be checked in PTIME.

(4) Assuming that either (a) P_S is empty, or else (b) $\mathsf{Update}(p, p')$ has the form (2) in Thm. 6 the satisfiability of $F_q^{\mathsf{update}} \wedge \mathsf{Def}$ can be checked in PTIME.

If we consider $|Q|$ and $|P|$ to be constant and the number of terms of sort p in Φ_{safe}, and the maximal number of variables in the update axioms as a parameter, the problems can be considered to be fixed parameter tractable.

Theorem 15 (Parametric Systems). *The complexity results in Thms. 9–12 and 14, as well as the small model property also hold for parametric SFLHA in which only the bounds in Φ_{entry} and Φ_{safe}, $\mathsf{guard}_e, \mathsf{jump}_e$, and Update are parameters. For systems in which parameters are allowed as coefficients or appear in the flow conditions the complexity is exponential.*

Theorem 16. *Under Assumptions 1–3, the complexity of synthesizing constraints on parameters which guarantee that a parametric SFLHA satisfies a safety condition with exhaustive entries (using quantifier elimination) is exponential.*

Remark. Similar methods can be used for showing that under Assumptions 1–3 the problem of checking conditions (i) and (ii) in the definition of exhaustive entry conditions is in NP. We can also express Φ_{entry} and S parametrically and infer constraints on parameters under which conditions (i) and (ii) hold.

6 Tool Support

In order to perform automatically the verification tasks we used H-PILoT [15], which performs stepwise hierarchical reductions of proof tasks in chains of local theory extensions to satisfiability problems in a combination of linear arithmetic over $\mathbb{R}$ and pure equality, which are then solved using Z3 [26]. Results of experiments with our running example are summarized in Fig. 2. We considered the safety conditions Φ_{safe}^g and variants of Φ_{safe}^l (cf. Ex. 6), as well as $\Phi = \forall i.i \neq \mathsf{nil} \to \mathsf{front}(i) \neq i$ and we provided constraints for all parameters.

	flow	init	jump	upd	flow_MR	init_MR	jump_MR	upd_MR
Φ	unsat	unsat	unsat	unsat	unsat	unsat	unsat	unsat
time	0.332	0.296	1.252	0.520	0.352	0.312	22.221	1.292
Φ^l_safe	unsat	unsat	unsat	sat	unsat	unsat	unsat	unsat
time	0.568	0.884	1.988	1.604	0.644	0.924	28.637	3.480
Φ^y_safe	sat	unsat	sat	unsat	unsat	unsat	sat	unsat
time	0.360	0.276	5.568	0.516	0.392	0.296	22.641	1.288

Fig. 2. Proof times in seconds

As can be seen, pure invariance checking is not always sufficient (for example Φ^l_safe is not invariant under all updates); we checked also invariance under *mode reachable* jumps/updates (tests indexed with MR; thus we could prove that Φ^l_safe holds in all runs). For satisfiable formulae H-PILoT returns models which can be used to visualize the counterexamples to the invariance properties. Further details can be found in [3]. Formalizations of the hybrid automata and the proof tasks presented here as well as the verification tools used can be found at userp.uni-koblenz.de/~horbach/haha.html along with formalizations of several of the examples from the Passel benchmark suite [20].

7   Conclusions

We proved that safety properties with exhaustive entry conditions for spatial families of similar linear hybrid automata can be verified efficiently: We reduced the proof task to invariant checking for certain mode reachable states and analyzed the complexity of such problems. As a by-product, we obtained a modularity result for checking safety properties. The results can also be used for invariant checking (for this the information about mode reachability in the formulae is ignored). Another important class of properties, related to timely completion of maneuvers, are bounded reachability properties. They state that for every run starting in a suitable initial configuration Φ_entry, a maneuver completion condition Φ_complete becomes true in a given bounded time frame. Similar methods can be used for efficiently checking also this type of properties if we guarantee that the number of jumps and topology updates in any fixed interval is bounded. We did not include such considerations here due to lack of space.

Acknowledgments. This work was partly supported by the German Research Council (DFG) as part of the Transregional Collaborative Research Center "Automatic Verification and Analysis of Complex Systems" (SFB/TR 14 AVACS) www.avacs.org

References

1. Abdulla, P.A., Haziza, F., Holík, L.: All for the price of few. In: Giacobazzi, R., Berdine, J., Mastroeni, I. (eds.) VMCAI 2013. LNCS, vol. 7737, pp. 476–495. Springer, Heidelberg (2013)
2. Alur, R., Henzinger, T.A., Ho, P.: Automatic symbolic verification of embedded systems. IEEE Trans. Software Eng. 22(3), 181–201 (1996)
3. Damm, W., Horbach, M., Sofronie-Stokkermans, V.: Decidability of verification of safety properties of spatial families of linear hybrid automata. Tech. Rep. 111, SFB/TR 14 AVACS (2015). http://www.avacs.org

4. Damm, W., Ihlemann, C., Sofronie-Stokkermans, V.: PTIME parametric verification of safety properties for reasonable linear hybrid automata. Mathematics in Computer Science 5(4), 469–497 (2011)
5. Damm, W., Peter, H., Rakow, J., Westphal, B.: Can we build it: formal synthesis of control strategies for cooperative driver assistance systems. Mathematical Structures in Computer Science 23(4), 676–725 (2013)
6. Emerson, E.A., Srinivasan, J.: A decidable temporal logic to reason about many processes. In: Dwork, C. (eds.) Proc. PODC 1990, pp. 233–246. ACM (1990)
7. Faber, J., Ihlemann, C., Jacobs, S., Sofronie-Stokkermans, V.: Automatic verification of parametric specifications with complex topologies. In: Méry, D., Merz, S. (eds.) IFM 2010. LNCS, vol. 6396, pp. 152–167. Springer, Heidelberg (2010)
8. Frehse, G., Jha, S.K., Krogh, B.H.: A counterexample-guided approach to parameter synthesis for linear hybrid automata. In: Egerstedt, M., Mishra, B. (eds.) HSCC 2008. LNCS, vol. 4981, pp. 187–200. Springer, Heidelberg (2008)
9. Frese, C.: A comparison of algorithms for planning cooperative motions of cognitive automobiles. In: Proc. 2010 Joint Workshop of Fraunhofer IOSB and Institute for Anthropomatics, Vision and Fusion Laboratory. No. IES-2010-06 in Karlsruher Schriften zur Anthropomatik, vol. 7, pp. 75–90. KIT Scientific Publishing (2010)
10. Frese, C., Beyerer, J.: Planning cooperative motions of cognitive automobiles using tree search algorithms. In: Dillmann, R., Beyerer, J., Hanebeck, U.D., Schultz, T. (eds.) KI 2010. LNCS, vol. 6359, pp. 91–98. Springer, Heidelberg (2010)
11. Fribourg, L., Kühne, U.: Parametric verification and test coverage for hybrid automata using the inverse method. Int. J. Found. Comput. Sci. 24(2), 233–250 (2013)
12. Hilscher, M., Linker, S., Olderog, E.-R., Ravn, A.P.: An abstract model for proving safety of multi-lane traffic manoeuvres. In: Qin, S., Qiu, Z. (eds.) ICFEM 2011. LNCS, vol. 6991, pp. 404–419. Springer, Heidelberg (2011)
13. Hungar, H., Grumberg, O., Damm, W.: What if model checking must be truly symbolic. In: Camurati, P.E., Eveking, H. (eds.) CHARME 1995. LNCS, vol. 987, pp. 1–20. Springer, Heidelberg (1995)
14. Ihlemann, C., Jacobs, S., Sofronie-Stokkermans, V.: On local reasoning in verification. In: Ramakrishnan, C.R., Rehof, J. (eds.) TACAS 2008. LNCS, vol. 4963, pp. 265–281. Springer, Heidelberg (2008)
15. Ihlemann, C., Sofronie-Stokkermans, V.: System description: H-PILoT. In: Schmidt, R.A. (ed.) CADE-22. LNCS(LNAI), vol. 5663, pp. 131–139. Springer, Heidelberg (2009)
16. Ihlemann, C., Sofronie-Stokkermans, V.: On hierarchical reasoning in combinations of theories. In: Giesl, J., Hähnle, R. (eds.) IJCAR 2010. LNCS(LNAI), vol. 6173, pp. 30–45. Springer, Heidelberg (2010)
17. Jacobs, S., Bloem, R.: Parameterized synthesis. Logical Methods in CS 10(1) (2014)
18. Jacobs, S., Kuncak, V.: Towards complete reasoning about axiomatic specifications. In: Jhala, R., Schmidt, D. (eds.) VMCAI 2011. LNCS, vol. 6538, pp. 278–293. Springer, Heidelberg (2011)
19. Johnson, T.T., Mitra, S.: Parametrized verification of distributed cyber-physical systems: An aircraft landing protocol case study. In: Proc. ICCPS 2012, pp. 161–170. IEEE (2012)
20. Johnson, T.T., Mitra, S.: A small model theorem for rectangular hybrid automata networks. In: Giese, H., Rosu, G. (eds.) FORTE/FMOODS 2012. LNCS, vol. 7273, pp. 18–34. Springer, Heidelberg (2012)
21. Kaiser, A., Kroening, D., Wahl, T.: Dynamic cutoff detection in parameterized concurrent programs. In: Touili, T., Cook, B., Jackson, P. (eds.) CAV 2010. LNCS, vol. 6174, pp. 645–659. Springer, Heidelberg (2010)

22. Khachian, L.: A polynomial time algorithm for linear programming. Soviet Math. Dokl. 20, 191–194 (1979)
23. Koubarakis, M.: Tractable disjunctions of linear constraints: basic results and applications to temporal reasoning. Theo. Comp. Sci. 266(1–2), 311–339 (2001)
24. McPeak, S., Necula, G.C.: Data structure specifications via local equality axioms. In: Etessami, K., Rajamani, S.K. (eds.) CAV 2005. LNCS, vol. 3576, pp. 476–490. Springer, Heidelberg (2005)
25. Mickelin, O., Ozay, N., Murray, R.M.: Synthesis of correct-by-construction control protocols for hybrid systems using partial state information. In: Proc. ACC 2014, pp. 2305–2311. IEEE (2014)
26. de Moura, L., Bjørner, N.S.: Z3: An efficient SMT solver. In: Ramakrishnan, C.R., Rehof, J. (eds.) TACAS 2008. LNCS, vol. 4963, pp. 337–340. Springer, Heidelberg (2008)
27. Nebel, B., Bürckert, H.J.: Reasoning about temporal relations: A maximal tractable subclass of Allen's interval algebra. J. of the ACM 42(1), 43–66 (1995)
28. Platzer, A.: Differential dynamic logic for hybrid systems. J. Autom. Reasoning 41(2), 143–189 (2008)
29. Platzer, A.: Quantified differential dynamic logic for distributed hybrid systems. In: Dawar, A., Veith, H. (eds.) CSL 2010. LNCS, vol. 6247, pp. 469–483. Springer, Heidelberg (2010)
30. Sofronie-Stokkermans, V.: Hierarchic reasoning in local theory extensions. In: Nieuwenhuis, R. (ed.) CADE 2005. LNCS (LNAI), vol. 3632, pp. 219–234. Springer, Heidelberg (2005)
31. Sofronie-Stokkermans, V.: Hierarchical reasoning for the verification of parametric systems. In: Giesl, J., Hähnle, R. (eds.) IJCAR 2010. LNCS (LNAI), vol. 6173, pp. 171–187. Springer, Heidelberg (2010)
32. Sofronie-Stokkermans, V.: Hierarchical reasoning and model generation for the verification of parametric hybrid systems. In: Bonacina, M.P. (ed.) CADE 2013. LNCS(LNAI), vol. 7898, pp. 360–376. Springer, Heidelberg (2013)
33. Sontag, E.: Real addition and the polynomial hierarchy. Inf. Proc. Letters 20(3), 115–120 (1985)

Rewriting and Constraint Solving

A Completion Method to Decide Reachability in Rewrite Systems

Guillaume Burel[1], Gilles Dowek[2], and Ying Jiang[3]

[1] Ensiie, 1 square de la Résistance, 91000 Évry, France
guillaume.burel@ensiie.fr
[2] Inria, 23 avenue d'Italie, CS 81321, 75214 Paris Cedex 13, France
gilles.dowek@inria.fr
[3] State Key Laboratory of Computer Science, Institute of Software,
Chinese Academy of Sciences, 100190 Beijing, China
jy@ios.ac.cn

Abstract. The Knuth-Bendix method takes in argument a finite set of equations and rewrite rules and, when it succeeds, returns an algorithm to decide if a term is equivalent to another modulo these equations and rules. In this paper, we design a similar method that takes in argument a finite set of rewrite rules and, when it succeeds, returns an algorithm to decide not equivalence but reachability modulo these rules, that is if a term reduces to another. As an application, we give new proofs of the decidability of reachability in finite ground rewrite systems and in pushdown systems.

1 Introduction

The Knuth-Bendix method [13,10] takes in argument a finite set of equations and rewrite rules and, when it succeeds, returns an algorithm to decide if a term is equivalent to another modulo these equations and rules. In this paper, we design a similar method that takes in argument a finite set of rewrite rules and, when it succeeds, returns an algorithm to decide not equivalence but reachability modulo these rules, that is if a term reduces to another.

As an application, we give new proofs of the decidability of reachability in finite ground rewrite systems [3] and in pushdown systems [1].

Like the Knuth-Bendix method, this method proceeds by completing a finite rewrite system into an equivalent one, by adding derivable rules. In the completed system, when a proposition $t \longrightarrow^* u$ has a proof, it also has a proof of the form

$$t = t_0 \longrightarrow t_1 \longrightarrow \dots \longrightarrow t_p = w = u_q \longrightarrow \dots \longrightarrow u_1 \longrightarrow u_0 = u$$

where $t_0 \succ t_1 \succ \dots \succ t_p$ and $u_q \prec \dots \prec u_1 \prec u_0$ for some reduction order $\prec$, that is a proof formed with a decreasing sequence followed by an increasing one. We can write such a proof

C. Lutz and S. Ranise (Eds.): FroCoS 2015, LNAI 9322, pp. 205–219, 2015.
DOI: 10.1007/978-3-319-24246-0_13

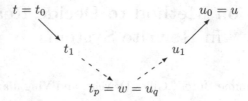

using the unusual convention to write the larger terms for the order $\prec$ on the top of the diagram and the smaller ones on the bottom, hence drawing an arrow oriented from the bottom to the top, when a smaller term reduces to a larger one.

In order to transform proofs into proofs of this form, we should consider critical steps of the form

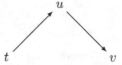

with $t \prec u \succ v$ and add a rule reducing directly t to v, avoiding the detour via u. If the reduction from t to u uses a rule $l_1 \longrightarrow r_1$ and that from u to v a rule $l_2 \longrightarrow r_2$, the terms r_1 and l_2 would have to be compared, to determine if one term unifies with a subterm of the other. We would therefore need to design a forward completion method that compares the left-hand side of a rule with the right-hand side of another.

An alternative method is to reverse the rules whose left-hand side is smaller than the right-hand side, and keep track that such reversed rules must be used backwards. Thus, we distinguish two kinds of rules: *negative* rules that are as usual, and *positive* rules that must be used backwards: $u_1 \longrightarrow_+ u_2$ means that $u_2 \longrightarrow u_1$ in the original system and $u_2 \prec u_1$. This way, in the completed system, when a proposition $t \longrightarrow^* u$ has a proof, it also has a proof of the form

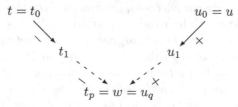

and the critical steps have the form

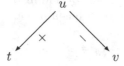

so that only left-hand side of rules need to be compared.

In the completed system, the proposition $t \longrightarrow^* u$ has a proof if and only if there exists a term w such that $t \longrightarrow^*_- w$ and $u \longrightarrow^*_+ w$. Thus reachability boils down to the existence of a common reduct. In a terminating system, reachability is obviously decidable and easy to check because reduction trees are always finite. In the same way, in a terminating system, the existence of a common reduct of two terms is decidable and easy to check because reduction trees are finite.

The reader familiar with polarized sequent calculus modulo theory [6,8] will remark that many ideas in this paper, in particular the idea to distinguish two kinds of rules, come from this calculus. But the paper is presented independently of polarized sequent calculus modulo theory.

2   Polarized Rewrite Systems

Terms, substitutions, rewrite rules, and rewrite systems are defined as usual. A rewrite rule $l \longrightarrow r$ is said to be *left-linear* if the term l is linear in each of its variables, that is if each variable of l occurs exactly once in l.

A *context* $C[X_1, ..., X_n]$ is an ordered pair formed with a term C, and a sequence of variables $X_1, ..., X_n$ each occurring exactly once in C. The term $(t_1/X_1, ..., t_n/X_n)C$ is written $C[t_1, ..., t_n]$.

Definition 1 (Polarized Rewrite System). *A polarized rewrite system $\mathcal{P}$ is a pair $\langle \mathcal{P}_-, \mathcal{P}_+ \rangle$ of rewrite systems. The rules of $\mathcal{P}_-$ are called* negative *and are written $l \longrightarrow_- r$, the rules of $\mathcal{P}_+$ are called* positive *and are written $l \longrightarrow_+ r$. The one step reduction relations $\longrightarrow_-$ and $\longrightarrow_+$ are defined as usual: $t \longrightarrow_- u$ (resp. $t \longrightarrow_+ u$) if there exists a negative rule $l \longrightarrow_- r$ (resp. a positive rule $l \longrightarrow_+ r$), a context $C[X]$ and a substitution σ, such that $t = C[\sigma l]$ and $u = C[\sigma r]$.*

Definition 2 (The Relation $\longrightarrow$). *The relation $\longrightarrow$ is $\longrightarrow_- \cup\ _+\longleftarrow$, that is $t \longrightarrow u$ if $t \longrightarrow_- u$ or $u \longrightarrow_+ t$.*

Definition 3 (Proof). *Let $\mathcal{P}$ be a polarized rewrite system. A proof (or a reduction sequence) in $\mathcal{P}$ is a sequence of terms $t_0, t_1, ..., t_n$, such that for all i, $t_i \longrightarrow t_{i+1}$, that is $t_i \longrightarrow_- t_{i+1}$ or $t_{i+1} \longrightarrow_+ t_i$.*

A proof is a proof of the proposition $t \longrightarrow^* u$ if $t = t_0$ and $u = t_n$.

Definition 4 (Polarization). *The polarized rewrite system $\mathcal{P}$ is said to be a polarization of a non-polarized rewrite system $\mathcal{R}$ if*

- *for each rule $l \longrightarrow r$ of $\mathcal{R}$, the system $\mathcal{P}$ contains either the rule $l \longrightarrow_- r$ or the rule $r \longrightarrow_+ l$,*
- *for each rule $l \longrightarrow_- r$ of $\mathcal{P}$, the system $\mathcal{R}$ contains the rule $l \longrightarrow r$,*
- *and, for each rule $l \longrightarrow_+ r$ of $\mathcal{P}$, the system $\mathcal{R}$ contains the rule $r \longrightarrow l$.*

Lemma 1. *Let $\mathcal{R}$ be a rewrite system, and $\mathcal{P}$ be a polarization of $\mathcal{R}$, then a proposition $t \longrightarrow^* u$ has a proof in $\mathcal{R}$ if and only if it has a proof in $\mathcal{P}$.*

Example 1. Let $\mathcal{R}$ be the rewrite system

$$f(g(a)) \longrightarrow b$$
$$f(f(a)) \longrightarrow c$$
$$b \longrightarrow g(g(f(f(a))))$$
$$c \longrightarrow h(a)$$

The polarized rewrite system $\mathcal{P}$

$$f(g(a)) \longrightarrow_- b$$
$$f(f(a)) \longrightarrow_- c$$
$$g(g(f(f(a)))) \longrightarrow_+ b$$
$$h(a) \longrightarrow_+ c$$

is a polarization of $\mathcal{R}$. The proposition $f(g(a)) \longrightarrow^* g(g(h(a)))$ has the following proof in $\mathcal{R}$

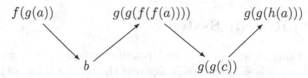

and the following proof in $\mathcal{P}$

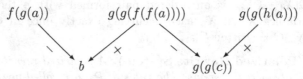

Definition 5 (Termination). *A polarized rewrite system is* terminating *if the relation* $\longrightarrow_- \cup \longrightarrow_+$ *is well-founded.*

Note that this does not imply that the relation $\longrightarrow$, that is $\longrightarrow_- \cup {}_+\!\longleftarrow$, is well-founded.

Definition 6 (Reduction Order). *A* reduction order $\prec$ *is an order such that*

 − *if* $t \prec u$, *then for all function symbols* f *and terms* $t_1, ..., t_{i-1}, t_{i+1}, ..., t_n$

$$f(t_1, ..., t_{i-1}, t, t_{i+1}, ..., t_n) \prec f(t_1, ..., t_{i-1}, u, t_{i+1}, ..., t_n)$$

 − *if* $t \prec u$, *then for all substitutions* σ

$$\sigma t \prec \sigma u$$

 − $\prec$ *is well-founded.*

Lemma 2. *Let* $\prec$ *be a reduction order and* $\mathcal{P}$ *be a polarized rewrite system such that* $l \succ r$ *for each rule* $l \longrightarrow_- r$ *or* $l \longrightarrow_+ r$ *of* $\mathcal{P}$. *Then, the system* $\mathcal{P}$ *terminates.*

3   Cut-Elimination

Definition 7 (Cut). *A* cut *(or a peak) in a proof* $\pi = t_0, t_1, ..., t_n$ *is a subsequence* t_{i-1}, t_i, t_{i+1} *such that*

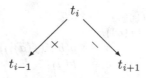

A proof is cut-free (or a valley *proof) if it contains no cuts, that is if it is formed
with a sequence of negative steps followed by a sequence of positive steps.*

A polarized rewrite system has the cut-elimination property *(or is confluent)
if every proposition* $t \longrightarrow^* u$ *that has a proof has a cut-free proof.*

Example 2. In the polarized rewrite system $\mathcal{P}$ of Example 1, the proposition
$f(g(a)) \longrightarrow^* g(g(h(a)))$ has the proof

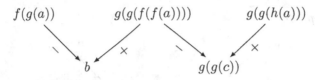

but no cut-free proof.

The reader familiar with polarized sequent calculus modulo theory will remark
that the proposition $t \longrightarrow^* u$ has a proof (resp. a cut-free proof) in $\mathcal{P}$ if and only
if the sequent $P(t) \vdash P(u)$, where P is a predicate symbol, has a proof (resp. a
cut-free proof) in polarized sequent calculus modulo $\mathcal{P}$.

Lemma 3. *Let $\mathcal{P}$ be a terminating finite polarized rewrite system. Then, the
existence of a cut-free proof in $\mathcal{P}$ of a proposition $t \longrightarrow^* u$ is decidable.*

Proof. The proposition $t \longrightarrow^* u$ has a cut-free proof if and only if the reducts
of t in $\mathcal{P}_-$ and those of u in $\mathcal{P}_+$ have a term in common. As $\mathcal{P}$ terminates, both
reduction trees are finite.

Definition 8 (Proof Reduction). *A proof π reduces to a proof π', if π' is
obtained by replacing a cut in π by a cut-free proof, that is if*

$$\pi = t_0, ..., t_{i-1}, t_i, t_{i+1}, ..., t_n$$

with

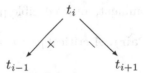

and

$$\pi' = t_0, ..., t_{i-1} = u_0, u_1, ..., u_p = w = v_q, ..., v_1, v_0 = t_{i+1}, ..., t_n$$

with

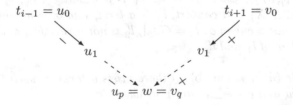

Definition 9 (Local Confluence). *A polarized rewrite system is locally confluent if every cut is reducible, that is if for each proof*

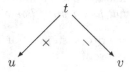

there exists a proof

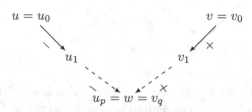

Newman's lemma can be seen as a termination lemma for proof-reduction [7], following an idea that is already in [11].

Lemma 4 (Newman). *If $\mathcal{P}$ is terminating and locally confluent, then it has the cut-elimination property.*

Proof. As $\mathcal{P}$ is terminating, the transitive closure of the relation $\longrightarrow_- \cup \longrightarrow_+$ is a well-founded order. Thus, its multiset extension $<$ [5] is also well-founded. A proof-reduction step replaces the multiset $\{t_1, ..., t_{i-1}, t_i, t_{i+1}, ..., t_n\}$ with the multiset $\{t_1, ..., t_{i-1}, u_1, ..., u_{p-1}, w, v_{q-1}, ..., v_1, t_{i+1}, ..., t_n\}$ and

$$\{t_1, ..., t_{i-1}, u_1, ..., u_{p-1}, w, v_{q-1}, ..., v_1, t_{i+1}, ..., t_n\} < \{t_1, ..., t_{i-1}, t_i, t_{i+1}, ..., t_n\}$$

because each term $u_1, ..., u_{p-1}, w, v_{q-1}, ..., v_1$ is smaller than t_i. Thus, proof-reduction terminates.

Finally, as $\mathcal{P}$ is locally confluent, an irreducible proof contains no cuts.

Definition 10 (Critical Pair). *A critical pair is a pair of terms of the form*

- *$\langle \sigma r_1, (\sigma C)[\sigma r_2] \rangle$, where $l_1 \longrightarrow_- r_1$ is a negative rule, $l_2 \longrightarrow_+ r_2$ is a positive rule, $C[X]$ is a context, l_1' is a term, and σ is a substitution, such that X does not occur in σ, $l_1 = C[l_1']$, l_1' is not a variable, and σ is the most general unifier of l_1' and l_2,*
- *or $\langle (\sigma C)[\sigma r_1], \sigma r_2 \rangle$, where $l_1 \longrightarrow_- r_1$ is a negative rule, $l_2 \longrightarrow_+ r_2$ is a positive rule, $C[X]$ is a context, l_2' is a term, and σ is a substitution, such that X does not occur in σ, $l_2 = C[l_2']$, l_2' is not a variable, and σ is the most general unifier of l_1 and l_2'.*

A critical pair $\langle u, v \rangle$ is joinable if there exists a term w, such that the propositions $u \longrightarrow_+^* w$ and $v \longrightarrow_-^* w$ are provable.

We now would like to prove that if all the critical pairs of a polarized rewrite system $\mathcal{P}$ are joinable, then $\mathcal{P}$ is locally confluent. Unfortunately, this property does not hold in general, as shown by the following counter-example

$$f(x,x) \longrightarrow_{-} g(x)$$

$$a \longrightarrow_{+} b$$

that contains no critical pairs, but that is not locally confluent, as the cut

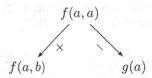

cannot be reduced: the term $g(a)$ reduces positively to $g(b)$ only, and the term $f(a,b)$ cannot be reduced negatively. It indeed reduces to $f(b,b)$, but not negatively. N. Hirokawa [9] has found a similar counter-example independently, in a different context. Fortunately, this property holds for left-linear rewrite systems.

We start by recalling two well-known classification lemmas [13,10].

Lemma 5. *Let $C_1[X]$ and $C_2[Y]$ be contexts, and u_1 and u_2 be terms such that $C_1[u_1] = C_2[u_2]$ then*

- *either the occurrences of X and Y are disjoint, that is there exists a context $D[X,Y]$ such that $C_1[X] = D[X,u_2]$ and $C_2[Y] = D[u_1,Y]$*

- *or the occurrence of X is higher than that of Y, that is there exists a context $D[Y]$ such that $C_2[Y] = C_1[D[Y]]$*

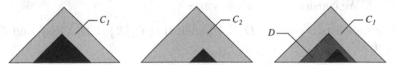

- *or the occurrence of Y is higher than that of X, that is there exists a context $D[X]$ such that $C_1[X] = C_2[D[X]]$*

Lemma 6. *Let t and u be terms, τ be a substitution and $D[Y]$ be a context such that the variable Y does not occur in τ and $\tau t = D[u]$. Then*

− *either the occurrence of Y in D is not an occurrence of t, that is there exist a variable x and contexts $E_1[X]$ and $E_2[Y]$, such that $t = E_1[x]$, $\tau x = E_2[u]$, and $D[Y] = (\tau E_1)[E_2[Y]]$*

− *or the occurrence of Y in D is an occurrence of t, that is there exist a context E and a term t' such that $t = E[t']$ and $D[Y] = (\tau E)[Y]$*

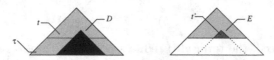

Lemma 7. *If all the critical pairs of a left-linear polarized rewrite system $\mathcal{P}$ are joinable, then $\mathcal{P}$ is locally confluent.*

Proof. Consider three terms t, u, and v such that

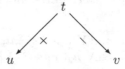

where t reduces to u by a rule $l_1 \longrightarrow_+ r_1$, and to v by a rule $l_2 \longrightarrow_- r_2$. Assume, without loss of generality, that l_1 and l_2 have no variables in common.

Thus, there exist two contexts $C_1[X]$ and $C_2[Y]$ and a substitution τ, such that X and Y do not occur in τ, $t = C_1[\tau l_1] = C_2[\tau l_2]$, $u = C_1[\tau r_1]$, and $v = C_2[\tau r_2]$. Thus, by Lemma 5, either there exists a context $D[X,Y]$ such that $C_1[X] = D[X, \tau l_2]$ and $C_2[Y] = D[\tau l_1, Y]$, or there exists a context $D[Y]$ such that $C_2[Y] = C_1[D[Y]]$, or there exists a context $D[X]$ such that $C_1[X] = C_2[D[X]]$. We consider these three cases.

− If there exists a context $D[X,Y]$ such that $C_1[X] = D[X, \tau l_2]$ and $C_2[Y] = D[\tau l_1, Y]$

we have $u = D[\tau r_1, \tau l_2]$, and $v = D[\tau l_1, \tau r_2]$, let $w = D[\tau r_1, \tau r_2]$. We have

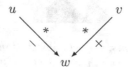

– If there exists a context $D[Y]$ such that $C_2[Y] = C_1[D[Y]]$

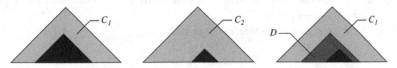

we have $t = C_1[\tau l_1] = C_1[D[\tau l_2]]$, $u = C_1[\tau r_1]$, and $v = C_1[D[\tau r_2]]$. As $C_1[\tau l_1] = C_1[D[\tau l_2]]$, we have $\tau l_1 = D[\tau l_2]$. Therefore, by Lemma 6, either there exist a variable x and contexts $E_1[X]$ and $E_2[Y]$, such that $l_1 = E_1[x]$, $\tau x = E_2[\tau l_2]$, and $D[Y] = (\tau E_1)[E_2[Y]]$, or there exist a context $E[Y]$ and a term l_1' such that $l_1 = E[l_1']$ and $D[Y] = (\tau E)[Y]$. We consider these two cases.

• If $l_1 = E_1[x]$, $\tau x = E_2[\tau l_2]$, and $D[Y] = (\tau E_1)[E_2[Y]]$, then we let $\tau' = \tau_{|\mathcal{V}\setminus\{x\}}$, and we have $\tau = (\tau', E_2[\tau l_2]/x)$. The term l_1 is linear and x does not occur in E_1, thus $\tau E_1 = \tau' E_1$. Let $w = C_1[(\tau', E_2[\tau r_2]/x)r_1]$. We have

$$u = C_1[\tau r_1] = C_1[(\tau', E_2[\tau l_2]/x)r_1] \longrightarrow^*_- C_1[(\tau', E_2[\tau r_2]/x)r_1] = w$$

$$v = C_1[D[\tau r_2]] = C_1[(\tau E_1)[E_2[\tau r_2]]] = C_1[(\tau' E_1)[E_2[\tau r_2]]]$$

$$= C_1[(\tau', E_2[\tau r_2]/x)(E_1[x])] = C_1[(\tau', E_2[\tau r_2]/x)l_1]$$

$$\longrightarrow^*_+ C_1[(\tau', E_2[\tau r_2]/x)r_1] = w$$

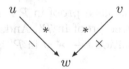

• If $l_1 = E[l_1']$ and $D[Y] = (\tau E)[Y]$, then $\tau l_1 = (\tau E)[\tau l_1'] = D[\tau l_1']$. As we have $\tau l_1 = D[\tau l_2]$, we get $D[\tau l_1'] = D[\tau l_2]$, thus $\tau l_1' = \tau l_2$. Let σ be the most general unifier of l_1' and l_2 and η such that $\tau = \eta \circ \sigma$. We have $u = C_1[\tau r_1] = C_1[\eta\sigma r_1]$ and $v = C_1[(\eta\sigma E)[\eta\sigma r_2]] = C_1[\eta((\sigma E)[\sigma r_2])]$. We know that the critical pair $\langle \sigma r_1, (\sigma E)[\sigma r_2] \rangle$ closes on a term, say w_0. Let $w = C_1[\eta w_0]$. We have

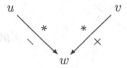

– The third case is similar to the second.

Definition 11 (Polarized Knuth-Bendix Method). *Let $\mathcal{P}$ be a left-linear finite polarized rewrite system and $\prec$ a reduction order, such that $l \succ r$ for each rule $l \longrightarrow_- r$ or $l \longrightarrow_+ r$ of $\mathcal{P}$.*
   While there is a non-joinable critical pair

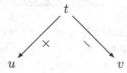

if $u \succ v$ and $u \longrightarrow_- v$ is a left-linear rewrite rule, add this rule to close the critical pair, if $v \succ u$ and $v \longrightarrow_+ u$ is a left-linear rewrite rule, add this rule to close the critical pair, otherwise fail.

Lemma 8. *Let $\mathcal{P}$ be a left-linear finite polarized rewrite system and $\prec$ a reduction order, such that $l \succ r$ for each rule $l \longrightarrow_- r$ or $l \longrightarrow_+ r$ of $\mathcal{P}$. If the polarized Knuth-Bendix method applied to $\mathcal{P}$ succeeds, then reachability in $\mathcal{P}$ is decidable.*

Proof. Let $\mathcal{P}'$ be the left-linear finite polarized rewrite system built by the polarized Knuth-Bendix method. The rules of $\mathcal{P}'$ are all derivable in $\mathcal{P}$, thus a proposition $t \longrightarrow^* u$ has a proof in $\mathcal{P}$ if and only if it has a proof in $\mathcal{P}'$.
   As all the critical pairs of $\mathcal{P}'$ are joinable, by Lemma 7, $\mathcal{P}'$ is locally confluent. By construction, $l \succ r$ for each rule $l \longrightarrow_- r$ or $l \longrightarrow_+ r$ of $\mathcal{P}'$. Thus, by Lemma 2, $\mathcal{P}'$ terminates. By Lemma 4, as $\mathcal{P}'$ is locally confluent and terminating, it has the cut-elimination property.
   Thus, a proposition $t \longrightarrow^* u$ has a proof in $\mathcal{P}$ if and only if it has a proof in $\mathcal{P}'$ if and only if it has a cut-free proof in $\mathcal{P}'$. And, by Lemma 3, the existence of a cut-free proof for a proposition $t \longrightarrow^* u$ in $\mathcal{P}'$ is decidable.

Example 3. Let $\mathcal{P}$ be the system defined in Example 1 and $\prec$ be the Knuth-Bendix order [13] with an equal weight 1 for all symbols and any precedence. For all rules $l \longrightarrow_- r$ or $l \longrightarrow_+ r$ of $\mathcal{P}$, we have $l \succ r$. The only non-joinable critical pair is

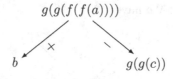

and it closes with the rule

$$g(g(c)) \longrightarrow_+ b$$

Let $\mathcal{P}'$ be the system obtained by adding this rule to $\mathcal{P}$. The proposition $f(g(a)) \longrightarrow^* g(g(h(a)))$ has the proof in $\mathcal{P}'$

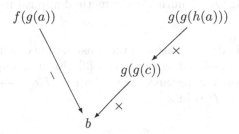

Theorem 1. *Let $\mathcal{R}$ be a (non-polarized) finite rewrite system, $\mathcal{P}$ be a polarization of $\mathcal{R}$ and $\prec$ be a reduction order. If $\mathcal{P}$ is a left-linear polarized rewrite system, for all rules $l \longrightarrow_- r$ or $l \longrightarrow_+ r$ of $\mathcal{P}$, $l \succ r$, and the polarized Knuth-Bendix method applied to $\mathcal{P}$ succeeds, then reachability in $\mathcal{R}$ is decidable.*

Proof. From Lemmas 1 and 8.

4   Ground Finite Rewrite Systems

A ground rewrite system is a rewrite system such that for all rules $l \longrightarrow r$, both terms l and r are ground.

D. Lankford [14,4] has observed that if $\prec$ is the Knuth-Bendix order [13] with an equal weight 1 for all symbols and any precedence, $\mathcal{R}$ is a finite ground rewrite system, $\mathcal{R}'$ is the equivalent system obtained by removing the rules of the form $l \longrightarrow l$ and reversing the rules $l \longrightarrow r$ such that $l \prec r$ into $r \longrightarrow l$, then the Knuth-Bendix method always succeeds on $\mathcal{R}'$, and therefore equivalence in $\mathcal{R}$ is decidable.

We now want to prove that, in a similar way, reachability in a finite ground rewrite system is decidable [3].

Theorem 2 (Dauchet-Tison). *Let $\mathcal{R}$ be a finite ground rewrite system. Then, the existence of a proof in $\mathcal{R}$ of a proposition $t \longrightarrow^* u$ is decidable.*

Proof. Let $\prec$ be the Knuth-Bendix order [13] with an equal weight 1 for all symbols and any precedence. This order is a reduction order and it is total on ground terms.

Without loss of generality, we can assume that $\mathcal{R}$ does not contain trivial rules of the form $l \longrightarrow l$. Let $\mathcal{P}$ be the polarization of $\mathcal{R}$ obtained by transforming each rule $l \longrightarrow r$ of $\mathcal{R}$ such that $l \succ r$, into a negative rule $l \longrightarrow_- r$, and reversing each rule $l \longrightarrow r$ such that $l \prec r$ into a positive rule $r \longrightarrow_+ l$. By construction, $l \succ r$ for each rule $l \longrightarrow_- r$ or $l \longrightarrow_+ r$ of $\mathcal{P}$.

Let T be the finite set containing the left-hand sides of the rules of $\mathcal{P}$ and T' be the set of ground terms t such that there exists a term u in T such that $t \prec u$ or $t = u$. As, for the Knuth-Bendix order, if u is a ground term, the set of ground terms t such that $t \prec u$ is always finite, the set T' is finite.

Then, the polarized Knuth-Bendix method applied to $\mathcal{P}$ generates rules whose left-hand sides and right-hand sides are in T'. As there is only a finite number of such rules, the polarized Knuth-Bendix method applied to $\mathcal{P}$ terminates successfully.

Note that the original proof based on the construction of automata recognizing left-hand sides and right-hand sides of rules [3] also uses implicitly the idea of reversing rewrite rules. For instance, with the rule $f(a) \longrightarrow g(b)$, it builds an automaton recognizing $f(a)$ in s

$$a \longrightarrow s_1$$

$$f(s_1) \longrightarrow s$$

another recognizing $g(b)$ in s'

$$b \longrightarrow s_1'$$

$$g(s_1') \longrightarrow s'$$

and takes the rewrite rule

$$s \longrightarrow s'$$

This construction can be decomposed in two steps, one transforming the rule $f(a) \longrightarrow g(b)$ into the rewrite system

$$a \longrightarrow s_1$$

$$f(s_1) \longrightarrow s$$

$$s \longrightarrow s'$$

$$s_1' \longrightarrow b$$

$$s' \longrightarrow g(s_1')$$

where $f(a) \longrightarrow f(s_1) \longrightarrow s \longrightarrow s' \longrightarrow g(s_1') \longrightarrow g(b)$ and then reversing the two rules

$$s_1' \longrightarrow b$$

$$s' \longrightarrow g(s_1')$$

The first step is in fact not needed.

5   Pushdown Systems

As another corollary of our result, we also get the decidability of reachability for pushdown systems [1].

Definition 12 (Pushdown System). *Consider a language containing a set S of unary function symbols called* stack symbols, *a set Q of unary function symbols called* states *and a constant ε. A pushdown system is a finite rewrite system with rules of the form:* pop rules

$$p(\gamma(x)) \longrightarrow q(x)$$

where γ is a stack symbol and p and q are states, push rules

$$p(x) \longrightarrow q(\gamma(x))$$

where γ is a stack symbol and p and q are states, and neutral rules

$$p(x) \longrightarrow q(x)$$

where p and q are states.

Theorem 3 (Bouajjani-Esparza-Maler). *Let $\mathcal{R}$ be a pushdown system. Then, the existence of a proof in $\mathcal{R}$ of a proposition $t \longrightarrow^* u$ is decidable.*

Proof. Consider a total precedence on function symbols such that stack symbols are larger than states and let $\prec$ be the lexicographic path order [12] relative to this precedence. The order $\prec$ is a reduction order and $p(\gamma(x)) \succ q(x)$ for all γ, p and q.

Pop rules are polarized as

$$p(\gamma(x)) \longrightarrow_- q(x)$$

push rules as

$$q(\gamma(x)) \longrightarrow_+ p(x)$$

and neutral rules according to the precedence.

Critical pairs have the form

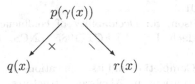

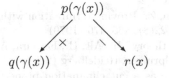

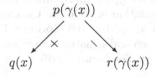

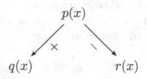

all these critical pairs are closed by adding a pop rule, a push rule, or a neutral rule. As there are a finite number of such rules, the polarized Knuth-Bendix method always terminates successfully.

Thus reachability in pushdown systems is decidable.

Note that we get, in this way, the decidability of reachability in pushdown systems, but not of alternating pushdown systems [1], that requires moving from polarized rewrite systems to polarized sequent calculus modulo [2].

Acknowledgements. The authors want to thank Nao Hirokawa, Gérard Huet, Jean-Pierre Jouannaud, Claude Kirchner, and Vincent van Oostrom, for useful discussions on this paper and bibliographical indications. This work is supported by the ANR-NSFC project LOCALI (NSFC 61161130530 and ANR 11 IS02 002 01) and the Chinese National Basic Research Program (973) Grant No. 2014CB340302.

References

1. Bouajjani, A., Esparza, J., Maler, O.: Reachability analysis of pushdown automata: Application to model-checking. In: Mazurkiewicz, A., Winkowski, J. (eds.) CONCUR 1997. LNCS, vol. 1243, pp. 135–150. Springer, Heidelberg (1997)
2. Burel, G., Dowek, G., Jiang, Y.: Automata, resolution and cut-elimination (manuscript) (2015)
3. Dauchet, M., Tison, S.: Decidability of confluence for ground term rewriting systems. In: Budach, L. (ed.) FCT 1985. LNCS, vol. 199, pp. 80–89. Springer, Heidelberg (1985)
4. Dershowitz, N.: Completion and its applications. In: Aït-Kaci, H., Nivat, M. (eds.) Resolution of Equations in Algebraic Structures, vol. 2, chapter 2, pp. 31–86. Academic Press (1989)
5. Dershowitz, N., Manna, Z.: Proving termination with multiset orderings. Communications of the ACM 22(8), 465–476 (1979)
6. Dowek, G.: What is a theory? In: Alt, H., Ferreira, A. (eds.) STACS 2002. LNCS, vol. 2285, pp. 50–64. Springer, Heidelberg (2002)
7. Dowek, G.: Confluence as a cut elimination property. In: Nieuwenhuis, R. (ed.) RTA 2003. LNCS, vol. 2706, pp. 2–13. Springer, Heidelberg (2003)
8. Dowek, G.: Polarized resolution modulo. In: Calude, C.S., Sassone, V. (eds.) TCS 2010. IFIP AICT, vol. 323, pp. 182–196. Springer, Heidelberg (2010)
9. Hirokawa, N.: Commutation and signature extension. In: Tiwari, A., Aoto, T. (eds.) International Workshop on Confluence (2015)

10. Huet, G.: Confluent reductions: abstract properties and applications to term rewriting systems. Journal of the Association of Computing Machinery 27(4), 797–821 (1980)
11. Jouannaud, J.-P., Kirchner, H.: Completion of a set of rules modulo a set of equations. SIAM Journal of Computing 15(4), 1155–1194 (1986)
12. Kamin, S., Lévy, J.-J.: Attempts for generalizing the recursive path ordering (unpublished manuscript)
13. Knuth, D., Bendix, P.: Simple word problems in universal algebras. In: Computational Problems in Abstract Algebra, pp. 263–297, Pergamon (1970)
14. Lankford, D.S.: Canonical inference. Technical report, Louisiana Tech. University (1975)

Axiomatic Constraint Systems
for Proof Search Modulo Theories

Damien Rouhling[1], Mahfuza Farooque[2],
Stéphane Graham-Lengrand[2,4], Assia Mahboubi[3], and Jean-Marc Notin[2]

[1] École Normale Supérieure de Lyon, France
[2] CNRS - École Polytechnique, France
[3] INRIA, Centre de Recherche en Informatique Saclay-Île de France
[4] SRI International, USA

Abstract. Goal-directed proof search in first-order logic uses meta-variables to delay the choice of witnesses; substitutions for such variables are produced when closing proof-tree branches, using first-order unification or a theory-specific background reasoner. This paper investigates a generalisation of such mechanisms whereby *theory-specific constraints* are produced instead of substitutions. In order to design modular proof-search procedures over such mechanisms, we provide a sequent calculus with meta-variables, which manipulates such constraints abstractly. Proving soundness and completeness of the calculus leads to an axiomatisation that identifies the conditions under which abstract constraints can be generated and propagated in the same way unifiers usually are. We then extract from our abstract framework a component interface and a specification for concrete implementations of background reasoners.

1   Introduction

A broad literature studies the integration of theory reasoning with generic automated reasoning techniques. Following Stickel's seminal work [16], different levels of interaction have been identified [2] between a theory-generic *foreground reasoner* and a theory-specific *background reasoner*, with a specific scheme for the *literal level* of interaction. In absence of quantifiers, the DPLL($\mathcal{T}$) architecture [11] is an instance of the scheme and a successful basis for SMT-solving, combining SAT-solving techniques for boolean logic with a procedure that decides whether a conjunction of ground literals is consistent with a background theory $\mathcal{T}$.

Our contribution falls into such a scheme, but in presence of quantifiers, and hence of non-ground literals. When given a conjunction of these, the background reasoner provides a means to make this conjunction inconsistent with $\mathcal{T}$, possibly by instantiating some (meta-)variables [2]. Technically, it produces a $\mathcal{T}$-*refuter* that contains a substitution.

Beckert [5] describes how this approach can be applied to *analytic tableaux*, in particular *free variable tableaux*: $\mathcal{T}$-refuters are produced to extend and eventually close a tableau branch, while the substitutions that they contain are globally applied to the tableau, thus affecting the remaining open branches. In fact, the

© Springer International Publishing Switzerland 2015
C. Lutz and S. Ranise (Eds.): FroCoS 2015, LNAI 9322, pp. 220–236, 2015.
DOI: 10.1007/978-3-319-24246-0_14

only way in which closing a branch affects the other branches is the propagation of these substitutions, as it is the case for tableaux without theory reasoning. This is well-suited for some theories like equality, for which *rigid E-unification* provides a background reasoner (see e.g. [4]), but maybe not for other theories. For instance, the case of Linear Integer Arithmetic (LIA) was addressed by using arithmetic constraints, and quantifier elimination, in the Model Evolution calculus [1] and the Sequent Calculus [14] (which is closer to the above tableaux).

This paper develops sequent calculi with a more general *abstract* notion of constraints so that more theories can be treated in a similar way, starting with all theories admitting quantifier elimination. But it also covers those total theories (total in the sense that $\mathcal{T}$-refuters are just substitutions) considered by Beckert [5] for free variable tableaux, for which constraints are simply substitutions.

Sect. 2 presents a sequent calculus LK_1 with ground theory reasoning (as in $\mathsf{DPLL}(\mathcal{T})$) and various target theories that we intend to capture. Sect. 3 introduces our abstract systems of constraints. Sect. 4 presents a sequent calculus $\mathsf{LK}_1^?$ similar to Rümmer's $\mathsf{PresPred}_\mathcal{G}^\mathcal{C}$ calculus [14], but generalised with abstract constraints. It collects constraints from the parallel/independent exploration of branches, with the hope that their combination remains satisfiable. Sect. 5 and 6 present a variant $\mathsf{LK}_1^{?}$ where the treatment of branching is asymmetric, reflecting a sequential implementation of proof search: the constraint that is produced to close one branch affects the exploration of the next branch, as in free variable tableaux [5]. Each time, we prove soundness and completeness relative to the reference sequent calculus LK_1. From these proofs we extract an axiomatisation for our background theory reasoner and its associated constraints. In Sect. 7 this axiomatisation is used to define a component interface with a formal specification, for our quantifier-handling version 2.0 of the PSYCHE platform for theorem proving [12]. We conclude by discussing related works and future work.

2 Ground Calculus and Examples

The simple sequent calculus that we use in this paper uses the standard first-order notions of term, literal, eigenvariable, and formula. Following standard practice in *tableaux* methods or the linear logic tradition, we opt for a compact one-sided presentation of the sequent calculus, here called LK_1. Its rules are presented in Fig. 1, where Γ is a set (intuitively seen as a disjunction) of first-order formulae (in negation-normal form) and Γ_{lit} is the subset of its literals; $A[x := t]$ denotes the substitution of term t for all free occurrences of variable x in formula A; finally, $\models$ denotes a specific predicate, called the *ground validity predicate*, on sets of *ground* literals (i.e. literals whose variables are all eigenvariables). This predicate is used to model a given theory $\mathcal{T}$, with the intuition that $\models \Gamma_{\mathsf{lit}}$ holds when the disjunction of the literals in Γ is $\mathcal{T}$-valid. Equivalently, it holds when the conjunction of their negations is $\mathcal{T}$-inconsistent, as checked by the decision procedures used in SMT-solving. Likewise, checking whether $\models \Gamma_{\mathsf{lit}}$ holds is performed by a background reasoner, while the bottom-up application of the rule of LK_1 can serve as the basis for a *tableaux*-like foreground reasoner.

$$\frac{}{\vdash \Gamma} \models \Gamma_{\text{lit}} \qquad \frac{\vdash \Gamma, A \qquad \vdash \Gamma, B}{\vdash \Gamma, A \wedge B} \qquad \frac{\vdash \Gamma, A, B}{\vdash \Gamma, A \vee B}$$

$$\frac{\vdash \Gamma, A\,[x := t], \exists x A}{\vdash \Gamma, \exists x A} \qquad \frac{\vdash \Gamma, A\,[x := \mathrm{x}]}{\vdash \Gamma, \forall x A}$$

where x is a fresh eigenvariable

Fig. 1. The LK_1 sequent calculus modulo theories

But a realistic proof-search procedure is in general unable to provide an appropriate witness t "out of the blue" at the time of applying an existential rule. We shall use *meta-variables* (called *free variables* in tableaux terminology) to delay the production of such instances until the constraints of completing/closing branches impact our choice possibilities. The way this happens heavily depends on the background theory, and below we give a few examples (more background on the technical notions can be found for instance in Beckert's survey [5]):

Example 1 (Pure first-order logic). In the empty theory, closing a branch $\vdash \Gamma$ is done by finding a literal l and its negation $\bar{l}$ in Γ or, if meta-variables were used, by finding a pair l and $\bar{l'}$ and a substitution σ for meta-variables that *unifies l* and l'. Such a *first-order unifier* σ may be produced by the sole analysis of $\vdash \Gamma$, or by the simultaneous analysis of the branches that need to be closed. Since the latter problem is still decidable, a global management of unification constraints is sometimes preferred, avoiding the propagation of unifiers from branch to branch.

Example 2 (First-order logic with equality). When adding equality, closing a branch $\vdash \Gamma$ is done by finding in Γ either an equality $t = u$ such that $\Gamma_E \models_E t = u$, or a pair of literals $p(t_1, \ldots, t_n)$ and $\bar{p}(u_1, \ldots, u_n)$ such that $\Gamma_E \models_E t_1 = u_1 \wedge \cdots \wedge t_n = u_n$, where Γ_E is the set of all equalities $a = b$ such that $a \neq b$ is in Γ, and $\models_E$ is entailment in the theory of equality. *Congruence closure* can be used to check this entailment. If meta-variables were used, then a substitution σ for meta-variables has to be found such that e.g. $\sigma(\Gamma_E) \models_E \sigma(t) = \sigma(u)$, a problem known as *rigid E-unification*. While this problem is decidable, finding a substitution that simultaneously closes several open branches (*simultaneous rigid E-unification*) is undecidable. A natural way to use rigid E-unification is to produce a *stream* of substitutions from the analysis of one branch and propagate them into the other branches; if at some point we have difficulties closing one of these, we can try the next substitution in the stream.

The idea of producing streams of substitutions at the leaves of branches (advocated by Giese [8]) can be taken further:

Example 3 (Theories with ground decidability). Any theory whose ground validity predicate is decidable has a semi-decision procedure that "handles" meta-variables: to close a branch $\vdash \Gamma$ with meta-variables, enumerate as a stream all substitutions to ground terms (i.e. terms whose variables are all eigenvariables), and filter out of it all substitutions σ such that $\not\models \sigma(\Gamma)_{\text{lit}}$. Stream productivity -and therefore decidability- may thus be lost, but completeness of proof search in first-order logic already requires fairness of strategies with e.g. iterative deepening methods, which may as well include the computation of streams.

While this mostly seems an impractical theoretical remark, heuristics can be used (e.g. first trying those ground terms that are already present in the problem) that are not far from what is implemented in SMT-solvers (like *triggers* [6]).

The enumeration strategy can also be theory-driven, and also make use of substitutions to non-ground terms: An interesting instance of this is higher-order logic expressed as a first-order theory, λ-terms being encoded as first-order terms using De Bruijn's indices, and $\beta\eta$-equivalence being expressed with first-order axioms. Similarly to Example 1, closing a branch with meta-variables requires solving (higher-order) unification problems, whose (semi-decision) algorithms can be seen as complete but optimised enumeration techniques.

All of the above examples use substitutions of meta-variables as the output of a successful branch closure, forming *total background reasoners* for the tableaux of [5]. But by letting successful branch closures produce a more general notion of theory-specific *constraints*, we also cover examples such as:

Example 4 (Theories with quantifier elimination). When a theory satisfies quantifier elimination (such as linear arithmetic), the provability of arbitrary formulae can be reduced to the provability of quantifier-free formulae. This reduction can be done with the same proof-search methodology as for the previous examples, provided successful branch closures produce other kinds of data-structures. For instance with p an uninterpreted predicate symbol, $l(x, y) := 3x \leq 2y \leq 3x+1$ and $l'(x, y) := 99 \leq 3y+2x \leq 101$, the foreground reasoner will turn the sequent

$$\vdash (\exists xy(p(x, y) \wedge l(x, y))) \vee (\exists x'y'(\overline{p}(x', y') \wedge l'(x', y'))$$

into a tree with 4 branches, with meta-variables $?X$, $?X'$, $?Y$, and $?Y'$:

$$\vdash p(?X, ?Y), \overline{p}(?X', ?Y') \quad \vdash l(?X, ?Y), \overline{p}(?X', ?Y')$$
$$\vdash p(?X, ?Y), l'(?X', ?Y') \quad \vdash l(?X, ?Y), l'(?X', ?Y')$$

While it is clear that the background reasoner will close the top-left leaf by producing the substitution identifying $?X$ with $?X'$, $?Y$ with $?Y'$, it is hard to see how the analysis of any of the other branches could produce, on its own and not after a lengthy enumeration, a substitution that is, or may be refined into, the unique integer solution $?X \mapsto 15, ?Y \mapsto 23$. Hence the need for branches to communicate to other branches more appropriate data-structures than substitutions, like *constraints* (in this case, arithmetic ones).

In the rest of this paper, all of the above examples are instances of an abstract notion of theory module that comes with its own system of constraints.

3   Constraint Structures

Meta-variables (denoted $?X$, $?Y$, etc) can be thought of as place-holders for yet-to-come instantiations. Delayed though these may be, they must respect the freshness conditions from System LK_1, so dependencies between meta-variables and eigenvariables must be recorded during proof search.

While Skolem symbols are a convenient implementation of such dependencies when the theory reasoner is unification-based (*occurs check* ruling out incorrect instantiations for free), we record them in a data-structure, called *domain*, attached to each sequent. Two operations are used on domains: adding to a domain d a fresh eigenvariable x (resp. meta-variable $?X$) results in a new domain $d; \mathsf{x}$ (resp. $d; ?X$). The use of the notation always implicitly assumes x (resp. $?X$) to be fresh for d. An *initial domain* d_0 is also used before proof search introduces fresh eigenvariables and meta-variables.[1]

Definition 1 (Terms, Formulae with Meta-Variables). *A* term *(resp. formula) of domain d is a term (resp. formula) whose variables (resp. free variables) are all eigenvariables or meta-variables declared in d. A term (resp. formula) is* ground *if it contains no meta-variables. Given a domain d, we define T_d to be the set of ground terms of domain d. A context of domain d is a multiset of formulae of domain d. In the rest of this paper, a* free variable *(of domain d) means either an eigenvariable or a meta-variable (declared in d).*

In this setting, the axiom rule of system LK_1 is adapted to the presence of meta-variables in literals, so as to produce theory-specific *constraints* on (yet-to-come) instantiations. We characterise the abstract structure that they form:

Definition 2 (Constraint Structures). *A constraint structure is:*

- *a family of sets $(\Psi_d)_d$, indexed by domains and satisfying $\Psi_{d;\mathsf{x}} = \Psi_d$ for all domains d and eigenvariables x; elements of Ψ_d are called* constraints *of domain d, and are denoted σ, σ', etc.*
- *a family of mappings from $\Psi_{d;?X}$ to Ψ_d for all domains d and meta-variables $?X$, called* projections, *mapping constraints $\sigma \in \Psi_{d;?X}$ to constraints $\sigma_\downarrow \in \Psi_d$.*

A meet constraint structure *is a constraint structure $(\Psi_d)_d$ with a binary operator $(\sigma, \sigma') \mapsto \sigma \wedge \sigma'$ on each set Ψ_d.*

A lift constraint structure *is a constraint structure $(\Psi_d)_d$ with a map $\sigma \mapsto \sigma^\uparrow$ from Ψ_d to $\Psi_{d;?X}$ for all domains d and meta-variables $?X$.*

Intuitively, each mapping from $\Psi_{d;?X}$ to Ψ_d projects a constraint concerning the meta-variables declared in $(d; ?X)$ to a constraint on the meta-variables in d. Different constraints can be used for different theories:

Example 5. 1. In Examples 1 and 2, it is natural to take Ψ_d to be the set whose elements are either $\bot$ (to represent the unsatisfiable constraint) or a

---

[1] For instance, a domain may be implemented as a pair $(\Phi; \Delta)$, where Φ is the set of declared eigenvariables and Δ maps every declared meta-variable to the set of eigenvariables on which it is authorised to depend. With this implementation, $(\Phi; \Delta); \mathsf{x} := (\Phi, \mathsf{x}; \Delta)$ and $(\Phi; \Delta); ?X := (\Phi; \Delta, ?X \mapsto \Phi)$. We also set $d_0 = (\Phi_0, \emptyset)$, with Φ_0 already containing enough eigenvariables so as to prove e.g. $\exists x (p(x) \vee \overline{p}(x))$.

substitution σ for the meta-variables in d.[2] Projecting a substitution from $\Psi_{d;?X}$ is just erasing its entry for $?X$. The meet of two substitutions is their most general unifier, and the lift of $\sigma \in \Psi_d$ into $\Psi_{d;?X}$ is $\sigma, ?X \mapsto ?X$.

2. In Example 3, the default constraint structure would restrict the above to substitutions that map meta-variables to either themselves or to ground terms, unless a particular theory-specific enumeration mechanism could make use of non-ground terms (such as higher-order unification).

3. In Example 4, $\Psi_{d;x} = \Psi_d$ for any d, and we take Ψ_{d_0} (resp. $\Psi_{d;?X}$) to be the set of quantifier-free formulae of domain d_0 (resp. $d; ?X$). Quantifier elimination provides projections, the meet operator is conjunction and the lift is identity.

4   A System for Proof Search with Constraints

In the rest of this section $(\Psi_d)_d$ denotes a fixed meet constraint structure.

4.1   The Constraint-Producing Sequent Calculus $\mathsf{LK}_1^?$

This sequent calculus is parameterised by a background theory reasoner that can handle meta-variables. The reasoner is modelled by a *constraint-producing predicate* that generalises the ground validity predicate used in System LK_1.

Definition 3 ($\mathsf{LK}_1^?$ Sequent Calculus). *A constraint-producing predicate is a family of relations $(\models^d)_d$, indexed by domains d, relating sets $\mathcal{A}$ of literals of domain d with constraints σ in Ψ_d; when it holds, we write $\models^d \mathcal{A} \to \sigma$.*

Given such a predicate $(\models^d)_d$, the constraint-producing sequent calculus $\mathsf{LK}_1^?$ manipulates sequents of the form $\vdash^d \Gamma \to \sigma$, where Γ is a context and σ is a constraint, both of domain d. Its rules are presented in Fig. 2.

$$\frac{\models^d \Gamma_{\mathsf{lit}} \to \sigma}{\vdash^d \Gamma \to \sigma} \qquad \frac{\vdash^d \Gamma, A \to \sigma \qquad \vdash^d \Gamma, B \to \sigma'}{\vdash^d \Gamma, A \wedge B \to \sigma \wedge \sigma'} \qquad \frac{\vdash^d \Gamma, A, B \to \sigma}{\vdash^d \Gamma, A \vee B \to \sigma}$$

$$\frac{\vdash^{d;?X} \Gamma, A\,[x := ?X]\,, \exists x A \to \sigma}{\vdash^d \Gamma, \exists x A \to \sigma_\downarrow} \qquad \frac{\vdash^{d;x} \Gamma, A\,[x := x] \to \sigma}{\vdash^d \Gamma, \forall x A \to \sigma}$$

where $?X$ is a fresh meta-variable   where x is a fresh eigenvariable

Fig. 2. The constraint-producing sequent calculus $\mathsf{LK}_1^?$

In terms of process, a sequent $\vdash^d \Gamma \to \sigma$ displays the inputs Γ, d and the output σ of proof search, which starts building a proof tree, in system $\mathsf{LK}_1^?$, from the root. The sequent at the root would typically be of the form $\vdash^{d_0} \Gamma \to \sigma$, with $\sigma \in \Psi_{d_0}$ to be produced as output. The constraints are produced at the leaves, and propagated back down towards the root.

---

[2] Technically, the term $\sigma(?X)$, if defined, features only eigenvariables among those authorised for $?X$ by d, and meta-variables outside d or mapped to themselves by σ.

Example 6. In Examples 1, 2, 3, the constraint-producing predicate $\models^d \mathcal{A} \to \sigma$ holds if, respectively, σ is the most general unifier of two dual literals in $\mathcal{A}$, σ is an output of rigid E-unification on $\mathcal{A}$, σ is a ground substitution for which $\sigma(\mathcal{A})$ is $\mathcal{T}$-inconsistent. In Example 4, $\models^d \mathcal{A} \to \sigma$ holds if the quantifier-free formula σ (of appropriate domain) implies $\mathcal{A}$ (as a disjunction). For our specific example, which also involves uninterpreted predicate symbols, proof search in system $\mathsf{LK}_1^?$ builds a tree

$$\frac{\vdash^d p(?X, ?Y), \overline{p}(?X', ?Y') \to \sigma_1 \quad \vdash^d l(?X, ?Y), \overline{p}(?X', ?Y') \to \sigma_2}{\vdash^d p(?X, ?Y), l'(?X', ?Y') \to \sigma_3 \quad \vdash^d l(?X, ?Y), l'(?X', ?Y') \to \sigma_4}$$

$$\cdots$$

$$\frac{}{\vdash^d (p(x,y) \wedge l(x,y)), (\overline{p}(x',y') \wedge l'(x',y')) \to \sigma}$$

$$\cdots$$

$$\frac{}{\vdash^{d_0} (\exists xy(p(x,y) \wedge l(x,y))) \vee (\exists x'y'(\overline{p}(x',y') \wedge l'(x',y'))) \to \sigma_{\downarrow\downarrow\downarrow\downarrow}}$$

where $d := ?X; ?Y; ?X'; ?Y'$, the background reasoner produces $\sigma_1 := \{?X = ?X'; ?Y = ?Y'\}$, $\sigma_2 := \{3?X \le 2?Y \le 3?X + 1\}$, $\sigma_3 := \{99 \le 3?Y' + 2?X' \le 101\}$, and $\sigma_4 := \sigma_2$ ($\sigma_4 := \sigma_3$ also works); then $\sigma := (\sigma_1 \wedge \sigma_2) \wedge (\sigma_3 \wedge \sigma_4)$ and finally $\sigma_{\downarrow\downarrow\downarrow\downarrow}$, obtained by quantifier elimination from σ, is the trivially true formula.

System $\mathsf{LK}_1^?$ is very close to Rümmer's PresPred_S^C System [14], but using abstract constraints instead of linear arithmetic constraints. Using $\mathsf{LK}_1^?$ with the constraint structure of Example 5.3 implements Rümmer's suggestion [14] to eliminate quantifiers along the propagation of constraints down to the root.

4.2 Instantiations and Compatibility with Constraints

Notice that, in system $\mathsf{LK}_1^?$, no instantiation for meta-variables is actually ever produced. Instantiations would only come up when reconstructing, from an $\mathsf{LK}_1^?$ proof, a proof in the original calculus LK_1. So as to relate constraints to actual instantiations, we formalise what it means for an instantiation to satisfy, or be compatible with, a constraint of domain d. Such an instantiation should provide, for each meta-variable, a term that at least respects the eigenvariable dependencies specified in d, as formalised in Definition 4. Beyond this, what it means for an instantiation to be compatible with a constraint is specific to the theory and we simply identify in Definition 5 some minimal axioms. We list these axioms, along with the rest of this paper's axiomatisation, in Fig. 4 on page 232.

Definition 4 (Instantiation). *The set of instantiations of domain d, denoted Σ_d, is the set of mappings from meta-variables to ground terms defined by induction on d as follows:*

$$\Sigma_{d_0} = \emptyset \qquad \Sigma_{d;x} = \Sigma_d \qquad \Sigma_{d;?X} = \{\rho, ?X \mapsto t \mid t \in T_d, \rho \in \Sigma_d\}$$

For a term t (resp. a formula A, a context Γ) of domain d and an instantiation $\rho \in \Sigma_d$, we denote by $\rho(t)$ (resp. $\rho(A)$, $\rho(\Gamma)$) the result of substituting in t (resp. A, Γ) each meta-variable $?X$ in d by its image through ρ.

Definition 5 (Compatibility relation). *A compatibility relation is a (family of) relation(s) between instantiations $\rho \in \Sigma_d$ and constraints $\sigma \in \Psi_d$ for each domain d, denoted $\rho \epsilon \sigma$, that satisfies Axiom* **Proj** *of Fig. 4.*

If the constraint structure is a meet constraint structure, we say that the compatibility relation distributes over $\wedge$ *if it satisfies Axiom* **Meet** *of Fig. 4.*

Another ingredient we need to relate the two sequent calculi is a mechanism for producing instantiations. We formalise a *witness builder* which maps every constraint of $\Psi_{d;?X}$ to a function, which outputs an "appropriate" instantiation for $?X$ when given as input an instantiation of domain d:

Definition 6 (Witness). *A witness builder for a compatibility relation ϵ is a (family of) function(s) that maps every $\sigma \in \Psi_{d;?X}$ to $f_\sigma \in \Sigma_d \to T_d$, for every domain d and every meta-variable $?X$, and that satisfies Axiom* **Wit** *of Fig. 4.*

Example 7. For the constraint structure of Example 5.1, we can define: $\rho \epsilon \sigma$ if ρ is a (ground) instance of substitution σ. Given $\sigma \in \Psi_{d;?X}$ and $\rho \epsilon \sigma_\downarrow$, we have $\rho = \rho' \circ \sigma_\downarrow$, and we can take $f_\sigma(\rho)$ to be any instance of $\rho'(\sigma(?X))$ in Σ_d.

In the particular case of Example 5.2, $\rho \epsilon \sigma$ if ρ coincides with σ (on every meta-variable not mapped to itself by σ). To define $f_\sigma(\rho)$, note that $\rho'(\sigma(?X))$ is either ground or it is $?X$ itself (in which case any term in Σ_d works as $f_\sigma(\rho)$).

For the constraint structure of Example 5.3, we can take: $\rho \epsilon F$ if the ground formula $\rho(F)$ is valid in the theory. From a formula $F \in \Psi_{d;?X}$ and an instantiation ρ, the term $f_F(\rho)$ should represent an existential witness for the formula $\rho(F)$, which features $?X$ as the only meta-variable. In the general case, we might need to resort to a Hilbert-style choice operator to construct the witness: $\epsilon(\exists x((\rho, ?X \mapsto x)(F)))$. For instance in the case of linear arithmetic, $\rho(F)$ corresponds to a disjunction of systems of linear constraints, involving $?X$ and the eigenvariables $\overrightarrow{Y}$ of d. Expressing how $?X$ functionally depends on $\overrightarrow{Y}$ to build a solution of one of the systems, may require extending the syntax of terms. But note that proof search in $\mathsf{LK}_1^?$ does not require implementing a witness builder.

A meet constraint structure can also be defined by taking constraints to be (theory-specific kinds of) sets of instantiations: the compatibility relation ϵ is just set membership, set intersection provides a meet operator and the projection of a constraint is obtained by removing the appropriate entry in every instantiation belonging to the constraint. Witness building would still be theory-specific.

To relate Systems $\mathsf{LK}_1^?$ and LK_1, we relate constraint-producing predicates to ground validity ones: intuitively, the instantiations that turn a set $\mathcal{A}$ of literals of domain d into a valid set of (ground) literals should coincide with the instantiations that are compatible with some constraint produced for $\mathcal{A}$ (a similar condition appears in Theorem 55 of [5] with $\mathcal{T}$-refuters instead of constraints):

Definition 7 (Relating Predicates) *For a compatibility relation ϵ, we say that a constraint-producing predicate $(\models^d)_d$ relates to a ground validity predicate $\models$ if they satisfy Axiom* **PG** *of Fig. 4.*

A constraint-producing predicate may allow several constraints to close a given leaf (finitely many for Example 1, possibly infinitely many for Examples 2 and 3, just one for Example 4). So in general our foreground reasoner expects a *stream* of constraints to be produced at a leaf, corresponding to the (possibly infinite) union in axiom PG: each one of them is sufficient to close the branch. The first one is tried, and if it later proves unsuitable, the next one in the stream can be tried, following Giese's suggestion [8] of using streams of instantiations.

4.3 Soundness and Completeness

System $\mathsf{LK}_1^?$ can be proved equivalent to System LK_1, from the axioms in the top half of Fig. 4 [13]. To state this equivalence, assume that we have a compatibility relation that distributes over $\wedge$, equipped with a witness builder, plus a constraint-producing predicate $(\models^d)_d$ related to a ground validity predicate $\models$.

Theorem 1 (Soundness and Completeness of $\mathsf{LK}_1^?$)
For all contexts Γ of domain d:
If $\vdash^d \Gamma \to \sigma$ is derivable in $\mathsf{LK}_1^?$, then for all $\rho\epsilon\sigma$, $\vdash \rho(\Gamma)$ is derivable in LK_1.
For all $\rho \in \Sigma_d$, if $\vdash \rho(\Gamma)$ is derivable in LK_1, then there exists $\sigma \in \Psi_d$ such that $\vdash^d \Gamma \to \sigma$ is derivable in $\mathsf{LK}_1^?$ and $\rho\epsilon\sigma$.

We will usually start proof search with the domain d_0, so as to build a proof tree whose root is of the form $\vdash^{d_0} \Gamma \to \sigma$ for some constraint $\sigma \in \Psi_{d_0}$. Since the only instantiation in Σ_{d_0} is $\emptyset$, and since $\emptyset(\Gamma) = \Gamma$, soundness and completeness for domain d_0 can be rewritten as follows:

Corollary 1 (Soundness and Completeness for the Initial Domain)
There exists $\sigma \in \Psi_{d_0}$ such that $\vdash^{d_0} \Gamma \to \sigma$ is derivable in $\mathsf{LK}_1^?$ and $\emptyset\epsilon\sigma$, if and only if $\vdash \Gamma$ is derivable in LK_1.

5 Sequentialising

The soundness and completeness properties of System $\mathsf{LK}_1^?$ rely on constraints that are satisfiable. A proof-search process based on it should therefore not proceed any further with a constraint that has become unsatisfiable. Since the meet of two satisfiable constraints may be unsatisfiable, branching on conjunctions may take advantage of a sequential treatment: a constraint produced to close one branch may direct the exploration of the other branch, which may be more efficient than waiting until both branches have independently produced constraints and only then checking that their meet is satisfiable. This section develops a variant of System $\mathsf{LK}_1^?$ to support this sequentialisation of branches, much closer than System $\mathsf{LK}_1^?$ to the free variable tableaux with theory reasoning [5].

In the rest of this section $(\Psi_d)_d$ is a fixed lift constraint structure.

5.1 Definition of the Proof System

Thus, the proof rules enrich a sequent with *two* constraints: the input one and the output one, the latter being "stronger" than the former, in a sense that we will make precise when we relate the different systems. At the leaves, a new predicate $(\dashv\vdash^d)_d$ is used that now takes an extra argument: the input constraint.

Definition 8 ($\mathsf{LK}_1^{?\rangle}$ Sequent Calculus). *A constraint-refining predicate is a family of relations $(\mapsto^d)_d$, indexed by domains d, relating sets $\mathcal{A}$ of literals of domain d with pairs of constraints σ and σ' in Ψ_d; when it holds, we write $\sigma \to\mapsto^d \mathcal{A} \to \sigma'$.*

Given such a predicate $(\mapsto^d)_d$, the constraint-refining sequent calculus, denoted $\mathsf{LK}_1^{?\rangle}$, manipulates sequents of the form $\sigma \to\vdash^d \Gamma \to \sigma'$, where Γ is a context and σ and σ' are constraints, all of domain d. Its rules are presented in Fig. 3.

$$\frac{\sigma \to\mapsto^d \Gamma_{\text{lit}} \to \sigma'}{\sigma \to\vdash^d \Gamma \to \sigma'} \qquad \frac{\sigma \to\vdash^d \Gamma, A, B \to \sigma'}{\sigma \to\vdash^d \Gamma, A \vee B \to \sigma'}$$

$$\frac{\sigma \to\vdash^d \Gamma, A_i \to \sigma'' \qquad \sigma'' \to\vdash^d \Gamma, A_{1-i} \to \sigma'}{\sigma \to\vdash^d \Gamma, A_0 \wedge A_1 \to \sigma'} \ i \in \{0, 1\}$$

$$\frac{\sigma^\uparrow \to\vdash^{d;?X} \Gamma, A\,[x := ?X]\,, \exists x A \to \sigma'}{\sigma \to\vdash^d \Gamma, \exists x A \to \sigma'_\downarrow} \qquad \frac{\sigma \to\vdash^{d;\mathsf{x}} \Gamma, A\,[x := \mathsf{x}] \to \sigma'}{\sigma \to\vdash^d \Gamma, \forall x A \to \sigma'}$$

$$\text{where } ?X \text{ is a fresh meta-variable} \qquad\qquad \text{where } \mathsf{x} \text{ is a fresh eigenvariable}$$

Fig. 3. The sequent calculus with sequential delayed instantiation $\mathsf{LK}_1^{?\rangle}$

The branching rule introducing conjunctions allows an arbitrary sequentialisation of the branches when building a proof tree, proving A_0 first if $i = 0$, or proving A_1 first if $i = 1$.

Example 8. In Examples 1, 2, 3, constraints are simply substitutions, and the constraint-refining predicate $\sigma \to\mapsto^d \mathcal{A} \to \sigma'$ is taken to hold if the constraint-producing predicate $\models^d \sigma(\mathcal{A}) \to \sigma'$ (as given in Example 6) holds. Here we recover the standard behaviour of free variable tableaux (with or without theory [5]) where the substitutions used to close branches are applied to the literals on the remaining branches. Of course in both cases, an implementation may apply the substitution lazily. In Example 4, the constraint-refining predicate $\sigma \to\mapsto^d \mathcal{A} \to \sigma'$ is taken to hold if $\models^d (\sigma \wedge \mathcal{A}) \to \sigma'$ holds. Proof search in $\mathsf{LK}_1^{?\rangle}$ builds, for our specific example and a trivially true constraint σ_0, the proof-tree

$$\frac{\begin{array}{ll} \sigma_0 \to\vdash^d p(?X, ?Y), \overline{p}(?X', ?Y') \to \sigma_1' & \sigma_1' \to\vdash^d l(?X, ?Y), \overline{p}(?X', ?Y') \to \sigma_2' \\ \sigma_2' \to\vdash^d p(?X, ?Y), l'(?X', ?Y') \to \sigma_3' & \sigma_3' \to\vdash^d l(?X, ?Y), l'(?X', ?Y') \to \sigma' \end{array}}{\cdots}$$

$$\frac{\sigma_0 \to\vdash^d (p(x, y) \wedge l(x, y)), (\overline{p}(x', y') \wedge l'(x', y')) \to \sigma'}{\cdots}$$

$$\sigma_0 \to\vdash^{d_0} (\exists x y (p(x, y) \wedge l(x, y))) \vee (\exists x' y' (\overline{p}(x', y') \wedge l'(x', y'))) \to \sigma'_{\downarrow\downarrow\downarrow\downarrow}$$

similar to that of Example 6, where $\sigma_1' := \sigma_1$, $\sigma_2' := \sigma_1' \wedge \sigma_2$, $\sigma_3' := \sigma_2' \wedge \sigma_3$ and $\sigma' := \sigma_3'$, projected by quantifier elimination to the trivially true formula $\sigma_{\downarrow\downarrow\downarrow\downarrow}'$.

5.2 Soundness and Completeness

We now relate system $\mathsf{LK}_1^{?\rangle}$ to system $\mathsf{LK}_1^?$. For this we need some axioms about the notions used in each of the two systems. These are distinct from the axioms that we used to relate system $\mathsf{LK}_1^?$ to LK_1, since we are not (yet) trying to relate system $\mathsf{LK}_1^{?\rangle}$ to LK_1. In the next section however, we will combine the two steps.

Definition 9 (Decency). *When* $\leqslant$ *(resp.* $\wedge$, P*) is a family of pre-orders (resp. binary operators, predicates) over each* Ψ_d*, we say that* $(\leqslant, \wedge, P)$ *is decent if the following axioms hold:*

D1 $\forall \sigma, \sigma' \in \Psi_d$, $\sigma \wedge \sigma'$ *is a greatest lower bound of* σ *and* σ' *for* $\leqslant$

D2 $\forall \sigma \in \Psi_d \, \forall \sigma', \sigma'' \in \Psi_{d;?X}$, $\sigma'' \simeq \sigma^\uparrow \wedge \sigma' \;\Rightarrow\; \sigma_\downarrow'' \simeq \sigma \wedge \sigma_\downarrow'$

P1 $\forall \sigma \in \Psi_{d;?X}$, $P(\sigma) \Leftrightarrow P(\sigma_\downarrow)$ P2 $\forall \sigma, \sigma' \in \Psi_d$, $\begin{cases} P(\sigma) \\ \sigma \leqslant \sigma' \end{cases} \Rightarrow P(\sigma')$

where $\simeq$ *denotes the equivalence relation generated by* $\leqslant$.

Notice that this makes $(\Psi_d/\simeq, \wedge)$ a meet-semilattice that could equally be defined by the associativity, commutativity, and idempotency of $\wedge$.

Definition 10 (Relating Constraint-Producing/Refining Predicates)
Given a family of binary operators $\wedge$ *and a family of predicates* P*, we say that a constraint-refining predicate* $(\mapsto^d)_d$ *relates to a constraint-producing predicate* $(\models^d)_d$ *if, for all domains* d*, all sets* $\mathcal{A}$ *of literals of domain* d *and all* $\sigma \in \Psi_d$,

A1 $\forall \sigma' \in \Psi_d$, $\sigma \to \mapsto^d \mathcal{A} \to \sigma' \;\Rightarrow\; \exists \sigma'' \in \Psi_d, \begin{cases} \sigma' \simeq \sigma \wedge \sigma'' \\ P(\sigma \wedge \sigma'') \\ \models^d \mathcal{A} \to \sigma'' \end{cases}$

A2 $\forall \sigma' \in \Psi_d$, $\begin{cases} P(\sigma \wedge \sigma') \\ \models^d \mathcal{A} \to \sigma' \end{cases} \Rightarrow \exists \sigma'' \in \Psi_d, \begin{cases} \sigma'' \simeq \sigma \wedge \sigma' \\ \sigma \to \mapsto^d \mathcal{A} \to \sigma'' \end{cases}$

In the rest of this sub-section, we assume that we have a decent triple $(\leqslant, \wedge, P)$, and a constraint-refining predicate $(\mapsto^d)_d$ that relates to a constraint-producing predicate $(\models^d)_d$. In this paper we only use two predicates P, allowing us to develop two variants of each theorem, with a compact presentation: $P(\sigma)$ is always "true", and $P(\sigma)$ is "σ is satisfiable", both of which satisfy P1 and P2.

System $\mathsf{LK}_1^{?\rangle}$ can then be proved sound with respect to System $\mathsf{LK}_1^?$ [13]:

Theorem 2 (Soundness of $\mathsf{LK}_1^{?\rangle}$)
If $\sigma \to \vdash^d \Gamma \to \sigma'$ *is derivable in* $\mathsf{LK}_1^{?\rangle}$, *then there exists* $\sigma'' \in \Psi_d$ *such that* $\sigma' \simeq \sigma \wedge \sigma''$, $P(\sigma \wedge \sigma'')$ *and* $\vdash^d \Gamma \to \sigma''$ *is derivable in* $\mathsf{LK}_1^?$.

Notice that the statement for soundness of Theorem 2 is merely a generalisation of axiom R2P where the reference to $\models^d$ and $\mapsto^d$ have respectively been replaced by derivability in $\mathsf{LK}_1^?$ and $\mathsf{LK}_1^{?\rangle}$.

A natural statement for completeness of $\mathsf{LK}_1^{?)}$ w.r.t. $\mathsf{LK}_1^?$ comes as the symmetric generalisation of axiom P2R:

Theorem 3 (Weak completeness of $\mathsf{LK}_1^{?)}$). *If $\vdash^d \Gamma \to \sigma'$ is derivable in $\mathsf{LK}_1^?$, then for all $\sigma \in \Psi_d$ such that $P(\sigma \wedge \sigma')$, there exists $\sigma'' \in \Psi_d$ such that $\sigma'' \simeq \sigma \wedge \sigma'$ and $\sigma \dashv\vdash^d \Gamma \to \sigma''$ is derivable in $\mathsf{LK}_1^{?)}$.*

This statement can be proved, but it fails to capture an important aspect of system $\mathsf{LK}_1^{?)}$: the order in which proof search treats branches should not matter for completeness. But the above statement concludes that there *exists* a sequentialisation of branches that leads to a complete proof tree in $\mathsf{LK}_1^{?)}$, so the proof-search procedure should either guess it or investigate all possibilities. We therefore proved [13] the stronger statement of completeness (below) whereby, *for all* possible sequentialisations of branches, there exists a complete proof tree. Therefore, when the proof-search procedure decides to apply the branching rule, choosing which branch to complete first can be treated as "don't care non-determinism" rather than "don't know non-determinism": if a particular choice proves unsuccessful, there should be no need to explore the alternative choice.

Theorem 4 (Strong Completeness of $\mathsf{LK}_1^{?)}$)
If $\vdash^d \Gamma \to \sigma'$ is derivable in $\mathsf{LK}_1^?$, then for all $\sigma \in \Psi_d$ such that $P(\sigma \wedge \sigma')$, and for all sequentialisations r of branches, there exists $\sigma'' \in \Psi_d$ such that $\sigma'' \simeq \sigma \wedge \sigma'$ and $\sigma \dashv\vdash^d \Gamma \to \sigma''$ is derivable in $\mathsf{LK}_1^{?)}$ with a proof tree that follows r.

6   Relating $\mathsf{LK}_1^{?)}$ to LK_1

Now we combine the two steps: from LK_1 to $\mathsf{LK}_1^?$ and from $\mathsf{LK}_1^?$ to $\mathsf{LK}_1^{?)}$, so as to relate $\mathsf{LK}_1^{?)}$ to LK_1. For this we aggregate (and consequently simplify) the axioms that we used for the first step with those that we used for the second step.

Definition 11 (Compatibility-Based Pre-order). *Assume we have a family of compatibility relations ϵ for a constraint structure $(\Psi_d)_d$. We define the following pre-order on each Ψ_d:*
$$\forall \sigma, \sigma' \in \Psi_d, \ \sigma \leqslant_\epsilon \sigma' \Leftrightarrow \{\rho \in \Sigma_d \mid \rho \epsilon \sigma\} \subseteq \{\rho \in \Sigma_d \mid \rho \epsilon \sigma'\}$$
and let $\simeq_\epsilon$ denote the symmetric closure of $\leqslant_\epsilon$.

We now assume that we have a lift constraint structure and a constraint-refining predicate $(\bumpeq^d)_d$ used to define $\mathsf{LK}_1^{?)}$, and the existence of

- a binary operator $\wedge$
- a compatibility relation ϵ that distributes over $\wedge$ (Proj and Meet in Fig. 4)
- a binding operator for ϵ (Wit in Fig. 4)
- a constraint-producing predicate $(\models^d)_d$ that relates to $\models$ (PG in Fig. 4)
- a predicate P

satisfying the axioms of Fig. 4. These entail decency [13]:

Lemma 1. *Given the axioms of Fig. 4, $(\leqslant_\epsilon, \wedge, P)$ is decent.*

Hence, we have soundness and completeness of $\mathsf{LK}_1^{?}$ w.r.t. LK_1 on the empty domain, as a straightforward consequence of Corollary 1 and Theorems 2 and 4:

Theorem 5 (Soundness and Completeness on the Empty Domain)
If $\sigma \rightarrow \vdash^{do} \Gamma \to \sigma'$ is derivable in $\mathsf{LK}_1^{?}$ and $\emptyset \epsilon \sigma'$, then $\vdash \Gamma$ is derivable in LK_1. In particular when P is the predicate "being satisfiable", if $\sigma \rightarrow \vdash^{do} \Gamma \to \sigma'$ is derivable in $\mathsf{LK}_1^{?}$, then $\vdash \Gamma$ is derivable in LK_1.

Assume P is always true or is "being satisfiable". If $\vdash \Gamma$ is derivable in LK_1, then for all $\sigma \in \Psi_{do}$ such that $\emptyset \epsilon \sigma$ and for all sequentialisations r, there exists $\sigma' \in \Psi_{do}$ such that $\emptyset \epsilon \sigma'$ and $\sigma \rightarrow \vdash^{do} \Gamma \to \sigma'$ is derivable in $\mathsf{LK}_1^{?}$ with a proof tree that follows r.

Remark 1 (Soundness of $\mathsf{LK}_1^{?}$). Soundness of $\mathsf{LK}_1^{?}$ on an arbitrary domain is a direct consequence of Theorem 1 and Theorem 2: If $\sigma \rightarrow \vdash^d \Gamma \to \sigma'$ is derivable in $\mathsf{LK}_1^{?}$, then $P(\sigma')$ holds and for all $\rho \epsilon \sigma'$, $\vdash \rho(\Gamma)$ is derivable in LK_1. For the sake of brevity, we omit the general statement of completeness on an arbitrary domain, which is quite long to write.

As we shall see in Sect. 7, it is useful to have a "top element" $\top$ in Ψ_{do} with $\emptyset \epsilon \top$, which we feed to a proof-search procedure based on $\mathsf{LK}_1^{?}$, as the initial input constraint σ mentioned in the soundness and completeness theorems.

Proj	$\forall \sigma \in \Psi_{d;?X}, \forall t \forall \rho, (\rho, ?X \mapsto t) \epsilon \sigma \Rightarrow \rho \epsilon \sigma_\downarrow$
Wit	$\forall \sigma \in \Psi_{d;?X}, \forall \rho, \quad \rho \epsilon \sigma_\downarrow \Rightarrow (\rho, ?X \mapsto f_\sigma(\rho)) \epsilon \sigma$
Meet	$\forall \sigma \sigma' \in \Psi_d, \forall \rho, \begin{cases} \rho \epsilon \sigma \\ \rho \epsilon \sigma' \end{cases} \Leftrightarrow \rho \epsilon (\sigma \wedge \sigma')$
PG	$\forall l, \forall \mathcal{A}, \quad \{\rho \mid \models \rho(\mathcal{A})\} = \bigcup_{\{\sigma \mid \models^l \mathcal{A} \to \sigma\}} \{\rho \mid \rho \epsilon \sigma\}$

Lift	$\forall \sigma \in \Psi_d, \forall \sigma' \in \Psi_{d;?X}, \forall \rho, (\rho, ?X \mapsto f_{\sigma'}(\rho)) \epsilon \sigma^\uparrow \Leftrightarrow \rho \epsilon \sigma$
P_1	$\forall \sigma \in \Psi_{d;?X}, \qquad P(\sigma) \Leftrightarrow P(\sigma_\downarrow)$
P_2	$\forall \sigma \sigma' \in \Psi_d, \qquad \begin{cases} P(\sigma) \\ \sigma \leqslant_\epsilon \sigma' \end{cases} \Rightarrow P(\sigma')$
R2P	$\forall d, \forall \mathcal{A}, \forall \sigma, \sigma' \in \Psi_d, \quad \sigma \rightarrow \not\models^d \mathcal{A} \to \sigma' \Rightarrow \exists \sigma'' \in \Psi_d, \begin{cases} \sigma' \simeq_\epsilon \sigma \wedge \sigma'' \\ P(\sigma \wedge \sigma'') \\ \models^d \mathcal{A} \to \sigma'' \end{cases}$
P2R	$\forall d, \forall \mathcal{A}, \forall \sigma, \sigma' \in \Psi_d, \quad \begin{cases} P(\sigma \wedge \sigma') \\ \models^d \mathcal{A} \to \sigma' \end{cases} \Rightarrow \exists \sigma'' \in \Psi_d, \begin{cases} \sigma'' \simeq_\epsilon \sigma \wedge \sigma' \\ \sigma \rightarrow \not\models^d \mathcal{A} \to \sigma'' \end{cases}$

Fig. 4. Full Axiomatisation

7   Implementation

PSYCHE is a platform for proof search, where a *kernel* offers an API for programming various search strategies as *plugins*, while guaranteeing the correctness of the search output [10]. Its architecture extensively uses OCaml's system of modules and functors. In order to modularly support theory-specific reasoning (in presence of quantifiers), the axiomatisation proposed in the previous sections was used to identify the signature and the specifications of *theory components*. In version 2.0 of PSYCHE [12], the kernel implements (the *focused* version of) System $\mathsf{LK}_1^{?}$, and a theory component is required to provide the implementation of the concepts developed in the previous sections, as shown in the module type above. It provides a lift constraint structure in the form of a module `Constraint`,

```
module type Theory = sig
 module Constraint: sig
  type t
  val topconstraint:t
  val proj : t -> t
  val lift : t -> t
  val meet : t -> t -> t option
  ...
 end
 val consistency :
  ASet.t -> (ASet.t,Constraint.t) stream
end
```

Theory component signature in PSYCHE 2.0

with a type for constraints, the projection and lift maps, as well as a top constraint (always satisfied) with which proof search will start. We also require a meet operation: While the theory of complete proofs in $\mathsf{LK}_1^{?}$ does not need it, the meet operation is useful when implementing a backtracking proof-search procedure: imagine a proof tree has been completed for some sequent $\mathcal{S}$, with input constraint σ_0 and output constraint σ_1; at some point the procedure may have to search again for a proof of $\mathcal{S}$ but with a different input constraint σ_0'. We can check whether the first proof can be re-used by simply checking whether $\sigma_0' \wedge \sigma_1$ is satisfiable. The `meet` function should output `None` if the meet of the two input constraints is not satisfiable, and `Some sigma` if the satisfiable meet is `sigma`.

Finally, the function that is called at the leaves of proof trees is `consistency`, which implements the constraint-refining predicate; `ASet.t` is the type for sets of literals with meta-variables and the function returns a stream: providing an input constraint triggers computation and pops the next element of the stream if it exists. It is a pair made of an output constraint and a subset of the input set of literals. The latter indicates which literals of the input have been used to close the branch, which is useful information for *lemma learning* (see e.g. [10]).

While our axiomatisation immediately yields the specification for theory components, it does not provide instances and so far, the only (non-ground) instance implemented in PSYCHE is that of pure first-order logic (based on unification).

8   Related Works and Further Work

The sequent calculi developed in this paper for theory reasoning in presence of quantifiers, are akin to the free variable tableaux of [5] for total theory reasoning. But they use abstract constraints, instead of substitutions, and our foreground reasoner is able to propagate them across branches while being ignorant of their nature. This allows new theories to be treated by the framework, such as those satisfying quantifier elimination, like linear arithmetic. In this particular case, the asymmetric treatment of $\mathsf{LK}_1^{?)}$ formalises an improvement, in the view of an effective implementation, over System $\mathrm{PresPred}_S^C$ [14] for LIA. A novel point of our paper is to show that the propagation of substitutions in tableaux and the propagation of linear arithmetic constraints follow the same pattern, by describing them as two instances of an abstract constraint propagation mechanism.

Constraints have been integrated to various tableaux calculi: In the nomenclature proposed in Giese and Hähnle's survey [9], our approach is closest to *constrained formula tableaux* or *constrained branch tableaux* which propagate constraints between branches (rather than *constrained tableaux* which have a global management of constraints). But the *tableaux* calculi cited by [9] in these categories are for specific theories and logics (pure classical logic, equality, linear temporal logic or bunched implications), in contrast to our generic approach.

When classes of theories are generically integrated to automated reasoning with the use of constraints, as for the Model Evolution Calculus [3], these are usually described as first-order formulae over a particular theory's signature (as it is the case in [1,14] for LIA). Our abstract data-structures for constraints could be viewed as the semantic counter-part of such a syntactic representation, whose atomic construction steps are costless but which may incur expensive satisfiability checks by the background reasoner. Our semantic view of constraints, as shown in Section 7, more directly supports theory-tuned implementations where e.g. the meet and projection operations involve computation. Our specifications for theory-specific computation also seems less demanding than deciding the satisfiability of any constraint made of atoms (over the theory's signature), conjunction, negation, and existential quantification [3].

The semantic approach to constraints was explored by a rich literature in (Concurrent) Constraint Programming [15], but the applicability of constraint systems to programming usually leads to more demanding axioms as well (requiring e.g. complete lattices) and to a global management of constraints (with a global store that is reminiscent of *constrained tableaux*). Our local management of constraints allows for more subtle backtracking strategies in proof search, undoing some steps in one branch while sticking to some more recent decisions that have been made in a different branch.

In the case of ground theory reasoning, the field of SMT-solving has evolved powerful techniques for combining theories (see e.g. the unifying approach of [7]). A natural question is whether similar techniques can be developed in presence of quantifiers, combining constraint-producing or constraint-refining procedures. We did not provide such techniques here, but we believe our modular and abstract approach could be a first step towards that end, with our axiomatisation identifying what properties should be sought when engineering such techniques, i.e. serving as a correctness criterion.

Finally, SMT-solvers usually adopt a heuristic approach for handling quantifiers, often involving incomplete mechanisms, with slimmer theoretical foundations than for their ground reasoning core. A notable exception is a formalisation of *triggers* mechanisms by Dross et al. [6], which we hope to view as particular instances of our constraint systems. Moreover, the way in which triggers control the breaking of quantifiers appears as the kind of structured proof-search mechanisms that PSYCHE can specify (based on focusing).

Acknowledgements. This research was supported by ANR projects PSI and ALCOCLAN, as well as by DARPA under agreement number FA8750-12-C-0284. The views and conclusions contained herein are those of the authors and should not be interpreted as necessarily representing the official policies or endorsements, either expressed or implied, of DARPA, or the U.S. Government.

References

1. Baumgartner, P., Fuchs, A., Tinelli, C.: ME(LIA) – Model evolution with linear integer arithmetic constraints. In: Cervesato, I., Veith, H., Voronkov, A. (eds.) LPAR 2008. LNCS (LNAI), vol. 5330, pp. 258–273. Springer, Heidelberg (2008)
2. Baumgartner, P., Furbach, U., Petermann, U.: A unified approach to theory reasoning. Technical report, Inst. für Informatik, Univ. (1992)
3. Baumgartner, P., Tinelli, C.: Model evolution with equality modulo built-in theories. In: Bjørner, N., Sofronie-Stokkermans, V. (eds.) CADE 2011. LNCS, vol. 6803, pp. 85–100. Springer, Heidelberg (2011)
4. Beckert, B.: Chapter 8: Rigid *E*-unification. In: Bibel, W., Schmitt, P.H. (eds.) Automated Deduction – A Basis for Applications. Foundations. Calculi and Methods, vol. I, pp. 265–289. Kluwer Academic Publishers (1998)
5. Beckert, B.: Equality and other theories. In: Handbook of Tableau Methods, pp. 197–254. Kluwer Academic Publishers (1999)
6. Dross, C., Conchon, S., Kanig, J., Paskevich, A.: Reasoning with triggers. In: Fontaine, P., Goel, A. (eds.) 10th Int. Work. on Satisfiability Modulo Theories, SMT 2012. EPiC Series, vol. 20, pp. 22–31. EasyChair, June 2012
7. Ganzinger, H., Rueß, H., Shankar, N.: Modularity and refinement in inference systems. Technical Report SRI-CSL-04-02, SRI (2004)
8. Giese, M.: Proof search without backtracking using instance streams, position paper. In: Baumgartner, P., Zhang, H. (eds.) 3rd Int. Work. on First-Order Theorem Proving (FTP), pp. 227–228. Univ. of Koblenz, St. Andrews (2000)
9. Giese, M., Hähnle, R.: Tableaux + constraints. In: Cialdea Mayer, M., Pirri, F. (eds.) TABLEAUX 2003. LNCS, vol. 2796, pp. 37–42. Springer, Heidelberg (2003)
10. Graham-Lengrand, S.: PSYCHE: A proof-search engine based on sequent calculus with an LCF-Style architecture. In: Galmiche, D., Larchey-Wendling, D. (eds.) TABLEAUX 2013. LNCS, vol. 8123, pp. 149–156. Springer, Heidelberg (2013)
11. Nieuwenhuis, R., Oliveras, A., Tinelli, C.: Solving SAT and SAT Modulo Theories: From an abstract Davis–Putnam–Logemann–Loveland procedure to DPLL(*T*). J. of the ACM Press 53(6), 937–977 (2006)

12. Psyche: the Proof-Search factorY for Collaborative HEuristics
13. Rouhling, D., Farooque, M., Graham-Lengrand, S., Notin, J.-M., Mahboubi, A.: Axiomatisation of constraint systems to specify a tableaux calculus modulo theories. Technical report, Laboratoire d'informatique de l'École Polytechnique - CNRS, Microsoft Research - INRIA Joint Centre, Parsifal & TypiCal - INRIA Saclay, France, December 2014
14. Rümmer, P.: A constraint sequent calculus for first-order logic with linear integer arithmetic. In: Cervesato, I., Veith, H., Voronkov, A. (eds.) LPAR 2008. LNCS (LNAI), vol. 5330, pp. 274–289. Springer, Heidelberg (2008)
15. Saraswat, V.A., Rinard, M., Panangaden, P.: The semantic foundations of concurrent constraint programming. In: Wise, D.S. (ed.) 18th Annual ACM Symp. on Principles of Programming Languages (POPL 1991), pp. 333–352. ACM Press, January 1991
16. Stickel, M.E.: Automated deduction by theory resolution. J. of Automated Reasoning 1(4), 333–355 (1985)

Transformations between Symbolic Systems

Formalizing Soundness and Completeness of Unravelings*

Sarah Winkler and René Thiemann

Institute of Computer Science, University of Innsbruck, 6020 Innsbruck, Austria
{sarah.winkler,rene.thiemann}@uibk.ac.at

Abstract. Unravelings constitute a class of program transformations to model conditional rewrite systems as standard term rewrite systems. Key properties of unravelings are soundness and completeness with respect to reductions, in the sense that rewrite sequences in the unraveled system correspond to rewrite sequences in the conditional system and vice versa. While the latter is easily satisfied, the former holds only under certain conditions and is notoriously difficult to prove. This paper describes an Isabelle formalization of both properties. The soundness proof is based on the approach by Nishida, Sakai, and Sakabe (2012) but we also contribute to the theory by showing it applicable to a larger class of unravelings.

Based on our formalization we developed the first certifier to check output of conditional rewrite tools. In particular, quasi-decreasingness proofs by AProVE and conditional confluence proofs by CorCon can be certified.

1 Introduction

Conditional term rewriting is a natural extension of standard rewriting in that it allows to specify conditions for rules to be applied. This is useful in many applications, for instance to reason about logic programs [14,16]. However, the addition of conditions severely complicates the analysis of various properties. This led to the development of transformations that convert conditional rewrite systems (CTRSs) into standard rewrite systems (TRSs). Provided certain requirements are fulfilled, one can then employ criteria for standard rewrite systems to infer e.g. termination and confluence of the conditional system. Unravelings are the most widely considered class of such transformations [2,7,11,14].

Tools to analyze CTRSs often exploit unravelings. For example, the conditional confluence tool CorCon [17] may unravel a given CTRS R into a TRS R'. It then invokes a confluence tool for TRSs to get a confluence proof P for R', in order to eventually conclude confluence of R. Similarly, AProVE [3] generates operational termination proofs for CTRSs by first applying an unraveling and then trying to prove termination of the resulting TRSs.

Like all tools for program analysis, rewrite tools are inherently complex and error-prone. In the following we describe our IsaFoR/CeTA [18]-based certification

---

* This research was supported by the Austrian Science Fund (FWF) projects I963 and Y757.

C. Lutz and S. Ranise (Eds.): FroCoS 2015, LNAI 9322, pp. 239–255, 2015.
DOI: 10.1007/978-3-319-24246-0_15

approach to validate confluence and termination proofs for CTRSs, which combines three different systems: an analyzer, a certifier, and a proof assistant.

1. A proof certificate is generated by an automatic analysis tool like AProVE or CorCon. The certificate consists of a CTRS R, an unraveled TRS R', and the termination (or confluence) proof P.
2. Our certifier CeTA can then be invoked on (R, R', P) to validate the certificate. To this end, CeTA first checks that $R' = U(R)$ for some unraveling U. Next, it verifies that P is a valid termination (or confluence) proof for R', for which it has a variety of techniques at its disposal [9,18]. Finally, it checks whether U satisfies certain syntactic criteria which ensure that termination (or confluence) of R' also implies termination (or confluence) of R.
3. Soundness of CeTA is guaranteed as it is based on the Isabelle [10] framework IsaFoR (Isabelle Formalization of Rewriting). To that end we formalized[1] two properties in IsaFoR: (a) if U satisfies the syntactic requirements then termination (or confluence) of R' implies termination (or confluence) of R; and (b) CeTA, a functional program written within Isabelle, is sound.

To the best of our knowledge, our contribution constitutes the first work on certified program verification for conditional rewriting. This paper describes the formalization done for task (3), giving rise to a certifier for task (2). Here the vast amount of effort goes into part (3a), after which (3b) can be achieved by applying Isabelle's code generator.

In the remainder of this paper we thus focus on (3a), primarily on formalizing two properties of an unraveling U which are of crucial importance: (i) every rewrite sequence admitted by the transformed TRS $U(R)$ (among terms over the original signature) should be possible with the CTRS R, and (ii) every rewrite sequence allowed by R should be preserved in $U(R)$. These properties are known as soundness and completeness with respect to reductions. While completeness imposes only mild restrictions on such a transformation, soundness is much harder to satisfy, and the respective proofs in the literature are involved and technical.

The remainder of this paper is structured as follows. We first recall some background on TRSs and CTRSs in § 2. In § 3 we describe our formalization of basic results on conditional rewriting, before we introduce unravelings in § 4. The formalization of completeness results of unravelings in combination with the certifier for termination proofs for CTRSs is the topic of § 5. In § 6 we describe the formalized soundness proof, covering a large class of unravelings. Building upon these results, in § 7 we outline a result connecting confluence of the unraveled system with confluence of the original system. Finally, in § 8 we conclude and shortly mention the experimental results.

The full formalization and the certifier (IsaFoR and CeTA) as well as details on the experiments are available on the following website:

http://cl-informatik.uibk.ac.at/software/ceta/experiments/unravelings/

For each lemma, theorem, and definition in this paper, the website also contains a link to our Isabelle formulation (and proof) of that lemma, etc.

---

[1] Here, the notion *formalized* always refers to a machine checked proof in Isabelle.

2   Preliminaries

We refer to [1] for the basics on term rewriting. In the sequel, letters $\ell, r, s, t, \ldots$ are used for terms, $f, g, \ldots$ for symbols, σ, θ for substitutions, and C for contexts. The set of terms over signature $\mathcal{F}$ and variables $\mathcal{V}$ is $\mathcal{T}(\mathcal{F}, \mathcal{V})$, and $\mathcal{S}ub(\mathcal{F}, \mathcal{V})$ denotes the set of substitutions of type $\mathcal{V} \to \mathcal{T}(\mathcal{F}, \mathcal{V})$. The set of variables in a term t is denoted by $\mathcal{V}ar(t)$. We write $\rhd$ for the strict subterm relation. The rewrite relation for some TRS R is denoted by $\to_R$, and the parallel rewrite relation is $\rightrightarrows_R$, where sometimes R is omitted if it is clear from the context. Rewrite relations may be restricted by positions, such as root steps ($\to_\epsilon$) or parallel rewriting where all steps are below the root ($\rightrightarrows_{>\epsilon}$). Given a binary relation $\to$, the reflexive transitive closure, the transitive closure, and the n-fold composition of the relation are denoted by $\to^*$, $\to^+$, and $\to^n$, respectively. A relation $\to$ is *confluent on* A if for all $y \in A$ and all x and z, whenever $x \;{}^*\!\leftarrow y \to^* z$, there is some u such that $x \to^* u \;{}^*\!\leftarrow z$; and $\to$ is *confluent* if it is confluent on the set of all elements. A TRS R is confluent if its rewrite relation $\to_R$ is confluent. A rewrite rule $\ell \to r$ is *left-linear* if no variable occurs more than once in ℓ, and a TRS is left-linear if so are all its rules.

An (oriented) conditional rewrite rule ρ over signature $\mathcal{F}$ is of the form $\ell \to r \Leftarrow s_1 \to t_1, \ldots, s_k \to t_k$ where $\ell, r, s_1, t_1, \ldots, s_k, t_k \in \mathcal{T}(\mathcal{F}, \mathcal{V})$. The condition $s_1 \to t_1, \ldots, s_k \to t_k$ is sometimes abbreviated by c. Every standard rewrite rule $\ell \to r$ can be considered a conditional rewrite rule where $k = 0$. A CTRS over $\mathcal{F}$ is a set R of conditional rules over $\mathcal{F}$.

Definition 1 (Conditional Rewriting [15, Def. 7.1.4]). *Let R be a CTRS. The unconditional TRSs R_n and the rewrite relation $\to_R$ are defined as follows.*

$$R_0 = \varnothing$$
$$R_{n+1} = \{(\ell\sigma, r\sigma) \mid \ell \to r \Leftarrow s_1 \to t_1, \ldots, s_k \to t_k \in R, \; \forall i. \; s_i\sigma \to^*_{R_n} t_i\sigma\}$$
$$\to_R = \bigcup_{n \in \mathbb{N}} \to_{R_n}$$

A CTRS R is of *type 3* if every rule $\ell \to r \Leftarrow c$ in R satisfies $\mathcal{V}ar(r) \subseteq \mathcal{V}ar(\ell) \cup \mathcal{V}ar(c)$. A CTRS of type 3 is *deterministic* if for every rule $\ell \to r \Leftarrow s_1 \to t_1, \ldots, s_k \to t_k \in R$ and every $1 \leqslant i \leqslant k$ it holds that $\mathcal{V}ar(s_i) \subseteq \mathcal{V}ar(\ell) \cup \bigcup_{j=1}^{i-1} \mathcal{V}ar(t_j)$. In the sequel, we will only deal with deterministic CTRSs of type 3 (abbreviated 3DCTRSs).

Example 2. Let $\mathcal{F}$ be the signature consisting of constants $0, \mathsf{T}, \mathsf{F}, []$, unary symbols s, qs, and binary symbols $\leqslant, :, @, \langle \cdot, \cdot \rangle, \mathsf{split}$. The following 3DCTRS R_1 over $\mathcal{F}$ encodes quicksort [15]:

$$0 \leqslant x \to \mathsf{T} \qquad \mathsf{s}(x) \leqslant 0 \to \mathsf{F} \qquad \mathsf{s}(x) \leqslant \mathsf{s}(y) \to x \leqslant y$$
$$[] @ x \to x \qquad (x : xs) @ ys \to x : (xs @ ys) \qquad \mathsf{split}(x, []) \to \langle [], [] \rangle$$
$$\mathsf{qs}([]) \to []$$
$$\mathsf{split}(x, y : ys) \to \langle xs, y : zs \rangle \;\Leftarrow\; \mathsf{split}(x, ys) \to \langle xs, zs \rangle, \; x \leqslant y \to \mathsf{T}$$
$$\mathsf{split}(x, y : ys) \to \langle y : xs, zs \rangle \;\Leftarrow\; \mathsf{split}(x, ys) \to \langle xs, zs \rangle, \; x \leqslant y \to \mathsf{F}$$
$$\mathsf{qs}(x : xs) \to \mathsf{qs}(ys) @ (x : \mathsf{qs}(zs)) \;\Leftarrow\; \mathsf{split}(x, xs) \to \langle ys, zs \rangle$$

3   Formalizing Conditional Rewriting

Instead of Def. 1, IsaFoR defines conditional rewriting as introduced in [12], where intermediate rewrite relations are used rather than auxiliary unconditional TRSs.

Definition 3 (Conditional Rewriting [12]). *Let R be a CTRS. The rewrite relation $\to_R$ is defined as follows.*

$$\overset{0}{\to}_R = \varnothing$$

$$\overset{n+1}{\to}_R = \{(C[\ell\sigma], C[r\sigma]) \mid \ell \to r \Leftarrow s_1 \to t_1, \ldots, s_k \to t_k \in R,\ \forall i.\ s_i\sigma \overset{n}{\to}{}_R^* t_i\sigma\}$$

$$\to_R = \bigcup_{n \in \mathbb{N}} \overset{n}{\to}_R$$

It is easy to see that $\overset{n}{\to}_R = \to_{R_n}$, and therefore $\to_R$ is the same relation in both Def. 1 and Def. 3.

In IsaFoR we used Def. 3 since it constitutes a stand-alone inductive definition, whereas Def. 1 additionally requires the notion of unconditional rewriting. The use of Def. 3 thus simplified proofs in that it avoided auxiliary results involving standard rewriting. In particular, every rewrite step according to Def. 1 is associated with a rule, a context, and *two substitutions*, where the first substitution originates from the definition of the unconditional TRS R_{n+1}, and the second one stems from the rewrite relation $\to_{R_{n+1}}$ of this unconditional TRS. In contrast, a rewrite step according to Def. 3 involves only one substitution.

Besides the definition of $\to_R$, based on $\overset{n}{\to}_R$ defined as a recursive function on n, we also added several basic results on $\to_R$ to IsaFoR, which were mainly established by first proving them component-wise for $\overset{n}{\to}_R$ by induction on n. For instance, $\overset{n}{\to}_R$ is closed under contexts and substitutions, $\overset{n}{\to}_R \subseteq \overset{m}{\to}_R$ for $n \leqslant m$, etc., and these properties are then easily transferred to $\to_R$. Moreover, we added some extraction results, e.g., for finite derivations $s \to_R^* t$ one can always find a suitable n such that $s \overset{n}{\to}{}_R^* t$. This made it easy to switch between the full relation $\to_R$ and some approximation $\overset{n}{\to}_R$ in proofs.

Recall that the notion of termination is not as important for CTRSs as it is for TRSs. For a CTRS R one is rather interested in operational termination [6], where in addition to strong normalization of $\to_R$ one ensures that there will be no infinite recursion required when evaluating conditions. For example, the CTRS $R = \{f(x) \to f(x) \Leftarrow f(f(x)) \to f(x)\}$ terminates as it satisfies $\to_R = \varnothing$, but it is not operationally terminating.

We formalized the following two sufficient criteria for operational termination.

Definition 4 (Quasi-Reductive). *A CTRS R is* quasi-reductive *for $\succ$ if $\succ$ is a strongly normalizing partial order which is closed under contexts, and for every $\ell \to r \Leftarrow s_1 \to t_1, \ldots, s_k \to t_k$ in R, every σ, and $0 \leqslant i < k$ it holds that*

- *if $s_j\sigma \succeq t_j\sigma$ for every $1 \leqslant j \leqslant i$, then $l\sigma\,(\succ \cup \rhd)^+\,s_{i+1}\sigma$, and*
- *if $s_j\sigma \succeq t_j\sigma$ for every $1 \leqslant j \leqslant k$, then $l\sigma \succ r\sigma$.*

A CTRS R is quasi-reductive *if it is quasi-reductive for some $\succ$.*

Definition 5 (Quasi-Decreasing). *A CTRS R is* quasi-decreasing *for $\succ$ if $\succ$ is a strongly normalizing partial order, $\rightarrow_R \cup \rhd \;\subseteq\; \succ$, and for every $\ell \rightarrow r \Leftarrow s_1 \rightarrow t_1, \ldots, s_k \rightarrow t_k$ in R, every substitution σ, and $0 \leqslant i < k$ it holds that if $s_j\sigma \rightarrow^*_R t_j\sigma$ for every $1 \leqslant j \leqslant i$ then $l\sigma \succ s_{i+1}\sigma$. A CTRS R is* quasi-decreasing *if there exists some $\succ$ such that R is quasi-decreasing for $\succ$.*

Definitions 4 and 5 are exactly the same as Definitions 7.2.36 and 7.2.39 in [15], respectively, except that our definitions do not mention signatures. This deviation is motivated by the fact that neither the conditional rewrite relation nor the unconditional rewrite relation in IsaFoR take signatures into account.

IsaFoR further includes the crucial proof of [15, Lemma 7.2.40], namely that whenever R is quasi-reductive for $\succ$, then R is also quasi-decreasing for $(\succ \cup \rhd)^+$. And since a 3DCTRS is quasi-decreasing if and only if it is operational terminating [6, Thms. 2 and 3], we provide a criterion for operational termination.

4   Unravelings

An unraveling is a computable transformation U which maps a CTRS R over some signature $\mathcal{F}$ to a TRS $U(R)$ over some signature $\mathcal{F}' \supseteq \mathcal{F}$.[2] An unraveling U is *sound with respect to reductions* for R if $s \rightarrow^*_{U(R)} t$ implies $s \rightarrow^*_R t$ for all terms $s, t \in \mathcal{T}(\mathcal{F}, \mathcal{V})$. It is *complete with respect to reductions* for R if $s \rightarrow^*_R t$ implies $s \rightarrow^*_{U(R)} t$ for all $s, t \in \mathcal{T}(\mathcal{F}, \mathcal{V})$. In order to be independent of concrete unravelings used by tools, our certifier is based on the following more flexible notion of *standard* unravelings.

To that end, two conditional rules $\ell \rightarrow r \Leftarrow s_1 \rightarrow t_1, \ldots, s_k \rightarrow t_k$ and $\ell' \rightarrow r' \Leftarrow s'_1 \rightarrow t'_1, \ldots, s'_{k'} \rightarrow t'_{k'}$ are called *prefix equivalent* up to m if $m \leqslant k$, $m \leqslant k'$, and there is a variable renaming τ such that $\ell\tau = \ell'$, $s_i\tau = s'_i$ for all $1 \leqslant i \leqslant m$, and $t_i\tau = t'_i$ for all $1 \leqslant i < m$. For instance, the first two conditional rules in Ex. 2 are prefix equivalent up to 2, with τ being the identity. For a finite set of variables $V = \{x_1, \ldots, x_n\}$, let $\vec{V}$ denote the sequence $x_1, \ldots, x_n$ such that $x_1 < \cdots < x_n$ for some arbitrary but fixed ordering $<$ on $\mathcal{V}$.

Definition 6 (Standard Unraveling). *A* standard unraveling *U maps a rule ρ of the form $\ell \rightarrow r \Leftarrow s_1 \rightarrow t_1, \ldots, s_k \rightarrow t_k$ to the set of rules $U(\rho)$ given by*

$$U(\rho) = \left\{ \ell \rightarrow U^\rho_1(s_1, \vec{Z_1}), \; U^\rho_1(t_1, \vec{Z_1}) \rightarrow U^\rho_2(s_2, \vec{Z_2}), \; \ldots, \; U^\rho_k(t_k, \vec{Z_k}) \rightarrow r \right\}$$

where $X_i = \mathcal{V}ar(\ell, t_1, \ldots, t_{i-1})$, $Y_i = \mathcal{V}ar(r, t_i, s_{i+1}, t_{i+1} \ldots, s_k, t_k)$, and Z_i is an arbitrary set of variables satisfying $X_i \cap Y_i \subseteq Z_i$, for all $1 \leqslant i \leqslant k$, and $U^\rho_1, \ldots U^\rho_k \notin \mathcal{F}$. Furthermore, we require that $U^\rho_i = U^{\rho'}_j$ only if $i = j$ and ρ and ρ' are prefix equivalent up to i, for all $\rho, \rho' \in R$.

The definition of U is extended to a CTRS R by setting $U(R) = \bigcup_{\rho \in R} U(\rho)$.

---

[2] Definitions of unravelings in the literature typically demand that $\rightarrow_R \;\subseteq\; \rightarrow^*_{U(R)}$ and $U(R \uplus R') = U(R) \cup R'$ hold for any TRS R'. We do not require this by definition but all considered transformations enjoy these properties.

Note that setting $Z_i = X_i$ yields Ohlebusch's unraveling U_{seq} [13,15], while by taking $Z_i = X_i \cap Y_i$ one obtains the optimized unraveling U_{opt} [2,11], both of which are thus standard unravelings in our setting.[3] In addition, we allow—but do not enforce—the reuse of U symbols as proposed for the variant of Ohlebusch's unraveling U_{conf} [4] (and already mentioned in [15, page 213]). The set of symbols $\mathcal{F}'$ denotes the signature which extends $\mathcal{F}$ by all U_ρ^i symbols introduced by U.

Example 7. Let R_2 be $U_{conf}(R_1)$, where the standard unraveling U_{conf} is applied to the CTRS R_1 from Ex. 2. Then R_2 contains all unconditional rules of R_1, and the following rules which replace the conditional rules of R_1:

$$\mathsf{split}(x, y : ys) \to U_1(\mathsf{split}(x, ys), x, y, ys)$$
$$U_1(\langle xs, zs \rangle, x, y, ys) \to U_2(x \leqslant y, x, y, ys, xs, zs)$$
$$U_2(\mathsf{T}, x, y, ys, xs, zs) \to \langle xs, y : zs \rangle$$
$$U_2(\mathsf{F}, x, y, ys, xs, zs) \to \langle y : xs, zs \rangle$$
$$\mathsf{qs}(x : xs) \to U_3(\mathsf{split}(x, xs), x, xs)$$
$$U_3(\langle ys, zs \rangle, x, xs) \to \mathsf{qs}(ys) @ (x : \mathsf{qs}(zs))$$

Note that the first four rules can simulate both of the first two conditional rules.

Alternatively, a standard unraveling may produce the TRS R_3 where the conditional rules are transformed into:

$$\mathsf{split}(x, y : ys) \to U_1(\mathsf{split}(x, ys), x, y) \qquad U_1(\langle xs, zs \rangle, x, y) \to U_2(x \leqslant y, y, xs, zs)$$
$$U_2(\mathsf{T}, y, xs, zs) \to \langle xs, y : zs \rangle \qquad\qquad U_2(\mathsf{F}, y, xs, zs) \to \langle y : xs, zs \rangle$$
$$\mathsf{qs}(x : xs) \to U_3(\mathsf{split}(x, xs), x) \qquad\qquad U_3(\langle ys, zs \rangle, x) \to \mathsf{qs}(ys) @ (x : \mathsf{qs}(zs))$$

Here, R_3 corresponds to $U_{opt}(R_1)$, except that U symbols are reused for the two prefix equivalent rules. For both R_2 and R_3, the extended signature is $\mathcal{F}' = \mathcal{F} \cup \{U_1, U_2, U_3\}$.

Reusing U symbols is often essential to obtain confluent unraveled systems, e.g., both $U_{opt}(R_1)$ and $U_{seq}(R_1)$ are non-confluent TRSs, whereas the TRSs $R_2 = U_{conf}(R_1)$ and R_3 in Ex. 7 are orthogonal and hence confluent. Also termination provers can benefit from the repeated use of U symbols since for locally confluent overlay TRSs it suffices to prove innermost termination [5].

5   Completeness of Unravelings

Completeness of an unraveling U demands that derivations of R can be simulated by $U(R)$, i.e., $\to_R^* \subseteq \to_{U(R)}^*$ holds. This result is not hard to prove but has limited applicability. For example, it does not entail that termination of $U(R)$ implies strong normalization of $\to_R$ or quasi-reductiveness of R. Therefore, we first formalized a more general, technical result (Lem. 9) which is helpful to derive many of the other properties that we are interested in.

---

[3] The unraveling U_D proposed by Marchiori [8] differs from U_{seq} in that it admits multiple occurrences of the same variable in $\vec{Z_i}$. In general, it is hence not a standard unraveling, but U_D and U_{seq} coincide in the setting of left-linear unraveled systems.

The notion of a standard unraveling does not cover Marchiori's unraveling U_D. In order to cover U_D and also to keep our results as widely applicable as possible, we introduce an even more general notion of unravelings: Instead of demanding that the left- and right-hand-sides of unraveled rules are exactly of the form $U_i^\rho(t_i, \overrightarrow{Z_i})$ and $U_i^\rho(s_i, \overrightarrow{Z_i})$, we only assume that they are of the shape $C[t_i]$ and $C[s_i]$ for some context C.

Definition 8 (Generalized Unraveling). *A generalized unraveling U maps a rule ρ of the form $\ell \to r \Leftarrow s_1 \to t_1, \ldots, s_k \to t_k$ to the set of rules $U(\rho)$ given by*

$$U(\rho) = \{\ell \to C_1^\rho[s_1], \ C_1^\rho[t_1] \to C_2^\rho[s_2]), \ \ldots, \ C_k^\rho[t_k] \to r\}$$

where each C_i^ρ is an arbitrary context. As in Def. 6, $U(R) = \bigcup_{\rho \in R} U(\rho)$.

In the remainder of this section, we assume that U is a generalized unraveling.

Lemma 9. *Let $\ell \to r \Leftarrow s_1 \to t_1, \ldots, s_k \to t_k$ be a rule in R, and $1 \leqslant i \leqslant k+1$. For $i = k+1$, define $s_{k+1} := r$ and $C_{k+1}^\rho = \Box$. If $s_j\sigma \to_{U(R)}^* t_j\sigma$ for all $1 \leqslant j < i$, then $\ell\sigma \to_{U(R)}^+ C_i^\rho[s_i]\sigma$.*

Proof. $\ell\sigma \to_{U(R)} C_1^\rho[s_1]\sigma \to_{U(R)}^* C_1^\rho[t_1]\sigma \to_{U(R)} C_2^\rho[s_2]\sigma \to_{U(R)}^* \cdots \to_{U(R)}^* C_{i-1}^\rho[t_{i-1}]\sigma \to_{U(R)} C_i^\rho[s_i]\sigma.$ $\qquad\Box$

Theorem 10 (Completeness). $\to_R \subseteq \to_{U(R)}^+$

Proof. We prove $\overset{n}{\to}_R \subseteq \to_{U(R)}^+$ by induction on n. The base case is trivial. So let $s \overset{n+1}{\to}_R t$, i.e., there is some $\ell \to r \Leftarrow s_1 \to t_1, \ldots, s_k \to t_k$ in R where $s = C[\ell\sigma]$, $t = C[r\sigma]$ and $s_i\sigma \overset{n}{\to}_R^* t_i\sigma$ for all $1 \leqslant i \leqslant k$. By the induction hypothesis, we conclude $s_i\sigma \to_{U(R)}^* t_i\sigma$ for all i. Hence, $\ell\sigma \to_{U(R)}^+ r\sigma$ by applying Lem. 9 for $i := k + 1$. But then $s = C[\ell\sigma] \to_{U(R)}^+ C[r\sigma] = t$ immediately follows. $\qquad\Box$

Theorem 11 (Termination Implies Quasi-Reductiveness). *If $U(R)$ is terminating then R is quasi-reductive for $\succ := \to_{U(R)}^+$.*

Proof. From termination of $U(R)$ we conclude that $\succ$ is a strongly normalizing partial order, which is obviously also closed under contexts. Let $\ell \to r \Leftarrow s_1 \to t_1, \ldots, s_k \to t_k$ be a rule in R, let i satisfy $0 \leqslant i \leqslant k$, and let $s_j\sigma \succeq t_j\sigma$ for every $1 \leqslant j \leqslant i$. By definition of $\succ$, the preconditions can be reformulated as $1 \leqslant i + 1 \leqslant k + 1$ and $s_j\sigma \to_{U(R)}^* t_j\sigma$ for all $1 \leqslant j < i + 1$. Hence, by Lem. 9 we get $\ell\sigma \to_{U(R)}^+ C_{i+1}^\rho[s_{i+1}\sigma]$, i.e., $\ell\sigma \succ C_{i+1}^\rho[s_{i+1}\sigma]$ where in case $i = k$ we have $C_{i+1}^\rho = \Box$ and $s_{i+1} = r$. Thus, for $i < k$ we obtain $\ell\sigma \succ C_{i+1}^\rho[s_{i+1}\sigma] \trianglerighteq s_{i+1}\sigma$, and for $i = k$ we get $\ell\sigma \succ C_{i+1}^\rho[s_{i+1}\sigma] = r\sigma$, so all conditions of Def. 4 hold. $\qquad\Box$

To model generalized unravelings within IsaFoR, we assume U to be given as a function which takes a conditional rule ρ and an index i, and returns the context C_i^ρ. All proofs have been formalized as described above, with only a small overhead: for example, in becoming explicit in the "$\cdots$" within the statement and the proof of Lem. 9 (via quantifiers and inductive), or in manually providing the required substitutions and contexts when performing conditional rewriting.

Example 12. The TRS R_3 from Ex. 7 is terminating. According to Thm. 11, R_1 is thus quasi-reductive. A corresponding proof is automatically generated by APROVE and certified by CeTA.

6   Soundness of Unravelings

After having formalized simple proofs on unravelings like completeness, in this section we describe the following more challenging soundness result.

Theorem 13 (Soundness of Standard Unravelings). *Consider a 3DCTRS R and a standard unraveling U such that $U(R)$ is left-linear. Then U is sound with respect to reductions for R.*

Our formalization of this result follows the line of argument pursued in [12, Theorem 4.3]. However, Thm. 13 constitutes an extension in several respects. First, it is not fixed to the unraveling U_{opt}. Instead, it only assumes U to be a standard unraveling, thereby in particular covering U_{seq}, U_{conf}, and U_{opt}. Second, it does not rely on the assumption that R is non-left variable or non-right variable, i.e., that either no left- or no right-hand side of R is a variable. In [12] this restriction is used to simplify the decomposition of $U(R)$-rewrite sequences. Instead, we introduced the notion of partial and complete ρ-step simulations below. Finally, in contrast to the proof of [12, Lemma 4.2], we devised an inductive argument to prove the Key Lemma 18 in its full generality, instead of restricting to rules with only two conditions.

A number of preliminary results were required in order to prove Thm. 13.

Definition 14 (Complete and Partial Simulation). *Let $\rho = \ell \rightarrow r \Leftarrow s_1 \rightarrow t_1, \ldots, s_k \rightarrow t_k$. A rewrite sequence $s \Rightarrow^n_{U(R)} t$ contains a complete ρ-step simulation if it can be decomposed into a $U(R)$-rewrite sequence*

$$s \Rightarrow^{n_0} \ell\sigma_1 \rightarrow_\epsilon U_1^\rho(s_1, \overrightarrow{Z_1})\sigma_1$$
$$\Rightarrow^{n_1}_{>\epsilon} U_1^\rho(t_1, \overrightarrow{Z_1})\sigma_2 \rightarrow_\epsilon U_2^\rho(s_2, \overrightarrow{Z_2})\sigma_2$$
$$\vdots \tag{1}$$
$$\Rightarrow^{n_k}_{>\epsilon} U_k^\rho(t_k, \overrightarrow{Z_k})\sigma_{k+1} \rightarrow_\epsilon r\sigma_{k+1} \Rightarrow^{n_{k+1}} t$$

for some $n_0, \ldots, n_{k+1}$ and substitutions $\sigma_1, \ldots, \sigma_{k+1}$ such that $n = n_{k+1} + \sum_{i=0}^k (n_i + 1)$. Moreover, $s \Rightarrow^n_{U(R)} t$ contains a partial ρ-step simulation up to m if it can be decomposed as

$$s \Rightarrow^{n_0} \ell\sigma_1 \rightarrow_\epsilon U_1^\rho(s_1, \overrightarrow{Z_1})\sigma_1$$
$$\Rightarrow^{n_1}_{>\epsilon} U_1^\rho(t_1, \overrightarrow{Z_1})\sigma_2 \rightarrow_\epsilon U_2^\rho(s_2, \overrightarrow{Z_2})\sigma_2$$
$$\vdots \tag{2}$$
$$\Rightarrow^{n_{m-1}}_{>\epsilon} U_{m-1}^\rho(t_{m-1}, \overrightarrow{Z_{m-1}})\sigma_m \rightarrow_\epsilon U_m^\rho(s_m, \overrightarrow{Z_m})\sigma_m \Rightarrow^{n_m}_{>\epsilon} t$$

for some $m \leqslant k$ as well as $n_0, \ldots, n_m$ and substitutions $\sigma_1, \ldots, \sigma_m$ such that $n = n_m + \sum_{i=0}^{m-1} (n_i + 1)$.

The proof of the following result is technical but straightforward, applying induction on the length of the rewrite sequence A.

Lemma 15. *Suppose* $s \in \mathcal{T}(\mathcal{F}, \mathcal{V})$ *admits a rewrite sequence* $A\colon s \Rightarrow^n_{U(R)} t$ *which contains a root step. Then A contains a complete or a partial ρ-step simulation for some $\rho \in R$.* $\square$

Lemma 16 ([12, Lemma A.1]). *Consider a 3DCTRS R, a rule $\rho \in R$ of the form $\ell \to r \Leftarrow s_1 \to t_1, \ldots, s_k \to t_k$ such that $U(\rho)$ is left-linear, and substitutions $\theta_1, \ldots, \theta_{k+1}$. If $s_i \theta_i \to^*_R t_i \theta_{i+1}$ and $\overrightarrow{Z_i} \theta_i \to^*_R \overrightarrow{Z_i} \theta_{i+1}$ for all $1 \leqslant i \leqslant k$ then $\ell \theta_1 \to^*_R r \theta_{k+1}$.* $\square$

Here $\overrightarrow{Z_i} \theta_i \to^*_R \overrightarrow{Z_i} \theta_{i+1}$ denotes $z_j \theta_i \to^*_R z_j \theta_{i+1}$ for all $1 \leqslant j \leqslant n$, given $Z_i = \{z_1, \ldots, z_n\}$. The following lemma follows from the properties of 3DCTRSs.

Lemma 17. *A rule $\ell \to r \Leftarrow s_1 \to t_1, \ldots, s_k \to t_k$ in a 3DCTRS satisfies*

1. $\mathcal{V}ar(s_{m+1}) \subseteq \mathcal{V}ar(t_m) \cup (X_m \cap Y_m)$ *for all $m < k$, and*
2. $\mathcal{V}ar(r) \subseteq \mathcal{V}ar(t_k) \cup (X_k \cap Y_k)$. $\square$

Lemma 18 (Key Lemma). *Consider a 3DCTRS R and a standard unraveling U such that $U(R)$ is left-linear. Let $s, t \in \mathcal{T}(\mathcal{F}, \mathcal{V})$ and t be linear such that $s \Rightarrow^n_{U(R)} t\sigma$ for some substitution $\sigma \in \mathcal{S}ub(\mathcal{F}', \mathcal{V})$. Then there is some substitution θ such that (i) $s \to^*_R \ell\theta$, (ii) $x\theta \Rightarrow^n_{U(R)} x\sigma$ and $x\theta \in \mathcal{T}(\mathcal{F}, \mathcal{V})$ for all $x \in \mathcal{V}ar(t)$, and (iii) if $t\sigma \in \mathcal{T}(\mathcal{F}, \mathcal{V})$ then $t\theta = t\sigma$.*

Before proving the key lemma, we show that it admits a very short proof of the main soundness result. The lemma will also be used in § 7 to prove confluence.

Proof (Proof of Thm. 13). Consider $s, t \in \mathcal{T}(\mathcal{F}, \mathcal{V})$ such that $s \to^*_{U(R)} t$. Let $x \in \mathcal{V}$ and $\sigma := \{x \mapsto t\}$. Hence $s \Rightarrow^*_{U(R)} x\sigma$ holds, and from Lem. 18 it follows that $s \to^*_R x\sigma = t$. $\square$

The following four pages describe a complete paper proof of the key lemma. We present it for the following reasons: In contrast to the proof of [12, Theorem 3.8], it devises an argument for the general case instead of restricting to two conditions. It is also structured differently, as it makes use of the notion of complete and partial ρ-step simulations and prefix equivalence. The latter differences in particular allowed us to show a more general result. And finally, the paper proof served as a detailed and human-readable proof plan for the proof within IsaFoR: the formalized proof contains even more details and is over 800 lines long.

At this point we want to emphasize the advantage of having a formalized proof within a proof assistant like Isabelle: in order to verify the proof's correctness, one can simply check whether the statement of the key lemma from the paper corresponds to the one in the formalization, because the (even more detailed) formalized proof is validated automatically.

Proof (of key lemma). The proof is by induction on (n, s), compared lexicographically by $>$ and $\rhd$. If $n = 0$ then $s = t\sigma \in \mathcal{T}(\mathcal{F}, \mathcal{V})$, and one can set $\theta = \sigma$. The remainder of the proof performs a case analysis on a rewrite sequence

$$s \Rrightarrow_{U(R)}^{n+1} t\sigma \tag{3}$$

To enhance readability, the subscript in $\Rrightarrow_{U(R)}$ will be omitted; all steps denoted $\Rrightarrow$ and $\rightarrow_\epsilon$ are in $U(R)$.

Case (i): The sequence (3) *does not contain a root step.* Then s cannot be a variable so, $s = f(s_1, \ldots, s_m)$ for some $f \in \mathcal{F}$. In this case, the result will easily follow from the induction hypothesis. Still, we have to consider two cases.

1. Suppose $t \notin \mathcal{V}$. As (3) does not contain a root step we may write $t = f(t_1, \ldots, t_m)$, and have $s_i \Rrightarrow^{n+1} t_i\sigma$ for all $1 \leqslant i \leqslant m$. (Here we employ the fact that $\Rrightarrow^k \subseteq \Rrightarrow^{n+1}$ for all $k \leqslant n + 1$, which will be freely used in the sequel of this proof.) For all i such that $1 \leqslant i \leqslant m$, $s_i, t_i \in \mathcal{T}(\mathcal{F}, \mathcal{V})$ and t_i is linear. Hence the induction hypothesis yields a substitution θ_i such that $s_i \rightarrow_R^* t_i\theta_i$, $x\theta_i \Rrightarrow^{n+1} x\sigma$ and $x\theta_i \in \mathcal{T}(\mathcal{F}, \mathcal{V})$ for all $x \in \mathsf{Var}(t_i)$, and $t_i\theta_i = t_i\sigma$ if $t_i\sigma \in \mathcal{T}(\mathcal{F}, \mathcal{V})$. By linearity of t, $\theta := \bigcup_{i=1}^m \theta_i|_{\mathsf{Var}(t_i)} \in \mathcal{T}(\mathcal{F}, \mathcal{V})$ is a substitution which satisfies $t_i\theta_i = t_i\theta$ for all i. Hence we obtain

$$s = f(s_1, \ldots, s_m) \rightarrow_R^* f(t_1, \ldots, t_m)\theta = t\theta \Rrightarrow^{n+1} f(t_1, \ldots, t_m)\sigma = t\sigma$$

   and if $t\sigma \in \mathcal{T}(\mathcal{F}, \mathcal{V})$ then $t_i\sigma \in \mathcal{T}(\mathcal{F}, \mathcal{V})$ implies $t_i\theta = t_i\theta_i = t_i\sigma$, such that $t\theta = t\sigma$.

2. We have $t = x \in \mathcal{V}$, hence $x\sigma = f(t_1, \ldots, t_m)$. Let $x_1, \ldots, x_m$ be distinct variables and σ' be a substitution such that $x_i\sigma' = t_i$ for all $1 \leqslant i \leqslant m$. As $s = f(s_1, \ldots, s_m)$ and (3) does not contain a root step, we have $s_i \Rrightarrow^{n+1} t_i = x_i\sigma'$. For all i such that $1 \leqslant i \leqslant m$, the induction hypothesis yields a substitution θ_i such that $s_i \rightarrow_R^* x_i\theta_i$, $x_i\theta_i \Rrightarrow^{n+1} x_i\sigma'$ and $x_i\theta_i \in \mathcal{T}(\mathcal{F}, \mathcal{V})$, where $x_i\theta_i = x_i\sigma'$ if $x_i\sigma' \in \mathcal{T}(\mathcal{F}, \mathcal{V})$. Let $\theta := \{x \mapsto f(x_1\theta_1, \ldots, x_m\theta_m)\}$. One thus obtains

$$s = f(s_1, \ldots, s_m) \rightarrow_R^* f(x_1\theta_1, \ldots, x_m\theta_m) = x\theta \Rrightarrow^{n+1} f(x_1, \ldots, x_m)\sigma' = x\sigma$$

   and if $t\sigma \in \mathcal{T}(\mathcal{F}, \mathcal{V})$ then $t_i = x_i\sigma' \in \mathcal{T}(\mathcal{F}, \mathcal{V})$ implies $x_i\theta_i = x_i\sigma'$, so $t\theta = t\sigma$.

Case (ii): The sequence (3) *contains a root step.* Then according to Lem. 15, (3) contains a partial or a complete ρ-step simulation for some $\rho \in R$ where ρ is of the shape $\ell \rightarrow r \Leftarrow s_1 \rightarrow t_1, \ldots, s_k \rightarrow t_k$, and $s \Rrightarrow^{n_0} \ell\sigma_1$ for some $n_0 < n+1$. As $\ell \in \mathcal{T}(\mathcal{F}, \mathcal{V})$ is linear by the assumption of left-linearity, the induction hypothesis yields a substitution θ_1 such that $s \rightarrow_R^* \ell\theta_1$, $x\theta_1 \Rrightarrow^{n_0} x\sigma_1$ and $x\theta_1 \in \mathcal{T}(\mathcal{F}, \mathcal{V})$ for all $x \in \mathsf{Var}(\ell)$, and if $\ell\sigma_1 \in \mathcal{T}(\mathcal{F}, \mathcal{V})$ then $\ell\theta_1 = \ell\sigma_1$ ($\star$).

1. Suppose (3) contains a partial ρ-step simulation up to m of the form

$$s \Rrightarrow^{n_0} \ell\sigma_1 \rightarrow_\epsilon U_1^\rho(s_1, \overrightarrow{Z_1})\sigma_1 \Rrightarrow_{>\epsilon}^{n_1} \cdots \rightarrow_\epsilon U_m^\rho(s_m, \overrightarrow{Z_m})\sigma_m \Rrightarrow_{>\epsilon}^{n_m} t\sigma$$

for $m \leqslant k$, such that $\mathsf{root}(t\sigma) = U_m$. Since $t \in \mathcal{T}(\mathcal{F}, \mathcal{V})$ by assumption it must be the case that $t = x \in \mathcal{V}$. Let $\theta = \{x \mapsto \ell\theta_1\}$. In combination with $(\star)$ it follows that $s \to_R^* \ell\theta_1 = x\theta$, $x\theta = \ell\theta_1 \Rrightarrow^{n_0} \ell\sigma_1 \Rrightarrow^{n+1-n_0} t\sigma = x\sigma$ and consequently $x\theta \Rrightarrow^{n+1} x\sigma$, $x\theta = \ell\theta_1 \in \mathcal{T}(\mathcal{F}, \mathcal{V})$ and $x\sigma \notin \mathcal{T}(\mathcal{F}, \mathcal{V})$ which shows the claim.

2. Suppose (3) contains a complete ρ-step simulation

$$s \Rrightarrow^{n_0} \ell\sigma_1 \to_\epsilon U_1^\rho(s_1, \overrightarrow{Z_1})\sigma_1 \Rrightarrow^{n_1}_{>\epsilon} U_1^\rho(t_1, \overrightarrow{Z_1})\sigma_2 \to_\epsilon U_2^\rho(s_2, \overrightarrow{Z_2})\sigma_2 \Rrightarrow^{n_2}_{>\epsilon} \cdots$$
$$\to_\epsilon U_k^\rho(s_k, \overrightarrow{Z_k})\sigma_k \Rrightarrow^{n_k}_{>\epsilon} U_k^\rho(t_k, \overrightarrow{Z_k})\sigma_{k+1} \tag{4}$$
$$\to_\epsilon r\sigma_{k+1} \Rrightarrow^{n_{k+1}} t\sigma$$

The key step is now to establish existence of a substitution θ' such that

$$s \to_R^+ r\theta', \qquad r\theta' \in \mathcal{T}(\mathcal{F}, \mathcal{V}), \text{ and} \qquad r\theta' \Rrightarrow^n t\sigma \tag{5}$$

First, suppose ρ is an unconditional rule $\ell \to r$. Then one can take $\theta' := \theta_1$: By $(\star)$ one has $s \to_R^* \ell\theta_1$, and for all $x \in \mathcal{V}ar(\ell)$ it holds that $x\theta_1 \in \mathcal{T}(\mathcal{F}, \mathcal{V})$, $x\theta_1 \Rrightarrow^{n_0} x\sigma_1$ and $x\theta_1 \in \mathcal{T}(\mathcal{F}, \mathcal{V})$. Obviously there is also the rewrite sequence $s \to_R^* r\theta_1$. As $\mathcal{V}ar(r) \subseteq \mathcal{V}ar(\ell)$ because R is a DCTRS, the properties of θ_1 imply $r\theta_1 \in \mathcal{T}(\mathcal{F}, \mathcal{V})$. Together with $(\star)$, $\mathcal{V}ar(r) \subseteq \mathcal{V}ar(\ell)$ also implies $r\theta_1 \Rrightarrow^{n_0} r\sigma_1$. Combined with the complete simulation, $r\theta_1 \Rrightarrow^n t\sigma$ holds.

Second, in the case of a conditional rule the following claim is used: there are substitutions $\theta_1, \ldots, \theta_{k+1}$ such that θ_1 is as derived in $(\star)$, and it holds that

(a) $s_i\theta_i \to_R^* t_i\theta_{i+1}$ (c) $\theta_j|_{V_j} \in \mathcal{S}ub(\mathcal{F}, \mathcal{V})$

(b) $\overrightarrow{Z_i}\theta_i \to_R^* \overrightarrow{Z_i}\theta_{i+1}$ (d) $x\theta_{i+1} \Rrightarrow^{N_i} x\sigma_{i+1} \; \forall x \in \mathcal{V}ar(t_i) \cup Z_i$

for all $1 \leqslant i \leqslant k$ and $1 \leqslant j \leqslant k+1$. Here $N_i = \sum_{j=0}^i n_j$, and V_j denotes the variable set defined by $V_1 = \mathcal{V}ar(\ell)$ and $V_{j+1} = \mathcal{V}ar(t_j) \cup (X_j \cap Y_j)$ for $j > 0$. We conclude the main proof before showing the claim. In particular, the claim yields substitutions $\theta_1, \ldots, \theta_{k+1}$ with properties (a)–(d). Due to (a), (b), and Lem. 16, there is a rewrite sequence $\ell\theta_1 \to_R^* r\theta_{k+1}$. In combination with $(\star)$ it follows that $s \to_R^* \ell\theta_1 \to_R^* r\theta_{k+1}$. According to Lem. 17 (2), $\mathcal{V}ar(r) \subseteq \mathcal{V}ar(t_k) \cup (X_k \cap Y_k) = V_{k+1}$, so with (c) it holds that $r\theta_{k+1} \in \mathcal{T}(\mathcal{F}, \mathcal{V})$. Moreover, in combination with (d) and the fact that $X_k \cap Y_k \subseteq Z_k$ one has $x\theta_{k+1} \Rrightarrow^{N_k} x\sigma_{k+1}$ for all $x \in \mathcal{V}ar(r)$, and hence $r\theta_{k+1} \Rrightarrow^{N_k} r\sigma_{k+1} \Rrightarrow^{n_{k+1}} t\sigma$. Now since $N_k + n_{k+1} \leqslant n$ one has $r\theta_{k+1} \Rrightarrow^n t\sigma$, so the substitution θ_{k+1} satisfies all properties of θ' as demanded in (5).

So suppose there is a substitution θ' which satisfies the properties (5). Applying the induction hypothesis to the rewrite sequence $r\theta' \Rrightarrow^n t\sigma$ yields a substitution θ such that $r\theta' \to_R^* t\theta$ (and hence $s \to_R^* t\theta$), $x\theta \Rrightarrow^n x\sigma$ and $x\theta \in \mathcal{T}(\mathcal{F}, \mathcal{V})$ for all $x \in \mathcal{V}ar(t)$, and if $t\sigma \in \mathcal{T}(\mathcal{F}, \mathcal{V})$ then $t\theta = t\sigma$. This concludes the case of a complete ρ-step simulation, it only remains to prove the above claim.

Proof of the claim. We perform an inner induction on k. In the base where $k = 0$, the singleton substitution list containing θ_1 vacuously satisfies properties (a), (b), and (d), and (c) holds as $\theta_1|_{V_1} \in \mathcal{S}\mathsf{ub}(\mathcal{F}, \mathcal{V})$ according to $(\star)$.

So consider the case for $k = m+1$. From the induction hypothesis one obtains substitutions $\theta_1, \ldots, \theta_k$ which satisfy properties (a)–(d) for all $1 \leqslant i \leqslant m$ and $1 \leqslant j \leqslant k$. In the sequel, they will be referred to by (a')–(d'). Let θ'_k be defined as follows:

$$\theta'_k(x) = \begin{cases} x\theta_k & \text{if } k = 1 \text{ and } x \in \mathcal{V}\mathsf{ar}(\ell), \text{ or } x \in \mathcal{V}\mathsf{ar}(t_m) \cup Z_m \\ x\sigma_k & \text{otherwise} \end{cases}$$

In the first place

$$s_k\theta'_k \Rightarrow^{N_m} s_k\sigma_k \quad \text{and} \quad s_k\theta'_k \in \mathcal{T}(\mathcal{F}, \mathcal{V}) \tag{6}$$

is established by means of a case analysis. First, suppose $k = 1$. As R is deterministic, $\mathcal{V}\mathsf{ar}(s_1) \subseteq \mathcal{V}\mathsf{ar}(\ell)$. According to $(\star)$, $x\theta_1 \Rightarrow^{n_0} x\sigma_1$ and $x\theta_1 \in \mathcal{T}(\mathcal{F}, \mathcal{V})$ hold for all $x \in \mathcal{V}\mathsf{ar}(\ell)$. By definition of θ'_1 and $\mathcal{V}\mathsf{ar}(s_1) \subseteq \mathcal{V}\mathsf{ar}(\ell)$ we get $s_1\theta'_1 = s_1\theta_1$. Hence $s_1\theta'_1 \Rightarrow^{n_0} s_1\sigma_1$ and thus $s_1\theta'_1 \Rightarrow^{N_0} s_1\sigma_1$, and $s_1\theta'_1 \in \mathcal{T}(\mathcal{F}, \mathcal{V})$. Second, suppose $k > 1$. By Lem. 17 (1) one has $\mathcal{V}\mathsf{ar}(s_k) \subseteq \mathcal{V}\mathsf{ar}(t_m) \cup (X_m \cap Y_m) = V_k$. Due to $X_m \cap Y_m \subseteq Z_m$ it also holds that $\mathcal{V}\mathsf{ar}(s_k) \subseteq \mathcal{V}\mathsf{ar}(t_m) \cup Z_m$. By (d'), $x\theta_k \Rightarrow^{N_m} x\sigma_k$ and $x\theta_k \in \mathcal{T}(\mathcal{F}, \mathcal{V})$ for all $x \in \mathcal{V}\mathsf{ar}(t_m) \cup Z_m$, such that also $s_k\theta_k \Rightarrow^{N_m} s_k\sigma_k$ holds. From $\mathcal{V}\mathsf{ar}(s_k) \subseteq \mathcal{V}\mathsf{ar}(t_m) \cup Z_m$ it also follows that $s_k\theta_k = s_k\theta'_k$ such that $s_k\theta'_k \Rightarrow^{N_m} s_k\sigma_k$ holds. Moreover, $\mathcal{V}\mathsf{ar}(s_k) \subseteq V_k$ and (c') imply $s_k\theta'_k \in \mathcal{T}(\mathcal{F}, \mathcal{V})$, so (6) is satisfied.

According to derivation (4) $s_k\sigma_k \Rightarrow^{n_k} t_k\sigma_{k+1}$ holds, so with (6) it follows that $s_k\theta'_k \Rightarrow^{N_k} t_k\sigma_{k+1}$. Now the outer induction hypothesis can be applied to this rewrite sequence: as $U(R)$ is left-linear also t_k must be linear, $s_k\theta'_k, t_k \in \mathcal{T}(\mathcal{F}, \mathcal{V})$, and $N_k < n + 1$ so one obtains a substitution θ_s such that

$$s_k\theta'_k \to_R^* t_k\theta_s, \qquad x\theta_s \Rightarrow^{N_k} x\sigma_{k+1}, \text{ and} \qquad x\theta_s \in \mathcal{T}(\mathcal{F}, \mathcal{V}) \tag{7}$$

for all $x \in \mathcal{V}\mathsf{ar}(t_k)$.

Next, we show that for every $z \in Z_k$ there is a substitution θ_z such that

$$z\theta'_k \to_R^* z\theta_z, \qquad z\theta_z \Rightarrow^{N_k} z\sigma_{k+1}, \text{ and} \qquad z(\theta_z|_{V_k}) \in \mathcal{T}(\mathcal{F}, \mathcal{V}). \tag{8}$$

holds, by a case analysis. First, in the case where either $k = 1$ and $z \notin \mathcal{V}\mathsf{ar}(\ell)$, or $k > 1$ and $z \notin \mathcal{V}\mathsf{ar}(t_m) \cup Z_m$, it suffices to take $\theta_z = \{z \mapsto z\theta'_k\} = \{z \mapsto z\sigma_k\}$ as according to derivation (4) one has $z\sigma_k \Rightarrow^{n_k} z\sigma_{k+1}$ and hence $z\sigma_k \Rightarrow^{N_k} \sigma_{k+1}$. Both $z(\theta_z|_{V_k}) \in \mathcal{T}(\mathcal{F}, \mathcal{V})$ and $z\theta'_k \to_R^* z\theta_z$ trivially hold, so (8) is satisfied.

Second, if $k = 1$ and $z \in \mathcal{V}\mathsf{ar}(\ell)$, or $k > 1$ and $z \in \mathcal{V}\mathsf{ar}(t_m) \cup Z_m$. Then

$$z\theta'_k \Rightarrow^{N_m} z\sigma_k \quad \text{and} \quad z(\theta'_k|_{V_k}) \in \mathcal{T}(\mathcal{F}, \mathcal{V}) \tag{9}$$

holds, as can be seen by a case analysis on k. If $k = 1$ and $z \in \mathcal{V}\mathsf{ar}(\ell)$, then by $(\star)$ it holds that $z\theta_1 \Rightarrow^{n_0} z\sigma_1$ and $z\theta_1 \in \mathcal{T}(\mathcal{F}, \mathcal{V})$, so also $z\theta_1 \Rightarrow^{N_0} z\sigma_1$ is satisfied, and $z\theta_1' = z\theta_1$ holds by definition. If $k > 1$ then $z\theta_k' \Rightarrow^{N_m} z\sigma_k$ and $z(\theta_k'|_{V_k}) \in \mathcal{T}(\mathcal{F}, \mathcal{V})$ hold according to (c'), (d') and as $z\theta_k' = z\theta_k$.

So in both cases (9) is satisfied. Now the derivation (4) implies $z\sigma_k \Rightarrow^{n_k} z\sigma_{k+1}$, and together with (9) it holds that $z\theta_k' \Rightarrow^{N_k} z\sigma_{k+1}$. Applying the outer induction hypothesis to this rewrite sequence yields a substitution θ_z that satisfies (8).

Since $U(R)$ is left-linear, $\mathcal{V}\mathsf{ar}(t_k)$ and Z_k are disjoint. Therefore, $\theta_{k+1} := \theta_s|_{\mathcal{V}\mathsf{ar}(t_k)} \cup \bigcup_{z \in Z_k}\{z \mapsto z\theta_z\}$ is a well-defined substitution. It can be verified that the sequence of substitutions $\theta_1, \ldots, \theta_m, \theta_k', \theta_{k+1}$ satisfies all desired properties (a)–(d):

First, note that $\theta_1, \ldots, \theta_m, \theta_k'$ also satisfy the properties corresponding to (a')–(d'): from (a') one has $s_m\theta_m \to_R^* t_m\theta_k'$ because $t_m\theta_k = t_m\theta_k'$; $\vec{Z}_m\theta_m \to_R^* \vec{Z}_m\theta_k'$ and $\theta_k'|_{V_k} \in \mathcal{S}\mathsf{ub}(\mathcal{F}, \mathcal{V})$ hold by (b'), (c'), and the definition of θ_k'. By the definition of θ_k', $x\theta_k' = x\theta_k$ for all $x \in \mathcal{V}\mathsf{ar}(t_m) \cup Z_m$, so (d') also holds for $\theta_1, \ldots, \theta_m, \theta_k'$.

In summary, one can conclude

(a) $s_i\theta_i \to_R^* t_i\theta_{i+1}$ (c) $\theta_j|_{V_j} \in \mathcal{S}\mathsf{ub}(\mathcal{F}, \mathcal{V})$

(b) $\vec{Z}_i\theta_i \to_R^* \vec{Z}_i\theta_{i+1}$ (d) $x\theta_{i+1} \Rightarrow^{N_i} x\sigma_{i+1}$ $\forall x \in \mathcal{V}\mathsf{ar}(t_i) \cup Z_i$

for all $1 \leqslant i \leqslant k$ and $1 \leqslant j \leqslant k+1$, where (a) follows from (a') and as $s_k\theta_k' \to_R^* t_k\theta_{k+1}$ follows from (7). Next, (b) holds because of (b') and (8), which entails $\vec{Z}_k\theta_k' \to_R^* \vec{Z}_k\theta_{k+1}$ as $z\theta_z = z\theta_{k+1}$ for all $z \in Z_k$. Finally, (7) and (8) imply $\theta_{k+1}|_{V_{k+1}} \in \mathcal{S}\mathsf{ub}(\mathcal{F}, \mathcal{V})$ and $x\theta_{k+1} \Rightarrow^{N_k} x\sigma_{k+1}$ for all $x \in \mathcal{V}\mathsf{ar}(t_k) \cup Z_k$, which together with (c') and (d') induce (c) and (d). $\square$

Thm. 13 and its preliminary lemmas are formalized in IsaFoR as presented in the proofs above. As already mentioned, the notions of partial and complete ρ-step simulations are used to circumvent the restriction to non-left or non-right variable CTRSs (and a respective duplication of the main proof steps). At some places the formalization induces some technical overhead, for instance to construct a substitution by taking the union of a set of domain-disjoint substitutions.

7   Applying Unravelings to Confluence

It is known that confluence of an unraveled system $U(R)$ implies confluence of the conditional system R under certain conditions [4]. In order to verify proof certificates by ConCon, a respective result was added to IsaFoR, and the following paragraphs describe our formalized proof.

We call a standard unraveling *source preserving* if for all rules $\rho \in R$ of the form $\ell \to r \Leftarrow s_1 \to t_1, \ldots, s_k \to t_k$ it holds that $\mathcal{V}\mathsf{ar}(\ell) \subseteq Z_i$ for all $i \leqslant k$. The intuition behind this notion is that then each term $U_i^\rho(t, \vec{Z}_i)\sigma$ completely determines σ on $\mathcal{V}ar(\ell)$. For instance, R_2 in Ex. 7 is source preserving, but R_3 is not since the information on x gets lost in U_2.

Lemma 19. *Let R be a deterministic, non-left variable 3DCTRS, and let U be a source preserving unraveling such that $U(R)$ is left-linear. Suppose $s, t \in \mathcal{T}(\mathcal{F}, \mathcal{V})$ such that $s \rightarrow^*_{U(R)} u \; {}_{U(R)}{}^*{\leftarrow} t$ for some $u \in \mathcal{T}(\mathcal{F}', \mathcal{V})$. Then there is some $v \in \mathcal{T}(\mathcal{F}, \mathcal{V})$ such that $s \rightarrow^*_R v \; {}_R^*{\leftarrow} t$ holds.*

Proof. By induction on u. If $u \in \mathcal{V}$ then $u \in \mathcal{T}(\mathcal{F}, \mathcal{V})$, so using Thm. 13 one can directly conclude $s \rightarrow^*_R u \; {}_R^*{\leftarrow} t$.

Otherwise, suppose for a first case that $\text{root}(u) \in \mathcal{F}$, so let $u = f(u_1, \ldots, u_m)$. Let u' be the linear term $f(x_1, \ldots, x_m)$, and $\sigma := \{x_i \mapsto u_i \mid 1 \leqslant i \leqslant m\}$, i.e., $u = u'\sigma$. We have $s \Rightarrow^{n_s}_{U(R)} u'\sigma$ and $t \Rightarrow^{n_t}_{U(R)} u'\sigma$ for some n_s and n_t. From Lem. 18 we thus obtain substitutions θ_s and θ_t such that $s \rightarrow^*_R u'\theta_s$, $t \rightarrow^*_R u'\theta_t$, and $u'\theta_s, u'\theta_t \in \mathcal{T}(\mathcal{F}, \mathcal{V})$. Moreover, for all variables $x_i \in \{x_1, \ldots, x_m\}$ we have $x_i\theta_s \rightarrow^*_{U(R)} x_i\sigma$ and $x_i\theta_t \rightarrow^*_{U(R)} x_i\sigma$; and since $u \rhd x_i\sigma$, we can apply the induction hypothesis to obtain $x_i\theta_s \rightarrow^*_R v_i \; {}_R^*{\leftarrow} x_i\theta_t$ for some $v_i \in \mathcal{T}(\mathcal{F}, \mathcal{V})$. Joinability of s and t follows because of

$$s \rightarrow^*_R u'\theta_s \Rightarrow^*_R f(v_1, \ldots, v_m) \; {}_R^*{\Leftarrow} u'\theta_t \; {}_R^*{\leftarrow} t$$

Second, assume $\text{root}(u) \notin \mathcal{F}$, so by the assumption $u \in \mathcal{T}(\mathcal{F}', \mathcal{V})$ we have $u = U_i^\rho(u_1, \vec{Z}_i\nu)$ for some $\rho \in R$ of the form $\ell \rightarrow r \Leftarrow s_1 \rightarrow t_1, \ldots, s_k \rightarrow t_k$ and $1 \leqslant i \leqslant k$, some term u_i and some substitution ν. Let $x \in \mathcal{V}$ be some variable, so we have $s \Rightarrow^{n_s}_{U(R)} x\{x \mapsto u\}$ for some n_s. By Lem. 18, there is a substitution θ_s such that $s \rightarrow^*_R x\theta_s$, and $x\theta_s \in \mathcal{T}(\mathcal{F}, \mathcal{V})$.

As u is rooted by U_i^ρ an analysis of the proof of Lem. 18 for this case shows the following:[4] The rewrite sequence $s \Rightarrow^{n_s}_{U(R)} x\{x \mapsto u\}$ contains a partial ρ'-step simulation up to i, for some rule $\rho' \in R$ prefix equivalent to ρ, and there are a substitution σ_0 such that $x\theta_s = \ell\sigma_0$ as well as substitutions $\sigma_1, \ldots, \sigma_i$ such that

1. $z\sigma_0 \Rightarrow^*_{U(R)} z\sigma_1$ for all $z \in \mathcal{V}ar(\ell)$,
2. $z\sigma_j \Rightarrow^*_{U(R)} z\sigma_{j+1}$ for all $z \in Z_j$ and $1 \leqslant j < i$, and
3. $z\sigma_i \Rightarrow^*_{U(R)} z\nu$ for all $z \in Z_i$.

Consider some variable $z \in \mathcal{V}ar(\ell)$. Since U is source preserving, $z \in Z_j$ for all $j \leqslant i$. Therefore, the properties of the substitutions σ_j yield a rewrite sequence $z\sigma_0 \Rightarrow^*_{U(R)} z\nu$.

In the same way the rewrite sequence $t \Rightarrow^{n_t}_{U(R)} x\{x \mapsto u\}$ gives rise to substitutions θ_t, τ_0 such that $t \rightarrow^*_R z\theta_t$, $z\theta_t \in \mathcal{T}(\mathcal{F}, \mathcal{V})$, $z\theta_t = \ell\tau_0$, and $z\tau_0 \Rightarrow^*_{U(R)} z\nu$ holds for all $z \in \mathcal{V}ar(\ell)$.

Consider again some $z \in \mathcal{V}ar(\ell)$. We have $z\sigma_0 \Rightarrow^*_{U(R)} z\nu$ and $z\tau_0 \Rightarrow^*_{U(R)} z\nu$, where $z\sigma_0, z\tau_0 \in \mathcal{T}(\mathcal{F}, \mathcal{V})$. But as we have $u \rhd z\nu$, the induction hypothesis shows $z\sigma_0 \downarrow_R z\tau_0$. Hence $\ell\sigma_0$ and $\ell\tau_0$ are joinable to some common reduct $\ell\nu' \in \mathcal{T}(\mathcal{F}, \mathcal{V})$.

In summary, joinability of s and t follows from the rewrite sequence

---

[4] Within IsaFoR this fact is made explicit by adapting the statement of Lem. 18.

$$s \to_R^* x\theta_s = \ell\sigma_0 \Rrightarrow_R^* \ell\nu' {}_R^* \! \Lleftarrow \ell\tau_0 = x\theta_t {}_R^* \! \leftarrow t \qquad \Box$$

Theorem 20 (Confluence). *Let R be a non-left variable 3DCTRS over signature $\mathcal{F}$, and U be a source preserving unraveling such that $U(R)$ is left-linear. Then confluence of $U(R)$ implies confluence of R.*

Proof. Consider a peak $s {}_R^* \! \leftarrow u \to_R^* t$ with $u \in \mathcal{T}(\mathcal{F}, \mathcal{V})$. Then also $s, t \in \mathcal{T}(\mathcal{F}, \mathcal{V})$ since R has signature $\mathcal{F}$. By completeness of U, we also have $s {}_{U(R)}^* \! \leftarrow u \to_{U(R)}^* t$. Confluence of $U(R)$ yields a join $s \to_{U(R)}^* v' {}_{U(R)}^* \! \leftarrow t$ for some term $v' \in \mathcal{T}(\mathcal{F}', \mathcal{V})$. By Lem. 19 there is also a term $v \in \mathcal{T}(\mathcal{F}, \mathcal{V})$ such that $s \to_R^* v {}_R^* \! \leftarrow t$. Hence R is confluent on terms in $\mathcal{T}(\mathcal{F}, \mathcal{V})$. A further technical renaming suffices to prove confluence on all terms u, where we refer to the formalization for details. $\qquad \Box$

Example 21. The TRS $R_2 = U_{\mathsf{conf}}(R_1)$ from Ex. 7 is confluent since it is orthogonal. According to Thm. 20, R_1 is thus confluent as well. Due to our formalization, the confluence proof generated by CorCon can be certified by CeTA.

The following example shows that U_{conf} is not necessarily an optimal choice when it comes to confluence analysis.

Example 22. Consider the CTRS R_4 consisting of rules

$$\mathsf{a} \to \mathsf{b} \Leftarrow \mathsf{c} \to x, \; \mathsf{d}_i(x) \to \mathsf{e} \qquad \mathsf{d}_i(\mathsf{c}) \to \mathsf{e}$$

for $i \in \{1, 2\}$. We obtain the following unraveled TRSs:

$$
\begin{array}{lllll}
U_{\mathsf{conf}}: & \mathsf{a} \to U_1(\mathsf{c}) & U_1(x) \to U_2^i(\mathsf{d}_i(x), x) & U_2^i(\mathsf{e}, x) \to \mathsf{b} & \mathsf{d}_i(\mathsf{c}) \to \mathsf{e} \\
U_{\mathsf{opt}}: & \mathsf{a} \to U_1^i(\mathsf{c}) & U_1^i(x) \to U_2^i(\mathsf{d}_i(x)) & U_2^i(\mathsf{e}) \to \mathsf{b} & \mathsf{d}_i(\mathsf{c}) \to \mathsf{e} \\
U_{\mathsf{seq}}: & \mathsf{a} \to U_1^i(\mathsf{c}) & U_1^i(x) \to U_2^i(\mathsf{d}_i(x), x) & U_2^i(\mathsf{e}, x) \to \mathsf{b} & \mathsf{d}_i(\mathsf{c}) \to \mathsf{e}
\end{array}
$$

U_{conf} admits the non-joinable peak $U_2^1(\mathsf{d}_1(x), x) \leftarrow U_1(x) \to U_2^2(\mathsf{d}_2(x), x)$, but U_{seq} (as well as U_{opt}) is confluent, so R_4 is confluent by Thm. 20.

8 Conclusion

We presented a formalization of soundness and completeness results of unravelings. We used these results to certify quasi-reductiveness proofs by AProVE [3] and conditional confluence proofs by CorCon [17]. As a test bench we used all 3DCTRSs from Cops (problems 1–438) and TPDB 9.0,[5] duplicates removed. In this way we obtained 85 problems from Cops and 31 problems from TPDB.

AProVE produces termination proofs for 84 input problems, and CeTA could certify these termination proofs for 83 problems. CorCon could prove confluence for 58 problems, and nonconfluence for 28 problems. CeTA could certify 38 confluence proofs. Around 17 % of the confluence proofs of CorCon required sharing

---

[5] See http://cops.uibk.ac.at/ and http://termination-portal.org/wiki/TPDB

of U symbols. All proofs that CeTA could not certify contain some techniques which are not yet formalized. Detailed experimental results are provided on the website.

In summary, we consider our contribution threefold. On the *formalization* side, we provided to the best of our knowledge the first formalization framework for conditional rewriting and unravelings. Besides basic definitions it comprises the crucial soundness and completeness results for the wide class of standard unravelings. *Theoretically,* we contribute a comprehensive proof for soundness of standard unravelings. It is based on [12, Theorem 3.8], but we could generalize it in several respects. *Practically,* we provide a certifier for CTRSs. It is able to certify quasi-decreasingness for all but one of the proofs generated by AProVE, and it confirms 65% of the examples where ConCon claims confluence.

Potential future work includes the integration of further (non)confluence techniques or termination techniques for CTRSs into IsaFoR.

References

1. Baader, F., Nipkow, T.: Term Rewriting and All That. Cambridge University Press (1998)
2. Durán, F., Lucas, S., Meseguer, J., Marché, C., Urbain, X.: Proving termination of membership equational programs. In: Proc. PEPM 2004, pp. 147–158 (2004)
3. Giesl, J., Brockschmidt, M., Emmes, F., Frohn, F., Fuhs, C., Otto, C., Plücker, M., Schneider-Kamp, P., Ströder, T., Swiderski, S., Thiemann, R.: Proving termination of programs automatically with AProVE. In: Demri, S., Kapur, D., Weidenbach, C. (eds.) IJCAR 2014. LNCS, vol. 8562, pp. 184–191. Springer, Heidelberg (2014)
4. Gmeiner, K., Nishida, N., Gramlich, B.: Proving confluence of conditional term rewriting systems via unravelings. In: Proc. IWC 2013, pp. 35–39 (2013)
5. Gramlich, B.: Abstract relations between restricted termination and confluence properties of rewrite systems. Fundamenta Informaticae 24, 3–23 (1995)
6. Lucas, S., Marché, C., Meseguer, J.: Operational termination of conditional term rewriting systems. IPL 95(4), 446–453 (2005)
7. Marchiori, M.: Unravelings and ultra-properties. In: Hanus, M., Rodríguez-Artalejo, M. (eds.) ALP 1996. LNCS, vol. 1139, pp. 107–121. Springer, Heidelberg (1996)
8. Marchiori, M.: On deterministic conditional rewriting. Technical Report Computation Structures Group Memo 405. MIT (1997)
9. Nagele, J., Thiemann, R.: Certification of confluence proofs using. In: Proc. 3rd IWC, pp. 19–23 (2014)
10. Nipkow, T., Paulson, L.C., Wenzel, M.: Isabelle/HOL. LNCS, vol. 2283. Springer, Heidelberg (2002)
11. Nishida, N.: Transformational Approach to Inverse Computation in Term Rewriting. PhD thesis, Nagoya University (2004)
12. Nishida, N., Sakai, M., Sakabe, T.: Soundness of unravelings for conditional term rewriting systems via ultra-properties related to linearity. LMCS 8(3), 1–49 (2012)
13. Ohlebusch, E.: Transforming conditional rewrite systems with extra variables into unconditional systems. In: Ganzinger, H., McAllester, D., Voronkov, A. (eds.) LPAR 1999. LNCS, vol. 1705, pp. 111–130. Springer, Heidelberg (1999)

14. Ohlebusch, E.: Termination of logic programs: Transformational methods revisited. AAECC 12(1–2), 73–116 (2001)
15. Ohlebusch, E.: Advanced Topics in Term Rewriting. Springer (2002)
16. Ohlebusch, E., Claves, C., Marché, C.: TALP: A tool for the termination analysis of logic programs. In: Bachmair, L. (ed.) RTA 2000. LNCS, vol. 1833, pp. 270–273. Springer, Heidelberg (2000)
17. Sternagel, T., Middeldorp, A.: Conditional confluence (System description). In: Dowek, G. (ed.) RTA-TLCA 2014. LNCS, vol. 8560, pp. 456–465. Springer, Heidelberg (2014)
18. Thiemann, R., Sternagel, C.: Certification of termination proofs using. In: Berghofer, S., Nipkow, T., Urban, C., Wenzel, M. (eds.) TPHOLs 2009. LNCS, vol. 5674, pp. 452–468. Springer, Heidelberg (2009)

Proofs and Reconstructions

Nik Sultana[1], Christoph Benzmüller[2], and Lawrence C. Paulson[1]

[1] Computer Lab, Cambridge University
[2] Department of Mathematics and Computer Science, Freie Universität Berlin

Abstract. Implementing proof reconstruction is difficult because it involves symbolic manipulations of formal objects whose representation varies between different systems. It requires significant knowledge of the source and target systems. One cannot simply re-target to another logic. We present a modular proof reconstruction system with separate components, specifying their behaviour and describing how they interact. This system is demonstrated and evaluated through an implementation to reconstruct proofs generated by Leo-II and Satallax in Isabelle/HOL, and is shown to work better than the current method of rediscovering proofs using a select set of provers.

Keywords: Proof reconstruction, Higher-order logic, Abstract machines.

1 Introduction

The case for interfacing logic tools together has been made countless times in the literature, but it is still an important research question. There are various logics and tools for carrying out formal developments, but practitioners still lament the difficulty of reliably exchanging mathematical data between tools.

Writing proof-translation tools is hard. The problem has both a theoretical side (to ensure that the translation is adequate) and a practical side (to ensure that the translation is feasible and usable). Moreover, the source and target proof formats might be less documented than desired (or even necessary), and this adds a dash of reverse-engineering to what should be a system integration task.

We suggest that writing such tools can be made easier by relying on a suitable modular framework. Modularity can be used to *isolate* the translation of different kinds of formulas, inferences, and logics from one another. This has significant practical benefits. First, the translations can be developed separately. Second, if the reconstruction of an inference fails, it does not affect the reconstruction of other inferences in the proof. This makes it easier to localise debugging efforts. Third, it improves usability. The diversity between proof systems means that inference-specific code can hardly ever be reused to reconstruct proofs from other theorem provers. Thus, proof reconstruction is difficult to scale to reconstruct proofs from different systems. The framework carves out the functionality that *can* be reused between systems. This code is often fairly general, and used to store and query formulas, inferences, and their metadata. We believe that

© Springer International Publishing Switzerland 2015
C. Lutz and S. Ranise (Eds.): FroCoS 2015, LNAI 9322, pp. 256–271, 2015.
DOI: 10.1007/978-3-319-24246-0_16

this divide-and-conquer approach is crucial to ease the implementation of proof reconstruction for different systems.

In this paper we propose a framework structured as a compiler. The compiler's target is specified as an abstract proof-building machine, which captures essential features of the target logic. This framework is designed to be efficient and extensible. Both compiler and abstract machine are implemented as an extension of the Isabelle/HOL proof assistant [14], to import proofs produced by the Leo-II [4] and Satallax [7] theorem provers.

Paper structure. The series of functions applied to a proof in our framework is outlined in §2. Our abstract model of a proof translator is described in §3, before returning to describe our framework in more detail in §4. Our implementation is described and evaluated in §5, before contrasting with related work in §6. We conclude in §7 with a description of what we learned from this project.

2   Reconstruction Workflow

Proof reconstruction consists of a series of steps, or workflow, applied to some representation of a proof. As a result of this workflow, a proof in a *source* logic is transformed into a proof (of the same theorem) in the *target* logic.

Before giving a detailed description of the workflow in later sections, we summarise our framework by outlining what needs to be implemented at each step of the translation. If an implementation of the framework already exists, then this description summarises what needs to be added or changed to translate proofs between different theorem provers.

1. **Parse the proof.**
2. **Interpret the logical signature.** We use a mapping from *types* and *constants* of the source logic, into types and constants of the target logic. This mapping might not be total if the source language cannot be fully interpreted in the target language. This mapping is lifted to map terms and formulas from the source to target. If one of the logics is not typed, then suitable encodings could be used [5].
3. **Analyse and transform the proof.** We often want to change the representation of the proof before translating it, to remove redundant information, or restore information that was not included when the proof's representation was produced.
4. **Generate a trace.** We linearise the proof into a series of inferences. These inferences are changed into instructions to an abstract proof-building machine, which we describe in the next section.
5. **Emulate inferences.** There are two kinds of *interpretations* at play when translating proofs. The first kind was encountered in step 2, when we interpreted expressions, mapping them from the source to the target language. The second kind of interpretation, which we call *emulation*, involves interpreting *inferences* of formulas, from the source to the target logic. As a result of emulation, we generate a finite set of admissible rules in the target logic.

This set forms a calculus that will be complete for the purpose of translating the source proof into the target logic.

6. **Play the trace.** This is done on the abstract machine, and supported by the emulated rules, to yield a proof in the target logic.

To use our framework, one must implement each of these steps. To handle a new source language we must change steps 1-5. Step 6 provides an interface to the target logic, in the form of an abstract proof-building machine. This machine is an intermediate target in our framework, between the source and target logics. We describe this machine next before describing the rest of the workflow in detail.

3   Cut Machines

The key observation of our approach is that while proof search abhors the cut rule [2], proof translation benefits from it. We describe a simple abstract machine for mapping proofs from one logic into another. It serves as an abstract model of proof translation. A similar method was used by de Nivelle [10] to describe the generation of proof terms that validate clausifications. It is also inspired by how generic proof checking is done in Isabelle [15].

The purpose of using such a machine in our framework is to isolate the source and target logics. We believe that this will make it easier to modify or repurpose the front-end and back-end of implementations of the framework, to reconstruct proofs from, or to, different logics. Such modifications would not affect other parts of the framework; this is inspired by how compilers are structured.

A *cut machine* is defined in terms of two features:

1. The machine's **state** consists of a tuple (ρ, σ, F), where ρ is a finite set of ground assumption sequents (that can include axioms of a particular theory). Symbol σ represents a stack of proof *subgoal* sequents, and F is the goal formula. Proving all the subgoals is sufficient for proving the goal. The proofs presented to the cut machine are translated to the target system. Translating the proofs of all the subgoals is sufficient for translating the proof of the goal.

2. **Instructions** given to the machine may consist of the following:
   - 'PROVE F' states that F is the goal formula. A goal formula may only be set once per proof.
   - 'CUT r' applies the sequent $r \in \rho$ to the stack of subgoals in the machine's state. This will be described in more detail below.
   - 'END' asserts that a machine is in a terminal state. A terminal state is one where the subgoal stack σ is empty. The goal formula F in that state has been shown to follow from ρ using the instructions presented to the machine, which result in a proof in the target logic.

We call them 'cut machines' because they mainly rely on applying instances of the Cut rule to splice together inferences. These are inferences in the target logic that emulate the inferences made in the source logic proof. Splicing together the emulated inferences produces a proof in the target logic. Specifically, consider the instruction 'CUT r', where $r \in \rho$ is a sequent, such that $r = \frac{A_1,\ldots,A_n}{B}$. (We overload the rule notation to express sequents, since the resulting notation is more pleasant to read. We use the symbol $\vdash_\rho$ to denote the finite proof system contained in ρ.) Then 'CUT r' can be interpreted as the following rule:

$$\frac{\vdash_\rho \frac{A_1,\ldots,A_n}{B} \qquad \vdash_\rho A_1 \qquad \ldots \qquad \vdash_\rho A_n}{\vdash_\rho B}$$

Let the symbol $\rhd$ represent the single-step transition relation between states. We will use '$-$' to describe an empty stack, and right-associative '$:$' to describe the push operation. The formal semantics of the machine's instructions are as follows:

$$\text{PROVE } F: \quad (\rho, -, \text{True}) \rhd (\rho, F, F)$$

$$\text{CUT } r: \quad (\rho, B:\sigma, F) \rhd (\rho, A_1:\ldots:A_n:\sigma, F)$$
$$\text{where } r \in \rho \text{ and } r = \frac{A_1,\ldots,A_n}{B}$$

$$\text{END}: \quad (\rho, -, F) \rhd (\rho, -, F).$$

A *cut program* consists of a finite sequence of instructions. A *well-formed* cut program consists of a single PROVE instruction, zero or more CUT instructions, and finally a single END. An *initial state* consists of any state of the form $(\rho, -, \text{True})$. A *terminal state* consists of any state of the form $(\rho, -, F)$.

A cut program describes the proof of some statement $\vdash_\rho F$ in the source logic, and the cut machine uses this description to build a proof in the target logic. Note that a cut program without a PROVE instruction only describes the tautology $\vdash_\rho$ True. A cut machine running a well-formed cut program can get stuck in two ways: (i) when executing 'CUT r' if $r \notin \rho$ or if the conclusion of r does not match the top element in σ, or (ii) when executing END if the machine is not in a terminal state.

3.1   Validating the Model

Use of the model relies on the assumption that ρ contains all the rules needed by the cut program. The finite set ρ contains a restricted inference system, consisting of inference rules in the target logic. This set is a parameter to the model, and the generation of these rules takes place externally—this will involve emulating the inference rules of the source logic in terms of the target logic, as described in §4.4.

A cut program that does not get stuck is called *well-going*. Provided that a suitable ρ exists, the model has the following properties. Provided it is given a well-going cut program, the cut machine has the following invariant: if the subgoals are valid, then the goal is valid too. We can also show that if a cut program reaches a terminal state then its proof goal is valid. Thus a well-going cut program always produces a theorem in the target logic. Moreover, this can be verified by inspecting a proof in the target logic.

3.2 Using the Model

This section will describe how this model interacts with the workflow described in §2. Let L_1 represent a source logic, and L_2 represent a target logic. 'Logic' here is used to describe essentially the syntactical features of a logic: the syntax of its formulas, and the formation rules of its proofs. To use the model we require three functions:

1. A mapping from formulas of L_1 into formulas of L_2, such that semantics is preserved. We rely on the interpretation of formulas for this, mentioned in point 2 in §2, and described further in §4.3.
2. A mapping from *inferences* in the source proof to inferences in the target logic. We call this mapping an *emulation*. This was mentioned in point 5 in §2, and will be described further in §4.4.

   The resulting inferences are not necessarily primitive inferences—they could be admissible rules. These rules make up the contents of ρ, one of the parameters of the machine described in this section.
3. A compiler that takes proofs encoded in L_1 and produces a cut program. This was mentioned in point 4 in §2, and will be described further in §4.5, which includes example output of such a compiler.

If the functions above are total and preserve semantic properties, then any proof in the source logic can be translated into a proof in the target logic. The translation can be carried out by running the cut program on an implementation of the cut machine.

3.3 Extending the Model

Reliance on the cut rule gives this framework its generality. A cut machine can be specialised by lifting features of the source logic to the level of the machine. This involves extending the definition of the machine and its instruction set. The lifted feature would then be simulated at the machine level, like the CUT instruction, rather than relying on opaque derivations in ρ.

This can be useful for features such as *splitting* [21]. Recall that splitting is a rule scheme used in clausal calculi to make clauses smaller. We will base the description of splitting on the implementation of this concept in Leo-II. Without loss of generality, we will look at an example starting with a binary clause $\{A, B\}$ such that A and B do not share free variables. We can split this clause into singleton clauses $\{A\}$ and $\{B\}$, but separate refutations must be obtained for each element of the split—that is, $\{A\}$ cannot be used in a refutation derived from $\{B\}$, and vice-versa.

Using the current definition of the machine, such a rule could be used outside the machine to populate ρ (remember that ρ is a parameter to the model) with the rule $\frac{A \vee B}{\mathsf{False}}$. We would then use this rule via CUT as before.

Instead, we could modify the machine's definition to *lift* the rule to the machine level, to specialise the machine to support splitting.

Logically, this is the following rule:

$$\frac{\vdash_\rho \frac{A}{\mathsf{False}} \qquad \vdash_\rho \frac{B}{\mathsf{False}} \qquad \vdash_\rho A \vee B}{\vdash_\rho \mathsf{False}}$$

The semantics of the new instruction $\text{SPLIT}(A \vee B)$ is:

$$\left(\rho, \ \frac{C}{\mathsf{False}} : \sigma, \ F \right) \quad \triangleright \quad \left(\rho, \ \frac{C \wedge A}{\mathsf{False}} : \frac{C \wedge B}{\mathsf{False}} : \frac{C}{A \vee B} : \sigma, \ F \right)$$

Such a machine has been implemented for interpreting Leo-II proofs in Isabelle/HOL. Interpreting Satallax proofs only relies on the basic machine, without splitting.

4 Framework

Our approach to proof reconstruction is made up of two phases: the *shunting* and *emulation* of inferences. The first phase (steps 1-4 in §2) transforms a proof and generates a cut program, while the second phase (step 5 in §2) assists in the execution of this program. The second phase populates the set ρ that will be used when executing the cut program (step 6 in §2). Executing the cut program will yield a proof in the target logic.

The two phases are related, but have different purposes:

- The *shunting* of inferences involves (globally) meaning-preserving transformations being applied to a proof, to facilitate its reconstruction.
- Emulation maps inferences of one calculus to chains of inferences in another calculus. In our implementation, the inferences made by Leo-II and Satallax are emulated as Isabelle/HOL-admissible rules.

It is advantageous to separate the two phases since some details of one can be encapsulated from the other. Furthermore, the emulation of each inference rule takes place independently of the others. Failure to reconstruct an inference will mean that we cannot reconstruct the entire proof, but would *not* affect the reconstruction of other inferences in the proof. This isolation in emulation is advantageous since it localises debugging, and could allow humans to assist in reconstructing inference rules that currently cannot be emulated by the implementation.

We will concretise our description of the framework to a specific proof being translated between two specific logics: from the classical higher-order logic clausal calculus of Leo-II to the classical higher-order logic of Isabelle/HOL. Despite their conceptual similarity, non-trivial manipulation is required to have the proofs of Leo-II checked by Isabelle/HOL: some information needs to be pruned away, and other information reconstructed, as will be explained below. Despite the specificity of this explanation, this method is applicable to other varieties of formal logic, such as the higher-order tableau calculus used by Satallax.

For a running example, let us take the TPTP problem SEU553^2. In this problem, we use individuals, whom we represent by the type symbol ι, to model sets of elements. The powerset function therefore has the type $\iota \to \iota$. The problem conjectures that if two arbitrary sets, A and B, containing individuals, are equal, then their powersets are equal too. This is formalised as follows:

$$\forall A : \iota, B : \iota. \ A = B \longrightarrow \mathsf{powerset}\,A = \mathsf{powerset}\,B$$

Leo-II proves this to be a theorem. Its proof output is shown in Figure 1, and rendered as a graph in Figure 2.

4.1 Proof Generation

Böhme and Weber [6] recommend that proofs intended for reconstruction should be sufficiently detailed to facilitate this task. We came to appreciate the validity of their advice based on our experience with different versions of Leo-II's proof output. By default, Leo-II proofs may contain instances of *compound rules*, such as those for clausification and unification. Using compound rules often results in shorter proofs since the details of member inferences are elided. Unfortunately, this loses information that can be very expensive to recompute. This is described in more detail and quantified in the first author's dissertation [19]. Fortunately Leo-II can be instructed to expand compound rules into primitive inferences in its proof output. We found this to be essential. Satallax does not use compound rules in its proofs.

4.2 Formula Interpretation

After the proof is parsed, its logical signature—consisting of a set of types, and a set of constants—is extracted. The signature is interpreted in the target logic—in this case, it consists of the types ι and $\iota \to \iota$, and the constants $\mathsf{powerset}$, $\mathsf{sK1_A}$, and $\mathsf{sK2_{SY2}}$, following the signature described on lines 1-3 in the proof shown in Figure 1. The constants $\mathsf{sK1_A}$ and $\mathsf{sK2_{SY2}}$ do not appear in the problem's formulation, because they are Skolem constants [11], and they are scoped in the proof, not in the original problem.

After interpreting the signature, the formulas contained in inferences (lines 4-29) are interpreted in the target logic relative to this signature. This leaves us with a skeleton of the proof consisting of the inferred formulas, but so far does not include the inferences themselves, other than metadata—such as the names of inference rules, and their parameters (e.g., which inferences they derive from).

This step is identical for both Satallax and Leo-II proofs encoded in TPTP. The approach will differ significantly for the two provers in the next steps, before converging again when the cut programs (resulting from their proofs) are executed.

4.3 Proof Analysis and Transformation

Some preprocessing and transformation of inferences is carried out on the proof skeleton. The inferences form a directed acyclic graph where the vertices are

```
1   - thf( tp_powerset, type, (powerset: ($i>$i))).

2   - thf( tp_sK1_A, type, ( sK1_A : $i)).

3   - thf( tp_sK2_SY2, type, ( sK2_SY2 : $i)).

4 ★ thf( 1 , conjecture, (![A:$i,B:$i]: ((A = B) => ((powerset@A) = (powerset@B)))),
5     file('SEU553^2.p',powerset__Cog)).

6 ★ thf( 2 , negated_conjecture, (((![A:$i,B:$i]: ((A = B) => ((powerset@A) = (powerset@B))))=$false)),
7     inference(negate_conjecture,[status(cth)],[1])).

8 ★ thf( 3 , plain, (((![A:$i,B:$i]: ((A = B) => ((powerset@A) = (powerset@B))))=$false)),
9     inference(unfold_def,[status(thm)],[2])).

10 ★ thf( 4 , plain, (((![SY2:$i]: (( sK1_A = SY2) => ((powerset@ sK1_A ) = (powerset@SY2))))=$false)),
11     inference(extcnf_forall_neg,[status(esa)],[3])).

12 ★ thf( 5 , plain, (((( sK1_A = sK2_SY2 ) => ((powerset@ sK1_A ) = (powerset@ sK2_SY2 )))=$false)),
13     inference(extcnf_forall_neg,[status(esa)],[4])).

14 ★ thf( 6 , plain, ((( sK1_A = sK2_SY2 )=$true)),
15     inference(standard_cnf,[status(thm)],[5])).

16 ★ thf( 7 , plain, (((powerset@ sK1_A ) = (powerset@ sK2_SY2 ))=$false)),
17     inference(standard_cnf,[status(thm)],[5])).

18 ★ thf( 8 , plain, (((~ ((powerset@ sK1_A ) = (powerset@ sK2_SY2 )))=$true)),
19     inference(polarity_switch,[status(thm)],[7])).

20 ★ thf( 9 , plain, ((( sK1_A = sK2_SY2 )=$true)),
21     inference(clause_copy,[status(thm)],[6])).

22 ★ thf( 10 , plain, (((~ ((powerset@ sK1_A ) = (powerset@ sK2_SY2 )))=$true)),
23     inference(clause_copy,[status(thm)],[8])).

24 ★ thf( 11 , plain, ((((powerset@ sK1_A ) = (powerset@ sK2_SY2 ))=$false)),
25     inference(extcnf_not_pos,[status(thm)],[10])).

26 ★ thf( 12 , plain, ((($false)=$true)),
27     inference(fo_atp_e,[status(thm)],[9,11])).

28 ★ thf( 13 , plain, ($false),
29     inference(solved_all_splits,[solved_all_splits(join,[]],[12])).
```

Fig. 1. Leo-II's proof of SEU553^2. Leo-II encodes its proofs in TPTP format [20], where each line is structured as follows: language(id, role, fmla, annotation), where the annotation is optional. Here the language is 'THF' [3], used to encode formulas in higher-order logic. Some information in the proof has been marked up: the grey-boxed text, such as tp_powerset and 1, are unique identifiers for inference steps; and the boxed text, consisting of sK1_A and sK2_SY2 are Skolem constants. Lines prefixed by a star ★ are annotation lines, and the underlined words in those lines are names of inference rules used by Leo-II.

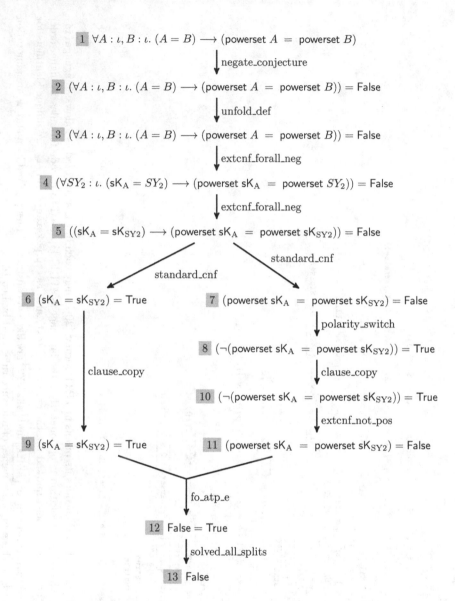

Fig. 2. Graph for Leo-II's proof of SEU553^2. Vertices consist of formulas derived during the proof, except for the topmost formula, labelled 1, which is obtain from the problem's formulation. The numeric labels adjacent to formulas, such as 1, are used by Leo-II to uniquely identify clauses it generates. We use these labels to index clauses during proof reconstruction. These labels correspond to the labels in Figure 1. Note that this proof contains inferences that do not materially advance the proof. We can see this between formulas 6 and 9, and between formulas 7-11. A simple static analysis could erase formulas 9 and 8-11, and adjust the edges from 6 and 7 to point to 12.

formulas, and the edges are labelled with inference names. The proof from Figure 1 is shown as such a graph in Figure 2.

The analysis and transformation of the inferences might be done to simplify the proof, or to facilitate further analyses or transformations. There are three proof transformations that we found to be useful for processing Leo-II proofs:

1. *Eliminating redundant parts of the proof.* Occasionally Leo-II includes redundant chains of inferences that do not materially contribute to the proof. We can see two examples of this in Figure 2, as explained in its caption.
2. *Extracting subproofs related to splitting.* Recall from §3.3 that each subproof of a split yields a refutation, and the set of inferences made during a subproof of a split is kept apart from the inferences made in other splits. Each subproof is used to construct a lemma that produces a premise to the disjunction-elimination rule.
3. *Separating instantiation from other inferences.* Leo-II sometimes overloads inferences with instantiation of variables. This makes it harder to emulate an inference. Rather than emulating this complex behaviour, we transform the proof to extract instantiations into separate inferences. This allows us to handle instantiations and other inferences separately.

A useful transformation in Satallax consisted of inlining assumption formulas to produce the actual inferences made at each step. Satallax does not explicitly encode an inference formula. Instead, each proof line produced by Satallax refers to formulas involved in that inference, and the formulas are stored separately. Combining these to give the actual inference is straightforward.

A useful analysis to carry out on both Leo-II and Satallax proofs involves discovering the definitions of Skolem constants. These definitions are necessary to emulate their ∃-elimination inferences. Both provers' proofs generally contain the declarations of Skolem constants (as can be seen for Leo-II on lines 2 and 3 of Figure 1), but not their definitions. These definitions are implicit in the proof, and can be extracted by analysing the syntax. Skolemisation occurs on lines 4 and 5 in Figure 1, and the equations extracted by our analysis are:

$$\mathsf{sK1_A} = (\varepsilon A : \iota.\ (\forall B : \iota.\ (A = B) \longrightarrow (\mathsf{powerset}\ A = \mathsf{powerset}\ B)) = \mathsf{False})$$
$$\mathsf{sK2_B} = (\varepsilon B : \iota.\ (\mathsf{sK1_A} = B) \longrightarrow (\mathsf{powerset}\ \mathsf{sK1_A} = \mathsf{powerset}\ B) = \mathsf{False})$$

These are then added as axioms to the theory. One might feel justifiably squeamish about adding axioms to a theory, but the axioms concerned here are definitional axioms for Skolem constants.

Note that here we assume that the target theory validates the Axiom of Choice (and can interpret Hilbert's ε operator). This arises from the specific features of our implementation targetting Isabelle/HOL (which is a classical logic) and it is not a feature or requirement of the cut-machine model.

4.4   Emulation of Inference Rules

We now turn to the inferences themselves. Inferences are emulated to yield admissible rules in the target calculus. Emulation might be implemented using rule schemes or proof-building functions, which could consist of calls to provers whose output we can already reconstruct. This was done previously between Leo-II, Satallax and Isabelle/HOL [18]. For instance, the Leo-II inference described in line 26 of Figure 1 can be emulated by the Isabelle/HOL-admissible rule

$$\frac{(\mathsf{sK1}_A = \mathsf{sK2}_{SY2}) = \mathsf{True}\ \wedge\ (\mathsf{powerset}\ \mathsf{sK1}_A = \mathsf{powerset}\ \mathsf{sK2}_{SY2}) = \mathsf{False}}{\mathsf{False} = \mathsf{True}}$$

where, as specified in Figure 1, the first premise is contributed from the conclusion of the inference labelled 9 (occurring in line 20), and the second premise from the inference labelled 11 (line 24). The proof text also indicates that this inference was made using the E theorem prover [17], with which Leo-II cooperates. The resulting rule in Isabelle/HOL is labelled "12", consistent with the name used in the TPTP encoding of the proof. Once all inference rules have been emulated, then the proof skeleton has been extended to include all the information necessary to produce a proof in the target logic.

4.5   Generating a Cut Program

So far we have imported all of the proof information—consisting of signature, formulas, and inferences—from the source logic into the target logic. We now need to combine the inferences to reconstruct the theorem in the target logic. The proof graph is traversed depth-first, to produce a trace, or cut program, of the proof. Running this on an implementation of a cut machine (described in §3) should produce the reconstructed proof.

For the example proof above, the program consists of 18 instructions, essentially a traversal of Figure 2:

```
1   [Cut "13", Cut "12", Unconjoin,
2     Cut "11", Cut "10", Cut "8", Cut "7",
3       Cut "5", Cut "4", Cut "3", Assumed,
4     Cut "9", Cut "6",
5       Cut "5", Cut "4", Cut "3", Assumed,
6   End]
```

4.6   Executing a Cut Program

The cut program is interpreted according to the semantics given in §3. We use some additional instructions in our implementation. We describe them next; they can both be seen in the example code snippet given above.

The *Unconjoin* instruction eliminates a conjunction, and behaves like the right-conjunction rule in the sequent calculus. This is needed since the proof graph is not a tree in general—it recombines. For example, this command is applied to step 12, formalised in Isabelle/HOL in §4.4, to break up the conjoined premises into two premises. This step consumes one subgoal, and produces two subgoals. Each subgoal relates to a path to the root of the graph. The root of the graph consists of the conjecture formula. Finally, the *Assumed* instruction discharges a subgoal using an identical element of ρ.

Note that in the program shown earlier, lines 3 and 5 are duplicates. We could extract a lemma that fuses together the contents of line 3 into another admissible rule, then replace line 5 with an application of this lemma. There are different ways of implementing this. One way is a proof analysis that produces commands to create and use a lemma (in which case the machine needs to be extended to interpret these commands). Another is a proof transformation that adds the lemmas to ρ and simply produces a 'Cut' command to use the lemma.

For both Leo-II and Satallax we execute this program on the double-negated conjecture, since they both work by refutation. If all emulation steps are successful, then the execution should yield an Isabelle/HOL theorem corresponding to that proved by Leo-II or Satallax.

5 Implementation

We implemented this system as an extension to Isabelle, and it consists of around 8600 lines (including comments) of Standard ML and Isabelle definitions—such as the formalisation of Leo-II and Satallax inference rules as Isabelle rules.[1] The cut machine described in this paper is implemented as an interface to Isabelle's kernel; ultimately all the reconstructed proofs are validated by Isabelle's kernel.

The preceding sections described the design of the framework and its components, and how it was implemented to import Leo-II and Satallax proofs into Isabelle/HOL. These are the limitations of the implemented prototype:

1. Currently we do not handle the rules for the Axiom of Choice in both Leo-II and Satallax. Emulating those rules is a natural extension to this work.
2. Recall that Leo-II collaborates with E to find a refutation. In our implementation, E's proofs are re-found by using Metis [12], whose proofs can already be reconstructed in Isabelle/HOL. Reconstructing E's proofs separately, and reconstructing hybrid Leo-II+E proofs, are discussed elsewhere [19].
3. Our Satallax reconstruction code currently does not support the use of axioms in proofs. Supporting axioms is logically straightforward: using an axiom involves drawing it from ρ and adding a Cut step for that axiom.

5.1 Evaluation

A set of test proofs was first obtained by running Leo-II 1.6 for 30 seconds on all THF problems in the TPTP 5.4.0 problem set. In these experiments, Leo-II cooperated with version 1.8 of the E theorem prover. Leo-II produced 1537 proofs. We used a repository version of Isabelle2013, the versions of Metis and Z3 packaged for Isabelle2013, and the experiments were done on a 1.6GHz Intel Core 2 Duo box, with 2GB RAM, and running Linux.

---

[1] All the code can be downloaded from
http://www.cl.cam.ac.uk/~ns441/files/frocos_2015_code.tgz

The translator was then run with a timeout of 10 seconds. By using Metis to emulate E, 1262 (82.1%) proofs were reconstructed entirely. If we treat E as an oracle (i.e., assuming E is sound, and that we have a perfect reconstruction for its proofs), then the number of reconstructed proofs increases to 1442 (93.8%). Currently, in Sledgehammer [16]—Isabelle's interface for external provers—Leo-II proofs are reconstructed by refinding using Metis and Z3 [9]. On the same problem set, Metis and Z3 were able to reconstruct 57.3% and 68.9% of the proofs respectively. Our scripts and data for this evaluation are available online.[2]

To evaluate the reconstruction of Satallax proofs we ran Satallax 2.8 in proof-generating mode on all THF problems in the TPTP 6.1.0 problem set, with a 30-second timeout for each problem. This set contains 3036 THF problems, 2458 of which are classified as theorems. Satallax provided proofs for 1860 THF problems. After removing proofs that involve axioms (because of the limitation described in §5 point 3) we are left with 1383 proofs.

Our reconstruction code was then run on each of these proofs, with a timeout of 10 seconds, and succeeded in reconstructing 1149 proofs (82%). On the same problem set, Metis and Z3 were able to reconstruct 51% and 67% of the proofs respectively. We used a repository version of Isabelle2014, and ran these experiments on a 2GHz Intel Core i7 machine, with 16GB RAM, and running OSX. Our scripts and data for this evaluation are available online.[3]

6   Related Work

There is a fairly large literature on proof translation and reconstruction. We focus on two recent projects that are similar in spirit and setup to ours. A more detailed survey is given in the first author's dissertation [19].

Keller [13] uses an extension of the Calculus of Constructions (as implemented in Coq) as the host logic for theorems proved by SAT and SMT solvers. She develops a trusted SMT proof checker and uses it to check proofs produced by other SMT solvers, or to interpret those proofs in Coq's logic. Keller's checker follows the design of an SMT solver: it mediates between theory-specific solvers to refute a conjecture. The theory-specific solvers in Keller's work consist of theory-specific decision-procedures implemented using Coq. In order to use Keller's system, a proof from an SMT solver must first be translated into a form that can be processed by the trusted checker. (We think that this is not unlike the generation of cut programs, at least in spirit.) This is done as a preprocessing step, and this realises an embedding of the source calculus in the target calculus. The pure logic component of SMT is identical to that of SAT: proofs consist of refutations expressed using resolution. This means that the pure logic component of Keller's system is much simpler than the systems developed in our work: for one thing, SMT lacks quantification. In a related respect, Keller's system is more complex than the systems developed in our work, since Keller's system supports a range of theories—as is expected in SMT. Currently, the state of the

---

[2] http://www.cl.cam.ac.uk/~ns441/files/recon_framework_results.tgz
[3] http://www.cl.cam.ac.uk/~ns441/files/frocos_2015_eval.tgz

art in higher-order theorem proving does not interpret any theories other than equality [1].

Chihani et al. [8] describe an architecture based on higher-order logic programming for checking proof certificates. These certificates can take different forms, depending on the proof calculus of the source logic they relate to. Checking these certificates involves interpreting them into a form that can be checked as a proof in LKU, a linear logic they devised.

The system designed by Chihani et al. consists of three components: The *kernel* is an implementation of LKU's proof system; the *client* is the proof-producing theorem prover, which encodes its proofs in some format chosen by the authors of the theorem prover; and *clerks and experts* are two types of agent-like functions that carry out proof construction in LKU. They correspond to the two phases of proof-construction in a focussed proof system. This component serves to interpret the proof certificate into an LKU proof, that can then be checked by the kernel.

Together, clerks and experts seem to constitute an embedding of the source logic into a fragment of LKU. The clerks and experts seem to carry out a similar role to that of Keller's preprocessor, described above. (Recall that a different preprocessor might be needed for each theorem prover whose proofs we want to import.) In our work, this role is carried out by the emulations of inference rules, described in §4.4.

Using Keller's approach does not require the embedding to be described in the host system (i.e., Coq in that case). In contrast, the approach taken by Chihani et al., and us, do require this: emulation takes inferences in the source logic and produces inferences in the target logic.

7   Conclusions

A modular framework for translating proofs between two logics, based on cut machines, can accomplish efficient and robust proof reconstruction. However, detailed proofs are essential; otherwise, reconstructing proofs requires excessive search, which can be very expensive. Our implementation of the framework outperforms the existing method for reconstructing Leo-II and Satallax proofs in Isabelle/HOL.

Modularity is achieved partly by breaking up the translation process into steps (such as interpreting formulas, and emulating inferences) but also by using an abstract proof-building machine to mediate between the source and target logics. Our modular design is intended to facilitate reuse and modification. The extent to which this is the case remains to be seen, but we are encouraged that similar concepts were used by Keller and Chihani et al.

Acknowledgments. We thank Trinity College, Cambridge University Computer Lab, Cambridge Philosophical Society, and DAAD (the German Academic Exchange Service) for funding support. The anonymous reviewers and Chad Brown provided feedback, for which we are grateful.

References

1. Benzmüller, C.: Equality and Extensionality in Higher-Order Theorem Proving. PhD thesis, Naturwissenschaftlich-Technische Fakultät I, Saarland University (1999)
2. Benzmüller, C., Brown, C.E., Kohlhase, M.: Cut-Simulation and Impredicativity. Logical Methods in Computer Science 5(1:6), 1–21 (2009)
3. Benzmüller, C.E., Rabe, F., Sutcliffe, G.: THF0 – The core TPTP language for classical higher-order logic. In: Armando, A., Baumgartner, P., Dowek, G. (eds.) IJCAR 2008. LNCS (LNAI), vol. 5195, pp. 491–506. Springer, Heidelberg (2008)
4. Benzmüller, C., Theiss, F., Paulson, L.C., Fietzke, A.: LEO-II – A cooperative automatic theorem prover for higher-order logic. In: Armando, A., Baumgartner, P., Dowek, G. (eds.) IJCAR 2008. LNCS (LNAI), vol. 5195, pp. 162–170. Springer, Heidelberg (2008)
5. Blanchette, J.C.: Automatic Proofs and Refutations for Higher-Order Logic. PhD thesis, Institut für Informatik, Technische Universität München (2012)
6. Böhme, S., Weber, T.: Designing proof formats: A user's perspective. In: Fontaine, P., Stump, A. (eds.) International Workshop on Proof Exchange for Theorem Proving, pp. 27–32 (2011)
7. Brown, C.E.: Satallax: An automatic higher-order prover. In: Gramlich, B., Miller, D., Sattler, U. (eds.) IJCAR 2012. LNCS, vol. 7364, pp. 111–117. Springer, Heidelberg (2012)
8. Chihani, Z., Miller, D., Renaud, F.: Foundational proof certificates in first-order logic. In: Bonacina, M.P. (ed.) CADE 2013. LNCS, vol. 7898, pp. 162–177. Springer, Heidelberg (2013)
9. de Moura, L., Bjørner, N.S.: Z3: An efficient SMT solver. In: Ramakrishnan, C.R., Rehof, J. (eds.) TACAS 2008. LNCS, vol. 4963, pp. 337–340. Springer, Heidelberg (2008)
10. de Nivelle, H.: Extraction of proofs from clausal normal form transformation. In: Bradfield, J.C. (ed.) CSL 2002. LNCS, vol. 2471, pp. 584–598. Springer, Heidelberg (2002)
11. Dowek, G.: Skolemization in simple type theory: the logical and the theoretical points of view. In: Benzmüller, C., Brown, C.E., Siekmann, J., Statman, R. (eds.) Festschrift in Honour of Peter B. Andrews on his 70th Birthday. Studies in Logic and the Foundations of Mathematics. College Publications (2009)
12. Hurd, J.: First-order proof tactics in higher-order logic theorem provers. In: Archer, M., Di Vito, B., Muñoz, C. (eds.) Design and Application of Strategies/Tactics in Higher Order Logics, number CP-2003-212448 in NASA Technical Reports, pp. 56–68, September 2003
13. Keller, C.: A Matter of Trust: Skeptical Communication Between Coq and External Provers. PhD thesis, École Polytechnique, June 2013
14. Nipkow, T., Paulson, L.C., Wenzel, M.: Isabelle/HOL. LNCS, vol. 2283. Springer, Heidelberg (2002)
15. Paulson, L.C.: Isabelle. LNCS, vol. 828. Springer, Heidelberg (1994)
16. Paulson, L.C., Blanchette, J.C.: Three years of experience with Sledgehammer, a practical link between automatic and interactive theorem provers. In: International Workshop on the Implementation of Logics. EasyChair (2010)
17. Schulz, S.: E – A Brainiac Theorem Prover. Journal of AI Communications 15(2/3), 111–126 (2002)

18. Sultana, N., Blanchette, J.C., Paulson, L.C.: LEO-II and Satallax on the Sledge-hammer test bench. Journal of Applied Logic (2012)
19. Sultana, N.: Higher-order proof translation. PhD thesis, Computer Laboratory, University of Cambridge, Available as Tech Report UCAM-CL-TR-867 (2015)
20. Sutcliffe, G.: The TPTP Problem Library and Associated Infrastructure: The FOF and CNF Parts, v3.5.0. Journal of Automated Reasoning 43(4), 337–362 (2009)
21. Weidenbach, C.: Combining superposition, sorts and splitting. In: Robinson, J.A., Voronkov, A. (eds.) Handbook of Automated Reasoning, vol. 2, pp. 1965–2013. MIT Press (2001)

Combination Methods

A Rewriting Approach to the Combination of Data Structures with Bridging Theories

Paula Chocron[1], Pascal Fontaine[2,*], and Christophe Ringeissen[2]

[1] IIIA-CSIC, Bellaterra, Catalonia, Spain
[2] INRIA, Université de Lorraine and LORIA, Nancy, France

Abstract. We introduce a combination method à la Nelson-Oppen to solve the satisfiability problem modulo a non-disjoint union of theories connected with bridging functions. The combination method is particularly useful to handle verification conditions involving functions defined over inductive data structures. We investigate the problem of determining the data structure theories for which this combination method is sound and complete. Our completeness proof is based on a rewriting approach where the bridging function is defined as a term rewrite system, and the data structure theory is given by a basic congruence relation. Our contribution is to introduce a class of data structure theories that are combinable with a disjoint target theory via an inductively defined bridging function. This class includes the theory of equality, the theory of absolutely free data structures, and all the theories in between. Hence, our non-disjoint combination method applies to many classical data structure theories admitting a rewrite-based satisfiability procedure.

1 Introduction

The modular construction of reasoning engines appears very often in logic and automated deduction, for instance to check whether a property still holds in a union of theories when this property holds in component theories. Working with signature-disjoint theories obviously simplifies the problem, e.g. in the Nelson-Oppen combination method where a satisfiability procedure for $T_1 \cup T_2$ is built from the satisfiability procedures for the two signature-disjoint theories T_1 and T_2. Even in that case, the signature-disjointness of T_1 and T_2 is not sufficient for the combination since additional "semantic" requirements on theories are required to get a complete satisfiability procedure. A first solution by Nelson and Oppen was to require stably infinite theories. This condition can be refined, and several other classes of *kind* theories have been recently investigated: shiny [20], polite [15] and gentle theories [10]. The Nelson-Oppen combination method is

* This work has been partially supported by the project ANR-13-IS02-0001 of the Agence Nationale de la Recherche, by the European Union Seventh Framework Programme under grant agreement no. 295261 (MEALS), and by the STIC AmSud MISMT.

C. Lutz and S. Ranise (Eds.): FroCoS 2015, LNAI 9322, pp. 275–290, 2015.
DOI: 10.1007/978-3-319-24246-0_17

now well-understood for disjoint unions of theories, and it is widely adopted to solve Satisfiability Modulo Theories (SMT) problems. It has become the core component of modern SMT solvers. But there is still an increasing demand on non-disjoint combinations. The extension of the Nelson-Oppen combination method to unions of non-disjoint theories has been already investigated during the last decade [11, 19]. This has led to the design of non-disjoint combination methods requiring some strong "semantic" assumptions on theories. However, these assumptions are difficult to meet in practical applications. For this reason, the use of non-disjoint combination methods in SMT solving is currently very limited.

We focus on simple techniques for non-disjoint combinations where the notions of polite and gentle theories [8] initially introduced for the disjoint case are also useful. In this paper, we consider a simple but meaningful non-disjoint case where the two theories T_1 and T_2 are connected by a *bridging* theory, whose axioms can be easily processed for any combined satisfiability problem. In this way, these non-disjoint combinations are reducible to disjoint ones. This avoids the need for complicated non-disjoint combination methods. Practical applications often involve a data structure theory T_1 and an arithmetic theory T_2. This particular union has been extensively studied, especially to combine an equational theorem prover processing (the axioms of) T_1 with an arithmetic solver for T_2 [7, 21]. This problem was first studied for disjoint combinations, but non-disjoint unions naturally arise when considering a bridging theory to relate the data structure theory T_1 to the arithmetic theory T_2, e.g. the length function for the data structure of lists [13, 14, 16]. The Ghilardi non-disjoint combination method [11] has been already applied to handle some connections between theories [3, 13, 14]. In [13, 14], the idea is to use superposition-based satisfiability procedures to process theory extensions of T_2. In that context, it is always a difficult and tedious task to design a new superposition calculus incorporating T_2 as a built-in theory.

In this paper, we develop a lightweight approach which is sufficient to handle the special case of bridging theories. This work is clearly inspired by the locality-based approach presented in [16] to handle bridging functions in local theory extensions. We consider the same problem by introducing a combination-based approach using a slight adaptation of the Nelson-Oppen disjoint combination method. Our approach has been initiated in [9] by studying the case of absolutely free data structures, with a particular focus on the adaptation required by the restriction to standard interpretations [6, 18, 22]. Like a locality-based satisfiability procedure applies to other theories of constructors [17], the combination method is actually applicable beyond the case of absolutely free data structures. In this paper, we investigate the constructor-based theories for which the combination method is sound and complete.

The main contribution of this paper is to identify a class of data structure theories for which our combination method is complete. In this class, theories are many-sorted, with disjoint sorts to denote respectively the data instances and the structure instances. Our combination method solves the satisfiability problem in a union of a data structure theory plus a target theory and a bridging theory. With this method, the target theory can be arbitrary. Actually, this is due to the fact that we are focusing on data structure theories that fulfill a form of politeness [12, 15]. Hence, our work can be considered as a way to extend the use of polite theories to some simple non-disjoint combinations. The class of data structure theories is clearly of practical interest since it includes well-known theories for which a rewriting approach to satisfiability can be successfully applied [1, 2]. In this class, one can find the theory of equality, the theory of (acyclic) lists, the theory of absolutely free data structures (with or without selectors).

The completeness of our combination method requires the construction of a combined model from the models available in the component theories. For that purpose, we introduce the notion of basic data structure theory, for which a satisfiable input admits a Herbrand model with a very particular *basic* congruence relation E. The originality of our approach is to define a bridging theory as a convergent term rewrite system F, and to analyse the interplay between F and E. The careful study of $F \cup E$ as a convergent rewrite system modulo E leads to the construction of the combined model.

Section 2 recalls the classical notations and concepts used for the equational reasoning and the combination problem. In Section 4, we present the class of *basic* data structure theories. Section 3 introduces a combination procedure for extensions of basic data structure theories with bridging functions. By using a rewriting approach, the completeness of this combination procedure is proved in Section 5. Finally, Section 6 reports directions for future work.

2   Preliminaries: Notations and Combinations

We assume an enumerable set of variables $\mathcal{V}$ and a first-order many-sorted signature Σ given by a set of sorts and sets of function and predicate symbols (equipped with an arity ar). Nullary function symbols are called constant symbols. We assume that, for each sort σ, the equality "$=_\sigma$" is a logical symbol that does not occur in Σ and that is always interpreted as the identity relation over (the interpretation of) σ; moreover, as a notational convention, we omit the subscript for sorts and we simply use the symbol $=$. The notions of Σ-terms, atomic Σ-formulas and first-order Σ-formulas are defined in the usual way. In particular an atomic formula is either an equality, or a predicate symbol applied to the right number of well-sorted terms. Formulas are built from atomic formulas, Boolean connectives ($\neg$, $\wedge$, $\vee$, $\Rightarrow$, $\equiv$), and quantifiers ($\forall$, $\exists$). A literal is an atomic formula or the negation of an atomic formula. A flat equality is either of the form $t_0 = t_1$ or $t_0 = f(t_1, \ldots, t_n)$ where each term $t_0, \ldots, t_n$ is a variable or a constant. A disequality $t_0 \neq t_1$ is flat when each term t_0, t_1 is a variable or a constant. A flat literal is either a flat equality or a flat disequality. An *arrangement* over a finite set of variables V is a maximal satisfiable set of well-sorted equalities and disequalities $x = y$ or $x \neq y$, with $x, y \in V$. Free variables are defined in the usual way, and the set of free variables of a formula φ is denoted by $Var(\varphi)$. Given a sort σ, $Var_\sigma(\varphi)$ denotes the set of variables of sort σ in $Var(\varphi)$. A formula with no free variables is closed, and a formula without variables is ground. A universal formula is a closed formula $\forall x_1 \ldots \forall x_n.\varphi$ where φ is quantifier-free. A (finite) Σ-theory is a (finite) set of closed Σ-formulas. Two theories are disjoint if no predicate symbol or function symbol appears in both respective signatures.

From the semantic side, a Σ-*interpretation* $\mathcal{I}$ comprises non-empty pairwise disjoint domains I_σ for every sort σ, a sort- and arity-matching total function $\mathcal{I}[f]$ for every function symbol f, a sort- and arity-matching predicate $\mathcal{I}[p]$ for every predicate symbol p, and an element $\mathcal{I}[x] \in I_\sigma$ for every variable x of sort σ. By extension, an interpretation defines a value in I_σ for every term of sort σ, and a truth value for every formula. We may write $\mathcal{I} \models \varphi$ whenever $\mathcal{I}[\varphi] = \top$. A Σ-structure is a Σ-interpretation over an empty set of variables. Given a Σ-interpretation $\mathcal{I}$ and signature $\Sigma' \subseteq \Sigma$, the Σ'-reduct of $\mathcal{I}$ is the Σ'-interpretation, denoted by $\mathcal{I}^{\Sigma'}$, obtained from $\mathcal{I}$ by restricting it to interpret only the symbols in Σ'.

A model of a formula (theory) is an interpretation that evaluates the formula (resp. all formulas in the theory) to true. A formula or theory is satisfiable (or consistent) if it has a model; it is unsatisfiable otherwise. A formula G is T-satisfiable if it is satisfiable in the theory T, that is, if $T \cup \{G\}$ is satisfiable. A T-model of G is a model of $T \cup \{G\}$. A formula G is T-unsatisfiable if it has no T-models. In our context, the T-satisfiability problem for any set of literals can be equivalently defined as establishing the consistency of $T \cup \{G\}$ for a set of ground literals G expressed over the signature extended with some fresh constants.

A theory T is *stably infinite* if any T-satisfiable set of literals is satisfiable in a model of T whose domain is infinite. A Σ-theory T can be equivalently defined as a pair $T = (\Sigma, \mathbf{A})$, where $\mathbf{A}$ is a class of Σ-structures, and given a signature $\Sigma' \subseteq \Sigma$, the Σ'-reduct of T is $T^{\Sigma'} = (\Sigma', \{\mathcal{A}^{\Sigma'} \mid \mathcal{A} \in \mathbf{A}\})$. Given a set of Σ-equalities E, the relation $=_E$ denotes the *equational theory of E* which is defined as the smallest relation including E which is closed by reflexivity, symmetry, transitivity, congruence and substitutivity. As usual, the equivalence classes of ground Σ-terms modulo E defines the Σ-structure of ground terms modulo E, denoted by $T(\Sigma)/=_E$. A term rewrite system R is a set of oriented equalities. A convergent term rewrite system R is defined in the usual way [4], and it implies the existence and the unicity of a normal form, denoted by $t\downarrow_R$ for each equivalence class of a term t modulo $=_R$.

Let us now introduce some key notions for the combination problem [15].

Definition 1 (Smoothness). *Let Σ be a signature and $S = \{\sigma_1, \ldots, \sigma_n\}$ a set of sorts in Σ. A Σ-theory T is* smooth *with respect to S if:*

- *for every T-satisfiable quantifier-free Σ-formula φ,*
- *for every T-interpretation $\mathcal{A}$ satisfying φ,*
- *for every cardinal number $\kappa_1, \ldots, \kappa_n$ such that $\kappa_i \geq |A_{\sigma_i}|$, for $i = 1, \ldots, n$,*

there exists a T-interpretation $\mathcal{B}$ satisfying φ such that

$$|B_{\sigma_i}| = \kappa_i \text{ for } i = 1, \ldots, n$$

Definition 2 (Self Witnessability). *Let Σ be a signature, S a set of sorts in Σ, and T a Σ-theory. A quantifier-free Σ-formula φ is S-populated if $Var_\sigma(\varphi)$ is non-empty for each $\sigma \in S$. A T-satisfiable S-populated quantifier-free Σ-formula φ is self witnessable in T with respect to S if there exists a T-interpretation $\mathcal{A}$ satisfying φ such that $A_\sigma = \{\mathcal{A}[v] \mid v \in Var_\sigma(\varphi)\}$ for each $\sigma \in S$. T is self witnessable with respect to S if any T-satisfiable S-populated quantifier-free Σ-formula φ is self witnessable in T with respect to S.*

Definition 3 (Perfect Politeness). *Let Σ be a signature and S a set of sorts in Σ. A Σ-theory T is perfectly polite with respect to S if it is both smooth and self witnessable with respect to S.*

A typical example of a perfectly polite theory is the theory of equality. A perfectly polite theory is a particular polite theory [12,15]. As shown in [12,15], there exists a combination method to decide the satisfiability problem in a union of theories $T_s \cup T_t$ if

- T_s and T_t do not share function symbols but share a set of sorts S;
- T_s is polite with respect to S;
- and the satisfiability problem is decidable in both T_s and T_t.

In this paper, the considered polite theories are perfectly polite.

3   Combination with Bridging Theories

We investigate the satisfiability problem modulo a non-disjoint union $T_s \cup T_f \cup T_t$, where T_s is a data structure theory, e.g., the theory of absolutely free data structures [16]. The source and target theories T_s and T_t are connected with some theory T_f specifying a bridging function f by structural induction over the "constructors" of T_s. A typical example is trees of sort struct over elements of sorts in Elem, with tree size as bridging function. We now define these theories.

Definition 4. *Consider a set of sorts Elem, and a sort struct $\notin$ Elem. Let Σ be a signature whose set of sorts is $\{struct\} \cup Elem$ and whose function symbols $c \in \Sigma$ (called constructors) have arities of the form:*

$$c : \sigma_1 \times \cdots \times \sigma_m \times struct \times \cdots \times struct \to struct$$

where $\sigma_1, \ldots, \sigma_m \in Elem$. To each n-ary constructor c, we associate the selectors $s_1^c, \ldots, s_n^c$ that are disjoint from Σ and such that $s_i^c = s_j^d$ iff $i = j$ and $c = d$. Let $\Sigma^+ = \Sigma \cup \{s_i^c \mid c \in \Sigma, i = 1, \ldots, ar(c)\}$. Consider the following axioms (where upper case letters denote implicitly universally quantified variables)

$$
\begin{cases}
(Inj_c) & c(X_1, \ldots, X_n) = c(Y_1, \ldots, Y_n) \Rightarrow \bigwedge_{i=1}^n X_i = Y_i \\
(Dis_{c,d}) & c(X_1, \ldots, X_n) \neq d(Y_1, \ldots, Y_m) \\
(Acyc_\Sigma) & X \neq t[X] \text{ if } t \text{ is a non-variable } \Sigma\text{-term} \\
(Proj_{c,i}) & s_i^c(c(X_1, \ldots, X_n)) = X_i
\end{cases}
$$

The Σ-theory of Absolutely Free Data Structures is

$$AFDS_\Sigma = \left(\bigcup_{c\in\Sigma} Inj_c \right) \cup \left(\bigcup_{c,d\in\Sigma, c\neq d} Dis_{c,d} \right) \cup Acyc_\Sigma$$

and the Σ^+-theory of Absolutely Free Data Structures with selectors is

$$AFDS_\Sigma^+ = AFDS_\Sigma \cup \bigcup_{c\in\Sigma} \left(\bigcup_{i=1}^{ar(c)} Proj_{c,i} \right)$$

The class of Data Structure Theories **DST**$^+$ *consists of all theories T_s such that T_s is any union of axioms among Inj_c, $Dis_{c,d}$, $Acyc_\Sigma$, and $Proj_{c,i}$. The subclass* **DST** *of* **DST**$^+$ *consists of all theories without axioms $Proj_{c,i}$.*

DST$^+$ includes inductive data structures (with selectors) such as lists and trees, but also, e.g., the theory of equality or injective functions alone.

Given a tuple e of terms of sorts in `Elem` and a tuple t of terms of sort `struct`, the tuple e, t may be written $e; t$ to distinguish terms of sort `struct` from the other ones. Hence, a Σ-term is denoted by $c(e; t)$.

Definition 5. *Consider two signatures Σ and Σ_t possibly sharing sorts except* `struct` *but no function symbols, where Σ complies with Definition 4. Let f be a new function symbol f with arity* `struct` $\to$ `t`*, where* `t` *is a sort in Σ_t. A bridging theory T_f associated to f has the form:*

$$T_f = \bigcup_{c\in\Sigma} \left\{ \ \forall e \forall t_1, \dots, t_n \ . \ f(c(e; t_1, \dots, t_n)) = f_c(e; f(t_1), \dots, f(t_n)) \ \right\}$$

where $f_c(x; y)$ denotes a Σ_t-term.

Notice that the notation $f_c(x; y)$ does not enforce all elements of $x; y$ to occur in the term $f_c(x; y)$: in particular only elements in x of sort in Σ_t are allowed in $f_c(x; y)$. Throughout the paper, we assume that for any constant c in Σ, f_c denotes a constant in Σ_t, and the equality $f(c) = f_c$ occurs in T_f. For instance, in the case of length of lists, $\ell(nil) = \ell_{nil} = 0$.

For the rest of this section, let $T = T_s \cup T_f \cup T_t$ where

- T_s is a Σ_s-theory in **DST**$^+$;
- T_t is a stably infinite Σ_t-theory such that Σ_s and Σ_t do not share function symbols, and `struct` does not occur in Σ_t;
- T_f is a bridging theory.

We describe below a decision procedure for checking the T-satisfiability of sets of literals. As usual, the input set of literals is first purified to get a separate form.

Definition 6. *A set of literals φ is in separate form if $\varphi = \varphi_{struct} \cup \varphi_{elem} \cup \varphi_t \cup \varphi_f$ where:*

- φ_{struct} *contains only flat literals of sort* struct
- φ_{elem} *contains only literals of sorts in* $\Sigma_s \backslash (\Sigma_t \cup \{\text{struct}\})$
- φ_t *contains only* Σ_t-*literals*
- φ_f *contains only flat equalities of the form* $f_x = f(x)$, *where* f_x *denotes a variable associated to* $f(x)$, *such that* f_x *and* $f(x)$ *occur once in* φ_f *and each variable of sort* struct *in* φ_{struct} *occurs in* φ_f.

It is easy to convert any set of literals into an equisatisfiable separate form by introducing fresh variables to denote impure terms.

Unlike classical disjoint combination methods, guessing only one arrangement on the shared variables is not sufficient to get a modular decision procedure. An additional arrangement on variables of sort struct is considered and the resulting set of flat Σ-equalities E is translated to a set of Σ_t-literals CP_E.

Definition 7. *Given a bridging theory* T_f, *the* target encoding *of a set of flat* Σ-*equalities* E *is the set of* Σ_t-*literals*

$$
\begin{aligned}
CP_E = \ & \{f_{x'} = f_c(e; f_{x_1}, \ldots, f_{x_n}) \mid c(e; x_1, \ldots, x_n) = x' : \text{struct} \in E\} \\
& \cup \{f_{x'} = f_x \mid x = x' : \text{struct} \in E\}
\end{aligned}
$$

The combination procedure below is presented in [9] for the particular case of absolutely free data structures.

Lemma 1. *Let* $\varphi = \varphi_{struct} \cup \varphi_{elem} \cup \varphi_t \cup \varphi_f$ *be a set of literals in separate form,* $V = Var(\varphi_{struct} \cup \varphi_{elem}) \cup Var_{struct}(\varphi_f)$, *and* $V_t = Var(\varphi_t) \cup Var_t(\varphi_f)$. *The formula* φ *is* T-*satisfiable if and only if there exist an arrangement* Arr_t *over* $V \cap V_t$ *and an arrangement* Arr_{struct} *over the set of variables of sort* struct *in* V, *such that*

- $\varphi_{struct} \cup \varphi_{elem} \cup Arr_t \cup Arr_{struct}$ *is* T_s-*satisfiable,*
- $\varphi_t \cup Arr_t \cup CP_E$ *is* T_t-*satisfiable,*
  where E *is the set of equalities in* $\varphi_{struct} \cup Arr_{struct}$.

Proof. (Only if direction: soundness) Straightforward, since $T_f \cup T_t \cup \varphi \models CP_E$. (If direction: completeness) See Lemma 2 in Section 5.

$\qquad\qquad\qquad\qquad\qquad\qquad\qquad\qquad\qquad\qquad\qquad\qquad\qquad\qquad\qquad\qquad$ □

For the sake of simplicity in Lemma 1, we have chosen to use arrangements to fix E. In practice however another solution would be to use a saturation-based T_s-satisfiability procedure with the capability to deduce E, like the one introduced in Section 4.

Example 1. Let T_t be the theory of integers and a theory of binary trees over integers, with Elem $= \{\text{int}\}$, constructors $\Sigma = \{nil : \text{struct}, cons : \text{int} \times \text{struct} \times \text{struct} \to \text{struct}\}$, and selectors $val, left, right$, formally defined by $T_s = \{val(cons(I,X,Y)) = I, left(cons(I,X,Y)) = X, right(cons(I,X,Y)) = Y\}$. The bridging theory for the function $sum : \text{struct} \to \text{int}$ is $T_{sum} = \{sum(nil) = 0, sum(cons(I,X,Y)) = I + sum(X) + sum(Y)\}$.

Consider the T-satisfiability of

$$\varphi = \{a = cons(e, b, c), d = cons(0, left(a), right(a)), a \neq d,$$
$$sum(a) \leq sum(left(a)) + sum(right(a)), e \geq 0\}$$

or in separate form $\varphi_{struct} \cup \varphi_t \cup \varphi_{sum}$ with

$$\varphi_{struct} = \{a = cons(e, b, c), d = cons(e', a_1, a_2),$$
$$a_1 = left(a), a_2 = right(a), a \neq d\}$$

$$\varphi_t = \{sum_a \leq sum_{a_1} + sum_{a_2}, e' = 0, e \geq 0\}$$

$$\varphi_{sum} = \{sum_x = sum(x) \mid x \in \{a, a_1, a_2, b, c, d\}\}$$

Let us compute the arrangements used in Lemma 1. First, Arr_{struct} relates a, b, c, d, a_1 and a_2; notice that $a_1 = left(a) = left(cons(e, b, c)) = b$ and similarly $a_2 = c$, so these equalities should belong to Arr_{struct}, as well as $a \neq d$ (from φ_{struct}). Second, Arr_t should be $\{e \neq e'\}$, since otherwise $a = cons(e, b, c) = cons(e', b, c) = cons(e', a_1, a_2) = d$ holds, in contradiction with Arr_{struct}.

The target encoding CP_E will contain $sum_a = e + sum_b + sum_c$, as well as $sum_b = sum_{a_1}$, $sum_c = sum_{a_2}$, derived from the equalities in Arr_{struct}. From $sum_a \leq sum_{a_1} + sum_{a_2}$ in φ_t, we get $e = 0$, contradicting Arr_t since $e' = 0$. ∎

Example 2. Assume that T_{sum} and T_t are defined as in Example 1. The formula

$$\varphi = \{a = cons(e, b, c), a = cons(e', a_1, a_2), sum(a) \leq sum(a_1) + sum(a_2), e > 0\}$$

can easily be shown unsatisfiable modulo $AFDS_\Sigma \cup T_{sum} \cup T_t$. However, in the combination $EQ_\Sigma \cup T_{sum} \cup T_t$ where EQ_Σ is the theory of equality over Σ, Arr_{struct} can be such that a, a_1, a_2, b, c are all different, and $Arr_t = \{e \neq e'\}$:

- $\varphi_{struct} \cup \varphi_{elem} \cup Arr_t \cup Arr_{struct}$ is trivially EQ_Σ-satisfiable
- $\varphi_t \cup Arr_t \cup CP_E$ is satisfiable in the theory of integers, e.g. with $e' = 0$.

Consequently, φ is satisfiable modulo $EQ_\Sigma \cup T_{sum} \cup T_t$. ∎

The combination method requires only few restrictions on the target theory to be sound and complete (cf. Section 5). Actually, T_t could be also a data structure theory obtained from a previous application of the combination method. Consider the case $T = T_{tree} \cup T_{sz} \cup T_t$ where T_{tree} denotes a theory of trees and T_{sz} denotes the bridging theory defining the tree size thanks to a target theory $T_t = T_{list} \cup T_\ell \cup T_\mathbb{Z}$ corresponding to a theory of lists extended with a bridging function ℓ computing the list length. Applying twice the combination method is a way to build a T-satisfiability procedure where T corresponds to the union of two disjoint data structure theories extended with their respective bridging functions to $T_\mathbb{Z}$: $T = (T_{tree} \cup T_{sz} \cup T_\mathbb{Z}) \cup (T_{list} \cup T_\ell \cup T_\mathbb{Z})$. In the same vein, the combination method applied twice yields a satisfiability procedure for a theory of lists of trees extended with tree size sz and list length ℓ. The above examples illustrate the generality of our combination method.

4   Basic Data Structure Theories

The class $\mathbf{DST}^+$ introduced above includes theories of practical interest worth considering for non-disjoint combinations with bridging functions. It contains the theory of Absolutely Free Data Structures, but also the theory of equality and other theories for which a rewriting approach to satisfiability can be successfully applied [2]. It appears that those theories satisfy a nice model-theoretic property, instrumental to prove the completeness of the above combination procedure. They admit some particular Herbrand models similar to the ones we can build for the theory of equality. Hence, it is another way to consider data structure theories that can be "reduced" to the theory of equality. In the same vein, one could use the locality approach [17] to get a "reduction" to the theory of equality through a finite instantiation of axioms. Our model-based approach eases the construction of a model for data structures extended with bridging functions.

Rather than handling a set of literals and a theory, we will consider the theory extension including a set of (ground) literals.

Definition 8. *Consider a finite constant expansion $\Sigma_s \cup C$ of a signature Σ_s such that C_σ is non-empty for each sort σ in Σ_s, and a Σ_s-theory T_s. A ground flat T_s-extension is a $\Sigma_s \cup C$-theory defined as the union $\mathfrak{T}_s = T_s \cup G$ such that G is a finite set of ground flat $\Sigma_s \cup C$-literals. $\mathfrak{T}_s = T_s \cup G$ is said to be subpopulated if C contains for each sort a constant not occurring in G.*

The consistency of a ground flat T_s-extension $\mathfrak{T}_s$ corresponds to a T_s-satisfiability problem of a set of flat literals. We focus on theories admitting models defined as structures of terms generated by some constructors and (a superset of) the free constants occurring in $\mathfrak{T}_s$. We will see in the proof of Proposition 1 that the unused constant generators in subpopulated $\mathfrak{T}_s$ are required to build the models in the presence of selectors.

The model-theoretic properties of $\mathbf{DST}^+$ theories are essential for combinations: models can be generated from some of their symbols (i.e., the constructors). The following definition captures these properties:

Definition 9. *Consider a set of sorts* Elem, *and a sort* struct $\notin$ Elem. *Let Σ_s be a signature whose set of sorts is* {struct} $\cup$ Elem. *Let $\Sigma \subseteq \Sigma_s$ be a signature containing only function symbols whose codomain sort is* struct. *Let $\mathfrak{T}_s = T_s \cup G$ be a ground flat T_s-extension whose signature is $\Sigma_s \cup C$. A Σ-basic Herbrand model of $\mathfrak{T}_s$ is a model $\mathcal{H}$ of $\mathfrak{T}_s$ such that $\mathcal{H}^{\Sigma \cup C}$ is $T(\Sigma \cup C)/=_E$, where E is a finite set of ground flat $\Sigma \cup C$-equalities defined as the set of $\Sigma \cup C$-equalities in G plus some additional equalities between constants of C occurring in G.*

A consistent Σ_s-theory T_s is a Σ-basic (resp., perfect Σ-basic) data structure theory if any subpopulated (resp., arbitrary) consistent ground flat T_s-extension admits a Σ-basic Herbrand model.

A Σ-basic Herbrand model is constructed on a subsignature Σ of T_s. This introduces a natural distinction between *constructors* in Σ and defined symbols in $\Sigma_s \setminus \Sigma$. The constructors are used to build the domain of the basic Herbrand model whilst the defined symbols are interpreted as operators on this domain. A classical example is $AFDS_\Sigma^+$ where the selectors are the defined symbols. From now on, we assume that function symbols $c \in \Sigma$ have arities as in Definition 4:

$$c : \sigma_1 \times \cdots \times \sigma_m \times \texttt{struct} \times \cdots \times \texttt{struct} \to \texttt{struct}.$$

Notice also that the above definition is suitable for a deductive approach in contrast to a guessing approach. In a guessing approach, the set E of equalities would be maximal (obtained from an arrangement) and in that case no additional equality would be needed.

We now prove that all the source theories T_s considered in Section 3, ranging from the theory of equality to $AFDS_\Sigma^+$, are Σ-basic data structure theories. For any of these source theories T_s, a saturation-based calculus (see Figure 1) provides a T_s-satisfiability procedure. As a side effect, the saturated set computed by this calculus yields a Σ-basic Herbrand model.

Proposition 1. *Theories in* **DST**$^+$ *are Σ-basic data structure theories, and theories in* **DST** *are perfect Σ-basic data structure theories.*

Proof. Consider any finite set of ground flat $\Sigma_s \cup C$-literals G and $\mathfrak{T}_s = T_s \cup G$. To check the consistency of $\mathfrak{T}_s$, we can use a (simplified) superposition calculus. It can be viewed as an abstract congruence closure procedure for the theory of equality extended with additional simplification rules on ground clauses to take into account the axioms listed above. In Figure 1, we provide a version of this calculus instantiated for the case of $AFDS_\Sigma^+$. One may remark that there is a one to one correspondence between the axioms of $AFDS_\Sigma^+$ and inference rules of this calculus. If we want to omit an axiom of $AFDS_\Sigma^+$, we just have to remove the corresponding inference rule, to get a satisfiability procedure. Hence, if we omit **Inj**$_c$, **Dis**$_{c,d}$, **Acyc**$_\Sigma$ and **Proj**$_{c,i}$, we retrieve the inference system for the satisfiability problem in the theory of equality. This inference system is parametrised by an ordering on constants.

For any considered T_s, the calculus terminates by computing a finite saturation. If this finite saturation does not contain the empty clause, $\mathfrak{T}_s$ is consistent. Moreover, it is possible to construct a model using the model-generation technique introduced by Bachmair and Ganzinger [5]: the set of equalities in the finite saturation leads to a convergent term rewrite system R such that the structure of R-normal forms $T(\Sigma_s \cup C){\downarrow}_R$ is a model of $\mathfrak{T}_s$. Let E be the set of equalities corresponding to ground flat rules in R. Then, we must distinguish two cases:

- If T_s does not include the *Projection* axiom, R only consists of ground flat rules. In that case, we can take $\Sigma = \Sigma_s$, and $T(\Sigma_s \cup C){\downarrow}_R$ is isomorphic to $T(\Sigma \cup C)/ =_E$.
- Otherwise, we consider the signature Σ obtained from Σ_s by removing selectors, and a structure whose domain is $T(\Sigma \cup C){\downarrow}_R$. By assumption on the constants used in G, there is a constant $u_s \in C$ not occurring in $\mathfrak{T}_s$, for each s in Σ_s. On this domain, the selector s_i^c with s as codomain sort is interpreted as follows:

- For any normal form which is a constant x, $s_i^c(x) = x'$ if $s_i^c(x){\downarrow_R} = x' \in C$, otherwise $s_i^c(x) = u_{\mathbf{s}}$.
- For any normal form which is a term $t = c(t_1, \ldots, t_n)$, $s_i^c(t) = t_i$
- For any other normal form t, $s_i^c(t) = u_{\mathbf{s}}$.

Using this interpretation, we get a structure of the desired form that is still a model of $\mathfrak{T}_s$, when $\mathfrak{T}_s$ includes the $Proj_{c,i}$ axiom. □

$$
\begin{aligned}
&\textbf{Sup}: \quad x = x', x = y \vdash x' = y \quad \text{if } x > x', x > y \\
&\textbf{Cong1}: x_j = x_j', x = f(\ldots, x_j, \ldots) \vdash x = f(\ldots, x_j', \ldots) \quad \text{if } x_j > x_j' \\
&\textbf{Cong2}: x = f(x_1, \ldots, x_n), x' = f(x_1, \ldots, x_n) \vdash x = x' \\
&\textbf{Param}: x = x', x \neq y \vdash x' \neq y \quad \text{if } x > x', x > y \\
&\textbf{Ref}: \quad x \neq x \vdash \square \\
&\textbf{Inj}_c: \quad x = c(x_1, \ldots, x_n), x = c(x_1', \ldots, x_n') \vdash x_1 = x_1' \ldots x_n = x_n' \text{ if } c \in \Sigma \\
&\textbf{Dis}_{c,d}: \ x = c(x_1, \ldots, x_n), x = d(y_1, \ldots, y_m) \vdash \square \text{ if } c, d \in \Sigma, c \neq d \\
&\textbf{Acyc}_\Sigma: x = t_1[x_1], \ldots, x_{n-1} = t_n[x] \vdash \square \text{ if } t_1, \ldots, t_n \text{ are } \Sigma\text{-terms of depth 1} \\
&\textbf{Proj}_{c,i}: x = c(x_1, \ldots, x_n) \vdash x_i = s_i^c(x)
\end{aligned}
$$

Fig. 1. T_s-satisfiability procedure

Proposition 2. *Theories in* **DST** *are perfectly polite with respect to* Elem.

Proof. Self witnessability directly follows from the definition of a perfect Σ-basic data structure theory. The smoothness is a consequence of the fact that sorts in Elem are only inhabited by constants in C. Thus, the set of generators C can be extended to any set of generators whose cardinality is larger than the cardinality of C, and the related term-generated structure remains a model. □

5 Completeness Proof

We study the satisfiability problem modulo $T = T_s \cup T_f \cup T_t$ where T_f is a bridging theory between a source theory T_s and a target theory T_t fulfilling the following assumption:

Assumption 1 (Theories) *The Σ_s-theory T_s and the Σ_t-theory T_t share no function symbol. The set of sorts in Σ_s is* Elem $\cup$ {struct}, *and* struct *does not occur in Σ_t. One of the following three cases hold:*

- *sorts in Σ_s and Σ_t are disjoint, T_s is a Σ-basic data structure theory and T_t is arbitrary*
- *Σ_s and Σ_t share sorts, and either*
  - *$T_s \in$ **DST** and T_t is arbitrary*
  - *$T_s \in$ **DST**$^+\backslash$**DST** and T_t is stably infinite.*

The combination procedure described in Section 3 is sound and complete also for the cases listed above. We prove the completeness of the combination procedure thanks to a combined model constructed using rewriting techniques. Given a bridging function $f : \texttt{struct} \to \texttt{t}$ where $\texttt{t}$ is a sort from the target theory, we define a bridging theory via a convergent term rewrite system F such that for any term s of sort $\texttt{struct}$, its normal form $f(s)\downarrow_F$ corresponds to a term that can be interpreted in a model of the target theory. To solve this problem, we must carefully study the interplay between the equational theory E related to a Σ-basic Herbrand model and the term rewrite system F.

For convenience, we will consider theory extensions including the sets of (ground) literals rather than handling literals and theories separately.

Assumption 2 (Input formulas) *Let T_s and T_t be theories as in Assumption 1. The signatures $\Sigma_s \cup C$ and $\Sigma_t \cup C_t$ are finite constant expansions of Σ_s and Σ_t, respectively.*

1. *$\mathfrak{T}_s$ is a consistent $\Sigma_s \cup C$-theory defined as a subpopulated ground flat extension of T_s. It admits a Σ-basic Herbrand model $\mathcal{H}$ such that $\mathcal{H}^{\Sigma \cup C}$ is $T(\Sigma \cup C)/ =_E$. The set of $C \cap C_t$-literals occurring in $\mathfrak{T}_s$ is an arrangement denoted by Arr_t.*
2. *$\mathfrak{T}_t$ is a $\Sigma_t \cup C_t$-theory defined as the union of T_t and some finite set of ground $\Sigma_t \cup C_t$-literals, such that $\mathfrak{T}_t \cup Arr_t$ is consistent.*

From now on, we assume a context where Assumption 1 and Assumption 2 hold.

A bridging theory T_f (from Definition 5 above) is an equational theory. It happens that it can naturally be oriented as a term rewrite system F.

Proposition 3. *Let T_f be a bridging theory as introduced in Definition 5, and let $\mathfrak{T}_F = T_f \cup \{f(x) = f_x \mid x : \texttt{struct} \in C\}$. The term rewrite system $F = \{f(l) \to r \mid f(l) = r \in \mathfrak{T}_F\}$ is convergent and satisfies the following properties:*

- *$f(c(e; t_1, \ldots, t_n)) \downarrow_F = f_c(e; f(t_1)\downarrow_F, \ldots, f(t_n)\downarrow_F)$ for any non-constant constructor $c \in \Sigma$;*
- *$f(c)\downarrow_F = f_c$ for any constant c in Σ, where f_c is a constant in Σ_t;*
- *$f(x)\downarrow_F = f_x$ for any constant $(x : \texttt{struct}) \in C$, where $(f_x : \texttt{t}) \in C_t$.*

Example 3. Consider the length function ℓ from lists to integers, and let $\mathfrak{T}_s = \{a = cons(e, b), b = cons(e', c), c = nil, a \neq c\}$. The set of constants of sort $\texttt{struct}$ in $\mathfrak{T}_s$ is $\{a, b, c\}$ and the related term rewrite system F is given by $\{\ell(cons(W, X)) \to 1 + \ell(X), \ell(nil) \to 0\} \cup \{\ell(a) \to \ell_a, \ell(b) \to \ell_b, \ell(c) \to \ell_c\}$. ∎

We focus on the problem of checking the $\mathfrak{T}_s \cup \mathfrak{T}_F \cup \mathfrak{T}_t$-consistency. To get a well-defined interpretation for $f : \texttt{struct} \to \texttt{t}$, we need a $\mathfrak{T}_t$-model in which f returns the same value of sort $\texttt{t}$ for all E-equal input terms of sort $\texttt{struct}$. This motivates the following definition of E-compatibility. Below, a $\texttt{struct}$-term denotes a Σ-term in which constants of sort $\texttt{struct}$ are in C.

Definition 10. *F is E-compatible in a model $\mathcal{A}$ of $\mathfrak{T}_t$ if for any $\texttt{struct}$-terms s and t, $s =_E t \Rightarrow \mathcal{A}[f(s)\downarrow_F] = \mathcal{A}[f(t)\downarrow_F]$.*

Proposition 4. *If F is E-compatible in a model of $\mathfrak{T}_t$, then $\mathfrak{T}_s \cup \mathfrak{T}_F \cup \mathfrak{T}_t$ is consistent.*

Proof. Consider the set of sorts S shared by Σ_s and Σ_t. Let us first assume $S = \emptyset$. We know that F is E-compatible in a model $\mathcal{A}$ of $\mathfrak{T}_t$, and there exists a model $\mathcal{H}$ of $\mathfrak{T}_s$ such that $\mathcal{H}^{\Sigma \cup C}$ is $T(\Sigma \cup C)/ =_E$. Given $\mathcal{A}$ and $\mathcal{H}$, let us define an interpretation $\mathcal{M}$ as follows. The domains of $\mathcal{M}$ are:

- $M_t = A_t$ for any sort t in Σ_t
- $M_s = H_s$ for any sort s in Σ_s

The function symbols are interpreted as follows[1]:

- For any g in $\Sigma_t \cup C_t$, $\mathcal{M}[g] = \mathcal{A}[g]$
- For any g in $\Sigma_s \cup C$, $\mathcal{M}[g] = \mathcal{H}[g]$
- For any struct-term t, $\mathcal{M}[f](\llbracket t \rrbracket) = \mathcal{A}[f(t) \downarrow_F]$

$\mathcal{M}$ is well-defined due to the assumption that F is E-compatible in $\mathcal{A}$. Let us check that $\mathcal{M}$ is a model of $\mathfrak{T}_s \cup \mathfrak{T}_F \cup \mathfrak{T}_t$.

- $\mathcal{M}^{\Sigma_s \cup C} = \mathcal{H}$, which is a model of $\mathfrak{T}_s$ by assumption.
- $\mathcal{M}^{\Sigma_t \cup C_t} = \mathcal{A}$, which is a model of $\mathfrak{T}_t$ by assumption.
- For any struct-term t, we have that

$$\mathcal{M}[f(t)] = \mathcal{M}[f](\llbracket t \rrbracket) = \mathcal{A}[f(t) \downarrow_F] = \mathcal{M}[f(t) \downarrow_F]$$

by definition of $\mathcal{M}$. Therefore $\mathcal{M}$ is a model of $\mathfrak{T}_F$.

Consider now the case $S \neq \emptyset$. By Assumption 1, T_s is smooth with respect to Elem, and more precisely there exists also a larger model $\mathcal{H}$ of $\mathfrak{T}_s$ such that $\mathcal{H}^{\Sigma \cup C}$ is $T(\Sigma \cup C \cup D)/ =_E$, where

- D is a set of elements of sort in $S \subseteq$ Elem,
- $H_\sigma = A_\sigma$ for each sort $\sigma \in S$.

Then the construction of $\mathcal{M}$ follows directly from the case $S = \emptyset$. In particular, $\mathcal{M}$ is well-defined on $C \cap C_t$ due to the arrangement Arr_t.   □

The missing piece of the method is to provide a way to check E-compatibility of F in a model of $\mathfrak{T}_t$. In the following, we show that this property can be reduced to a $\mathfrak{T}_t$-satisfiability problem.

Proposition 5. *F is E-compatible in a model of $\mathfrak{T}_t$ if the theory $\mathfrak{T}_t \cup Arr_t \cup CP_E$ is consistent, where CP_E is the target encoding of E (Definition 7).*

Proof. Let $\mathcal{A}$ be a model of $\mathfrak{T}_t \cup Arr_t \cup CP_E$. Let R be the convergent term rewrite system associated to E. Since $\mathcal{A}$ satisfies Arr_t, we have that $\mathcal{A}[e \downarrow_R] = \mathcal{A}[e]$ for any constant e of sort in $\Sigma_s \cap \Sigma_t$. We first prove by structural induction that for any struct-term u, $\mathcal{A}[f(u \downarrow_R) \downarrow_F] = \mathcal{A}[f(u) \downarrow_F]$.

(Inductive case) Assume $u = c(e; u_1, \ldots, u_n)$.

---

[1] For any struct-term t, $\llbracket t \rrbracket$ is the equivalence class of t modulo $=_E$.

- If $c(e; u_1, \ldots, u_n)\!\downarrow_R = c(e\!\downarrow_R; u_1\!\downarrow_R, \ldots, u_n\!\downarrow_R)$, then we have:

$$
\begin{aligned}
&\mathcal{A}[f(c(e; u_1, \ldots, u_n)\!\downarrow_R)\!\downarrow_F] \\
&= \mathcal{A}[f(c(e\!\downarrow_R; u_1\!\downarrow_R, \ldots, u_n\!\downarrow_R))\!\downarrow_F] \\
&= \mathcal{A}[f_c(e\!\downarrow_R; f(u_1\!\downarrow_R)\!\downarrow_F, \ldots, f(u_n\!\downarrow_R)\!\downarrow_F)] \\
&= f_c(\mathcal{A}[e\!\downarrow_R]; \mathcal{A}[f(u_1\!\downarrow_R)\!\downarrow_F], \ldots, \mathcal{A}[f(u_n\!\downarrow_R)\!\downarrow_F)] \\
&= f_c(\mathcal{A}[e]; \mathcal{A}[f(u_1\!\downarrow_R)\!\downarrow_F], \ldots, \mathcal{A}[f(u_n\!\downarrow_R)\!\downarrow_F)] \\
&= f_c(\mathcal{A}[e]; \mathcal{A}[f(u_1)\!\downarrow_F], \ldots, \mathcal{A}[f(u_n)\!\downarrow_F]) \\
&= \mathcal{A}[f_c(e; f(u_1)\!\downarrow_F, \ldots, f(u_n)\!\downarrow_F)] \\
&= \mathcal{A}[f(c(e; u_1, \ldots, u_n))\!\downarrow_F]
\end{aligned}
$$

- Otherwise, $c(e; u_1, \ldots, u_n)\!\downarrow_R$ is necessarily a constant x', and $u_1, \ldots, u_n$ are constants $x_1, \ldots, x_n$. Then, by assumption on $\mathcal{A}$, we have

$$
\mathcal{A}[f(x')\!\downarrow_F] = \mathcal{A}[f_{x'}] = \mathcal{A}[f_c(e; f_{x_1}, \ldots, f_{x_n})] = \mathcal{A}[f(c(e; x_1, \ldots, x_n))\!\downarrow_F]
$$

(Base case) Assume u is a constant x. If $x\!\downarrow_R = x$, then we have $f(x\!\downarrow_R)\!\downarrow_F = f(x)\!\downarrow_F$, and so $\mathcal{A}[f(x\!\downarrow_R)\!\downarrow_F] = \mathcal{A}[f(x)\!\downarrow_F]$. Otherwise, we have $x\!\downarrow_R = x'$. Then, by assumption on $\mathcal{A}$, we have $\mathcal{A}[f(x')\!\downarrow_F] = \mathcal{A}[f_{x'}] = \mathcal{A}[f_x] = \mathcal{A}[f(x)\!\downarrow_R]$.

To conclude the proof, let s and t be any **struct**-terms. If $s =_E t$, then $s\!\downarrow_R = t\!\downarrow_R$ and $\mathcal{A}[f(s)\!\downarrow_F] = \mathcal{A}[f(s\!\downarrow_R)\!\downarrow_F] = \mathcal{A}[f(t\!\downarrow_R)\!\downarrow_F] = \mathcal{A}[f(t)\!\downarrow_F]$. This means F is E-compatible in the model $\mathcal{A}$ of $\mathfrak{T}_t$. $\qquad\square$

Example 4. (Example 3 continued). Let $\mathfrak{T}_t$ be the theory of integers. We have $E = \{a = cons(e, b), b = cons(e', c), c = nil\}$ and so $CP_E = \{\ell_a = 1 + \ell_b, \ell_b = 1 + \ell_c, \ell_c = 0\}$. Since $\mathfrak{T}_t \cup CP_E$ is consistent, we get the consistency of $\mathfrak{T}_s \cup \mathfrak{T}_F \cup \mathfrak{T}_t$ by applying Proposition 5 and then Proposition 4. ∎

As a side remark, in the trivial case of $F = \{f(x_k) \to f_{x_k}\}_{k \in K}$, the combination becomes disjoint, and the consistency of $\mathfrak{T}_s \cup \mathfrak{T}_F \cup \mathfrak{T}_t$ corresponds to the consistency of the union of three disjoint theories, including the theory of equality for f.

Proposition 4 and Proposition 5 are instrumental to prove the completeness of the combination procedure. We thus get this result, subsuming Lemma 1:

Lemma 2. *Let $T = T_s \cup T_f \cup T_t$, where T_s, T_t follow Assumption 1 and T_f is a bridging theory according to Definition 5. The combination procedure introduced in Lemma 1 is sound and complete for T-satisfiability.*

Proof. The soundness is straightforward just like in Lemma 1. Let us focus on the completeness. Consider the separate form φ and the sets of variables V and V_t given in Lemma 1. By viewing φ as a set of ground literals in a constant expansion of $\Sigma_s \cup \Sigma_f \cup \Sigma_t$, we can introduce the same theories $\mathfrak{T}_s$, $\mathfrak{T}_t$ and $\mathfrak{T}_F$ as in Assumption 2 and Proposition 3:

- the $\Sigma_s \cup C$-theory $\mathfrak{T}_s$ is $T_s \cup \varphi_{struct} \cup \varphi_{elem} \cup Arr_t \cup Arr_{\mathbf{struct}}$,
- the $\Sigma_t \cup C_t$-theory $\mathfrak{T}_t$ is $T_t \cup \varphi_t$,
- $\mathfrak{T}_F = T_f \cup \varphi_f \cup \bigcup_{x:\mathbf{struct} \in C \setminus V}\{f(x) = f_x\}$,

where C and C_t are as follows:

- $C = V$ when $T_s \in \mathbf{DST}$. Otherwise, C is equal to V plus one fresh constant for each sort in T_s.
- $C_t = V_t \cup \bigcup_{x:\mathtt{struct} \in C \setminus V} \{f_x\}$.

Assume $\varphi_{struct} \cup \varphi_{elem} \cup Arr_t \cup Arr_{\mathtt{struct}}$ is T_s-satisfiable and $\varphi_t \cup Arr_t \cup CP_E$ is T_t-satisfiable. Equivalently, $\mathfrak{T}_s$ and $\mathfrak{T}_t$ are consistent. By applying Proposition 4 and Proposition 5, we get that $\mathfrak{T}_s \cup \mathfrak{T}_F \cup \mathfrak{T}_t$ is consistent, and so $T_s \cup T_f \cup T_t \cup \varphi$ is consistent, or equivalently, φ is T-satisfiable. $\qquad\square$

6 Conclusion

In this paper, we present a combination method to solve the satisfiability problem in some particular non-disjoint union of three theories including a source, a target and a bridging theory from the source to the target. The combination method is sound and complete for a large class of source data structure theories, ranging from the theory of equality to the theory of absolutely free data structures. For all these axiomatized theories, the satisfiability problem can be solved by using an off-the-shelf equational theorem prover.

We envision several further investigations. First, we would like to consider the case of non-absolutely free constructors, e.g., associative-commutative constructors, to allow a more general congruence relation E in the definition of a data structure theory. Second, it would be interesting to allow non-convex data structure theories, such as the theory of possibly empty lists [1]. Third, to go beyond the considered bridging axioms, a natural continuation is to identify other "simple" connecting axioms that could be compiled into a combination method à la Nelson-Oppen.

References

1. Armando, A., Bonacina, M.P., Ranise, S., Schulz, S.: New results on rewrite-based satisfiability procedures. ACM Trans. Comput. Log. 10(1) (2009)
2. Armando, A., Ranise, S., Rusinowitch, M.: A rewriting approach to satisfiability procedures. Inf. Comput. 183(2), 140–164 (2003)
3. Baader, F., Ghilardi, S.: Connecting many-sorted theories. J. Symb. Log. 72(2), 535–583 (2007)
4. Baader, F., Nipkow, T.: Term rewriting and all that. Cambridge University Press (1998)
5. Bachmair, L., Ganzinger, H.: Rewrite-based equational theorem proving with selection and simplification. J. Log. Comput. 4(3), 217–247 (1994)
6. Barrett, C., Shikanian, I., Tinelli, C.: An abstract decision procedure for a theory of inductive data types. JSAT 3(1–2), 21–46 (2007)
7. Baumgartner, P., Waldmann, U.: Hierarchic superposition with weak abstraction. In: Bonacina, M.P. (ed.) CADE 2013. LNCS, vol. 7898, pp. 39–57. Springer, Heidelberg (2013)

8. Chocron, P., Fontaine, P., Ringeissen, C.: A gentle non-disjoint combination of satisfiability procedures. In: Demri, S., Kapur, D., Weidenbach, C. (eds.) IJCAR 2014. LNCS, vol. 8562, pp. 122–136. Springer, Heidelberg (2014)
9. Chocron, P., Fontaine, P., Ringeissen, C.: A polite non-disjoint combination method: theories with bridging functions revisited. In: Felty, A.P., Middeldorp, A. (eds.) CADE 2015. LNCS, vol. 9195, pp. 419–433. Springer, Heidelberg (2015)
10. Fontaine, P.: Combinations of theories for decidable fragments of first-order logic. In: Ghilardi, S., Sebastiani, R. (eds.) FroCoS 2009. LNCS, vol. 5749, pp. 263–278. Springer, Heidelberg (2009)
11. Ghilardi, S.: Model-theoretic methods in combined constraint satisfiability. Journal of Automated Reasoning 33(3-4), 221–249 (2004)
12. Jovanović, D., Barrett, C.: Polite theories revisited. In: Fermüller, C., Voronkov, A. (eds.) LPAR-17. LNCS, vol. 6397, pp. 402–416. Springer, Heidelberg (2010)
13. Nicolini, E., Ringeissen, C., Rusinowitch, M.: Combinable extensions of abelian groups. In: Schmidt, R.A. (ed.) CADE 2009. LNCS (LNAI), vol. 5663, pp. 51–66. Springer, Heidelberg (2009)
14. Nicolini, E., Ringeissen, C., Rusinowitch, M.: Combining satisfiability procedures for unions of theories with a shared counting operator. Fundam. Inform. 105(1–2), 163–187 (2010)
15. Ranise, S., Ringeissen, C., Zarba, C.G.: Combining data structures with nonstably infinite theories using many-sorted logic. In: Gramlich, B. (ed.) FroCoS 2005. LNCS (LNAI), vol. 3717, pp. 48–64. Springer, Heidelberg (2005)
16. Sofronie-Stokkermans, V.: Locality results for certain extensions of theories with bridging functions. In: Schmidt, R.A. (ed.) CADE 2009. LNCS (LNAI), vol. 5663, pp. 67–83. Springer, Heidelberg (2009)
17. Sofronie-Stokkermans, V.: Automated reasoning in extensions of theories of constructors with recursively defined functions and homomorphisms. In: Ball, T., Giesl, J., Hähnle, R., Nipkow, T. (eds.) Interaction Versus Automation: The Two Faces of Deduction. number 09411 in Dagstuhl Seminar Proceedings. Schloss Dagstuhl - Leibniz-Zentrum fuer Informatik, Germany (2010)
18. Suter, P., Dotta, M., Kuncak, V.: Decision procedures for algebraic data types with abstractions. In: Hermenegildo, M.V., Palsberg, J. (eds.) Principles of Programming Languages (POPL), pp. 199–210. ACM (2010)
19. Tinelli, C., Ringeissen, C.: Unions of non-disjoint theories and combinations of satisfiability procedures. Theoretical Comput. Sci. 290(1), 291–353 (2003)
20. Tinelli, C., Zarba, C.G.: Combining non-stably infinite theories. Journal of Automated Reasoning 34(3), 209–238 (2005)
21. Tran, D., Ringeissen, C., Ranise, S., Kirchner, H.: Combination of convex theories: Modularity, deduction completeness, and explanation. J. Symb. Comput. 45(2), 261–286 (2010)
22. Zhang, T., Sipma, H.B., Manna, Z.: Decision procedures for term algebras with integer constraints. Inf. Comput. 204(10), 1526–1574 (2006)

Unification and Matching in Hierarchical Combinations of Syntactic Theories

Serdar Erbatur[1], Deepak Kapur[2], Andrew M. Marshall[3], Paliath Narendran[4], and Christophe Ringeissen[5]

[1] Ludwig-Maximilians-Universität, München, Germany
[2] University of New Mexico, USA
[3] University of Mary Washington, USA
[4] University at Albany, SUNY, USA
[5] LORIA – INRIA Nancy-Grand Est, France

Abstract. We investigate a hierarchical combination approach to the unification problem in non-disjoint unions of equational theories. In this approach, the idea is to extend a base theory with some additional axioms given by rewrite rules in such way that the unification algorithm known for the base theory can be reused without loss of completeness. Additional techniques are required to solve a combined problem by reducing it to a problem in the base theory. In this paper we show that the hierarchical combination approach applies successfully to some classes of syntactic theories, such as shallow theories since the required unification algorithms needed for the combination algorithm can always be obtained. We also consider the matching problem in syntactic extensions of a base theory. Due to the more restricted nature of the matching problem, we obtain several improvements over the unification problem.

1 Introduction

A critical question in matching and unification is how to obtain an algorithm for the combination of non-disjoint equational theories when there exist algorithms for the constituent theories. In recent work [7], a new "hierarchical" approach to the unification problem in the combination of non-disjoint theories is developed and classes of theories are identified for which the method can be applied. The main property of these classes is a hierarchical organization of the two equational theories E_1 and E_2, where E_1 is a set of axioms extending a base theory E_2. The method is successful in providing a unification method to the combination of theories for which no previous combination method was applicable. However, the main difficulty in applying the new combination method is that a new type of unification algorithm, denoted by A_1, is required to incorporate the axioms of E_1. The A_1 algorithm is not actually a black box unification algorithm. Rather the algorithm constructs a specific type of solved-form which has the property of reducing an $E_1 \cup E_2$ unification problem to one or more E_2-unification problems. A general A_1 method is developed in [7], based on the general E-unification methods studied in [10,19]. However, as with the general unification methods,

© Springer International Publishing Switzerland 2015
C. Lutz and S. Ranise (Eds.): FroCoS 2015, LNAI 9322, pp. 291–306, 2015.
DOI: 10.1007/978-3-319-24246-0_18

there is no general termination proof for an arbitrary theory. Termination must be proven for A_1 to satisfy the restrictions of [7].

Here we are able to overcome this limitation by showing that for some classes of theories, such as shallow equational theories, the unification *algorithms* for those theories can be used for the A_1 algorithm. This replaces the need to construct a dedicated unification algorithm via the method presented in [7] and allows one to use an "off the shelf" available algorithm.

In this paper, we also consider the matching problem in this new hierarchical framework and obtain a new non-disjoint combination method for the matching problem. Due to the more restricted nature of the matching problem, the combination method introduced in [7] for unification can be simplified. For the matching problem, we are not restricted to shallow theories but syntactic theories [5, 11, 12] are allowed. By assuming a resolvent presentation of a syntactic theory E_1, we are able to construct in a modular way a matching algorithm for hierarchical combination. The matching algorithm we present can be seen as an extension of the one known for disjoint unions of syntactic (finite) theories [15] and a variation of the one existing for disjoint unions of regular theories [16, 17]. A preliminary version of this algorithm has been presented in [8]. Compared to [8], we now rely on the standard definition of syntactic theory.

Let us give a brief preview of the remaining portions of the paper. Section 2 presents the preliminary background material. Section 3 presents an overview of the hierarchical combination. The overview given here is actually an improvement via simplification to the original hierarchical presentation in [7]. Section 4 applies hierarchical combination to shallow theories. Section 5 extends the hierarchical approach from the unification problem to the matching problem by considering a syntactic theory E_1.

2   Preliminaries

We use the standard notation of equational unification [3] and term rewriting systems [1]. Given a first-order signature Σ and a (countable) set of variables V, the set of Σ-terms over variables V is denoted by $T(\Sigma, V)$. The set of variables in a term t is denoted by $Var(t)$. A term t is *ground* if $Var(t) = \emptyset$. For any position p in a term t, $t|_p$ denotes the subterm of t at position p, and $t[u]_p$ denotes the term t in which $t|_p$ is replaced by u. Given a set E of Σ-axioms (i.e., pairs of Σ-terms, denoted by $l = r$), the *equational theory* $=_E$ is the congruence closure of E under the law of substitutivity. For any Σ-term t, the equivalence class of t with respect to $=_E$ is denoted by $[t]_E$. The E-free algebra over V is denoted by $T(\Sigma, V)/=_E$. By a slight abuse of terminology, E will be often called an equational theory. An axiom $l = r$ is *variable-preserving* (also called *regular*) if $Var(l) = Var(r)$. An axiom $l = r$ is *linear* (resp., *collapse-free*) if l and r are linear (resp. non-variable terms). An equational theory is *variable-preserving* (resp., regular/linear/collapse-free) if all its axioms are variable-preserving (resp., regular/linear/collapse-free). An equational theory E is *finite* if for each term t, there are only finitely many terms s such that $t =_E s$.

A theory E is *subterm collapse-free* if and only if for all terms t it is not the case that $t =_E u$ where u is a strict subterm of t. A theory E is *syntactic* if it has a finite *resolvent presentation* S, that is a presentation S such that each equality $s =_E t$ has an equational proof $s \leftrightarrow^*_S t$ with at most one step $\leftrightarrow_S$ applied at the root position. A theory E is *shallow* if variables can only occur at a position at most 1 in axioms of E. When E is both subterm collapse-free and shallow, variables can only occur at position 1 in axioms of E. Shallow theories are known to be syntactic theories [6]. Let us recall some results connecting syntactic theories and unification. First, shallow theories admit a mutation-based unification algorithm [6]. Second, finite syntactic theories admit a mutation-based matching algorithm [16]. We will reuse both of these algorithms in this paper. In addition, any collapse-free and finitary unifying theory is syntactic [12]. For instance the Associative-Commutative (AC) theory is syntactic, as well as the $\mathcal{E}_{AC}$ theory introduced in [9] as a finitary unifying theory of distributive exponentiation.

A Σ-equation is a pair of Σ-terms denoted by $s =^? t$. An E-unification problem is a set of Σ-equations, $\mathcal{S} = \{s_1 =^? t_1, \ldots, s_m =^? t_m\}$. The set of variables of $\mathcal{S}$ is denoted by $Var(\mathcal{S})$. When $t_1, \ldots, t_n$ are ground, $\mathcal{S}$ is called a matching problem, also denoted by $\{s_1 \leq^? t_1, \ldots, s_m \leq^? t_m\}$, where $s_i \leq^? t_i$ denotes a match-equation. A solution to an E-unification problem $\mathcal{S}$, called an E-*unifier*, is a substitution σ such that $s_i\sigma =_E t_i\sigma$ for all $1 \leq i \leq m$. A substitution σ is *more general modulo* E than θ on a set of variables V, denoted as $\sigma \leq^V_E \theta$, if there is a substitution τ such that $x\sigma\tau =_E x\theta$ for all $x \in V$. Two substitutions θ_1 and θ_2 are *equivalent modulo* E on a set of variables V, denoted as $\theta_1 \equiv^V_E \theta_2$, if and only if $x\theta_1 =_E x\theta_2$ for all $x \in V$. A *Complete Set of E-Unifiers* of $\mathcal{S}$ is a set of substitutions denoted by $CSU_E(\mathcal{S})$ such that each $\sigma \in CSU_E(\mathcal{S})$ is an E-unifier of $\mathcal{S}$, and for each E-unifier θ of $\mathcal{S}$, there exists $\sigma \in CSU_E(\mathcal{S})$ such that $\sigma \leq^{Var(\mathcal{S})}_E \theta$. An inference rule $\mathcal{S} \vdash \mathcal{S}'$ is sound (resp. complete) for E-unification if $CSU_E(\mathcal{S}) \subseteq CSU_E(\mathcal{S}')$ (resp. $CSU_E(\mathcal{S}) \supseteq CSU_E(\mathcal{S}')$). An inference system is sound (resp. complete) for E-unification if all its inference rules are sound (resp. complete). A set of equations is said to be in *dag-solved form* (or *d-solved form*) if they can be arranged as a list $x_1 =^? t_1, \ldots, x_n =^? t_n$ where (a) each left-hand side x_i is a distinct variable, and (b) $\forall 1 \leq i \leq j \leq n$: x_i does not occur in t_j. Each x_i in this case is called a *solved variable*. We call a term (e.g., a variable) *fresh* if it is created by applying an inference rule (or a unification algorithm) and did not previously exist.

Consider the union $\Sigma_1 \cup \Sigma_2$ of two disjoint signatures Σ_1 and Σ_2. A term t is called a Σ_i-rooted term if its root symbol is in Σ_i. Variables, Σ_i-terms and Σ_i-equations are *i-pure*. We also use the notion of an *alien subterm*. An alien subterm of a Σ_i-rooted term t is a Σ_j-rooted subterm s $(i \neq j)$ such that all superterms of s are Σ_i-rooted. A *purification* procedure can be defined that uses *variable abstraction* [2] to replace any alien subterm u in a term t by a fresh variable x and adds the equation $x =^? u$. Then, equations $s =^? t$ between a 1-pure term s and a 2-pure term t are split into two pure equations $x =^? s$ and $x =^? t$ where x is a new variable. An equation between two variables is always both 1-pure and 2-pure. Given a set of pure equations P, we denote by $P|_{\Sigma_i}$ the set of i-pure equations in P (for $i = 1, 2$), and we say that P is in Σ_i-*solved form* (*partial* solved form) if $P|_{\Sigma_i}$ is in dag-solved form.

A *term rewriting system* (TRS) is a pair (Σ, R), where Σ is the signature and R is a finite set of rewrite rules of the form $l \to r$ such that l, r are Σ-terms, l is not a variable and $Var(r) \subseteq Var(l)$. Given a TRS $R = (\Sigma, R)$, the signature Σ is often partitioned into two disjoint sets $\Sigma := C \uplus D$, where $D := \{f | f(t_1, \ldots, t_n) \to r \in R\}$ and $C := \Sigma \setminus D$. Symbols in C are called *constructors*, and symbols in D are called *defined functions*. A term s *rewrites* to a term t, denoted by $s \to_R t$ (or simply $s \to t$), if there exist a position p of s, $l \to r \in R$, and substitution σ such that $s|_p = l\sigma$ and $t = s[r\sigma]_p$. A term s is a *normal form with respect to the relation* $\to_R$ (or simply a normal form), if there is no term t such that $s \to_R t$. This notion is lifted to substitutions as follows: a substitution σ is *normalized* if, for every variable x in the domain of σ, $x\sigma$ is a normal form. A TRS R is *terminating* if there are no infinite reduction sequences with respect to $\to_R$. A TRS R is *confluent* if, whenever $t \to_R s_1$ and $t \to_R s_2$, there exists a term w such that $s_1 \to_R^* w$ and $s_2 \to_R^* w$. A confluent and terminating TRS is called *convergent*. In a convergent TRS, we have the existence and the unicity of R-normal forms, denoted by $t\downarrow_R$ for any term t. We define an *inner constructor* to be a constructor f that satisfies the following additional restrictions: (1) f does not appear on the left-hand side on any rule in R; (2) f does not appear as the root symbol on the right-hand side of any rule in R; (3) there are no non-constant function symbols below f on the right-hand side of any rule in R. We consider a $\Sigma_1 \cup \Sigma_2$-theory E_1 and a Σ_2-theory E_2. The $\Sigma_1 \cup \Sigma_2$-theory E_1 is given by a Σ_1-*rooted TRS* R_1 such that for each $l \to r \in R_1$, l and r are Σ_1-rooted terms. Moreover, Σ_2-symbols do not occur in left-hand sides of R_1. We use the notion of *convergence modulo an equational theory*. When R_1 is convergent modulo E_2, we have that for any terms s and t, $s =_{R_1 \cup E_2} t$ if and only if $s\downarrow_{R_1} =_{E_2} t\downarrow_{R_1}$.

3   Hierarchical Combination

Our hierarchical combination has been introduced in [7]. We present a simplified version in Definition 1. The motivation is to simplify the relationships between the theories and allows for an easier notation. However, the new definition follows the one presented in [7]. For completeness, we also repeat several results proven in [7] on hierarchical combination. These results will prove useful in showing the applicability of hierarchical combination to shallow theories, and then more generally to syntactic theories.

Definition 1. *A* hierarchical combination *is a pair* (E_1, E_2) *such that*

- $\Sigma_1 \cap \Sigma_2 = \emptyset$;
- E_1 *is a subterm collapse-free equational* $\Sigma_1 \cup \Sigma_2$-*theory given by a TRS* R_1 *which is* Σ_1-*rooted and convergent modulo* E_2;
- E_2 *is a finite equational* Σ_2-*theory*;
- Σ_2-*symbols are inner constructors in* R_1.

A hierarchical combination (E_1, E_2) *is finite (resp., shallow/syntactic) if* E_1 *is finite (resp., shallow/syntactic). The equational theory of* (E_1, E_2) *is* $E_1 \cup E_2$.

Since a finite theory is subterm collapse-free, we have that both E_1 and E_2 are subterm collapse-free.

Proposition 1. *[7] If* (E_1, E_2) *is a hierarchical combination, then* $E_1 \cup E_2$ *is subterm collapse-free.*

Let us now introduce a key notion of great interest to relate combined equational proofs with pure ones. The notion of variable abstraction is widely used in the context of combined equational theories [2, 4, 18]. In the following, we use a slight adaptation to abstract ground terms by constants ($\mathcal{C}$) and non-ground terms by variables ($\mathcal{Y}$). According to our assumptions, theories are regular and so a ground term cannot be equal to a non-ground one.

Definition 2 (Variable Abstraction). *Let* $\mathcal{Y}$ *be a countably infinite set of variables,* $\mathcal{C}$ *be a countably infinite set of constants such that* V, $\mathcal{Y}$ *and* $\mathcal{C}$ *are pairwise disjoint. We consider a bijection*

$$\pi : (T(\Sigma_1 \cup \Sigma_2 \cup V)_{\downarrow R_1} \smallsetminus V)/ =_{E_2} \longrightarrow \mathcal{Y} \cup \mathcal{C}$$

such that $\pi([t\downarrow_{R_1}]_{E_2}) \in \mathcal{C}$ *if and only if* t *is ground. For* $i = 1, 2$, *the* π_i-*abstraction of* t *is denoted by* t^{π_i} *and defined as follows:*

- *If* $t \in V$, *then* $t^{\pi_i} = t$.
- *If* $t = f(t_1, \ldots, t_n)$ *and* $f \in \Sigma_i$, *then* $t^{\pi_i} = f(t_1^{\pi_i}, \ldots, t_n^{\pi_i})$.
- *Otherwise,* $t^{\pi_i} = \pi([t\downarrow_{R_1}]_{E_2})$.

An inverse mapping of π *is a mapping* $\pi^{-1} : \mathcal{Y} \cup \mathcal{C} \longrightarrow (T(\Sigma_1 \cup \Sigma_2 \cup V) \smallsetminus V)$ *such that* $\pi([\pi^{-1}(z)\downarrow_{R_1}]_{E_2}) = z$ *for any* $z \in \mathcal{Y} \cup \mathcal{C}$.

In a hierarchical combination, a key feature is the ability to reuse an E_2-unification algorithm, say A_2, to solve 2-pure unification problems without loss of completeness.

Lemma 1. *[7] Let* (E_1, E_2) *be any hierarchical combination.*

- *For any terms* s *and* t, *if* $s \longleftrightarrow_{E_1 \cup E_2} t$, *then* $s^{\pi_2} =_{E_2} t^{\pi_2}$.
- E_2-*unification is a sound and complete method to solve 2-pure* $E_1 \cup E_2$-*unification problems.*

Let us now present the combination procedure.

3.1 Combination Procedure for Hierarchical Combination

We describe the combination procedure in an abstract way. By applying variable abstraction, we split the input set of equations P into two sets of 1-pure and 2-pure equations, denoted respectively by P_1 and P_2. Two algorithms A_1 and A_2 aim at solving P_1 and P_2:

- A_1 returns a Σ_1-solved form of 1-pure $E_1 \cup E_2$-unification problems. Thus, A_1 is a special type of algorithm that returns a "partial" solved form. We address the problem of building such a procedure in Section 4.
- A_2 is an E_2-unification algorithm.

Lemma 1 shows that an E_2-unification algorithm is the right tool for solving 2-pure problems. For unification problems that are not 2-pure, the idea is to use a rule-based unification procedure A_1. The role of A_1 is to reduce the problem to a form for which A_2 can be applied. The approach taken is as follows:

1. Run A_1 on P_1 to obtain P_1'.
2. Run A_2 on P_2 to obtain P_2'.
3. Combine P_1' and P_2' into a set of equations P'.
4. If P' is not solved, then iterate the procedure with P' as input.

In comparison with the combination algorithm presented in [7], the above description represents the core procedure of hierarchical combination. The algorithm of [7] can be seen as a single iteration of the loop in the above procedure. To ensure a single iteration is sufficient there are some additional technical restrictions present in [7], such as restricting the occurrence of "ping-pong variables". Additionally, some machinery, such as variable identification, is also required.

4   Unification in Shallow Hierarchical Combination

In this section we show that shallow theories are another class of theories for which a hierarchical combination approach can be applied. Let E_1 be a shallow equational theory [6] and E_2 an equational theory, both satisfying Definition 1. Thus, R_1 is a rewrite system where variables occur in rules at depth 1 (a variable cannot occur at depth 0 since R_1 is collapse-free). In this particular case, an inner constructor can only occur in a right hand side of a rule and as the root symbol of a ground flat term. By applying constant abstraction on right-hand sides of rules, we can build an "equivalent" shallow rewrite system which is disjoint from E_2. As shown below, we can rely on a unification algorithm for shallow equational theories [6,13,14] to build an A_1 procedure.

Let $R_1^\pi = \{l \to r^{\pi_1} \mid l \to r \in R_1\}$. Obviously, R_1^π is also a shallow rewrite system.

Lemma 2. *Let s be a Σ_1-rooted term such that its alien subterms are R_1-normalized. If $s \to_{R_1} t$, then*

- *t is a Σ_1-rooted term such that its alien subterms are R_1-normalized,*
- *$s^{\pi_1} \to_{R_1^\pi} t^{\pi_1}$.*

Proof. Let $s \to_{R_1} t$.

1. E_1 is subterm collapse free and Σ_2 symbols in R_1 appear as inner constructors. Thus, if s is Σ_1-rooted then t is Σ_1-rooted.

2. If $s = s[l\sigma]_p \to_R s[r\sigma]_p = t$ for some R-normalized σ and position p, then p must not occur in an alien subterm of s since we assume s has R_1-normalized alien subterms. This implies, $s^{\pi_1} = s^{\pi_1}[(l\sigma)^{\pi_1}]_p$ and $t^{\pi_1} = s^{\pi_1}[(r\sigma)^{\pi_1}]_p$. Let $(\sigma)^{\pi_1} := \{x \mapsto (x\sigma)^{\pi_1} \mid x \in Var(l)\}$. Note, l contains only Σ_1 symbols and any Σ_2 symbols in r must be roots of ground terms. Thus, $(l\sigma)^{\pi_1} = l(\sigma)^{\pi_1}$ and $(r\sigma)^{\pi_1} = r^{\pi_1}(\sigma)^{\pi_1}$. This implies

$$s^{\pi_1} = s^{\pi_1}[(l\sigma)^{\pi_1}]_p = s^{\pi_1}[l(\sigma)^{\pi_1}]_p \to_{R_1^\pi} s^{\pi_1}[r^{\pi_1}(\sigma)^{\pi_1}]_p = s^{\pi_1}[(r\sigma)^{\pi_1}]_p = t^{\pi_1}$$

$\square$

Lemma 3. *Let s and t be Σ_1-rooted terms. If $s =_{E_2} t$ then $s^{\pi_1} = t^{\pi_1}$.*

Proof. Let $s =_{E_2} t$. For each pair of alien subterms $s' \in s$ and $t' \in t$ such that $s' \leftrightarrow^*_{E_2} t'$, $\pi(s') = \pi(t')$. In addition, s and t have the same root symbol. Therefore, $s^{\pi_1} = t^{\pi_1}$. $\square$

Proposition 2. *Let $s =^? t$ be a Σ_1-equation, and σ be a R_1-normalized substitution. If $s\sigma =_{E_1 \cup E_2} t\sigma$, then $s\sigma^{\pi_1} =_{R_1^\pi} t\sigma^{\pi_1}$.*

Proof. Since $s\sigma =_{E_1 \cup E_2} t\sigma$, we have $s\sigma \to^*_{R_1} (s\sigma){\downarrow}_{R_1} =_{E_2} (t\sigma){\downarrow}_{R_1} \leftarrow^*_{R_1} t\sigma$. By Lemma 2, we have $s\sigma^{\pi_1} \to^*_{R_1^\pi} ((s\sigma){\downarrow}_{R_1})^{\pi_1}$ and $t\sigma^{\pi_1} \to^*_{R_1^\pi} ((t\sigma){\downarrow}_{R_1})^{\pi_1}$. By Lemma 3, $((s\sigma){\downarrow}_{R_1})^{\pi_1} = ((t\sigma){\downarrow}_{R_1})^{\pi_1}$, and so $s\sigma^{\pi_1} =_{R_1^\pi} t\sigma^{\pi_1}$. $\square$

Proposition 2 shows that the problem of solving 1-pure equations can be reduced to a R_1^π-unification problem. Let us now show that the hierarchical combination approach initiated in [7] can be applied to the theories under consideration. It is shown in [7] that if three restrictions are satisfied by the combined theory, there exists a combined unification algorithm. We present those restrictions below, rephrased as to conform to the current presentation.

Restriction 1. *(Algorithm A_1) Let P_1 be a set of 1-pure equations. Algorithm A_1 applied to P_1 computes a set of problems $\{Q_k\}_{k \in K}$ such that*

$$\bigcup_{k \in K} CSU_{E_1 \cup E_2}(Q_k) \text{ is a } CSU_{E_1 \cup E_2}(P_1) \text{ and for each } k \in K:$$

(i) Q_k is in Σ_1-solved form.
(ii) No fresh variable occur under Σ_2-rooted terms.

Restriction 2. *(Algorithm A_2)*
Algorithm A_2 computes a finite complete set of $E_1 \cup E_2$-unifiers of 2-pure unification problems.

Restriction 3. *(Errors)*

(i) A Σ_2-rooted term cannot be $E_1 \cup E_2$-equal to a Σ_1-rooted term.
(ii) $E_1 \cup E_2$ is subterm collapse-free. Therefore, an $E_1 \cup E_2$-unification problem including a cycle has no solution.

Lemma 4. *Shallow hierarchical combination (E_1, E_2) satisfies Restrictions (1) through (3).*

Proof. Let us consider the different restrictions.

- Restriction 1: Since R_1^π is shallow, R_1^π-unification is finitary and a unification algorithm for shallow theories is known. Given a set of Σ_1-equations P_1, it computes a finite complete set of R_1^π-unifiers of P_1, say $\{\sigma_k\}_{k \in K}$. By Proposition 2, $\{\sigma_k \pi^{-1}\}_{k \in K}$ is a $CSU_{E_1 \cup E_2}(P_1)$. By purification, each σ_k can be equivalently written as a unification problem Q_k such that Q_k is in Σ_1-solved form, and Q_k contains only ground Σ_2-rooted terms.
- Restriction 2: This restriction follows directly from Lemma 1.
- Restriction 3: $E_1 \cup E_2$ is subterm collapse-free due to Proposition 1. Since E_1 and E_2 are both subterm collapse-free, Σ_2-rooted terms cannot be $E_1 \cup E_2$-equal to Σ_1-rooted terms without contradicting Lemma 1. $\square$

Directly from Lemma 4 and [7] we have the following.

Theorem 1. *For any shallow hierarchical combination* (E_1, E_2), *there exists a combined* $E_1 \cup E_2$-*unification algorithm, provided that an* E_2-*unification algorithm is known.*

Proof. In [6], unification is shown decidable and finitary in shallow theories. In addition, they provide a method for constructing a unification algorithm for an arbitrary shallow theory. Thus, we can construct a finitary unification algorithm, A_1, from the shallow equational theory of R_1^π. By Lemma 4, the result follows. $\square$

Example 1. Consider the (ground) hierarchical combination (E_1, E_2) where the *TRS* R_1 associated with E_1 is $\{f(a,b) \to g(a+b), f(b,a) \to g(b+a)\}$ and $E_2 = \{x + y = y + x\}$. The *TRS* R_1 is convergent modulo E_2. The *TRS* R_1^π is $\{f(a,b) \to g(c), f(b,a) \to g(c)\}$ where $c = \pi([a+b]_{E_2})$. A R_1^π-unification algorithm can be obtained by adding to a syntactic unification algorithm some mutation rules [6]. Then, most general $E_1 \cup E_2$-unifiers of a 1-pure unification problem can be derived from most general R_1^π-unifiers by replacing the constant c with $a + b$.

Shallow theories are particular syntactic theories admitting a terminating mutation-based unification procedure. In [13], Lynch and Morawska have investigated a larger class of syntactic theories admitting a terminating mutation-based unification procedure. In Section 5, we consider a mutation-based approach for the matching problem. This particular unification problem is particularly interesting with respect to our combination method since there will be no termination issue due to the fact that solutions are necessarily ground.

5   Matching in Finite Syntactic Hierarchical Combination

In this section we consider the matching problem in any finite syntactic hierarchical combination. Due to the more restricted nature of the matching problem we obtain several improvements over the unification problem. One of the improvements is that we are able to relax several restrictions we assumed for the unification problem. In the unification setting it was necessary to restrict variables which could cause reapplication of the first unification algorithm, denoted as "ping pong" variables in [7]. This restriction can be easily fulfilled if most general solutions can be expressed without any new variable. Considering matching problems in regular theories, there are only ground solutions, and so no ping pong variables. Since subterm collapse-free theories are regular, the theories we are interested in seem well-suited for a hierarchical approach to the matching problem.

The combination algorithm we propose is similar to the one existing for matching in disjoint unions of regular theories [16, 17]. In that context, matching algorithms A_1 and A_2 are applied repeatedly until reaching normal forms that correspond to most general solutions. The key principle of the combination algorithm for matching is to purify only the left-hand sides of matching problems. Thus, this purification introduces a "pending" equation $s =^? X$ that will lead to a match-equation: since X occurs in a match-equation solved by A_1 or A_2, X will be instantiated by a ground term, say u, transforming eventually $s =^? X$ into a match-equation $s \leq^? u$.

Definition 3. *Let P be a conjunction of match-equations and equations.*
The set of ground-solved variables in P is the smallest set of variables in P such that

1. *variables occurring in left-hand sides of match-equations are ground-solved.*
2. *if $t =^? t'$ is an equation in P such that variables in t' are ground-solved, then variables in t are also ground-solved.*

When P contains only ground-solved variables, it is called an extended matching *problem. A matching problem is an extended matching problem containing no equations. For any match-equation in an extended matching problem, we assume that the right-hand side is R_1-normalized. Hence, there will be an implicit normalization of right-hand sides when new match-equations are generated by some inference rules.*

In the following, we present a rule-based combination method to solve $E_1 \cup E_2$-matching problems. Let us briefly introduce the main steps of that combination method. On the one hand, solving match-equations with 2-pure left-hand sides generate solved match-equations. On the other hand, solving match-equations whose left-hand sides are Σ_1-rooted generate new equalities while preserving the syntactic form of an extended matching problem. Then, there are some combination rules to remove successively the equations introduced during the purification and the solving phases. Eventually, we obtain a matching problem in solved form. As shown below, this method is sound and complete when (E_1, E_2) is a finite syntactic hierarchical combination, which means that E_1, E_2 are finite and E_1 admits a resolvent presentation denoted by S_1. If E_1 and E_2 are finite, then $E_1 \cup E_2$ is finite according to the result below.

Proposition 3. *(E_1, E_2) is a finite hierarchical combination if and only if $E_1 \cup E_2$ is finite.*

Proof. (If direction) Straightforward.

(Only if direction) Assume that this is not the case, that is, there exists a term $t \in T(\Sigma_1 \cup \Sigma_2, \mathcal{X})$ with an infinite set of terms S such that $t =_{E_1 \cup E_2} s$ for each $s \in S$. Since there exists a convergent rewrite system R_1 which is equivalent to E_1, we can consider the unique R_1-normal form of each term $s \in S$. Let $S' = \{s{\downarrow}_{R_1} \mid s \in S\}$. The set of terms S' is also infinite, otherwise it would contradict that E_1 is finite. Since R_1 is convergent modulo E_2, $t{\downarrow}_{R_1} =_{E_2} s'$ for each $s' \in S'$. This implies the existence of an infinite E_2 equivalence class $[t{\downarrow}_{R_1}]_{E_2}$, which contradicts our assumption that E_2 is finite.   □

Since matching is finitary in a finite theory, we could take a brute for approach to construct an $E_1 \cup E_2$-matching algorithm [15]. Actually, a match-equation $s \leq^?_{E_1 \cup E_2} t$ has the same set of (ground) $E_1 \cup E_2$-solutions as the syntactic matching problem

$$\bigvee_{\{t' \mid t' =_{E_1 \cup E_2} t\}} s \leq^?_\emptyset t'$$

where $\emptyset$ denotes the empty equational theory. However, similarly to [15], we can also proceed in a modular way, by using some "pure" matching algorithms, say A_1 and A_2 dedicated respectively to E_1 and E_2. In the context of matching, A_1 aims at handling match-equations whose left-hand sides are Σ_1-rooted, whilst A_2 denotes an E_2-matching algorithm to solve match-equations whose left-hand sides are 2-pure.

Restriction 4. (E_1, E_2) *is a finite syntactic hierarchical combination with the following constituent algorithms:*

1. A_1 *is given by the mutation-based algorithm* $\mathcal{M}$ *depicted in Fig. 1, where* S_1 *denotes a resolvent presentation of the finite syntactic theory* E_1.
2. A_2 *is an* E_2*-matching algorithm.*

Lemma 5. E_2*-matching is a sound and complete method to solve* $E_1 \cup E_2$*-matching problems whose left-hand sides are 2-pure, provided that the right-hand sides are replaced by their* π_2*-abstractions.*

Proof. Let $s \leq^? t$ be a match-equation such that s is 2-pure term, and consider the corresponding 2-pure match-equation $s \leq^? t^{\pi_2}$, where t^{π_2} can be effectively computed (up to a renaming). The soundness is obvious: any E_2-solution σ of $s \leq^? t^{\pi_2}$ leads to an $E_1 \cup E_2$-solution $\sigma\pi^{-1}$ of $s \leq^? t$. For the completeness, consider an $E_1 \cup E_2$-solution σ of $s \leq^? t$ where s is 2-pure. By Lemma 1 (and induction on the length of derivation), $s\sigma =_{E_1 \cup E_2} t$ implies $s\sigma^{\pi_2} =_{E_2} t^{\pi_2}$ where $\sigma =_{E_1 \cup E_2} \sigma^{\pi_2}\pi^{-1}$.   □

5.1   Mutation-Based Procedure

We now consider the question of applying a mutation-based inference system to simplify match-equations whose left-hand sides are Σ_1-rooted. The mutation inference is known to be complete for syntactic theories [5,11,12], and so for E_1. The next lemma shows that this property is preserved when considering $E_1 \cup E_2$.

Lemma 6. *Let S_1 be a resolvent presentation of E_1, and let s and t be Σ_1-rooted terms such that t is R_1-normalized. If $s =_{E_1 \cup E_2} t$, then there exists an equational proof of $s =_{E_1 \cup E_2} t$ with at most one S_1-equational step applied at the root position.*

Lemma 6 justifies the eager R_1-normalization of the right-hand sides of match-equations, and it implies the completeness of the inference system $\mathcal{M}$ (Fig. 1).

Mutate

$$\{f(s_1, \ldots, s_m) \leq^? g(t_1, \ldots, t_n)\} \cup P$$
$$\longrightarrow \{r_1 \leq^? t_1, \ldots, r_n \leq^? t_n, \; s_1 =^? l_1, \ldots, s_m =^? l_m\} \cup P$$

If $f(l_1, \ldots, l_m) = g(r_1, \ldots, r_n)$ is a fresh variant of an axiom in S_1.

Matching Decomposition

$$\{f(s_1, \ldots, s_m) \leq^? f(t_1, \ldots, t_m)\} \cup P$$
$$\longrightarrow \{s_1 \leq^? t_1, \ldots, s_m \leq^? t_m\} \cup P$$

Where $f \in \Sigma_1$.

Matching Clash

$$\{f(s_1, \ldots, s_m) \leq^? g(t_1, \ldots, t_n)\} \cup P$$
$$\longrightarrow \; Fail$$

Where $f \in \Sigma_1$, $f \neq g$ and **Mutate** does not apply.

Fig. 1. Mutation-based inference system $\mathcal{M}$ for Matching

Lemma 7. *$\mathcal{M}$ (Fig. 1) is sound, complete and terminating.*

Proof. The soundness is straightforward. The completeness is a consequence of Lemma 6. Let us now prove the termination. The multiset consisting of the sizes of the right-hand sides of match-equations can be used as a complexity measure. The three rules of $\mathcal{M}$ decrease this complexity measure, and so $\mathcal{M}$ terminates. □

Corollary 1. *Let P be a set of match-equations whose left-hand sides are Σ_1-rooted. There exists a finite derivation $P \vdash \cdots \vdash P'$ in $\mathcal{M}$ such that P and P' have the same set of solutions, and P' is in normal form w.r.t. $\mathcal{M}$.*

Lemma 8. *If P is an extended matching problem in normal form w.r.t. $\mathcal{M}$, then P does not contain match-equations whose left-hand sides are Σ_1-rooted.*

Proof. By contradiction. Let P_1 be the set of match-equations in P whose left-hand sides are Σ_1-rooted. If P_1 is non-empty, then some rule in $\mathcal{M}$ must apply, which means that P is not a normal form w.r.t. $\mathcal{M}$. □

To conclude this section we introduce a complexity measure, which will be useful to prove the termination of the combined matching procedure (Fig. 2). Since $E_1 \cup E_2$ is finite, any extended matching problem P has only finitely many ground solutions, and each non-ground right-hand side of an equation in P, say t, can only be instantiated among a (possibly empty) finite set of ground terms $Gnd(t)$. Then, the set of match-equations *encoded by* P is inductively defined as follows:

$$ms(\{s =^? t\} \cup P) = \bigcup_{t' \in Gnd(t)} \{s \leq^? t'\} \cup ms(P) \text{ if } t \text{ is non-ground}$$
$$ms(\{s =^? t\} \cup P) = \{s \leq^? t\} \cup ms(P) \text{ if } t \text{ ground}$$
$$ms(\{s \leq^? t\} \cup P) = \{s \leq^? t\} \cup ms(P)$$

To compare match-equations we use the ordering: $(s \leq^? t) \prec (s' \leq^? t')$ if

- s is a strict subterm of s',
- or $Var(s) \cap Var(s') = \emptyset$ and t is a strict subterm of t',
- or $t = t'$ and s strictly subsumes s'.

The ordering $\prec$ is well-founded and so its multiset extension $\prec_m$ is well-founded.

Lemma 9. *Any rule in $\mathcal{M}$ strictly decreases ms with respect to $\prec_m$.*

The above lemma is another way to prove the termination of $\mathcal{M}$.

5.2   Combination Procedure

Based on the restrictions related to A_1 and A_2, we can give a new matching procedure for the hierarchical combination.

Consider $\mathfrak{C}_\mathcal{M}$ the inference system depicted in Fig. 2, with the following inferences rules $\{\textbf{Solve}_1, \textbf{Solve}_2, \textbf{VA}, \textbf{RemEq}, \textbf{Rep}, \textbf{Merge}, \textbf{Clash}\}$. We can easily verify that each rule in $\mathfrak{C}_\mathcal{M}$ preserves the set of $E_1 \cup E_2$-solutions. This is clear for the rules in $\{\textbf{VA}, \textbf{RemEq}, \textbf{Rep}, \textbf{Merge}, \textbf{Clash}\}$. Moreover, this is true by Lemma 7 for $\textbf{Solve}_1$, and by Lemma 5 for $\textbf{Solve}_2$. The inference system $\mathfrak{C}_\mathcal{M}$ aims at computing matching problems in solved form.

Lemma 10. *Normal forms with respect to $\mathfrak{C}_\mathcal{M}$ are matching problems in solved form.*

Proof. Assume P is an extended matching problem which is not a matching problem in solved form. Then we can always show that a rule in $\mathfrak{C}_\mathcal{M}$ can be applied:

1. If there is some equation $t =^? t'$ in P, we have two possible cases. First, if t' is ground, then **RemEq** applies. Second, if t' contains some ground-solved variable, then a match-equation containing some fresh variable must also occur in P. If this match-equation is solved, then **Rep** applies. Otherwise, just like in the third case below, either **Solve**$_1$ or **Solve**$_2$ or **VA** applies on this unsolved match-equation.

Solve₁:

$$\frac{P_1 \cup P}{A_1(P_1) \cup P} \qquad P_1 \text{ is a set of match-equations with } \Sigma_1\text{-rooted left-hand sides}$$

Solve₂:

$$\frac{P_2 \cup P}{A_2(P_2) \cup P} \qquad P_2 \text{ is a set of match-equations with 2-pure left-hand sides}$$

VA:

$$\frac{\{s[u] \leq^? t\} \cup P}{\{s[X] \leq^? t, u =^? X\} \cup P} \qquad \text{if } s \text{ is } \Sigma_2-\text{rooted, } u \text{ is an alien subterm}$$

RemEq:

$$\frac{\{t =^? t'\} \cup P}{\{t \leq^? t'\} \cup P} \qquad \text{if } t' \text{ is ground}$$

Rep:

$$\frac{\{Y \leq^? u, \ t =^? t'[Y]\} \cup P}{\{Y \leq^? u, \ t =^? t'[u]\} \cup P}$$

Merge:

$$\frac{\{X \leq^? t, \ X \leq^? s\} \cup P}{\{X \leq^? t\} \cup P} \qquad \text{if } s =_{E_1 \cup E_2} t$$

Clash:

$$\frac{\{X \leq^? t, \ X \leq^? s\} \cup P}{Fail} \qquad \text{if } s \neq_{E_1 \cup E_2} t$$

Fig. 2. $\mathfrak{C}_{\mathcal{M}}$: inference system for the combination of matching

2. If there are $X \leq^? t$ and $X \leq^? s$ in P, then either **Merge** or **Clash** can be applied.
3. If there is some match-equation $s \leq^? t$ in P where s is not a variable, then either **Solve₁** or **Solve₂** or **VA** can be applied.

$\square$

To show the soundness and completenes of $\mathfrak{C}_{\mathcal{M}}$, it remains to show that $\mathfrak{C}_{\mathcal{M}}$ terminates for any input.

Lemma 11. *Let P be any input matching problem. Any repeated application of rules in $\mathfrak{C}_{\mathcal{M}}$ on P terminates.*

Proof. Consider the complexity measure ms introduced for Lemma 9 plus the following ones:

- m_1: number of equations (denoted by $=^?$)
- m_2: number of Σ_2-rooted match-equations
- m_3: number of match-equations
- m_4: number of variables occurring in equations (denoted by $=^?$)

Then, the termination of $\mathfrak{C}_{\mathcal{M}}$ can be obtained by considering a lexicographic combination of these complexity measures, more precisely the one given by the tuple (ms, m_1, m_2, m_3, m_4), as shown in the table below.

	ms	m_1	m_2	m_3	m_4
Solve₁	↓				
VA	↓				
RemEq	↓=	↓			
Solve₂	↓=	↓=	↓		
Merge/Clash	↓=	↓=	↓=	↓	
Rep	↓=	↓=	↓=	↓=	↓

□

Theorem 2. *For any finite syntactic hierarchical combination* (E_1, E_2), *there exists a combined* $E_1 \cup E_2$-*matching algorithm (Fig. 1 and Fig. 2), provided that an* E_2-*matching algorithm is known.*

Proof. Direct consequence of Lemmas 10 and 11.   □

5.3   Example: Matching in a Theory of Distributive Exponentiation

As an example of the above combination method for matching algorithms we consider in this section a theory of distributive exponentiation, namely $\mathcal{E}_{AC}$ for which a rule-based unification algorithm is presented in [9]. We recall that $\mathcal{E}_{AC} = (E_1, E_2)$, where $E_2 = AC(\circledast) = \{(x \circledast y) \circledast z = x \circledast (y \circledast z), x \circledast y = y \circledast x\}$ and E_1 is given by the following convergent rewrite system modulo E_2:

$$R_1 = \begin{cases} exp(exp(x,y),z) \to exp(x, y \circledast z) \\ exp(x * y, z) \to exp(x,z) * exp(y,z) \end{cases}$$

Lemma 12. $\mathcal{E}_{AC}$ *is a finite syntactic hierarchical combination* $(E_1, AC(\circledast))$ *where* E_1 *admits the following resolvent presentation:*

$$S_1 = \begin{cases} exp(exp(x,y),z) = exp(x, y \circledast z) \\ exp(x * y, z) = exp(x,z) * exp(y,z) \end{cases}$$

Note that Restriction 4(2) is addressed trivially since there are well-known AC-matching algorithms. Therefore, the main task is to instantiate the inference system $\mathcal{M}$ (Fig. 1). This leads to the mutation rules for $\mathcal{E}_{AC}$-matching shown in Fig. 3.

Example 2. Consider the equational theory $\mathcal{E}_{AC}$ and the matching problem

$$exp(X, V \circledast c_1) \leq^? exp(b, c_1 \circledast c_2 \circledast c_3)$$

The combination algorithm $\mathfrak{C}_{\mathcal{M}}$ works as follows with this input. First, **Matching Decomposition** is applied and leads to $\{X \leq^? b, V \circledast c_1 \leq^? c_1 \circledast c_2 \circledast c_3\}$. Then **Solve₂** applies and provides a first solved form $\{X \leq^? b, V \leq^? c_2 \circledast c_3\}$. Another possibility is to apply the first **Mutate** rule from Fig. 3, yielding $\{Y \circledast V \circledast c_1 \leq^? c_1 \circledast c_2 \circledast c_3, X =^? exp(b, Y)\}$. By **Solve₂**, the above 2-pure match-equation has two solutions. The first solution is $\{Y \leq^? c_2, V \leq^? c_3\}$. After **Rep** and **RemEq**, we obtain a new solved form: $\{V \leq^? c_3, X \leq^? exp(b, c_2)\}$. Similarly, for the second solution $\{Y \leq^? c_3, V \leq^? c_2\}$, we get the solved form $\{V \leq^? c_2, X \leq^? exp(b, c_3)\}$. The other **Mutate** rules lead to a failure thanks the application of **Matching Clash**.

Mutate

$\{exp(s_1, s_2) \leq^? exp(t_1, t_2)\} \cup P \longrightarrow \{Y \circledast s_2 \leq^? t_2, s_1 =^? exp(t_1, Y)\} \cup P$

$\{exp(s_1, s_2) \leq^? exp(t_1, t_2)\} \cup P \longrightarrow \{exp(s_1, Y) \leq^? t_1, s_2 =^? Y \circledast t_2\} \cup P$

$\{exp(s_1, s_2) \leq^? t_1 * t_2\} \cup P$
$\longrightarrow \{exp(X, s_2) \leq^? t_1, exp(Y, s_2) \leq^? t_2, s_1 =^? X * Y\} \cup P$

$\{s_1 * s_2 \leq^? exp(t_1, t_2)\} \cup P$
$\longrightarrow \{X * Y \leq^? t_1, s_1 =^? exp(X, t_2), s_2 =^? exp(Y, t_2)\} \cup P$

Fig. 3. Mutation rules for $\mathcal{E}_{AC}$-matching

6   Conclusion

We have presented a collection of new results about our hierarchical combination approach for solving unification problems. First we defined a simpler reformulation of the combination method, which is sufficient for the problems we focus on in this paper. Our application to shallow extensions complement and improve our earlier work on hierarchical combination presented in [7,9]. Hierarchical combination requires a solver A_1, taking in account the axioms of E_1, to produce partial solved forms. Although a general sound and complete method is available to construct A_1, the problem of termination still remains. We solve this problem for shallow theories by showing how to exploit unification algorithms known for them. Second, we have shown another combination method for the matching problem in finite syntactic extensions. Future work includes applying the general method developed here to partly ground unification problems and finding conditions which allow us to combine unification algorithms of larger classes of equational theories.

References

1. Baader, F., Nipkow, T.: Term rewriting and all that. Cambridge University Press, New York (1998)
2. Baader, F., Schulz, K.U.: Unification in the union of disjoint equational theories: Combining decision procedures. Journal of Symbolic Computation 21(2), 211–243 (1996)
3. Baader, F., Snyder, W.: Unification theory. In: Robinson, J.A., Voronkov, A. (eds.) Handbook of Automated Reasoning, pp. 445–532. Elsevier and MIT Press (2001)
4. Boudet, A.: Combining unification algorithms. Journal of Symbolic Computation 16(6), 597–626 (1993)
5. Boudet, A., Contejean, E.: On n-syntactic equational theories. In: Kirchner, H., Levi, G. (eds.) ALP 1992. LNCS, vol. 632, pp. 446–457. Springer, Heidelberg (1992)

6. Comon, H., Haberstrau, M., Jouannaud, J.: Syntacticness, cycle-syntacticness, and shallow theories. Inf. Comput. 111(1), 154–191 (1994)
7. Erbatur, S., Kapur, D., Marshall, A.M., Narendran, P., Ringeissen, C.: Hierarchical combination. In: Bonacina, M.P. (ed.) CADE 2013. LNCS, vol. 7898, pp. 249–266. Springer, Heidelberg (2013)
8. Erbatur, S., Kapur, D., Marshall, A.M., Narendran, P., Ringeissen, C.: Hierarchical combination of matching algorithms. In: Twentyeighth International Workshop on Unification (UNIF 2014), Vienna, Austria (2014)
9. Erbatur, S., Marshall, A.M., Kapur, D., Narendran, P.: Unification over distributive exponentiation (sub)theories. Journal of Automata, Languages and Combinatorics (JALC) 16(2–4), 109–140 (2011)
10. Gallier, J.H., Snyder, W.: Complete sets of transformations for general E-unification. Theoretical Computer Science 67(2–3), 203–260 (1989)
11. Jouannaud, J.-P.: Syntactic theories. In: Rovan, B. (ed.) MFCS 1990. LNCS, vol. 452, pp. 15–25. Springer, Heidelberg (1990)
12. Kirchner, C., Klay, F.: Syntactic theories and unification. In: Proceedings of the Fifth Annual IEEE Symposium on Logic in Computer Science Logic in Computer Science, LICS 1990, pp. 270–277, June1990
13. Lynch, C., Morawska, B.: Basic syntactic mutation. In: Voronkov, A. (ed.) CADE 2002. LNCS (LNAI), vol. 2392, pp. 471–485. Springer, Heidelberg (2002)
14. Nieuwenhuis, R.: Decidability and complexity analysis by basic paramodulation. Inf. Comput. 147(1), 1–21 (1998)
15. Nipkow, T.: Proof transformations for equational theories. In: Proceedings of the Fifth Annual IEEE Symposium on Logic in Computer Science Logic in Computer Science, LICS 1990, pp. 278–288, June 1990
16. Nipkow, T.: Combining matching algorithms: The regular case. J. Symb. Comput. 12(6), 633–654 (1991)
17. Ringeissen, C.: Combining decision algorithms for matching in the union of disjoint equational theories. Inf. Comput. 126(2), 144–160 (1996)
18. Schmidt-Schauß, M.: Unification in a combination of arbitrary disjoint equational theories. Journal of Symbolic Computation 8, 51–99 (1989)
19. Snyder, W.: A Proof Theory for General Unification. Progress in Computer Science and Applied Logic, vol. 11. Birkhäuser (1991)

Combining Forward and Backward Propagation

Amira Zaki[1,2], Slim Abdennadher[1], and Thom Frühwirth[2]

[1] German University in Cairo, Egypt
{amira.zaki,slim.abdennadher}@guc.edu.eg
[2] Ulm University, Germany
thom.fruehwirth@uni-ulm.de

Abstract. Constraint Handling Rules (CHR) is a general-purpose rule-based programming language. This paper studies the forward and backward propagation of rules, and explores the combination of both execution strategies. Forward propagation transforms input to output, while backward propagation uncovers input from output. This work includes a source-to-source transformation capable of implementing a backward propagation of the rules. Furthermore with the addition of annotating trigger constraints, CHR programs can be executed in a strictly-forward, strictly-backward or combined interleaved quasi-simultaneous manner. A programmer should only write one program and then the annotated transformation empowers the multiple execution strategies. The proposed work is useful for automatic implementation of bidirectional search for any search space through the combined execution strategies. Moreover, it is advantageous for reversible bijective algorithms (such as lossless compression/decompression), requiring only one algorithm direction to be implemented.

Keywords: Forward/Backward, Constraint Handling Rules, Bidirectional Search, Combined Propagation, Source-to-source transformation.

1 Introduction

A program P can be defined as a series of transitions transforming an input state to an output state, while an inverse (or backward) program P^{-1} is one that uncovers the input given the output [11]. The transition rules transforming input to output are known as forward rules, whereas those reversing output to input are known as backward rules. For example, compression can be considered as a forward program, and decompression is its backward program.

The study of transition directions for the same program captures some interesting program pairs, such as encryption/decryption, compression/decompression, invertible arithmetic functions and roll-back transactions. Despite the relation between inverse computations, it is common practice to maintain two separate programs to perform each transition direction. The two programs are similar and essentially related to one another, however two disjoint programs have to be written. Furthermore, maintaining the relationship between the programs can be a

© Springer International Publishing Switzerland 2015
C. Lutz and S. Ranise (Eds.): FroCoS 2015, LNAI 9322, pp. 307–322, 2015.
DOI: 10.1007/978-3-319-24246-0_19

source of errors and inconsistency, since any changes must be reflected in both programs.

To avoid duplication of effort, a user ideally wants to write and maintain a single program. This work facilitates a combination of forward and backward propagation directions automatically for any given program. Programs are written using Constraint Handling Rules (CHR), which is a high-level programming language based on guarded rewrite rules [7]. The language was originally designed to write constraint solvers, however it is a strong and elegant general-purpose language with a large spectrum of applications. Source-to-source transformations extend CHR programs to ones with additional machinery [8]. This work presents a source-to-source transformation, to generate a combined program which is more expressive and complex, featuring two-way execution.

Programming languages themselves vary in the inference direction used; backward chaining languages are highly non-deterministic compared to committed-choice forward chaining languages. Languages supporting deterministic forward and backward computation are known as reversible languages such as the imperative language Janus [16]. Recently, [10] proposed a class of programming languages that generalizes both Constraint Logic and Concurrent Constraint Programming to combine forward and backward chaining, however the work lacks a proper implementation. Prolog uses backward chaining, and can be used to implement two-way programs whose arguments maybe used for input or output. However, implementing such programs is quite tricky, and special care must be taken while implementing with two-way predicates and operators.

For example, the run-length encoding algorithm is a simple data compression technique, where consecutive runs of characters within a text are packed and stored as a single character followed by its count. The text 'aaaaabccc' (wrapped in a compress/1 constraint) is compressed into 'a5b1c3' (in a result/1 constraint). The run-length encoding algorithm can be expressed in CHR as shown below, where pack/2 is used to pack consecutive letter runs and comp/3 to accumulate the encoding. This program encapsulates the combined forward and backward nature of the algorithm, and two-way execution is explored through the transformations described this work.

```
start @ compress(In) <=> comp(In,[],[]).
run-end @ comp([H1,H2|T],Run,Acc) <=> H1\=H2 | Run2=[H1|Run],
    pack(Run2,PackRun), append(Acc,[PackRun],Acc2), comp([H2|T],[],Acc2).
run-cont @ comp([H1,H2|T],Run,Acc) <=> H1=H2
    | Run2=[H1|Run],comp([H2|T],Run2,Acc).
last-char @ comp([H],Run,Acc) <=> Run2=[H|Run],
    pack(Run2,PackRun), append(Acc,[PackRun],Acc2), result(Acc2).
end @ comp([],_,_) <=> result([]).
```

This work presents a source-to-source transformation that captures the backwards operational semantics of CHR for range-restricted programs. The transformation was introduced earlier [17] however in this work it is revisited and expressed more formally. The previously mentioned run-length encoding program is transformed into a combined form as presented in this work. Then for a string 'aaaaabccc', the program can be forwardly run by: 'fwd, compress([a,a,a,a,a,b, c,c,c])' to produce the compressed form: 'result([[a,5], [b,1],[c,3]])'. Similarly, a backward run can be attained through a query: 'bck, result([[a,5], [b,1],[c,3]])' to decompress the sub-lists to: 'compress([a,a,a,a,a,b,c,c,c])'.

Furthermore this work introduces the addition of annotating trigger constraints, to empower the execution of CHR programs in a strictly-forward, strictly-backward or interleaved quasi-simultaneous bidirectional manner. This means that only one program is written and the annotated transformation enables multiple execution schemes. This is useful for solving bijective algorithms and the aforementioned inverse computation pairs. The paper extends by showing how the combined programs can be extended to facilitate bidirectional search.

Previous work, such as [1], tend to use CHR as a language for abduction. However, the problem is that the user has to write two different programs for deductive and abductive reasoning. This work presents a technique to write a program once, then facilitate different reasoning directions.

The paper proceeds by recalling background information about CHR in Section 2. In Section 3, the combined two-way programs are presented through source-to-source transformations, and then the extension for bidirectional search is given in Section 4. This is followed by an application in Section 5. The paper concludes by some remarks and future work in Section 6.

2 Constraint Handling Rules

2.1 Syntax

Constraint Handling Rules (CHR) [7,9] is a high level, committed choice, rule-based programming language. It consists of guarded rewrite rules that perform conditional transformation of a multi-set of constraints. It distinguishes between two types of constraints; built-in constraints which are predefined by the host language and other user-defined CHR constraints which are declared as functor/arity pairs. A generalized CHR simpagation rule is given as:

$$rule\text{-}id \text{ @ } H_k \setminus H_r \Leftrightarrow G \mid B$$

Every rule has an optional unique identifier preceding it given by $rule\text{-}id$. H_k and H_r are a conjunction of one or more CHR constraints; known as the kept and removed head constraints respectively. The guard G is an optional conjunction of built-in constraints. The body of the rule B consists of a conjunction of both built-in and CHR constraints.

Simplification and propagation rules are two other rule types which are special cases of simpagation rules. Simplification rules have no kept head constraints, and propagation rules have no removed head constraints. They are of the forms:

$$simplification\text{-}id \text{ @ } H_r \Leftrightarrow G \mid B$$

$$propagation\text{-}id \text{ @ } H_k \Rightarrow G \mid B$$

Constraint Handling Rules with Disjunction (CHR$^\vee$) [2] is an extension of CHR featuring disjunctive rule bodies to allow a backtrack search over alternatives. The rules are similar to the rule forms described above, however the rule body can be composed of two or more disjunctive bodies $(B_1 \vee B_2)$. For example a CHR$^\vee$ simpagation rule is of the form:

$$disjuntive\text{-}id \ @ \ H_k \setminus H_r \ \Leftrightarrow \ G \mid B_1 \ ; \ B_2$$

2.2   Operational Forward Semantics

The behavior of a CHR program is modeled through an operational semantics, in terms of a state transition system. The very abstract semantics (ω_{va}) is a state transition system, where a transition corresponds to a rule application and states represent goals consisting of a conjunction of CHR and built-in constraints. An initial state is an arbitrary one and a final state is a terminal one where no further transitions are possible. The ω_{va} semantics includes one rule which is shown below, where P is a CHR program and $\mathcal{CT}$ is the constraint theory for the built-in constraints. The body of a rule (B) and C consist of both built-in and CHR constraints, moreover H_k and H_r are a conjunction of CHR constraints, while G is a conjunction of built-in constraints.

Apply
$$(H_k \wedge H_r \wedge C) \mapsto^r_{apply} (H_k \wedge G \wedge B \wedge C)$$
if there is an instance of a rule r in P with new local variables $\bar{x}$ such that:
$$r \ @ \ H_k \setminus H_r \Leftrightarrow G \mid B \text{ and } \mathcal{CT} \models \forall(C \to \exists \bar{x} G)$$

The extended transition system for CHR$^\vee$ operates on a disjunction of CHR states known as a configuration: $S_1 \vee S_2 \vee \cdots \vee S_n$. The original apply transition is applicable to a single state. An additional split transition is applicable to any configuration containing a disjunction. It leads to a branching derivation entailing two states, where each state can be processed independently.

Split
$$((H_1 \vee H_2) \wedge C) \vee S \mapsto_\vee (H_1 \wedge C) \vee (H_2 \wedge C) \vee S$$

However, these semantics are highly non-deterministic and thus more refined semantics are needed for the actual implementation of CHR compilers[5]. The order of constraint execution and rule application determine how a derivation proceeds and is defined by the implemented operational semantics. Starting with the same initial query, multiple derivations are possible. If all derivations ultimately lead to the same goal, then the program is known as a confluent one.

2.3   Operational Backwards Semantics

The forward ω_{va} semantics models a forward rule application on an initial state to a final state. The inverse of this rule application is defined by a *backwards* semantics ω_b that reverses a final state to an initial state. This semantics was formally introduced in [17], and it is typically the same as the apply transition but with exchanging the left and right hand side states of the transition.

Backwards
$$(H_k \wedge G \wedge B \wedge C) \mapsto^r_{back} (H_k \wedge H_r \wedge C)$$
if there is an instance of a rule r in P with new local variables $\bar{x}$ such that:
$$r @ H_k \setminus H_r \Leftrightarrow G \mid B \text{ and } \mathcal{CT} \models \forall(C \rightarrow \exists \bar{x} G)$$

The semantics works by undoing each step of the forward execution. However without any external knowledge on how to proceed with the inverse tree, the backwards semantics only shows that any original state can be uncovered. In fact, inverse programs are normally non-confluent ones.

3   Combined CHR Programs

This work builds upon the K.U. Leuven system [9], which uses CHR with Prolog as the host language. To introduce the two-way execution, the contribution of the existing Leuven system is presented and source-to-source transformations are given to augment additional machinery on-top of the existent CHR system.

3.1   General Formulation

The first part of this work is to define a transformation of a CHR program for forward/backward execution. Programs are intended to be written once and then executed in several ways; data supplied is considered as input or output depending on the program direction used. Figure 1 represents the relation between input and output and the expected transitions of the two-way program.

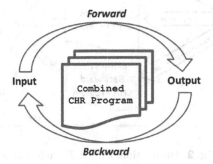

Fig. 1. Transitions between input and output

The cardinality of the program that transforms the input to output, decides on the properties of the two-way program required. If the relation is one-to-one, then for every output there exists only one input and vice versa. This makes the backward transition quite straight-forward, since for every output there is only one possible input that caused it. These relations would require a direct forward/backward execution mechanism. This is especially useful for bijective functions such as loss-less compression/decompression and encryption/decryption.

On the other hand, a list sorting program transforms several permutations into the same sorted output. Hence the forward transition has a many-to-one cardinality, and therefore its backward transition (shuffling a sorted list) is one-to-many. Due to the committed-choice nature of CHR and the deterministic implementation of the Leuven system, it would never reach all transition possibilities. Thus, it requires using a source-to-source transformation [6] that fully explores the search-space to reach all final states.

Therefore, for every transition direction two execution strategies are required; a direct one-way execution and an exhaustive execution. Annotations are added to the combined program, to decide on the chosen execution strategy. The annotation involves adding a kept head constraint to each program rule, where its presence will denote the activation of this rule. The annotation will involve four CHR constraints: fwd/0, fwd-ex/0, bck/0 and bck-ex/0. The following subsections highlight the necessary changes that are needed to transform a CHR program into a combined two-way one with control terms that steer the direction. The summary of the transformations can be depicted in Figure 2.

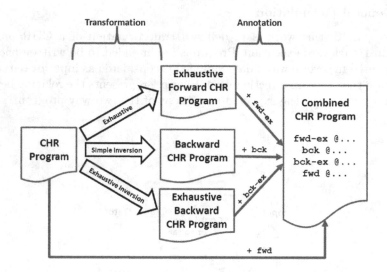

Fig. 2. Bidirectional CHR Transformations

3.2 Forward CHR

In order to change the program execution flow, source-to-source transformations are used to facilitate a straight-forward implementation on top of existing CHR implementations whilst exploiting the optimizations of current CHR compilers [15]. The normal execution of a committed-choice CHR program can be transformed into one featuring exhaustive completion to fully explore a goal's search space [6].

Directly Forwards. The CHR Leuven system follows a refined operational semantics with additional fixed orders for explored goals and chosen program rules. It applies the program rules on a goal, until a fixed point is reached. Thus this provides the direct forwards execution of the combined program.

A constraint `fwd/0` is introduced as a kept head constraint to every program rule. Thus for every generalized CHR simpagation rule, a corresponding annotated rule is added of the form shown below. For other rules, the missing constraints are non-existent accordingly (i.e H_k or H_r).

$$fwd\text{-}simpagation \text{ @ } \texttt{fwd} , \ H_k \setminus H_r \Leftrightarrow G \mid B$$

Example 1. Run-length Encoding *The compression algorithm presented in the introduction can be rewritten using forward annotation as shown below. For a string* '`aaaaabccc`', *the program is forwardly run by:* '`fwd,compress([a,a,a,a,a,b,c,c,c])`' *to yield the compressed form:* '`result([[a,5], [b,1],[c,3]])`'.

```
start @ fwd \ compress(In) <=> comp(In,[],[]).
run-end @ fwd \ comp([H1,H2|T],Run,Acc) <=> H1\=H2 | Run2=[H1|Run],
    pack(Run2,PackRun), append(Acc,[PackRun],Acc2), comp([H2|T],[],Acc2).
run-cont @ fwd \ comp([H1,H2|T],Run,Acc) <=> H1=H2
    | Run2=[H1|Run],comp([H2|T],Run2,Acc).
last-char @ fwd \ comp([H],Run,Acc) <=> Run2=[H|Run], pack(Run2,PackRun),
    append(Acc,[PackRun],Acc2), result(Acc2).
end @ fwd \ comp([],_,_) <=> result([]).
```

Exhaustive Forward. For non-confluent programs, overlapping sets of rule constraints and the order of constraints within rules and queries entail different derivation paths to several possible outputs. The exhaustive transformation [6] was proposed to allow full space exploration for any CHR program to reach all possible solutions to a query. It changes a CHR derivation into a search tree with disjunctive branches to reach all leaves.

A `depth/1` constraint is added to represent the current depth of the search tree. The transformation annotates constraint occurrences within the rules with two additional arguments; one to denote the occurrence number and the other to represent the current depth within the search tree. Details of the transformation for forward execution will not be revisited here due to space limitations, and can be directly referred to in [6]. However it will be presented for backward execution in the next section, since it is a modification of [6]. Thus for a forward CHR program, the transformation is applied and the resulting CHR rules are annotated with a `fwd-ex/0` kept head constraint.

Example 2. Sets of Cards *Given N cards, each represented with a* `card/1` *constraint, a simple program can be written to select three cards whose sum equals 12, to form a set* (`set/3`) *using the predefined* `sumlist/2` *list predicate.*

```
select @ card(A), card(B), card(C) <=> sumlist([A,B,C],12) | set(A,B,C).
```

Running the program with a query '`card(1),card(2),card(3),card(4),card(5),`
`card(6),card(7),card(8),card(9),card(10)`', will result in: '`card(10), card(8),`

card(7),card(6),set(5,4,3),set(9,2,1)'. Due to the implementation of the CHR compiler, only one result is reached. However there are multiple other sets that can be assembled from those 10 cards. The forward program is transformed according to the exhaustive transformation to produce the below program (where card(X,_,_) is equivalent to card(X)):

```
src-mod @ fwd-ex \ depth(Z), card(A,1,Z), card(B,2,Z), card(C,3,Z)
    <=> sumlist([A,B,C],12) | set(A,B,C).
assign @ fwd-ex, depth(Z) \ card(A)
    <=> card(A,0,Z); card(A,1,Z); card(A,2,Z); card(A,3,Z).
rest @ fwd-ex, depth(Z) \ card(A,0,Z1) <=> Z1 < Z | card(A).
pruning @ fwd-ex \ end, card(A,_,_), card(B,_,_), card(C,_,_)
    <=> sumlist([A,B,C],12) | fail.
```

The exhaustive forward program can be run with the same query as before but adding the appropriate fwd-ex trigger. The query's execution gets transformed into a derivation tree, producing all possible card set combinations.

3.3   Backward CHR

Directly Backwards. The backwards semantics ω_b can be achieved through a source-to-source transformation of the CHR program. The transformation idea was introduced in [17] but will be formalized in this paper.

Definition 1. Backwards Transformation *Every range restricted rule of the form $(r \ @ \ H_k \setminus H_r \Leftrightarrow G \mid B)$ in program P (where $B = B_b \wedge B_c$ representing the built-in and CHR constraints respectively), an inverse rule* in-r *is added to the transformed program P^{-1} of the form (where* bck *is an annotating trigger constraint):*

$$in\text{-}r \ @ \ bck, \ H_k \setminus B_c \Leftrightarrow B_b, \ G \mid H_r$$

Applying the backwards transformation on the cards example, would require one backward rule as shown below:

```
bck-select @ bck \ set(A,B,C)<=>sumlist([A,B,C],12)|card(A),card(B),card(C).
```

Similarly, the previous run-length encoding program (Example 1) can be transformed using the backwards transformation as follows:

```
bck-start @ bck \ comp(In,[],[]) <=> compress(In).
bck-run-end @ bck \ comp([H2|T],[],Acc2) <=>
    Run2=[H1|Run], pack(Run2,PackRun), append(Acc,[PackRun],Acc2), H1\=H2
    | comp([H1,H2|T],Run,Acc).
bck-run-cont @ bck \ comp([H2|T],Run2,Acc) <=> Run2=[H1|Run], H1=H2
    | comp([H1,H2|T],Run,Acc).
bck-last-chr @ bck \ result(Acc2) <=>
    Run2=[H|Run], pack(Run2,PackRun), append(Acc,[PackRun],Acc2)
    | comp([H],Run,Acc).
bck-end @ bck \ result([]) <=> comp([],_,_).
```

Decompression of the encoded message can be easily attained by a backwards transition from output to input. Thus a query 'bck, result([[a,5], [b,1],[c,3]])' decompress the sub-lists to: 'compress([a,a,a,a,a,b,c,c,c])'.

Exhaustive Backward. The completeness of the backwards transformation relies on the high-level non-determinism of the ω_{va} semantics. The completion fails when implementing on top of current CHR systems. Thus for implementation, the backwards transformation is coupled with an exhaustive execution transformation [6]. To illustrate why this is necessary consider the next sorting example.

Example 3. *(Exchange sort) In CHR, constraints of the form* n(Index,Value) *can be sorted by exchanging any pair of constraints with an incorrect order. This is possible through a forward program consisting of a single simplification rule:*

```
sort @ fwd \ n(I,V),n(J,W) <=> I>J,V<W | n(I,W),n(J,V).
```

Using the defined transformation, the program becomes:

```
in-sort @ bck \ n(I,W),n(J,V) <=> I>J,V<W | n(I,V),n(J,W).
```

The two-way program sorts a query 'fwd,n(0,9),n(1,1), n(2,5)' to ordered numbers represented as 'n(0,1),n(1,5), n(2,9)'. On the other hand, a query 'bck,n(0,1),n(1,5),n(2,6) uncovers the permutation 'fwd,n(0,9),n(1,4),n(2,1)'. This is a correct input, but not necessarily the exact one used in the forward run. The reason is that sorting is a many-to-one function, where permutations of unsorted lists derive the same sorted list. The inverse of sorting problem is a shuffle operation which generates all possible permutations of the ordered list. This cannot be achieved here as the backwards transition generates only one permutation.

The transformation required to generate exhaustive backward program rules is shown next. All the generated rules are annotated with a `bck-ex` constraint to distinguish them within the two-way program. All unannotated inverse rules $(\text{in-r} @ H_k \setminus B_c \Leftrightarrow B_b, G \mid H_r)$ in program P^{-1} are transformed as described by the upcoming Definition 2.

Definition 2. Exhaustive Backwards Transformation *A transformed inverse exhaustive program P^{-T} is defined for a program P by the three following steps (adapted from [6] but with no pruning of intermediate states).*

1. *Each constraint $c(X_1, ..., X_n)$ in a forward program's B_c constraints is changed to $c^t(X_1, ..., X_n, y, Z)$, such that constraint occurrences within the program (where m is the total number of occurrences) are annotated with an argument y and depth Z. y represents the yth occurrence of the constraint c, i.e. $y \in [1, m]$. Thus, for every constraint $c(X_1, ..., X_n)$ that appears in the forward program's rule body, an assignment rule is added to the transformed program, defined as follows:*
   $\text{assign}_c @ \text{bck-ex}, \; depth(Z) \setminus c(X_1, ..., X_n)$
   $\Leftrightarrow c^t(X_1, ..., X_n, 0, Z) \vee ... \vee c^t(X_1, ..., X_n, m, Z)$
2. *For every rule $(H_r \Leftrightarrow G \mid B_b, B_c)$ in a forward program, with $B_c = c_1(X_{11}, ..., X_{1n_1}), ..., c_l(X_{l1}, ..., X_{ln_l})$, a modified source rule is added to the transformed program, as follows:*
   $\text{in-r}_t @ \text{bck-ex} \setminus depth(Z), c_1{}^t(X_{11}, ..., X_{1n_1}, y_1, Z), ...,$
   $c_l{}^t(X_{l1}, ..., X_{ln_l}, y_l, Z) \Leftrightarrow B_b, G \mid H_r, depth(Z + 1)$

3. *An additional rule is needed to reset unmatched constraints if a newly state in the tree is derived. Hence, for every constraint $c(X_1, ..., X_n)$ that appears in B_c, a reset rule is added to the transformed program:*
   $$reset_c @ \ bck\text{-}ex, \ depth(Z) \setminus c^t(X_1, ..., X_n, 0, Z') \Leftrightarrow Z' < Z \ | \ c(X_1, ..., X_n)$$

Example 4. *(Exchange sort - Revisited) Applying the newly defined transformation on the exchange sort of Example 3, will generate the following rules:*

```
assign-a @ bck-ex, depth(Z) \ n(X,Y)
     <=> n_t(X,Y,0,Z); n_t(X,Y,1,Z); n_t(X,Y,2,Z).
in-sort-t @ bck-ex \ depth(Z),n_t(I,W,1,Z),n_t(J,V,2,Z)
     <=> I>J, V<W | n(I,V), n(J,W), depth(Z+1).
reset-a @ bck-ex, depth(Z) \ n_t(X,Y,0,Z1) <=> Z1 < Z | n(X,Y).
```

The transformed rules can be run with the sorted input: `bck-ex`, `depth(0)`, `n(0,1)`, `n(1,5)`,`n(2,9)`. It generates several results, which form the complete set of all permutations of those three numbers. However there exists several redundancies; the intensive use of disjunction produces several duplicate states which are revisited multiple times. The backward run is terminating, and the use of a breadth-first strategy covers the entire search space. The reason for this is that the number of permutations of a list is finite.

4   Interleaved Forward/Backward Propagation

The combined two-way program enables either a strictly forward or strictly backward execution depending on the used trigger. However, we further propose an additional transformation towards a combined interleaved execution, which is inspired from bidirectional search. Bidirectional search tries to find the shortest path to a node/element by running two simultaneous searches. It involves one forward search from the initial state, and one backward search from the goal state. The search stops when the two searches reach the same state, somewhere in the middle. In many problems, bidirectional search can dramatically reduce the amount of required exploration [14]. The two-way CHR programs can be modified to implement a bidirectional search for a goal. Instead of running a transition in a strictly forward or strictly backward manner, we introduce a technique to have an interleaved forward and backward manner to achieve a combined quasi-simultaneous two-way execution.

For clarity, bidirectional search is exemplified with direct forwards and backwards transitions. The technique can also be applied to the exhaustive variants, but it makes the presentation too long for the scope of this paper.

Example 5. List Searching *Determining whether an element is found within a list can be performed in CHR as shown below. A constraint* `find/2` *is used to search in the first argument (a list) for the second argument and a constraint* `found/1` *denotes that it has been found. A query* `fwd, find([0,1,2,3,4],3)` *would reach the goal* `found(3)`.

```
end @ fwd \ find([X],Y) <=> X=Y, found(Y).
middle @ fwd \ find([X|_],Y) <=> X=Y | found(Y).
search @ fwd \ find([X|Xs],Y) <=> X\==Y | find(Xs,Y).
```

The backward search from a found element, constructs arbitrary lists containing this element. The direct backward rules are given as:

```
in-end @ bck \ found(Y) <=> X=Y | find([X],Y).
in-middle @ bck \ found(Y) <=> X=Y | find([X|_],Y).
in-search @ bck \ find(Xs,Y) <=> X\==Y | find([X|Xs],Y).
```

Due to the chosen direct (non-exhaustive) execution, the second rule (`in-middle`) becomes unreachable in this context and these rules form a non-confluent program; the first two rules have the exact same rule heads and guards. One way to resolve this problem is to use the previously introduced exhaustive execution. Alternatively, since these rules are single-headed with the same guards, then it is sufficient to use Clark's completion and merge the two rules into one. For clarity and to save writing space, the second representation is preferred here over the exhaustive execution. Thus the rules `in-end` and `in-middle` are equivalent to:

```
in-end-middle @ bck \ found(Y) <=> X=Y | find([X],Y) ; find([X|_],Y).
```

Due to the lossy nature of the program the other un-found values are lost. Thus a query `bck,found(3)` would reach several lists with unknown filler values. Some of the backward goals reached are: `find([3],3)`, `find([3,_],3)`, `find([_,3,_],3)`, etc.

For the automatic implementation of a bidirectional search, the idea is to change the execution of these rules such that it follows alternating forward and backward transitions.

Definition 3. Bidirectional Transform *A combined two-way program P^{-T} can be transformed to enable quasi-simultaneous bidirectional search by the following steps:*

1. *Trigger constraints* bck *and* fwd *should not be kept head constraints. They must be consumed by the rules, and on rule application, the opposite direction trigger is added. Thus forward rules (*fwd *,* $H_k \setminus H_r \Leftrightarrow G \mid B$*) should be changed into:*

$$H_k \setminus \text{fwd}, H_r \Leftrightarrow G \mid B, \text{bck}$$

*Similarly, backward rules (*bck*,* $H_k \setminus B_c \Leftrightarrow B_b, G \mid H_r$*) become:*

$$H_k \setminus \text{bck}, B_c \Leftrightarrow B_b, G \mid H_r, \text{fwd}$$

2. *Constraints of the backward rules must be differentiated from the forward rules, such that each search direction operates on different goals until they meet. Thus every constraint* $c(X_1, ..., X_n)$ *in the backward rules is changed to* $c^b(X_1, ..., X_n)$.
3. *A unification rule must be added to halt the execution once both search goals can be unified with one another. Thus given a forward goal* $c(X_1, ..., X_n)$ *and a backward goal* $c^b(Y_1, ..., Y_n)$*, a possible unifying rule would be of the form:*

$$\text{unify} @ c(X_1, ..., X_n), c^b(Y_1, ..., Y_n) \Leftrightarrow unifiable(c(X_1, ..., X_n), c^b(Y_1, ..., Y_n), \_)$$
$$\mid write(\text{'Bidirectionally found!'}).$$

Therefore the interleaved quasi-simultaneous bidirectional list search program becomes as shown below; all constraints of backward rules are distinguished with (`_b`).

```
end @ fwd, find([X],Y) <=> X=Y, found(Y), bck.
middle @ fwd, find([X|_],Y) <=> X=Y | found(Y), bck.
search @ fwd, find([X|Xs],Y) <=> X\==Y | find(Xs,Y), bck.
unify @ find(X,Y), find_b(Z,Y) <=> unifiable(Z,X,_)
    | write('Bidirectionally found!').
in-end-middle @ bck, found_b(Y) <=> X=Y
    | (find_b([X],Y); find_b([X|_],Y)), fwd.
in-search @ bck, find_b(Xs,Y) <=> X\==Y
    | find_b([X|Xs],Y), fwd.
```

Searching for an element 3 in a list $[0, 1, 2, 3, 4]$ can be performed by the bidirectional search program, with a query find([0,1,2,3,4],3), found_b(3), fwd. The derivation for this query would be as shown below, while underlining the matched constraints (a trace is also shown in Figure 3): <u>fwd, find([0,1,2,3,4],3)</u>, found_b(3)

$\mapsto_{search}$ find([1,2,3,4],3), <u>bck, found_b(3)</u>

$\mapsto_{in\text{-}middle}$ <u>find([1,2,3,4],3), fwd</u>, find_b([3,_],3)

$\mapsto_{search}$ find([2,3,4],3), <u>bck, find_b([3,_],3)</u>

$\mapsto_{in\text{-}search}$ <u>find([2,3,4],3), fwd, find_b([_,3,_],3)</u>

$\mapsto_{unify}$ write('Bidirectionally found!').

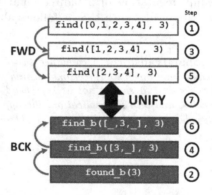

Fig. 3. Bidirectional search trace: 'fwd, find([0,1,2,3,4],3), found_b(3)'

5 Application for Combined Programs

Another application of the proposed work is for reasoning. Reasoning is the process of using existing knowledge to infer conclusions, speculate predictions, and create explanations. The philosopher C. S. Pierce distinguished between three kinds of reasoning; deduction, induction and abduction [13]. Deduction involves applying rules to specific cases to deduce a certain result, while induction is reasoning which infers a rule from a case and result. Abduction is a kind of backward reasoning which infers a case from the rule and result.

The relation between abduction and reverse deduction has been studied in several works to highlight the difference between them [12]. However, it has also been argued that abduction is a form of reversed deduction and that there is a duality in the explanation of abduction and deduction [3].

The combined two-way programs capture the duality relation between deduction and abduction, and produce a powerful reasoning program. The reasoner exploits existent knowledge to infer conclusions and speculate predictions for observed phenomena. Logic theories that describe the real world are modeled in CHR. Then the exhaustive forward transformation facilitates exhaustive exploration of a query's search space and thus enables deductive reasoning. Furthermore, an exhaustive backward execution of the modeled CHR programs empowers abductive reasoning.

It is not the first time that CHR has been used for abductive reasoning. In [1], logic programs containing Horn clauses are expressed in CHR while differentiating between intensional predicates and extensional ones to perform abductive reasoning. However in this work, all logic clauses including non-Horn ones can be modeled in CHR. Moreover the framework empowers both abductive and deductive reasoning. This is not possible with [1] since the used representation relied heavily on the underlying meaning of abduction and manually gathered similar rule bodies as disjunctive rule bodies.

5.1   Modeling

In order to use the annotated transformations for two-way reasoning, the modeling of logic theories in CHR must first be formalized. A logic theory T is a set of well-formed formulae, where each formula is an implication of the form $A \to B$, and A and B are conjunctions of one or more literals. Logic implications are mapped in a one-to-one manner to CHR simplification rules. The mapping is quite similar to [1], nonetheless in our model both A and B can be conjunctions.

The model is defined by representing literals with CHR constraints and built-ins. Due to the syntax of CHR, two filtering functions are also defined: a `chr/1` function that extracts the predicates/constraints from a set of literals and a `built/1` function that extracts the built-in expressions from a set of literals.

Thus, every implication of the form $A \to B$ is modeled as a forward CHR simplification rule of the form:

$$\texttt{fwd} \setminus chr(A) \Leftrightarrow built(A) \mid B$$

Given the following logic theory which defines some family relations [1]:

Example 6. $father(F, C) \to parent(F, C)$, $mother(M, C) \to parent(M, C)$, $parent(P, C1), parent(P, C2), C1 \neq C2 \to sibling(C1, C2)$

It is transformed into the following annotated forward CHR rules:

```
fwd \ father(F,C) <=> parent(F,C).
fwd \ mother(M,C) <=> parent(M,C).
fwd \ parent(P,C1), parent(P,C2) <=> C1\=C2 | sibling(C1,C2).
```

Integrity constraints can be added to the modeled program to provide semantic optimization to the reasoner. Since these rules ensure the integrity, they are not involved in any of the transformations and thus should not be annotated with any trigger constraints. For Example 6, the following integrity constraints can be added:

```
father(F1,X) \ father(F2,X) <=> F1=F2.
mother(M1,X) \ mother(M2,X) <=> M1=M2.
person(P,G1)\ person(P,G2) <=> G1=G2.
father(F,X) ==> person(F,male), person(X,_).
mother(M,X) ==> person(M,female), person(X,_).
```

An extensional (trigger-less) introduction rule is required to add all the facts into the constraint store, to be introduced with a `start` constraint in any query:

```
start ==> parent(john,mary), father(john,peter), mother(jane,mary),
          person(john,male), person(mary,female), person(paul,male),
          person(peter,male), person(jane,female).
```

To ensure a closed world, the set of hypothesis facts for a given predicate need to be pruned. Closing rules (also without trigger constraints) are added for these predicates [1]. For a predicate p/n defined by $p(t_1^1, \ldots, t_n^1), \ldots, p(t_1^k, \ldots, t_n^k)$, a closing rule is required as a propagation rule shown below:

$$p(x_1, \ldots, x_n) \Rightarrow (x_1 = t_1^1, \wedge, \ldots, \wedge x_n = t_n^1) \quad \vee \cdots \vee (x_1 = t_1^k, \wedge, \ldots, \wedge x_n = t_n^k)$$

To restrict the $person/2$ predicate of Example 6, a closing rule would be added as shown below:

```
person(X,Y) ==> (X=john, Y=male);(X=peter, Y=male); (X=paul, Y=male);
                (X=jane, Y=female);(X=mary, Y=female).
```

5.2   Strictly Forward

Due to the modeling of non-Horn clauses, the normal execution of CHR would not yield deductive reasoning. However, transforming the program to an exhaustive variant would ensure the completeness of the search-space. Using the transformation, it is possible to start from an initial query and deduce all possible derivations to goals.

Thus for deductive reasoning, only rules representing the main transformed implications (i.e. those annotated with `fwd`) are transformed into rules featuring exhaustive execution using the exhaustive transformation. These other rules maintain certain properties for the modeling, hence they need not be transformed.

The three implication rules of the family example can be modeled into CHR and then transformed into their exhaustive executing variant with the constraint trigger `fwd-ex`. Using the initial knowledge that John is the father of Peter and Mary and that Jane is the mother of Mary, one can deduce that Mary and Peter are siblings and that Paul, Jane, Peter, Mary and John are all persons. This deduction can be reached using a query '`fwd-ex`, `start`, `father(john,peter)`, `father(john,mary)`, `mother(jane,mary)`,`depth(0)`', to produce the final state:

```
sibling(mary,peter), person(paul,male), person(jane,female),
person(peter,male),  person(mary,female), person(john,male).
```

5.3 Strictly Backward

For abductive reasoning, the exhaustive backwards transformation is performed for, again, only the main annotated CHR rules representing transformed implications from the logic theory.

Abductive reasoning involves deriving hypotheses about certain predicates that are incompletely defined; these are known as abducible predicates. Thus to include the notion of abducibles in the proposed model, only the closing rules of non-abducible predicates are retained (as forward and untransformed rules); other closing rules are completely removed from the program. All other integrity constraint rules and extensional introduction rules are also kept unchanged in the abductive program.

In the family example, predicates `father` and `mother` are abducible but not `person`. Thus the abductive program should contain only one closing rule for `person`. Executing the query 'sibling(paul,mary),bck-ex' with the abductive program, arrived to the following two possibilities: `father(john,paul)`, or `mother(jane,paul)`.

The goals present two different abductive explanations as to how Paul and Mary are siblings, i.e. either John is the father of Paul or that Jane is the mother of Paul. Furthermore, the abductive query 'sibling(goofy,mary)' fails because `person` is not abducible. These results match those reached by the abductive CHR modeling of [1].

6 Conclusion

The paper presents a combined perspective for Constraint Handling Rules based on a source-to-source transformation. It involves transforming CHR programs into ones capable of both forward and backward propagation, either in a direct committed-choice manner or in an exhaustive full-space explorative manner. The combination is especially useful for implementing high-level bijective functions, such as encryption/decryption and compression/decompression algorithms, for implementing quasi-simultaneous bidirectional search algorithms and for exploiting dual definitions of reasoning, such as for deduction and abduction.

For future work, an evaluation of the bidirectional search is needed to determine how bidirectionality reduces the amount of required exploration. The search implementations can also be extended to experimenting with different search directions, such as the breadth-first traversal of CHR [4]. Moreover, the proposed reasoning framework is to be compared with other abductive and deductive systems and to evaluate the attained results. Moreover, it could be possible to include the notion of probabilistic abduction by encoding the probabilities in the search tree generated by the exhaustive transformation. Then once the transformation is defined, it would be compared with other implementations of probabilistic abductive logic programs.

References

1. Abdennadher, S., Christiansen, H.: An experimental CLP platform for integrity constraints and abduction. In: Larsen, H.L., Andreasen, T., Christiansen, H., Kacprzyk, J., Zadrożny, S. (eds.) FQAS 2000. ASC, vol. 1, pp. 141–152. Springer, Heidelberg (2000)
2. Abdennadher, S., Schütz, H.: CHR $^\vee$: A flexible query language. In: Andreasen, T., Christiansen, H., Larsen, H.L. (eds.) FQAS 1998. LNCS (LNAI), vol. 1495, pp. 1–14. Springer, Heidelberg (1998)
3. Console, L., Dupr, D.T., Torasso, P.: On the relationship between abduction and deduction. J. Log. Comput. 1(5), 661–690 (1991)
4. De Koninck, L., Schrijvers, T., Demoen, B.: Search strategies in CHR(Prolog). In: Schrijvers, T., Frühwirth, Th. (eds.) Proceedings of the 3rd Workshop on Constraint Handling Rule, pp. 109–124. K.U.Leuven, Department of Computer Science, Technical report CW 452 (2006)
5. Duck, G.J., Stuckey, P.J., de la Banda, M.G., Holzbaur, C.: The refined operational semantics of constraint handling rules. In: Demoen, B., Lifschitz, V. (eds.) ICLP 2004. LNCS, vol. 3132, pp. 90–104. Springer, Heidelberg (2004)
6. Elsawy, A., Zaki, A., Abdennadher, S.: Exhaustive execution of chr through source-to-source transformation. In: Proietti, M., Seki, H. (eds.) LOPSTR 2014. LNCS, vol. 8981, pp. 59–73. Springer, Heidelberg (2015)
7. Frühwirth, T.: Constraint Handling Rules. Cambridge University Press (2009)
8. Frühwirth, T., Holzbaur, C.: Source-to-source transformation for a class of expressive rules. In: Buccafurri, F. (ed.) Joint Conference on Declarative Programming APPIA-GULP-PRODE 2003 (AGP 2003), pp. 386–397 (2003)
9. Frühwirth, T., Raiser, F. (eds.): Constraint Handling Rules: Compilation, Execution, and Analysis. Books on Demand, March 2011
10. Haemmerlé, R.: On combining backward and forward chaining in constraint logic programming. In: Proceedings of 16th International Symposium on Principles and Practice of Declarative Programming (PPDP 2014) (2014)
11. Hou, C., Vulov, G., Quinlan, D., Jefferson, D., Fujimoto, R., Vuduc, R.: A new method for program inversion. In: O'Boyle, M. (ed.) CC 2012. LNCS, vol. 7210, pp. 81–100. Springer, Heidelberg (2012)
12. Mayer, M.C., Pirri, F.: Abduction is not deduction-in-reverse. Logic Journal of the IGPL 4(1), 95–108 (1996)
13. Peirce, C.S.: Collected Papers of Charles Sanders Peirce, vol. 2. Harvard University Press (1931)
14. Pohl, I.S.: Bi-directional search. Machine Intelligence 6, 127–140 (1971)
15. Sneyers, J., Van Weert, P., Schrijvers, T., De Koninck, L.: As time goes by: constraint handling rules – a survey of CHR research between 1998 and 2007. In: Theory and Practice of Logic Programming, pp. 1–47 (2010)
16. Yokoyama, T.: Reversible computation and reversible programming languages. Electronic Notes in Theoretical Computer Science 253(6), 71–81 (2009). Proceedings of the Workshop on Reversible Computation (RC 2009)
17. Zaki, A., Frühwirth, T.W., Abdennadher, S.: Towards inverse execution of constraint handling rules. In: Theory and Practice of Logic Programming, 13(4-5-Online-Supplement) (2013)

Reasoning in Large Theories

Random Forests for Premise Selection

Michael Färber and Cezary Kaliszyk

University of Innsbruck, Austria
{michael.faerber,cezary.kaliszyk}@uibk.ac.at

Abstract The success rates of automated theorem provers in large
theories highly depend on the choice of given facts. Premise selection
is the task of choosing a subset of given facts, which is most likely to
lead to a successful automated deduction proof of a given conjecture.
Premise selection can be viewed as a multi-label classification problem,
where machine learning from related proofs turns out to currently be the
most successful method. Random forests are a machine learning technique known to perform especially well on large datasets. In this paper,
we evaluate random forest algorithms for premise selection. To deal with
the specifics of automated reasoning, we propose a number of extensions to random forests, such as incremental learning, multi-path querying, depth weighting, feature IDF (inverse document frequency), and
integration of secondary classifiers in the tree leaves. With these extensions, we improve on the k-nearest neighbour algorithm both in terms of
prediction quality and ATP performance.

1 Introduction

An increasing number of interactive theorem provers (ITPs) provide proof automation based on translation to automated theorem provers (ATPs): A user given
conjecture together with a set of known facts in a more complicated logic of the
ITP is translated to the logic of an ATP. If a proof is found by the ATP, it can be
used to prove the conjecture in the ITP either by providing a precise small set of
facts sufficient to prove the conjecture or the ATP proof can be used to recreate
a skeleton of an ITP proof. To increase the success rate of the procedure, it is
useful to identify a subset of theorems[1] that is most likely to produce a proof.
This process is called *premise selection* (or *relevance filtering*) and is used in
most ATP translation tools [AHK+14], e.g. Sledgehammer/MaSh [KBKU13] for
Isabelle/HOL [NPW02], or HOL(y)Hammer [KU15] for HOL Light [Har96], or
MizAR [KU13a] for Mizar [NK09].

Premise selection is also used in ATPs, for example the Sumo Inference Engine (SInE) [HV11] improves the prediction quality of the Vampire theorem
prover [KV13] when working with large theories and its algorithm has also been
implemented as a part of E-Prover [Sch13]. Nonetheless, as the complexity of

---

[1] As in premise selection we do not distinguish between axioms and lemmas, we denote their union as *theorems*. Furthermore, we denote the theorems used in a proof
attempt as *premises*.

© Springer International Publishing Switzerland 2015
C. Lutz and S. Ranise (Eds.): FroCoS 2015, LNAI 9322, pp. 325–340, 2015.
DOI: 10.1007/978-3-319-24246-0_20

the translations to ATP highly depends on the lemmas to be translated, often only a subset of the lemmas is translated: For example in higher-order logic, if a constant f is always used with the same arity, e.g. $f(a, b)$ and $f(c, a)$, it can be directly translated as FOL function $f(x, y)$. However, if f appears with different arities, e.g. in $f(a)$ and $f(a, b)$, f cannot be translated as FOL function, and apply functors are necessary. Similarly, if a polymorphic constant only appears fully instantiated, its translation can be a FOL constant rather than a FOL function. Furthermore, the success rates of the ATPs depend significantly on the translation applied [BBP11], so avoiding unnecessary lemmas can shorten proof time by a better than linear factor. Premise selection for automated reasoning in ITPs is also different from that in ATPs due to a large knowledge base of previously proven theorems. The dependencies extracted both from ITP and ATP proofs can be used to further enhance premise selection.

Many algorithms used for premise selection stem from machine learning. To the best of our knowledge, one popular machine learning algorithm not yet tried in premise selection are random forests. In this paper we evaluate offline and online random forests for premise selection and propose a number of extensions to random forests that improve final ATP performance. Specifically we:

- investigate offline [AGPV13] and online [SLS+09] random forests for premise selection,
- improve an offline random forest algorithm with incremental learning,
- add multi-path querying and depth weighting to improve multi-label output,
- integrate k-NN in the leaves of the random forest trees,
- evaluate the proposed extensions experimentally, confirming that random forests offer better prediction quality than previously used algorithms, and more theorems can be proven automatically by the ATPs.

Related work. The Meng-Paulson relevance filter (MePo) [MP06] integrated in Isabelle/HOL as part of Sledgehammer was one of the first premise selectors for ITPs. It is an iterative algorithm, which counts function symbols in clauses and compares them to the function symbols in the conjecture to prove. In contrast to many other premise selectors, MePo does not consider the dependencies used to prove similar theorems.

Naive Bayes as implemented by the SNoW framework [CCRR99] was the first machine learning algorithm used in an automated reasoning loop, and thanks to dependencies, the prediction quality improved upon syntactic tools [Urb04]. Simple Perceptron networks have also been evaluated for HOL(y)Hammer predictions [KU14], and their results are weak but complementary to other methods.

Machine learning algorithms such as k-nearest neighbours [ZZ05] and Naive Bayes were integrated into Sledgehammer as part of MaSh (Machine learning for Sledgehammer) [KBKU13], significantly improving ATP performance on the translated problems. The single most powerful method used for premise selection in HOL(y)Hammer, MizAR, and Sledgehammer/MaSh is a customized implementation of k-NN [KU13b]. Stronger machine-learning methods that use kernel-based multi-output ranking (MOR [AHK+14] and MOR-CG [KBKU13]) were

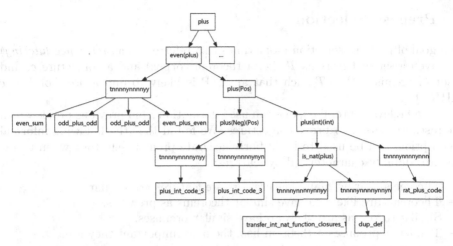

Fig. 1. Excerpt from a decision tree trained on the Isabelle dataset. Leaf nodes have unique identifiers t[yn]*, which encode their position in the tree. The branch node with feature even(plus) has a positive leaf node with four theorems, namely even_sum, odd_plus_odd (two times), and odd_plus_even – all having features plus and even(plus). The theorem plus_int_code_3 has features plus and plus(Pos), but neither even(plus) nor plus(Neg)(Pos).

found to perform better, but were too slow to be of practical use for premise selection in large theories so far.

Decision trees are another machine learning method that can be used for premise selection: A binary decision tree is either a leaf $L(S)$ with data S or a branch $B(l, f, r)$ with a criterion (also called feature) f and two subtrees l and r. Querying a branch $B(l, f, r)$ involves querying l if the criterion f is fulfilled, otherwise querying r. Querying a leaf $L(S)$ returns S. A part of an example tree used in premise selection is shown in figure 1: Here, a criterion is the presence of certain symbols in a theorem, such as plus, and the data in the leaves are theorems that are relevant if the tree path to them corresponds to the symbols of the conjecture we seek to prove. We explain building and querying of decision trees in more detail in sections 3 and 4.

Random forests [Bre01] are a family of bagging algorithms [Bre96] known for fast prediction speed and high prediction quality for many domains [CNm06]. Many different versions of random forests [AGPV13,Bre96,LRT14,SLS+09] have been proposed. In general, a random forest chooses random subsets of data to build independent decision trees, whose combined predictions form the prediction of the forest. Random forests are used in applications where large amounts of data needs to be classified in a short time, such as the automated proposal of advertisement keywords for web pages [AGPV13] or prediction of object positions in real-time computer graphics [SLS+09].

2   Premise Selection

The goal of premise selection (sometimes also referred to as *relevance filtering*) is: Given a set of theorems T (i.e. a theorem corpus) and a conjecture c, find a set of premises $P \subseteq T$ such that an ATP is likely to find a proof of $P \vdash c$ [AHK+14].

To find relevant premises, one can use information from previous proofs which premises were used to prove conjectures. We found that the following informal assumptions can be used to build fairly accurate premise selectors, when theorems are suitably characterised by features:

- Theorems sharing many features or rare features are similar.
- Theorems are likely to have similar theorems as premises.
- Similar theorems are likely to have similar premises.
- The fewer premises a theorem has, the more important they are.

The above assumptions can be encoded as a multi-label classification problem in machine learning. First we encode a given theorem corpus T as machine learning input: Every proven theorem $s \in T$ gives rise to a training *sample* $\langle s, \varphi(s), \lambda(s) \rangle$, which consists of the theorem s, the set of *features* $\varphi(s)$ and the set of *labels* $\lambda(s)$. The labels are the premises that were used to prove s.

The features $\varphi(s)$ are a characterisation of a theorem s. For example we can choose to characterise theorems by the constants and types present in their statements. The features of a set of samples S are $\varphi(S) := \bigcup_{s \in S} \varphi(s)$. We define those samples of S having or not having a certain feature f as

$$S_f := \{s \mid f \in \varphi(s)\},$$
$$S_{\neg f} := S \backslash S_f.$$

Example 1. The sample corresponding to the HOL Light theorem ADD_SYM stating $\vdash \forall m\, n.\, m + n = n + m$ is $\langle$ADD_SYM, φ(ADD_SYM), λ(ADD_SYM)$\rangle$ with:

φ(ADD_SYM) $= \{+, =, \forall, \texttt{num}, \texttt{bool}\}$

λ(ADD_SYM) $= \{$ADD_CLAUSES,ADD,ADD_SUC,REFL_CLAUSE,FORALL_SIMP,num_INDUCTION$\}$

Samples encode the relationship between features and labels, i.e. which features occur in conjunction with which labels, both of which can be represented internally as sparse vectors. With this representation, we can view premise selection as an instance of a multi-label classification problem [TK07].

Definition 1 (Multi-label classifier). *Given a set of samples S, a multi-label classifier trained on S is a function r that takes a set of features φ and returns a list of labels $[l_1, \ldots, l_n]$ sorted by decreasing relevance for φ.*

Using multi-label classification, we can obtain suitable premises from a set of theorems S for a conjecture c as follows:

1. Obtain a multi-label classifier r for S.
2. Compute $\varphi(c)$, the features of the conjecture.
3. Return $r(\varphi(c))$, the list of labels predicted by the classifier.

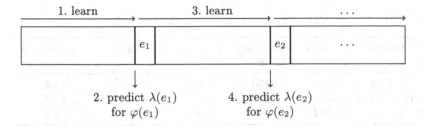

Fig. 2. In an evaluation, an arbitrary number of samples is learned in a white block until an evaluation sample e is encountered, for which labels $\lambda(e)$ are predicted.

2.1 Quality Measures

To evaluate the quality of predicted premises, we can compare them to the actual premises from our training samples. We first introduce a notation: Given a sequence of distinct elements $X = [x_1, \ldots, x_n]$, we denote $X_i^e = [x_i, x_{i+1} \ldots, x_e]$. Furthermore, when it is clear from the context, we treat sequences as sets, where the set elements are the elements of the sequence.

The first quality measure is n-Precision, which is similar to Precision [Sor10], but considers only the first n predictions. It computes the percentage of premises from the training sample appearing among the first n predicted premises, which corresponds to our passing only a fixed maximal number of premises to ATPs. If not stated otherwise, we use 100-Precision in our evaluations.

Definition 2 (n-Precision). *n-Precision for a sequence of predictions P and a set of labels L is*

$$\mathrm{Prec}_n(P, L) = \frac{|L \cap P_1^n|}{|L|}.$$

The second measure, AUC, models the probability that for a randomly drawn label $l \in L$ and a randomly drawn label $m \notin L$, l appears in the predictions before m.

Definition 3 (AUC [Faw04]). *Given a sequence of predictions P and a set of labels L, the area under ROC curve (AUC) for the predictions is*

$$\mathrm{AUC}(P, L) = \begin{cases} \frac{\sum_{n=1}^{|P|} |L \cap P_1^n|}{|L| \cdot |P \backslash L|} & if\ |L| \cdot |P \backslash L| > 0 \\ 1 & if\ |L| \cdot |P \backslash L| = 0. \end{cases}$$

2.2 Evaluation

We now explain how to evaluate predictor performance on a set of samples. For this, we define a subset of the samples as *evaluation samples*, for which the classifier will predict premises by iterating over all samples in order and predicting $\lambda(e)$ for each evaluation sample e before learning e, as illustrated in figure 2. We can evaluate the quality of the predictions in two ways: First, they

Table 1. Datasets used in the evaluation

Dataset	Samples	Evaluation samples	Features	Avg. labels per sample	Avg. features per sample
Mizar	3221	2050	3773	8.8	14.2
HOL Light	2548	2247	4331	2.6	13.4
Isabelle	23442	1656	31308	4.2	23.1

can be compared to the actual labels of the evaluation samples, using the a quality measure from section 2.1. Second, the predictions can be translated to an ATP problem and given to an automated prover.

2.3   Used Datasets

We use the Mizar MPTP2078 dataset [AHK+14] updated to Mizar 8.1.02 [KU13a] using α-normalised subterms as features, the Isabelle 2014 theory HOL/Probability together with its dependencies [KBKU13], and the core library of HOL Light SVN version 193 [KU15]. The statistics are shown in table 1.

3   Existing Algorithms

In this section we describe offline and online random forests and evaluate them in the context of ITP premise selection.

Multi-Label Learning with Millions of Labels. Agrawal et al. [AGPV13] use random forests to learn large amounts of data, in order to obtain relevant advertising keywords for web pages. Their algorithm builds several decision trees on random subsets of the data as follows: Given a set of samples S to learn and the minimal number of samples μ which a leaf has to contain (we describe this in section 4.3), it returns a decision tree. The algorithm first determines a splitting feature (explained in section 4.4) for S, which is a feature f that splits S in two sets S_f (samples having f) and $S_{\neg f}$ (samples not having f). If $|S_f| < \mu$ or $|S_{\neg f}| < \mu$, the algorithm returns a leaf node containing S, otherwise the algorithm recursively calculates subtrees for S_f and $S_{\neg f}$ and combines them into a branch node with the splitting feature f.

This approach has several disadvantages when used for premise selection: While we need to learn data quickly and query only a few times after each learning phase, the algorithm of Agrawal is optimised to answer queries in logarithmic time, whereas its learning phase is relatively slow. Furthermore, the algorithm is an *offline* algorithm, meaning that in order to learn new samples, it is necessary to rebuild all trees. We found that our implementation of this method was several magnitudes slower than k-NN even for small datasets, rendering it impracticable for incremental learning. Furthermore, the prediction quality was lower than expected: For the first 200 evaluation samples of the Mizar dataset, a random forest with 4 trees and 16 random features evaluated at every tree branch achieved an AUC of 82.96% in 1m22sec, whereas k-NN achieved an AUC of 95.84% in 0.36sec. In section 4, we show how to improve the prediction quality and speed of this algorithm for premise selection.

On-line Random Forests. Saffari et al. [SLS+09] present an online random forest algorithm, in which all trees in the forest are initially leaf nodes. When learning a new sample, it is added to all trees with a probability determined by a Poisson distribution with $\lambda = 1$ [OR01]. Adding a sample to a leaf node consists of adding the sample to the samples in the leaf node. As soon as the number of samples in a leaf node exceeds a certain threshold or a sufficiently good splitting feature for the sample set is found, the leaf node splits into a feature node and two leaf nodes. When adding a sample to a feature node, the sample gets added to the left or to the right child of the node, according to whether or not it has the node's feature.

The method introduces a bias in that features which appear in early learned samples will be at the tree roots. Saffari et al. solve this problem by calculating the quality of predictions from each tree (OOBE, out-of-bag error) and by periodically removing trees with a high OOBE. However, this introduces a bias towards the latest learned samples, which is useful for computer graphics applications such as object tracking, but undesirable for premise selection, as the advice asked from a predictor will frequently not correspond to the last learned theorems. Therefore, we do not use the approach of [SLS+09], but adapt its use of probability distributions to create online versions of bagging algorithms in section 4.2.

4 Adaptations to Random Forests for Premise Selection

In this section, we describe the changes we made to the algorithms described in section 3 to obtain better results for premise selection.

4.1 Sample Selection

When learning new samples S, one needs to determine which trees learn which samples. In [AGPV13], each tree in a forest randomly draws n samples from S. This approach may introduce a bias, namely that some samples are drawn more often than others, while some samples might not be drawn (and learned) at all. Therefore, instead of each tree drawing a fixed number of samples to learn, in our approach, each sample draws a fixed number of trees by which it will be learned, where we call this fixed number *sample frequency*. This approach has the advantage that by definition, every sample is guaranteed to be learned as often as all other samples.

4.2   Incremental Update

We present two methods to efficiently update random forests incrementally: The first one is a method applicable to all kinds of classifiers, the second one is an optimised update procedure for decision trees.

Onlining Bagging Algorithms. Given a bagging algorithm (such as random forests) whose individual predictors (in our scenario the decision trees of the forest) learn a random subset of samples offline, we show a method for decreasing the runtime of learning new data incrementally. The method is based on the observation that, when learning only a small number of new samples (compared to the number of samples already learned), most predictors will not include any of those new samples, thus they do not need to be updated. To model this, let r be a binomially distributed random variable $r \sim B(s, P)$, where s is the number of samples in each predictor and $P = \frac{n_{new}}{n_{new}+n_{old}}$ is the probability of drawing a new sample from the common pool of new and old samples. r then models the number of new samples drawn by a predictor. Each predictor evaluates the random variable r, and if its value r_p is 0, the predictor can remain unchanged. Only if r_p is greater than 0, the predictor is retrained with r_p samples from the set of new samples and $s - r_p$ samples from the set of old samples.

While this method gives a performance increase over always rebuilding all predictors, it still frequently retrains whole predictors. As training a decision tree is a very expensive operation, this method is clearly suboptimal for our setting, therefore we present a method to update trees efficiently in the next section.

Tree Update. We show an improved version of the first algorithm given in section 3, which updates trees with new samples. Given a tree t and a set of new samples S, the algorithm calculates S', which is the union of S with all the samples in the leaf nodes of t, and a splitting feature f for S'. If t is a node with f as a splitting feature, we recursively update both subtrees of t with S_f and $S_{\neg f}$ respectively. Otherwise, we construct a new tree for S': If $|S'_f| < \mu$ or $|S'_{\neg f}| < \mu$, we return a leaf node with S', otherwise we construct subtrees for S'_f and $S'_{\neg f}$ and return a branch node with f as splitting feature.

This algorithm returns the same trees as the original algorithm, but can be significantly faster in case of updates; for example, predicting advice for the whole Mizar dataset takes 21m27sec with this optimisation and 57m22sec without.

4.3   Tree Size

At each step of the tree construction, the given set of samples S is split in two by a splitting feature. A leaf containing S is created if one of the two resulting sets contains fewer samples than the minimum number of samples μ. We evaluated three functions to calculate μ, which depend on the samples of the whole tree, namely $\mu_{\log}(S) = \log|S|$, $\mu_{\mathrm{sqrt}}(S) = \sqrt{|S|}$, and $\mu_{\mathrm{const}}(S) = 1$. In [AGPV13] only $\mu_{\log}$ is used.

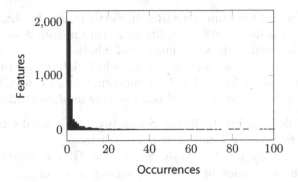

Fig. 3. Feature histogram for the Mizar MPTP2078 dataset [AHK+14]. For example, there are 2026 features which occur only a single time among all samples, and only 34 that occur ten times.

4.4   Feature Selection

We determine a splitting feature for a set of samples S in two steps: First, one selects a set of features $F \subseteq \varphi(S)$ to evaluate, then, one evaluates each of the features in F to obtain a suitable splitting feature.

Obtaining Evaluation Features. In [AGPV13], the evaluation features are obtained by randomly drawing with replacement (meaning you draw an element from a set, then place it back in the set) a set of features φ_R from $\varphi(S)$, where $n_R = |\varphi_R|$ is a user-defined constant. When we applied the method in the context of premise selection, we frequently obtained trees of small height with many labels at each leaf, because many features occur relatively rarely in our datasets, see figure 3. Taking larger subsets of random features alleviates this problem, but it also makes the evaluation of the features slower. To increase performance, we determine for each feature in φ_R how evenly it divides the set of samples in two, by evaluating

$$\sigma(S, f) := \frac{||S_f| - |S_{\neg f}||}{|S|}.$$

The best output of $\sigma(S, f)$ for a feature is 0, which is the case when a feature splits the sample set S in two sets of exactly the same size, and the worst output is 1, when the feature appears either in all samples or in none. In the evaluation phase, we consider only n_σ features φ_σ of φ_R that yield the best values for $\sigma(S, f)$. The motivation behind this is to preselect features which are more likely candidates to become splitting features, thus saving time in the evaluation phase.

Evaluating Features. The best splitting feature for a set of samples S should be a feature f which makes the samples in S_f and $S_{\neg f}$ more homogenous compared to S [AGPV13]. Common measures to determine splitting features are information gain and Gini impurity [RS04]. Furthermore, to obtain a tree that is not too high, it is desirable for a splitting feature to split S evenly, such that S_f and $S_{\neg f}$ have roughly the same number of labels.

In general, we look for a function $s(S, f)$, which determines the quality of f being a splitting feature for S. The best splitting feature can then be obtained by $\arg\min_{f \in \varphi_\sigma} s(S, f)$. We evaluated two concrete implementations for $s(S, f)$:

1. $\sigma(S, f)$: While σ optimally divides S into two evenly sized sets S_f and $S_{\neg f}$, it does not take into account their homogenicity.
2. $G(S, f) = \frac{1}{|S|} \left(|S_f| g(S_f) + |S_{\neg f}| g(S_{\neg f}) \right)$: The Gini impurity [AGPV13] g measures the frequency of each label among a set of samples, and gives labels with very high or very low frequency a low value. That means that the more similar the samples are (meaning they possess similar labels), the lower the Gini impurity.

Definition 4 (Gini impurity). *Gini impurity $g(S)$ of a set of samples S is*

$$g(S) = \sum_{l \in \lambda(S)} p_S(l) \left(1 - p_S(l)\right)$$

$$p_S(l) = \sum_{s \in S} p_S(l|s) p(s), \quad p_S(l|s) = \frac{|\lambda(s) \cap \{l\}|}{|\lambda(s)|}, \quad p_S(s) = \frac{|\lambda(s)|}{\sum_{s' \in S} |\lambda(s')|}$$

4.5 Querying a Tree

Querying a tree with features F corresponds to finding samples S from the tree maximising $P(S|F)$. We show a multi-path querying algorithm, as well as a method to obtain labels from the samples with classifiers such as k-NN.

Multi-path Querying. To query a decision tree with features F, a common approach is to recursively go to the left subtree l of a branch node $B(l, f, r)$ if $f \in F$ and to the right if not, until encountering a leaf $L(S)$, upon which one returns S. We found that this approach frequently missed samples with interesting features when these did not completely correspond to the features we queried for. This is why we considered a different kind of tree query, which we call *multi-path querying* (MPQ) in contrast to *single-path querying* (SPQ). MPQ considers not only the path with 100% matching features, but also all other paths in the tree. At each branch node where the taken path differs from that foreseen by the splitting feature of the node, we store the depth d of the node, as illustrated in figure 4. The output of a multi-path query for a tree t and features F is $mq_F(t, 0, \emptyset)$, defined as follows:

$$mq_F(t, d, E) = \begin{cases} (S, d, E) & t = L(S) \\ mq_F(l, d+1, E) \cup mq_F(r, d+1, E \cup \{d\}) & t = B(l, f, r) \wedge f \in F \\ mq_F(r, d+1, E) \cup mq_F(l, d+1, E \cup \{d\}) & t = B(l, f, r) \wedge f \notin F \end{cases}$$

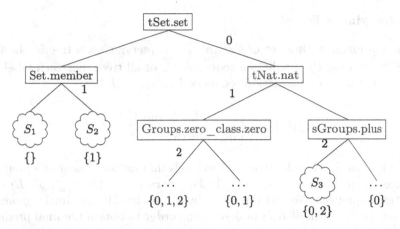

Fig. 4. Multi-path query example, where the tree is an excerpt from an actual random forest tree generated from the Isabelle/HOL Probability dataset. Query features are {tSet.set, Set.member}. The numbers next to the branches indicate the depth of wrongly taken decisions, which are accumulated and shown below the samples at the bottom.

Depth Weighting. We want to assign to each tree leaf a weight, which indicates how well the features F correspond to the features along the path from the root of the tree to the leaf. To do this, we consider the depths of the branch nodes where we took a different path than foreseen by F, and calculate for each of the depths a weight, which we later combine to form a branch or sample weight.

For each $e \in E$, where $(S, d, E) \in mq_F(t, 0, \emptyset)$, we calculate a depth weight, where the constant μ represents the minimal weight: $e_{\text{ascending}}(d, e) = \mu + (1 - \mu)\left(\frac{e}{d}\right)$, $e_{\text{descending}}(d, e) = 1 - (1-\mu)\left(\frac{e}{d}\right)$, $e_{\text{inverse}}(d, e) = 1 - \frac{1-\mu}{e+1}$, and $e_{\text{const}}(d, e) = \mu$. Using the depth weights, we calculate a weight for each sample:

$$w_t(s) = \sum_{(S,d,E) \in mq_F(t,0,\emptyset),\, s \in S} \prod_{e \in E} e_i(d, e).$$

Classifier in Leaves. Regular decision trees with single-path querying return all the labels of the chosen branch. To order the results from multiple branches in a tree, which is necessary with multi-path querying, we run a secondary classifier on all the leaf samples of the tree. The secondary classifier is modified to take into account the weight of each branch. In our experiments, the secondary classifier is a k-NN algorithm adapted for premise selection (IDF, premise relevance inversely proportional to the number of premises [KU13b]), which we modified to accept sample weights: k-NN will give premises that appear in samples with higher weights precedence over those from samples with lower weights. In default k-NN, all samples would have weight 1, while in our secondary classifier the weight of a sample s is given by $w_t(s)$, which stems from the path to s in the decision tree.

4.6   Querying a Forest

We query a forest with a set of features F by querying each tree in the forest with F, combining the prediction sequences $\overrightarrow{L}$ of all trees. For each label l, we calculate its rank in a prediction sequence $L = [l_1, \ldots, l_n]$ as:

$$\varrho(l, L) = \begin{cases} i & \text{if } l = l_i \text{ and } l_i \in L \\ m & \text{otherwise} \end{cases}$$

Here, m is a maximal rank attributed to labels that do not appear in a prediction sequence. Then, for each label, we calculate its ranks $R(l) = \biguplus_{L \in \overrightarrow{L}} \varrho(l, L)$ for all prediction sequences. We sort the labels by the arithmetic, quadratic, geometric, or the harmonic mean of $R(l)$ in descending order to obtain the final prediction sequence.

5   Experiments

We implemented the algorithms from section 4 in Haskell.[2] Our experimental results for the Mizar dataset are given in table 2: Random forests give best results when combined with multi-path querying and path-weighted k-NN+IDF classifier in the leaves. Both considering Gini impurity and taking random subsets of features decrease the prediction quality, while having a very negative impact on runtime. Different sample selection methods (samples draw trees vs. trees draw samples) have a large impact when using small sample frequencies, but when using higher sample frequencies, the difference is negligible. In this evaluation, we simulated single-path querying (SPQ) by a constant depth weight with $\mu = 0$ (meaning that all non-perfect tree branches receive the minimal score 0). Running this method takes longer than real SPQ, but gives a good upper bound on SPQ's prediction quality. Random forests have a longer runtime than k-NN, but still, the average prediction time for our test set is below one second, which is sufficient for premise selection.

To produce the number of proven theorems in table 3, we predict max. 128 (for Mizar, for HOL Light 1024) premises for each conjecture, translate the chosen facts (if no PS: all previous facts) together with the conjecture to TPTP first-order formulas [Sut09] and run E-Prover 1.8 [Sch13] using automatic strategy scheduling with 30 seconds timeout.

Alama et al. [AHK+14] have reported 548 proven theorems with Vampire (timeout = 10s) without external premise selection, which their best premise selection method (MOR-40/100) increases to 824 theorems (+50.4%). On our data, E (timeout = 10s) without premise selection proves only 414 theorems, increasing with timeout = 30s to 653 theorems (+57.7%) and with timeout = 10s and RF premise selection to 962 (+132.3%).

---

[2] Source and detailed statistics (also for HOL Light and Isabelle datasets) are available at http://cl-informatik.uibk.ac.at/~mfaerber/predict.html.

Table 2. Results for Mizar dataset. By default, we use 4 trees with a sample frequency of 16, samples draw trees. The minimal sample function is $\mu_{\log}$, we do not use Gini impurity, and we use e_{Inverse} with $\mu = 0.8$. The final prediction is obtained by running k-NN with IDF over the weighted leaf samples of each tree, combining results with the harmonic mean.

Configuration	100-Prec [%]	AUC [%]	Runtime [min]	Avg. time per prediction [s]
k-NN + IDF	87.5	95.39	**0.5**	**0.02**
RF (IDF)	88.0	95.68	32	0.93
RF (no IDF)	77.8	91.40	25	0.75
RF (single-path query)	53.7	60.86	37	1.07
RF (sample freq. = 2, trees draw s.)	65.6	72.76	2	0.05
RF (sample freq. = 2, samples draw t.)	88.0	95.59	4	0.10
RF (random features $n_R = 32$)	88.0	95.65	151	4.41
RF (Gini impurity, $n_\sigma = 2$)	88.0	95.65	97	2.84
RF (Gini impurity, $n_\sigma = 16$)	88.0	95.62	220	6.44
RF ($e_{\text{ascending}}$)	88.0	95.72	36	1.07
RF ($e_{\text{descending}}$)	88.1	95.66	39	1.15
RF (e_{inverse})	88.0	95.68	38	1.12
RF (e_{const})	88.1	95.81	37	1.08
RF (arithmetic mean)	87.5	95.49	33	0.98
RF (geometric mean)	88.0	95.67	35	1.01
RF (quadratic mean)	87.4	95.34	33	0.97
RF (100 trees, sample freq. = 50)	88.5	95.85	137	4.01
RF (24 trees, sample freq. = 12)	88.5	95.83	31	0.90
RF (24 trees, sample freq. = 12, e_{const})	**88.6**	**95.91**	22	0.66

Table 3. Results of k-NN and random forest predictions for two different datasets. For random forests, we used the best configuration from table 2, i.e. 24 trees, sample frequency 12, and constant depth weight.

	k-NN AUC	RF AUC	k-NN Prec	RF Prec	k-NN proved	RF proved	Total
Mizar	0.9539	0.9591	0.875	0.886	931	959 (+3.0%)	2050
HOL Light	0.9565	0.9629	0.919	0.929	789	823 (+4.3%)	2247

Table 4. Comparison of runtime necessary to achieve the same number of proven theorems (969) for the Mizar dataset

Classifier	Classifier runtime	E timeout	E runtime	Total runtime
k-NN	0.5min	15sec	341min	341min
RF	22min	10sec	252min	272min

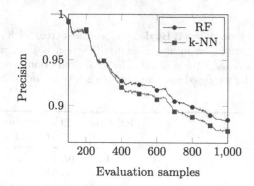

Fig. 5. Comparison of k-NN with random forests by number of evaluation samples on Mizar dataset

In table 4, we compare ATP runtime required to prove the same number of theorems using k-NN and RF predictions. While RF classification requires more runtime than k-NN, the ATP timeout can be decreased by more than 25%, resulting in overall runtime reduction of about 20%.

Number of Evaluation Samples. In figure 5, we show how the prediction quality develops for the Mizar dataset as more data is learned: For this purpose, we calculated statistics for the predictions of just our first evaluation sample, then for the first two, etc. When comparing the output of our random forest predictor (24 trees, sample frequency 12, constant depth weight) with k-NN, we see that it consistently performs better.

6   Conclusion

We evaluated several random forest approaches for ATP premise selection: Without modifications, the algorithms return worse predictions than the current state-of-the-art premise selectors included in HOL(y)Hammer, MizAℝ, and Sledgehammer/MaSh, and the time needed to select facts from a larger database is significant. We then proposed a number of extensions to the random forest algorithms designed for premise selection, such as incremental learning, multi-path querying, and various heuristics for the choice of samples, features and size of the trees. We combined random forests with a k-NN predictor at the tree leaves of the forest, which increases the number of theorems from the HOL Light dataset that E-Prover can successfully reprove over the previous state-of-art classifier k-NN by 4.3%. We showed that to attain the same increase with k-NN, it is necessary to run E-Prover for 50% longer.

In scenarios where the number of queries is large in comparison with the number of learning phases, the random forest approach is an effective way of improving prediction quality while keeping runtime acceptable. This is the case for usage in systems such as HOL(y)Hammer and MizAℝ, but not for Sledgehammer, where data is relearned more frequently. The performance of random forests could still be improved by recalculating the best splitting feature only after having seen a certain minimal number of new samples since the last calculation of the best feature. This would improve learning speed while not greatly altering prediction results, because it is relatively unlikely that adding few samples to a big tree change the tree's best splitting feature. Further runtime improvements could be made by parallelising random forests.

Acknowledgements. We thank Josef Urban as well as anonymous CADE and FroCoS referees for their valuable comments. This work has been supported by the Austrian Science Fund (FWF) grant P26201.

References

AGPV13. Agrawal, R., Gupta, A., Prabhu, Y., Varma, M.: Multi-label learning with millions of labels: recommending advertiser bid phrases for web pages. In: Proceedings of the 22nd International Conference on World Wide Web, WWW 2013, pp. 13–24 (2013)

AHK⁺14. Alama, J., Heskes, T., Kühlwein, D., Tsivtsivadze, E., Urban, J.: Premise selection for mathematics by corpus analysis and kernel methods. Journal of Automated Reasoning 52(2), 191–213 (2014)

BBP11. Blanchette, J.C., Böhme, S., Paulson, L.C.: Extending sledgehammer with SMT solvers. In: Bjørner, N., Sofronie-Stokkermans, V. (eds.) CADE 2011. LNCS, vol. 6803, pp. 116–130. Springer, Heidelberg (2011)

Bre96. Breiman, L.: Bagging predictors. Machine Learning 24(2), 123–140 (1996)

Bre01. Breiman, L.: Random forests. Machine Learning 45(1), 5–32 (2001)

CCRR99. Carlson, A.J., Cumby, C.M., Rosen, J.L., Roth, D.: SNoW user guide (1999)

CNm06. Caruana, R., Niculescu-mizil, A.: An empirical comparison of supervised learning algorithms. In: 23rd Intl. Conf. Machine Learning (ICML 2006), pp. 161–168 (2006)

Faw04. Fawcett, T.: ROC graphs: Notes and practical considerations for researchers. Technical report, HP Laboratories, March 2004

Har96. Harrison, J.: HOL Light: A tutorial introduction. In: Srivas, M., Camilleri, A. (eds.) FMCAD 1996. LNCS, vol. 1166, pp. 265–269. Springer, Heidelberg (1996)

HV11. Hoder, K., Voronkov, A.: Sine qua non for large theory reasoning. In: Bjørner, N., Sofronie-Stokkermans, V. (eds.) CADE 2011. LNCS, vol. 6803, pp. 299–314. Springer, Heidelberg (2011)

KBKU13. Kühlwein, D., Blanchette, J.C., Kaliszyk, C., Urban, J.: MaSh: Machine learning for sledgehammer. In: Blazy, S., Paulin-Mohring, C., Pichardie, D. (eds.) ITP 2013. LNCS, vol. 7998, pp. 35–50. Springer, Heidelberg (2013)

KU13a. Kaliszyk, C., Urban, J.: MizAR 40 for Mizar 40. CoRR (2013)

KU13b. Kaliszyk, C., Urban, J.: Stronger automation for Flyspeck by feature weighting and strategy evolution. In: PxTP 2013. EPiC Series, vol. 14, pp. 87–95. EasyChair (2013)

KU14. Kaliszyk, C., Urban, J.: Learning-assisted automated reasoning with Flyspeck. Journal of Automated Reasoning 53(2), 173–213 (2014)

KU15. Kaliszyk, C., Urban, J.: HOL(y)Hammer: Online ATP service for HOL Light. Mathematics in Computer Science 9(1), 5–22 (2015)

KV13.   Kovács, L., Voronkov, A.: First-order theorem proving and Vampire. In: Sharygina, N., Veith, H. (eds.) CAV 2013. LNCS, vol. 8044, pp. 1–35. Springer, Heidelberg (2013)

KBKU13.   Kühlwein, D.A.: Machine Learning for Automated Reasoning. PhD thesis, Radboud Universiteit Nijmegen, April 2014

LRT14.   Lakshminarayanan, B., Roy, D., Teh, Y.W.: c. In: Advances in Neural Information Processing Systems (2014)

MP06.   Meng, J., Paulson, L.C.: Lightweight relevance filtering for machine-generated resolution problems. In: ESCoR: Empirically Successful Computerized Reasoning, pp. 53–69 (2006)

NK09.   Naumowicz, A., Korniłowicz, A.: A brief overview of MIZAR. In: Berghofer, S., Nipkow, T., Urban, C., Wenzel, M. (eds.) TPHOLs 2009. LNCS, vol. 5674, pp. 67–72. Springer, Heidelberg (2009)

NPW02.   Nipkow, T., Paulson, L.C., Wenzel, M.: Isabelle/HOL. LNCS, vol. 2283. Springer, Heidelberg (2002)

OR01.   Oza, N.C., Russell, S.J.: Online bagging and boosting. In: Proceedings of the Eighth International Workshop on Artificial Intelligence and Statistics, AISTATS 2001, January 4-7, vol. Key West, Florida, US (2001)

RS04.   Raileanu, L.E., Stoffel, K.: Theoretical comparison between the Gini index and information gain criteria. Annals of Mathematics and Artificial Intelligence 41(1), 77–93 (2004)

Sch13.   Schulz, S.: System description: E 1.8. In: McMillan, K., Middeldorp, A., Voronkov, A. (eds.) LPAR-19 2013. LNCS, vol. 8312, pp. 735–743. Springer, Heidelberg (2013)

SLS⁺09.   Saffari, A., Leistner, C., Santner, J., Godec, M., Bischof, H.: On-line random forests. In: 3rd IEEE ICCV Workshop on On-line Computer Vision (2009)

Sor10.   Sorower, M.S.: A literature survey on algorithms for multi-label learning. Oregon State University, Corvallis (2010)

Sut09.   Sutcliffe, G.: The TPTP problem library and associated infrastructure. Journal of Automated Reasoning 43(4), 337–362 (2009)

TK07.   Tsoumakas, G., Katakis, I.: Multi-label classification: An overview. Int. J. Data Warehousing and Mining, 1–13 (2007)

Urb04.   Urban, J.: MPTP - motivation, implementation, first experiments. J. Autom. Reasoning 33(3-4), 319–339 (2004)

ZZ05.   Zhang, M.-L., Zhou, Z.-H.: A k-nearest neighbor based algorithm for multi-label classification. In: Proceedings of the 1st IEEE International Conference on Granular Computing (GrC 2005), Beijing, China, pp. 718–721 (2005)

Lemmatization for Stronger Reasoning
in Large Theories

Cezary Kaliszyk[1], Josef Urban[2], and Jiří Vyskočil[3]

[1] University of Innsbruck, Austria
[2] Radboud University Nijmegen
[3] Czech Technical University in Prague

Abstract. In this work we improve ATP performance in large theories by the reuse of lemmas derived in previous related problems. Given a large set of related problems to solve, we run automated theorem provers on them, extract a large number of lemmas from the proofs found and post-process the lemmas to make them usable in the remaining problems. Then we filter the lemmas by several tools and extract their proof dependencies, and use machine learning on such proof dependencies to add the most promising generated lemmas to the remaining problems. On such enriched problems we run the automated provers again, solving more problems. We describe this method and the techniques we used, and measure the improvement obtained. On the MPTP2078 large-theory benchmark the method yields 6.6% and 6.2% more problems proved in two different evaluation modes.

1 Introduction

When solving many problems in a certain theory, mathematicians usually remember and re-use the important lemmas found in related problems. *Lemma* usually denotes a statement that was useful or crucial for proving a (important) theorem, often an important technical step. For example commutativity or distributivity of some algebraic operations under certain assumptions might greatly simplify proofs in algebra.

This paper describes several experiments that attempt to improve the efficiency of automated theorem proving (ATP) over a larger theory by designing *automated* methods for re-using lemmas from related problems. We are interested in proving theorems (and re-using lemmas) in general large-theory mathematics represented in the first-order TPTP format and giving rise to thousands of related problems, containing many formulas. We assume that there are many symbols in such problems and that they are named consistently across all the problems. Such problems are typically neither purely equational nor Horn nor EPR, and the strongest existing tools for them are refutational first-order ATPs such as Vampire [10] and E [18]. Hence our task revolves around the refutational proofs obtained from such ATPs. The important topics that need to be addressed are:

– How do we generate re-usable lemmas automatically from such ATP proofs?
– How do we automatically choose a set of good lemmas from related problems?

© Springer International Publishing Switzerland 2015
C. Lutz and S. Ranise (Eds.): FroCoS 2015, LNAI 9322, pp. 341–356, 2015.
DOI: 10.1007/978-3-319-24246-0_21

- What are good lemmas for a particular new ATP problem?
- How do we evaluate the usefulness of re-using lemmas in ATP?
- How much ATP performance can we gain by re-using lemmas?

There have been several lines of work in ATP related to these questions, we briefly mention those that are most relevant to our work. So far the most successful technique for re-using lemmas from ATP proofs has been Veroff's *hints* method [26]. It extracts lemmas from the (manually selected and semi-manually re-oriented) proofs produced by Prover9 and uses them for internally directing Prover9's given-clause loop on related problems. The main application have so far been problems in equational algebra [15]. A recent example where very long proofs of open conjectures are found thanks to this technique is the project **AIM**-ed at characterizing loops with **A**belian **I**nner **M**appings groups [9]. A similar technique that extracts and generalizes lemmas from previous proofs and uses them for proof guidance was implemented by Schulz in E prover as a part of his PhD thesis [17].

We have tried to experiment with this E technique on large-theory problems, so far without success.[1] Our very initial experiments (done with Veroff) with hints on large-theory problems have shown that unlike the equational proofs, the proofs of large-theory problems contain many (incompatible) skolem constants and steps depending on the negated conjecture, and thus are harder to re-orient into the *strictly-forward* proofs [9] from which lemmas derived only from the axioms and containing only known symbols can be extracted. A related issue is that the large-theory proofs seem to be much more heterogeneous than e.g. the AIM problems, likely requiring targeted selection of hints for a particular problem rather than unrestricted use of all available lemmas as hints. To address such issues, we instead proceed here as follows:

1. We extract all the direct (axiom-derived) skolem-free lemmas used in the proofs. These lemmas can be immediately re-used in other proofs.
2. To make other lemmas re-usable, we first attempt to heuristically *redirect* general refutational ATP proofs into Jaśkowski-style natural deduction proofs using the recent tools developed for Sledgehammer by Blanchette and Smolka [2,19], so that the proof steps (later translated into lemmas) only depend on axioms.
3. Then we *extract* and heuristically *deskolemize* lemmas from the redirected natural-deduction proofs, so that the lemmas only speak about symbols that are known in the original large-theory problems (and thus are re-usable).
4. We verify and optionally interreduce the lemmas.
5. Given a new conjecture C, we use several AI methods to estimate which of the previously extracted lemmas might be most useful for proving C. Various numbers of the best lemmas are then added to the axioms with which we try to prove C.

The evaluation is done on the large-theory MPTP2078 benchmark [1], containing 2078 related problems in general topology (and related fields) extracted

---

[1] Schulz confirms that the code has not been maintained and might need various updates.

from Mizar. Note that large-theory techniques developed on one large-theory benchmark or corpus typically transfer well to other large-theory corpora [22,3]. In the following sections, we first describe in more detail the scenario and the techniques involved, and then we run ATPs on the benchmark with and without using such lemmatization methods, and evaluate their performance.

2   Lemmatization Scenario and Initial Statistics

Our goal is to prove as many problems over a large theory as possible. Concretely on the MPTP2078 benchmark, E prover (version 1.8) can prove in 60 seconds 569 of the 2078 *large* problems containing all previous premises (theorems, definitions and axioms). E can prove 1208 of the *small* versions of these problems, obtained by only giving E the premises that were needed for the (human-assisted) Mizar proofs.

The problems are chronologically ordered by their appearance in the Mizar library. We can assume that for a given problem P in the benchmark, all the lemmas found in all the previous proofs can be used for proving P. We can use both the lemmas from the large problems and from the small (human-assisted) problems, assuming that the mathematician needs to write the human-assisted formal proof regardless, even when the automation fails him, and that such human-assisted proofs can then be given to an ATP, which then may produce useful lemmas when running on such small problems.

The initial statistics of unmodified lemmas extracted from the 1208 proofs of the small problems is shown in Table 1. There are 75044 total lemmas when counting the same lemma multiple times (if it was created in multiple proofs). Only about half of them (38058) do not depend on the negated conjecture. About 60% (43995) of all lemmas contain a skolem symbol. Practically all those (96%) which depend on the negated conjecture contain a skolem symbol, but that is also the case for 22% of those that do not depend on the negated conjecture. This leaves only about 40% (29554) lemmas (with repetition) that are derived without the use of the negated conjecture and that do not contain any skolem symbol. After approximate merging of the same lemmas from different problems,[2]

Table 1. Initial statistics of lemmas from the small problems

	lemmas	neg.-conj.-dependent	neg.-conj.-independent
all	75044	36986	38058
all skolem	43995	35671	8324
all no skolem	31049	1315	29554
unique	23764	13660	10104
unique skolem	18189	13616	4573
unique no skolem	5575	44	5531

---

[2] This merging is only approximate because for the purpose of this initial statistics we do not try to detect if the (serial) skolem names used in the different problems come from the same first-order formula or not.

these numbers are even smaller: the ratio of usable lemmas that are independent of the negated conjecture and do not contain skolem symbols drops to 23% of all lemmas, while 77% do contain skolem symbols and 57% depend on the negated conjecture.

This is a good motivation for trying methods that make the lemmas independent of the negated conjecture and remove the skolem symbols, thus making many more lemmas generally applicable in the next problems.

3   Extracting Reusable Lemmas from Refutational Proofs

The task of making proof steps independent of the negated conjecture is closely related to the task of human-level presentation of ATP proofs. There have been several tools attempting such human-level presentation, for example Tramp [13] and P.rex [4]. The most recent one that has been tested on a large number of problems is Blanchette and Smolka's ATP proof presentation toolchain made for the Isabelle/Sledgehammer framework [19]. This toolchain relies on Blanchette's *proof redirector* [2], which tries to reverse proofs by contradiction into direct proofs.

In more detail, Blanchette's tool takes a refutational TPTP proof and creates a natural deduction (Isabelle/Isar) proof which has as many forward steps as possible, i.e., as many steps derived from the axioms as possible. This is roughly done by reversing the part of the derivation graph that depends the negated conjecture. For example, a final step that derives $\perp$ from two lemmas ϕ_1 and ϕ_2 depending on the negated conjecture:

$$\phi_1, \phi_2 \vdash \perp \tag{1}$$

is redirected into:

$$\vdash \phi_1 \wedge \phi_2 \rightarrow \perp \tag{2}$$

Assuming further that ϕ_1 was derived using ϕ_0 which is also dependent on the negated conjecture and using some other lemmas that are not conjecture-dependent, we further get:

$$\vdash \phi_0 \wedge \phi_2 \rightarrow \perp \tag{3}$$

The inference step on the redirected lemmas (2,3) is then justified by referring to the exact same conjecture-independent lemmas that were used in the original proof to derive ϕ_1 from ϕ_0. This mechanism propagates through the lemmas dependent on the negated conjecture, ultimately deriving that the negated conjecture implies $\perp$, i.e., deriving the unnegated conjecture in a forward style.

While Blanchette's redirection tool works on propositional level, the whole framework (due to Blanchette and Smolka) also translates the ATP skolemization steps into natural deduction steps that fix universally or existentially quantified variables as local constants for parts of the proof. In general, the redirected Jaśkowski-style natural deduction proofs may also introduce assumptions.

3.1   Extracting Lemmas from the Natural Deduction Proofs

The above framework assumes that the first-order TPTP problems are a result of translating higher-order facts and conjectures written in Isabelle/HOL, and it ultimately tries to create a legal higher-order natural-deduction proof from the first-order TPTP proof that justifies the higher-order conjecture. In order to instead process an arbitrary first-order TPTP proof and to generate standard first-order lemmas, we do the following:

- We modify the tool to be able to start with arbitrary first-order TPTP proofs that have no Isabelle origin, by using empty internal Isabelle translation tables, not typechecking the terms and formulas in the resulting natural deduction proof, and writing a separate TPTP printer that prints such untyped proofs.
- We add flattening of the assumption and local-constant block structure of the natural deduction proofs, producing globally valid TPTP lemmas. This step is in principal similar to the earlier translation of the Jaśkowski-style Mizar proofs into TPTP derivations [23], however there are several differences discussed below.
- The modified functionality is then compiled into a standalone tool,[3] which can be used as an initial lemma extractor for any TPTP proof.

The flattening of the natural-deduction proofs proceeds by tracking the assumption and quantification structure leading to a particular statement in the natural-deduction proof, and performing universal quantification for each local constant introduced by Isar's "fix" step, implication for each supposition ("assume") step, and existential quantification for each local constant introduced by Isar's "obtain" step, changing the corresponding Isar local constants to the quantified variables.

This procedure is correct, i.e., it cannot generate a lemma that would not be provable from the initial axioms, and it has the desired property that the generated lemma will not contain new skolem symbols, thus making the lemma usable for proving the next conjectures. In order to achieve this, we however sacrifice completeness in some cases.[4] For example, when in the natural deduction proof a local constant c such that $q(c)$ is obtained from $\exists X : q(X)$, and in its scope statements $p(c)$ and $r(c)$ are proved, the extracted lemmas will be $\exists X : p(X)$ and $\exists X : r(X)$ instead of the stronger version $\exists X : (p(X) \wedge r(X))$. In the Mizar proof export this is handled via additional Henkin axioms about the local constants, however that means proliferation of such new constants in the lemmas, which we want to avoid here. A related completeness issue comes from the fact that proper TPTP skolem functions (not constants) are translated into higher-order constants by the proof presentation framework. During the flattening we currently just skip generating all such lemmas instead of trying

---

[3] http://cl-informatik.uibk.ac.at/users/cek/frocos15/redirector/

[4] We obviously do not lose completeness in general, because all the lemmas can be derived from the axioms, however we weaken or lose some of the lemmas during the translation process.

more advanced transformations. Figures 1,2,3 show a side-by-side example of the transformations done on a simple propositional proof. Figure 1 shows the TPTP proof starting with the conjecture g and eight axioms. The conjecture is negated, and the contradiction (final line) is derived in eight inference steps. In the corresponding Isar proof (Figure 2) we use a compressed notation: the numbers in brackets refer to the serially numbered assumptions (corresponding to the TPTP axioms), that are used to justify a particular step. There are various imperfections (acknowledged by Blanchette), for example $f \Rightarrow g$ is proved (and then extracted by us as a lemma in Figure 3) despite being an axiom. Note that many of the extracted lemmas in Figure 3 are implications whose antecedents correspond to the Isar assumptions (Isar keyword **assume**).

```
fof(0, conjecture, (g)).
cnf(25,axiom,(h|g)).
cnf(26,neg_conj,(~g), [0]).
cnf(32,axiom,(a|~h)).
cnf(33,neg_conj,(h), [25,26]).
cnf(39,axiom,(~a|~b)).
cnf(40,neg_conj,(a), [32,33]).
cnf(45,axiom,(c|b)).
cnf(46,neg_conj,(~b), [39,40]).
cnf(48,axiom,(g|~f)).
cnf(50,axiom,(d|~c)).
cnf(51,neg_conj,(c), [45,46]).
cnf(52,axiom,(f|~e)).
cnf(53,neg_conj,(~f), [48,26]).
cnf(54,axiom,(e|~d)).
cnf(55,neg_conj,(d), [50,51]).
cnf(56,neg_conj,(~e), [52,53]).
cnf(57,neg_conj,(),[54,55,56]).
```

```
lemma assumes
  "a ∨ ¬h" "a ⟹ ¬b"
  "¬b ⟹ c" "c ⟹ d"
  "d ⟹ e" "e ⟹ f"
  "f ⟹ g" "¬h ⟹ g"
shows "g"
proof -
  have "d ⟶ f" (5,6)
  moreover
  { assume f
    hence g (7) }
  moreover
  { assume "¬ d"
    hence "¬ c" (4)
    hence b (3)
    hence "¬ a" (2)
    hence "¬ h" (1)
    hence g (8) }
  ultimately show g
qed
```

```
fof(53___55_0,plain,(d=>f)).

fof(9_0,plain,(f=>g)).

fof(51_0,plain,(~(d)=>~(c))).
fof(46_0,plain,(~(d)=>b)).
fof(40_0,plain,(~(d)=>~(a))).
fof(33_0,plain,(~(d)=>~(h))).
fof(9_0,plain,(~(d)=>g)).
fof(0_0,plain,g).
```

Fig. 1. Original proof   **Fig. 2.** Isabelle proof   **Fig. 3.** Lemmas

4   Filtering Lemmas

We run the lemma extractor on all TPTP proofs obtained from all the small MPTP2078 problems, taking 260 s in total. For five proofs the redirection phase runs out of memory, and from the rest we extract altogether 3394 *plain* (derived from axioms only) lemmas and 6328 *negated* (originally depending on negated conjecture) lemmas. The plain lemmas are in general much smaller (178 bytes on average) than the negated ones (526 bytes), typically because the redirection process adds assumptions to such lemmas.

Note that the number of plain lemmas produced by the redirector is much less than the 29554 plain skolem-free lemmas obtained by the direct extraction in Section 2. This is mainly due to de-duplication (not) applied at different stages and other small differences.

Re-proving and tautology removal: The first filter that we apply is fast (1 second) proving of each lemma from its problem's axioms, removing those that do not need any axiom (tautologies), and ending up with 5183 unique directly extracted provable lemmas (**pla**), 961 unique plain redirected lemmas (**plr**), 3538 unique negated lemmas (**neg**) of which 1617 are unique negated lemmas that do not contain conjunctions (**nmu**). In total there are 4377 unique redirected lemmas (**red**), and combined with pla there are 9057 lemmas in total (**all**). 768 of these lemmas are (after α-normalization) identical to some of the 4564 original MPTP2078 formulas.

The re-proving is done to be sure that we do not introduce unsoundness (which could then prove all the remaining problems) in the extraction phase. In Isabelle, an occasional error in the proof translation would not be an issue, because the translated proofs are ultimately checked by Isabelle's LCF kernel. Another reason for the re-proving is that we want to determine the exact proof dependencies of each lemma. This is an important information for learning how to use the lemmas and other formulas for future proofs.

Making lemmas usable for future problems: Each lemma is inserted into the chronological sequence of all premises, right *after* the theorem in which it proved for the first time (and possibly other lemmas generated in its proof). Even though the lemmas were proved *before* their theorem, inserting them before it would often result in very simple new proofs of the lemma-enriched large problems, because some of the new lemmas are very close to their theorems. In general, the lemma only becomes known after the proof is found, so we only allow to use the lemma for the theorems that follow the problem from which the lemma was first extracted.

Updating the dependencies: One of the main factors when selecting the most suitable lemmas for a problem is the information about how each lemma was previously used, and also how it was proved. This *dependency information* is added to the set of proof dependencies that we already have for the main theorems and lemmas. After this addition, we have three sets of dependencies for further experiments:

old: We add the new lemmas (if any) into the chronological sequence as described above, but do not add any information about their dependencies neither about dependencies on them.

all: For each new lemma, we also add the dependency on the axioms from which it was proved. So far we do not use dependencies between the lemmas.

fut: For each original proved theorem, we also add its dependency on all the lemmas that were extracted from its proof. We call these *future* dependencies, because as mentioned above, we allow these lemmas to be used only after the theorem is proved.

4.1   Additional Filters

On the set of all (possibly redirected) reproved lemmas (**all**) combined with the original MPTP2078 formulas we further apply the three additional filters explained below. We do not filter the other sets (**pla, plr, red, neg, nmu**) here because they are already sufficiently small.

Forward subsumption: We use the MoMM [21] subsumption tool derived from E's perfect discrimination trees on the lemmas in their order, disallowing backward subsumption, so that future stronger lemmas cannot remove earlier weaker versions. Such weaker version might be useful before the stronger lemma is proved later. This optional filter can remove 6956 of the new lemmas which are subsumed by another (older) lemma or by an existing axiom/theorem. 2101 of the **all** lemmas are left after this optional phase (**mom**). The disadvantage of such interreduction is that suitable frequently derived instances disappear in this way, and that such instances may contain symbols that make them more eligible for selection when using further similarity-based filters.

PageRank: One of the graph-based filters we experiment with is PageRank [14] used on the three graphs of direct proof dependencies (each lemma/theorem points to those used in its proof). It takes 0.574 s to compute the ranks of all the (about 13k) nodes. We then choose only the best 2048 new lemmas according to their PageRanks (**pgr**), which are then handed over to the final problem-specific premise selectors.

AGIntRater [16] is a tool that tries to compute important characteristics of the lemmas in ATP proofs, producing an aggregated *interestingness* rating for each lemma. AGIntRater fails to rate the complete set of new lemmas with dependencies (fut), likely because of the size of the dependency graph. Instead, we run AGIntRater on all the small proofs. We have considered computing the sums, averages and maximums of the lemma ratings across all the proofs for each unique lemma, however it turns out that many of the positive ratings are for the CNF transformations that do not give rise to new lemmas. Only 3564 of the new lemmas ever have nonnegative rating (**ag0**). We have also created an even more strict selection (**ag5**), where only the 1150 lemmas with average interestingness rating at least 0.5 were added.

5   Problem-Specific Premise Selection

Each of the above dependency sequences (**old, all, fut**) restricted to the preselected lemmas (**all, pla, plr, red, neg, nmu, mom, pgr, ag0, ag5**) provides information about how theorems and lemmas were proved. This information, together with suitable characterization (features) of the theorems and lemmas is incrementally learned from and used for each MPTP2078 theorem T to rank the preceding theorems and lemmas according to their estimated relevance for proving T.

For this we run two fast and scalable learning-based premise selectors: our currently strongest version of distance-weighted k-nearest-neighbor (k-NN) learner and our implementation of the naive Bayes learner [3]. Both methods use an IDF-weighted combination of symbol and term features for formula characterizations [5]. For each original MPTP2078 theorem we thus obtain (by training the learners on the previous proof dependencies) a ranking of the set of previously available MPTP2078 formulas and the added lemmas. Table 2 shows how often

Table 2. Ratio (in %) of the new lemmas in the first n k-NN predictions for several lemma-selection methods and the **all** sequence

Lemma selection	first	10-first	100-first	1000-first
pla	0.57	3.46	16.64	32.56
red	0.48	4.06	22.44	40.61
ag0	0.68	4.94	20.89	36.09
mom	0.72	3.61	15.32	28.91
pgr	0.34	5.18	20.43	32.78

the k-NN predicts the new lemmas among the first n predictions when using the **all** proof dependencies (only several interesting sequences are shown). For comparison we also add to the evaluation the normal non-lemmatizing premise selection method (**non**).

6   Evaluation

All the data, tools, and statistics for this paper are available at our web page.[5] In particular, the full versions of the tables shown in this section are online.[6]

There are several approaches to evaluating the improvement. First, we can compare the ATP performance of the best methods with and without lemmas, i.e., in both cases after choosing the best-performing combination of learning-based selection with the underlying lemmatizing method. To find such best combinations, we try to prove each theorem with the best-ranked selections (segments) of 16, 32,64,...,2048 MPTP2078 formulas and lemmas, using a 30 s time limit. As the underlying ATP we always use E 1.8 running in its automated mode. Note that E itself runs many ATP strategies for each problem in its automated mode. These strategies are selected for each problem individually by a machine-learning system developed by Schulz, based on suitable problem characteristics and performance of the strategies on a large set of problems.

Table 3 compares the best results achieved with and without lemmas for each number of the best-ranked premises tried, showing also the relative improvement for each premise number. The complete table of the 336 combinations is available online.[7] The best lemma-based method (k-NN, fut, all lemmas, 128 best-ranked premises) proves 936 theorems, while the best non-lemmatizing method (k-NN, old, no lemmas, 128 best-ranked premises) proves 878 theorems, i.e., 6.6% less.

The improvement from lemmatization is relatively low – 3.5% – when using only 16 best-ranked premises (618 by k-NN/all/ag0 versus 597 by k-NN/old/non). This rises to 14.8% when using 256 premises and peaks at 20.9% when using 512 premises (851 by k-NN/fut/all versus 705 by NB/old/non), which is a very significant improvement. Figure 4 shows the success rates for these premise numbers

---

[5] http://cl-informatik.uibk.ac.at/users/cek/frocos15/

[6] http://cl-informatik.uibk.ac.at/users/cek/frocos15/statistics/

[7] http://cl-informatik.uibk.ac.at/users/cek/frocos15/
statistics/all-single-statistics.html

Table 3. Comparison of the best methods for the 8 premise-selection sizes

Premises	16	32	64	128	256	512	1024	2048
Lemmas	618	820	926	**936**	915	851	724	657
Old	597	797	877	**878**	797	705	627	551
Improvement (%)	3.5	2.9	5.6	6.6	14.8	**20.7**	15.5	19.2

for the different lemmatizing strategies, each aggregated across the two premise selectors and the various methods of constructing the dependencies.

There are several effects involved in these results. At the low premise selection numbers, the main challenge is to select premises that really justify the conjecture, i.e., which do not leave any countermodels left (see e.g., SRASS [20] and MaLARea-SG1 [24] for more detailed experiments). For this, the original Mizar library theorems seem to be quite well designed, and only a few of the strongest lemmas – in particular the ones chosen by AGIntRater and PageRank – help to increase the performance by 3.5%. On the other hand, when allowing many premises, insufficient logical power of the premises is usually no longer an issue, and the main problem is to focus the proof search towards the conjecture. Such focusing is the core of Veroff's hints method, which is likely to some extent being emulated at the higher premise numbers by adding some previously useful conclusions of the main library theorems. A related effect that we have quite often observed, is that during the premise selection the more conjecture-related or more instantiated lemmas replace some less related or more general library theorems, which in the no-lemma case more easily confuse the proof search. Lastly, even if no new lemma is eventually used in a proof, it happens quite often that the new proof dependencies created with the help of the added lemmas make it easier for the machine learners to choose the right Mizar theorems for the proof. The latter effects – useful instantiations, many conjecture-related lemmas replacing other theorems, and more data for learning – likely also explain the relatively low performance of the lemmas interreduced by forward subsumption (MoMM) compared to only α-normalized lemmas (all).

Another way to compare the methods is to look at the aggregated results (unions of problems solved) across the two machine learners and the eight premise numbers. This is shown in Table 4. The best new method – k-NN/ag0 – solves in total 1268 problems, compared to 1217 solved without lemmas, i.e., 4.2% more. Note that just using all lemmas, relying only on learning-based premise selection without any further filtering does not perform much worse (1262 problems). In total, the union of all problems solved by the new and old methods is 1375 problems, compared to 1217 without lemmas, i.e., 13.0% more. Such comparison is however unrealistic, because the total time spent on all the new combinations together is much higher than the total time spent on the old ones.

A fairer way how to do such total comparison is to give the new methods only as much time as is needed to solve the 1217 problems by the old methods, i.e., in our case allowing only 14 most complementary new methods, see Table 5.

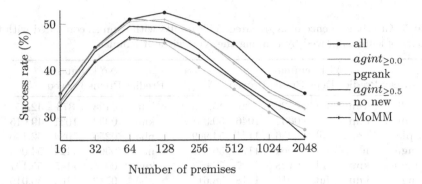

Fig. 4. ATP success rates over 8 premise-selection sizes for several strategies

As common in such evaluations [6,8,12] the most complementary methods are computed by a greedy algorithm, and the resulting greedy sequences are shown from top to bottom in the table. The total improvement is in this case 6.2%, i.e. a comparable result to the 6.6% improvement obtained by comparing only the best single methods.

Table 4. Aggregated ATP results across the premise-selection sizes

Strategy	Dependencies	Proved	%	Unique
ag0	fut	1268	61.020	3
all	fut	1262	60.731	1
all	all	1253	60.298	1
ag0	all	1247	60.010	1
pla	all	1247	60.010	0
pgr	all	1242	59.769	5
pgr	fut	1240	59.673	3
pla	fut	1236	59.480	2
ag5	fut	1235	59.432	1
ag5	all	1233	59.336	0
red	fut	1230	59.192	0
red	all	1228	59.095	0
neg	fut	1227	59.047	1
plr	fut	1225	58.951	1
mom	all	1222	58.807	1
plr	all	1222	58.807	2
non	old	1217	58.566	0
all	old	1216	58.518	3
neg	all	1215	58.470	0
any		1375	66.169	

Table 5. Greedy sequence of aggregated ATP results with lemmas compared with the numbers of lemmas proved by running the ATP without lemmas.

	With lemmas						No lemmas			
Strategy	Predict	Deps	Prems	Proved	%		Predict	Prems	Proved	%
all	knn	fut	0128	936	45.043		knn	0128	878	42.252
all	knn	all	0032	1046	50.337		knn	0032	1031	49.615
pla	knn	all	0256	1141	54.909		nba	0256	1084	52.166
ag5	nba	fut	0064	1175	56.545		nba	0064	1124	54.090
mom	knn	all	0128	1197	57.603		knn	0016	1145	55.101
ag0	knn	fut	0016	1218	58.614		nba	0512	1164	56.015
all	knn	fut	2048	1235	59.432		knn	0064	1176	56.593
pgr	nba	fut	0512	1248	60.058		nba	0016	1185	57.026
nmu	nba	fut	0064	1258	60.539		nba	0128	1193	57.411
pgr	knn	all	0064	1267	60.972		nba	0032	1200	57.748
nmu	nba	fut	0256	1274	61.309		knn	2048	1207	58.085
all	knn	old	0016	1280	61.598		knn	0256	1213	58.373
nmu	knn	fut	0064	1286	61.886		knn	0512	1215	58.470
pla	knn	all	0128	1292	62.175		nba	1024	1217	58.566

7   Examples of New Lemmas

While the statistics in the previous section gives an global overview of the strength of the methods, it is also interesting to inspect several examples of new proofs found thanks to the added lemmas.

1. The first Mizar theorem about basic set operations (in this case symmetric difference), XBOOLE_0:1,[8] states that:

   x in X \+\ Y iff ((x in X & not x in Y) or (x in Y & not x in X)).

   The ATP proof of this fact includes a CNF statement that in the Mizar syntax would read:

   X1 in X3 implies not X1 in X2 \ X3.

   This lemma could be easily derived as a consequence of more general facts already present in the Mizar library, however it does help in a number of future ATP proofs. For examples it lets the ATPs prove XBOOLE_1:40,[9] which states:

   (X \/ Y) \ Y = X \ Y,

---

[8] http://mizar.cs.ualberta.ca/~mptp/7.11.07_4.160.1126/
html/xboole_0.html#T1

[9] http://mizar.cs.ualberta.ca/~mptp/7.11.07_4.160.1126/
html/xboole_1.html#T40

and to prove ZFMISC_1:72:[10]

{x,y} \ X = {x,y} iff (not x in X & not y in X).

2. Another example is a new lemma derived by the ATP in the proof of XBOOLE_1:1:[11]

X1 \ (X2 \ X1) = X1,

which is useful in the proofs of four more theorems (three of them in XBOOLE_1, one in TOPS_1).

3. A more complicated new lemma is derived in WAYBEL_7:9:[12]

with_infima(BoolePoset X).

This is a simple consequence of two facts already present in the Mizar library, but it enables three new ATP proofs in the formalization of prime ideals and filters in WAYBEL_7. This is likely because a large number of such simple facts can be derived in this rich domain, and pointing out the relevant one makes the three proofs achievable.

8   Related Work

Some relevant related work such as Veroff's and Schulz's work is already mentioned in the introduction. A more extensive summary of the related methods is given in our paper on extracting and re-using the millions to billions lemmas arising in Interactive Theorem Proving (ITP) [7]. Some issues discussed here overlap to some extent with the ITP setting: for example the need for fast methods for filtering a large number of lemmas. The need for further fast filters is however not so big here: we can easily handle all lemmas (thousands) by the learning-based premise selectors and only use the additional filters to get better predictions, whereas in ITP (millions to billions lemmas) fast pre-filtering is crucial.

A number of further issues differ in the ATP setting: the lemmas need re-orienting and deskolemizing, and the ATP proofs are short and suitable for ATP-style tools like AGIntRater. It is also worth mentioning that even in the ITP setting, ATP proofs are typically a valuable source of training data for learning premise selection [11,6]. This means that the ATP and ITP lemma extraction could likely be fruitfully combined in the various strong [AI]TP "hammer" systems.

---

[10] http://mizar.cs.ualberta.ca/~mptp/7.11.07_4.160.1126/
html/zfmisc_1.html#T72
[11] http://mizar.cs.ualberta.ca/~mptp/7.11.07_4.160.1126/
html/xboole_1.html#T1
[12] http://mizar.cs.ualberta.ca/~mptp/7.11.07_4.160.1126/
html/waybel_7.html#T9

9   Conclusion and Future Work

We have introduced a toolchain for re-using lemmas across many related ATP problems, and evaluated it on the MPTP2078 large-theory benchmark. The main challenges are extraction of reusable context-independent lemmas from the ATP proofs, their subsequent filtering, and extracting suitable proof dependencies for learning premise selection. To make lemmas reusable, we first redirect them, using a modified version of the Isabelle/Isar proof presentation tools, and then we heuristically deskolemize them. The subsequent filtering is done by several tools – AGIntRater, PageRank, MoMM – that make use of different aspects of the proofs and lemmas. The filtered lemmas and their proofs result in modified proof dependencies, from which we learn along with the old proof dependencies, and use such learned knowledge to select premises for each MPTP2078 theorem. The 30 s improvement over the best old method is 6.6% more problems proved, and the improvement when using 14 most complementary methods is 6.2%. This comparison is done against the strategy-scheduling E prover, which itself runs a customized selection of strategies on each problem, choosing these strategies from a large portfolio. This means that the lemmatizing strategies add nontrivial performance to the E strategies. We have found that the new lemmas are particularly useful when using many premises, improving over the no-lemma case by about 15% and 20% when using 256 and 512 premises, respectively.

In the future we would like to experiment with running the toolchain on consistently pre-skolemized problems and on harder problems that miss some of the original MPTP2078 theorems. Another direction is to combine the filters and to use more of them, possibly on a larger dataset such as the whole MPTP-translated MML, using also methods for selecting lemmas from the ITP (Mizar) proofs [25,7]. We can also try more MaLARea-style iterations of the lemma-enrichment, i.e., extracting lemmas from the newly found problems and trying unsolved problems with such new lemmas added. And yet another direction is to re-use the filtering methods for Veroff-style hints selection and for improving given-clause guidance in ATPs by a large pool of previous lemmas.

Acknowledgments. We thank the CADE-25 referees for a number of useful comments to an early version of this paper. Kaliszyk was supported by the Austrian Science Fund (FWF): P26201, Urban's work was funded by NWO grant 612.001.208: *Knowledge-based Automated Reasoning*, Vyskočil's work was supported by institutional resources for research by the Czech Technical University in Prague, Czech Republic.

References

1. Alama, J., Heskes, T., Kühlwein, D., Tsivtsivadze, E., Urban, J.: Premise selection for mathematics by corpus analysis and kernel methods. J. Autom. Reasoning 52(2), 191–213 (2014)
2. Blanchette, J.C.: Redirecting proofs by contradiction. In: Blanchette, J.C., Urban, J. (eds.) PxTP@CADE. EPiC Series, vol. 14, pp. 11–26. EasyChair (2013)

3. Blanchette, J.C., Kaliszyk, C., Paulson, L.C., Urban, J.: Hammering towards QED. J. Formalized Reasoning (in press, 2015)
4. Fiedler, A.: *P.rex*: An interactive proof explainer. In: Goré, R.P., Leitsch, A., Nipkow, T. (eds.) IJCAR 2001. LNCS (LNAI), vol. 2083, pp. 416–420. Springer, Heidelberg (2001)
5. Kaliszyk, C., Urban, J.: Stronger automation for Flyspeck by feature weighting and strategy evolution. In: Blanchette, J.C., Urban, J. (eds.) PxTP 2013. EPiC Series, vol. 14, pp. 87–95. EasyChair (2013)
6. Kaliszyk, C., Urban, J.: Learning-assisted automated reasoning with Flyspeck. J. Autom. Reasoning 53(2), 173–213 (2014)
7. Kaliszyk, C., Urban, J.: Learning-assisted theorem proving with millions of lemmas. Journal of Symbolic Computation 69, 109–128 (2015)
8. Kaliszyk, C., Urban, J.: MizAR 40 for Mizar 40. J. Automated Reasoning (in press, 2015)
9. Kinyon, M., Veroff, R., Vojtěchovský, P.: Loops with abelian inner mapping groups: An application of automated deduction. In: Bonacina, M.P., Stickel, M.E. (eds.) Automated Reasoning and Mathematics. LNCS, vol. 7788, pp. 151–164. Springer, Heidelberg (2013)
10. Kovács, L., Voronkov, A.: First-order theorem proving and Vampire. In: Sharygina, N., Veith, H. (eds.) CAV 2013. LNCS, vol. 8044, pp. 1–35. Springer, Heidelberg (2013)
11. Kuehlwein, D., Urban, J.: Learning from multiple proofs: First experiments. In: Fontaine, P., Schmidt, R.A., Schulz, S. (eds.) PAAR 2012. EPiC Series, vol. 21, pp. 82–94. EasyChair (2013)
12. Kühlwein, D., Blanchette, J.C., Kaliszyk, C., Urban, J.: MaSh: Machine learning for Sledgehammer. In: Blazy, S., Paulin-Mohring, C., Pichardie, D. (eds.) ITP 2013. LNCS, vol. 7998, pp. 35–50. Springer, Heidelberg (2013)
13. Meier, A.: System description: TRAMP: transformation of machine-found proofs into nd-proofs at the assertion level. In: McAllester, D. (ed.) CADE 2000. LNCS(LNAI), vol. 1831, pp. 460–464. Springer, Heidelberg (2000)
14. Page, L., Brin, S., Motwani, R., Winograd, T.: The PageRank citation ranking: Bringing order to the Web. Technical report, Stanford Digital Library Technologies Project (1998)
15. Phillips, J.D., Stanovský, D.: Automated theorem proving in quasigroup and loop theory. AI Commun. 23(2–3), 267–283 (2010)
16. Puzis, Y., Gao, Y., Sutcliffe, G.: Automated generation of interesting theorems. In: Sutcliffe, G., Goebel, R. (eds.) FLAIRS, pp. 49–54. AAAI Press (2006)
17. Schulz, S.: Learning search control knowledge for equational deduction. DISKI, vol. 230. Infix Akademische Verlagsgesellschaft (2000)
18. Schulz, S.: System description: E 1.8. In: McMillan, K., Middeldorp, A., Voronkov, A. (eds.) LPAR-19 2013. LNCS, vol. 8312, pp. 735–743. Springer, Heidelberg (2013)
19. Smolka, S.J., Blanchette, J.C.: Robust, semi-intelligible Isabelle proofs from ATP proofs. In: Blanchette, J.C., Urban, J. (eds.) PxTP 2013. EPiC Series, vol. 14, pp. 117–132. EasyChair (2013)
20. Sutcliffe, G., Puzis, Y.: SRASS - A semantic relevance axiom selection system. In: Pfenning, F. (ed.) CADE 2007. LNCS (LNAI), vol. 4603, pp. 295–310. Springer, Heidelberg (2007)
21. Urban, J.: MoMM - fast interreduction and retrieval in large libraries of formalized mathematics. Int. J. on Artificial Intelligence Tools 15(1), 109–130 (2006)
22. Urban, J.: BliStr: The Blind Strategymaker. CoRR, abs/1301.2683 (2014) (accepted to PAAR 2014)

23. Urban, J., Sutcliffe, G.: ATP-based cross-verification of Mizar proofs: Method, systems, and first experiments. MCS 2(2), 231–251 (2008)
24. Urban, J., Sutcliffe, G., Pudlák, P., Vyskočil, J.: MaLARea SG1 - machine learner for automated reasoning with semantic guidance. In: IJCAR, pp. 441–456 (2008)
25. Urban, J., Sutcliffe, G., Trac, S., Puzis, Y.: Combining Mizar and TPTP semantic presentation and verification Tools. Studies in Logic, Grammar and Rhetoric 18(31), 121–136 (2009)
26. Veroff, R.: Using hints to increase the effectiveness of an automated reasoning program: Case studies. J. Autom. Reasoning 16(3), 223–239 (1996)

Author Index

Printed in the United States
By Bookmasters